BY
DEBORAH COHEN

LAST CALL
AT THE
HOTEL IMPERIAL

RANDOM HOUSE

NEW YORK

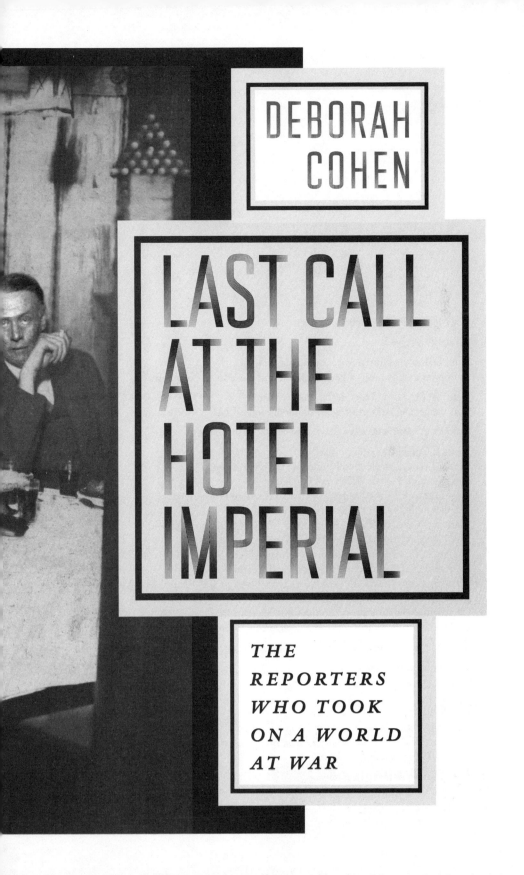

DEBORAH COHEN

LAST CALL AT THE HOTEL IMPERIAL

THE REPORTERS WHO TOOK ON A WORLD AT WAR

Published in the United States by Random House,
an imprint and division of Penguin Random House LLC, New York.

RANDOM HOUSE and the HOUSE colophon are
registered trademarks of Penguin Random House LLC.

LIBRARY OF CONGRESS CATALOGING-IN-PUBLICATION DATA

NAMES: Cohen, Deborah, author.
TITLE: Last call at the Hotel Imperial : the reporters who
took on a world at war / Deborah Cohen.
DESCRIPTION: First edition. | New York : Random House, [2022] |
Includes bibliographical references and index.
IDENTIFIERS: LCCN 2021035621 (print) | LCCN 2021035622 (ebook) |
ISBN 9780525511199 (hardcover) | ISBN 9780525511205 (ebook)
SUBJECTS: LCSH: Foreign correspondents—United States—Biography. |
Journalism—United States—History—20th century.
CLASSIFICATION: LCC PN4871 .C594 2022 (print) | LCC PN4871 (ebook) |
DDC 070.922 [B]—dc23/eng/2021121
LC record available at https://lccn.loc.gov/2021035621
LC ebook record available at https://lccn.loc.gov/2021035622

Printed in the United States of America on acid-free paper

randomhousebooks.com

1st Printing

First Edition

*Title page image: An evening out in Vienna. From left to right:
John Gunther, M. W. Fodor, Martha Fodor, Frances Gunther,
Dorothy Thompson, Sinclair Lewis.*

Book design by Barbara M. Bachman

CONTENTS

PERSONAE

the inaugural National Book Award for Biography. Married to Dinah Forbes-Robertson Sheean.

DOROTHY THOMPSON: Born in Lancaster, New York, 1893. First woman chief of a major American overseas news bureau (Berlin), widely syndicated political columnist for the *New York Herald Tribune*. First husband: Joseph Bard; second husband, Sinclair Lewis; third husband, Maxim Kopf.

OUTER CIRCLE

MARCEL FODOR: b. 1890, Hungarian foreign correspondent, Vienna correspondent for the *Manchester Guardian,* central European correspondent for American papers, including the Philadelphia *Public Ledger* and New York *Evening Post*.

EMILY (MICKEY) HAHN: b. 1905, St. Louis, writer for the *New Yorker,* reporting from Shanghai as of 1935, author of *China to Me* (1944) and dozens of other books.

JAWAHARLAL NEHRU: b. 1889, Allahabad (British India). Leader of the Indian freedom struggle, first prime minister of India.

HAROLD NICOLSON: b. 1886, Tehran. British diplomat, Member of Parliament and writer (including *Some People* and *Peacemaking 1919*). Husband of Vita Sackville-West.

EDWARD (EDDY) SACKVILLE-WEST: b. 1901, London. Music critic and heir to Knole, 5th Baron Sackville.

WILLIAM (BILL) SHIRER: b. 1904, Chicago, reared in Cedar Rapids, Iowa. Foreign correspondent for the *Chicago Tribune,* including stints in Vienna and India, later broadcasting for CBS. Author of *The Rise and Fall of the Third Reich* (1960).

REBECCA WEST: b. 1892, London. Writer, *The Return of the Soldier* (1918) and *Black Lamb and Grey Falcon* (1941), among many others.

MAP I. THE TRAVELS OF JOHN GUNTHER, H. R. KNICKERBOCKER, VINCENT SHEEAN, AND DOROTHY THOMPSON, 1926–1928

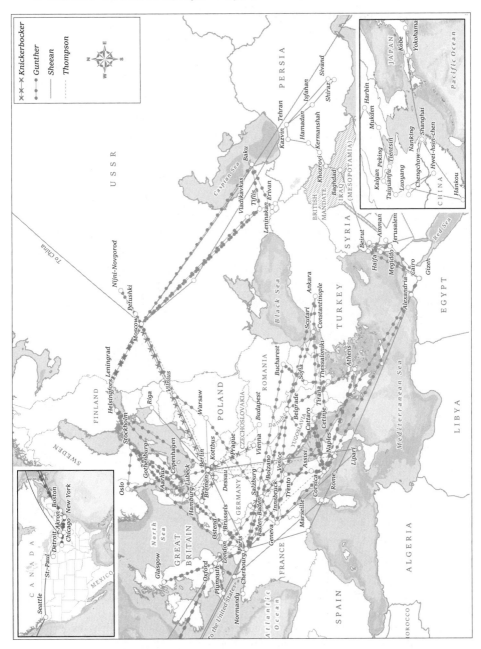

This map uses the historic place names conventional in American cartography during the years 1926–1928.

SOURCES: Newspaper cutting books of John Gunther, H. R. Knickerbocker, and Dorothy Thompson; Sheean's *Personal History,* and articles from newspapers.com. The maps accurately reflect the order and destinations of the reporters' trips, though not necessarily the precise routes followed.

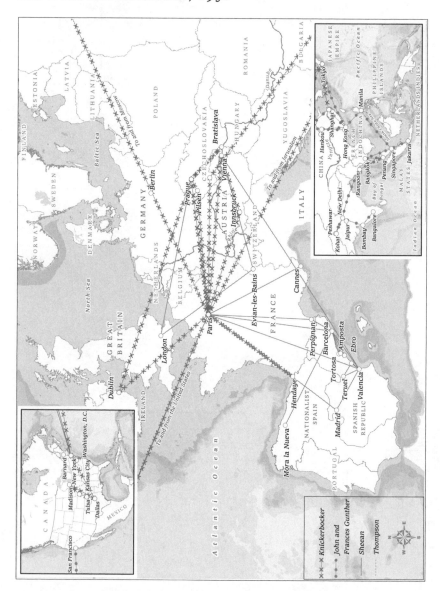

This map uses the historic place names conventional in American cartography during the year 1938. Boundary lines are fixed in February 1938.

SOURCES: Newspaper cutting books of John Gunther and H. R. Knickerbocker, Frances Gunther's travel diary, articles from newspapers.com. The maps accurately reflect the order and destinations of the reporters' trips, though not necessarily the precise routes followed.

MAP 3. JOHN GUNTHER'S *INSIDE U.S.A.* TRAVELS,
1944–1945

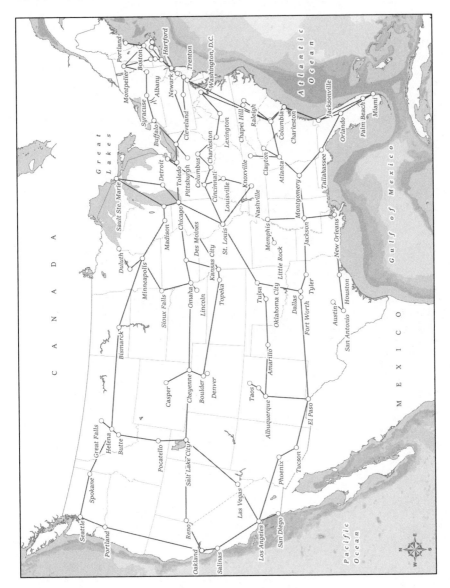

PROLOGUE

—

THE NAZI SPIES WERE WATCHING FROM THE SHORE AS THE passengers boarded the Dutch liner in Southampton, England, bound for New York. The war was a few weeks old, and every transatlantic ship was full. England would be bombed from the air—that was a certainty. Prepare for poison gas attacks, the British government had instructed its populace. To accommodate the crowds scrambling for berths, the ship's crew had set up cots in the gymnasium and filled the Delft-tiled swimming pool with makeshift bunks.

At the harbor, newly minted security officials, zealous in their duties, were screening every traveler. *Overzealous,* judged some of the passengers, especially the well-heeled ones, as the guards picked through their valises and badgered them with questions about their plans abroad and their acquaintances in America. The security officials had been warned about smugglers and saboteurs trying to get on board. At this rate, it would be hours before all the passengers had made their way through the long lines onto the ship.

The name of the boat, the *Nieuw Amsterdam,* was painted on the side of the hull in huge white letters. The Dutch, for now, were still a neutral power. Would it be enough to dissuade a trigger-happy German U-boat commander? That was the subject—to be joked or fretted about, according to one's disposition—as the first-class passengers settled into the smoking room to calm their nerves.

On its maiden transatlantic crossing the previous year, the Holland-America Line had boasted that its new flagship was a "Ship of Peace," built with luxury—not conversion to military use—in mind. The irony was already apparent well before the *Nieuw Amsterdam* left Rotterdam. In March 1938, the Third Reich's soldiers had marched over the Austrian border. In Munich six months later, the British prime minister, Neville Chamberlain, sacrificed the Czechs to Hitler in the name of "peace for our time." When it came to wishful thinking, the directors of the Holland-America Line had plenty of company. That included many of the ship's American passengers, who had nonchalantly dismissed the war clouds, departing their homes in Cleveland and Rochester for business trips that summer to Frankfurt or London, jaunting to Florence to see the Old Masters or to Salzburg for the music.

The Nazi spies kept an eye on the passengers in line. The shabby ones traveling third class were mostly Jews—merchants from Odessa or Warsaw who'd paid for their family's passage to New York with pieces of jewelry or cash smuggled out in the lining of their coats or the hems of wives' dresses. There were illustrious personages waiting to board, too, the sort whom the Holland-America Line's directors had envisioned when they outfitted the boat with a full-sized air-conditioned theater, satinwood dining chairs, and gold-leafed ceilings hung with Murano chandeliers. The son of the Chinese leader Chiang Kai-shek was sailing on the *Nieuw Amsterdam*. So, too, was the eighty-two-year-old widow of steel tycoon Andrew Carnegie. Winston Churchill's confidant, Conservative Party politician Sir Ronald Tree, was aboard. He'd been dispatched to America to shore up the British propaganda effort. And there was Hollywood royalty in the person of the actress Merle Oberon, who'd dazzled that year as the tormented heroine of *Wuthering Heights*.

Still more famous, though, were the two men whom the Nazi spies were tailing. Their bylines had appeared all around the globe, reporting on bank collapses, peace conferences, uprisings, assassinations. Their voices were familiar from newsreels and radio. Between them, they'd interviewed Mussolini, Gandhi, Nehru, and Hitler. They had tête-à-têtes with FDR at the White House, shared cigars with Churchill, and traveled on a paddleboat from Constantinople to the island of Prinkipo for an audience with Leon Trotsky, the exiled prophet of worldwide revolution. Their predictions headlined newsreels and their exploits were written up in the gossip columns. "Knights-errant of our time, rescuers of nations in distress, Champions of the downtrodden and oppressed," groused one envious English reporter.

The Nazis already had thick files on both men. John Gunther was thirty-eight years old, tall, and well-built, with deep-set blue eyes, blond hair, and a high forehead. A few years earlier, he'd written the sort of book that, like Hemingway's *The Sun Also Rises*, made a young man's future, not least because of the scandal it caused. Published in 1936, *Inside Europe* was a daringly frank account of the doings in the Continent's chancelleries and palaces. With dash and insight, Gunther had drawn an acid portrait of the dipsomaniacs and neurotics who were driving the Continent full throttle toward catastrophe, and the septuagenarians who were trying, impotently, to avert the crash. He'd done more than any other reporter to raise the alarm about the European crisis. The book was banned in Germany, a fact that Gunther's publishers elsewhere played up in their advertising. It sold a million copies worldwide.

The spies' real quarry, though, was Gunther's traveling companion, H. R. Knickerbocker—Knick to his friends. Red-haired and wiry, Knick had shot out of Yoakum, Texas, snapping at facts like a terrier, to win the Pulitzer Prize for his reporting on Stalin's first Five-Year Plan. On the eve of the war, he was, at forty-one, reportedly one of the best-paid correspondents in the world. He was always rushing, Hermes featherweight typewriter in hand, to the places other people were fleeing. Was it true that the great H. R. Knickerbocker was on the train? a Jewish passenger on the Vienna-bound service had inquired just before Nazi tanks rolled into Austria. "With the foreign press here they won't dare to do anything wrong, will they? Will they?" the man pleaded.

Neither Knick's fame nor his passport could insulate him from what was coming. A few days before boarding the *Nieuw Amsterdam,* Knick had filed the biggest scoop of his career. Now Hitler's propaganda minister, Joseph Goebbels, was baying for his blood.

"WE WERE SCAVENGERS, BUZZARDS, out to get the news, no matter whose wings got clipped," John Gunther wrote years later of his world-famous coterie of American correspondents. In the 1920s and 1930s, millions of Americans got their foreign news from a very small number of international reporters. Among them were John's closest friends: Knick, Vincent (Jimmy) Sheean, and Dorothy Thompson.

Jimmy and Dorothy, like John and Knick, had arrived in Europe in the early 1920s as young reporters, just as the dust of the Great War was settling. Sent by their editors to Bucharest, Prague, and Vienna, they saw—more clearly than most—the practical failings of the peace treaty signed at Versailles in 1919. The new democracies created from the shards of defeated empires were frail things, their economies shattered, their politics riven. Lacking tidy ethnic frontiers, the states midwifed at the Paris Peace Conference proved no match for the nationalist passions incubating within their borders.

At first, the reporters had cracked jokes, as everyone did, about the strongmen rising in Italy and Germany and across east-central Europe: Mussolini posturing under a steel helmet, on a horse, striding atop a cannon. Hitler strutting and bellowing and a whole battalion of little Hitlers in lockstep behind him. But it didn't take long before they realized how close these gangsters were to taking power. As Americans, they had imagined that people wanted freedom: that the whole thrust of human history, in fact, was toward liberty. But what if the leaders people freely chose were dictators rather than democrats?

As irrationality replaced progress as the leitmotif of the era, the ideas about unconscious drives that Sigmund Freud had developed in prewar Vienna gained new currency. At bohemian dinner parties in Greenwich Village or Chicago's Towertown, all the talk was of complexes and repression, of neuroses to which sexual liberation provided the cure. Americans were particularly enthusiastic about psychoanalysis, though Freud complained that they made a "hodge podge" of his theories. The self was becoming the new frontier of human experience and explaining the world required looking inward as well as out.

In the interwar years, American foreign correspondents became the kings of the hill. Shouting questions in ministerial briefing rooms, bragging in bars, they comprised the largest contingent of foreign reporters in most world capitals. Their outsize role doesn't accord with the old stereotype of an isolationist United States, barricaded behind its oceans. However, it helps to explain the monumental turnabout in the 1940s, when the United States went from hemispheric power to global hegemon.

Decades before American military bases dotted the globe, the correspondents saw the world as a whole: Europe, Asia, and the United States, colliding at warp speed. Armed with a peculiarly American obsession with personalities, they sounded an early warning about the rise of the dictators. At a time when appeasement and isolationism held sway, theirs were the voices prophesying the Second World War, garnering audiences in the millions for their efforts. The storm, they said, was just over the horizon. It was high time for Americans to engage with foreign affairs.

Of the marquee names in foreign correspondence, Knickerbocker, Sheean, Thompson, and Gunther were the undisputed stars. Knickerbocker's were the only foreign dispatches that Mussolini bothered to read all the way through. Sheean wrote *the* coming-of-age memoir of the 1930s, *Personal History,* turning his experiences reporting from revolutionary China and Soviet Russia into a call for young people in the West to embrace the world's struggles. On the eve of the Second World War, *Time* magazine described Thompson and Eleanor Roosevelt as the most influential women in the United States. From the mid-1930s through the 1950s, Gunther had more American bestsellers, fiction or nonfiction, than any other author save the romance novelist Daphne du Maurier.

Unlike the conventional portrait of the Lost Generation—F. Scott Fitzgerald and Ernest Hemingway, drinking their anomie away at a Parisian café—the reporters turned to, not away from, the world. They relayed the global struggles of their era in a new kind of journalism, both more subjective and more intimate; they conceived, too, a new sort of memoir, delving into previously unexplored areas of love and death. Hollywood fictionalized them in movies, including *Woman of the Year*, a send-up of Dorothy Thompson's career that was the first Katharine Hepburn and Spencer Tracy picture. Sheean's *Personal History* was the original inspiration for the movie that became Alfred Hitchcock's 1940 *Foreign Correspondent*. They began the decade by reporting the story, but by 1939, they were the story.

THEY HAD COME TO Europe at a moment when the Continent was war-torn and poor, and the United States in its stumbling global ascendancy. Over the next two decades, the question of what, if anything, the New World owed the Old became a hard-fought issue. By 1939, the dispute between those who thought the United States should join the Allied fight and the so-called isolationists (as the interventionists branded them) was bitter. Knick was all for the European war and thought that the United States ought of course to be in it. John, an equally fervent anti-Nazi, didn't agree. All options struck him as bad—either Nazi domination of Europe, which he abhorred, or war, the prospect of which he also dreaded. And it seemed entirely possible that the world would go to war and the Nazis would win anyway.

That put John, queasily, in a different state of mind not just from Knick but from Jimmy and Dorothy, too. Jimmy had been lecturing across America that summer, condemning Chamberlain as a villain and a bungler. Dorothy was equally vehement. The first American correspondent to be expelled from Nazi Germany, she had an audience estimated at eight to ten million for her thrice-weekly, pro-intervention syndicated columns. "What right does such a nitwit woman, her brains must be made of straw, have to speak out publicly against such a great man as the Führer," Goebbels ranted. At stake—right now—is the future of civilization, Dorothy exhorted her readers.

There was something shameful about not wanting the war, John felt. According to Dorothy, people who knew the evils of fascism shouldn't be fainthearted about the need to stop Hitler. John tended to keep quiet in these discussions. It wasn't that he and his friends had always agreed. They argued all the time. About Communism and the Spanish Civil War, for instance. They'd debated what Franco really wanted and quarreled about FDR and the New Deal.

Until the summer of 1939, the arguments had been short-lived and outweighed by their camaraderie. They'd seen each other coming and going from one trouble spot to another: nights together at the Hotel Imperial in Vienna, working over leads from the Bulgarian tipsters; trips on the wagons-lits, arriving early in the morning after an attempted coup, greeted by sandbags and machine-gun nests in the streets. Above all else, they shared a common cause: the conviction that the ideal of journalistic objectivity revered by their elders and editors had to yield to a different, more personal sort of reporting. They wrote what they thought about the events in Europe and Asia and, just as importantly, what they felt. The truth, as Jimmy put it, mattered more than a litany of facts. For Americans, it required a new way of imagining oneself in the world.

But now John was boarding the *Nieuw Amsterdam,* going the wrong way. He was heading home to America just as war was starting in Europe. Home to his wife who needed him, he told himself. John had left the United States ten weeks earlier, racing through all the places he and Frances had once reported from together. He'd started in Holland and Belgium, then to France and Switzerland, across Italy, Yugoslavia, Hungary, the Baltic States and Denmark, dipping into Germany, the Soviet Union, and finally to Britain.

Frances—who'd had her own career as a foreign correspondent—had opted to stay home.

He was at odds with himself. He didn't agree with Frances's attitude toward the war, but she'd influenced him more than he liked to admit. "Cry peace," Frances had wired John in Riga, disgusted by the bellicose turn she thought his radio broadcasts were taking. What the hell was wrong with their friends that they were all shrieking for war? Frances fumed. Couldn't they see that the real problem was the British Empire? Slight and wide-eyed with blond hair that was fluffy and soft as a chick's down, Frances looked delicate, but she had a yen for dominance. When she met someone for the first time, her stare was frank, unflinching. The trouble with the British, she pronounced, was that they talked of liberty but practiced conquest. They were also, she added, lousy Europeans.

From New York, Frances was fomenting an American-led rebellion against the British Empire. She had her sights on Indian independence. Now's the "time to hold up England for Indian freedom," she urged the nationalist leader Jawaharlal Nehru. She'd met Nehru the previous year in Bombay and long, flirtatiously argumentative letters had been flying between New York and Allahabad ever since. Nehru was making plans to visit her in the United States. That was another reason why she was staying home, she told John flatly.

Many years after the war, John came to believe that his trip on the *Nieuw Amsterdam* that September was the start of the end. The idea that a dispute about world politics could finish off a marriage wasn't by then a surprise to him. The fault lines that ran through a crumbling Europe, he and his friends had found, ran through their own lives as well. "If I ever divorce Dorothy, I'll name Adolf Hitler as co-respondent," Thompson's husband, the Nobel laureate Sinclair Lewis, liked to say. It was only half in jest.

BECAUSE THE REPORTER'S MÉTIER is the moment, their names are largely forgotten today. However, they left behind archives of an astonishing nature, both personal and professional. Notes scribbled in little spiral-bound books as they were interviewing Hitler, Gandhi, and Mussolini. Letters to and from lovers, some preserved with the careful notation at the top: "unsent." Diaries of rigorous, chiding introspection, full of desires and jealousies and gossip. Volumes of dream journals kept at the behest of a psychoanalyst, to be scoured for clues as to the workings of the unconscious. Thousands and thousands of candy-hued slips of paper, bound together with rusty paper clips or stuffed into envelopes. On one scrap, a confession of infidelity, on another, a rumor about Stalin's family life.

This archival jumble of private and public is a useful metaphor, a hallmark of their moment: the collapse of the boundaries between the geopolitical and the personal. As they immersed themselves in the world crisis, they found themselves channeling it in their own lives. Whirled around Europe and Asia, plunged into successive public nightmares, they could no longer separate themselves from the turmoil that surrounded them, and they spoke to readers whom they presumed couldn't either. "Do you feel as I do—a fantastic, dreamlike, unreal quality?" Thompson wrote in her column a few weeks before the *Nieuw Amsterdam* raced across the Atlantic. "A sense of sickness—as though all the world and everybody in it, and you and I, were sick in our nerves and in our brains and in our hearts?"

These extraordinary records make it possible to capture the texture and the course of their thought at very close hand. Of course, every archive, no matter how voluminous, contains only fragments of the past standing in for whole existences. About some crucial events, there is little evidence, while others generated mountains of contradictory accounts. What was saved was in some measure self-serving. Caught between the dictates of Victorian rationalism and Freud, the people in this book would grapple for years with the difficulty of rendering an adequate account of their emotions.

My aim as author has been to follow their own lead as journalists— to convey how it felt to live so exposed to history in the making.

When I indicate what a person felt or thought, I am always drawing upon archival documents. Their reportorial method was intimate and immediate, and as I worked in their papers, it often felt like walking in on an argument. Even when they were far apart, even after they fell out, they kept right on talking and arguing, long after the actual conversations had ended.

PART
ONE

WHY NOT GO?

—

A "YOUNG-MAN-GOING-SOMEWHERE" WAS THE WAY THE OLD-timers at the *Chicago Daily News* described overeager cub reporters like John Gunther. In 1924, a couple of years out of the University of Chicago, John was dashing between bank robberies, fires, gangster shoot-outs, and Rotary club luncheons. Those were the sorts of stories the lowest guy on the totem pole got assigned at the city's main afternoon paper, but John had already set his sights much higher: he wanted a job at the *Daily News*'s bureau in London. He was fed up with America, its hypocrisy, philistinism, and cant: the Prohibition that didn't really prohibit, the moral regeneration spearheaded by charlatans like the evangelist Aimee Semple McPherson, the corruption and graft bubbling up under the veneer of postwar "normalcy."

But the postwar disillusionment that had settled over much of American youth was only part of what was ailing John. For more than two years—two fruitless, unavailing years—he'd been trailing around after Helen Hahn, a local belle. He made small talk with her father, ate dinners with her family, sent her letters and books when he was away. John was constant but Helen, a blond stunner, was fickle. Mostly she liked to string him along, touching his arm while they talked, her big blue eyes gazing into his. He'd paid for one of her abortions though the kid definitely wasn't his, which even at the time struck him as the sort of thing only a chump would do. He knew he had to flee.

The arrival of the British writer Rebecca West in Chicago in November 1923 was a beacon from the sophisticated Old World beckoning to the New. West was Britain's most notorious modern woman, a novelist, journalist, and feminist who had just wrenched herself free from an affair with the writer H. G. Wells, immensely famous, twenty-six years her senior, and married.

When John and Rebecca met one evening at the University of Chicago, she was a well-seasoned thirty; he a decidedly tender twenty-two. She was on her first American lecture tour, addressing audiences on such racy subjects as polygamy. There wasn't a man living who could gratify four or five women, Rebecca had insisted: "There are many men who cannot make even one woman happy."

For years Rebecca had been eager to see America, but when she arrived in New York she wasn't all that impressed. "This whole place strikes me as a greedy children's party," she wrote her sister, appalled by the relentless getting and spending. Chicago was different. In its swagger and newness, it wasn't like any place she had ever seen. From her room at the Drake Hotel, she marveled at the never-ending lake, its gray-green wintry water tugged by millions of waves. The skyscrapers looked like enormous gasoline cans, stolid but lacking in grace. A wholly new shopping street, Michigan Avenue, had been whipped up as swiftly as a Hollywood set. Between the business district and the miles upon miles of identical brick houses rising raw out of the prairie wobbled an elevated railway north, south, and west.

And the people, with their curious addiction to introspection and self-analysis. It was a Midwestern quality, Rebecca thought: this touching eagerness to take one on a tour of their inner lives. Such a creature was John Gunther. Rebecca nicknamed the young man "John Silence" because he never stopped talking during the weeks she spent in Chicago. John had the "vitality of seven cart-horses," she later wrote. A "Gothic angel—tall and slender and golden-haired." That was, she added, until he discovered European cooking.

She'd later introduce him to her friends in London by saying: "This is John Gunther who comes from Chicago in fact he *is* Chicago, he is a moral imbecile but a darling."

It was all her doing, Rebecca always said, that John finally left his hometown. She didn't know whether he had any talent at all, but he'd be better off, she told him, if he ceased writing those atrocious short stories and novels and caught a steamer to Europe. Maybe he could earn his living as a foreign correspondent. She thought he was a little in love with her.

John's bosses refused his entreaties to go to London. He was much too green to be entrusted with a position abroad, his editor informed him. He decided to quit his job and leave anyway; the $150 he'd saved would go further in Europe. He had a clutch of letters of introduction from powerful literary agents and publishers to writers such as Rafael Sabatini and Aldous Huxley. Rebecca had promised to show him the town. He booked his passage on the White Star Line's SS *Olympic,* departing New York for Southampton in October 1924.

It was a lucky break that the Prince of Wales was on the same boat, returning home to England from his six-week tour of North America. Now John had a story to sell. With a $100 advance from the United Press, he traded up from steerage to a first-class cabin, a necessary luxury to track the prince's activities. The palace's humorless courtiers tried to quarantine His Majesty—"like a Hindu virgin or a case of leprosy," reported John. The prince needed guarding both from the reporters on board and from ambitious Long Island dowagers with unmarried daughters. Nevertheless, John found plenty to send the UP.

Who was that magnificent girl swathed in furs, who sat alone in the Parisian restaurant the first two nights and was seen with the prince every night thereafter? (John knew: it was a married American newspaperwoman, who caught the prince's fancy and reported their conversations to John every night.) The whole ship was abuzz, he wrote, with rumors that the prince might renounce his right to the throne. (As indeed, twelve years later, he did for Wallis Simpson.) If there was nothing in the rumor, John noted, the prince's courtier wouldn't have bothered to issue an official denial. John's story ricocheted through the American and British papers.

John was running away from Helen, but still, he saw every sight through her eyes. How she would have laughed at the dress of the Britishers on board. "Mauve spats, taupe knickers wide enough to drive a Ford through, dinky caps, rugs for capes, monocles . . ."There was the ancient duke who promenaded on deck in his rose-colored bedroom slippers, another who appeared in sparkly purple bow ties. Too bad she wasn't there to stroll with him through the *Olympic*'s vast acres of floating grandeur. Did Helen realize that there were palm gardens and swimming pools and tennis courts on the ship? He'd asked the one pretty girl on board to dance. The girl's family had country houses on Long Island and Rolls-Royces, too; her hair was marcelled and jet-black, her eyes wide-set, and she let him talk and talk.

In those years, the 1920s, hundreds of thousands of Americans set off from the New World's docks to live for a spell on the Continent. The trip from New York to Southampton was a swift five or six days by liner, short enough to return home if a parent became ill or the home office required managing, and with the money you saved over in Europe, where the living was cheap, you could afford plenty of return journeys. American entrepreneurs settled on the Right Bank in Paris, hoping to hook the French on imported sweet corn or shredded wheat biscuits or elastane corsets. American engineers struck out for the brand-new industrial cities proliferating in the Soviet steppes; they'd show Stalin's workers how to build harvesters and steel foundries. In Europe's leading cabarets, the music was jazz, and American performers taught the king of Spain and the Aga Khan the latest dance steps. There were American bankers who trumpeted Wall Street's ever-buoyant securities and American heiresses who husband-hunted among Europe's titled but hard-up nobility. Everywhere there were American dentists who retailed New World methods for polishing and straightening teeth.

The writers who went to Europe, though, had a different purpose in mind. They'd sell the experience of the Continent—the condoms advertised in every druggist, the sewage stink of Naples, the Tanqueray cocktail, the long creamy sticks of French bread, the azure waters of the Riviera, the anti-colonial politics, the charred battlefields of Belgium—back to an America that was scandalously isolated, moralized, and teetotaling because of Holy Rollers, and raised on canned food and the Bible. John had gone to Europe because of Helen and maybe because of Rebecca and definitely because of his family. For those reasons, and because he wanted to write.

"ALWAYS I HAD DREAMS of Europe," he wrote later, when recounting this part of his life. "These must have started (my mother's influence) when I was a child." In the roomy kitchen of the old house on Chicago's North Side, John's mother would read Keats, propping her book open with one hand and stirring the soup with the other. She cut a stately figure, tall and shapely, with soft, lovely hair, and elegant long fingers. Lizette Schoeninger's family was cultivated, solid, German. The women played bridge in the long afternoons, had heavy, well-polished silver tea sets, and their houses smelled of beeswax and warm coffee strudel. For Christmas they gave each other stacks of leather-bound books, and their trees glittered with hundreds of candles.

Why had she married Eugene Gunther? It was a mystery to John. Could his mother really have loved his father? Eugene had once been handsome, even a little dashing. She was nearly thirty, getting old to be a bride. John supposed she must have once been fond of him.

But later, how she suffered the shame of the man. Eugene had one disreputable job after another: peddling cigars and fake liquor; fishy dealings in real estate; and, worst of all, managing a garage, home every night with grease-stained pants. He was a cheat in poker as in everything else, and a glad-hander, the type who in low-down bars made a show of bonhomie by throwing his arms around the bartender. Crooked through and through, Eugene was nonetheless a stickler for decorum: he did not tolerate curse words at the dinner table and condemned the new fashions in underwear; funerals had to be arranged according to his rigid sense of correctness.

The house was outwardly peaceful, but the tensions within were impossible to ignore. Lizette cultivated herself and her children, John and his sister, Billi (but especially John), not just as defense but as a weapon against her husband. To the Art Institute or to improving lantern lectures at the local public library they went, sailing out of the house the three of them, Lizette and her two children, irreproachably attired. She read the *Iliad* to John and they cried together over the death of Hector.

Lizette kept John at home with her until he was nine. He couldn't go to school yet because of his asthma, she said. There was never enough fresh air in his childhood, he thought in retrospect. His hobby was writing encyclopedias: drawing up entries for battleships and his favorite poems, for momentous dates in history and the animals of the world classified species by species. When his mother finally enrolled him in school, he worried that he would address his teachers as "Mama."

As a small boy, John had pined when his father was away. "Papa, do you like me?" he wrote when he was five and Eugene was traveling. "I wish you would come home." He sent samples of the colors of his Crayola box and listed all of the animals he could think of. But more and more, he took on his mother's fastidiousness, shuddering when his father mispronounced names or repeated his old stories. He saw that his father was a braggart who couldn't stand to be wrong and didn't want to be outdone by his son. Eugene used his pudgy fingers to push food onto his fork. He *chewed* his ice cream. He got heavy and ill with dropsy, chain-smoking cigars, so corpulent that he could no longer cross his legs.

One evening, when he was twelve, John broke the still surface of a family dinner to declare that he wished he had been born an Englishman. Not an American. His father stormed away from the table, detecting Lizette's influence over the boy. To be English was to be high-toned, cosmopolitan, literary, better than Chicago. Eugene started to accuse his wife of turning the children against him. Like other German Americans caught between pride in their heritage and loyalty to the United States, the family's claim to Americanness was fraying. The Guenthers, as they were known then, were too close for comfort to the Kaiser's Germans, with their spiked iron helmets and their rape of Belgium. A year or so after the dinner table incident, Eugene and Lizette changed the spelling of their surname. During the First World War, the Germanic Guenthers became the unobtrusively American Gunthers.

"You must be a success, a success," John's mother urged him. By high school, John was devouring books, one every few days, an appetite that encompassed Edna St. Vincent Millay's *A Few Figs from Thistles* as well as *Keeping Fit at 50*, with plenty of cowboy stories and worthy classics in between. Arthur Conan Doyle's *The Sign of the Four* was "one peach of a book" and Scott's *Ivanhoe* was the sort of story that "suits me better than any other sort." *Tom Sawyer*, by contrast, didn't live up to *Huckleberry Finn*. George Eliot's *Silas Marner* was "almost as bad" as Dickens's *David Copperfield*, both dust-dry. "Shaw may be pessimistic, unclean, too cynical for youthful minds, but believe me, I'm going to read him," he pronounced after a first encounter with the author of *Pygmalion*. "Conrad at last!" he noted on reading the novel *Victory*. "I never before imagined that such a concentrated, awful force of action could be wholly transmitted to the printed page."

He had his own opinions but the ones that mattered, he knew, belonged to other people: the scathing Chicago critic, Burton Rascoe; the dramatist George Nathan, editor of *The Smart Set*, the literary magazine for fashionable youth; and most important, H. L. Mencken, the iconoclast of Baltimore, who flayed the sham moralism of the American "booboisie" and the pettiness and provincialism of what passed for culture in the United States. To the young literary striver, devotion to Nathan and especially Mencken was as essential as a porkpie hat and a long raccoon coat. Even measured by that rigorous standard, John's apprenticeship to his idols was notably systematic. Alongside a forty-six-page loose-leaf list of obscure words he'd plucked from the dictionary ("triune," "hypocaust," "systolic"), he recorded Mencken's judgments (Conrad's short story "The Return" was "no good") and listed Nathan's likes (the curmudgeonly comic, W. C. Fields, the Ziegfeld Follies) and dislikes (*Tosca*, the movies).

By his final year of high school, John figured he was finally making something of himself. His stock of clippings, information filed away to be made use of, was accumulating. He started taking notes on 5 x 7 filing cards, methodical in his drive for self-knowledge. Observations about his family members, about his personal emotions, about his friends, about fraternities and sororities. Lists of original phrases, of epigrams, notes on plots for novels, lists of dresses, cards about girls. "Growing realization that I was meant for something <u>big</u>," he put down on a Personal Emotions card. Already he had plans to write his autobiography. It would have to be ruthlessly frank, everything bared, but he would write it in the third person.

IN THE FALL OF 1918, when he was seventeen, John enrolled at the University of Chicago, "that mountain range of twentieth-century Gothic near the shores of Lake Michigan," as Jimmy Sheean, a fellow student, described it. The campus in Hyde Park was barely two decades old, an arriviste university decked out in full medieval regalia, its gray limestone buildings arranged in quadrangles and studded with gargoyles, topped with crenellated towers, and draped with the requisite ivy. It was as if a dignified assortment of Oxford or Cambridge colleges had been muscled onto a transatlantic liner and deposited several miles south of the central business district. The oil money of John D. Rockefeller had built the new campus, and Chicago's ambitions for a world-class university to rival the East Coast propelled the scheme forward. The idea was to combine the best of the German university tradition, with its emphasis on graduate education, with the hustle and bustle of the American college. From its founding, in 1890, the university, like many other Midwestern institutions of higher education, was coeducational.

That fall, most of the male students were in army khaki though German troops were deserting their regiments en masse and the war, everyone knew, was nearly over. John wasn't in uniform as he was still too young to enlist. He was working his way through college. His father disapproved of the University of Chicago in particular and college in general as a waste of time; he couldn't have afforded the tuition anyway. To save money, John was living at home and commuting to campus, a trip that often took two hours on the train each way. In the student popularity contest otherwise known as fraternity rush, he was therefore at a double disadvantage. A couple of fraternities offered him bids, but according to the anxious hierarchies that regulated such things, both were "bad," so he accepted neither—becoming a "barbarian" (or "barb") as opposed to a fraternity man.

He knew of Jimmy Sheean, who was a year ahead of him at the university. But as Jimmy would later say, John was "a real barb in those days," and they didn't have much to do with each other.

John studied chemistry in his first years at the university, a major he had elected for practical reasons. That proved a mistake as he had no aptitude for it. What rescued him was literature—in particular, the extraordinary set of American books published in 1919 and 1920: James Branch Cabell's sex-steeped *Jurgen,* Carl Sandburg's gritty *Smoke and Steel* poems, Sherwood Anderson's psychological portraits in *Winesburg, Ohio,* and of course always Mencken, whose defense of the pungency of Americanisms in the English language was followed by two volumes of his collected essays in *Prejudices.* "I was inflamed by them as by a case of malaria," John wrote. In a sketch of himself titled "Original Portrait of a Young Man," John tried to boil down his personality into a series of wise-cracking, semi-lacerating one-liners.

"He likes to talk about books to his mother, who knows more about them than he does." "He has decided, with Mencken and most of the great writers of the world, 'that life, after all, essentially, is meaningless.'" "He frequently becomes so obsessed with an idea, that he almost can think coherently of nothing else for days &

days & must needs tell everyone else about his great discovery." "He makes few friends, but he is fairly affable & easy to get along with. Very few people, however, really like him." "It is his invariable luck that the mother of the girls he takes out like him better than the girls themselves." "He is as yet a virgin. It is neither religion, nor ideals, nor self-respect, nor the thought of another girl, nor the thought of future marriage, that has left him chaste, but merely fear of possible infection."

That fear—of gonorrhea, specifically—came from his mother, but there was plenty in what John found at the University of Chicago to reinforce Lizette's lurid warnings on the subject. Girls these days, a fellow student told him, were ashamed of not being kissed. Too much hair below the waist, a student named Marj informed him, was a "big handicap" to a girl. The casualness about petting (three-quarters of Northwestern University girls did it on a first date, Marj said), the easy espousal of free love as an ideal, was not at all what he had been expecting, and the notes he took on his Girls cards attest to his bewilderment. This was not the prudery that Mencken had been decrying. He had nearly fainted, he recorded, when a prim, demure coed named Lucile dropped the word "intercourse" nonchalantly into her conversation. "Girls in halls talk constantly about 'it'," she said to John. "Why, you didn't think this was the first time I talked about this."

The chemistry major now abandoned for the study of English and history, a room near campus secured, girls to kiss: John increasingly felt himself superior to the mindless copycats in the fraternities on campus. What originality had they with their Oxford brogues, their loud scarves, snug coats, and droopy trousers? John managed to get himself appointed to the college newspaper, the *Daily Maroon,* as its first ever literary editor. When the literary magazine *The Smart Set* went looking for an undergraduate to anatomize the University of Chicago for a series on college campuses, he landed the assignment. The other articles in the series ranged from the affectionate— Gilbert Seldes's portrait of Harvard—to the unabashedly worshipful

(John Peale Bishop's account of Princeton). John, by contrast, took out his knives and set to work.

With its brightly polished doorknobs and its hankering after tradition, the University of Chicago, John began, could be accused of a certain vulgarity. There was a standing order that the windows in the Harper Quadrangle were not to be washed, he wrote, in order that the building might rapidly acquire the grime of distinction. Never refer to the University of Chicago man as a Chicago University man: anything less than the university's full title he would receive as an affront. Then there were the girls who occupied the peak of the social pyramid, successfully pledging the clubs that, with the fraternities, ruled over social life. What did they learn in their exclusive societies? To dress in "clothes that fit tightly as frankfurter skins" and— a shocking claim—the latest birth control techniques.

The article made John infamous on campus. It was an exercise in score-settling by an outsider who wanted in. The depiction was "unfair" went the murmur, and certainly in bad taste. But now everyone knew John Gunther's name. That summer, he wrote to the editors of the Midwestern newspapers, sending out more than a thousand queries, asking them if they'd like to syndicate the weekly literary column he wrote in the *Maroon*. Three papers agreed, and that tactic, together with the *Smart Set* piece, landed him a regular job on the *Daily News* when he graduated. He didn't bother to attend the university convocation, for after a year of terse entries in his pocket diary, crossing off the days, there was finally something worth recording: "I AM GOING TO EUROPE THIS SUMMER." He'd signed on to work on a cattle boat bound for Southampton. He'd be back in the fall, to start his job on the *Daily News*.

ANXIOUS AS JOHN WAS to leave, Chicago was—in the view of his hero Mencken—the "Literary Capital of the United States." The atmosphere was one of experimentation, of striving after an authentic, modern American form that was as close to the soil as thousands of dusty Podunk towns and as virile and raw as the city's slaughter-houses and blast furnaces. What was known in retrospect as the "Chicago Renaissance" encompassed an astonishing efflorescence of talent: the novelist Theodore Dreiser, whose *Sister Carrie* (1900) was the first really important novel to be set in urban America, and the poet Carl Sandburg, who gave Chicago the moniker "City of the Big Shoulders"; the reporter, playwright, and later screenwriter Ben Hecht, whose comedy *The Front Page* paid homage to the rollicking newsroom, its hard-boiled characters, and the quick double knocked back in a bar at midnight; the novelists Sherwood Anderson, Edna Ferber, and Edgar Lee Masters, author of *Spoon River Anthology*.

This was bohemia with hayseed in its hair and dirt under its fingernails: cheap lodgings behind batik curtains, dinners in a goulash house or a greasy spaghetti joint, the evening passed in a gambling parlor. Meanwhile, Chicago's more decorous citizens sustained its coarser elements without trying to tame them. At Harriet Monroe's poetry evenings, the genteel founder of *Poetry Magazine* coaxed modernistic verse from her acolytes, among them Sandburg—his stony Swedish face and chopped-up white hair, a leather cap in all weathers, and his cigar chewed pulpy. "You know my city, Chicago triumphant—factories and marts and the roar of machines—horrible, terrible, ugly and brutal," declaimed Anderson, who'd abandoned his paint business and family in Elyria, Ohio: "Can a singer arise and sing in this smoke and grime?" The chief merit of the Midwestern school of literature, according to Anderson, "was that it had made fucking respectable in fiction."

For the literary types who gathered in Towertown, the district near the old stone Water Tower that had survived Chicago's Great Fire, the lack of refinement was the point. Squeezed between the limestone mansions of the Gold Coast and the crime-ridden Italian slums of "Little Hell," they'd made this neighborhood their own; the bootleggers and the gangsters followed them there. Towertown's haunts included the Dill Pickle Club, entered off an alley, through an orange door, above which was scrawled DANGER, with two arrows jutting downward. "Step High, Stoop Low, Leave Your Dignity

Outside" was the motto on the door. If you took the flight of stairs down, as a clientele that included anarchists, Gold Coast socialites, and tourists did, there would, depending upon the evening, be a debate about the evils of private property or the ecstasies of free love under way in the cavern below.

The catalyst for Chicago's literary renaissance was its newspapers. They offered a steady income for writers: Sandburg, Hecht, Ring Lardner and Nelson Algren, among many others, all earned their living by working as reporters. But more important still was the role that reporting played in fashioning the trademark Chicago style: irreverence tempered by disdain and married to a genuine curiosity about the variety of types—the mob boss and the numbers-runner, the Ukrainian and the Galician—to be found in this Midwestern boomtown with its population of more than 3.3 million.

Reporters poked their noses into the ossuary of city life and learned how to extract the marrow from the bones. A few hours later, they wrote it up in the wise-guy style: the man in Colosimo's restaurant with a knife stuck in his belly, the society dame jumping to her death from the top of the Masonic Temple, racetrack rackets, embezzlement schemes, graft, and swindlers. The trick was to find the right blazing image, words that shone a torch in a few sharp sentences. Cynicism looked a lot like literary realism. The newspaper was the place, according to the *Chicago Daily News*'s editor Henry Justin Smith, where a man could get more of life than anywhere else.

Among Chicago's dozens of papers in the 1920s, the biggest was the *Tribune,* with a circulation of 450,000 daily and 800,000 on Sundays. For the *Tribune*'s proprietor, Colonel McCormick, the paper served as a vengeance-extracting megaphone. Then there were the weeklies, such as the Black paper, the *Chicago Defender,* with its pioneering investigations of subjects, such as lynching and segregation, which the white press largely ignored. But the most storied and literary paper was the *Chicago Daily News,* which could claim Hecht and Sandburg among its veterans. The *Daily News*'s style was akin to a "daily novel," said its editor. Its old building was on North Wells Street, a warren of fun-house rooms serviced by an unreliable elevator. To reach some floors, you had to go up three steps and down two. The sooty newsroom was ninety feet long and thirty wide, with room for forty or so men, their typewriter cylinders banging back and forth and the ceaseless buzz of the telegraph and the din of the linotypes echoing in the background. Starting at seven A.M., the beginning of the workday, the phones never stopped ringing.

In 1922, John was the kid whom the tobacco-chewing veterans joshed mercilessly. On his first day, he'd asked to change a quarter to make a call in the newsroom not knowing it was free. Yet they slapped his back when his story about the insane fireman who saved his fellow inmates the night the Dunning Asylum burned was named one of the nation's best news articles. John tagged along when the reporters dined out at Schlogl's, a block away from the *Daily News* building, where a literary roundtable gathered. Schlogl's was always choked with smoke from pipes and cigars. A cut-glass chandelier illuminated the murky green of the tin ceiling, casting a dull glare on the gloomy oil paintings of wine-drinking monks, and the Bernkastel lithographs. The reporters crowded around a big round black walnut table in a corner. No one ever ordered the owls on the menu, but there was plenty of sweet white Rüdesheimer to drink and you ate what the waiter served up, especially the stewed chicken and the hamburger steak fried in butter. Unlike the more famous New York Algonquin Hotel roundtable frequented by Dorothy Parker, the literary circle at Schlogl's was for men only.

Despite Mencken's praise, Chicago's literati had a chip on their shoulder. They boasted about the Muses that coughed and hacked their way to authenticity in what Hecht called the "chewing gum center of the world." New York, by contrast, according to Hecht's short-lived *Chicago Literary Times*, was a "National Cemetery of Arts and Letters," which evoked Art mournfully, decorously, "as if it were their dead grandmother."

To a whippersnapper like John, all that protesting gave itself away. He sold an article about the collapse of Literary Chicago to Mencken's new publication, the *American Mercury*. Chicago's writers— John alleged—had gone soft. They'd lost their vigor, indulged in "excessive experimentalism," or, still more damning, sold out in pursuit of bigger audiences. They'd arrived in the city riding rough on freight trains and were now departing in sumptuous Pullman sleeping cars. Mrs. Monroe's best years were behind her; Carl Sandburg's "sociological" preoccupations (with the labor movement, with poverty) had choked his "purely lyrical strain"; the talents of Ben Hecht, it turned out, were best suited to the newspaper business; Sherwood Anderson had gotten self-conscious and long-winded. One by one, John shoved all the idols off their pedestals. But then he talked up the article so much that Mencken caught wind of the gossip all the way in Baltimore and refused to publish it. By "blabbing," Mencken rebuked John, "you gave away the whole substance of it." For John, it was shattering, like a chastisement from God.

Chicago wasn't in fact finished, though Hecht himself was preparing to decamp for New York and, a few years later, for a career in a place he despised even more—Hollywood. There was another renaissance afoot in Chicago, this one in the African American neighborhood of Bronzeville, of which Gwendolyn Brooks and Richard Wright would become the most famous exemplars. At Hecht's going-away party at Schlogl's in 1924, however, Chicago's Black Renaissance was a world away. Nineteen white men are captured by the camera, a few bow-tied, all in suits, fedoras suspended from hooks in the alcove, bottles of Lea & Perrins cluttering the table. There are broad smiles to commemorate the moment, stogies in hands. John is solemn-faced and in profile, as if he weren't really part of the festivities. He would be going away soon enough himself, to New York first and then on to London.

Seeing John off at the train station, his mother cried, but reconciled herself to his departure by considering it the culmination of all her efforts. He would send her word sketches of places they'd read about. She and her son would correspond about literature. Which Henry James novel to try next? she'd asked him. (Not *Wings of a Dove*, she hadn't liked it.) Maybe she would even save up her money and come to see him—and Europe. That would be something to dream about.

"All the things I have longed to do, you are doing," she wrote him. "You are the dearest thing in the world to me." And: "By the way, I wish you'd notice the spelling of receive and leisure!" Unless he wanted to get fat like Papa, he would have to watch his diet. Cut out the bread and potatoes. Take more exercise. Weigh himself and send her those numbers.

Her letters reached him at American Express in Paris and Rome or the *poste restante* boxes in Jerusalem and Damascus. "What a store of memories you are laying up!" his mother exclaimed. A store of memories, presumably, for when he returned to Chicago to scale the heights of the *Tribune* or the *Daily News,* steward the papers to Pulitzers, drum up more advertisements, sweat over the accounting ledgers. Perhaps she hoped that one day he would have a gray stone house in Lakeview down the street from where he'd grown up, and blond, stocky children to whom she could read the *Iliad.*

She was a remarkable woman, a passionate woman, John recorded on one of his cards. "Complete & absolute sympathy & understanding & love of mamma—always." She was, he'd note, the "Biggest infl. in my life," as if he couldn't quite bring himself to write out the word "influence" in full. He wasn't ever coming back to Chicago.

LIKE JOHN, JIMMY SHEEAN lived in his books. As a boy, he built himself a seat up in a silver maple not far from his house and there he took his apples and his books. He read one author at a time— George Eliot when he was ten, George Meredith when he was twelve. By the first year of high school, he'd ingested all of Shake-speare, all of Stevenson, then all of Austen and all of the Dickens he could find in Pana, Illinois, a coal town in the south of the state, population 7,500, a half day's train journey from Chicago. Enough books to choke a horse, as Jimmy put it. When it was too cold for the maple, he sat on a wooden box in the parlor next to the potbellied stove. After school, he liked to impart his knowledge to classmates, a "gang of midwestern small-town molluscs," as he later described them. Walking backward like a tour guide, he told them, inter alia, that Queen Elizabeth was one of the first to have false teeth and related the latest news of the pope. Jimmy knew the meaning of more words than he could pronounce.

For Jimmy, the characters in books, fictional or historical, were as real as his family. More real, in fact: he barely noticed the death of his grandmother but hung on the drama of poor, persecuted Marie Antoinette. His mother encouraged him in his reading. His Irish family had much in common with John's Germanic upbringing. His father was a commercial traveler who sold flavoring extracts, had to be dragged out of saloons, but was a stickler for church attendance and other people's propriety. William Sheean was crueler than Eugene Gunther, too. One Christmas he gave Jimmy, the youngest of his four sons, a newfangled toy train, only to smash it to pieces when it made too much noise. He bestowed upon his wife leather-bound books only to rage when she dared to read them, rather than to entertain her husband, in the evenings.

Jimmy's mother left his father on a few occasions, once taking Jimmy and his older brothers back to Denver where her relations lived. There, she had everything she desired: theater, opera, quiet, the company of Jimmy, who invented an imaginary Balkan country when he was six and proceeded to fill out the details. But then she returned to Pana to try the marriage again and her health broke down. Now she was stuck. "Something of the flat disaster of his mother's life penetrated early," wrote Jimmy in an autobiographical story.

Father Fox, an Irish priest in Pana who had studied at the seminary in Tours, took it upon himself to teach the boy French; Jimmy learned Italian from the local Sicilian fruit merchant, to which he added a smattering of German from a Lutheran pastor. When he was a junior in high school, a young woman named Helen Mills— unkempt, unfashionable, nervous—arrived from the University of Chicago to teach English. Jimmy was tall and gangly, with long blond hair that hung down, greasy and uncombed; his conversation ranged from Moses to the theosophist Madame Blavatsky, from Tolstoy to the Jacobite Bonnie Prince Charlie. Miss Mills told him:

"Your second-hand information is so far ahead of your first-hand knowledge that if you spend another five years like the last you'll be ruined so far as doing anything real is concerned." He spent evenings with Miss Mills, whom he learned to call Helen; they stayed out in the park until one A.M. despite the rain. The principal of the high school demanded that they stop seeing each other. When Miss Mills defied the principal, he fired her.

Having become the center of small-town gossip, Jimmy sought to live up to the romantic part. In his senior year of high school, he cut his hair and became the editor of the school newspaper. He wrote a prize essay on literature that won him a scholarship at the University of Chicago. When Jimmy left Pana, Father Fox prayed for him every day for the next five decades.

JIMMY'S WAS A PROVINCIAL upbringing, not unlike that of other men who distinguished themselves as foreign correspondents in the 1920s and 1930s. The leading lights of international reporting didn't come from the boarding schools of the East Coast or the Ivy League. Rather, they hailed from America's Babbitt towns and the rich agricultural plains of the Midwest, the provincial heartland. The revolutionary changes in technology and transport that brought Model Ts to rural America also delivered mail-order books, those cloth-bound sets of Shakespeare and Dickens, as well as the big-city papers that traveled hundreds of miles through the night to be delivered before breakfast.

For young people chafing at the rounds of Sunday sermons and ice-cream socials, those papers and books represented an escape, or the promise of escape. Yet even after they'd left Pana, Illinois, or Dowagiac, Michigan, or Velva, North Dakota, they never forgot the open skies and narrow horizons of their birthplaces. Or the audience back home. They had the finely honed sense of the recently arrived for the sort of stories Americans would want to read. The Mowrer brothers, Paul and Edgar, both of whom won Pulitzer Prizes for their foreign reporting, came from Bloomington, Illinois, not far from Pana. Junius Wood, with his shaved head and corncob pipe and his talent for vexing the Soviet secret police, was the son of a watch factory machinist in Elgin, Illinois, whose farthest travel from home was a single visit to the Chicago World's Fair of 1893. Bill Shirer, a little younger than John and Jimmy, grew up in Cedar Rapids, Iowa, bridling at the stultifying combination of chapel and Chamber of Commerce.

When Jimmy arrived at the University of Chicago in the fall of 1917, his sights were already set on the pantheon of campus celebrity. First, though, he had to acquire some firsthand experience of life. He'd never, for instance, met a Jew except in books. That was how he came to pledge a so-called Jewish fraternity without realizing it was Jewish. When a girl he knew explained that choosing a Jewish house would ruin his reputation, he fled in the middle of the night and surrendered his membership by letter the following day. Next he tried the Poetry Club, but he couldn't help sniggering at the spectacle of Wisconsin farm boys spouting unintelligible modernistic verse to an indulgent Harriet Monroe.

By his junior year, Jimmy had managed to become the sort of individual whom people talked about, eccentric enough to merit singling out, but (unlike John) still clubbable. An invitation to join Phi Gamma Delta, a "good" fraternity, followed the Jewish fraternity debacle, his hometown now identified as Denver, Colorado, rather than Pana. He wrote dramatic plays—"The Lady with the Midnight Hair"—and comic opera. His opinions figured in front-page headlines. He deemed the new student magazine worth reading: "Phoenix Deserving of Attention Says J. Vincent Sheean." His fellow students told stories about him. He'd come up to college clutching a typewriter under each arm. He was *just* like the egotistical hero of F. Scott Fitzgerald's *This Side of Paradise*. The tremblings on campus? That was the sound of Jimmy Sheean dropping a course, reported the *Maroon*.

In a notebook from those years, which survived Jimmy's habit of forgetting suitcases on trains or throwing things away, he recorded his friendship with Fred Millett. He'd met Millett, a graduate student in English, through his high school teacher, Helen Mills. Millett's rooms were dimly lit, with red-painted bookcases; he read Edward Carpenter and Compton Mackenzie. Millett's favorites soon became Jimmy's own: "analysis, analysis, emotions, books, poetry, emotions, analysis, sensation—the round has not let me much alone," Jimmy wrote. "Should I be sorry? I do not know. It is a world. To be in a world is better than to be standing at the threshold of all the world with no key to enter."

For those with the keys, the Carpenter and Mackenzie volumes were a giveaway: Fred's was a world of men who loved men. Jimmy sang Laurence Hope's "Indian Love Lyrics"—"Pale hands I loved beside the Shalimar"—and Fred accompanied him on the piano. They went to Jane Addams's Hull House to see amateur theatricals and slummed in Halsted Street, touring through the crowded enclaves of Jewtown and Little Italy. Millett became the repository for Jimmy's confidences: his crushes (some reciprocated) on various Phi Gam boys; a visit to a brothel; a love affair with a gruff fellow student, a banker's son, who detested demonstrativeness and "went in for the masculine stuff."

Jimmy would have had his eyes opened anyway, he said later, "but the fact is that Fred B. Millett did it." Millett committed his own portrait of Jimmy to his diary. The boy was a wreck: "emotionally, he has the fluidity of dry sand; nervously, he is a chameleon; intellectually, he is a prodigy." In addition to the young men who came to Jimmy's room, talking for hours about "love, and the world, the Flesh and the Devil," Jimmy squired around debutantes, who asked him to tea dances and concerts. According to Millett: "He is brilliant socially; he can be, and usually is, very charming but his egotism and his heartlessness make him frequently and thoughtlessly brutal to people."

From the standpoint of book learning, Jimmy's college years were a bust. He rarely bothered to attend class. Intellectual developments on campus—most prominent among them the "Chicago School" of sociology, which probed the relation between the individual and the mass, self and society—passed him by. There was an exception or two: he immersed himself in a course on the decline of the Ottoman Empire, fascinated by the personage of Ibn Saud, who preached holy war for a purified Islam and would become the founder of Saudi Arabia and its first monarch. But on the whole, Jimmy treated the place like a country club, enrolling in classes that he could ace without trying. "Snaps," they were called then.

Later on, when he came to reflect on his time at the University of Chicago, what struck him was how insulated he'd been from world events. In that sense, he was a typical American young person of the era, he supposed. He learned to fox-trot but knew nothing of the Bolshevik revolution that erupted his first year at college. As the war's victors gathered in 1919–20 at the Paris Peace Conference to dispose of the problems of defeated states and broken empires, Jimmy was composing "Barbara, Behave!" for the Blackfriars' annual student revue. It was still alarmingly easy to live your life ignorant of the world's affairs.

In 1920 Jimmy considered breaking off his education because he'd run up piles of debt and didn't see the point any longer. He left to work, first for the *Detroit Times,* then as the tutor to the son of a Chicago meatpacking tycoon. He'd write a novel, he decided, and had a long talk with the publisher Alfred Knopf, who urged him to be quick about it as "the novel of youth by youth happens to be tremendously in vogue now." He would title the book, *The Passionate Years: A Book of Preludes.*

His mother wanted him to return to the university and sold the last of her shares in Colorado oil stocks to fund another couple of terms. But she hadn't been well for some time, and in January 1921, she died. The cause of death was anemia; she was fifty-two. The night of her death, Jimmy locked himself in her sitting room and pounded out on the piano Liszt's transcription of the Rigoletto quartet again and again. At her funeral, he remained standing during the prayers, refusing to kneel. Everyone in Pana was shocked by Jimmy's behavior. Years later, whenever he heard the first verse of the Illinois state song—"By thy rivers gently flowing, Illinois, Illinois"—he broke down in tears.

———

THE NEW YORK PAPER that hired Jimmy in 1921 was a fledgling enterprise with a people-pleasing idea. Give the masses the stories they want, the more ghoulish or titillating, the better. Lead with pictures—plenty of them, especially on the front page. A murderess, masked and strapped into the electric chair at Sing-Sing. Spice up the look with thundering typography and cracking headlines (Dead!, with a baseball bat–sized exclamation point). And advertise the novelty of the venture with a new format: a newspaper that the ordinary straphanger could read on the subways, its pages little more than half the size of the standard broadsheet.

Founded in 1919, the New York *Daily News* was America's first tabloid. The idea that sensation sells wasn't, of course, new in the 1920s. From the 1880s, the buccaneers of yellow journalism—Joseph Pulitzer and William Randolph Hearst—had been trading shrieking headlines. For those theorists who'd hoped that newspapers would foster a national intelligence, the advent of the tabloid, on the heels of the yellow press, proved a worrying development. If newspapers were the medium through which people experienced the world, then what sort of world did the sensational press offer its readers? Part brothel, part variety show, part advertising gimmick, answered its critics. Rather than educating the public to be responsible citizens, the tabloid played on people's worst instincts.

From the start, the *Daily News* had its detractors but it soon had many more imitators. By 1926, the paper was selling more than a million copies a day, and new tabloids were mushrooming across the country. Unlike most of its Victorian yellow press predecessors, the tabloid had staying power with a mass readership. Personalities were the thing, the more dazzling the better: Babe Ruth's gargantuan sexual appetites, the gangster "Legs" Diamond's skill in bullet-dodging, the shameless graft of Chicago's mayor "Big Bill" Thompson, and New York's Jimmy Walker. Within the decade, tabloids had become as essential a part of urban life as the jazz band, the cocktail, and the skyscraper.

The editors who took on Jimmy figured (correctly) that the handsome young man with the curled lip would prove an asset in courting the confessions of murderesses and philandering wives. Not long after he started at the *Daily News*, the quarrel between a prominent New York banker and his wife made its first appearances in the headlines. Mrs. Stillman was a sweet-faced society beauty with notably slim ankles who had made the bandanna her trademark headdress. Her husband James was a millionaire and president of the National City Bank of New York. Stillman alleged that the couple's toddler son was in fact the progeny of a Mohawk guide whom his wife had met at the family's lodge in the Quebec wilderness. Mrs. Stillman countersued, accusing her husband of maintaining a stable of hennaed mistresses and having his own illegitimate offspring.

It didn't take long for Jimmy to win Mrs. Stillman's confidence. Her pictures didn't begin to do her smoky hair or haughty prettiness justice, he reported. He was soon filing exclusive interviews with her, dispatches from a Hudson Valley wheat field and the subdued, tasteful drawing room of her Fifth Avenue apartment. My husband is worse than a Bolshevik, she insisted. Just look at the damage he is inflicting on American morality and family life. In Jimmy's telling, Mrs. Stillman was a charming innocent, a demure and devoted mother, emblematic of all the women done wrong. He so thoroughly championed her side that there was talk that he, too, would be named a co-respondent in the trial.

The final act in the drama was a twist Jimmy's readers could not have anticipated. On a trip into the North Woods of Canada to try to clear Anne Stillman's name, Jimmy became friendly with the Mohawk guide. The man had in his possession four love letters that proved the affair beyond a doubt. Now Jimmy switched sides, acting on behalf of the wronged husband. Following a hasty series of conferences called in a Montreal hotel room, he purchased the letters from the guide and turned them over to Stillman's private detective. Mrs. Stillman's lover wanted $25,000 for the letters but Jimmy bargained him down to $15,000. Even for a tabloid reporter acting in what the *New York Times* called "a purely personal capacity," it was a cool piece of betrayal. In the spring of 1922, Jimmy left in a big hurry for Paris.

WHY NOT GO? IN the early 1920s, that was the question that many young women in America were asking themselves. For the previous generation, it would have been nearly unthinkable for a young lady, on her own say-so and unchaperoned, to catch a steamer bound for Europe. But after the war, American girls were piling into high schools and then proceeding to colleges. They cast ballots. Some of them also jettisoned their corsets, bobbed their hair, drank Manhattans, and procured cervical caps. They didn't ask anyone's permission to go where they wanted.

It was in that spirit that twenty-six-year-old Frances Fineman left New York in the summer of 1924, bound for Moscow via Paris, Berlin, and Vienna. Unlike John and Jimmy, her trip was something of a return journey. Frances's parents were Russian Jews who had immigrated to America several decades earlier. The story of her family, Frances said, was transplantation, upheaval, and an unavailing search for soft earth into which to plant their roots. Every time, including in America, they'd hit stone instead, and clung on, buffeted by the storms.

Frances was born in New York City on the thirteenth of September, 1897, but her mother, Sonia, fearing the date unlucky, insisted that her father register the birth three days later. Sonia Fineman had fled her village south of Kiev after the Cossack raiders had jeered that they'd be back to take the blond Jewess. Sonia had eyes that were blue as the dawn, and, like Frances herself, smooth, pale skin and curly hair the color of pale amber. Into her trunks Sonia packed her goose-down pillows, not trusting in the bedding of the New World. Her elder sister, the village bluestocking, accompanied her to America.

Sonia met her first husband, Frances's father, in New York. He loved her; she tolerated him. She was vital and vigorous, practically illiterate but a capable businesswoman. In her fabric store on Second

Avenue and 102nd Street, she sold the finest silks and muslins and velvets; customers traveled all the way from Madison Avenue for one of Mrs. Fineman's bargains. Frances's father was a mustachioed dreamer, a chaser of utopias: he'd come to America because he'd read of Emerson and the Transcendentalists at Brook Farm. He ought to have married Sonia's sister, a fellow intellectual—she was actually in love with him—but he wanted the younger girl. On the night of her marriage, Sonia had prayed to her dead father, a rabbinical scholar, to watch over her.

"Papa is a philosopher. You must always have respect for your papa," insisted her mother when Frances was a child. He didn't drink, he didn't gamble. But his children could tell that he considered them an encumbrance: "I like the cow, but I don't care for the calves," he said. Her parents divorced when Frances was three and her brother, Bernie, was five. The children trundled between their parents' shops: his, in a poorer district far uptown, sold cigars, newspapers, and candy. All day long, her father sat, smoking Sweet Caporals and reading the newspapers, his chair in the doorway. He lived in a room at the back: a table and two chairs, a bed, a gas stove. He made the children lunch, scrambled eggs with pink rounds of wurst. Frances wanted to talk to him but never could.

Her mother had three rooms behind her store. Until Frances was thirteen, she slept in the big double bed with her mother, her back against Mama's soft body. "Do you want to go back into Mama's belly?" her mother would ask. Frances's answer was always yes. One night she awoke to find her mother gone. In the next room, there Mama was, stretched out, asleep, on a makeshift bed made of the parlor chairs. Sleeping beside her was a strange man. Soon enough, Frances had a stepfather.

FOR FRANCES AND HER friends, the lives of their mothers appeared unfathomable. What did those careworn women have to show for themselves? Thirty years of married life, with two husbands, and yet never any pleasure, her mother admitted to her. What Sonia knew of the sex act was far worse than ignorance would have been, Frances noted. She had been told it was for men to enjoy and for women to suffer through. Was there a woman of her own generation, Frances wondered, who had questioned her mother about sex and *not* been appalled by the answers?

When her mother moved the family to Texas to join her new husband, Frances finished high school in Galveston. But at the very first opportunity, she was on a midnight train back to New York. She enrolled at Barnard College in the winter of 1916. Like the University of Chicago, Barnard was a relatively new institution, founded in 1889 after Columbia's board of trustees refused to admit women who had petitioned for higher education. Unlike the University of Chicago, Barnard was poor, as were all women's colleges then. The college's first class of students, all nine of them, matriculated in a four-story brownstone on Madison Avenue, taking their lessons in makeshift classrooms fashioned from bedrooms and making do with a couple of shelves of books in a front room in place of a library. A few decades later, when Frances and her 150 or so classmates arrived at Barnard, most of the trappings of collegiate life were in place, though the facilities still didn't bear comparison to those at nearby Columbia. There was now a small campus in Morningside Heights and a library with tens of thousands of volumes. Barnard students were even permitted to attend Columbia classes. The college had developed traditions such as the Greek Games, at which the freshman and sophomore classes, wearing billowing togas, competed in chariot racing, discus throwing, poetry composition, and other classical arts. A roster of student clubs vied for members, among them the Socialist Club and the Journalism Club, both of which Frances joined in her first year.

That Frances would attend university had never been in doubt. Opting for a university education was no longer the flame-throwing or even eccentric decision that it had been for an earlier generation. By 1920, nearly half of the college students in the United States were women, a development decades in the making. Having kicked over some of the barriers to a full life, the others seemed surmountable. A few months after arriving at Barnard, Frances addressed the Journalism Club on the subject of Rabindranath Tagore's play *Chitra*, the story of a warrior princess who finds love without surrendering anything of herself. Over late-night mugs of cocoa, Frances and her classmates swore that they, too, would live for themselves. Their galoshes unbuckled, stockings rolled down, hair clipped close, they would partake of all the forbidden experiences. Half of the brainpower of the world was still a virtually untapped resource.

Compared to the other women's colleges, Barnard had a reputation for radicalism. By 1916, debates about American neutrality were sparking up on campus. Should the United States take sides in the conflict engulfing Europe? In February 1917, after Germany and the United States broke off diplomatic ties, Columbia's men approved a resolution calling for the university to put its full resources at the disposal of the American government. Barnard's women retorted by passing a measure condemning war. They "had been taught to think," noted the college's official history, "and thinking is painful in wartime."

Once the United States entered the war, 80 percent of Barnard's women came around to the cause. They labored on farms, bringing in the summer harvest; they raised money for the Red Cross and a Columbia ambulance unit; they rolled bandages. But not Frances. By now the secretary-treasurer of the Socialist Club, reading Marx and Lenin, she was attending meetings, agitating against militarism and for world peace. She was also consorting with radical professors at Columbia, whose anti-war activities would lead to their dismissal.

In the spring and summer of 1917, the campus in Morningside Heights was awash in protest. Columbia's president, Nicholas Murray Butler, suspended academic freedom for the duration of the war, one of the few university leaders to do so. Butler defined pacifism as sedition: "What had been folly, was now treason," he declared. Students and faculty members gathered on the steps of the library to rally against the university administration. Soon there would be a wholesale purge of pacifist faculty, they cried. The renowned historian Charles Beard resigned his position in protest, denouncing Columbia's leadership as "reactionary and visionless in politics, narrow and medieval in religion."

That June, Nicholas Murray Butler himself insisted on Frances's expulsion. She was one of five Barnard troublemakers whose presence on Morningside Heights the dictatorial Butler could no longer abide. The Barnard dean, Virginia Gildersleeve, a protégée of Butler's, tried to save her. Frances, Dean Gildersleeve pleaded, was merely irresponsible and had been led astray by others. She wasn't "guilty of any overt act serious enough to actually warrant our dropping her from College." Better not to wait around until Miss Fineman did something outrageous, Butler retorted. It was unwise to waste a Barnard education on such an "undesirable person." Frances was booted out.

Getting expelled from colleges would become something of a point of pride for Frances. She enrolled for a year at the Rice Institute in Houston, near her mother. She was tossed out of Rice when the president there learned more about the circumstances of her dismissal from Barnard. That was fine, Rice didn't suit her. So many inane rules: "Tennis shoes shall be put on and taken off in the building and not on the Quadrangle. Students must not go off the College grounds without hats on . . ." It was as if they'd admitted women to colleges only to corset them more tightly than ever before.

Still, Frances wanted an education and managed to talk her way into Radcliffe, where the dean extracted a pledge of good behavior in exchange for admission on a trial basis. She made this allowance because of the very promising nature of Miss Fineman's academic work. "You will enjoy talking with her if you take her in," Dean Gildersleeve had written her Radcliffe counterpart. "She is rather conceited, decidedly clever, and a somewhat interesting character."

In a series of tiny leatherette, college-issued diaries, Frances kept track of the ways that life might sweep her away. At Barnard in 1916, Mr. Laidlaw of the International Socialist Society—she was a regular at the Wednesday evening meetings—spoke winningly to her over the telephone. Three years later, there was the little navy ensign

from Yale. He announced to her: "You arouse my natural instinct—
I want to spank you."

Then there was the boy who told her he'd ceased to love her, chiding: you can't hold on to a man's love.

"Perhaps—I don't care to?" she replied.

She wrote love letters to the journalist Lewis Gannett whom she'd known in New York and received in return, a poem from his new bride:

> *Frances, whom I've never seen*
> *Gray-eyed maiden of nineteen . . .*
> *For he who should write verse to me*
> *Spends dawns on gray eyes, not on brown.*

Her height, Frances recorded, was five feet, one inch, her weight was 110. She needed to acquire a black georgette dinner dress and a pair of black satin pumps.

A night with the socialist Dorothy Day, luncheon with the best-selling novelist Fanny Hurst, an interview with Mrs. Vincent Astor, a socialite. Frances's days were a whirl. The Labour Party intellectual Harold Laski, who was teaching at Harvard, took a shine to her. Tea at the Laskis with a handful of other students, "all very stiff and formal and stupid," she judged. The *Radcliffe Magazine* wanted an article from her.

Working on a play, Turgenev with a twist: "First Love & Well What Are You Going to Die For." Reading F. Scott Fitzgerald's *This Side of Paradise*. A marvel! How perfectly a Princeton boy of twenty-three had understood the psychology of the flapper. "If I could only turn out something like that this summer." One night very late, a soul-to-soul with a Radcliffe friend. "I've been evading such encounters—they eat me out." The friend had a sharpness about her and understood Frances better than anyone else. "There's something masculine about her," Frances reflected. "She kissed me good night a lot."

Frances would later claim she'd gotten kicked out of Radcliffe, too, but there's no evidence of that in her student file. Instead, after her trial year in Cambridge, she moved back to New York. Dean Gildersleeve quietly reinstated Frances as a student at Barnard College in the fall of 1920. A formidable advocate for women's advancement, Gildersleeve had been toiling to open Columbia's professional schools to women, a battle she eventually won (everywhere but the Engineering School) when she offered to handpick the female matriculants herself. Now women college graduates could go to law school or medical school, train as architects, engage in the field of public policy. Among Frances's fellow students at Barnard were Margaret Mead, who would become the most important anthropologist of her generation; Freda Kirchwey, who later became the editor of the left-wing weekly, the *Nation;* and the actor and politician Helen Gahagan Douglas, the first woman Democrat elected to the Congress from California. Theirs was the first generation of college-educated women who could fail professionally because they had the chance, however slim, to succeed.

When Frances finally graduated from Barnard in 1921, at the age of twenty-four, she had a battle cry: "Muddle-headedness is the only immorality." And an aim: "Life's ultimate goal: love in a cottage." But first she'd see the great Soviet experiment for herself.

OVER THERE

—

WHEN FRANCES ARRIVED IN EUROPE IN THE SUMMER OF
1924, she called herself a journalist, which was a bit of a
stretch since she'd never worked on a newspaper and no editor had
sent her there. She'd done publicity for a vaudeville troupe, labored
in a brassiere factory in Newark, and, after graduating from Barnard,
had gone out to Hollywood for six months to try her hand at script-
writing. But until she left for the Continent, a few hundred dollars
in her pocketbook, her experience in reporting was confined to student efforts. She was no innocent abroad, though. Unlike John and
Jimmy, who liked to emphasize their American freshness and ignorance, Frances had read the classic texts of Marxism with Harold
Laski and the Wednesday Socialist Club, attended Dadaist art shows
and constructivist theater, and undergone a yearlong psychoanalysis
at the hands of Dr. Philip Lehrman in New York. She was paying
attention to the world.

But what was the story that needed telling? There were so many
in those years immediately after the war, with the old world shattered and new possibilities on every horizon. One could take an in-
ventory of the ruins: the millions of dead and wounded, the
empires—Habsburg, German, Russian, and Ottoman—swept away
in the war's wake. The better choice for a young reporter was to try

to predict what was to come. Was the future being made in Geneva at the League of Nations, where an experiment in world government was under way? Or was it happening, instead, in the capitals of the fledgling democracies—in Prague, Vienna, and Berlin? Empires surely were on their last legs. Or were they? The British and French empires were now bigger than ever.

Choosing the right story could make a young reporter's reputation, and stringers had no need to hedge their bets. Would the Bolshevik revolution catch fire beyond Russia as Lenin and Trotsky had so confidently predicted? If that was what one believed, then Moscow or Budapest or even Shanghai was the place to go. On the other hand, perhaps reaction, and not revolution, was the future. The autocratic Romanoffs of Russia were dead and gone, but could the other deposed monarchs of Europe manage to scramble back onto their thrones?

For Frances, the choice had been clear since her student days. Her destination was Moscow. She put her wager on the spread of Bolshevism. The success of the Russian Revolution, so it was thought, would spark communist revolutions in other industrialized countries, as the socialist parties of Germany, France, and Britain shook off their complacent reformism and seized power violently. But with a few exceptions—chief among them, the journalist Béla Kun's soviet regime in Hungary, which had lasted all of 133 days—the worldwide dictatorship of the proletariat seemed, by the early 1920s, at the very least delayed. Perhaps socialism would have to be built in one country first.

In Berlin, awaiting a visa to visit the Soviet Union, Frances arranged to interview the dancer Isadora Duncan, who had left the ballet school she'd established in New York for a new life in Moscow. "I love the people," Duncan told her, recounting her experiences performing a dance for the Red Army set to the tune of the Internationale. Duncan was dressed in a demure, lilac-colored Chinese mandarin coat, but her conversation was bloodcurdling. She'd told a noblewoman who'd brought her a box of chocolates: People like you in Russia are stood against the wall and shot. "I always say things like that to such people," she boasted to Frances. Duncan's vengeful talk was "bitter and foolish," Frances thought, but she nevertheless found the dancer captivating. The Soviet Union needed journalists, Duncan told Frances: "You will be our Joan of Arc." At the door, she pressed her fur coat on Frances. "Take it," she said, "I have another"— and kissed her goodbye.

Frances's first glimpse of Leningrad, where she arrived by train on a wet, windy day in October, seven years after the Revolution, wasn't encouraging. What was there to write about in such a drab, gloomy place? This was hardly a paradise. The people were poorly dressed, the cobblestone streets torn up and muddy because of a flood the previous month; there was nothing at all in the shops worth buying; and the entire city was plastered in hectoring signs. "Stop Fascism!" "Stop leftist capitalism-social-democracy!" Leningrad smelled like the steerage class on a ship: sweat plus coal smoke plus dank grime. And she only had $25 to her name.

Although Frances looked frail—like an orphaned child with the croup, as a friend put it—she wasn't at all shy about asking favors of strangers, even famous ones. In Moscow, she went backstage to see the director Vsevolod Meyerhold, proposing to write an article about him. She knew an editor at the *New York Times* who would be interested. Come to the rehearsal, see how we work, yes, tomorrow— come, Meyerhold told her. Her Russian was no good but they could converse in German. Hailed today as a pioneer of modern theater, Meyerhold was then at the height of a career that had jettisoned every convention of the realistic stage. Mechanical poses and gestures, he decided, conveyed much more than words. He branded his experiments of the early 1920s "biomechanics," and demanded that his actors vault, puppet-like, around the stage at his command. Fired by revolutionary ideals, Meyerhold sought to use untrained workers rather than professional actors in his productions and gave away tickets; the sets were sparse and mechanical in flavor, with scaffolding and ladders the main props.

It was a novel and thrilling way of seeing the new world the Russian Revolution had wrought and it proved the fuel Frances required.

In a country where the theater excited as much commentary as the World Series did in America, the Soviet stage, she wrote, conveyed something of the thoroughgoing newness of the place. The devotion to the machine, the rethinking of human emotion: these were evident in work of Meyerhold; the set designer Isaac Rabinovich; the young film director Sergei Eisenstein, with whom Frances had also started to keep company. She couldn't help but to be impressed by the audacity of the experiments, the way that theater audiences, given all the changes they'd witnessed in daily life, were prepared to entertain any innovation, at least once. "Besides, everything in Russia is drama," she wrote a friend.

She used to laugh at people who felt after a few months in Russia that they had to write a book about it but now she was thinking along those same lines. The combination of material privation and the headiness of intellectual life, the sense of communal purpose. The West ought to take heed of what was happening in the Soviet Union. "I think this thread of unity is what we miss so much at home, for all our boasting of our individualistic freedom." Moreover, she owed it to geniuses like Meyerhold to make them known worldwide. She wrote up her impressions of the performances she'd seen and sent them to the *Times,* which ran the articles. By comparison to the triumph of American capital across Europe, the dictatorship of the Russian proletariat was "child's play," she joked with Meyerhold in a letter, including a clipping of her *Times* article. Oh, yes, and send my greetings to Frau Meyerhold, Frances added. I know she doesn't like me, but that's because she doesn't know me.

After four months in the Soviet Union, Frances had encountered many of the other American correspondents there: the burly Louis Fischer, an intellectual bruiser dressed in the collarless, homespun shirt of the Soviet worker, who called her "an impertinent and charming rascal"; Walter Duranty, who reported for the *New York Times,* later to become notorious for his denial of the Ukrainian famine; Junius Wood, the *Daily News* man with a shaved head, who once sent an opened piece of his mail, spotted with the censor's green ink, back to the Moscow post office with the note, "Fire this fellow, he's careless." The correspondents comprised "one big, almost permanent poker party," as Louis Fischer put it, and there was hardly a woman at the table. But in Vienna, before leaving for Moscow, Frances had met one reporter who had the career she imagined for herself.

Dorothy Thompson had invited Frances over to the apartment she shared with her Hungarian husband, Joseph Bard. Dorothy looked like a sports teacher at a girl's school: a healthy complexion, a square, friendly face, the modern woman's bob, and sturdy legs in white stockings. Four years earlier, in 1920, she'd started out as Frances had, with little more than a university degree, a brief stint as a publicist, a pocketbook of savings, and the ambition to succeed in a profession for which she had practically no training. "A young girl like that," Dorothy's Methodist minister father had marveled, equal measures disapproval and astonishment, "and running around Europe." He didn't know the half of it. The Reverend Thompson had understood that Dorothy was going to stay with his cousin in England, but then she'd written to tell him she was off to Russia. "I shall write and forbid her," he said but didn't. "My impatient child. Fly away little bird," he'd teased when she was a little girl, sitting on his knee. Now Dorothy was the Vienna correspondent for the Philadelphia *Public Ledger*, and even the grizzled reporters had to admit that the stories she'd broken had plenty of red meat.

"I HAVE BEEN A 'wild cat walking by my wild lone self' most of my life since 16," wrote Dorothy Thompson to a friend in 1921. When Dorothy was seven, her mother had died of septicemia. The Reverend Thompson remarried a couple of years later, but when Dorothy didn't get along with her new stepmother, he sent her to Chicago to live with his sisters and attend a private school. She went to dances but, as befitted a minister's daughter, didn't dance. Instead, she read voraciously: the Bible, of course, George Eliot, Walt Whitman,

Dickens, Mark Twain, Shakespeare, and history by the barrowful. According to a classmate, Dorothy talked of tariffs while young men tried to romance her on moonlit balconies.

Her family didn't have the money for her to attend Bryn Mawr or Vassar, the colleges she might have hoped for. If Dorothy wanted a university education (and she was certain that she did), she'd have to take up the scholarship that Syracuse University offered to the children of the Methodist clergy. By her senior year, she was—as ran the title of a talk she gave on campus—"Outgrowing Things." Small-town life, formal religion, injunctions not to argue. Even in high school, she'd clambered out of her seat and proceeded through the aisles, gesticulating. What if man had invented God, and not vice versa? she wondered. Might science, she asked her father, be a better guarantor of progress than the church?

Yet moral certainties came easily to her, the inheritance, not un-common, of a preacher's child. "I used to feel, *really* feel, that the gods loved me," she remembered. She threw herself into the cam-paign for women's suffrage in New York state, cajoling, browbeating, and charming her audiences in upstate hamlets; speechifying from bunting-decorated stages before baseball games and Fourth of July parades; meeting the leading citizens of every town; drumming up local suffrage committees. After the New York franchise was won in November 1917, she moved to Cincinnati as director of publicity for a new venture in community organizing, the National Social Unit Organization. The Social Unit's aim was to deliver on the ideals of democracy by organizing the poor to demand medical care for their communities. But then Cincinnati's mayor accused the project of importing Bolshevism to his city, and when Dorothy fell in love with the Social Unit's founder, who was married, it was time to leave. She wanted to see the real Bolshevism, to tour the Soviet Union and write about it. Her gambit to secure a bank loan for the trip to Europe—pitched as a down payment on a career in foreign correspondence—failed, so she and a friend from the suffrage cam-paign combined their savings and went anyway.

When Dorothy arrived in Europe in 1920, American papers were just coming around to the notion that they ought to hire Americans to report from abroad. There had long been star "special" correspondents, especially in wartime, men such as Richard Harding Davis, whose good looks and jingoist tales of adventure from the Spanish-American War of 1898 had made him a sensation. But for regular dispatches from foreign countries, most American papers had relied on wire services such as Reuters and the Associated Press, which in turn drew on the local press. This changed with the war, the fifty thousand Doughboys dead in France, and the settlement at Versailles. Now Americans required their own eyes and ears abroad. Never again would the Europeans, particularly the British, trick naïve Yankees into a costly Continental entanglement. Seven papers were building up extensive foreign news services: the *Chicago Daily News,* the *New York Times,* the *New York Herald Tribune,* the *Christian Science Monitor,* the *Chicago Tribune,* and the Philadelphia *Evening Ledger.*

Nearly as soon as Dorothy arrived in Europe, legends began to gather around her. The woman's timing, it was said, was uncanny. Hours before the Lord Mayor of Cork, Terence MacSwiney, was dragged away by British police on charges of sedition, she stopped by his office for an interview—"long" and "exclusive," in her description. It turned out to be MacSwiney's last; he died two months later after a hunger strike in prison. For American papers, breathlessly reporting on MacSwiney's death by starvation, Dorothy's story was front-page news; she had detected a "flash of premonition" in the Martyred Mayor's eyes. Then there were the stories that circulated about her determination: she was a cross between "the Goddess Minerva and the engines of the S.S. Normandie," as John Gunther would later describe her.

You need a reporter in Vienna, she informed the Philadelphia *Public Ledger.* After a ten-day visit to the city, she had a hunch that the problems of east-central Europe—nationalist grievances combined with economic dislocation—were storing up trouble for the future. "You ought to send me there," she insisted. The terms weren't what she had hoped for. She could call herself a special correspondent, said the *Ledger,* but she'd only be paid for what she wrote, a glorified freelancer in fact. But together with publicity work she was doing for the Red Cross at 10 francs per 100 lines, it was enough, and it gave her a perch in Vienna.

Before the First World War, Vienna's Beaux-Arts palaces and chestnut-lined boulevards had anchored an empire of fifty-five million people. It was a cream-skimming capital, "the London of an empire which did not lie in far-off lands, but at its very door," as Dorothy put it. For centuries the Viennese had lived off the sweat of the Hungarians, the Croats, the Romanians; out of their scrabbling labor conjured jewels in velvet-lined cases and magnificently plumed teams of milky-gray stallions. In those days, the Habsburg Empire stretched from the sharp limestone coasts of the Adriatic to the northern coalfields of Silesia, from the eastern Carpathian Mountains in present-day Ukraine to the mountainous Tyrol in the west. For more than a half-millennium, starting in the fifteenth century, the empire had been ruled by the Continent's longest-lived dynasty. The Habsburg Empire had the third-largest population in Europe. At the start of the war, its army issued mobilization orders in fifteen languages.

The collapse of the empire at the end of the war came, fittingly, in a series of revolts and revolutions so strung out as to set a hundred arguments running about when (and if) Habsburg rule was finished. In Hungary, the socialist Red Count, Michael Károlyi, came to power in October 1918; a few weeks later, another revolution in Vienna declared an Austrian Republic; in Prague, in Zagreb, in Galicia, in Lemberg, in Bucharest people tore the imperial eagle, the symbol of the Crown, off of their uniforms and government buildings. In November, Emperor Karl of Habsburg relinquished the Austrian throne, departing Schönbrunn Palace as plain old Herr Habsburg in a taxi. When the empire was formally sawn apart at the Paris Peace Conference, the remnant called Austria was no bigger than the state of Illinois, its population just six million people, more than two million of whom lived in the capital. Vienna was a swollen head on a dismembered torso with exactly the prognosis to be expected in such a situation. Yoked to a reactionary countryside poor in farmland and other natural resources, the city was governed by Socialists, a party that was anathema to the hinterland.

It was impossible to do justice to the situation unfolding in east-central Europe, the newspapermen grumbled to their editors, all the more so as the Vienna beat, by convention, extended right down to the Black Sea: Albania, Bulgaria, Czechoslovakia, Hungary, Yugoslavia, Romania, Greece, and Turkey were all part of it. Each country had its own set of characters to master, though the problems were mostly the same: bankrupt treasuries, hatchet-faced veterans toting carbines, populations aflame with resentments. Reporting from the territory required at least four months of travel every year. Because no American paper had a formal bureau in Vienna, the work had to be managed without an office or even a secretary, and stringers couldn't be counted on for much. "Wolves had gotten into such and such a village in Herzegovina and had eaten up a 13-year-old girl," was the way that Dorothy characterized the Yugoslav stringer's annual spring dispatches. "Vienna Special Correspondent" became the job that editors assigned to energetic young men with ambition, a trial run for the most important posts in Paris, London, and Berlin. For Dorothy, it was a prize.

The trick of reporting, as Dorothy put it, was figuring out what you wanted to know, and then finding the people who could tell you. Much of the knowledge she acquired early on in Vienna came from Marcel Fodor, a Hungarian working for the *Manchester Guardian.* "Let me explain you," began Fodor, proceeding to a primer on the intrigues of Balkan politics or a disquisition on the decay of the Magyar aristocracy, culminating in the night at Sacher's Restaurant when Archduke Something-or-Other appeared stark naked, save for his fur cap. The scion of a banking family whose holdings included several Hungarian newspapers, Fodor's dandified ambitions as a young man—to paint, to live in Paris—had given way, under pressure from his parents, to more practical training as a chemical engineer. When the First World War came, he was living in England, and was interned there as an enemy alien. By the time he returned to Budapest in 1919, both of his parents were dead. With little in the way of training other than his prodigious knowledge of Habsburg history, acquired in evenings of reading on his father's yacht on the Dalmatian coast, he started filing pieces for the English-language press.

Dorothy and the owl-eyed Fodor soon made a reporting duo. Dapperly dressed when he could afford it, Fodor was short and running to fat. "Oh, the little dumplings of Vienna!" he would exclaim, patting his midsection with a sigh. Dorothy declined his offer of marriage without hard feelings on either side, and they were off. Fodor's connections opened doors. On a jaunt to Prague, Tomáš Masaryk, the founding father and first president of Czechoslovakia, gave the pair a five-hour interview. Then to parts east. In Belgrade, Dorothy scored exclusives with both Queen Marie of Romania and her daughter, the newly crowned queen of Yugoslavia. It was the young queen's first interview, and she confided to Dorothy that she was terrified. The business of a queen, she hazarded, was "to make a country more livable."

Articles about royalty became a staple of Dorothy's repertoire, and not just because she knew that Americans liked to read about eligible Romanian dukes and threadbare Russian princesses driving taxis. Although the First World War had swept away dynasties and courts, plumed stallions and gold-leafed throne rooms, the forces of reaction, she saw, were plotting a return, leaguing across borders in the "old militaristic, autocratic spirit." The Romanoffs, hauled out by the Bolsheviks and shot, wouldn't be returning: that was certain. But could the Hohenzollerns or the Habsburgs, not to mention the smaller dynasties—Prince Alexander of Serbia or King Carol II of Romania—connive their way back into power? They weren't giving up so easily. Maybe the counterrevolution, not the Bolshevik revolution, was the real story.

In particular, the restoration of the Habsburg monarchy was a possibility to be taken seriously in the early 1920s, far-fetched as the idea now seems. After a monumental sixty-seven years on the throne, the walrus-mustachioed emperor Franz Josef died in 1916. His great-nephew Karl understood that the empire needed to conciliate its subjects, but it was, by then, too late. When Karl departed Schönbrunn Palace in 1918, he hadn't formally abdicated the Hungarian crown but left a door open. Its borders slashed to barely one-third of their prewar size, Hungary had ricocheted in the course of two years from a Soviet Republic under the journalist Béla Kun to Admiral Horthy's right-wing military dictatorship. A Red Terror had given way to a White Terror that killed at least a thousand people identified as Socialists or Jews. Now monarchism was resurgent in Hungary.

When Karl sought to regain the Hungarian throne in 1921, then, he could plausibly claim that he was responding to his subjects' desperate pleas for help. An unlikely set of allies gathered around him: Social Democrats who loathed the reign of Admiral Horthy, irredentists who hankered for a return to Habsburg glories past. With the aid of a cadre of plotters, he flew to Hungary with his wife, Zita, on the twentieth of October, 1921; the couple's seven children remained behind in Switzerland. Within a few days, an entire regiment of the Hungarian army was swearing oaths of allegiance to Karl, and he and Zita proceeded to Budapest, accompanied by two thousand or so soldiers and cheering crowds on the way. On the outskirts of the city, the train halted. Admiral Horthy had called out the paramilitaries, forces he could count on, to battle with Karl's soldiers. Nineteen people died in the fighting that day. Fearing more violence, Karl decided to abandon his coup. Along with their fellow plotters, Karl and Zita were arrested and delivered to the Esterházy Castle in Tata, an hour's train ride from Budapest, to await Horthy's reckoning.

Dorothy had dashed off to Hungary on the Orient Express when she heard that Karl was en route to Budapest. So had the rest of the foreign press corps, but when they arrived, the news blackout was complete. The moated, gray stone castle at Tata rose from Lake Öreg, connected to land by a narrow drawbridge. While the reporters milled about on the shore, waiting impotently for snippets of gossip, Dorothy had an idea. Her boss at the American Red Cross was Captain James Pedlow, head of the organization in Hungary, and the man responsible for what little food the country's starving population was getting. Empress Zita was pregnant with her eighth child. Shouldn't a woman in the empress's fragile condition see a doctor? Dorothy asked. Pedlow took some persuading. But the next day, there was Pedlow, accompanied by Dorothy—dressed as a Red Cross nurse in a starched white uniform—driving across the narrow drawbridge to the Esterházy Castle.

For her readers, she set the scene. Her own trepidation, having stolen into the castle in disguise; the magnificent, romantic castle where Haydn had written the Habsburgs' anthem. Seated around the tea table were Karl, dressed in a Hungarian general's uniform, and Zita in navy-blue silk, dignified and serene; the aged Count Andrássy, a plotter, who was complaining that he'd been in the same dirty linen for four days; the daughter of the house, Lulu Esterházy, guileless and reckless, whose lover was one of the conspirators. Among the morose house-prisoners was Rakowsky, whom Karl had designated as his government's premier: a "puffy-eyed, heavy man who sipped his tea and ate scrambled eggs in gloomy silence." A few days earlier, as Karl proceeded to Budapest, Rakowsky had called the Hungarian prime minister on the phone to demand his resignation. "Steady old boy," the prime minister replied. "We will wait a few days before determining who shall do the hanging."

"I would not spill a drop of Hungarian blood for a thousand thrones," Karl told her, explaining why he'd abandoned his bid for the Hungarian crown. The Empress Zita asked Dorothy to send a telegram to her son in Switzerland, the nine-year-old Crown Prince Otto, reassuring him that his parents were unharmed: "We are all well. Please do not worry. We embrace you tenderly. Mama." The royal couple and their children would be exiled to the Portuguese island of Madeira, where Karl died the following year of pneumonia. The exclusive interview with the Habsburgs was Dorothy's, all the other newsmen caught flat-footed: "If I could scoop them all I felt I'd die happy," she told a friend.

At the Café Louvre in Vienna or in the bar at the Hotel Adlon in Berlin, Dorothy was the center of every circle of reporters, arguing, laughing, telling stories, her pink cheeks flushed with good health, able to hold any amount of liquor. She might have been wrong about the Habsburg restoration, but her adventure at Tata was just the start of the chase. She commandeered planes and found cars where no one else could. When she needed a visa to travel to the Balkans, she forged one and adorned it with the red seal from a coffee can. On another occasion, she got her dispatches past a censorship cordon by first wiring what she described as "a most intimately affectionate, not to say compromising message" to the country's leader. "She was a Richard Harding Davis in evening gown," observed a fellow reporter. "Nothing prosaic ever happened to her."

Late one night in 1926 she borrowed money from Sigmund Freud (whom she'd interviewed) so that she could travel to Poland to cover Marshal Piłsudski's seizure of power. Proceeding with a crisp briskness, she went on to interview Atatürk, Trotsky, Gustav Stresemann, Alexandra Kollontai, Hitler. She cultivated her own legend, of course, turning her talent for publicity to advantage but even the old-timers paid her a grudging respect. Whose brains, extracted and pickled in formaldehyde, would make the best paperweight? Dorothy's, chimed in the men whom she bested.

How had she done it? the editors of the *Nation* asked her, requesting an article on the difficulties ("if any") she had encountered in her ascent through the ranks.

That's a silly question, she replied. She had no truck with the "see-what-the-little-darling-has-done-now" attitude. Didn't everyone now agree on the general matter of women's intelligence? (Genius, she noted mischievously, wasn't a trait required of the newspaperman.) She'd needed to cultivate her intellect, of course. It helped, too, to have good nerves and a sense of humor, as well as the willingness to be an outsider. What she didn't say, but might have, is that it was easier for a woman to get a foothold in a new field. The European men she dealt with, Dorothy noted, weren't in the least bit surprised by her interest in politics or economics. It was only American editors who seemed to think female reporters were best employed on women's pages, writing of hairstyles and ladies' clubs.

If they tell you "you write like a man," Dorothy would later tell a group of women reporters, don't take it as a compliment. "That's only a man's badge of approval, and it doesn't mean anything."

ALTHOUGH DOROTHY AND FRANCES (and many others) arrived in Europe with barely a shred of reporting to their names, John's effort to get a job with the *Daily News*'s foreign service was a different matter. As his bosses in Chicago had explained, it was a plum post, one intended for the most experienced newsmen. The aim of the paper's foreign service was not just to chronicle events as they happened. That was a task that could be left to the wire services, such as the Associated Press, Reuters, or the United Press. Rather, the *Daily News* expected its correspondents to look forward—to anticipate those events or ideas or people "which seem likely to influence the destinies of nations."

Theirs was the work of interpretation: of explaining why an event had happened, and what it meant. "We have therefore to be clearer, more analytical, more thorough, less superficial, more cautious, more generally accurate, and perhaps more conscientious, than most of our competitors," proclaimed Paul Scott Mowrer, head of the paper's Paris bureau. The correspondent, Mowrer continued, was expected to exercise personal initiative, to be resourceful and energetic, to chase up "a big thing" of his own, thoroughly investigating it. If he had the prospect of scooping a competitor, he could cable the story to the New York office, remembering that it had to be received by eleven A.M. to make the early afternoon edition of the paper. If it wasn't a story that would go stale, though, he should instead write a "mailer," an article of 900 words dispatched by post, or if the subject merited it, a series of articles, though in that case the topic required vetting by Mowrer's Paris office.

Above all else, the *Daily News*'s correspondents were to consider the national interest. As Mowrer presented the matter, the paper's overseas reporting served a function that was part educative, part diplomatic. Americans needed to know about all manner of remote regions, even if they still didn't recognize that fact. Part of the job of the correspondent, then, was to raise the national intelligence by creating a demand for the news from abroad. They were to report how foreigners saw the world, "even when those viewpoints are unsympathetic to the United States." Taking sides "morally" was to be avoided, but the correspondent could, under certain limited conditions, offer his opinion—"if modestly formulated, and based on apparently sound data"—about the likely political or economic consequence of a given event or policy. The paper was particularly eager for stories about the unusual experiences of Chicagoans traveling abroad. To that end, the *Daily News*'s foreign offices were outfitted like men's clubs, with oriental rugs, potted palms, and leather armchairs; visiting Chicagoans were to be made welcome, especially if they had local contacts that could prove useful.

It was John's good fortune to turn up in the *Daily News*'s Trafalgar Square offices on a dreary fall day in 1924, when the correspondent there, Hal O'Flaherty, hadn't had a vacation in three years. O'Flaherty hired him immediately as a temporary helper. He had to talk the bosses back in Chicago into making an exception for a rookie like John.

After just a month in London, John informed his former flame Helen Hahn that he could already feel himself changing. English conversation was "appallingly brilliant" and London a charmingly elusive city, its gnarled medieval byways juxtaposed with the neon and glitz of Piccadilly Circus. However, the flappers were frumpy; none of the elevators had ceilings; the English apparently didn't believe in salting their food; and in London theaters, he had to sit like a spider, with his long legs practically folded under him. He was living in cold-water bachelor digs at a private men's club, the Connaught, with an enormous map of London tacked up on the wall, a photograph of Helen in an airplane hanging above his bureau, and his unfinished novel about her on his table.

"I am most extraordinarily aloof," he wrote Helen, "I am also most extraordinarily (for me) skeptical." Adding: "At any rate, I am achieving perspective."

At least in part, that was Rebecca West's doing. Shortly after arriving in London, he'd run into Rebecca at a party for the anarchist Emma Goldman. In Chicago, Rebecca had instructed him to look her up when he came to Europe. Now she renewed her invitation, and when a few weeks went by without a letter from him, she took the initiative. Why hadn't he come to see her? she demanded. Had he already starved to death? In that case, where should she send his bones? "Please consider me your mother, cousin, sister, and all other discreet female relatives during your stay in England."

In the white-paneled rooms of her South Kensington flat, she cooked him dinner, carelessly, leaving out the salt. He talked to her about his novel, provisionally titled "White Helen." He was taking as his subject the modern sort of girl who dallied with boys and worried she'd never fall in love. As John embarked upon a starstruck courtship of London's literary eminences, parlaying his letters of introduction into teas and lunches, Rebecca provided the necessary jaded counterpoint.

W. B. Yeats? Like an old walking stick parading among the umbrellas.

The playwright Michael Arlen, that pompous ass? She had named her icebox after him.

An embrace from Ford Madox Ford? Consider the plight of the toast under a poached egg.

See here, Rebecca said to John, we have to discuss those novels of yours. It took her, she told him, hours and hours to write two thousand words. Whereupon John returned to his room at the Connaught and burned the manuscript of his hastily drafted novel in the grate. "I like her," he confided to Helen. "I am also a little afraid of her."

When Rebecca met John, she was fresh out of the clutches of H. G. Wells. Their affair had started in 1913, after Wells invited the bold twenty-year-old critic to his house in Essex to discuss her slashing review of his last novel, *Marriage*. She had a decorous lunch with Wells and his wife. Within the year, she and H.G. were meeting in secret at his London flat. A "curious mixture of maturity and infantilism," he would describe her, noting "a big soft mouth" and "dark expressive troubled eyes." For nearly a decade, Rebecca had stuck with H.G.—for his sake, she told herself, even more for the sake of their son, Anthony, born just as the war started. She had tried to leave Wells a half-dozen times, only to have him hunt her down again, wheedling his way back. "Have I ever got in your arms to cry?" he pleaded when she left for Capri. "I would like to do that now."

The strain of the situation almost finished her. Dog-tired, taking care of a little boy on her own, her mother and sisters taking advantage of her, too. They'd all nearly bled her white, Rebecca said. Nonetheless, she'd written two well-regarded novels in the interval, *The Return of the Soldier* and *The Judge,* as well as tens of thousands of words of unsparing literary criticism in the *English Review,* the *New Statesman,* the *New Republic,* the *Daily News,* the *Daily Chronicle,* and *Time and Tide.* She had a knack for removing the "skin of her victims to the accompaniment of a happy laugh," as a friend put it. None of her contemporaries had to work under the conditions that she did, she complained. Hardly a surprise, then, that she succumbed to illness after illness: too many lung infections to count; an attack of colitis that caused agonies; a mouth full of aching teeth; an oozing, excruciating carbuncle on her hip.

During that winter and spring of 1924–25, John improved her spirits considerably. Unlike most men she knew, he didn't seem to mind playing second fiddle. They lunched at Claridge's with the courtesan Mrs. Melville, brows plucked high over her quizzical eyes, plastered in jewels, four snow-white Pomeranians lounging on the cream silk sofas. Rebecca is my only respectable friend, Mrs. Melville informed John. One afternoon they dreamed up ideas to torment a Hearst editor chasing Rebecca for a story. The editor was after scandal—the filthier and more sensational the better. He'd been sent to London to coax American-style first-person confessionals from the English. I know! Rebecca exclaimed, chortling. I'll propose: "How I Was Raped by the Archbishop of Canterbury."

The editor's proposals were no less ridiculous and much more insulting. He turned up at Rebecca's flat, proposing that she write essays on the following topics: "How It Feels to Be the Mistress of a Great Novelist" and "Why I Am Proud of My Bastard Son." No matter, Rebecca told John, who was outraged on her behalf. It was the Hearst enterprise. Can one complain, really, when a savage appears naked? "I Regard Marriage with Fear and Horror" was the essay she delivered and only because Hearst paid richly for it.

Just before John left for a holiday in France, one splendid spring afternoon in 1925, he and Rebecca swept through every shop in Mayfair, the tobacconists and the chinaware merchants, the perfumers and soap-makers. She tried on extravagant picture hats, John mugged with the guns at the colonial outfitters. On every street corner, they bought daffodils. They returned to Rebecca's flat in a tumult when she remembered she had a guest coming for tea. Rather unaccountably to her mind, he didn't try to take her to bed that night. She thought she'd made it quite clear to him that she was keen.

IF ONE WIELDED
THE LASH

—

THE FIRST NIGHT THAT JOHN SPENT WITH FRANCES, SHE PLAYED footsie with three different men, of whom he was one. It was a Saturday evening in May 1925, a couple of months after his daffodil afternoon with Rebecca. Back from his holiday on the French island of Porquerolles, John was on an assignment at the *Daily News* bureau in Paris. He'd met up with two friends larking on the Left Bank as would-be novelists. One of them was a college chum of his, the other, a fellow Chicagoan named Jerry Frank. After a course of psychoanalysis, Jerry would later abandon his novel, two-thirds finished, and become a New Dealer, a favorite of FDR's, and a federal Court of Appeals judge. Frances had just returned from Moscow and was writing a book about the revolution in Russian theater.

The evening started with dinner at the Savoyarde, where the Surrealists held court, on the terrace overlooking a Paris glimmering with lights. After dinner they moved on to cheap seats at the opera, then back up to Montmartre for a Russian cabaret before hitting two more nightclubs, the Canari and the Fantasio. The four Americans rounded out the evening with a midnight meal of greasy chicken and hours of driving in a taxicab through the Bois de Boulogne. A big talker, Jerry didn't shut up the whole night long.

Seven months after leaving Chicago, John still hadn't given up hope that he could spark some jealousy in the fickle Helen Hahn. He'd nearly finished a new novel, he informed her, much of which he'd written on his three-week holiday in Porquerolles. Titled *The Red Pavilion*, it told the story of a man shaking himself free from enslavement to the woman he loved. Oh, and the *Daily News* had offered him a job, he added. Also he'd met a girl. That last piece of information he mentioned casually, providing a teasing if not entirely alluring description ("a small corn-colored haired creature") and an account of the evening with Jerry Frank. "She was very good on that party, alone handling three men, and she did an excellent job, she should be congratulated," John noted.

He was more forthcoming when he turned that first dinner with Frances into a scene for a novel: "she tantalized him, excited him more than he'd been excited before." He took Frances out several more times, each occasion noted for Helen's benefit: to a party given by the novelist Ford Madox Ford ("England's most promising man for about forty years"), to an avant-garde performance of *Tristan*.

Then Helen's own announcement reached him. She was getting married. John tried to pretend he didn't mind but he stepped up the volley of news about Frances: "This Frances girl is fun. She is small and blond and has just returned from six months alone in Moscow whither she went looking for adventure." His friends started to call her the "fatal Frances." She barely came up to his shoulder.

That week, he sent the *Chicago Daily News* a profile of her for publication. "Miss Fineman lived alone in Moscow for six months and came out thinking that the bolsheviki are not so bad as they have been painted." "Of course prisoners are badly treated and non-communists are persecuted," he quoted her as saying. "But this is simply an evidence of Russia's temperament and tradition." Frances was furious about the article, John told Helen. "I am perhaps a little bit in love with this Frances child but that is possibly only reaction from your news."

To Frances, John seemed puzzlingly diffident. *You know, you could have had me that first night in the Bois de Boulogne*, she later told him. But as soon as he left Paris, his courtship became ardent. "Dear Lord, do come soon," he wrote her from England, where he'd returned to take up a post at the *Daily News*'s London bureau. "I think somehow we're in it, Frances. I'm yours, utterly & maybe forever yours." Shortly after she joined him in London that summer, John booked a weekend for them at the Mermaid Hotel, an old coaching inn in the town of Rye, where Henry James, prewar England's most famous expatriate literary American, had taken up residence. The Mermaid was a rambling Tudor establishment. With raftered ceilings and oak-paneled rooms, secret staircases, and thick rounds of glass that let in a greenish light, it was a place to lose one's way.

Their first night together in Rye was a painful, fumbling encounter, over practically before it had started. Nothing went right. "Shall we survive our bodies?" Frances had asked him before Rye, sensing something of the peril of the situation. It seemed to her that John needed to get himself psychoanalyzed. For years, she'd also suffered from "impotence," as she called it; her analysis in New York had cured her sexual difficulties. "Don't think I say this merely as a girl you did not satisfy," she wrote to John. "I know my own agony, and since knowing you I have known something of the agony I must have given to others."

For Frances, as for many young, freethinking Americans, confidence in psychoanalysis was part of the mental furniture. Imported to the United States before World War I, Freud's ideas fit well with the American penchant for reinvention, promising a saner and more self-aware society. Psychoanalysis turned many of the Victorian prescriptions with which John and Frances had been raised on their heads. Self-control—rebranded as repression—made a person sick. By the same token, the preservation of society demanded frankness, not reserve. The analyst became an authority figure to replace discredited parents or ministers. What started in bohemian urban circles soon spread far beyond them, as psychoanalysis became the preeminent way to explain human behavior. Among the mass-market, bestselling "Little Blue" booklets churned out in Girard, Kansas, in the 1920s, was a series of psychoanalytic titles, including "How to Psychoanalyze Your Neighbors."

Despite Frances's urging, John didn't go to psychoanalysis then, yet they carried on, somehow. The "strangest summer I have ever had," John later called it. Crazy, passionate nights followed by long, perplexing arguments. Frances's ideas about the proper relations between the sexes both intrigued and unsettled him. She wrapped up some very retrograde ideas in a glossy modern package. One moment she was addressing him as "my dear lord" and declaring that she wished to be "recessive to his dominance." The next, she was showing him up intellectually, talking about books he hadn't read, ideas he hadn't considered.

Like other young women who came of age just as the struggle for the vote was won, Frances took university education, the franchise, meaningful work, and sexual fulfillment as her due. She rejected the militant suffrage notion of a "sex antagonism": the idea that men and women held bitterly irreconcilable interests. That sort of thinking was for dried-up old maids, she figured. She was a new model feminist who expected marriage and a career, domesticity and adventure. As for the question roiling postwar feminism—were women the same as men or different?—Frances, courtesy of her time in analysis, had no doubt. Of course, they were different: she was a firm believer in biological imperatives, in women's drive to motherhood and the hazards of maladjustment if they deviated from that course.

She wanted a man who wasn't simply her equal, but her better. Feminism, she insisted, served as "a prod to urge on masculine superiority." It forced men to recognize they couldn't take their historical advantages for granted. If they wanted to maintain their position, they now had to write better books, paint better pictures, devise better political strategies, be more important or more famous. In that way, feminism would improve the world.

Was John a man she could look up to? From his vantage point, it seemed unlikely, given the dim view she'd taken of his talents. She composed a harsh assessment of his draft novel, deploying the mocking voice of a critical reviewer. *The Red Pavilion* was amusing, she wrote; it was light, it was motivated by the modern desire to offer an account of the changing mores of marriage. But how perceptive was Mr. Gunther? Not at all, she judged. He'd written a whole novel about the struggle for dominance between men and women without at all understanding the subject. Then, having cut him down to size, she was remorseful. "You see I can't do this thing gracefully like a woman. I hate like hell falling for you."

By the time she left for New York in September 1925, they had come to the understanding that it was over, at least for the moment. Her father was ill back in New York and she'd decided to go home and get a proper job. Sometime that summer, she had gotten pregnant and apparently had an abortion; they didn't talk of marriage. At the pier, John came to bid her goodbye, and she dressed up for the occasion: "I want to see you very beautiful, with your hair old powdery gold and your arms white." He had an expensive, perfect peach delivered from Fortnum & Mason to her cabin on the *Berengaria*. "And so the prologue ends," he wrote to her. "The intermission lasts a couple of months instead of a couple of minutes. But I suppose that is well also. And then—then!—the play begins."

The trouble was that he couldn't stop thinking about her during the so-called intermission, and the play was the sort where the hero and heroine circle each other warily, each eager to demonstrate that the other is more captivated. John played out his ambivalence for Frances's benefit, confessing both that he was daydreaming about her constantly and that he wasn't sure he wanted to marry her. Besides which there was the fact that he was in love with three other girls: Helen (of course); Helen's younger sister, Mickey; and Rebecca West. John assured Frances that she was leading that contest by a nose. Her own very small, pert nose.

"Lay off the hysteria," Frances replied from New York, where she'd taken a job as a publicity agent and was living on Barrow Street, a few doors down from the poet Edna St. Vincent Millay's narrow gabled house. All that nonsense he was writing her about waking up in the middle of the night, sweating blood at the thought of her.

"You don't understand anything about me—That seems incredible to me, but it's so." After a few months apart, she was absolutely no longer in love with him. "So far, you've only been a troublesome disturbance to me, nothing more." And she certainly wasn't interested in marrying him. "I want to work hard, and I want to live well—I don't want to mess around. See what I mean?"

But John kept writing her, even after she stopped answering. The fact that she kept him off-balance—that he never knew where he stood with her—drew him in. He was coming to America for a visit. Would she see him? Frances agreed, at first, to meet him at the train station in Chicago but then didn't show up. He waited for her for hours.

That afternoon she was supposed to meet him, Frances sat at her desk, tears rolling down her cheeks, wanting to go to the station, wanting to see him again, but afraid to. If she hadn't had the abortion, her baby would have been due that month. The letter John sent her as he departed for Europe only deepened her confusion. He wasn't in love with those other girls any longer, he insisted. "All I can say is that you mean more to me, in a very strange way, than anyone I know, that I think of you continually, unbearably, that I want you & yet am afraid to want you."

JOHN HAD ONLY BEEN home for two months when the *Daily News* sent him back to Europe in April 1926 to roam the globe as an independent correspondent. He wrote to Mickey Hahn, Helen's kid sister, straightaway. "Grand, isn't it? I feel a small excited child before such adventure." Two publishers, he informed Mickey—*two*—were bidding on *The Red Pavilion*. He wanted her to know, too, that when he last visited her, he hadn't managed to say everything he intended. Never mind, though: in a year's time, after she graduated from college, she would come to see him in Europe. She had pretty much agreed to that plan. Hadn't she?

Of the five Hahn girls, Helen was the undisputed beauty and Mickey by far the cleverest. The Hahns were of German-Jewish origin. Their mother was an ardent suffragist and freethinker who liked to argue about causes. Their father, a dry-goods salesman, was a quiet, recessive type. He steered clear of disputes, refusing, as Mickey put it, to give his wife's "restless spirit the exercise it craved."

In a family that merrily disregarded the conventional, it was Mickey who most exuberantly rushed the barricades. She enrolled at the University of Wisconsin's College of Engineering—the first woman to do so—and held on, even as the faculty appealed to the state legislature to have her thrown out. When her adviser at the College of Engineering assured her that "the female mind" couldn't grasp the subject of mining engineering, she immediately opted for that course of study.

Mickey wanted an adventure like the boys of her acquaintance were having, working the cattle boats to Europe, moonlighting as chauffeurs, hitchhiking across America, or riding the rails. But even the permissive Hahn parents wouldn't stand for that. Lake Kivu in the Belgian Congo, where she really wanted to go, was out of the question. So the summer before her senior year at the university in Madison, she and a friend equipped their Model T with rain curtains and a mosquito net, and in an era when roads were unpaved and full of mudholes, and motels didn't yet exist, they headed west, a pistol stowed away in the back seat.

When Helen, Mickey, and their youngest sister, Dauphine, were at home in Chicago, the Hahn family home teemed with boys. They crowded the halls, filled the parlor, and called incessantly on the phone. Mickey mostly treated them with mocking disregard—as a rule, her elder sister's castoffs held no appeal—though occasionally she indulged in the sport of swiping one of Helen's beaux. John, however, was very persistent and he liked to send her books and talk about them, though he did most of the talking.

He was the only one, Mickey told him, who "got away without listening to me at least now and then." She secretly suspected, though, that he was taking notes all the while. She'd once said to him, "People should be mirrors to oneself." A few hours later, he repeated the phrase, murmuring, "Yes. That's good." He *was* listening. "Then I knew more about him, suddenly. After all, he uses everything. He'll use that some day. Unless I do first," she recorded in her journal.

"Ask John. He Knows," became a favorite Hahn family saying, a joke at the expense of a young man who appeared to have all the answers.

IF JOHN FIGURED IN Hahn legend as an amiable know-it-all, the irony was that the longer he stayed abroad, the less he felt he knew. It was like the joke the reporters told about the Soviet Union. Come for two weeks and you'll have the place figured out. Stay for several months, and you won't understand a thing. As soon as he reached the Paris office, his editors sent him to Syria.

He arrived in June 1926 amid a tenacious uprising against French rule. For centuries, Syria had been part of the Ottoman Empire, but at the end of the First World War, Turkish forces had been forced out by Arab nationalist fighters and their British allies. Now Syria counted as the former imperial possession of a defeated power. As such, it was among those territories with which the League of Nations, charged with developing a workable form of world government, occupied itself in the 1920s.

What should be done with these people? the League's diplomats and functionaries wondered. Did Woodrow Wilson's principles of self-determination apply to them? To most Western observers, the answer seemed obvious. However many petitions the Hashemite Arabs or the Druze peoples of Syria—or for that matter the Togolese or the Cameroonians—submitted, arguing for the same rights to independence that the Poles and Czechs had gotten at Versailles, the League's diplomats concluded that they weren't yet fit for self-governance. The League would have to exercise "tutelage," or trusteeship, over these territories, with the lion's share of responsibility (and thus the bounty) going to the victors. Although Syria had operated for a few months as an independent kingdom, the League granted the French "mandatory control" over the region in 1920.

Officially, these mandates were to be administered in the interest of the subject peoples. But what if the local population, as in Syria, rose in rebellion? The French authorities had at first shrugged off the revolt, characterizing it as the work of a few disgruntled fanatics among the Druze "tribesmen." An ungovernable people, they insisted. But soon the French were bombing Damascus to bring the territory to heel, hanging rebels in the city's squares, plowing tanks through its narrow streets, and launching aerial attacks on undefended villages. The gravity of the situation had become undeniable. Eager to drum up favorable publicity in the American press, the French military permitted John to accompany a column of troops into the stronghold of the rebellion, the Jabal region in the far north of the country.

The Jabal is a six-thousand-foot plateau in the middle of the desert, and into this natural fortification the Druze built their houses of black volcanic rock with peepholes instead of windows. The French started shelling, and the black stone houses crumbled, then collapsed. After the bombardment, the French army, composed of troops from West Africa whom the Druze called "eggplants" because of the color of their skin, fought their way, street by street, through the village. It was 120 degrees in the shade and the only water the soldiers had was what they'd carried in. After the Druze men were killed, Druze women took their place, shooting German rifles, brandishing curved swords. For three days the fighting continued, but the end was foretold, John reported. In the name of civilization, rebellious villages would be burned to the ground.

The Syrian Rebellion was a story that John—unusually for the time—told from the perspective of the Druze. After his expedition with the French army, he wanted to hear the Druze side of things. Back in Damascus, he gained the confidence of young rebels whom he'd met through an American missionary. One of them, a law student, agreed to serve as his guide into Druze territories, apologizing that he'd have to return to the city to take his exams in a week's time. "I was amazed," John wrote in an eight-part series of articles on the Druze. "Were these the desperate savages who counted human sacrifice (as the French say) among their more childish amusements?" For his expedition, John dressed up in a white robe and a maroon fez, putting on tinted glasses to conceal his Nordic blue eyes. He wanted to see Emir Emin Arslan, the head of Druze rebel forces, but for the moment, he would have to settle for a visit to the Queen of the Druze.

The road to the Moukhtara Palace was a narrow ledge that dipped and rose, sickeningly. The palace, a gray-stone Moorish castle, hung on a slope thicketed with olive groves. There, on a divan, sat Lady Nazira, the widowed queen of the Druze. She motioned for John to sit down in a Western-style chair. Behind her purple veil laced with gold, he caught an impression of "her dense black hair, great, dark, sad eyes under arched brows and a glint of red lips and white teeth." On one side of the room, the queen's servants, holding heavy brass trays in outstretched arms, stood like soldiers, as he and the queen drank orangeade flavored with rose oil, followed by sweet, grainy coffee.

Beyond a few platitudes, the queen refused to talk about politics with him, and that was just as well, for John knew that it was the escapade, and the scene at Moukhtara that would appeal to readers. Instead, he made small talk with her about American women and American clothes. When John did finally find Emir Arslan, in Beirut, he spent nearly as many lines on his attire—"a Palm Beach suit, trimly cut, a silk-sport suit with the collar attached in the American style, a blue foulard tie, a Panama hat, and shoes—just shoes"—as he did on his political philosophy. The meeting was, as John admitted, a "sort of comic anticlimax." Arslan gave him the Druze's peace terms to transmit to America and asserted that his people would fight the French for generations.

Sympathetic as John was to the Druze, their plight didn't stick with him; he stayed entirely within the prescriptions—interpretation without advocacy—that his editor had laid down. Another American journalist who witnessed the bombing of Druze villages took his report directly to the League of Nations, protesting both the inhumanity of French rule and the League's complicity. For John, Syria was more an adventure story than a world-historical lesson. "Damascus," he said later that year, "is a city where guns pop almost as much as they do in Chicago." Plus the millions of fleas, of course, and the corpses swinging from gibbets in the town square. "As I say, Syria is a great deal like Chicago. Except that they actually do hang them in Syria." A hookah, he informed his readers, is the proper name for a water pipe. He compared apricots in Jerusalem (small, with a musky perfume) and Rome (fleshy and yellow) and kept track of the vast number of religions in the world. "I am as zestful with all my pretty new exciting scraps of information as a child with a set of letters glazed on wooden blocks," he exulted to Mickey.

When John returned from Syria via Italy, he had dreamed up an idea for a set of articles. Like every cub correspondent in Europe, he'd put in the requisite weeks sitting on the hard wooden benches in the second-floor press gallery at the League of Nations. The deliberations below mostly seemed a snooze, so much hot air. Sure, he had an instinctive fealty to democracy and high-minded ideas of world government. But the whole Wilsonian system created at Versailles—newborn republics, international relations regulated by open diplomacy, government by the consent of the governed—was faltering, it seemed to John, and possibly failing utterly. Stuck inside the League chambers in Geneva you might be able to wish away the real situation in Sofia or Warsaw or Istanbul. You might delude yourself into believing that any trouble was just a temporary way station on the road to liberal democracy. You might imagine that the neat borders of the new nations would be able to contain people's passions.

But if you visited those places, you could see how strongmen of every stripe—royal, military, nationalistic—were seizing power, with or without the assent of the populace. In countries like Hungary or Bulgaria, which had lost territory at the Paris Peace Conference, constitutional government was dead on arrival. Its prospects weren't much better in those nations, such as Romania and Poland, that had emerged as winners. In Romania, radicalized students wearing embroidered Moldavian peasant shirts rioted to restrict the number of

Jews in universities, then proceeded to carry out assassinations. In Poland, Marshal Piłsudski seized power from a squabbling parliament under the banner of "moral renovation," denouncing the delegates in speeches so obscenely scatological that no Western paper could print them.

The series John proposed would be entitled "The Rise of the Dictators." "Well, my idea is simply to cash in on the idea that instead of being made safe for democracy, etc, Europe has become made safe for dictatorship," he wrote to Mickey. "Now, dictatorship is a darned interesting thing. And there are dictators now ruling in Poland, Italy, Spain, Portugal, Greece, Turkey, Rumania, Hungary, and Albania."

"Isn't that rather a tremendous idea?" he exclaimed. "And a tremendous stunt?" It was 1926 and most people were still laughing Hitler off as a bad Austrian joke.

REBECCA WEST HAD SUSPECTED that Frances Fineman was in love with John when she'd met her the previous summer. But after Rebecca saw Frances in New York in the spring of 1926, a few months after the train station incident, she became certain of the fact. The question was what—if anything—Rebecca should do about it.

Rebecca was holed up in the Hotel Majestic on Central Park West. She'd come to New York with the aim of writing without distractions, but every other minute the phone was ringing, lecture agents, reporters, and other busybodies vying for her attention. To put them off the scent, she'd started to answer the phone with an assumed Scots brogue. But as soon as Frances identified herself, Rebecca thought *Oh Hell, might as well get this over with*, and invited her to come up to her room. She didn't bother changing out of her nightdress, and hastily pulled on a white satin kimono to get the door.

One look at Frances's face, strained and teary, and Rebecca settled in for a long conversation. Prior to her call, Frances had written a letter (very silly and morbid, according to Rebecca), the point of which was that regret about the abortion had consumed her, and she was tormenting herself. As she talked on and on about John, Rebecca came to the conclusion both that Frances was genuinely in love and that she was a hopeless sort of person. Frances wasn't spiteful, Rebecca thought, but she was determined to nab John and the fact that he wasn't interested wouldn't deter her.

The meeting dragged on the whole morning, and when Frances had finally gone, Rebecca sat down to write to John. Really, he ought to be ashamed of how he'd conducted himself. She meant for her letter to bring him up short. John wasn't Rebecca's type—she favored powerful men, not boys—but she did maintain a proprietary interest in his behavior. "I think the situation between you presents itself as a failure on your part to utilise the opportunity she gave you to make something good of both your lives." Maybe there was nothing John could do about it, but he ought at least to be kind to Frances: "If you can do anything nice to her do it. She'll never get anything out of life, poor child."

Rebecca observed that when it came to women, John had a "shepherding instinct." She surmised that it stemmed from a frustrated desire to protect his mother, and she was hoping to summon it up in him. But if John felt guilty, he was also liable to flee. When Frances answered his letter about being afraid to love her with a reverie—"I think of you twenty-five hours a day, and hug the pillow, and tremble with fear with wanting you"—he cut things off entirely. He was finished with love, he insisted: he didn't want to hurt her.

Still, the idea of doomed love, of a lost chance—the story of Daisy and Gatsby, published the previous year—was enthralling to them both. After John retreated, Frances took on the persona of the wised-up flapper who could take care of herself. She insisted he owed her nothing and she didn't regret a thing that had happened between them. Furthermore, she disclaimed all expertise with regard to Freudianism and neuroses. "And what's this about my still fighting? Me? Sir, my armor's in the woodpile, and I'm running naked in the sun and wind."

When freedom rather than obligation was Frances's offer, John was once again hooked. Did the lock of her hair still play tag with her forehead? he wondered. He had to smile, he told her, when he saw an envelope addressed in her neat, spidery handwriting waiting in his mailbox. Frances was coming to Europe as a publicity agent and they'd see each other in London in December for a couple of weeks. There was talk of finishing what they'd started at Rye.

ONE OF THE EFFECTS of all the Freudianism in the air was that gossiping about other people's private lives could no longer be dismissed simply as bad manners. Instead, discoursing about the Oedipus complexes and penis envy displayed by one's friends took on an air of scientific legitimacy. As Rebecca made the rounds in New York and Chicago, hearing gossip about Frances—and there was a great deal of it—she became more unsettled about the advice she'd given John.

Rebecca heard from John's old friend Jerry Frank that the critic Carl Van Doren was in love with Frances, but then when she saw Carl and asked him about Frances, he said he'd only seen her twice in his life and was utterly uninterested in her. According to Rebecca, that accorded with Frances's reputation in Chicago: she claimed that men whom she barely knew were besotted. Rebecca had heard it said that John had toyed with Frances, led her on and dropped her, and then picked up the affair once more.

So when Rebecca learned that Frances was sailing for London to meet John, all her apprehensions seemed justified. She'd had premonitions, Rebecca wrote John. "If I've sounded raucous it was only because you would shout, wouldn't you, if you saw somebody you were dearly fond of going over the edge of a precipice?" From New York, Rebecca had even cabled a warning to him in London. She had to send a wire because a letter wouldn't reach John before Frances did.

Rebecca feared that Frances would arrive in London and make a dramatic scene, perhaps even threaten suicide. What happened, though, was worse. The facts, as Rebecca gathered them up, like a detective picking fastidiously through the evidence in a trampled crime scene, were as appalling as could be.

In some foolhardy moment in London, John had pledged to marry Frances if she got pregnant again. An act of God, he'd told her, would decide the matter.

"Will of God," read the cable Frances sent him in late January 1927 when she'd returned home to New York.

"Marry me?" he cabled from Rome.

"If John Gunther turns up in London with a terrible blonde Jewess wife be good to him," Rebecca wrote to her sister. "He has been tricked into this marriage in the most dreadful way imaginable and is in a frightful state of mind."

THERE ARE AT LEAST two versions of the events that had precipitated the marriage of Frances Fineman and John Gunther: Rebecca's and John's. Each was self-serving, useful to their tellers. In the story that Rebecca recounted, there was no pregnancy. Frances had feigned the whole thing to force John to marry her.

For Rebecca, the story confirmed a favorite theme of hers: the propensity to self-destruction in human relations. It was a peculiar, terrible quality of human nature, she observed, that if one party wielded the lash, the other bowed willingly to it. This theme is threaded through her early book reviews to her later, 1941 masterpiece about the Balkans, *Black Lamb and Grey Falcon*. Faced with the choice of death and life, men will at least half of the time choose death. "There is nothing rarer than a man who can be trusted never to throw away happiness, however eagerly he sometimes grasps it," she would write. "In history we are as frequently interested in our own doom."

H.G. had insisted that Rebecca keep her own pregnancy a secret, petulantly batting away the suggestion that he divorce his wife. Instead, Wells shunted Rebecca and baby Anthony off to a redbrick, semidetached, bow-fronted house in Norfolk, where they would live as lodgers under the supervision of a postman and his wife. He told her: "It is your nature to darken your world and blacken every memory. So long as I love you you will darken mine."

Rebecca had not shied from the punishment meted out to her, for she knew the world blamed her, and not Wells for Anthony's existence. Of course, she had tried to pass herself off as the boy's aunt, claimed that she was in Norfolk to recuperate from an illness. But no one who mattered was fooled. The fact that H.G.'s wife played the saint—"Give her my dear love if you can," she told Wells—only deepened Rebecca's debacle.

Years later, when Rebecca and her son had broken with each other irretrievably, Anthony judged that his mother's enmity toward him stemmed from her mismanagement of the original fiasco. Pregnant by H.G. but unable to extract a commitment of marriage from him, Rebecca had "shown herself incompetent to make a go of the most banal and despicable of female maneuvers." As he said: "She was, in the vulgar phrase, stuck, with nothing to show for her trouble."

If Rebecca felt she had failed, then Frances, by contrast, had proven herself a virtuoso. For John to do anything other than marry Frances, said Helen Hahn, would have been, for him, unthinkable, a caddish disgrace. Even in their sophisticated circles, men proposed marriage under such circumstances, if only to placate their families. Anyway, Helen insisted that Frances *had* been carrying John's baby, only she had gotten rid of it in New York just before she sailed back across the Atlantic, to join him in Italy.

"I wish to God I could have saved you from all this," Rebecca wrote John.

It was too late. By then, Frances had arrived in Rome, her trousseau distributed over several trunks. At the old city hall on the Piazza del Campidoglio on the morning of March 16, 1927, she married John, the ceremony witnessed by a brigade of black-shirted *fascisti* and presided over by the flag-besashed representative of the governor of Rome, a gold medal agleam on his broad chest. Neither bride nor groom had any relatives present at the ceremony. Lizette, John's mother, would only learn of her son's marriage thirdhand: "John Gunther Is Wed After Cable Romance" read the headline in the *Chicago Daily News*.

Will of God, he'd called it. The lack of fetters—his generation's unimaginable freedom—made the idea of fate seductive. Before posting the banns, the notice that Italian law required before a marriage, John and Frances walked around the piazza: once, twice, three times. In his pocket John was carrying the ring he'd bought for five lira the night before.

BUT WAS THAT HOW it happened? Another telling of the events that preceded his wedding was supplied by John himself, thirty years later. At the time, he was turning out short stories as if under a compulsion, five and six in a month. Most of them languished, unpublished. It was a frustration to him. When it came to journalism, he couldn't miss. His fiction, though, was a different matter. His first novel, *The Red Pavilion,* published in 1926 while he was in Syria, had earned him a few overinflated comparisons to Aldous Huxley and many critics who disparaged the shallowness of the endeavor: "a tin-foil plow scraping a two-inch furrow through swift-moving acres of very sandy soil," in the *New Republic*'s assessment. He'd write six more novels, none of them more than a modest success. His characters were stilted, his dialogue contrived, and not enough happened in his plots.

There was another problem, too. Even by the forgiving standards of the roman à clef, he was very obviously writing about himself and his friends. When John found himself stuck on a story, he opened his diaries or excavated Frances's old letters from his closet. Among John's unpublished pieces, in box 154 of his archive at the University of Chicago, is a story entitled "Okay, Bliss." The protagonist is waiting on the station platform in Rome for a girl—Bliss—to arrive. He's miserable and angry. Over the past three years, he and the girl have given each other a vexed time. She's gotten pregnant twice, each time he said nothing about marriage, though it was clear to him that was what she wanted. She has had two abortions, the second worse and more sordid than the first. They've parted, fractiously, and reunited, he at first reluctantly and then avidly. He's written her passionate love letters, she's come to see him in London, staying in splendor at the Savoy rather than the run-down pension in Russell Square he reserved for her. When she wires him later—"Will of God"—there is no question in his mind but that he must now marry her.

John changed at least a few details. The protagonist and Bliss meet first in New York, not in Paris. Bliss tells his mother about the pregnancy. In fact, John's mother learned of his engagement when a *Daily News* reporter called her up for a comment on the whirlwind romance. But plenty else corresponds. Frances did send a Will of God telegram. She did say, "It's my damn hungry womb" after getting pregnant. She likely had at least one abortion, possibly two, before they married.

At the end of "Okay, Bliss," though, there is no trickery. When Bliss isn't on the train as planned, her fiancé thinks she's not coming. But then she steps out of a taxi at the station, composed and nonchalant; she'd arrived in Rome the day before without telling him. He informs her that he's had the banns posted so that they could marry on Tuesday. She becomes distracted over dinner, almost as if she isn't listening to anything he says. She appears even more defenseless than usual. "If only you could love me," she tells him. When he protests that he does love her, she turns away in disbelief. At the end of dinner, she hands him a small envelope.

Inside is a shriveled black thing, a fetus barely an inch in length: a miscarriage. You can unpost the banns and call the marriage off, Bliss tells him. Go ahead—throw it in the Trevi Fountain or in the Tiber. He reaches across the table and slaps her, full and hard in the face.

Decades after the wedding in Rome, John was still angry enough at Frances to deliver a fictional slap. Yet at the same time, he saw only too clearly the damage he'd inflicted in their relationship. After striking Bliss, the narrator acknowledged for the first time "the full extent of the injury he had done her, the immolating intolerable hurt." In John's version of events, he went willingly, fully conscious of the facts, to his destiny. The couple married on Tuesday, according to plan.

TO FIND
THE CENTER

—

THE FLAG THAT FLUTTERED ATOP NEOCLASSICAL, OFFICIAL Berlin was the black, red, and gold banner of the new Weimar Republic. In 1920s Germany, an experiment in democracy was under way. Weimar stood for modernity, progress, and equality, for women's rights, generous welfare benefits, and advanced ideas in education. But could a peaceable republic be wrested from Prussian militarism and autocracy? The reactionary old guard—the counts and the barons, the colonels and the generals—were bitterly hostile to the fledgling republic. From their yachts and country villas flew the black-and-white flag of the deposed Kaiser.

Weimar was a society out of kilter, punctuated by putsches and political assassinations. A "weird mixture of champagne, starvation, drugs and violence" as Jimmy Sheean described it. A catastrophic hyperinflation in 1923 had both bankrupted anyone with savings and unleashed a buying frenzy for automobiles, bicycles, bushels of potatoes, bedsheets, and any object whose value wouldn't evaporate overnight. The destruction of capital and stability proved vertiginous. If the world was topsy-turvy, then all the rules about right and wrong, about male and female, went out the window: the nightclubs were raunchier in Berlin, the sex wilder, the artists—especially the Expressionists—more scathing.

For Dorothy Thompson, the new Berlin correspondent for the Philadelphia *Public Ledger* and the *New York Evening Post,* this feverish atmosphere proved intoxicating. By day, she sniffed out would-be insurrectionists; in the evenings, she went to the theater, staying up through the night, if need be, to file her copy. In 1925, she had become the first American woman to lead a major overseas news bureau, beating out all the men vying for one of the best posts for a foreign correspondent. Her husband disliked Berlin but as attached as she was to him, Dorothy took the job. Joseph would be left to his own devices in Vienna and London.

Sleek, raven-haired, and primarily ornamental, Joseph was a Hungarian Don Juan. Like a "hairdresser, with a naïve passion for fancy vests," was Rebecca West's verdict. Joseph was writing in three languages at once what a friend of Dorothy's described as a "great, serious, unfinishable tome" entitled "The Mind of Europe." He was prodigiously unfaithful, making conquests of other women even on their honeymoon in 1923. For a few years, Dorothy told herself that she could put up with Joseph's overactive "glands," tolerable in a man as creative as her husband. But then he seduced her friend Edna St. Vincent Millay, and when Dorothy retaliated one night by sleeping with the war correspondent Floyd Gibbons, who'd ridden through Mexico with the revolutionary Pancho Villa, the marriage was well and truly over.

Part of Dorothy's greatness, wrote Jimmy many years later, was that "she could always step over the corpses and go on, steadily, resolutely, right to the end, with her head held very high indeed." The two had met for the first time in Berlin in 1926, though they didn't see each other again until a dinner party the next year. On that evening, Dorothy's indomitability was very much in evidence. The dinner took place at Dorothy's apartment in Berlin. She was living on the leafy Händelstrasse, overlooking the Tiergarten, in a thirteen-room Beaux-Arts house, which she shared with her friends Edgar and Lilian Mowrer. The brother of Paul Mowrer, who headed the *Chicago Daily News*'s Paris bureau, Edgar was the paper's Berlin correspondent, and his wife, Lilian, reported for the British press; they occupied the ground-floor rooms of Händelstrasse 8, with Dorothy and occasionally Joseph on the floor above.

At Dorothy's, one could always be certain of a good dinner, excellent wines, and conversation carried on in at least two or three languages by the personalities of the day. Choose an evening and the guests would include an eminent psychoanalyst, a decrepit aristocrat or two, refugees from the Balkans, a former prime minister, a spy— all useful to the correspondent's exercise in "brain-picking." The Hungarian Red Count Mihály Károlyi, leader of the country's first postrevolutionary republic, dined at Dorothy's, as did the novelist Thomas Mann and the playwright Bertolt Brecht.

On that particular evening, Dorothy's guests included the lawyer Helmuth James von Moltke, scion of the distinguished family of generals, and his mother, the South African–born Countess von Moltke. The novelist Sinclair Lewis—nicknamed "Red" for his carroty hair—was also there. The author of a pair of novels, *Main Street* and *Babbitt,* which, depending upon your perspective, were either a brilliant dissection of middle-class American conformity or a vicious libel on the entire Midwest, Lewis was an international celebrity and behaved the part: remote, dressed in Savile Row suits, an ironic bow. And Jimmy. A "very nice boy, with a wet lower lip, and a little too much prettiness, and he was, alas, *drunk,*" Dorothy commented the next day.

Red Lewis was restricting himself to beer and water. A notorious drunk himself, he was on a serious campaign to win Dorothy's affections; he'd been proposing marriage from the moment he met her. Because Red was stone-cold sober, Jimmy's conversation was all the more annoying to him. Jimmy had just returned from China via Moscow and was preparing to go back to the Soviet Union for the celebration of the tenth anniversary of the Bolshevik revolution. "All come to Moscow . . . you must *all* come to Moscow," Jimmy said over and over again, extolling the genius of Mikhail Borodin, the Communist agent who'd been sent to China to stiffen the spines of the Soviet-sympathizing forces there.

Finally, Red had enough. "O you *must* come to *Mos*cow for the

Seventh of November," he launched in, his thin, pockmarked face arranged in a grimace even when he was smiling. First he put Jimmy's enthusiasm in the words of the muscular Chicago poet Vachel Lindsay, known for his incantatory rhythms, boom boom BOOM. Then he proceeded to parody Longfellow, Swinburne, and finally Tennyson rhapsodizing about the Bolshevik anniversary. He didn't pause for breath. The words came out in great torrents. Though no one could afterward remember a word that Red had said, it was, they agreed, the most brilliant of improvisations, even for a man known for his astounding mimicry.

Red's purpose, as Jimmy well understood, was to mock the absurdity of his enthusiasm. And Jimmy, whose world historical sense of himself was always tempered by irony, knew that Red wasn't wrong. After all, when the Bolsheviks marched on Petrograd's Winter Palace in November 1917, he had been entirely consumed with the dramas of the fraternity rush season. But the year 1927 marked a turning point for him. It was then that the distinction between public and private, between the events of the world and his own inner life started to collapse. Why this had happened to him Jimmy could only ever explain as a strange sort of love story.

WHEN JIMMY FIRST MET Rayna Prohme in China, he figured her for a type he knew well enough: a well-bred girl, a graduate of the University of Illinois in Champaign, an idealist, susceptible to causes. One day, Jimmy supposed, she'd write a book about her adventures fomenting revolution in Hankou entitled *Up from Canton* or *China in Travail*. "Uplifters," Dorothy called them, Westerners who put their shoulders to the wheel in the service of the triumph of worldwide Bolshevism. Rayna's shoulders were very slight. Her hair was a wiry mass of red-golden curls. She'd divorced one husband, and was in China with a second, a would-be revolutionary named Bill Prohme.

Rayna thought she had Jimmy figured out, too. A newspaperman who prided himself on telling both sides. A spectator perched on the fence, dressed in the European-in-the-Orient's white silk suit, smoking Egyptian cigarettes, drinking Scotch.

"How's the weather up there?" she inquired of him on that first meeting. "Is it a nice fence?"

"It's comfortable and I get a good view," he retorted. "How do you like it down there where you are? You don't see much, do you?"

Jimmy wasn't quite as disinterested then as he later made out. For a fiery revolutionary like Rayna, he counted undeniably as a bystander. But by the early 1920s, Jimmy's sympathies were distinctly on the left even as his tastes for high living, the opera, and Italian clothes tended to the epicurean. He was a so-called pink in a white silk suit. "All the people who think my way are so disgusting, for the most part, and all the people with whom I cannot possibly agree are so charming, that there's very little point in keeping on with my 'views,'" he reflected.

In 1925, reporting from the Rif War, Jimmy had made a name for himself as a young man willing to do anything to get a story. In northern Morocco, the Berber peoples were in full revolt against their Spanish overlords. One of the earliest anticolonial struggles of the postwar years, the Rif War was viewed by all sides as a test case for the prospects of imperial rule. The Rifi, equipped only with a small artillery, were dealing blow after blow to the Spanish military, largely through guerrilla combat. Their leader, Mohammed ben Abd el-Krim, had established a republic based on Koranic law. He stood accused of fomenting a pan-Islamic movement to rally Muslim believers across North Africa against European imperialism.

Determined to interview el-Krim, Jimmy set out for the Rif against the better judgment of his *Tribune* editors. By the time he reached Morocco, the Spanish had blockaded the routes to the mountains that were the Rifi stronghold. He would continue anyway. Fitted out in a fine white woolen djellaba he'd purchased in Tangier, Jimmy mounted a mule, seated on a wooden saddle, to traverse the wide, arid plain. He survived capture by Metalza riflemen, Arab allies of the Rifi, and made his way over rugged terrain, following goat tracks, to arrive at the Rifi capital.

He was one of the few reporters to get through the blockade lines to Abd el-Krim—and he did it not once, but twice. The second time, seven months later, was still more perilous, as the French, guarding their Moroccan empire, had by then joined the Spaniards to crush the Rif uprising. The tracks to the mountains were under constant bombardment. Jimmy's articles left no doubt as to the brutality of the French onslaught. Armored tanks ran down men mounted on mules and donkeys; new model machine guns arrayed against rusty old rifles, poison gas seeping into the caves where villagers were hiding from the bombers overhead.

Like John in the Druze lands, Jimmy already knew that imperialism was wrong. The suspicion of European imperialism was common enough among Americans, especially Midwesterners. Unlike John, though, Jimmy saw the Rif War as a portent. It represented a "most persistent and heroic nationalism," akin to the European nationalisms and just as transformative in its consequences. Watching as Abd el-Krim, alone at the mouth of a cave, fired his rifle at a squadron of Spanish airplanes spraying machine-gun bullets, Jimmy marveled at the Rifi leader: he was both in the thick of the battle and above it. "You may say for me that we are not to be destroyed," el-Krim told Jimmy. "We represent a force which is unconquerable." Fixed in el-Krim's mind, Jimmy understood, was a future he wouldn't personally see: "I understood that nobody had ever felt more deeply than this man how far our hopes and dreams outrun us all."

One of the "views" with which Jimmy emerged from the Rif, then, was a still more fervent anti-imperialism. He'd acquired, too, the cachet of the adventurer. He could be the next coming of Richard Harding Davis, his bosses intimated. But Jimmy didn't want to be tramping from escapade to exploit. What could be more idiotic than seeking out adventure for adventure's sake? What stirred Jimmy's interest, rather, were those causes—anti-imperialism for one, Communism for another—that even after the disillusioning spectacle of the Great War, could still mobilize the masses to fight, even die, for an idea.

It was that curiosity which brought him in 1927 to the port city of Hankou, present-day Wuhan, in northern China. As the prospects for European Bolshevism had faded, the Soviets turned their attention to Asia, and particularly China, where Sun Yat-sen's revolution of 1911 was lagging, incomplete. The Manchu (Qing) dynasty, which had ruled China for more than two millennia, was destroyed. But what had taken its place was an ineffectual constitutional regime in Beijing, unable to control either the warlords who seized power across the country or the foreign capitalists—the American, British, Japanese, and French, with their gunboats patrolling Chinese waters—who sought to tighten their grip on the Chinese economy.

For the new Soviet regime in Moscow, China would become a battleground for the future: one that pitted two of Lenin's feuding heirs, Trotsky and Stalin, against each other. Without worldwide, permanent revolution, Trotsky insisted, the Bolshevik project would collapse. Stalin, the powerful party secretary, countered that the Soviet state could survive only by strengthening itself internally. The Chinese leaders whom the Soviets trained in Moscow started fighting among themselves. Would Communism on Soviet lines rule China or would the young general, Chiang Kai-shek—who insisted on his own nationalist vision and an accommodation with Chinese bankers—prevail? The success of Chinese Communism would prove that Bolshevism could triumph around the world, as Trotsky had argued. Its failure, conversely, would demonstrate that socialism had to be built first in the Soviet Union, the solution that Stalin urged.

Jimmy could see that the task set for Mikhail Borodin, the man whom the Comintern had sent out to China, was impossible. Hankou, the outpost of Soviet influence, was very far from being a "soviet" as anyone in Moscow would have understood the term: capitalism thrived there, virtually undisturbed, with the Western navies standing by to guarantee its security. By the time Jimmy arrived, in the spring of 1927, Hankou was moreover an isolated and increasingly beleaguered citadel, and Chiang was losing patience. Borodin was a canny, farsighted strategist, but the end of the Hankou experiment—and a civil war that pitted the left-wing, Communist faction of the Nationalist movement against Chiang's troops—was in sight.

It was a terrible disappointment, "and many of my ideas have been blown sky-high," Jimmy confessed to a friend after three weeks in China. He'd hoped that the Nationalists would stick together long enough to kick the warlords and foreign capitalists out of China. But instead, they'd turned on each other. Chiang he labeled a "traitor," and the other revolutionaries were imbecilic, spouting "half-educated studentisms and silly catchwords." The closer he got to any movement, the more disillusioned he became. "Nothing ever stands up under examination," he reflected. He went searching for epic poetry, and instead he got sloganeering.

These were the circumstances under which Jimmy met Rayna, and he quickly came to understand how wrong his initial impression of her had been. She was no dilettante, but a dedicated operator. As editor of the Hankou *People's Tribune,* the Nationalists' English-language organ, Rayna had gained the confidence both of Borodin and of Soong Ching-ling, the elegant young widow of the revolutionary Sun Yat-sen. Soon Jimmy was visiting Rayna every day, arguing about the logic of revolution. How could he rest, Rayna demanded, now that he'd seen the injustice of the world? She felt the cruelty inflicted on the Chinese coolie like a blow to her own body. Her own safety, her own future mattered little to her. As the fall of the Hankou government neared, she shrugged off Jimmy's pleas that she seek refuge at the American consulate.

Jimmy had to leave Hankou—his editors insisted. He owed the North American Newspaper Alliance, a newly founded syndicate that had taken him on, more personal adventures. The end battle in Hankou could be covered adequately enough by the wire agencies. He traveled through China, haunted by the reports of the terror Chiang Kai-shek's soldiers were inflicting on the Communists: the garroting of the leaders, the girl rebels broken on the rack. If Rayna had survived, she'd go to Moscow, he figured. He left Harbin in Manchuria for Moscow, spending nine interminable days on the

Trans-Siberian train. After several more days looking for her, he turned away from the hall porter's desk at the Hotel Metropole one afternoon to discover her walking toward him, laughing.

"I knew you'd turn up. I expected you any day," she told him.

She'd escaped Hankou, traveling from Shanghai to Vladivostok on a Russian merchant boat, accompanied by Madame Sun. Sun Yat-sen's widow had refused to bless Chiang's takeover, calling the general a traitor to her husband's memory. The Soviets wanted her in Moscow as a symbol of the cause. Rayna's husband had to stay behind in Shanghai; he'd soon be off to Manila for propaganda work. At three-thirty in the morning, Rayna and Madame stole away from Shanghai, speeding through deserted streets and reaching the boat by sampan. The ship was packed full but Madame—"a darling," Rayna called her—had offered her the couch in her cabin.

Between the time Jimmy left Hankou and the meeting at the Metropole in Moscow, Rayna had become the center of his world. He struggled to explain what he meant. It wasn't sexual, he later wrote, "at least, not as the phrase is currently understood." He would describe his talks with Rayna as the only real conversations he'd ever had in life. She had solved for herself the problem that beset him—how to integrate an individual life with the world's struggles.

The proper relationship between the individual and the collective wasn't just Jimmy's question, but one that plenty of other Americans were grappling with in that era. It had been provoked by the human costs of the world war and the ravages of unfettered capitalism, to which Bolshevism seemingly offered a solution. How did the outer world act on the personality? asked the philosopher John Dewey and his Chicago School colleagues, investigating the permeable boundaries between self and society. What duty did the individual owe to the collective? was the way that the Catholic bishops of the United States put the question in their 1919 call for a program of social reconstruction.

Rayna's solution was the revolutionary's surrender of self. Could Jimmy do that? Did he even want to? He would spend the winter in Moscow, he decided. But as usual, he was broke. He had to borrow money from Rayna to get back to London, where he'd persuade an editor or a publisher to advance him the funds for a stay in the Soviet Union. He'd bring Rayna some warm winter clothes when he returned. It would only be a few weeks, he promised. He left in a flurry on the Leningrad Express, barely catching the train. Rayna and the porter hurled his belongings into the carriage just as it pulled away from the station.

THAT AFTERNOON OF THEIR reunion at the Hotel Metropole, Jimmy was already sloshed on vodka. He was "embarrassingly enthusiastic about seeing me," Rayna wrote her husband Bill in Manila: "you remember his affectionate streak when he is tight." Jimmy had blathered on to a translator from the Russian news agency Tass about his devotion to Rayna and had insisted on taking her to the opera to see *Boris Godunov*, though he dozed off into a drunken sleep after fifteen minutes.

What a "disorganizing" man Jimmy was, Rayna observed. He was entertaining, in a self-centered sort of way. So like Raph—her first husband, the playwright Samson Raphaelson, author of *The Jazz Singer*—"only without a single complex." Rayna had been glad, though, for Jimmy's whirl of cabs and visitors and theaters, and missed him once he'd gone. She was desolate and lonely in Moscow, wrecked by the failure in Hankou. Although it had been rumored for weeks that Borodin was coming back, he was nowhere to be seen.

Her bravado had deserted her. She felt distracted and adrift, without any purpose. She'd been expected to look after Madame Sun but then—without warning—had been cast off, with hardly a kind word from the widow, who was ensconced in a palace that had once belonged to a sugar baron, with Roman baths, marble staircases, and curly maple furniture. Given the housing shortage in Moscow, finding a decent room for herself—or even a few feet in a room—was nearly impossible. What she would do for work was another puzzle. She'd barely learned any Russian at all; the language seemed to defy her.

She was suffering, too, with headaches that lasted for days, and her mind often seemed a fog. It was getting cold in Moscow, and Jimmy—that "selfish beast"—hadn't yet turned up with the promised winter clothes. Weeks and weeks went by without any sign from him. He'd certainly be there for the tenth-anniversary celebrations of the Bolshevik revolution. She'd heard that Jimmy was issuing invitations to Moscow at every booze-up in Europe; it was rumored that Sinclair Lewis himself was coming.

Jimmy made it back to Moscow on the morning of the seventh of November, just in time for the festivities. Dorothy (but not Red) arrived a few days ahead of him. He and Rayna went to Red Square to observe the pageant. The spectacle was undeniably impressive. Strung across the wall of the Kremlin was a huge sign that read "1917–1927" in electric lights; bands were blaring revolutionary anthems. Infinite columns of marchers from across the Soviet Union—soldiers on horseback, workers holding red banners aloft, peasants in their traditional costumes, women carrying babies—filed past, saluting Stalin and the Russian Communist leadership, positioned atop Lenin's mausoleum.

But she felt distant from it all, Rayna wrote her husband. She didn't say that she'd attended the celebrations with Jimmy. Nor did she tell Bill about the plans she was apparently making. According to Jimmy, she'd made up her mind to enter the Lenin Institute, the Communist International's elite academy for the education of a party cadre; students received instruction in Marxist theory as well as practical strategy. She'd forsake life as she'd formerly known it, every bourgeois pleasure, every scintilla of individualism, to be trained by the Comintern and dispatched to Asia to foment revolution.

Jimmy tried arguing with her, then pleading. Would she be prepared to do everything that the Comintern required of her? He accused her of romanticism, of preferring the exhilaration of plots and riots (worthy or not) to a staid life of orchestra attendance and ladies' club meetings in Chicago. "Don't be a damn fool, Jimmy," she replied. He kept her up late at night, remonstrating. He begged her for a final evening together of bourgeois pleasures: she'd wear the gold silk dress, austere and elegant, that Madame Sun had given her, and they'd dine in all splendor at the old Grand Hotel.

"Jimmy is kind, but hard," Rayna wrote Bill. "He knows what he wants and is very sure he will get it." Drinking and dashing about, Jimmy talked a blue streak, flirting all the while. He was selfish, entirely lacking in feeling for others: "I can't imagine him weeping at anything." She meant to put Bill's mind at ease: "He is a philanderer but not with me."

She danced with Jimmy, twice, after the dinner at the Grand Hotel. Dorothy had come by their table, flabbergasted at the decision that Rayna was making. By then, Dorothy had seen enough of the Soviet Union to know what she thought of it. She'd visited factories and clubs, schools and theaters, and what struck her was a contrast: the "grandiose scheme for the collective life—the pitiful meanness of the individual situation." Could the Soviet experiment succeed? Dorothy was doubtful. Look, for instance, at the communal kitchens, where the tenants all insisted on cooking on their own, one-burner oil stoves: "In the matter of kitchens all men are individualists." And Trotsky? Where was he during the tenth-anniversary festivities? There were rumors that Stalin had already had him locked up or killed. The Congress of the Soviets, ostensibly the supreme governing body of the USSR, hadn't met for a year and a half. Rayna was a nice girl, Dorothy wrote Red, but she "had balled up her life inextricably."

The next day, Rayna collapsed. Jimmy carried her, light as a child, through the streets to the Hotel Metropole. It seemed, at first, like a complete nervous breakdown, a result of strain and overwork. Or was it some sort of stomach trouble? Not trusting the Russian doctors, Rayna's friends sent for the German embassy's physician. The German doctor didn't wish to issue a diagnosis prematurely. In the meantime, he instructed that no one was to talk about politics to Rayna.

"Will you tell me what on earth anybody'd ever talk about in

Moscow if political discussion was forbidden?" Rayna inquired, laughing. "What do you suppose we can talk about? I can't remember any other subjects!"

Rayna seemed to improve that week. The curtains were opened and her room was light. She was lively and happy, talking about her childhood in Chicago, about her time in Berkeley and her friends there. She dictated cablegrams to her parents, to her best friend, to Raph. But then she had another bad night, and started to lose her grasp on reality, conversing with her parents or her first husband as if they were in the room. She died the morning of November 21, 1927, of an abscess on the brain. That night, it snowed in Moscow and Jimmy walked out in the storm, continuing his conversation with her, weeping.

Whether the cause of the abscess was encephalitis contracted in China or a brain tumor was something that Jimmy and Bill Prohme would later argue about. The case was a rare one, and the Moscow doctors, after the autopsy, kept a piece of her brain for further study.

Madame Sun Yat-sen attended Rayna's funeral, pitiful in a thin cloak against the icy Moscow weather. Dorothy was there, too, and with the other Americans, she insisted on following the hearse five miles out to the crematorium, walking, shivering the whole way. The icy cobblestones were slippery and it was snowing again. Over Rayna's coffin was draped the Soviet flag with hammer and sickle and the hearse was bright red, too. The band was switching between the revolutionary funeral anthem, off-key, and Chopin's dirge. There weren't any Russians in the procession to the crematorium, Dorothy took note, just Americans. "What a funny thing nationality is!" she wrote to Red. The prospect of dying as Rayna had—alone in a foreign hotel room—terrified Dorothy. She decided then that she'd go home and marry Red.

Rayna's coffin was heaped with flowers: the only forty roses that could be found in Moscow, pastel tea roses grown in the Crimea and purchased on behalf of Bill Prohme; and mounds of chrysanthemums, white and copper ones ordered by her father in Chicago and yellow from Raph. Jimmy's flowers were red and white. As the bier that held Rayna's coffin sank into the crematorium's furnace, Jimmy leaned forward, as if to pull her back from the flames.

EARLIER THAT SAME YEAR, as Jimmy arrived in Hankou, John and Frances were beginning their married life a world away, in Paris. John was hardly ever there, called away on one assignment or another. Frances opened every letter from him in a whirl of fear, steeling herself for whatever might be inside. In her cable accepting his marriage proposal, she'd offered an escape clause: "Marriage Rome Divorce Paris September." The idea, at least in theory, was that they'd divorce at a suitable interval after legitimating their child. Now that there was no baby, how long would he still consider himself bound to her?

Please don't say that, John begged her. It made him feel like a cad.

The *Daily News* sent John to Geneva and then his editor ordered him to Macedonia. In between he traveled to Tirana, Scutari, Belgrade, Bucharest, Athens, and Sofia for his series on dictators. It had taken John a few months to convince his editors that his idea was worth pursuing. Wasn't the subject of dictators now a little passé? they had objected. They'd already had plenty in the paper about Mussolini. John agreed to leave Italy out and focus on the East.

Dictators, John observed, came from border lands. Poland's Piłsudski was a Lithuanian, Stalin a Georgian, Turkey's Atatürk was born in Salonika. Why that was the case he didn't try to explain, instead telling the sorts of stories that would make newspaper readers in Chicago gawp or chuckle. The dictator of Albania had six hundred blood feuds against him. Amid his 1926 coup, Piłsudski had learned French so that he could swear in the language. Belgrade was as full of uniformed men as Rome. You never saw a woman in Albania who wasn't laden down with baskets or live chickens or bundles of wood; the men had to have their hands free to carry guns.

Be glad you're not here, he wrote Frances from Bucharest: the town was a bust, only one halfway decent hotel with indoor plumbing, and he was so busy she wouldn't have seen him, not even for meals. He had a chance of getting an interview with the queen of Romania, though it would be hard to arrange since that lady was in official mourning and had stashed herself away near the Black Sea. He was slaving away, running the gauntlet of ladies-in-waiting and plenipotentiaries, putting in an honest day's work.

This town is crawling with prostitutes, he added. In fact, the whole of Bucharest reeked of sex, "but so *dirty!*"

In Paris, Frances was shifting for herself, installed in a borrowed flat or at the Hotel Navigateur, carrying on aimless flirtations with bored husbands, making a point to drop hints to John. Tea was on for the afternoon with that playboy Pierre, she'd wear her scarlet dress and hat. John upped the ante in his old way. From Bulgaria, he informed her that he'd written nostalgic Christmas love letters to eight women, among them Rebecca, Helen, and Mickey. All nearly identical, God I hope they don't compare them. He'd saved the draft of his letter for her. How, by the way, was Pierre? he inquired.

"Well, remember, take along 2 rubbers when you go to call on the Queen," she replied. And no more pieces, darling, about "the Golden Curls of the Boy King." She was proving her usefulness to him, trying to steer his work in a more rigorous direction. She liked the idea of a general series about the Balkans "being au même temps so to speak fucked by France and pederasted by Italy." But what he *ought* to do was a behind-the-scenes book about European politics. "Note down all the 'inside' stories you hear and you'll have plenty of material in no time (not forgetting of course the fundamental magnetic pull of plain dirt economics)."

THE HAHN SISTERS DID of course compare John's Christmas love letters. Mickey's way of conducting a rivalry, though, was to keep her information to herself: "yes, from what you say I guess John wrote me the same letter exactly, as usual," she told Helen, "Except that he never says he loves me; quite the contrary."

In fact, John constantly told Mickey how much he loved her.

Before Frances sent him her "Will of God" telegram, Mickey had been planning to come out to Europe to meet him. He'd made arrangements for her to be hired as his assistant. She'd been working for nearly a year as a mining engineer—a victory she relished over the boys at the College of Engineering who'd assured her she would never have a job in the field. Nevertheless, she wrote John, she was ready to leave: "I don't want to grow important here. I don't approve of Oil."

When Frances's telegram arrived, John obviously had to tell Mickey their plan was off, but he went much further than that: "I've dreamed of winning you so long, that now my only reaction is that I've irretrievably lost." It was possible that he'd be happy in his marriage to Frances. But he doubted it. The situation in which he found himself was, he acknowledged, at least partly his own fault. The only consolation John saw in the whole mess was that Mickey didn't love him in return. In fact, maybe she didn't even care for him at all.

All this love business, Mickey sighed when she received his Christmas letter. Though John halved the number of love letters he acknowledged sending, Mickey saw through his ploy. If you're only writing four women, she replied, you can count yourself "an unusually restrained young man." Frances must be a real "humdinger" if John loved her. "Lord knows it's easy enough to love Helen and Rebecca and me, if you insist, the landlady's cat and the first queen of Egypt." John apparently liked to be in love. Her own method was different. She only fell in love if she was on her way someplace else. "Of course trains are sometimes late," she added.

"I do like states of indecision like what I'm in now—apartment unrented; half a dozen ragged relationships lying around spoiling for an artistic finish," Mickey had written her parents after John called off their European plans. She quit her job anyway and spent a drunken summer in New Mexico working as a tour guide. After a few months in New York, taking classes at Columbia and dining over at Helen's, complimenting her sister on how well-cooked the chicken was, she set out on her own, bound for Paris and later the Congo.

In his Christmas love letter to Rebecca, John adopted the persona of the naïf, puzzling over his own behavior. Here he was, newly married and yet writing love letters to six women. (Just the right number, he believed, to impress Rebecca.) "Am I a complete bounder," he wondered, "or the only honest man in the world?"

He felt he owed Rebecca an explanation on another score, too. Against the backdrop of Frances's straight talk about impotence, he now thought with chagrin of his lovemaking. On his way back from Syria, he'd stayed the weekend with Rebecca in Diano Marino, on the Italian Riviera. He'd met her in Antibes, too—"when you had more of me than anyone ever had had before." He knew he'd been lacking: "But you know—it's curious—I've never been a good lover to you—Oh yes—never. I can't tell why."

"Well—enough of this—and really I shouldn't write this way— it's wrong & unfair & useless. . . . And damn it I do care for Frances— like her—want her—mustn't hurt her."

FRANCES JOINED JOHN IN Constantinople for Christmas, 1927, on the heels of his love-letter barrage. But only after much dilly-dallying and exhortations from John to join him. They celebrated Christmas in a city that was, under the westernizer Atatürk's influence, full of Christmas trees and mistletoe, and unusually, snowbound. By the time they stood on the deck of the boat back to Romania, the minarets of the Hagia Sophia fading to faint traces, Frances was pregnant. "God's victory over rubber goods!" she told John.

Will of God—again—but this time, it righted the balance between them. They'd been playing at not being married since the wedding in Rome but now, it seemed, the fates had something different in store for them. She was thirty and he, twenty-six. John found that he wanted the baby, desperately so. "I'm prepared to argue I'm MUCH fonder of our child than you are," he wrote her. "I'm thinking of kites now, toy boats, Chanson de Roland, Homer, and Who is God? I'll need your help lady."

Even the news that the paper would be sending John to Russia for four months didn't dampen Frances's good cheer. John hadn't been given any say in the matter; he was to fill in for the *Daily News*'s Moscow correspondent, Junius Wood. Frances would stay in Paris. It was out of the question for her to travel to Russia: no milk, no anesthetics, those roads. He'd be back before the baby was born.

Send me pictures of you in your pajamas, John directed her from Moscow. He slept with those, and the nude photos she'd sent, too. "I miss you so—you're so deeply interwoven in the very texture of my mind." He relished fretting over her. Under no circumstances, he insisted, was she to run for a bus. Or unpack heavy trunks. Or sleep less than ten hours a night. Sit on the terrace in the sun! he urged her. Drink bottles of cream!

She no longer hid her books about baby care when their friends came around. Now, she put them right on the shelf. Don't worry about me, she reassured him. I'm in blooming good health and nut-brown from all of the sun baths. My belly looks like one of those gold Moscow church domes when I lay on the chaise longue. "What an immense step it is to use the word Mother about myself," she told him.

I have been such a silly, stupid, immature fool these last few years, he wrote her. "Not to have taken care of you better! Not to have adored you for all you were worth—from the beginning."

JOHN ARRIVED IN MOSCOW in June 1928. He was lodging in Junius Wood's rooms at the Grand Hotel, where Rayna and Jimmy had met for their final bourgeois evening of dining and dancing the winter before. Most of the Western correspondents and visiting dignitaries stayed at the Grand, which also functioned as a storehouse for the expropriated riches of Russia's former aristocracy. All the Louis Quinze, Sèvres porcelain, and coroneted napery a person could wish for, but just try to get a clean towel, Dorothy observed when she was a guest. In Bolshevik Russia, hotel employees were referred to as "officials," and it was said that the porters were, to a man, agents of the secret police. Through profligate tipping, Junius had somehow managed to install a Yale lock on his hotel room door to which he alone had the key.

Go to see Eisenstein, Frances instructed John from Paris. Ask him to show you his movies, take him to dinner. And Meyerhold: you must go to his theater and tell him I sent you. The Kremlin: it's imperative that you talk your way into a tour of the place, just raise hell until they let you in.

John was full of impressions. How surprising to be offered a cigarette by the chambermaid in your Moscow hotel: the social leveling wrought by the world's first proletarian revolution summed up in one interaction that was more telling than a hundred Politburo reports. The fact that servants now insisted on eating with the family. The existence of a food shop on the Tverskaya, the city's main avenue, as stupendously well stocked as any Parisian emporium. The absence of outdoor cafés—and cars, save a few rheumy specimens pressed into service as taxis and the government's flotilla of black Rolls-Royces. The complete lack of souvenirs, including postcards. The darkness of Moscow at night, a city with hardly any streetlights. The throngs gathered around loudspeakers mounted on telephone poles, listening to the news or broadcast speeches. The sour smell of black bread, cabbage soup, and sweat. Notes and notes but he couldn't pull them together into anything coherent.

The country, John admitted to Frances, was overwhelming him. Every morning, Junius's Russian assistant translated aloud the newspapers for him. He was taking Russian lessons twice a week, though he wasn't making any progress in the language. He'd been to see the official censor, a "charming fellow." But his efforts to extract basic statistics from the functionaries at the Soviet Foreign Office had been a flop: no one here seemed to know anything about crop yields. He'd barely managed to write a few cables. How on earth had Dorothy banged out mail stories after just a week in Moscow? To top it all off, he was feeling ridiculous in his Bond Street clothes, the new fedora, and the spit-polished boots, his walking stick tap-tapping over the cobbles while a hundred incredulous Muscovites pointed and stared. "I feel rather like the Eiffel Tower."

At loose ends, he was occupying himself with his usual diversions: drawing up lists of the characteristics that famous American novelists shared, taking in a Clara Bow movie, hosting a party at his hotel, to which he'd invited a few reporters and some of the representatives from the Swedish and Norwegian foreign legations. He was chewing over the problem of what to do with himself. Not politics: "I haven't an iota of public service in me." He was having doubts about novel-writing, too: imaginary characters were becoming less interesting to him than real ones. By contrast, journalism mattered in the world. "That is, it moves people and to a certain often variable extent influences actual events, with the result that the author achieves power. Which is tremendously what I want." In short: "I'd rather be Hoover than Thornton Wilder."

It had taken him weeks but finally, he wrote Frances, he was getting down to fundamentals and had an idea for a story: "the perfectly extraordinary resemblance" between Moscow and Rome. They looked the same, cobbled streets and decrepit buildings in shades of buff, and "a dank sort of hotness" in summer. In both capitals, the state indoctrinated youngsters early. In neither was there any liberty of the press. Certainly, the foreign society had a similar quality: tiny and inbred and gossipy. And Russians had that same amiable shiftlessness he'd observed in the Italians.

"Likens Moscow to Modern Rome; Daily News Man Finds Striking Similarities in Two Capitals," was the headline in the paper.

Think about it *harder,* Frances exhorted John from Paris. The similarities he saw between Moscow and Rome were undeniably there, but on the surface. What about the profound differences between the two regimes? What about labor laws? Women's rights? Schooling? Take Mussolini and Lenin. Benito had the personality of the actor, all ego and a hankering for personal power. Vlad had been a skeptic, a father figure, humorous.

John was a first-class describer of things—that was his strong suit. But he needed not just to see but to explain. He needed, insisted his wife, to sharpen his mind. Take his observation that Moscow had loudspeakers on every corner but no magazine stands. Such stuff deserved a whole article. People had to understand the Soviet ambition to leapfrog over entire historical eras.

And why in God's name was he spending his time in Moscow boozing it up with foreigners? Frances demanded. Had he seen Eisenstein yet? How many Russians had he met? Why was he eating dinners with well-mannered Swedes? "Jesus, you've spent all your life and will spend all the rest of your life with Nordics and fried chicken." Here she was in Paris, making do without him, and hoping that he'd get down to some serious, sustained thinking if he were on his own. Instead? "You seem to be leading the full life of the first social secretary of a liberian legation."

She felt contrite after berating him. Yet she meant every word of it. By the way, she added, every night I weep over your empty toothpaste tube.

He didn't have her gumption, he retorted. Maybe *she* would just barge in on Eisenstein, but he couldn't. Prodded by Frances, he did arrange to see the director, though. Eisenstein, John learned over dinner, was burning to get to Hollywood, where he could put aside aesthetics and make a first-class detective movie. He'd already had a bellyful of the Soviet government, which had wrecked his *Red October* by cutting out all the Trotsky footage. "Of course I'm a propagandist," Eisenstein told him, smiling. "So are all movie producers in America."

FRANCES WAS FAR MORE sympathetic than John to the Soviet experiment, and like Rayna Prohme and to some degree Jimmy himself, more enamored of the notion of a meaningful collective existence. But Frances hadn't been in the Soviet Union since 1924 and she did not appreciate how quickly the regime was changing. At the 15th Party Congress, convened in December 1927, a month after the revolutionary celebrations, all deviation from orthodoxy was condemned. Party doctrine would be decided by Stalin, whose grip on the machinery of power was tightening. The sorts of private ownership—of land, of shops, of light industry—that had been permitted under the New Economic Policy of 1921 would soon end, as the state reimposed control over industry and commerce.

John's feel for atmosphere yielded its own analysis. He sensed the watchful eyes on him, the oppression in the air. In comparing Rome and Moscow, his point was that Bolshevism and fascism, ostensibly at the "uttermost possible poles from each other," in fact shared much as a matter of practical government, including the "almost total extinction of personal liberty." His instincts were right. It wouldn't be long before foreign reporters were no longer free to wander where they wished or put locks on their hotel room doors. The scope of the terror to come was beyond imagining. In 1940, the theater director Meyerhold, aged sixty-five, would be arrested for his ideological nonconformity, beaten on the soles of his feet and his back with a rubber strap, and executed by firing squad.

As a matter of pure theory, John admired a lot of what the Russians were trying to do. Just not as much as Frances did. "I think that my emotions here are just what they would be had I lived in Paris in 1793," he wrote her after his nightly walk through Red Square. "That was Progress. With a big P. So is this. Anyone would be a fool to deny it." At the same time, though, when you picked up the telephone, there was the dispiriting, telltale click that indicated the secret police was listening in. "On the whole, I don't like it. Give me England. I believe in liberty. (A dreadful thing to confess—I still wish I was an Englishman.)"

As for her idea about how Russia was vaulting through the millennia: "oh Lord!—I need you here." He did write that piece, just as she had suggested, charting "this effort to skip overnight a hundred generations." It was his attempt to give the revolution its due. If the private market and capitalism hadn't yet been eradicated (and John doubted they would be), it was nonetheless the case that dramatic changes had been wrought. Before the Revolution, the illiteracy rate had been 85 percent. Now the country had some of the most advanced schools in the world. The restrictive social mores of a backward country had been swept away, replaced by divorce on demand and abortion, too. In the place of a domineering and superstitious religion, the Soviets had no religion at all. The calculating machine had supplanted the abacus.

It wasn't long now, just a month more, before he'd be home, he wrote her from the oil town of Baku in September 1928. The fields were mucky with oil; there was a new seven-story hotel *and* camels in the main street. Would she meet him at the station in Paris? He'd come hurdling over the gates. There were so many plans to make. He assumed the baby Frances was carrying would be a boy. "I have great times thinking of games to play, swimming (and teaching him to swim) on sunny silver beaches; the first Xmas trees and what my-thology is; Battle stories and tin solders; what is truth and plasticine. This <u>shall</u> be a child."

He still felt terrible about those other babies, she had to know that. Did she? Had she guessed? Now their lives would be different. They were starting all over again. "You shall have 3 babies & a house on a hill overlooking the sea: I shall have a library with all the books in the world in it & a big desk & one half of your warm delightful bed."

FILING THE
MINORITY REPORT

—

WHAT AN UPROAR JIMMY SHEEAN IS CAUSING, VIRGINIA Woolf gossiped to her sister, the painter Vanessa Bell. In the spring of 1929, little more than a year after he returned from Moscow, Jimmy had taken up with Woolf's friend Eddy Sackville-West, a music critic and heir to the estate of Knole, one of the largest houses in England. On account of Jimmy—"a wretched American who talks through his nose," as Woolf put it—Eddy had announced he would never, ever marry. Now the Sackville-Wests were in a state, fearing that their ancestral property would pass to a distant cousin. If Eddy's love interest had been more conventionally objectionable (say, an actress or a duke), his family probably wouldn't mind so much, Woolf added.

That Jimmy would embed himself in Woolf's Bloomsbury set was a feat nearly as surprising as his interviews with Abd el-Krim. The Bloomsbury Group, which included Woolf and Vanessa Bell, the writers E. M. Forster and Lytton Strachey, the economist John Maynard Keynes, and the Postimpressionist painters Duncan Bell and Roger Fry, was notoriously clubby and self-sustaining. Their London habitat was the terraced brick Regency houses on Gordon Square, then a raffish contrast to the tranquil, pristine Kensington neighborhoods of aproned servants and regular dinner hours in which they'd been raised. In Bloomsbury, before the First World War, Woolf, Bell, Strachey, and their friends established ménages where they could paint and write and argue, while forgoing table napkins and drinking coffee rather than tea. They "lived in squares" and "loved in triangles," said Dorothy Parker, a quip that aptly sums up Bloomsbury's pursuit of domestic pleasures and its embrace of unconventionality in personal relationships.

As Jimmy saw it, his Bloomsbury friendships served as the counterweight to his attachment to Rayna Prohm. She stood for the abnegation of self; they, for its worldly realization. Her individuality would be subsumed in the collective. Theirs would be nurtured by the company of a select few. Politics was everything to her. Bloomsbury was apolitical, detached from the world, he judged (somewhat unfairly). In Gordon Square, liberation came instead through self-fulfillment, shaking off Victorian repressions via honest talk. "We discussed copulation with the same excitement and openness that we had discussed the nature of good," remembered Woolf of Bloomsbury's early days. That drive to self-revelation continued to sustain the group's bonds after the First World War. At meetings of a semi-secret Memoir Club, founded in 1920, absolute candor on the part of the speaker was obligatory, and the rule was that no one was to be shocked or take offense at anything said.

The first of Jimmy's Bloomsbury friends were the literary critic and editor Raymond Mortimer and Harold Nicolson, a diplomat and writer. Nicolson was married to Virginia Woolf's sometime lover, the novelist Vita Sackville-West. He was also in love with the urbane, dark-haired, and dimple-chinned Mortimer, who for a little while, at least, had his own pash on Jimmy, before settling into the role of steadying confidant and moneylender. Through Raymond Mortimer, Jimmy came to know two of Bloomsbury's "demi-gods," as he called them: Duncan Grant and Vita's cousin, Eddy Sackville-West, both of whom became smitten with him. "Glad you had Jimmy," Vita teased her husband after one of Jimmy's visits. "No, I don't mean that; honi soit qui mal y pense."

None of these entanglements, it goes without saying, were intended for public consumption. In Britain, as in most American states, sex between men, whether in public or in private, was a criminal offense, to be punished by imprisonment. Harold Nicolson's recklessness in love affairs struck Jimmy as a dangerous indulgence. In his own line of work, exposure would be "simply fatal," Jimmy felt certain, noting: "I have to mind my p's and q's or starve to death."

Yet the innuendo about Jimmy piled up. It's there in Dorothy's comment about his prettiness and wet lower lip. And it had real costs: Jimmy was fired from his correspondent job at the *Chicago Tribune,* despite the success of his reporting in the Rif, for what the paper's publisher described in a letter to his cousin as "bad practices," adding in a penciled notation: "perverted." The Arabist George Antonius, a civil servant in the British Mandate of Palestine (and "not one of the fils de Sodome," Jimmy wrote Eddy), warned Jimmy to be careful about his mail in Jerusalem.

In the 1920s and 1930s, the concept of homosexuality as a distinct, exclusive identity was still in the making. Bisexuality was a term of art for Freudians, who believed it to be the natural state of humans, but for laypeople, there was simply a muddy, unlabeled middle. Even in circles such as Bloomsbury, in which homosexual desire was frankly acknowledged, it often coexisted with marriages or love affairs with the opposite sex. That was the case for Woolf and Vita Sackville-West, as well as Harold Nicolson, John Maynard Keynes, and Duncan Grant, whose relationship with Woolf's sister, Vanessa Bell, produced a daughter.

"Forgive me if this question displeases you," was the way that an acquaintance of Duncan's started a conversation with Jimmy: "'are you to any degree homosexual?'"

"I jumped a little," Jimmy related to Duncan, adding that he'd replied: "'To a very high degree, I think, but I've never had a really expert opinion.'"

If homosexuality was a matter of "degrees," it was also the open secret par excellence: often known, but in most cases, assiduously if imperfectly covered up. Vanessa Bell's son, Quentin, was shocked to find out about Jimmy, though as he admitted to his mother, "I'm no good at spotting the buggers." When an English acquaintance told Jimmy's friends in New York that he was "the most notorious bugger in Europe," they hooted with laughter. Their merriment only increased when the man indignantly produced the names of Jimmy's conquests. Like Duncan Grant, Jimmy was wildly attractive both to women and to men. He couldn't handle affairs with more than two ladies at a time, he remarked airily to Raymond Mortimer, and when they came in fives and sixes, he was finished.

In the year after Rayna died, Jimmy spent much of his time in Paris and in London, and soon enough, he was a regular visitor to Eddy's rooms at Knole, coming down for weekends and parties, staying at holiday time. Eddy lived in the fifteenth-century Gatehouse Tower, which stood sentry over the vast gray stone pile. His style was a mix of 1890s decadence and modernist fancy, skulls and a crucifix on the wall, a sword in the corner, an astrological ceiling painted in blue and gold, the modest rooms of the Tower distempered in chalky pink and mint green and sky blue.

It was all "rather awful," judged Vita, "Eddy himself mincing in black velvet," his wrists heavy with gold bracelets. Her father was the 3rd Baron Sackville but the estate, to Vita's bitterness, was entailed on the male line. She would never inherit it, which made Eddy's effeminacy all the more grating. Virginia Woolf, who liked Eddy, described him as a "tiny lap dog," with a girlish voice and "a face like a persian cats, all white and serious, with large violet eyes and fluffy cheeks." His eyes were sleepy, his manner languid; he had a hereditary bleeding disorder. He had arched eyebrows and a high forehead. He favored lipstick.

Eddy had published a novel, he wrote music criticism, and even as a child had played Chopin and Wagner by ear. He entertained Jimmy in the pink music room, its fire screen painted by Duncan Grant with flames resembling octopus tentacles. No matter how many fires they set, it was subarctic in the Tower in the winter; there was no central heating at Knole. Freezing cold, they listened to *Tristan* on Eddy's gramophone and did (in Jimmy's description) "what the music so clearly commands one to do." About his "carnal desires for my boneless, bodiless, wispy and exquisite Enfant Cheri," Jimmy wrote forthrightly. "Dearest, I love you," he declared when he left for a reporting assignment in Palestine. He was saving up for their "scappato," or run-away fund, he promised Eddy.

If only Eddy didn't insist on taking the whole thing so seriously, Jimmy complained to Raymond a few months later. "I adore him, but—helas!—tu me connais," he wrote. "Being in love with me is a dreadful waste of time." Fidelity had nothing to do with it: that wasn't expected on either side. Eddy told Jimmy of his escapades on a trip to Berlin and Jimmy mentioned to him a fling in Marseilles en route to Jerusalem. To Eddy, though, love apparently meant "Nordic transports, romantisme, melancholy," none of which were to Jimmy's liking, as he told Raymond. "My instability is not only in my character and emotions, but in the life I lead, so that you literally can't be sure where I am, in any sense at all."

Warned by his friends of Jimmy's "volage" nature, Eddy wrote his lover an uneasy letter. Was Jimmy really as fickle as Raymond and Harold were saying? "I'm a constant creature, really, when I get a chance to be," Jimmy assured him.

AGAINST THE LURES OF the outside world, the cloistered pleasures of Knole stood no chance at all with Jimmy. He set out for Palestine in the summer of 1929, traveling via Paris and Marseilles to Port Said and from there, on the Cairo express, to Jerusalem. He'd gotten the assignment to visit the country from the *New Palestine,* the official publication of the Zionist Organization of America. He had a romantic idea of Zionism; his subject would be life in the rapidly expanding Jewish settlements. His advance was $500, the equivalent of $7,400 today, with another $1,500 to come when he finished the series and gave a lecture tour on the subject. Sympathetic as he was to the idea of a Jewish nation, Jimmy told the *New Palestine*'s editor, he nevertheless stipulated that he would write no propaganda.

In the divvying up of seized enemy territories that followed the

First World War, the League of Nations had accorded Palestine, formerly an Ottoman possession, to the British to administer as a mandate. Since the Balfour Declaration of 1917, the British government had been publicly committed to the development of Palestine as a homeland for the Jewish people. But how could a national home for the Jews be created where other people, the Arabs of Palestine, had themselves also been living for generations? According to the Balfour Declaration, "nothing shall be done which may prejudice the civil and religious rights of existing non-Jewish communities in Palestine"—an answer that said nothing of the political or economic rights of those populations. And what about the separate, contradictory promises the British had already made? First to the sharif of Mecca in 1915, promising support for an independent Arab state in exchange for a wartime Arab uprising against Ottoman rule; second, the following year, to the French, dividing the Ottoman territories into British and French zones of influence, with coastal Palestine under international control.

Palestine, in short, was a first-class mess, even for reporters conversant with the vying nationalisms of east-central Europe. The situation was volatile, not least because the immigration of Jews from Eastern Europe to Palestine was booming. Jewish trusts were buying up land in Palestine, sowing still more dispossession and resentment. According to John Gunther, who arrived in Jerusalem a few months after Jimmy, the assignment was devilishly tough. Reporting from Palestine, John wrote to Frances, required "distilling fact out of the filthiest mess of rumor, slander, lies, prejudice I have ever run into. The way feeling runs here!"

Jimmy found the ancient city of Jerusalem enchanting. The streets resembled gently sloping staircases and its hills reminded him of early Italian paintings, in which the struggles with perspective lent a magical quality to the landscape. He was lodging at the Austrian Hospice, a vast, monastery-like structure of honeyed stone built in the mid-nineteenth century to house German-speaking pilgrims to the city. The rooms were domed and quiet. Even in the heat of a Jerusalem summer, it was cool. And from the roof of the Austrian Hospice, the biblical landscape lay just in the distance: the golden Dome of the Rock, with the Western Wall just below it; the Mount of Olives, a Jewish cemetery for three thousand years and, according to the New Testament, the place from which Jesus rose to heaven, to the east. At night, every star in the sky seemed to beckon just in reach.

Before he arrived in Jerusalem, Jimmy had known that the population of the old, walled city was mainly Arab, but to see the domes of the mosques and to hear the calls to prayer from all corners set him wondering. Were relations between Palestine's Arab inhabitants and the Jewish settlers in fact as harmonious as his Zionist informants had led him to believe? The Zionists told him that Arabs cared only about the money—that they would be pleased to sell their land for a good profit to the Jews and depart for Syria, Iraq, Transjordan, and Arabia, all Arab countries where they could live. But it seemed doubtful to Jimmy that the case was as clear as all that. For one thing, there was the Haram esh-Sharif, or the Temple Mount.

Just a few minutes' walk from the Austrian Hospice, the Haram esh-Sharif is the compound where the holiest places of Judaism and Islam nest together. Here is the octagonal Dome of the Rock, marking the spot from which Muhammad ascended to heaven. Here, too, is the Western (or Wailing) Wall, a southwestern section of the Haram, the giant blocks of limestone all that remained of the destroyed Second Temple. In 1919, Zionists had tried to buy the Wailing Wall outright, offering £80,000 for it. The Muslim authorities of the city had refused, and more and more, the Wall became a flash point, with Jews pushing for further prerogatives and the newly installed Grand Mufti of Jerusalem, the twenty-four-year-old Hajj Amin al-Husseini, in turn, placing new restrictions. Jews petitioned for the right to build screens to separate the men from the women at the Wall, as at a synagogue; they wanted to blow the shofar there; they objected to Arabs driving their mules on the pavement. In 1929, the Mufti, provocatively, opened a new passageway to the Haram, which meant that Muslims could leave and enter the mosque from the pavement in front of the Western Wall.

Jimmy took to visiting the Haram esh-Sharif compound, spending days in the Dome of the Rock, parts of which dated back to the seventh century. Unlike Islam's other sacred sites, the Dome of the Rock was then open to non-Muslims (it no longer is). Jimmy would sit on the perimeter of the stone floor of the mosque, marveling at the discordance between the passionate hatreds he felt around him and the glittering mosaics above, harmonies of sea-green, azure, and gold. Sometimes, he'd lie there on his back, quiet and still. An Arabic paper had attacked him for being in the pocket of the Jews, which made him wonder whether he could in fact write objectively when his employer was the *New Palestine*. He decided to renounce the contract with the Zionist Organization of America, saying that he'd take no more money and reiterating that he had to write as he pleased. His sympathies were shifting to the Arab population of Palestine. "All my interest in Zionism has completely evaporated," he reported to Eddy after a month in Jerusalem. He was spending his days in the Austrian Hospice, trying to finish an autobiographical novel about the attraction between a Red young woman and a bourgeois reporter.

On the afternoon of August 14, Jimmy was in his room, working on the last chapter of his novel about Rayna, when an American woman named Anne Goldsmith, a schoolteacher whom he knew slightly from Zionist circles, asked to see him downstairs. She was a friend of Gerson Agronsky, the former press director of the Palestine Zionist Executive, now stringing for *The Times* of London. As Jimmy told the story, Goldsmith warned him there would be a "bust-up" at the Western Wall that evening, the start of Tisha B'Av, the Jewish holiday that marked the destruction of the Temple. Gangs of young men from Eastern Europe, the so-called *halutzim* (or pioneers) of the settlements, were gathering at the Wall and they would be armed. Agronsky was in Zurich for the Zionist Congress, where a new agency—the United Jewish Agency—had just been created to unite world Jewry in support of Zionism. Would Jimmy accompany her to the Wall and report on the scene there? She'd heard that Hadassah, the Jewish hospital in Jerusalem, was preparing extra stretchers to deal with the casualties.

It would be a very good thing, Anne Goldsmith confided to Jimmy, if there were trouble between Zionists and Arabs. The sanctity of the Wall was the one thing that all Jews could agree on; a riot at the Wall would be a positive boon for Zionist fundraising efforts on behalf of the new United Jewish Agency. "We have to show them we are here." Jimmy was incredulous. Did the woman understand what she was implying? Were the young Zionists actually planning to provoke the Arabs? Everyone in Tel Aviv knew about the plans, she told him. "She was inconceivably cynical and flippant about the whole thing," Jimmy recorded in his diary, and "apparently enjoyed the impression of horror she was making on me."

It seemed to him impossibly far-fetched that Zionist leaders could have planned such a provocation. But the next evening the young settlers were once again on their way to the Wall, raising the Zionist national flag. Jimmy felt he ought to go to the British authorities and tell them what he'd heard. But who would believe such an outlandish story? His friend George Antonius, a Lebanese Christian and Arab patriot who worked for the British mandate, would have—but he was away on holiday. A crowd of two thousand or so Muslims were assembled at the Western Wall, pulling out the prayers that Jews had left between the stones of the wall and tearing them up. Brawls broke out in the streets between Arabs and Jews. A Jewish boy was stabbed in a fight with Arabs on a soccer field and died. "Every day I expect the worst. It can't go on like this without an outbreak," Jimmy wrote on the morning of August 23, 1929.

That afternoon came the disaster that Jimmy was fearing. The violence that started at the Wall was spreading. A mob of Arabs, armed with knives and clubs, attacked the houses of Georgian Jews near the Damascus Gate. Equipped only with truncheons, the British policemen were powerless to stop the assaults. Worse still was to come. Stoked by rumors that Jews had destroyed the Haram, Arab gangs massacred unarmed Jews in the town at Hebron, killing sixty-four and wounding another fifty-four, among them women and children, an atrocity all the more horrible, thought Jimmy, because the Jews of Hebron were a long-settled, devoutly religious people who had lived in peace with their neighbors for centuries. Palestine was in the throes of what the newspapers called a "racial war," and by the time that the fighting had ended, British authorities counted 133 Jews and 116 Arabs dead, 339 Jews and 232 Arabs wounded.

Jimmy's reports were among the earliest detailed accounts filed from Palestine. Jewish reporters could not leave their homes without risking their lives; British papers labored under their government's censorship regime; and American correspondents such as John Gunther, who traveled by boat from Genoa, took several days to arrive in Jerusalem. Detailing the horrors the Arabs had perpetrated at Hebron, Jimmy nonetheless laid blame on the "Zionist fascisti," whom he accused of having precipitated the crisis. The young Zionist settlers, he'd seen firsthand, were "spoiling for a fight" and bore a "fearful responsibility."

These were incendiary charges, and it wasn't long before the papers that printed Jimmy's dispatches were beset by protests. Outside the offices of the *New York Evening World,* angry demonstrators gathered to denounce Sheean's reporting. There were irate letters and Jewish businesses threatened to withdraw their advertising. The paper backed away from Jimmy's account, regretting the "injustice" his article had done the Zionists. From Louisville, Kentucky, a rabbi struck a characteristic note. He condemned Sheean as an Arab partisan and charged that his "cruel misrepresentations" amounted to blaming the victims of the attacks. Far from being fascists, the young Zionists—their settlements besieged at every turn by "predatory Arab barbarians"—were "heroes of the art of peace."

For a few days, Jimmy was unaware of the controversy that was whipping up around him. He'd gone to the hospitals in Jerusalem to visit survivors of the Hebron massacre and to report on the viciousness of the Arab attacks. Shaken by the screams of agony in the children's ward, he could barely hold his pencil. By the time he returned to the Austrian Hospice at two A.M., he was near collapse.

Feverishly he typed cablegram after cablegram to the North American News Agency, each one attempting to describe what he'd seen. In the morning, he crawled into bed, the floor littered with unsent cables. For four days, he could not even get out of bed. It was a "mental derangement unlike anything else I have ever known," he wrote.

Where was he? Why wasn't he sending cables? his editors demanded by telegram. Eventually Jimmy fired off his reply. Having observed the Zionist movement at close hand, he told them, he'd concluded it was "aggressive dangerous and unjust." While his Zionist friends would call him an anti-Semite, such an accusation was "nonsense." The point was that he could no longer claim to be impartial in the face of "the horrors created by political injustice." He'd provided the news agency with the "best non partisan service" he could offer during the immediate crisis, but demanded—for the good of the news agency—to be let go. When his editors petitioned for more dispatches, Jimmy refused. "Do Not Annoy Me by Further Cables," was his reply.

The result was that Jimmy would be savaged again in the Jewish press as ignorant and biased. The allegations of "Zionist fascisti" aroused especially bitter recriminations. But John, who arrived in Palestine in early September, after much of the fighting was over, came to many of the same conclusions. His articles were more dispassionate than Jimmy's. In a series of mailers, he explained what made Palestine such a conundrum. The contradictory promises the British had made during the war and their eagerness to keep hold of the Palestine mandate. The tenacity of Jewish settlers, who had indeed done much to raise the standard of living in Palestine, draining the swamps, improving the fertility of the land, building infrastructure. The dispossession of the Arabs, who still owned most of the land in the country, but feared with good cause that Jewish immigrants would eventually buy up the rest.

Like Jimmy, John emphasized the role that the "extreme fascist wing of Zionism" had played in provoking the August riots. "In each case, Zionist provocation came first." The actions of the *halutzim* at the Western Wall—the raising of the Zionist flag, the singing of the Jewish national anthem: "all of this exactly comparable to advancing to an annoyed and ravenous lion and sticking one's head inside his mouth." No longer was Zionism a "remote experiment plodding along in comparative obscurity," John observed. Now it had become a raging international issue that inflamed the passions of Jews and Muslims across the world. It was "a question with no solution." To Frances he wrote more frankly: "I should like to join the Arab army, that's all." He couldn't wait to leave.

After the Holocaust, when fascism became synonymous with anti-Semitism and mass murder, the term "Zionist fascisti" would become an almost unimaginable slur. But in 1929, to label Zionists (or segments of Zionism) as fascist was inflammatory but not uncommon. The right-wing Zionist leader Vladimir Jabotinsky had indeed been influenced by European fascist movements, modeling his own paramilitary force on Mussolini's blackshirts. Jabotinsky's Jewish opponents in the Zionist Labour movement regularly called him a fascist. When John and Jimmy invoked fascism, they meant that Zionism was expansionist, aggressive, nationalistic, and racially exclusive, all characteristics of the kind of fascism they had seen firsthand in Italy, Romania, and Hungary.

More significant still was the association they drew between Zionism and imperialism. They likened Zionism to the conquest of Native American territory by the land-grabbing settlers. Jimmy and John also thought that Zionism served the interests of British imperialism. By writing into the mandate the obligation to create a Jewish national home in accord with the Balfour Declaration, the British legitimated their own presence in Palestine. "Zionism," wrote John, "not only serves to give the British an anchor in the Middle East, it makes that anchor moral."

John left Jerusalem after a month there, but Jimmy stayed on for another six weeks. During that time, he saw more of George Antonius, and got to know the Grand Mufti. The Mufti was a fervent anti-Zionist, to be sure, but as Jimmy saw it, far from inciting the August violence (as Zionists alleged), he had sought to contain it.

God, what a mess, Jimmy wrote Eddy, "I've never seen such a thing in the course of a somewhat extensive experience with messes." Zionism, he had decided, was "a disreputable and thoroughly unjust experiment. Nothing will ever change my view of it now." He agreed to give evidence on behalf of the Palestine Arabs to the British Parliamentary commission, headed by the retired colonial judge Sir Walter Shaw, which had been appointed to investigate the causes of the violence.

When the Shaw Commission arrived in Jerusalem in late October, taking possession of all the available typewriters in the Mandate to do their work, Jimmy was the first nonofficial witness called to testify. He'd been suffering from malaria, was sick with feverish chills, and entirely unprepared for the grilling he was about to undergo. The Commission had taken the form of a court, with sworn testimony and counsel for the Palestine Zionist Executive and for the Palestine Arab Executive examining the witnesses.

Questioned by the lawyer for the Palestine Arab Executive, Jimmy related the story of his encounter with Anne Goldsmith and his observations about the behavior of the *halutzim* at the Western Wall. The Labour Member of Parliament on the Commission, seated just a few feet away, became disgruntled. He didn't see the point of soliciting Sheean's testimony. "Just a journalist out for a good story!" he exclaimed in a loud voice as Jimmy was talking.

Sir Boyd Merriman, counsel for the Zionists, rose to begin his cross-examination. Almost immediately he called into question Jimmy's objectivity.

"You did not seem very surprised when I put the suggestion to you, are your sympathies anti-Jewish?" Merriman asked him.

"Anti-Jewish, no. Anti-Zionist," Jimmy explained.

"Your sympathies with Zionism are at the moment imperfect."

"They are non-existent," Jimmy replied.

Given the gravity of Jimmy's accusations, Miss Anne Goldsmith had to be heard, Merriman said. Called to testify under oath that same afternoon, she denied nearly all of Jimmy's allegations. The term "bust-up" was one she had never in her life used. No, she wasn't a Zionist. She'd heard about the extra stretchers, yes, but only because she'd visited an upholsterer in the vicinity of the Hadassah Hospital. No, she hadn't said anything to Jimmy about the *halutzim* or trouble at the Wall helping the Zionist cause.

"I have made such a mess of things," Jimmy lamented to John, who was back in Paris. "I don't think my testimony in Jerusalem did an ounce of good to the Arabs, and it has probably marked me for life as an enemy of the Jews." He'd spoken plainly, he said—probably too plainly for the Commission members, who were more accustomed to hearing from equivocating, cautious civil servants.

Jimmy departed the day after he gave his second session of testimony. He would come to Knole directly from the train station in London, he informed Eddy, and they could celebrate his thirtieth birthday in the Tower. "I warn you to be prepared for a rather startling apparition." He'd shaved his head in Jerusalem because of the heat, and his hair was growing in with patches of gray. In Vienna, he'd had a winter overcoat made from a Bedouin cloak of prickly camel's hair. He hadn't been to bed with anyone during his five months in Palestine, he added.

There *might* have been opportunities with Arabs, Jimmy told Raymond Mortimer. But given his position, he couldn't take the risk of being compromised by his "private vices." Based on a few chance remarks, he suspected the Zionists already had something on him. When he got to London, he had an appointment to see the Labour Party prime minister, Ramsay MacDonald, to offer his views on the situation in Palestine. "I have (don't laugh) another Cause now," Jimmy wrote Raymond. "It's the Arabs. I do love them and I think they're getting an abominable swindling from everybody."

Doubtful as Jimmy was about the utility of his testimony, the Shaw Commission—much to the consternation of Zionists—came to conclusions not so different from his own. Drawing on evidence gathered from 123 witnesses in 47 open sittings and another 11 in private, the Commission largely exonerated the Grand Mufti, determining that the Arab attacks were not premeditated. It identified as a proximate cause of the unrest the demonstration of *halutzim* at the

Western Wall, organized by the right-wing Zionist Dr. Joseph Klausner and his Pro–Wailing Wall Committee. The conflict's deeper roots, claimed the Shaw Commission, stemmed from the immigration of Jews to Palestine, which understandably raised Arab apprehensions about their economic and political future.

Like much else about the Palestinian-Israeli conflict, there is considerable dispute about the Shaw Commission and, more broadly, who was to blame for the events of 1929. Controversial at the time, the Shaw report has since been both lauded as right-minded and condemned as a whitewash. The Grand Mufti in particular has come in for more criticism than either the Shaw report or Sheean allowed, accused of fomenting violence to further Arab nationalist claims and to shore up his own position vis-à-vis rivals. By blaming Zionism for the attacks, it has been argued, the British mandatory authorities sought to deflect attention from their own failures, most significantly the lack of a sufficient police force. That the British authorities were woefully unprepared for the trouble (a point soft-pedaled by the Shaw Commission) is one of the few subjects on which there is a consensus.

When the Shaw report was published in 1930, Jimmy was on a three-month lecture tour of America, with stops at Pasadena Junior College, the Sheboygan Women's Club, and the Pittsburgh YWCA. The title of his talk varied according to the audience: "The Road in the East," "Political Movements of the Old World," or (more pointedly, joining his various anti-imperial causes) "An Irishman Looks at Zion." At every stop, he was trailed by Zionists who alternately boycotted and heckled him. The Commission's findings were, he admitted, a surprise to him. The Shaw report told "truths of the most unpleasant and awkward nature," he wrote. Jimmy cautioned Arabs, though, not to indulge in too much rejoicing, for above all else, the report seemed to him evidence of a "sort of subconscious telepathy between Englishmen which tells them how to make the best move for the empire's good." At present the British Empire seemed intent on placating the Arabs. Tomorrow they might favor the Jews. This was a perspicacious analysis: the Shaw report's recommendation about limiting Jewish immigration and land purchases, written into a new government statement of policy, the 1930 Passfield White Paper, was itself overturned the following year.

Zionists, Jimmy observed to George Antonius, were the strangest combination of idealism and cynicism: "Fascists in their own affairs, with regard to Palestine, and internationalists in everything else." After his lecture in Pittsburgh, Jimmy was asked why Palestinian Arabs didn't just move to Syria or Mesopotamia if they didn't like Zionism. He had his answer prepared. What if New York City were given to the Jews for a national home? How would the non-Jewish population of the city and the surrounding areas feel about that solution?

Jimmy's latest cause was earning him something of a reputation as "a champion of the downtrodden, etc. etc.," he informed John. "Nearly everywhere I go there is some Hindu or Indian Moslem or Chinese or Arab who turns up, after the lecture, to thank me with tears in his eyes for 'helping' them as they can't help themselves."

JOHN AND JIMMY HAD known each other slightly at the University of Chicago and they'd met again on a sidewalk in Paris in 1922. But it wasn't until September 1929, when they were together in Palestine, that they became friends. They went up to the roof of the Austrian Hospice and talked and drank through the hot nights. John had a car, and they drove up to Damascus, taking stock of the reverberations of the Palestine riots in Syria and visiting the dig that the Rockefellers were sponsoring at Armageddon. Jimmy was the only person in Jerusalem with whom you could discuss something other than Zionists and Arabs and Palestine, John said. He's an "amusing beggar (not bugger)," John told Frances.

But there was one thing that John hadn't been able to talk to Jimmy about. It puzzled him why he'd withheld it. One ought to be able to discuss pretty much anything with one's friends, he felt. In that spirit, he'd unburdened himself to various comrades about his troubles with Frances. But through all those nights on the Austrian Hospice's roof, he'd kept quiet about what had happened to the baby Frances had conceived in Constantinople.

Their baby—a girl—was born in Paris in September 1928. They named her Judith. She'd arrived in time to claim a place on the Gunthers' Christmas card, caricatured as a bawling mouth and a lick of hair. In truth, she was a contented baby, with big velvety eyes. "Now you will have to begin steering her past Cape Oedipus, well to the left of Mother-fixation whirlpool, and to the right of the thousand complexes, repressions, inhibitions, etc. which so amply compensate the modern child for loss of the old thrills of sin and devil-dodging," offered one of Judy's godfathers.

A few months after Judy's birth, John's mother fell ill, and he hurried home to Chicago to see her. His father had died, unlamented, the previous year: "I have such a guilty conscience at being so free and cheerful," his mother had written. John was on the SS *Majestic* in the middle of the Atlantic when a radiogram arrived announcing Lizette's death. A few days later, Frances bundled Judy and her nurse onto the *Paris,* departing Le Havre for New York, where they'd see Frances's mother for a day, and then proceed to Chicago.

John scribbled a few notes on the trip over, memories of his mother, but it was all too painful to think about. Mostly he paced the decks of the *Majestic.* Had he disappointed his mother? he asked himself. Not when he was younger. Confronted with a choice of conduct, he had, his mother said, "invariably chosen the fine thing."

But what about later in life? His mother had been alarmed when she heard about his engagement to Frances. Lizette wasn't opposed to the marriage, she wanted her son to understand. But how could John have taken such an important step in life without consulting her? Relations between the two women were cordial but nothing more: Frances was "alarmingly frank," Lizette had opined, while her self-sacrificial never-mind-me manner grated on Frances's nerves.

Lizette and John's sister Billi came to Europe the summer that John was away in Russia. Frances was pregnant with Judy, and they'd stayed with her in Paris, trying to be helpful but mostly driving her crazy.

Frances and Judy arrived in Chicago too late for his mother's funeral. A few days later, he and Frances had a night out at the theater, taking Billi with them to try to cheer her up. They left the baby with a nursemaid in the house on Kenmore Avenue. When they returned home, Judy was dead.

"Did the nurse kill her?" Frances had cried. It was a thymic death, a doctor friend explained, what would today be called a crib death. The baby, said the doctor, was smothered by an enlarged gland resting on the trachea. No one could have detected anything wrong in a four-month-old baby. It was an unavoidable accident, a tragedy. There was nothing hereditary to worry about. "You should have no fear in bringing into this world another Judy," the doctor wrote Frances.

Their friends wrote to express their grief and sympathy, but no one really knew what to say. For the generation of their parents and grandparents, the death of a baby or a child under the age of five had been a common enough occurrence—sad, of course, but not unfathomable. It was God's will, people said to comfort each other: another angel for Heaven. In 1900, pneumonia, tuberculosis, enteritis, diphtheria, and influenza claimed the lives of one in every six babies in the United States; babies and small children comprised nearly a third of all deaths. By the 1920s, because of improvements in sanitation and medical treatment, writing a condolence letter about a baby was a much less familiar task. "My dear fellow—and my dear Frances," wrote a friend of John's. "I ought to be able to write a coherent letter but I just stumble around trying to think of words," adding, "There's just nothing I can say that would be adequate."

It is striking how often their friends—writers nearly all of them—acknowledged that words wouldn't help John and Frances. "There's nothing anyone can say that's of any help, I know," wrote the poet

Stephen Vincent Benét, whose *John Brown's Body* won the Pulitzer Prize for poetry that year. There was no talk of God in these letters; what solace there was in the world came through personal relationships, not religion.

"It's Judy's day," Frances would write on the baby's birthday in the years that followed. I know, darling, John replied. He hadn't forgotten, of course. "Whenever you do anything grand, I always want to tell her," she told him. I'd have been so much happier if my sweet little daughter hadn't died, she said of herself later.

They buried Judy in Chicago. Then they went to Carmel, where John's favorite aunt and uncle lived. It was there, in a cottage by the sea, that their second child, Johnny, was conceived. John had his doubts about whether they ought to rush into having another baby. But he kept those to himself.

LITTLE JOHNNY WAS BORN on the fourth of November, 1929, a few days after the Black Friday crash on Wall Street. As the American economy slid into depression, many of the expatriates the Gunthers knew in Paris began to clear out. The so-called Lost Generation—as they were already known—was heading home. The term referred to the cohort of young men (less often, women) who were born in the last decades of the nineteenth century and came of age during the First World War. Hemingway, who made the phrase famous, credited it to Gertrude Stein, who'd overheard it shouted at a young French mechanic by his boss, the garage owner, angry about the inept repair of Stein's Model T.

Eventually the term "Lost Generation" came specifically to denote the American writers and expatriates who, in the words of F. Scott Fitzgerald (a banner member of the club), had "grown up to find all Gods dead, all wars fought, all faiths in man shaken." Disillusioned by the Great War, alienated by American materialism, they'd moved to Europe in the 1920s, embracing what the critic Malcolm Cowley called "salvation by exile." They put their faith in artistic production, in a truth-telling "terrible honesty" delivered in a broadly modernist key. Now the dividends had evaporated, adult life beckoned, the half-finished novel would be put away. The "exiles" were returning, sobered-up and broke, newly conscious (perhaps) of the ties that bound them to other Americans.

Cowley's 1934 memoir *Exile's Return* would become the classic apologia of the Lost Generation. He wrote their generational saga as a two-act play: first exile, and then redemption. He interpreted the expatriate life of the 1920s as a detour—either into self-absorbed nostalgia or fruitless modernistic experimentation. But after a decade of living fast and hard abroad, the worthiest of his generation returned home to dedicate themselves to American problems, writing about rural poverty or racial oppression, with only the occasional glance toward Europe. They underwent a political awakening, discovered the class struggle, and aimed to speak to the masses. They'd solve the problem of the individual and the collective by embracing, if belatedly, their domestic responsibilities.

In his roster of Lost Generation writers, Cowley included very few reporters. John and Jimmy made the cut, but Frances and Dorothy Thompson did not, nor did H. R. Knickerbocker, William Shirer, Mickey Hahn, or the *New Yorker*'s Janet Flanner (among many others). By and large, the foreign correspondents didn't fit Cowley's pattern. For them, the 1930s marked not a retreat to America, but a more concerted engagement with international politics. Already they'd begun traveling beyond London, Paris, and Moscow to Shanghai, Addis Ababa, and Delhi. They were starting to see the world as a whole, to work out the interconnections between the different stories they were reporting. How an uprising against British rule in India shifted politics in the Kremlin. How the collapse on Wall Street fueled resurgent nationalisms in Eastern Europe.

After the Wall Street bust, there wasn't any question in either John's or Frances's mind that they would remain abroad. The *Chicago Daily News* had promised John a post of his own, in Vienna. There, they'd have a ringside seat at the European slugfest, and after five years of reporting, they'd gained a much better sense of the pugilists. There wouldn't be any revival of the monarchies, they knew now. The sixteenth century didn't stand a chance against the twentieth. As for the empires, the Gunthers agreed, they were down, but not yet out, especially the British. In the main ring, the big fight was just starting. Democracy was in one corner, fascism in another, and communism in the third. Two against one, was the way the reporter H. R. Knickerbocker put it.

PART
TWO

PART
TWO

LOST

—

E VEN FOR FERVENT BELIEVERS IN DEMOCRACY AND CAPITALISM, the years after the 1929 crash posed a test of faith. As the Western democracies slid into crisis—factories idling, breadlines lengthening, depositors panicking, and governments collapsing—the authoritarian states, both Left and Right, went from strength to apparent strength. In Italy, Mussolini was draining marshes and building train lines that ran on time. In the Soviet Union, full employment was the rule and industrial production soared, as beefy shock workers in newly built factories rushed to deliver socialism.

This contest of ideologies was, in the first instance, a battle for global public opinion, in which foreign correspondents would serve as the self-appointed referees. The matter to be decided was this: Which political system delivered the best life for its populace? The struggle would be played out before a global audience, many of whom were taking part for the first time in national politics—in the democracies because most citizens had gained the right to vote after the war, and in the authoritarian states because the legitimacy of those regimes depended upon constant public glorification.

With gusto, Knick mixed into the ideological fray. A wire of a man with a thick shock of hair, he was a vigorous, confident type. His first job had been at the *Newark Morning Ledger,* where he lit up the paper with stories of New Jersey's white slavery rings and jewel heists ("the revolver muzzle nudging his spine"), writing as many as five articles a day. He worked long hours and he worked fast, composing nearly as quickly as he talked. The *New York Sun* hired him as a "rewrite man," who turned the information provided by the "legman" into copy, to be snatched up by a messenger boy who delivered it, paragraph by paragraph, to the editorial desk for a once-over, before it was fed into a pneumatic tube, set in type, and returned to him for proofing. Any errors and he'd find himself out of a job. When Knick wasn't working, he danced the Charleston, skied, and played tennis. No movies, though: he couldn't sit still that long.

In 1923, when the German hyperinflation made medical school in that country practically free for those with dollars in their pockets, Knick had come to Munich to train as a psychiatrist. He'd had enough of the grind of reporting. Now he wanted perspective: he would survey man's foibles through the eyes of a scientist. One evening in November, he wandered into the beer hall where thousands of followers of an Austrian corporal with a toothbrush mustache had gathered, pistols in hand, to overthrow the Weimar Republic. For the next five weeks, he attended Hitler's trial for treason in the Beer Hall Putsch, and then, his money gone, he sprang back into full-time reporting.

Knick knew his economics and had a cynic's sixth sense about politics. He wrote with a vinegary panache, treating European politics irreverently—like a gilded police court. In Berlin, he served for a few months as Dorothy Thompson's assistant at the *Public Ledger*. Then he put in a couple of years in the Soviet Union at Hearst's wire agency, the International News Service. His wife, Laura, was also a reporter. They'd met as undergraduates at Southwestern University in Georgetown, Texas, and she'd followed him to Moscow, working as a stringer for the Hearst publications. At a briefing at the German Foreign Ministry in 1927, Knick had introduced Dorothy to Sinclair Lewis. When Dorothy married Lewis the following year, Knick got her job as Berlin bureau chief of the *Public Ledger*. He and Laura had a son, Conrad (named after the novelist Joseph Conrad), in 1929, born the same year as little Johnny Gunther.

Knick encountered John Gunther for the first time in Berlin, not long after Conrad was born. Knick figured the tall, friendly blond man chasing him around the tables at the El Dorado nightclub in the small hours of the morning was trying to pick him up. The El Dorado was that sort of establishment. A dimly lit corridor hung with paintings of men in compromising poses led to a long room with bars on both ends and a dance floor in the middle, where couples of the same sex clung to each other and a slim young "hostess" in an evening gown of black lace wafted from table to table, making small talk with the guests.

John was in town to fill in for Edgar Mowrer—"visiting firemen," such roving reporters were called—and Edgar's wife, Lilian, was showing him the sights. The cabaret scene in Berlin wasn't at all like it had been after the Revolution of 1918, Lilian said. Then, it was genuinely depraved, all the old inhibitions cast aside in the revelry and disorder of revolutionary upheaval. Now, places like the El Dorado were full of tourists. Knick was supposed to be meeting them at the cabaret, but it was after midnight, the dancer swathed in ostrich feathers and black chiffon had finished her act, and he still hadn't shown up. Lilian sent John off to look for Knick. You won't be able to miss him in *this* crowd, she said: he's red-haired and masculine. John pursued Knick all the way to his table.

John and Knick became fast friends. John couldn't remember the last time he relished someone's conversation so much. "Knick is a love," he declared to Frances. Though Knick was four years older than he was, there was something about the man that reminded John of himself when he was younger. "He is tied up and unhappy but has a nice extrovert detachment about it."

Laura had been operatically unfaithful, Knick told John. When Conrad was two, she picked up and left Europe, taking the boy with her. She went to Topeka, Kansas, where she began an analysis with the psychiatrist Karl Menninger. After she'd gone, Knick hired a prostitute for a week. He'd never let himself love another woman again. If he were a tribesman, Knick continued, he'd have a wife in every village and thousands of children.

"A rather oversexed young man," judged Dorothy. The son of a Southern Methodist minister, Knick had worked up an impressive repertoire of swear words in the major European languages and always carried a Bible. He'd been on the plane in 1927 when the Germans attempted the first transatlantic flight from Europe to the United States. It was meant to be the Old World's answer to Charles Lindbergh. Knick sat in the rear of the fuselage, coolly operating the radio communication system, and when the machine had to make an emergency landing before they'd even reached the North Sea, he climbed out of the wrecked plane and made a joke of the whole thing.

IN THE SUMMER OF 1930, Knick packed a hundred pounds of tinned German food, sardines mostly, into his suitcases and set out for the Soviet Union. He'd be gone for two months and cover ten thousand miles, traveling on crowded trains outfitted with triple-stacked sleeping berths of hard wooden shelves, without mattresses or blankets, suitcases pressed into service as pillows. The trip would take him from the gigantic open-faced asbestos mines of the Ural Mountains to the smooth concrete sidewalks of oil-producing Baku on the Caspian Sea. Along the way, he'd coax details about production costs out of mine managers and finagle the first ever interview with Stalin's mother, whom he located in a hamlet in the Caucasus. She insisted on changing into a black ceremonial dress, a black kerchief on her head and a white lace shawl around her shoulders, so that he could take her picture. Really, she told Knick, she had hoped her son would become a priest.

The Soviet Union was then barely two years into the Five-Year Plan that Stalin had launched in October 1928. The vision of headlong industrialization under state control had originally been Trotsky's, who also planned to force Russia's twenty-five million small family farms into larger, state-directed collectives as a means of solving the country's perpetual economic backwardness. Stalin's approach, Knick observed, was to banish or kill his opponents, "and then adopt their more useful suggestions." Now his rival Trotsky was in exile, and sluggish Russia was to become an industrial power-house. The Soviet comrades would be driving cars, promised Stalin, and its peasants, tractors: "let the worthy capitalists, who boast so much of their 'civilization,' try to overtake us!"

Knick had anticipated privations, but he wasn't prepared for the suffering he saw. Looking at the windows of Moscow's shops, empty and grimy save for a dusty French horn or a pair of skis, you'd think you were in a ghost town, not a city packed with millions of people. Three years earlier, peasant women at the railway stations had been selling roast chickens and sandwiches stuffed with plump beads of caviar; now all they had to peddle were wormy, hard green apples. The wait for a government-made bicycle was at least a year and a half; the used ones at the city's Sukharevsky market cost fifteen times as much as they did in Germany. The only men wearing decent leather boots were soldiers or members of the state security forces. The rest had tattered rubber boots or canvas sneakers with cardboard soles—and they were the lucky ones, for plenty went barefoot, their feet wrapped in rags.

This is a country at war, Knick informed his readers. The Soviets were financing their breakneck industrialization by stripping land from peasants and rudimentary consumer goods from the rest of the populace. A "colossal coercive savings plan," he called it. In Moscow, cynics had dismissed as a pipe dream Soviet plans for a vast complex of blast furnaces to rival Gary, Indiana. There were blueprints of the Magnitogorsk project, but no city, they said. Not true, Knick discovered when he rolled into the largest construction camp on earth, the first foreign reporter to visit Magnitogorsk. A dam three-quarters of a mile long had been built across the Ural River—in just four months. The furnaces would soon follow. He saw the inevitable inefficiencies, the shoddy workmanship, the machinery that didn't function or went missing. But skeptical as he was of the inflated statistics pumped out by the Moscow planners, the scale of the transformation was profound.

More than five thousand Westerners a year visited the Soviet Union during the era of the Five-Year Plans (1928–1937). Unlike Knick, many of them were sympathetic to the Communist project. Enthralled by the spectacle of high-speed industrialization, these Russia observers—diplomats, professors, artists, and reporters—tended to rationalize the misery they saw, justifying the suffering of the populace as the necessary by-product of a great stride forward. They did so even as forced collectivization plunged the Ukraine, Kazakhstan, the North Caucasus, and the Volga Valley into famine in 1932 and 1933. As many as eight million people starved to death while Western experts in Russia, including the majority of foreign correspondents, minimized the scale of the catastrophe. The people were hungry but they weren't starving, insisted the Englishman Walter Duranty, the *New York Times*'s man in Moscow from 1922 to 1936.

Duranty has become known as the most infamous of the famine-denying correspondents, not least because in his day he was a celebrated authority on the Soviet Union, who befriended visiting firemen (Knick and John among them), entertaining them in his four-room flat in Moscow with its well-stocked larder and liquor cabinet. But plenty of other reporters followed Duranty's lead, including Frances's friend Louis Fischer, who reported for the *Nation*. Years later, after he had repudiated the Soviet regime, Fischer would regret "glorifying steel and kilowatts and forgetting the human being." But in the early 1930s, Fischer was enchanted by the prospect of rapid modernization and as scathing about peasant resistance as Soviet officials were themselves. Russia's peasants were reactionary and apathetic, clinging to their medieval methods of farming, the horse and plow rather than the tractor, because that was what they knew. What was the Soviet state to do when faced with such intransigence?

Knick, by contrast, was affronted by the ruthless nature of the Five-Year Plan and much more alive to its human costs. Even in his 1930 articles he was issuing warnings, and documenting arrests and executions. "Zeal and terror are the two psychological instruments for accomplishment of the Plan," he observed. The Five-Year Plan, he saw, wasn't simply imposed upon the populace; in his travels, he had met plenty of Russians who wholeheartedly embraced the Soviet vision of the future. At the same time, the machinery of terror was penetrating farther into daily life, sweeping up technical experts who bucked Stalin's own cherished ideas. "The worst offence to-day in the Soviet Union is to doubt the Plan," wrote Knick. "Skepticism in Bolshevik Russia is more heinous than crimes of violence."

The Soviet system was "nothing short of horrible," Knick told his editor on his return to Berlin. If he didn't mention the names of his sources, that was because he didn't want to be responsible for "unnecessary bloodshed." "This may sound like an exaggeration but I assure you it is not." As critical as he was of the regime, he was nevertheless convinced that the Five-Year Plan would turn the Soviet Union into an industrial powerhouse. Anti-communists who talked about the system "going to pot" were fooling themselves. What they didn't understand was that the Soviet regime wasn't communism, certainly not as Marx had envisioned it. Instead, it was best understood as the most extractive sort of capitalism in which all profits belonged to the state.

Knick's series on Russia amounted to twenty-four articles, written with the "utmost objectivity," he assured his editor, but intended, of course, to bring the reader around to his own point of view. During the run of Knick's Russia series, the *New York Evening Post* added twenty thousand readers. "Stalin's Mother Talks!" promised the paper. "Russia—and You" ran the advertisement for the book that resulted from the series, promising an answer to the question: "What does this mean to you?" In 1931, Knick won the Pulitzer for foreign correspondence, a prize inaugurated only two years earlier.

On his trip, Knick had been permitted to travel freely in the Soviet Union, looking inside factories and workers' kitchens as he pleased, much as Dorothy had done a few years earlier. But after 1930 the Press Office of the People's Commissariat for Foreign Affairs would tighten restrictions on reporters, and in the spring of

1933, as reports of famine in Ukraine filtered out, the authorities forbade foreigners to travel within the USSR. Even as Moscow-bound reporters continued to downplay the rumors of starvation, a young Welshman named Gareth Jones, fluent in Russian and familiar with the country from three previous trips, defied the ban, got off a train in Kiev, and tramped alone forty miles through famine-stricken villages. When Jones brought back the news of starving peasants portioning out their cattle fodder, the oxen and horses already dead of famine, Knick was the first to interview him. He vouched for Jones's "reliability and impartiality."

The reports of famine are "mostly bunk," the *New York Times*'s Duranty grumbled from Moscow. Duranty had already done what he could to discredit Jones, repudiating his reporting as the feverish imaginings of a young man with scant knowledge of Russia. Conditions weren't nearly as bad as Jones made out. Moreover, the success of the Five-Year Plan, Duranty insisted, required some trade-offs, and the recalcitrant, premodern Russian peasantry would have to give way: "to put it brutally—you can't make an omelette without breaking eggs." As Duranty told Knick, "I'm a reporter not a humanitarian."

WHILE KNICK WAS OFF on his Russian tour, taking the measure of the brutal Soviet industrialization, John and Frances settled down in Vienna, an apparently sleepy city that harbored its own sort of menace. In May 1930, the *Daily News* had given John the Vienna beat. He'd become the paper's golden-haired boy wonder, a darling of the Chicago office. His editors praised him as scrupulously fair-minded in his reporting, and always punctual in delivering acres of lively copy. Now John's articles came accompanied by his photo: a good-looking young man with quizzical eyes. That summer, when Johnny was nine months old, John and Frances set up housekeeping on the second floor of a dilapidated villa with two bathrooms of their own—a great luxury in the city—and a big garden.

Send us pieces that "reflect human nature in its more amiable aspects," John's editor instructed him. In Vienna, that was a snap, for the city was chock-full of curiosities. No two clocks told the same time, he observed, with the exception of those in the railway stations, which were set five minutes fast, as if to rush their lackadaisical passengers, who refused on principle to hurry. It was said (and he believed it) that the horses idling in the city's shopping streets ate asparagus for breakfast. By depositing two ten-groschen pieces, you could ride an elevator up but not down. Were you expecting a balance statement from your bank? Tough luck. No bank in Austria ever issued statements on a regular schedule. Blame the *Föhn,* the warm, metallic-smelling wind that gusted over the Styrian hills and enervated the Viennese. It was a city of sleepwalkers, dozing over their strong black coffees.

Where had the legendary Viennese beauties gone? John asked. How are the displaced Habsburg aristocrats now spending their days? Step onto the Ringstrasse, the grand boulevard that collared Vienna's inner city, and it was as if Karl of Habsburg had just departed in his taxi. The streets were still lined with chestnuts and lilacs; the snorting stone stallions still cantered atop baroque palaces. The darkened premises of the Mühlhauser toy store told a different story, though. In better years, Mühlhauser had outfitted the nurseries of pint-sized Habsburg princesses and counts. Now, to save money on electricity, the shopgirls lit up one department after another as the customer moved through the store. Sometimes the whole place would be pitch-black and other times, an eerie spot of light fell here or there.

Remember, Walter Duranty told John, you're writing for the sort of people who think Prague is a ham. John's editor chimed in: American newspaper readers didn't have much interest in "political developments" in Europe. John became an expert in brightening his stories with picturesque details. An article about Hungary's discontents with the Treaty of Trianon could be pepped up by relating his conversations with revanchist barbers and bellboys peddling postcards of the country's shrunken borders. ("They are free, monsieur. Perhaps you will accept them and mail them to your friends. They mean much to Hungary.") Statistics about the number of heads of Hungarian cattle and the factories that had been lost to the Romanians or the Czechs: now that was the kind of information to make the Midwestern porkpackers snap to attention.

Still, John wasn't satisfied with the work he was doing. He envied Knick. The Texan had a "better head" than he did. "I wish I could get over being so annoyed that I have not got a good mind," John wrote to Frances.

From the start of their relationship, that was the fault she had identified in John: his inability to analyze. Her criticisms began with John's lack of interest in politics. You're right, he conceded. Politics bored him stiff; his interest was in human nature. Really? she retorted. What about those interviews of yours? You ask a man what he ate for breakfast and you write about the contours of his waxed mustaches, but why? Does any of it matter? If you're going to understand anything, she insisted, you can't glide along the surface.

And then there was the fact that John lacked moral sense, his wife said.

"What the hell is moral sense, anyway?" he wondered. "Please explain, in writing."

Try as he might, John feared that Frances was right: he had a two-dimensional mind. He didn't have it in him to penetrate to fundamentals the way Frances or Knick did. Perhaps he was nothing more than a first-class brain-picker. He was a good listener and, like a scavenger, made use of everything. Put him in a room with a source or another reporter and by the end of a couple of hours, he'd know what the man believed in and what he felt about his father—and yes, what he'd had for breakfast—and much more that the man didn't know that he knew. People, all sorts of people, laid their heads right down on the cushion of his personality and talked.

But was that enough? Frances thought not.

JOHN'S DAYS IN VIENNA quickly fell into a routine. Most mornings he met Dorothy Thompson's old friend Marcel Fodor at the Hotel

Imperial on the Kärntner Ring. Fodor was always generous about taking the American newcomers in hand and John had practically apprenticed himself to the man.

At the café on the ground floor, the jewel merchants shared the back room with the gamblers and the musicians. A smattering of turpentine and flax brokers colonized the front. Reporters took the low-ceilinged, paneled room facing the street. In the giant mirror that filled its far wall, you could see who was coming and going: former Ottoman potentates and Montenegrin bandits, schemers, gunrunners, the Outs conniving against the status quo. There was an aroma of conspiracy about the place; it was said that the assassination of Archduke Franz Ferdinand had been plotted there. A white-gloved waiter oversaw the wooden cupboard in which sixteen Austrian newspapers and sixty-odd foreign papers hung on rattan racks: Yugoslav and Bulgarian broadsheets; newspapers from Greece, the Netherlands, Spain, Sweden, and Denmark and a Cairo paper published in English. "I have the honor," said the waiter dispensing the papers, looking as if you'd demanded his kidney rather than Thursday evening's *Paris-soir*.

Over little ham sandwiches on poppy-seed rolls, Fodor spun his interpretations. The Austrian elections were set for November 1930 and all the talk was about the gains the fascists would make. Two months earlier, in Germany, the Nazis had blanketed the country in the final four weeks before the election, holding thirty-four thousand rallies in villages, towns, and cities, with Hitler himself drawing crowds of thousands. Parliamentary democracy, the Nazi leader fulminated, was exhausted, captive to "international finance spiders" (the Jews) and Marxist traitors (the Socialists). "Let's give a sound thrashing to all those who have an interest in deceiving the people," sloganeered the Nazis. When the ballots were counted, Hitler's party had won more than 18 percent of the vote (compared to their previous 2.6 percent) and 107 seats in the Reichstag, the German Parliament (up from 12). Now the Nazis were the second-largest party in Germany, behind the Socialists.

But Austria was different from Germany, Fodor insisted. The Socialists had been the biggest party in Austria since 1918. They could count on around 40 percent of the vote, most of it concentrated in Vienna, where a third of the country's population lived. From their commanding position in the City Hall, the Socialists had turned Red Vienna into a worker's paradise, rehousing sixty thousand slum-dwellers in a decade. They had built swimming pools for children, medical clinics for workers, and homes for tubercular children. They'd provided free milk for poor women who were pregnant and fixed the prices of gas, water, and electricity at cost. And they'd done it by taxing the rich, levying duties on villas and luxury flats, on households full of servants, on racehorses, on patrons of restaurants and hotels. Outside of Moscow, Vienna was the most advanced workers' society in the world.

For their efforts, the Socialists were heartily despised by Austria's rural hinterland, which was devoutly Catholic, poor, and conservative to its marrow. The Austrian countryside wanted no part of either Red Vienna's taxation regime or its welfare state. But according to Fodor, Austria's peasants and townspeople weren't Nazis—at least not yet. The Nazi Party of Austria was still small. Much more important was the so-called Heimwehr or Home Army, which had sprung up at the end of the war to defend Austria's border and guard against looting.

The Heimwehr was Austria's own homegrown brand of fascism. What began as a ragtag militia soon became a force in its own right. The Heimwehr stood for Austrian autonomy, rejecting the Nazi dream of absorbing the country into a Greater Germany, and for Catholicism, which was, according to the Heimwehr's leaders, under threat both from Austria's Socialists and from irreligious German Nazis. Vehemently anti-Socialist, the Heimwehr was increasingly contemptuous, too, of the other established Austrian parties. In the November 1930 elections, the Heimwehr would for the first time be fielding its own electoral candidates, and in the run-up to the vote, the countryside was rife with rumors of a Heimwehr coup.

A third of Austria's young men were out of work, and every one of them, it seemed, had a uniform at the ready: gray if you were a

Socialist of the Schutzbund militia, pledged to defend Red Vienna; apple green with a huge green, curled feather stuck in your hat if you were the Heimwehr; brown if you were a Nazi. "Our poor little Owstria," Fodor lamented.

In the afternoons, John and Fodor would settle into the back booth at the Café Louvre, the foreign correspondents' *Stammtisch*, right across the street from the Central Telegraph & Telephone Office. Most of the regulars at the Louvre were Americans. A decade earlier American correspondents had been relative newcomers on the international stage, but by 1930, they comprised the lion's share of foreign reporters in every European and Asian capital. They sent the news home to a public that had, courtesy of the Depression, become increasingly attuned to the interconnected nature of the world. As American correspondents doorstepped Chiang Kai-shek or trailed around after Gandhi in India, they faced surprisingly little competition from their European colleagues. The British and French papers were short on cash and hobbled by censors and cozy relationships between their editors and government officials. Practically the first step dictators took when they came to power was to cripple their own country's papers.

It was a motley crew at the Café Louvre. Whit Burnett of the *New York Sun*, skinny as a whippet, and nervous as one, too. Bill Shirer from the *Chicago Tribune*—a good sort but a bit dull and callow and on the make, in John's estimation. Greasy-faced Bob Best with the United Press wire service, two hundred pounds capped off with a Stetson. Dorothy, of course, when she came through Vienna.

The Louvre was large and dingy, its booths upholstered in a striped tapestry fabric furred by years of hard duty. Theodor Herzl and his Zionists had once spent their evenings there. To the Louvre came a louche Bulgarian diplomat peddling rumors about the Serbs, or a political refugee from the Ukraine hoping to gin up news stories sympathetic to his cause. Then there were the tipsters who for a few crumpled dollars would sell you tidbits about the palace intrigue in Romania or a sticky-palmed judge in Budapest. It was like living amid a detective novel, Dorothy observed: everyone who doled out information had an ulterior motive, and it was up to the reporter to figure out what exactly it was.

Perhaps politics was in fact best understood as another kind of human interest story, John was starting to think. He was bringing the novelist's sense of character to bear on the machinations he was supposed to be covering. He took note of snippets of the correspondents' conversation:

"Yugoslavia? . . . The dictatorship isn't doing too badly, but remember, no Serbian head of state ever died a natural death."

"Stalin? A lump of granite. If he has nerves, they are veins in rock. His contribution is, however, perfectly enormous—he's made the Russian Revolution work."

How the correspondents could talk—they'd be at it all night, talking and drinking, until the Louvre's waiters, yawning, rolled the iron shutters down over the windows. Tie another one on! All in the name of easing nerves stretched taut by the constant deadlines and the day's events. Then another. It was a professional vice, they readily admitted: seeing too much of the wicked ways of the world and trying to drown them in drink.

In Austria's November 1930 elections, the Socialists again won the largest number of votes, but not enough to make a majority in Parliament, so the stalemate between the conservatives and the Socialists dragged on. The Heimwehr's own candidates, though, fared worse than expected while the Hitlerites polled barely over 100,000. "Most of the putsch talk is an invention of foreign journalists," a former Austrian chancellor insisted to John.

JOHN'S PERSONAL CRISIS STARTED not with a failure, but with a success. In the spring of 1931, a little less than a year after arriving in Vienna, he and Fodor, tipped off by Edgar Mowrer, ferreted out that Germany and Austria were in secret talks about a customs union. The two countries were planning to institute a common set of external tariffs, allowing goods to flow freely across their borders. A customs union was an attempt to solve the economic problems of

Austria, shorn of its empire, starved of raw materials and fertile agricultural land. But to the French and Czechoslovak governments, it looked like a first step toward the unification of Germany and Austria. The plan was an outright violation of the Treaty of Versailles, they protested.

Within a few months, though, the issue of the customs union became entangled in another mess. In May, the Rothschild-directed Credit-Anstalt, the largest bank in Central Europe, announced that it was facing losses to the tune of 140 million shillings, as much as 85 percent of its equity. Desperate to prevent the failure of the bank, the Austrian state was scraping its own coffers bare.

The collapse of the Credit-Anstalt would set off a chain reaction that led to the devaluation of the British pound and runs on banks in Hungary, Germany, Czechoslovakia, Poland, and Romania. Desperate customers pounded on bank doors to withdraw their money before it was too late, and within a few months, banks were failing in Britain and the United States, too. This was the crisis that plunged the world economy into the depths of the Great Depression. The French now had the leverage to scotch the customs union because Austria needed a bailout.

Among Vienna's foreign correspondents, the failure of the Credit-Anstalt precipitated a further scandal. In November, the city's leading socialist paper revealed that the bank had been bribing reporters, both domestic and foreign, to keep news of its true position under wraps. Journalists who were on the take had played down the scale of the bank's losses, issuing reassurances about its viability. As president of the newly founded Anglo-American Press Association, John had to investigate which of his colleagues had been bought off. He and Bill Shirer burst into the Austrian Ministry of Finance, demanding to photograph the Credit-Anstalt's secret registers of reporters so that they could conduct their own inquiry—a "stink" of a business, as John put it.

This entire sequence of events from the secret customs union to the bribery scandal should have been a great story. But for reasons John couldn't explain, the reporting left him dissatisfied. Of course, he was ground down, he told himself. He was working fifteen-hour days, bolting his food as he devoted himself to the tedious details of the latest Danube tariff treaty or the ins and outs of reparations policy. But it wasn't just that.

In the novel John started to write later that year about the Credit-Anstalt affair, he concocted a more satisfying plot—one that foregrounded the reporter's role not simply as witness but as participant. He made a small but consequential change to the sequence of events, putting the bribery scandal before the Credit-Anstalt's failure rather than after it. In John's fictionalized version, Austria's largest bank is bribing reporters. When the ace reporter breaks that story, the money men in Chicago withdraw their short-term loans, setting off a chain of events that not only brings down the bank but means that the reporter had "caused, personally, the whole depression."

The subject John wanted to explore wasn't the obvious one of the journalist's responsibility, however inadvertent, for the epoch-making consequences of his stories. Rather, John put his hero in the middle of events to dramatize a different point: the ways in which corruption in public affairs was seeping into private lives. Twinned with the story of the bank's collapse were the troubles in the hero's marriage. The stories ran together, the outer world acting on the inner. This was the sea change in perception that Jimmy Sheean had detected: the moment when the line between the individual and the world around him began to dissolve.

AFTER JUDY DIED, FRANCES began talking of divorce. But then Johnny arrived, followed by the family's move to Vienna. One moment they were calmly discussing the prospect of separation, and the next, Frances became distraught. She wanted dozens of children, but not with John! If there was a baby growing inside her, she'd poke it out with a stick! He should make love to her again, immediately! No, she was going to demand a divorce! Why didn't he try his luck with the blond girl at the lido?

As dismal as things got between them, they came to no resolution, stalemated like the politicians in the Austrian parliament. He went away to Juan-les-Pins to work on his Credit-Anstalt novel and when he was gone, they wrote longing letters back and forth. "Do you think we ought to miss each other so much?" Frances asked him. When he returned, he typed up her sheets of longhand manuscript so she could send the short story she'd written off to a literary agent. They took Johnny for weekends of swimming and sunbathing in Edlach in the summer, the stony Rax mountains overlooking the bright green valley below. In the winter, they drove to the Semmering, where they climbed snow-covered mountains and skied, Frances exulting over the winter skies. They made love. "Gee, we're getting too fond of each other. We'll never manage that divorce," she told him.

That summer they moved from the elaborately plastered villa on the outskirts of Vienna to a modern flat that overlooked Modena Park in the city center. This apartment was more to their liking, four compact rooms opening onto each other. They turned the hallway over to rows of bookshelves and set up Johnny's little chrome table and chairs in the kitchen. They threw parties, ever aware that friendship, for a correspondent, was a way to obtain information; a tip from the chancellery was currency to be parlayed into more tips. In addition to the other reporters, they invited Heimwehr officers and Schutzbunders, and junior attachés and press officers from the various embassies. The Russians and the Americans and the French always showed up. Practicing the economies that the Depression made necessary, they mixed American cocktails with slivovitz rather than expensive gin. They had a Ping-Pong table and set out divans on the balcony so the parties spilled outside.

The Credit-Anstalt story kept John in Vienna for much of 1931, but the following year he was away five months, pursuing one news eruption after another. Hardly a day went by now in Central Europe without a bank failure or an attempted coup. In April and May 1932, he traveled with Knick to the Balkans and Turkey; in June to Dalmatia with Frances; in September to Bulgaria; and then in November to Spain with Knick again, plus his new girlfriend Agnes. While he was gone, Frances had an affair, maybe more than one. She didn't seem to mind—not obviously, at least—John's flirtations with Bill Shirer's wife, Tess. Bill was chasing all the other correspondents' wives, Frances included (unavailingly), so tit for tat.

John didn't learn that Frances had had another abortion until he was already in Madrid with Knick and Agnes. She'd done it in Vienna, in October 1932, without telling him. She'd been using her cervical cap, but it had failed her—again, and she recriminated about his unwillingness to wear a condom. Abortion was of course illegal in Austria, as it had been in London or New York or the other places she'd previously had them. As many as a fifth of educated, middle-class American women surveyed in the 1920s had aborted a pregnancy. They'd jumped off tables, thrown themselves down flights of stairs, taken boilingly hot baths, or ingested tonics of slippery elm or pennyroyal purchased at a druggist or cigar shop. If the usual home remedies failed, those with money and connections readily found doctors willing to perform a dilation and curettage.

An abortion was painful, possibly humiliating, but in those years it wasn't necessarily something that a woman had to feel shame about or keep quiet. The sexual license of the 1920s meant more accidental pregnancies, especially among the unmarried. During the Depression, the idea of abortion as a legitimate response to financial exigency gained ground. Abortion increasingly figured in novels and short stories by Ernest Hemingway, Edith Wharton, Dorothy Parker, F. Scott Fitzgerald, John Dos Passos, Sinclair Lewis, and Gertrude Stein, among many others—both as an actual practice and a metaphor for the individual's struggle against social constraints. At least some of the interwar American literary heroines who had abortions struck a defiant note, justifying the termination of a pregnancy as a matter of personal liberation: "It wasn't sin. What was it, then? It was—freedom."

John was familiar enough with this attitude. Helen Hahn made reference to the fact that she'd had an abortion the first day she met him, tossing that information over her shoulder as they parted. Her casualness bothered him. When Helen's sister Mickey showed up in

Paris in 1928, she was pregnant and needed an abortion, which John helped to arrange. Do you expect me to pay for yours, too? John had inquired, coldly. "Feeling better! It's wonderful to have an easy stomach and no emotions," Mick wrote him when it was over. Frances, by contrast, never forgave herself for her abortions or him, either.

The baby had been his, of that there was no doubt. And although he'd thought they'd agreed she was never to have another abortion— she'd nonetheless done it. And without telling him. Why? To punish him? That was the only thing he could figure. My darling, my darling, he wrote Frances. Didn't she know that he'd rather have a thousand children than for her to lose another baby? "Maybe you will say it is for 'my sake.' But don't you see that I am being destroyed by this, more even than you."

What an unspeakably awful year it had been, John wrote Bill and Tess Shirer that month. If he had acted lighthearted, it was only to fool himself. The worldwide crisis seemed to have got inside him, maybe because he'd spent so much time chasing it. Now he couldn't shut it out. How wretched it was to think that one's own fate depended on what some farmer in Iowa felt—or more to the point, how he voted. Still, if Herbert Hoover could be got rid of, if FDR prevailed in the November 1932 election in America, John would feel cheerier because there'd at least be the possibility of some sort of political change. "I think the crisis is mostly to blame for the sort of spiritual deadness I feel, and the insecurity in most of my personal life," he concluded.

JIMMY SHEEAN THOUGHT THE expression "Lost Generation" was idiotic, but in 1931 he pretty well fit the bill, for he was as adrift as the pejorative use of the term implied. Jimmy's objection to the idea of a "Lost Generation" started with the fact that Hemingway, in defining the type, had drawn the circle too narrowly, meaning chiefly people like himself, American writers and poets. The larger problem was that Hemingway apparently didn't understand *why* they were "lost." Like Fitzgerald and e.e. cummings and the other avatars of modernist disillusionment, Hemingway had in the 1920s turned away from politics at the very moment that foreign correspondents like Jimmy were running toward the fires. Where Jimmy was drawn to causes, Hemingway disdained the collective, viewing ideology (left or right) with contempt. He "shut out the whole world," Jimmy wrote, dwelling on subjects of the "narrowest individual significance": the tragedy of a man whose balls were blown off in the war (*The Sun Also Rises*), for instance. Hemingway wasn't haunted by the question of his place vis-à-vis the masses. In fact, he felt no need even to broach the subject.

But where had worrying about Chinese coolies or dispossessed Arabs gotten Jimmy? He was thirty and dead broke. Nearly every cent he had earned from his American lecture tour talking about Palestine had gone to pay his debts and he was still in hock to his agents for the $500 he'd had to return to the Zionist paper. His novel, *Gog and Magog*, about his relationship with Rayna, hadn't made him any money. He'd been to Hollywood to test his prospects, but the town that was proving a mecca for other washed-up writers wasn't for him. "The whole thing struck me as being rather Greek, these marvelous lads and lasses disporting themselves among the flowers in a classic (if monotonous) sunshine," he reported to Eddy.

America didn't suit him. The whole country was impossibly vulgar. You couldn't cross a hotel lobby in Los Angeles without stepping on chewing gum; the desserts came festooned with names like "Clara Bow Marshmallow Nut," and just try ordering a raw apple (No, not cooked!) in a diner. Unlike the repentant former expatriates like Malcolm Cowley, Jimmy wasn't the least bit apologetic that he preferred the civilization of the Old World. At the first opportunity, he booked a first-class passage back to Europe. A tour through the European capitals, recording interviews with personages such as King Carol in Bucharest and Monsignor Seipel in Vienna and Albert Einstein in Berlin, was lucrative but short-lived. He'd have to put off their *scappato* indefinitely, Jimmy informed Eddy: he didn't have the money to run away anywhere.

In fact, Jimmy was running away even from running away. He'd

Ben Hecht's farewell party at
Schlogl's, 1924, with John Gunther
in profile, fifth from the right

John Gunther in 1926, shortly
before the *Chicago Daily News*
sent him back to Europe as a
roving correspondent

Frances Fineman in 1916, when
she was a student at Barnard

A young Dorothy Thompson, from her yearbook

Vincent Sheean, publicity shot of the Rif adventurer, 1925

Frances Gunther, c. 1927, shortly after her wedding

John Gunther
in 1929

Dorothy Thompson in
the early 1930s

Jimmy Sheean,
photographed by
John Banting and
Barbara Ker-Seymer,
c. 1931

H. R. Knicker-
bocker with
Stalin's mother,
1930

Frances and Judy on the
SS *Paris*, 1929

Frances Gunther in
the early 1930s

Frances and Johnny
in the early 1930s

Anglo-American Press
Association in Vienna,
early 1930s. Fodor is standing fourth from the left;
Frances (seated) is the only
woman; John is second
from the right.

Knick talking to
German Chancellor
Heinrich Brüning at
the Foreign Press
Ball, 1932

Knick,
caricatured
in 1935

Press luncheon
with Chancellor
Engelbert Dollfuss
in Vienna, 1934:
Dollfuss at the head
of the table,
John far left.

Knick in
Abyssinia, 1935.

John after the
publication
of *Inside Europe*,
1936

Europe as bomb or deflating balloon? Two cover
designs for the British edition of *Inside Europe*.

Inside Europe on display in the
windows at Selfridge's, London

Johnny Gunther,
Jr., c. 1935

John and Johnny,
c. 1937

Mickey Hahn
in her role as
Lysistrata,
Shanghai, c. 1935

Lee Miller, John Gunther, and Frances Gunther
(left to right) at the pyramids, 1937

Dorothy with Sinclair Lewis, 1938, after the stage production of *It Can't Happen Here*

Knick and Agnes, December 1939. Knick had just returned home after his showdown with Goebbels.

TIME

THE WEEKLY NEWSMAGAZINE

DOROTHY THOMPSON
She rides in the smoking car.
(Press)

Dorothy on
the cover of
Time magazine,
June 1939

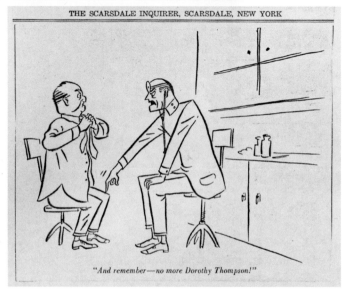

THE SCARSDALE INQUIRER, SCARSDALE, NEW YORK

The anxiety-
inducing
consequences
of Dorothy's
columns,
according to
the *Scarsdale
Inquirer*

"And remember—no more Dorothy Thompson!"

Dorothy at the German-American Bund meeting, February 1939: "Bunk, bunk, bunk!" she shouted. "*Mein Kampf*, word for word!"

The photo that Nehru sent to Frances in 1940

Jimmy (center) giving interviews in New York after returning home from the Battle of Britain, 1940

Jimmy and Knick, back home from the Blitz, 1940,
comparing the map of their American lecture tours

Dorothy with Free Czech troops in London, August 1941

Frances with
Johnny in
Madison,
Connecticut,
summer of
1946

Frances working
with the Emergency
Committee to Save
the Jewish People of
Europe, 1943

John in 1949 after the publication
of *Death Be Not Proud*

started posing for Duncan Grant in London, entertaining the painter by singing forty operas during a sitting one afternoon. For the failure of his love affair with Jimmy, Eddy would fault Duncan entirely: "you have shoved your nose in wrecked my happiness & the best dream of my life."

"Surely you and I can, without doing any harm to anybody, be together for a bit," Jimmy wrote Duncan from Rome, where by the spring of 1931 he was ensconced in a rose-silk upholstered suite in the Palazzo Lovatelli. "And I'll not say it's going to be perfect if you don't want me to, but it will." He'd gotten a job, of sorts, helping the deposed Grand Duchess Marie of Russia—daughter of King George I of Greece and Queen Olga of Russia, granddaughter of King Christian IX of Denmark, first cousin of Tsar Nicholas II of Russia—write her memoir.

The memoir didn't need to be as silly an enterprise as it turned out to be. Jimmy didn't mind the "altesses," as he termed the dethroned nobility, with their pompadours and diamond chokers, who had taken him up in Rome. And the grand duchess was a lively enough character, with plenty of good stories to tell about her august relations. But she refused to include any of them in the book. "'Sophie would be furious!' or else 'the King wouldn't like it' (*the King*, in royal conversations, almost always means your king)," Jimmy told Duncan. How had he become "a sort of quack fixer-up of old women's memoirs"? he wondered mournfully. "God! How I waste my time—my life!—I am really sorry I ever embarked on this ridiculous experiment."

Less than two weeks after Duncan arrived in Rome, Jimmy left him, packing his suitcases in a hurry and taking the train to Naples. "I simply cannot endure living with anybody, sharing the same bathroom, getting toothbrushes mixed up," he began. "I can't stand it, and never could, and I was a fool to think I could now." The fact that Duncan cried whenever Jimmy tried to explain himself was an impossible burden. "You know how I am," Jimmy would write him, "all flame and smoke for awhile, and then dirty cinders."

THESE MONSTERS

—

O NE NIGHT IN VIENNA IN THE EARLY 1930S, JOHN LIT INTO Knick. Knick was by then working for William Randolph Hearst's International News Service, lured by a big raise after he'd won the Pulitzer. No amount of money, John and Dorothy objected, was enough to sell your soul to the increasingly reactionary Hearst, but Knick had just laughed off their concerns and taken the job. Now he was back from Bulgaria, where he'd bagged an interview with King Boris. The monarch was notoriously reclusive and Knick was the first correspondent to get him to talk on the record. The previous month, Knick had interviewed Mussolini, too—his second interview with the Duce. Those were interviews that John had badly wanted, and after too many drinks, he assailed Knick as a "journalistic whore," who wrote flatteringly of people whom he otherwise loathed if they gave him an interview. The two men nearly came to blows.

Knick wasn't the only opportunist. For the reporters who gathered at the Hotel Imperial or the bar at Berlin's Hotel Adlon, the personages you'd landed—how many, how important—functioned as a proxy for status. "Has interviewed Lloyd George, President Masaryk of Czechoslovakia, King Carol of Rumania . . ." read the entry John submitted to *Who's Who*. The more important the reporter, the bigger the interviews as a rule, unless (like Jimmy with Abd el-Krim), you were prepared to traverse the desert barefoot, planes bombing overhead, to nab your prize. Who you got to see also depended on your paper. Some publications were willing to pay for interviews, some not. Politics entered into the matter, too. If you worked for Hearst, you had a better chance of meeting Mussolini or Hitler, whom the press baron—completing his conversion to right-wing causes—hired to write the occasional syndicated article. But by the same token, you'd be hard pressed to get an interview with the Russian revolutionary Leon Trotsky; he refused on principle to speak to Hearst reporters.

Reporters had long sought interviews with the great and the good in politics, figuring out how to get the story from the headline-hogging big-city boss or the charismatic senator without getting played in the process. But reckoning with Hitler or Stalin or Mussolini—or, for that matter, Abd el-Krim or the Grand Mufti of Jerusalem—was different. These figures had managed to redirect the stream of history, forcing the tide of events into different channels. How else could you explain their uncanny ability to bend events to their own will? What was their appeal and why were millions of people following them to the future they'd dreamed up?

Marxists had always claimed that individuals didn't matter; history was determined by impersonal economic and social forces that carried humanity onward, no matter the leaders bobbing along at the helm. Nor had liberals or conservatives devoted much attention to the transformative power of the individual leader. No matter how powerful politicians such as David Lloyd George or Raymond Poincaré were, they represented the distillation of the energies of their parties and their people. In that sense, they were interchangeable with another statesman.

But by the early 1930s, when Knick and John feuded in a Vienna café, it was clear that the "authority of personality," as Hitler put it, mattered more than it ever had in their lifetimes. One couldn't account for what was happening otherwise. The individual leader, as Knick wrote, now counted for "nearly everything." They were the ones fomenting the world crisis: it was happening within them and through them. When the fate of the world hinged upon a handful of men, personal pathologies became the stuff of geopolitics. The correspondents needed a new way of thinking about the role of the individual.

THE DICTATORS RISING ACROSS Europe were changing how politics, in its entirety, was done. They proclaimed their will as law, abolishing parliamentary governance, the legislature, and the independent civil service. They dispensed, too, with the normal mechanisms for securing the consent of the governed. They didn't need elections, they insisted, because they personally embodied the people. Bitter party conflicts are a thing of the past! We will punish the bloodsuckers who have drained our people dry! they roared to stadiums filled with their cheering throngs.

The very scripted nature of the dictators' personae made an in-person audience seem all the more valuable. What lay behind the military uniforms and spit-polished shoes, the jutting jaws displayed in the posters on every corner, the salutes on the newsreels, and the throaty radio addresses? A meeting with the man was a chance for the reporter to try to take his measure: to assess the subtle changes in the Führer's voice as he spoke of his subordinates; to joust with Mussolini, asking when he thought war would come.

In fact, what you learned if you met Hitler in person was that he was almost exactly the same in private as in public. He disliked interviews: he gave only a dozen or so to the foreign press between 1923 and 1933, including one to Dorothy and one to Knick. He recognized that he was much more persuasive to a stadium full of thousands than he was one-on-one. An interview with Hitler began normally enough, but after a few sentences, his eyes fixed on the ceiling, and he ranted through his usual litany. The German army had been stabbed in the back by profiteers on the home front. The iniquities of the Treaty of Versailles and the Allies' outrageous reparations payments. It was impossible for reporters to get a direct answer to any of the questions they posed: the man just repeated his speeches.

The fact that Hitler wouldn't carry on a conversation didn't stop the correspondents from clamoring to see him. Dorothy had been petitioning Hitler's foreign press chief, the half-American, Harvard-educated Putzi Hanfstaengl, for an interview since the Beer Hall Putsch. After marrying Sinclair Lewis in 1928, Dorothy had returned to America. She'd overseen the renovation of Twin Farms, the property Lewis bought in Vermont; planted thousands of flower bulbs in the gardens; gone on an unsatisfying lecture tour through the Midwest; and, in 1930, had a baby. But Red was drunk all the time. Like "a vampire," Dorothy wrote, "he absorbs all my vitality, all my energy, all my beauty—I get incredibly dull." In the pages of the *Pictorial Review,* they'd conducted a very public round of fisticuffs on the subject "Is America a Paradise for Women," with Red arguing "Yes," citing women's opportunities in American public life (including as "Lady Mussolini of the local study club"), and Dorothy "No," bemoaning the lack of sympathy and companionship in American marriage. After Red won the Nobel Prize for Literature in 1930, Dorothy returned to Germany for a stint of reporting, leaving their infant son Michael with her friend Rose Wilder Lane, a fellow journalist and the daughter of Laura Ingalls Wilder. She secured a contract with the *Saturday Evening Post,* the most prominent and widely circulated of American weekly magazines, for a series of articles.

In December 1931, when Dorothy finally met Hitler, he was fresh off the Nazi Party's surprise show of strength in the elections the previous year, and willing to offer an audience to a select few foreign reporters. In the 1930 election, all of Weimar's moderate and liberal parties had lost ground to the extremes, but the Nazis had scored the biggest gains of all. They stood on the brink of an electoral breakthrough that could mean real power in the government. Both the political and the economic situation in Germany, Dorothy recognized, were dire. Many of the people she met talked of the country's "ruin," a consequence of reparations she herself described as vindictive and damaging. She was all prepared, she would write, to be bowled over by Hitler. But less than a minute in his presence, and what struck her was his "startling insignificance."

"I Saw Hitler!" was the headline, and Dorothy's verdict was scathing. "He is the very prototype of the Little Man," she began, noting the dictator's boneless face, his awkward gestures, his shyness. She'd wondered if she would require smelling salts to face him down, but quite to the contrary. Hitler's manner was soft, "almost feminine." Given the Nazis' virile posturing, that was telling; she proceeded to let the air out of the inflated Hitler balloon. With a wink to the rumors about his homosexuality, she noted: "I bet he crooks his little finger when he drinks a cup of tea." She'd been informed that she could pose three questions, which had to be submitted twenty-four hours in advance of the interview. But that was all for show: Hitler didn't even pretend to reply. When she interrupted him in mid-rant, repeating her first question—"What will you do for the working masses of Germany?"—he told her he didn't intend to let his enemies in on the details of his program.

Could such a man rule Germany? He was an "agitator of genius," Thompson judged. Of course his theories made no sense, but she well knew, too, that "reason never yet swept a world off its feet." Millions of Germans had been taken in. They were little people, like Hitler himself, aggrieved and resentful, intent on revenge for the miseries that had been heaped upon them. "Listening to him they feel themselves exalted." No, Dorothy decided. Even if Hitler came to power, the Nazis would govern in coalition with the realists of the Catholic Center Party. "I predict that Hitler will be extinguished between two prelates." And: "If Hitler comes into power, he will smite only the weakest of his enemies."

It was, as John put it to Jimmy decades later, "her comico-terrible gaffe." As the chief of the *Public Ledger*'s bureau in Berlin, Dorothy had been well ensconced in German intellectual and political circles, which she rated as superior to those in the United States. Germany was the land of Einstein and Thomas Mann. How could a third-rate type like Hitler come to power in a country like that? To many other observers before 1933, the idea of a civilized people commanded by a little Austrian corporal turned house painter seemed just as farcical as it did to Dorothy.

Not to Knick, though. Knick interviewed Hitler a few months after Dorothy did. He'd been traveling around Germany to assess the situation, dressing up as a homeless tramp to stand in soup lines; putting on a freshly pressed suit to eavesdrop on the fat cats guzzling champagne in the nightclubs; talking to local Nazi leaders, industrialists like the steel tycoon Gustav Krupp, hungry schoolchildren. The debauchery amid want, the resentments, the inability of successive governments to manage the economy: every sign pointed to the fact that the German crisis was sharpening. The unemployment rate had soared to nearly 25 percent and at night, Nazis brawled with anti-fascists, mostly Communists, for control of the streets.

Courtesy of Putzi Hanfstaengl, whom he'd known since the Beer Hall Putsch, Knick arranged to see Hitler in Munich at the Nazi Party's "Brown House" headquarters. Hitler was courteous, insisting that Knick take a seat first. The Führer was dressed not in a uniform, but in a black suit, with a white shirt and a black tie. He looked, or so Knick observed, like a "rising young district attorney in a second class county in Texas." An ambitious mediocrity, in other words.

"What will happen to American property and investments when you come to power?" Knick began. (Not "if" but "when.")

As soon as Hitler began to talk, the mask of ordinariness fell away. Far from an idiot, the man was a talented, dangerous demagogue. It was just a matter of time before he came to power, Knick thought. Hitler's success in the July 1932 elections vindicated Knick's assessment. The Nazi Party won 37 percent of the vote, still a minority in the Reichstag, but now they had overtaken the Socialists to become the country's largest party. Still, there were plenty of observers who assumed that the Nazi danger would pass, especially after the National Socialists shed voters that fall in the November elections. Knick's critics accused him of undue alarmism, of whipping up a tabloid-style frenzy: "Mr. Knickerbocker is perhaps a little too susceptible to the magic of Hitler: it is part of his emphasis on the sensational."

In the years that followed, Dorothy was annoyed to be reminded of her error of judgment about Hitler. The fact that she wasn't alone in underestimating the Führer was hardly a consolation. She'd pay for the mistake in more ways than one. Her erroneous prediction jeopardized her ability to report from Germany. So livid was the Nazi leader about Dorothy's article that he refused to meet foreign reporters for an entire year. If Hitler ever did come to power, commented one Brooklyn paper, Mrs. Lewis had better steer clear of Germany.

CULTIVATING FASCISTS REQUIRED A certain measure of flattery. But how much was too much? What made someone a "journalistic whore"? More than any other figure, it was Mussolini, a onetime political journalist and editor himself, who precipitated that question. The Italian dictator liked bantering with reporters, especially pretty lady reporters. He made a point of seeing the foreign press at regular intervals, both to burnish his own image and to gather up crumbs of information about what was happening in other chancelleries. Knick would meet him four times, once in 1932, twice in 1934, and once in 1936. On the first occasion, the interview came as part of Knick's reporting on European responses to the Great Depression. "Your statements on my general thesis, 'Can Europe Recover Economically?' would be of more interest and value to me and my readers than those of any other statesman in Europe," Knick entreated.

At the gate of the Palazzo Venezia, the Renaissance mansion that Mussolini had taken for his office, Knick submitted his credentials at a guard station, walked up three flights of stairs, followed a corridor past more blue-liveried guards standing at attention, passed through a Renaissance door, traversing two more chambers before finding himself before an imposing door. The room on the other side was immense, and at a carved desk eighty feet away, virtually the only piece of furniture in the room, Mussolini was sitting, waiting for him.

The Duce wasn't at all what Knick was expecting. He was prepared for a "snooty, Prussian-officer dictator." Mussolini, by contrast, was a charmer, who rose from his desk and walked across the room, extending his hand. "Benevolent, agreeable, polite, intelligent, etc.," Knick wrote a colleague. Conversant with the reporter's trade, the Duce didn't permit anything he said to be quoted verbatim and if you ever hoped to interview him again, it was a rule to be followed to the letter. He preferred to answer, in writing, questions put to him in advance. That lent the conversation itself a gossipy, almost intimate flavor. His Excellency pumped the reporters he met for information, asking nearly as many questions as he answered.

"And what do you think of Hitler?" Mussolini asked Knick the year after the Nazis came to power. Did he still have the support of the Germans?

The Germans, Knick told Mussolini, wouldn't abandon Hitler, not even if thousands of them starved to death.

Knick could tell that Mussolini was thinking the same was true of his own fascist state in Italy. "Yes, I think you're right. They could even starve and it would make no difference. Nothing but death or a lost war would make the difference." However similar their grip over their respective populaces, it was also plain from his tone that the Duce regarded Hitler as a less imposing strongman than himself.

None of this made it into the articles that Knick wrote in the early 1930s. If Dorothy demolished Hitler's public presentation, Knick portrayed Mussolini much as he wanted to be seen. The Duce was knowledgeable, canny, and decisive. He was combatting the Depression with large-scale public works programs and an aggressive form of corporatism. He was rearming Italy but not looking for war. As Knick wrote, "No man has a better grasp of the menaces that threaten Europe." It was a description often used to praise Knick himself. In depicting the success of Italian fascism, Knick worried that he had overdone it. "I hope nobody interprets my report as a plea for Fascism or a defense of it in any country but Italy," he wrote his editor. "There is only one Italy and only one Mussolini."

———

THE YEAR AFTER KNICK first interviewed Mussolini, John got Trotsky. It had taken months of wheedling and letters full of promises (and probably an envelope full of cash), but on a dazzlingly bright day in April 1932, John stepped off the paddleboat on the island of Prinkipo in the Marmara Sea, off the coast of Constantinople. Expelled by Stalin from the Soviet Union, Trotsky had lived in exile since 1928, plotting a global revolution. Stalin might be willing to content himself with building socialism in one country but Trotsky continued to insist that Marxism would succeed only if it ushered in the permanent revolution—in every country.

At the Prinkipo pier, John was met by Trotsky's secretary, a slight young man in surprisingly bourgeois attire: gray striped trousers and a gray felt fedora. Before John could see Trotsky, said his secretary, they'd first of all sort out the translation of the interview. John had submitted his questions in advance, and these Trotsky had answered. But Trotsky, who'd worked as a journalist and a war correspondent before the Russian Revolution, was very particular about how he was quoted. Together, John and the secretary (who spoke no English) were to translate Trotsky's answers (which were in Russian) into English for Trotsky (who himself spoke little English) to approve. They'd have to make do with French. John and the secretary settled into a pier-side café. The hours crept by.

By the time Trotsky's secretary declared himself satisfied, it was midday, and they ambled slowly up the hill. The villa where Trotsky was staying was a secluded palazzo of rosy red plaster on the northern coast of the island, its rectangular garden surrounded by high stone walls and overgrown with bougainvillea and mimosa. Just past the iron gates, on the right, was a hut where a few Turkish policemen, equipped with dogs and pistols, stood guard. Trotsky's study occupied a large room on the second floor. When John entered, Trotsky was at work, behind a huge desk made of bricks and planks and loaded with stacks of paper.

"I am astounded at his face," John noted. It wasn't the way that he (or, he presumed, his readers) thought that the man who invented the modern coup d'état would look: "the thing that made an overwhelming first impression on me was Trotsky's lightness and cleanness." The revolutionary was scrubbed fresh, bright as a bubble, his manner gracious and precise. Surely it had taken a more menacing character to recognize that you could overthrow a state by taking control of technology, seizing the telephone and telegraph exchanges and the electrical plants. As John read the translated interview aloud, here and there Trotsky interjected a correction, plucking dictionaries off his shelves to get a word right. With a child's chuckle, he showed John the hiding places—books with their pages scooped out—where he kept his valuable documents.

"Will the capitalist system survive the present crisis?" John asked. Yes, Trotsky judged, the current crisis but not those that would follow. Trotsky brought up the World Disarmament Conference, which had opened in Geneva to great fanfare a couple of months earlier. The purpose of the Geneva Conference was to promote world peace by eliminating offensive weapons. Such efforts Trotsky deemed hopeless: the question was not whether war would come, but when.

"Is there any possibility of your returning to Russia?" If danger threatened the country, Trotsky pronounced, he'd be prepared to serve. But by sidestepping the question, he allowed it to hang there in the air: yet another shot aimed at Stalin. Trotsky left no doubt as to his contempt for the Soviet leader. Back in the old days in Moscow, as Stalin launched into one of his Politburo speeches, Trotsky used to pick up a book and start reading.

Incredible, really, how the hatred between the two men—visceral, profound—had shaped the course of Russia, John observed. And not just Russia. In the countries where John traveled, in Spain and Germany, he met fervent Trotskyites, pledged to the Fourth International, who took their orders from Prinkipo. Small wonder that the capitalist countries still shuddered when Trotsky—"a packet of dynamite, wrapped in asbestos," as John put it in *Harper's*—crossed their borders: "gingerly he was forked across frontiers as if the very elements of his person might spontaneously explode."

Stalin had kicked Trotsky out of the Soviet Union rather than having him shot, and given how many followers Trotsky had, perhaps that was shrewd. But it was only a matter of time before Trotsky's agitations, his *Bulletin of the Opposition,* became intolerable. When Trotsky came downstairs for meals, the members of the Prinkipo household barred the dining room's windows and doors with iron shutters. When he slept, they took turns standing guard armed with semiautomatic German Parabellums, the dapper secretary included, all night long.

Was Trotsky finished or was he just getting started? On that question, John rendered no judgment. There was no doubt in his mind, though, that the man was a genius: "A genius in the sense that Michelangelo was a genius." It wasn't just that Trotsky was a masterful tactician and a brilliant theorist. His career, as John put it, "couldn't be explained by any rationalization of the historical process." Contrary to Marx's vision of history, in which feudalism gave ineluctably onto capitalism and then, after the revolution, to communism, it seemed to John there wasn't anything inevitable about Trotsky's rise. And yet, the Russian Revolution was unthinkable without him.

The fact that Trotsky, Mussolini—and Goebbels, too—had all started as journalists created its own sort of dynamic with the correspondents. The politicians liked turning the tables, deploying the reporter's bag of tricks to their own advantage: turning on the charm, trading information without giving too much away, polishing the quotations attributed to them. For their part, the reporters put themselves, at least imaginatively, in the politicians' shoes. I want power, John had confessed to Frances from Moscow in 1928, and in that, he was hardly alone. Most newspapermen, John had noticed, quickly grew tired of witnessing events; they longed to play a part. Stories of reporters secretly brokering peace treaties made the rounds.

To interview a man like Trotsky was to ask oneself—could I have been him? After all, as John wrote, Trotsky had vaulted himself from journalistic oblivion to control of one-seventh of the world's land surface. What was that genius? John was grappling with what Jimmy called the fit between the man and history but unusually for him, ever a clear writer, he left the idea a stub in his article, elliptical and unexplored.

FRANCES WAS A MARXIST but she was also a Freudian, which meant that she thought that an investigation of personality in light of the formative experiences of childhood was imperative. But she thought John and his friends were going about it the wrong way. For one thing, they were far too cautious about what they put in print. Why wouldn't they just write the truth—that Poland's Marshal Piłsudski was subject to psychopathic temper tantrums and Turkey's Kemal Atatürk was a mother-fixated drunk? Tear the veil off the dictators, she urged her husband.

At the same time, Frances urged John to pay more attention to the powers behind the throne. The capitalists who were using the Nazis to prop up their own class interests. The industrialists filling up Nazi coffers. The arms dealers supplying the fascists with munitions. "Why should these powerful people, whose behavior can influence millions of lives, live behind a smoke-screen, while poor politicians like Hitler have their balls discussed in public?" she demanded. They ought to be unmasked, too. The better article, said Frances, wasn't "I Saw Hitler!" but "I Saw the Guy Who Pays for Hitler's Pants."

Frances had no shortage of ideas for John, but when she sat down to do her own work, she made little progress. She'd been working on a play entitled "Mothers and Lovers" when Johnny was a baby, but she couldn't figure out how it should end and spent fruitless days fretting over it. She helped John with his work, subbing for him when he was away, filing articles under his name, which was the common practice when an assistant filled in. The London *News Chronicle*, a liberal paper, hired her to report from Vienna, but the work was occasional, only when there was a big story afoot. She ought to have had plenty of time to write.

Of course, there was Johnny to worry about. From the moment that he was born, weeks earlier than expected, nose first and jaundiced, Frances kept a journal about him. On gridded pages, she charted his progress: Weight, Travel, Thumb-Sucking, Food, Social Behavior, Nurses. She was fastidious and watchful, recording a test done when he was two weeks old for the enlarged thymus blamed for Judy's death. At first, she wrote tersely, as if to ward off disaster, a checklist of attainments (standing up in playpen, ten months), but later on, the entries came more easily. It was important to manage his childhood correctly, she knew: as the years progressed, she looked for signs of an Oedipus complex, arranged for him to spend time alone with John, kept him in bed when he had colds, and instructed Milla, the Austrian nursemaid she hired, not to scold him for masturbating. She answered forthrightly when he asked about body parts and had informed him—it was crucial to do it early—about how babies were made. "But Mama," he replied, "that's not true at all."

What a darling child, people said to her: a blond cap of hair, his father's blue eyes, a tall boy with rounded, sturdy limbs. Mild-mannered and gentle, he could play for hours, sitting in one place, with his toys. Every morning he drew in his notebooks after completing his exercises. He danced to the Victrola, whether or not there was music playing. He was fond of the moon. At the age of three he showed his first sign of jealousy when Dorothy Thompson's son tried to take Milla's hand. He spoke always in German though she and John supposed that he understood a little English. I love you as much as Milla, he told Frances. I love you as much as Mama, he told John that same week. Perched up on John's shoulder, he said proudly that he'd be as tall as his papa one day. At night, she and John and Johnny kissed good night, which they called *Alle drei lieb haben*. All three of us loving.

"My Experiment in Johnny," she noted atop a sheet of blue paper: to create in him "a cooperative—not a competitive person."

Johnny is fine, said John. The apartment is fine. I am fine. Please do your work. Finish your play, write more for the *News Chronicle*. "I am a Penelope writer," she replied. By night she unpicked all that she'd done in the morning. She found news reporting straightforward enough: journalism was "premature emission" in her opinion. The problem came when she tried to write something more substantial. Stop making excuses, John reproached her. "I loathe it unendurably, much more than I've even told you, that you waste your talent so unendingly." No more lists of household chores, put away the cookbooks. Just wake up in the morning and start writing. I'll help you, he promised. "Talent is <u>so</u> damned rare, & <u>so</u> precious it seems to me nothing short of criminality to fritter it away."

WHILE FRANCES STRUGGLED WITH her work, Dorothy was writing more and better than ever before. The year after she interviewed Hitler, Dorothy put aside her essay, entitled "The End of Bourgeois Morality," and began a novel about her first marriage to Joseph Bard. In addition, she was turning out long, deeply researched pieces for the *Saturday Evening Post*. At the root of the trouble in Central Europe, Dorothy judged, was the settlement at Versailles that followed the 1914–1918 war. She briskly dissected its errors. It wasn't just the vindictive reparations payments. Peace treaties had often enough taken Carthaginian form. Far more destabilizing, she wrote, was its misplaced idealism. The most dangerous person at the Paris Peace Conference had been Woodrow Wilson, "the college professor with the not quite good enough intellect." Wilson's nineteenth-century liberal nationalism—his confidence in the principle of the self-determination of peoples—ignored both the economic interdependence of twentieth-century Europe and the impossibility of creating ethnically pure states where populations were "so hopelessly intermingled." Wilson's belief that democracy could be imposed upon a people had led, in short order, to the military dictatorships and corrupt cabals of the successor states; small states, it turned out, could be just as oppressive as large empires.

Dorothy's pieces were expansive, analytical, richly descriptive about daily life in Depression-era Europe but always rounding on a relevant point for Americans. She recognized she had to cultivate her audience, demonstrating why they should care about developments thousands of miles away. There was a wholesale retreat from internationalism now under way in Europe, she warned her readers. Xenophobia was ascendant. The British yammered on about buying British, extolling the virtues of local limestone over Italian marble for tombstones. The Germans, meanwhile, laid plans for autarchy and the French cried about the need for national defense. "The only international which seems to be winning these days is the international of the anti-internationalists," Dorothy observed. "So, if you are planning to go abroad in the next few months equip yourself with a thorough knowledge of the leading national anthems."

She was unsparing in her judgments, often sardonic. To point up the idiocy of trade barriers dividing up the old Habsburg lands, she envisioned the Austrians (left only with luxury industries) boiling their snakeskin handbags for soup while the Hungarians across the border (with their rich agricultural lands but little manufacturing) stuffed themselves with food but were reduced to wearing rags. Her articles put the reader there, with her, on the spot. Discussing the Depression, Germany's ex-chancellor Heinrich Brüning diagnosed an economic crisis "complicated by profound psychological disturbances." At the League of Nations's headquarters in Geneva, Dorothy cornered an English delegate to talk about the subject of national minorities. How do you determine which peoples count as a national minority? she asked him. Did the ethnic Ruthenians in the new state of Poland count? "Any group of more than six malcontents," he replied, not bothering, as Dorothy noted, to hide his boredom.

Crisscrossing Europe, she gathered up budget forecasts, personal stories, details of daily life. She extracted information from her colleagues. "She always was a diligent gold digger in a journalistic way but the Saturday Evening Post technic has got it down to a clinic basis where the patients are lined up and the old surgeon just passes along and whittles what he wants out of each one without wasting anytime," one of them complained to John. For his part, John felt only a dejected sort of admiration, comparing his own work—"all the smut and slime"—with Dorothy's dignified, serious articles that made Europe so relevant for Americans.

The *Saturday Evening Post* articles were turning Dorothy into a household name in America. She and Red had arranged to spend Christmas in the mountains of the Semmering, a two-hour train journey from Vienna. They were renting the Villa Sauerbrunn, comfortable like the Ritz but "a cuckoo clock in aspect." Promising tobogganing and skiing and tea dances, Dorothy invited a slew of their friends, old and new, for that Christmas week, 1932, among them Knick (who couldn't come), the Gunthers, and the Fodors; Edgar Mowrer, the *Daily News*'s man in Berlin, and his wife, Lilian; and Nicholas Roosevelt, the American ambassador to Hungary. At the Villa Sauerbrunn, they'd put on lunches and dinners. And at the house next door, an annex to a big hotel, they'd reserved rooms for their friends to stay.

The party on the Semmering was to become one of those occasions that people argued over, correcting each other's memories decades later as to what exactly had taken place. Had the lawyer Helmuth James von Moltke been present? Was there enough snow for skiing or was the weather, cold and rainy, a bust? What was beyond dispute was that John ended up confined to bed for practically the entirety of the week with a severe case of asthma; he thought he might die. Red was on the wagon and in a lethal temper. And Dorothy, who'd taken other lovers during her marriage to Red, fell in love with one of her guests, the writer Christa Winsloe, the former Baroness Hatvany, author of (among other books) *Das Mädchen Manuela*, now heralded as a classic lesbian novel.

Somewhere around this time, Frances and Dorothy compared their marriages. Frances was taking notes; she wanted to write a profile of Dorothy for the *New Yorker*. By that point, there were as many rumors about Dorothy and Red divorcing as there were about Nazi putsches in Austria. The truth was Dorothy wasn't sure how much more she could stand. "This year, sometimes I've thought I couldn't hold out any longer & I'd have to give up our marriage," she said to Frances. Red kept vowing to stay off the booze but couldn't. When he wasn't drinking, he was cold and resentful. When he was, he turned mean and violent, deriding Dorothy, tearing up furniture, smashing the crockery. He'd even hit her. That was the most awful moment, the time when she knew "I must save myself; I must really, now, save myself." But there had been other breaking points, before. When she was pregnant, she'd called Jimmy Sheean late one night to ask him to drive her to the Roosevelt Hotel; she had been making plans then to separate from Red.

At the root of the problem, as Dorothy explained to Frances, was jealousy. "A woman is proud of her man's achievement—she expands with it. But no man can bear to have his wife achieve anything apart from him." Red was the first American to win the Nobel Prize for Literature and his books had sold millions of copies. Yet he ran around lamenting: "I'll be known as Dorothy Thompson's Husband." Dorothy had enough of it. "Did you ever hear anything so ridiculous?" she asked Frances.

Feminism hadn't functioned as Frances had once imagined it would: there was no sign that men had taken competition from women as an incentive to better themselves. Instead, as Dorothy put it, women were improving but men were getting worse. Modern women, Dorothy observed a few years earlier, "will not let men swallow them up, because the swallowers aren't good enough." Maybe they'd willingly surrender to a bona fide genius, but to a man whose aspiration was to make a better toothpaste or move his money from one stock to another? They weren't going to snuff out their own flame for *that*.

She recognized that Red was a bona fide genius. But he also wanted her to be his mother, Dorothy told Frances. She wouldn't do it. She'd be his wife, or nothing. "Cock-Vanity—they're too proud of their cocks. I never wanted one. Do you know what I want? To live on a big estate and have lots & lots & lots of children." Having once disdained the suffragettes' notion of "sex antagonism"—of a war between the sexes—as antiquated, Dorothy and Frances now found themselves fighting its battles as individuals, within their own marriages.

"But do you *feel* stifled?" Dorothy asked Frances.

How else could Frances explain her inability to make progress in her work? When John wrote articles that grappled seriously with the paradoxes of Soviet modernization or, following her suggestion, investigated the links between the international arms firms ("as incestuous as white mice"), she was proud. But a vicarious pride in John's accomplishments wasn't the same thing as having the satisfaction of writing well herself. Had her ambition on John's behalf suppressed her own? Did you see John's pieces in *Foreign Affairs* and everywhere else? she asked their friend Jerry Frank. "Aren't you impressed. Haven't I done well by him?" Doing well by John meant helping to make him into the writer he could be. Whether she could have written the articles better herself, though, was another question.

A MONTH AFTER DOROTHY's party on the Semmering, Adolf Hitler, whose Nazi Party had scored electoral victories in the July and November 1932 elections, came to power in Germany. Following a succession of backstage intrigues presided over by the wily aristocrat, Franz von Papen, and the doddering hero of the First World War, General Field Marshal von Hindenburg, Hitler was named chancellor in January 1933. Arriving in a rush from Austria, still in his ski clothes, John met Knick and Edgar Mowrer, who were drinking with the other newspapermen at the bar in the Hotel Adlon in Berlin. Later that night, hundreds of thousands of men dressed in brown shirts and holding aloft torches and Nazi flags promenaded past the hotel and down the neoclassical boulevard, Unter den Linden.

The conservative grandees who smoothed Hitler's path to the Chancellery imagined they could contain him, divert the Nazi energies to their own nationalist and anti-Socialist cause. But that was folly, the reporters at the Adlon wagered, like "trying to tag on to a comet," according to John. "It is a shocking catastrophe for Germany, I do think, and for the world," he observed. "Those bloody people are likely to cause a war, deliberately, and then we all will be dished."

Within a few weeks, the purge of officials loyal to the old Weimar Republic had begun, a housecleaning of the police and the civil service. Enemies of the regime were refused passports for foreign travel. John attended a Hitler rally at the Sportpalast in Berlin, the immense arena seating eighteen thousand, with another sixty thousand huddled outdoors in front of loudspeakers despite the freezing February weather. The Führer shot out words "as if they were bolts of lightning"—he would not abandon Germany to ruin, he vowed. Though Hitler said nothing new, he burned up the crowd with the "absolute magic of his own person," John reported in the paper. The Nazis are "childish, hysterical, bumptious and dangerous," he wrote Frances. "Hitler very flabby and feminine, talks with his arms wound round his bosom husky throaty voice, great sex appeal."

See von Papen, she urged him. Get an interview with General Schleicher, ousted from the chancellery in von Papen's machinations. "See all the outs, quick, while they're easy to see." She pronounced Hitler's speeches "Sublime-Perfect Text Book Examples of What a Classical Demagogue Speech Should Be." The whole sequence of events fit together so perfectly it seemed to her nearly theatrical in form. A series of chancellors, striding onto the stage, each demanding a further concession from the victorious powers— the end to reparations, the expansion of the German military. Each, individually, had gotten more than any one of them could have on their own. It all fit together so perfectly, Frances quipped, mocking the Nazi propensity for finding Jewish villains in all circumstances. A "Jewish playwright must have had a hand in it."

John never saw von Schleicher but he met von Papen, who invited the press over for a *Bierabend:* a "charming fellow, rippling with suave, light laughter, whom I would not trust with a nickel five feet away." More useful were the meetings he and Knick had with Putzi Hanfstaengl. Sure, Knick said, Putzi was a revolting person, a court jester and an official bootlicker, but he knew who among the Nazis were fairies, which was useful coin to trade in. He might even be able to arrange an interview for the two of them with Hitler.

John and Knick took Putzi to dinner, buying bottles of wine at

20 marks apiece to soften him up. Even in a Savile Row suit Putzi looked like a boxer. His features were coarse and swollen; he had a permanent stoop. When the Führer had trouble sleeping, he summoned Putzi to play the piano for him. My piano-playing is Hitler's sole relaxation, Putzi told them.

But, Putzi, you play like an elephant, Knick needled. You knock the hell out of the piano. Does that soothe Adolf's Wagnerian soul?

At this mention of Hitler's Christian name, Putzi became flustered. "Putzi, what do <u>you</u> call Hitler to his face?" Knick inquired. "Herr Hitler, of course." He wouldn't dare call him anything else. They didn't get an interview with Hitler. And if the Führer was a "fairy," Putzi wasn't telling.

John left Berlin just before the Reichstag was gutted by a fire in late February 1933, the week before Germany went to the polls. He returned that fall to cover the trial of the supposed arsonist, the "half-wit" Dutchman Marinus van der Lubbe and a clutch of Communists. By the time that the German Supreme Court reviewed the Reichstag arson case, democracy had been extinguished. Hitler's government had shut down the socialist and communist newspapers, jailing their editors or driving them into hiding or out of the country. The Nazis outlawed parties other than National Socialists; restricted jobs in the civil service to "Aryans," firing Jewish teachers; and rounded up political opponents in a "Brown terror" that involved raiding their homes, then dragging them off to "Brown bases," where they were beaten, dosed with castor oil, urinated on, and had their teeth knocked out with the end of a revolver. "It is a glorious victory, indeed," Knick said sardonically, "of 65,000,000 more or less Aryans against 500,000 Jews, professors, and school-children."

If she hadn't seen the consequences of the Brown terror with her own eyes, Dorothy wrote a friend, she wouldn't have believed it, either. She'd been on her way to rendezvous with Christa Winsloe on the Italian Riviera when she made a detour to Germany. Dorothy was in Berlin when the Reichstag burned, and stayed on to gather evidence about the violence. The Jewish Telegraphic Agency commissioned her eyewitness reports. Working from tips, she and her colleagues in the foreign press—Americans, Danes, Swedes, French, English, Dutch, and Czech—divided the city into districts, fanning out to visit hospitals where casualties might have come in. They interviewed doctors (who often wouldn't talk) and interns and nurses (who sometimes did). They visited the homes of Communists and Jews who'd been beaten up, their families cowering in the corner. Then they met every night, pooling their information.

Make no mistake about it, Dorothy told the readers of the *Jewish Daily Bulletin* in May 1933, the aim of the Nazis was "utterly to destroy German Jewry." The Nazis were conducting an organized campaign of economic and social "strangulation," of legal and professional annihilation. The purpose of the violence, she argued, was to "break civil courage in Germany," to terrorize those who might resist to prepare the ground for the Nazi revolution of daily life. And look at how few Germans had openly protested the treatment of the Jews. That was proof the Nazi strategy was working. "Most discouraging of all is not only the defenselessness of the liberals but their incredible (to me) docility," she wrote Red. "There are no martyrs for the cause of democracy."

Hitler's government issued formal denials that there had been any violence. They summoned the leaders of the Socialist and Jewish organizations to make the victims themselves refute the charges. Repudiate the foreign correspondents' reports of atrocities, the Nazis demanded, or we won't answer for what the storm troopers might do to your people. The browbeaten organizations produced those statements, dismissing the articles as "pure inventions" and "irresponsible distortions." The foreign correspondents, they said, had greatly exaggerated their accounts of the Brown terror. (Understandable, but nonetheless disappointing, judged Dorothy.)

Pressing the point, the Nazi government told the Association of Foreign Correspondents to remove Mowrer as their president. By a vote of 60 to 7, the reporters refused. "There remains, therefore, a single agency in Germany, which has so far not been intimidated in telling the truth, and that is the corps of foreign correspondents," Dorothy noted.

The Nazi government alternated between outright intimidation and efforts to drum up favorable press coverage. After Knick's blistering series of articles on the Nazi revolution, including reporting on the effort to "destroy" the Jews, he received an invitation from Hermann Göring's press chief to visit the camp at Sonnenburg where political prisoners were held. The purpose was to demonstrate the regime's benevolence toward its enemies—a line that Knick wasn't buying. Soon after, Nazi propagandists began denouncing him as a secret Jew, a Meyer or a Levitsky hell-bent on destroying the Third Reich. In Memphis, Knick's father, pastor of the First Methodist Church, was besieged by wires requesting that he attest to the family's Aryan purity.

"The Nazi press yells for the blood of all who criticize their chief," Knick explained to his editor. The Nazis expelled Soviet reporters, as well as a British correspondent for the *Daily Telegraph* who dared to report that the storm troopers were carrying arms in a military parade. After Edgar Mowrer reported that Nazi thugs were attacking Jews in the street with steel rods, Putzi telephoned him: "Ah, and how are you today, my dear little Black Sheep," he breathed menacingly down the wire. The Mowrers woke up every morning to the sight of SS men posted outside their door.

What chance, then, did the accused in the Reichstag trial have of getting a fair hearing? Like many others in Germany, John observed, the Supreme Court's seven judges (some committed Nazis, others just sympathetic) were already convinced of the guilt of the Communists. While van der Lubbe had confessed to the crime, it was obvious that a partially blind Dutch drifter couldn't have simultaneously set twenty or thirty fires. He must have had accomplices. Because van der Lubbe was a Red, the Nazis had announced the night of the fire, the arson must have been a Communist plot. Immediately they had jailed a hundred Communist deputies, their fiercest political opponents, and seized, too, the Comintern official Georgi Dimitrov, whom they claimed was the ringleader of a larger Bolshevik plot. So confident were the government's prosecutors that they barely put together a case. Surely, it would be a quick proceeding.

As persuaded as the judges were of the guilt of the Communists, they nonetheless recognized the need for a trial that comported with international standards. They were playing to the foreign correspondents sitting in the press box. Very quickly the state's case against the purported arsonists began to unravel. Dimitrov, it turned out, had been in Munich, not Berlin, on the night of the fire. As each witness took the stand, the prosecution dug a deeper hole for itself, calling outright con men whom the judges dismissed. "With dreadful pertinacity, with true Teutonic thoroughness, the court plodded on," John wrote, "deeper every day in a morass of evidence that ineluctably proved just what it didn't want proved—the innocence of the accused."

The star of the trial was Dimitrov himself, who single-handedly, audaciously, prosecuted the prosecutors. Asking about a witness who couldn't be located, he inquired: "Have you looked for him in a concentration camp?" His exchange with Göring, during which he accused the Nazis of setting the fire themselves, "contributed deeply to the pure joy of living," John wrote. In his closing statement, facing execution by decapitation, Dimitrov demanded that the German government give him "compensation for his wasted time!" What had started as a frame-up was turning into a circus. After sitting for fifty-seven days, the Supreme Court called a halt to the proceedings, acquitting Dimitrov and sentencing van der Lubbe to death.

The rule of law in Germany was hanging by a thread. John tried to take the measure of the place. He counted how many times the movie crowd applauded when newsreels featuring Hitler were shown (sometimes clamorous applause and sometimes absolute silence, a mild clapping most frequent of all). He relayed what a hotel waiter had said to a friend: "Tell them in America that we're not ALL crazy." Militarism, he could see, was ramping up: the steady diet of war films in the theater; a showroom of weaponry entitled "The Front" on Unter den Linden, outfitted with a romanticized model trench from the last war. The opposition forces, mostly Socialists and Communists, were scattered, fragmented. Unable to muster an armed challenge to the Nazis, left-wing provocateurs shouted

"Death to fascism!" on a crowded street or painted THE RED FRONT LIVES in huge red letters on a bridge. Worst of all was the situation of the Jews, subjected to a vicious program of terror, the only campaign pledge the Nazis could fulfill.

From Chicago, John's editor sent a request for "more diversified" articles: "The whole paper has been loaded with anti-Hitler copy for two weeks." The time had come, his editor insisted, "to write about something else besides the infringement of personal liberty." The *Daily News* was laying itself open to the charge of bias; the news columns shouldn't be used "for the advocacy of a cause." He regretted holding up one of John's Berlin stories but reiterated that the paper couldn't continue to fill its pages solely with articles criticizing the Nazis. He chastised the reporters in Berlin for having "lost sight of our major purpose as a newspaper which is to publish a well rounded account of events without trying to advise foreign governments how to act or how to operate."

To report the persecution of the Jews, as John's editor understood the matter, was to risk the *Daily News*'s neutrality; he feared the charge of "distortion and overemphasis." His reluctance was typical enough. It's become commonplace that the American and British press downplayed the subject of the Holocaust, either neglecting it entirely or burying vague, sometimes skeptically written articles deep inside their pages. Having fallen for the propaganda of the First World War about Germans bayoneting babies, reporters and their editors had learned the wrong lesson—that reports of atrocities were often exaggerated for effect. In the face of hot Nazi denials, they tended to throw up their hands and assume that Jews were stretching the truth. The *New York Times*, historians have argued, was particularly remiss, as its Jewish owners, the Sulzbergers, fearing the accusation of special pleading on behalf of their co-religionists, went to great lengths to minimize the fact that Jews—as Jews—were particular targets of Nazi oppression.

Yet to follow the articles of Thompson, Knickerbocker, Gunther, Mowrer, Shirer, and many other reporters as they were printed and reprinted in papers across the nation is to see how much—and how early—Americans were in fact being informed about the Nazi crusade against the Jews. Although Dorothy's "Hitler the Menace" series was first published in the *Jewish Daily Herald,* her findings, like Knick's series for the *Public Ledger,* circulated widely, cited in the *Buffalo Evening News,* the *Cleveland Plain Dealer*, the *St. Cloud Times,* and the *Honolulu Advertiser,* among hundreds of other papers and magazines. To be sure, these accounts generated their own pushback. Both reporters would be accused of bias in reporting, of contravening the standards of objectivity. According to a columnist for the *Montclair Times,* Knickerbocker had gotten himself "quite excited" about Jews and failed to depict the German perspective. His reports were "hearsay," they were exaggerated, they could scarcely be believed. "There must be two sides to the question."

What was happening in Germany was indeed hard to comprehend and would only become more so. But in 1933, Dorothy, John, Knick, and Jimmy had no trouble tracing the main line: Jews were facing economic and social annihilation as well as a systematic campaign of physical violence. The reporters' dilemma, rather, was how to get the news out without jeopardizing their sources, opening them to further retaliation. Beg your journalist friends to report that "all is quiet and orderly in Germany," Christa Winsloe's comrades wrote her. Dorothy retorted: "Sure, I say, so it is in a cemetery." She refused to stop writing about what was happening inside the country. Were it not for the Nazis, she would have been "entirely happy," she wrote Red from Italy, where she and Christa were working in their rooms in the morning, lunching lightly, and drinking wine late into the evening in front of a fire. "I lie awake nights thinking what one could do," she said.

No, she and Red weren't divorcing, Dorothy told the reporters yet again when she and Christa returned to New York from Portofino. Just as her notebooks alternated between interviews with Nazi Gauleiters and musings about the place of sex in love, so, too, did Dorothy construe her relationship with Christa as part of her fight against fascism. The Baroness Hatvany, she told the waiting reporters, was a leader of the anti-Nazi cause. They'd join forces to combat the National Socialists from America.

AFTER THE REICHSTAG TRIAL, it was a relief, John said, to get back to Vienna. But how long would it be before Austria, too, went Nazi? In 1933, there were tens of thousands of homegrown Nazis stirring up trouble across the country, obeying Hitler's call—proclaimed in the very first paragraph of *Mein Kampf*—for the country's annexation to Germany. They'd bombed train lines and railway bridges, cut the telegraph wires, killed a Jewish jeweler and his customer with a bomb wrapped in a silk stocking, and hurled through a shop window in Vienna. At the frontier, Nazi cars were waiting to smuggle the plotters to safety in Germany. These days one could hardly sit in a café in Vienna without worrying whether that small paper sack on the next table was full of explosives.

Engelbert Dollfuss, Austria's chancellor, was defiant. His country would remain independent. Dollfuss's government was a coalition of parties (Catholics, right-wing agrarians, and the Heimwehr) united chiefly by their hatred of the Socialists. To fend off Hitler, the diminutive Dollfuss, four feet, eleven inches in his stockings, was courting Mussolini. The Duce abhorred the idea of a Greater Germany on Italy's border.

Jokes about Dollfuss and Mussolini made the rounds in Vienna: "Did you hear the new one about Dollfuss? No need for him to take a train to visit Mussolini. He was airmailed to Rome!"

From Munich, Nazi propagandists used the radio to broadcast attacks on Dollfuss across the Austrian border. Slave of the Jews, slave of the Catholic Church, slave of foreign capitalists! they raged.

Just a few weeks after the Reichstag fire in Berlin, on a March morning in 1933, Dollfuss had dissolved the Austrian Parliament, declaring an end to democracy. Henceforth, he would rule as a dictator by emergency decree. The Ringstrasse was blocked by barbed wire and punctuated by rifle rests. The grounds of the Hofburg, the seat of the old Habsburg court, swarmed with mounted police and steel-helmeted Austrian soldiers. Machine guns in the streets, "howling mobs" of Nazis gathered on the Ringstrasse, and "so many rumors of Putsches that even Fodor is satisfied," John wrote mordantly to Bill and Tess Shirer.

Dorothy's old friend Marcel Fodor was glum but not hopeless. "One must not have any illusions," he reported to his editor. "Dollfuss's regime is also Fascism. But it has one thing: it is Austrian Fascism." This was autocracy tempered by *Schlamperei*, by laziness and inefficiency. Dollfuss was at heart a reactionary, Fodor thought: he intended to take the country right back to 1914 when the Habsburgs reigned.

Vienna wasn't as bad as Berlin, Fodor reassured himself. There weren't storm troopers here to haul innocent people off to prison. And hadn't Dollfuss pointedly said that Austria could absorb other cultures besides the German one? Of the two million inhabitants of Vienna, more than two-thirds weren't even of German origin: there were two hundred thousand Jews, nearly as many Hungarians, a hundred thousand Czechs. Surely Hitler's fanatical racial theory couldn't work here.

Nevertheless, Fodor had to admit that the spying was getting to him. The police tracked his every movement, his telephone had been tapped, and they were opening his mail. The Central Telegraph & Telephone Office, where the correspondents sent their dispatches, was infested with Nazi spies.

Several months after Dollfuss abolished the Parliament, John and Fodor set off for one of their regular reporting trips to Prague. John was driving. He was annoyed when Fodor insisted on a detour. At Fodor's direction, they drove nearly all the way to the Czech border, bumping along rutted country roads in the Austrian hinterland. John looked over at Fodor with an expression he hoped would convey exasperation. No such luck. The man just sat there, placidly, giving nothing way.

But what could Fodor possibly want in this godforsaken place? The village, called Spital, was twenty or so whitewashed huts strung out on a muddy hill, two hundred souls living with their animals, front courtyards given over to dung heaps. A church with a squat tower. Finally, in front of a single-story, brown plaster cottage right in the middle of the village, Fodor gestured for John to stop the car. In this village here, said Fodor, among the lowest kind of peasants, he had found the kinfolk of Herr Hitler. No reporter had ever interviewed them.

Fodor knocked on the door of the cottage. The man who answered was bent almost in half, young still, but deformed. Hitler's first cousin, Eduard Schmidt, was a hunchback. A body encased in iron braces, and an intelligent face atop it, reminiscent of the star of a thousand newsreels. The same brown eyes tucked under the same shallow forehead. There was no art in getting Eduard to answer their questions: he was difficult to understand because of a speech impediment, but he talked on and on. He was a convinced Nazi, naturally, a true believer in his cousin's ideal of a Teutonic master race.

"No, we don't hear from him. Ah, but he is far too busy. He is the greatest man in the world and what are we but poor peasants!"

John and Fodor entered the house through the courtyard where the animals were quartered, beyond which was a single room for living and sleeping. The day was warm and the room, painted a pale light blue and pin-neat, with prints of the Madonna and saints on the wall, smelled of coal smoke from the tiled oven. The only furniture was two beds, a table, and a couple of rough chairs. Alerted to the visitors by the commotion of villagers, Eduard's mother came into the cottage with her husband, Herr Anton Schmidt, a toothless and sturdily built peasant.

Hitler's aunt, Frau Schmidt, was a mountain of a woman, draped in a black shawl. Her gray hair was covered by a kerchief. From a wrinkled face her blue eyes, alert, surveyed the situation. She had a vigorous, confident manner of speaking. She would require more managing than her son. "You look tremendously like Adolf," John began.

"Oh go on . . . !" the old woman demurred.

John's German wasn't good enough to follow Fodor's careful inquiries. Who her parents were and where they had lived and the same about Hitler's father's people, reaching back deep into the dim mists of time. Where they had come from before Spital. Her answers were a blur of Schicklgrubers and Hiedlers and Hüttlers and words to do with relatives and ancestors and forefathers and foremothers that left him stupefied. John did understand that Frau Schmidt wouldn't say one way or another whether Hitler's father had been illegitimate (there were a lot of rumors). She would take them to see the registers in the village church, and they could see for themselves.

When it was his turn, John asked Frau Schmidt in faltering German about her elder sister, Hitler's mother. Klara was Alois Hitler's third wife, twenty-three years younger than her husband. Klara had left home when she was just ten, Frau Schmidt said, first to a neighboring town, where she'd worked as a housemaid for Alois's first wife. Then to Vienna, a city that Frau Schmidt herself had never visited. When Klara returned to Spital a decade later, in 1884, she was nervous, not a word to say about her Vienna adventures. After old Alois Hitler buried his second wife that year, he came to Spital and proposed to Klara.

Why had her gentle, fine sister married a lump like Alois? He was a tyrant and a brute, dead drunk most nights in the tavern. Klara's salvation was Adolf. From the time he was six, she was sick with cancer, but Klara kept living for her son. "She told Adolf he must be ambitious, he must lift himself from his surroundings, he must be a great man so that she, in her old age, would be proud of him." They made an alliance of two against Alois's cruelties. "Adolf was the light of Clara's soul. She worshipped him and he worshipped her. Then just as his career might have begun . . . she died."

By the time that they had landed on the Pölzls, the Schicklgrubers, and the Hiedlers in the moldy church registers, dusk was settling over the village and they had to get on their way. They arrived in Prague long after dinner.

For Fodor, the trip was a disappointment: he'd wire some copy about Frau Schmidt's reminiscences of the Hitler family to the *New York Evening Post*, but it was far from the story he'd hoped for. In

Vienna there'd long been a lot of gossip about Hitler's family tree and, quite apart from all that, he had his own suspicions. To be precise, the surname is a common one among Polish Jews in Galicia and, as for Adolf's mother, Klara—that's a typical Jewish name in Austria though the gentiles use it freely in Germany and in Western Europe. It would have been interesting to prove this, would it not? Imagine: little Adolf, raving about the Jews, with a Jewish "parasite" in his own lineage!

It was not true—"unfortunately," Fodor went on. What they had seen and heard proved that our Adolf was as much an Aryan as he needs to be. The Austrian and Czech gutter press could keep digging. But he was now convinced there was nothing there and he wouldn't touch the story. At least their beds were waiting for them in Prague, feather pillows and a good golden beer, and their phones wouldn't be tapped there.

But was the trip so useless? John wondered. After all, they'd got something the reporters in Berlin had hankered after—good stories about Hitler. With Putzi, Knick and John had been pecking for crumbs, but in Spital he and Fodor had the cake to themselves. They had seen pictures of Hitler as a baby and a photo of his mother when she was sick, blond braids fading to gray, cheeks sunken. They'd heard his aunt's bile about Alois, Hitler's father.

"All this proves what?" John asked.

"I tell you the truth on it—nothing," admitted Fodor.

To John it all seemed important. But why, exactly, he didn't know. In the hotel in Prague, he started writing his articles about Spital but the point of the family stories kept eluding him. "There are many extraordinary things about Adolf Hitler," he began, "but surely the most amazing is that his mother was a servant girl in the household of his father's preceding wife!"

THE VISIT TO SPITAL emboldened John to try again to finagle a meeting with Sigmund Freud. To ask the great man for an interview was hopeless: Freud had declined his first entreaty on the ground that he refused to see reporters. This time, John requested that Herr Dr. Freud spare him just a few minutes of his time.

"It is simply that I have admired you and your work so profoundly that it seems cruel to live in the same city and never have seen you." He and Frances had met Freud's wife, an unexpected honor, when they visited the villa that the Freuds were occupying in Pötzleinsdorf. They'd been looking for a house to rent, only the villa was too far from town to be practical.

He mentioned that they shared H. G. Wells as a friend in common. He didn't say that he'd written a newspaper article about their chance encounter with Frau Dr. Freud, dressed all in lavender, who had conducted them around the house, discussing utility bills, careful not to disturb her husband at work behind the closed study door. "His wife spoke of him as if he were scarcely mortal, scarcely alive," he informed the readers of the *Daily News*. Who would have thought that the greatest living expert on sex would have such a tidy, capable housewife?

"Perhaps you are interested in the appalling things that are happening in Germany?" John continued. "I have recently returned from Berlin, and have some gossip."

Saving the best for last, John set his bait. "A few weeks ago I visited Hitler's surviving cousins, aunts, and so on in Upper Austria; we learned some interesting things about the psychological background of Hitler's childhood."

Freud wasn't interested. He had to stick to his rules and limit visitors only to those with truly urgent business, he replied. But by now John had a hunch there was a story to be told.

MASS AGAINST MASS

—

FRANCES HAD BEEN URGING JOHN TO GO FOR ANALYSIS PRACtically from the moment they met, but it wasn't until January 1934—when asthma had him flat on his back, pale and gasping for breath—that he presented himself at Dr. Wilhelm Stekel's consulting rooms in Vienna.

Tell me about the troubles that brought you here, Stekel always began. Where does the shoe pinch? The doctor was a man in his mid-sixties, with a twirled mustache and a gray beard trimmed to a sharp point.

John started with the asthma. Mustard brought it on. So did feathers and dander from cats and dogs, and fat blades of timothy weed. All of the usual remedies had been tried, none of which alleviated his illness. Just entering a room where there was a cat was enough to set off an attack.

But there were other problems, too. Problems with his wife. The return of the impotence that had afflicted him, off and on, for years. Dissatisfaction with his work. He'd squandered two years on a novel about the collapse of the Credit-Anstalt that now seemed, two hundred pages in, a dud.

Here is how we shall proceed, Stekel would say. First will come a trial period of a week. That was a step he always required. It allowed him time to assess the chances of a cure and, if necessary, to terminate an analysis that would be fruitless. In the meantime, Herr Gunther was to make a record of his dreams. Note them down in a dream journal within the first minutes of waking. The dream-book should always be brought to the analytical sitting. The patient must hold nothing back from the analyst. Remember what Goethe so wisely said: "I have never heard of a crime that I couldn't have committed myself under certain circumstances." Under no condition, Stekel insisted, was the patient to talk about the analysis with anyone when it was in progress. Afterward, he could tell whomever he liked.

CARL JUNG, ALFRED ADLER, MYSELF—we were all three Freud's disciples. That was the way Stekel told the story. He was a young doctor from Czernowitz on the eastern fringes of the Habsburg territories. Shortly after settling in Vienna, he was analyzed by Freud. The famous Wednesday evening discussion circle? That had been Stekel's idea. He'd proposed it to Freud in 1902. The conversation would be strictly informal; the men—Stekel and Adler and a few other disciples—would arrive at the Berggasse after the Freuds had finished their dinner. Enchanting evenings, Stekel said: none but a miner in the California Gold Rush could have known such a thrill of discovery, the talk of complexes and dreams and sex lives right there for the taking.

Before too long, though, he found himself at odds with Freud over matters of interpretation. They quarreled over autoeroticism (Stekel saw nothing wrong in it), about whether all neuroses (or as Stekel believed, only some) were caused by sexual repression, over who deserved credit for the idea of the death instinct. "Stekel is going his own way," Freud had announced in 1912. The break hadn't been his doing and he tried, over the years, to mend it. He certainly hadn't set out to become Freud's apostate. Without speaking against the great master, Stekel would only say that Freud wished to be the pope. He treated doubters as sinners and insisted on being quoted incessantly.

Painful as it was for him personally, perhaps it was better for psychoanalysis that he separated from Freud. Freed from Freud's orthodoxies, Stekel had analyzed thousands of patients. He had developed a technique he called "active analysis," a course of treatment of three to six months: three if the problem could be skimmed off the surface, six if he had to root out a deep-seated childhood conflict. With Freud, by contrast, you could sit for years with no improvement. Stekel didn't take on a patient unless he thought that he could do him some good; it was his responsibility to improve marriages, not just cause divorces, especially if there were children involved.

Stekel's books—among them, *Frigidity in Women, Impotence of the Male, Auto-erotism: A Psychiatric Study of Onanism and Neurosis, The Language of Dreams, Sadism and Masochism: The Psychology of Hatred and Cruelty*—had been translated into twenty-six languages and his name was very well known in America. He'd lectured there and treated cases in New York and Chicago in 1921. Psychoanalysis, he had to instruct his American audiences, was a science, "not a kissing-game."

Stekel's method was to start the analysis with a series of questions: What was Herr Gunther's favorite book? Was his parents' marriage happy? What terms was he on with his sister? What was his sexual history? Tell me about your wife.

JOHN FILLED UP HIS green notebooks trying to understand his wife. Frances's intelligence and capacity for deep thought, her low soft voice, the delight she took in moonlight and rocks polished smooth by the ocean. Her sweetness and dignity. The shocking things she said. At dinner, while eating salad, cool as could be: "Darling, please screw me tonight."

He took down her sayings, snippets of their conversation. She flashed onto his page like a character he was trying out.

He to her, amid one of their divorce talks: "I wonder if I ever *will* write a good book!"

"If you don't," she replied, "I'll come right back and re-marry you, as punishment."

"Frances is certainly the most intelligent woman I have ever met. It took me 3 years to realize this." He'd known her for nine years and had been married to her for seven and not once in that time had she uttered a trite thought. Her wit and her brightness still took him by surprise: he never knew what she'd do or think next. And when the facts didn't bear out her theories? "So, I'm wrong!" she would declare. She made it sound like a victory.

Why, then, in practical matters did she often seem so fragile, so undone? When it came to choosing a dessert from a restaurant menu, or a dress from a shop, she hung, paralyzed, unable to make a decision; it was maddening. In the kitchen, she was worse than incompetent. She could hardly scramble an egg. She was never on time and kept everyone waiting. "A tremendous paradox: F.'s absolutely sterling courage and strength in fundamentals, and her petty weakness in trivial things." If her aura of helplessness didn't quite square with her boldness in the Barnard Socialist Club, still less with her solo trip to the Soviet Union, it was, he knew, Frances's frailty as well as her intelligence that attracted him.

"My diaries get nothing of F's delicacy, grace, and occasional childishness, also her devotion to theory," John acknowledged. He also left out the habits of hers that other people remembered: how she sometimes locked herself into a room at parties, sitting there silently for hours, refusing to come out. Or her willingness to "let go," as Mickey Hahn admiringly put it, telling people exactly what she thought of them. She "was a B-I-T-C-H," pronounced Edgar Mowrer's wife, "one of those people who go for the jugular," according to Rebecca's son, Anthony.

John knew very well how much his work owed to Frances's influence. She'd fed him ideas and she never stopped exhorting him to improve. Why wouldn't he take a stronger stand in his writing? she continually demanded. "You've got to feel strongly & care yourself, or your readers won't care," she told him. Be fair to both sides, of course, but "care for one side." They argued about it when he filed his dispatches from the Soviet Union in 1928 and they fought more in the early 1930s, in Vienna. The job of a reporter, he protested, was neutrality. His task was to observe and to analyze, not to offer moral judgment. It was one of his strengths as a journalist that he could, almost reflexively, see both sides.

It had been drummed into John, as it was into every other cub reporter, that objectivity was the reputable American newspaper's life blood. Preserving the public's trust required a scrupulous distinction between fact and opinion; accuracy—and decency, too—were gospel. Those were the principles that separated dignified papers such as the *Chicago Daily News* or the *New York Times* from the yellow press of the 1890s. But if impartiality and the embrace of facts had seemed straightforward enough propositions at the turn of the twentieth century, that was no longer the case by the 1920s and 1930s. The development of public relations as a profession, the success of propaganda during the First World War, the uneasy sense that irrationality as much as reason drove the human psyche, the competition from the tabloids: all combined to cast doubt on whether objectivity was possible—or even desirable.

Just as John and Frances debated the merits of taking a stand, American newspapers—in pursuit of the ideal of objectivity—were wrestling with the subjectivity inherent in reporting the news. The rise of the syndicated political columnist in the 1930s was a means of providing interpretation beyond the editorial pages; increasingly, as well, news stories were signed, previously the rule only for foreign correspondence. The belief that facts carried viewpoints, that they (at the very least) needed explanation, bolstered calls for the professionalization of journalism. Reporters, argued the journalist and theorist Walter Lippmann, required a scientific method: they couldn't take their own disinterestedness for granted. Or was the right answer Henry Luce's? According to the publisher of *Time*, founded in 1923, the strict division between news and opinion needed to be relinquished.

Foreign correspondents had long had a wider field of endeavor than their fellow reporters at home. They were permitted to be "editorial" since it was understood that affairs abroad required explanation. The trick, though, was to offer interpretation without advocacy. For most of the old-timers reporting from Europe, this hadn't seemed a dilemma at all. With the exceptions of a few partisans, such as John Reed, whose reportage was avowedly political, most correspondents cultivated neutrality as though having no stake in the matter was the most superior position. Cynics and wise guys, they wandered from capital to capital, some dressed like dandies, others like tramps, turning wars and revolutions into inches of coolly detached newsprint. They were Americans and only there to see things, they said: that's the job.

A decade earlier, John had a cowed respect for his elders among the foreign correspondents. But by 1934, it wasn't enough to be a camera, not after what he'd seen of the fascists in Berlin. He cared too much about truth and decency and reason to treat the subject of Nazis evenhandedly. But if he abandoned the polestar of objectivity, how was he to explain what he was seeing in Austria? Put differently, what was *behind* the news? Frances's exhortations were finally taking hold. The deeper he got pulled into events, the less sense they made to him. It was as if he'd set out to explain the forces of gravity using a ruler and a compass. After several months of analysis with Stekel, John began to think that perhaps he'd been operating with the wrong tools all along.

AT THE CAFÉ LOUVRE, all the talk was of secret negotiations. Dollfuss had an ironclad commitment from Mussolini to defend Austria's borders against the Germans, it was said. But what had he given the Duce in return? Fodor had seen Dollfuss for a half-hour private conversation after he and John returned from Spital. The chancellor, Fodor reported to his editor, had lost his ebullience. He looked pale and seemed rattled. While Dollfuss pronounced himself committed to the anti-Nazi fight, he was also inclined, so thought Fodor, to take Hitler's peacemaking overtures seriously.

When Dollfuss proclaimed the death of Parliament and concentrated more power in his own hands that fall, filling his cabinet not simply with old-fashioned reactionaries but outright fascists, Fodor called it the "greatest disappointment in my life." Nevertheless, he continued to think the worst sorts of brutality could be avoided in Austria: "There is something terribly civilised in the Austrian nature which prevents them to be inhuman." On his own or under Fodor's tutelage, John had come to something of the same conclusion. Writing in *Foreign Affairs,* he marshaled the old Habsburg stereotypes: "The Austrian does not think that he is better than anyone else, he sometimes wonders if he is as good; his political nature is skeptical, lazy, and fatalistic; he thinks of the irredentism of Hungary or the chauvinism of Germany as simply ill-bred."

Whether the Austrian populace was energetic or listless hardly mattered at all to the story John wanted to tell. His focus was Dollfuss. John's aim was to explain how Dollfuss had become the bulwark against Nazism, and here, what counted was the man's personality. He wasn't a blusterer, like Hitler or Mussolini. He wasn't clever, like Metternich. Rather, the source of Dollfuss's authority, as John saw it, was an earnestness that, together with his religiosity, gave him "a curious innocence": the sort displayed by "old, wise priests." Dollfuss's foes—the Socialists as well as the Nazis—continually underestimated him, even as he succeeded in turning their errors to his own advantage. His political allies, meanwhile, behaved like "hypnotized sheep" around him.

Unlikely as it would seem, Dollfuss had become the "political darling of Western Europe," John observed. Though he didn't say so, the little chancellor was also a favorite of the foreign press corps, John included, as much for his personality as his stance against Hitler. In high political circles, his modesty made him a curiosity. He was known to laugh at the jokes traded about him. Have you heard of the latest attempt on the life of Dollfuss, Knick chortled from

Berlin: "Detectives found a mousetrap in his room!" John's articles about Dollfuss were evenhanded. To the publisher of the *Chicago Daily News,* though, John expressed himself more frankly: "He is pursuing a courageous and intelligent course and I hope he wins through."

For the spies in Vienna's Central Telegraph & Telephone Office, the reporters' fondness for Dollfuss presented an opportunity. On the whole, the spies took a dim view of the "Anglo Saxon" foreign correspondents, the Gunthers included: "Mr. John GUNTHER, an American, whose wife is half-Russian and who during his long stay in Moscow as a correspondent has acquired an undisguised sympathy for Soviet Russia." They condemned the whole Louvre bunch as naïve and inclined to sensationalist reporting, puffing up any rumor of coups or revolutions, and unremittingly hostile to the Heimwehr. But precisely because the correspondents respected Dollfuss, the spies thought that it might be possible to bring them around to a more sympathetic point of view.

It would be a fool's errand to try to predict the course of events in Austria, John acknowledged in *Foreign Affairs.* By the time that the reader opened the magazine—his piece appeared in the January 1934 issue—the little chancellor could be in hiding or in prison. And despite all of Dollfuss's talk of class harmony and a new era in industrial relations, Austrian fascism might well prove as much a "swindle" of the working class as Hitler's or Mussolini's regime. "One thing is certain. The Dollfuss system will not mean a terror," John declared.

THE NEXT MONTH, on a February morning a few weeks after John started his analysis, the streetcars that glided along their street came to a halt. The electricity in the apartment cut out, too.

Outside, the tram drivers and conductors were standing around the idled streetcars. They'd become wary as the reporter approached them, go silent and stare, but a greeting of Comrade! would soon get them talking. Had the Nazis possibly managed to sabotage the central power station? Or was it a general strike?

If it was a strike, the tram workers hadn't been told about it. The electricity had just gone out suddenly, they said. There were rumors, though, that Nazis had been shooting their comrades in Linz. They'd heard that Dollfuss had called out the government troops. And if Austrian soldiers or the Heimwehr fired on workers, there'd be civil war. They wouldn't be taken like cattle.

On the radio, the day before, the head of Vienna's Heimwehr, Major Fey, had addressed his troops. "The time has come to exterminate the Reds, once and for all!" he declared. Emil Fey had a widow's peak oiled black like Mussolini's and a jutting chin like the toe of a boot. But his smooth white dress gloves: that part was all Austrian, as homegrown as schnitzel. "Tomorrow," Fey proclaimed, equal parts menace and pomposity, "we are going to clean up Austria."

Maybe little Dollfuss will keep his head, John said hopefully.

There were preparations the Gunthers knew to make in situations such as these. The nanny would run over to fetch Johnny from kindergarten, and then Frances would talk her into staying for the rest of the afternoon. She filled the two bathtubs so that they'd have a supply of drinking water and laid in a store of candles, matches, and flour. In the meantime, John went to fetch the car.

They picked up Fodor first. In the city center where he lived, right around the corner from the Stock Exchange, the streets were quiet. There was a heavy stillness that set the heart racing. The Heimwehr men patrolling the streets had rifles slung across their chests. A bad sign: the government had opened the munitions depots to Fey's men. The Ringstrasse was already barricaded with tanks and tangles of barbed wire, troops pulling machine guns into place to guard the arterial roads. On the walls of buildings were posters proclaiming martial law.

The battles, apparently, were being fought in the Socialist housing projects, the Sandleiten, the Karl Marx-Hof, the Goethehof, and the other gigantic buildings on the outskirts of the city. Even from miles away, they heard the awful whistle and crash of mortar fire, the cold crack of the howitzers. But Dollfuss wouldn't order government troops to fire on Austrian workers, would he? Such a thing was unimaginable, the reporters told each other. Thousands of children and women lived in those buildings. Zigzagging through the city, avoiding the cordoned-off streets, the Gunthers and Fodor reached the Sandleitenhof by early afternoon.

John drove the Ford right up to the Sandleiten's allotment gardens. The ground was a hard crust, the buildings drawn up like fortresses behind hastily barred gates. In front of the arched entryways, garbage cans had been pulled into a line, a makeshift barricade. The police, wearing steel helmets, carbines at their sides, were dragging the cans away.

From the second-story windows of the Sandleiten, a flash of a rifle, and the crackle of a sniper's fire sent the police scuttling. The Socialists had orders not to fire first—that Frances and John had heard. But how long could the people inside hold on? How many weapons did they have? And what had happened to the Schutzbund, the Socialist militia?

The police had machine guns, the infantry had artillery. They'd bring in armored tanks to crash through the street barricades.

"John, drive on!" Frances cried out, determined to get as close as they could.

FRANCES HAD SEEN FEY up close at the Anglo-American Press Association meeting when he'd come to deliver the usual speech about the Bolshevik menace stalking the Austrian homeland. A bullet-headed clod, she decided, an implementer of other people's orders.

Prince von Starhemberg, the chief commander of the Heimwehr, was another matter. Cary Grant without the chin dimple, he was elegant and loose-limbed with a hedonist's mouth. He was the possessor of thirteen ancestral castles and the namesake of the von Starhemberg who'd fought back the Turks from Vienna's gates in 1683. It was said he was in hock up to his eyeballs to Jewish moneylenders. Von Starhemberg had the aristocrat's supercilious sense that social peace would reign in Austria only if the workers could be liberated from their "Jewish-Marxist betrayers." He was fond of saying that no one, absolutely no one, had more respect for Austria's workers than he did.

Sometimes von Starhemberg threw himself into politics, energetically marshaling the Heimwehr, intriguing against his rivals. But he also liked the company of actresses and women skiing champions, late evenings in the nightclubs. On a hot Vienna summer day, you could find him, stripped to his shorts, bathing on the Lido.

What sort of game was von Starhemberg playing, though? the correspondents wondered. For a few years he'd delivered tirades of the Nazi sort, not purple-faced like Hitler's, but with the well-bred cadences that wouldn't be out of order at his mother's dining table. "In 'the people' I do not include those foreign, flat-footed parasites from the East who exploit us," he'd declared. The time for compromise was finished; he was a man of action. "We know that the strength of our movement is not in parliament but in our militant formation." The future of Austria, he once said, was with Germany.

But more recently, von Starhemberg seemed to have acquired a different view. Ever since Dollfuss had allowed him a freer hand (at Mussolini's behest, claimed the sages of the Café Louvre), he'd bestirred himself to declarations about Austria's sovereignty. To Frances, he seemed a nasty opportunist in a charmer's body. He reminded her—strangely—of her stepfather. She took every chance she could to watch von Starhemberg in action.

"From my experience in fascist countries," Frances wrote a few months later, "I have come to one conclusion. Rules of democratic fair play should be reserved for democrats. Decencies of liberalism should be reserved for liberals. But the only way to treat a fascist is to treat him the way he intends to treat you—first. That means hitting him below the belt before he has a chance to hit you below the belt."

She knew her editor at the *News Chronicle,* a good London liberal, would object to those sentiments. He didn't know yet that laissez-faire liberalism was done for, as dead as horse-drawn carriages and hoopskirts. It was time to out-fascist the fascists. "At least, when you knock a fascist out, you will send him to a hospital or observation ward—but when he knocks you out, he sends you to a concentration camp or a crematorium."

The Socialists she and John knew—men like Oskar Pollak, the editor of Vienna's leading socialist paper, the *Arbeiter-Zeitung*— were good and decent. As an intellectual matter, they understood that you couldn't play a game of chess with an adversary whose sole purpose was to smash the board and scatter the pieces. But in their decency, Frances thought, they were making a fatal mistake. They still saw a future for Red Vienna stretching out in front of them.

She wouldn't deny for a minute that their ambitions were glorious. The Sandleiten's butter-colored façades, the arched entryways and windows with twelve big panes of glass: sun and light and air for the masses. Grassy courtyards for children to run and play. A kindergarten outfitted with miniature washstands and towels, a whole orchestra of musical instruments for the children. The gymnasium and swimming pool onsite. The communal laundry room. The workers' library, fifteen thousand volumes strong.

That was what it meant to have a fair government, Frances said. But all of that had to be defended and she didn't see a Lenin or even a Trotsky among Red Vienna's leaders.

NOW, THE BIG GLASS panes of the workers' paradise shook from the concussion of machine-gun fire. John edged the Ford up to the Sandleiten with Frances urging him on—keep going, just a little farther! Much to Fodor's relief, and probably John's, too, the police forbade them to drive on.

When they returned home that night, the streets were pitch-black. It was impossible to see the blockades. John ran the car into barbed wire, reversing directions, again and again. On the radio, there were all manner of lies: a criminal strike at the central electric power plant had started the trouble; the Bolshevik leaders, having provoked a revolution, had fled before a shot was fired, their trunks stuffed with stolen party funds. Let there be no doubt about it: the government would chase the "hyenas to the devil."

But this was no socialist revolution, it was clear to John and Frances. It was a right-wing coup. The government's troops and the Heimwehr had joined forces to crush the Socialists. At the Rathaus, seat of Red Vienna, Heimwehr fighters ran their green and white banner up the flagpole.

This was a government making war on its own people. This was a massacre. How could anyone possibly sleep? The rifle fire all night, the thud of shells, the bitter cold. Even from miles away, their windows were rattling in the frames. My God, there are children in those buildings, people would say all night long to each other, as if saying so could restore decency.

John left just after daybreak for the Goethehof. Waving his press pass, he'd gotten through a few hours after the bombardment. If you could only have seen the kindergarten, he reported. Little desks buried under collapsed beams. A child's rectangular, metal paint-box smashed up. Shards of blackboards. This was the vengeance meted out against people who dared to defend their homes. "Of course even the Heimwehr admits the Bolshevik foe fought bravely—especially the women and children," he wrote Bill Shirer.

John now knew why there had been no concerted defense of Vienna by the Socialist Schutzbund. Like the Heimwehr, the Schutzbund had storehouses of weapons—in pits buried deep in the courtyards of the Sandleiten, or bricked up in secret locations within the walls of the Karl Marx-Hof. They'd made contingency plans: the commander of the Schutzbund, his subordinate, and the next layer of underlings all knew where the guns were. But they hadn't counted on the efficiency of Dollfuss and Fey, who'd rounded up the Schutzbund leaders and their deputies, shooting some of them, arresting the others.

All Monday and Tuesday night, then, through Red Vienna's model housing blocks, Socialist men and women had searched for their cache of weapons, scratching in the dirt of the courtyards with their bare hands while Dollfuss's army blasted the buildings to rubble. They'd chipped away at the interior walls with picks where someone had heard that the munitions stores might be. As for the guns that might have made for a fair fight, the trunks of bullets and grenades intended for the defense of Vienna's socialist experiment: they were never found.

It was quick work for Dollfuss's troops to clean up Vienna. The entire thing lasted just four days, the Socialist dead numbered more than fifteen hundred, the wounded four times as many. Every hospital in the city was full. In the sewers of Vienna, injured Schutzbund men hid in the shadows, waiting for comrades who could smuggle them out, in darkness, wearing fresh, unbloodied suits. Inside one housing project, home to five hundred families, there were long red streaks where the bodies had been dragged down the halls, Fodor reported.

The Socialist Party is dissolved! proclaimed the radio. The trade unions are disbanded! The Bolshevik ringleaders will be hanged!

The trouble with the Austrian Socialists wasn't their radicalism, Frances declared. It was that they weren't Bolshevik enough. Why hadn't they nationalized Austria's largest industrial concerns, seized their assets back in 1918, when they'd had the chance? How could they not have seen that it was no time to obey the rules? During the fighting, the Socialist leaders took *pride* in the fact that there was no looting. It was rumored that one Schutzbund battalion surrendered to the Heimwehr because they didn't want to tread on the grass! Say what you like about Lenin and Trotsky, she told John: they wouldn't have made that mistake.

After the showdown in Austria was over, the correspondents spoke even more carefully at the Louvre and agreed that there was no telling, now, what might happen.

The police swooped down on newsstands and swept away the foreign newspapers. Austrian officials lodged bitter protests with the American chargé d'affaires in Vienna about the reporters' dispatches. Papers that carried "atrocity stories," Dollfuss's government threatened, would be banned in Austria. The correspondents consoled themselves that New York and Peoria and Richmond would hear about the massacre of the Socialists. On one evening in late February, some twenty thousand people gathered at Madison Square Garden to demonstrate against the Austrian government's actions.

Of course prisoners hadn't been beaten up, Dollfuss protested to the American and British reporters who assembled at the Anglo-American Press Association. "You know how gentle we are in Austria." He'd come for a parley with the correspondents, to correct misapprehensions. Now was the time to heal the wounds from the fighting, he said. The Socialists who had fought the government were not bad men, they were simply misled. "These men defended themselves so bravely that I am sure it is worth doing everything to try to win their full confidence and their help in building up a new Austria."

Prince von Starhemberg saw the reporters, too. His message was different from Dollfuss's in tone as well as content. He called the Social Democrats "Austro-Bolshevists," the Heimwehr's fighting words. "I have always deliberately fostered Fascism and fought democracy, and I believe that the democratic system is dying throughout the world. It cannot last much longer," said von Starhemberg. "We feel there is a Fascist wave." The Austrian government and the Nazis shared much in common, he continued. They were both enemies of democracy. But the Nazis' campaign against the churches he rejected as "crazy," and insisted: "We do not accept the exaggerated racial program of the Nazis."

And yet the Nazis, the reporters suspected, would be the beneficiaries of the events of February 1934. By destroying Red Vienna, Dollfuss had weakened the forces of resistance to a Nazi takeover. What the correspondents had witnessed was the first onslaught on the postwar European order. This was "mass murdering mass," wrote Rebecca West, one segment of the population turned assassins, the other victims. And from now on, the "embryos"—Rebecca's name for men like Mussolini, Dollfuss, and Hitler—would be in charge. Because "adults cannot be happily governed by embryos," as she later put it, "existence must decline from what ease and dignity it had attained to a hitherto unknown level of pain and humiliation."

AFTER THE FIGHTING WAS done, there was no longer any doubt in John's mind about the need to take sides. No one who walked through that kindergarten in the bombed-out Karl Marx-Hof could have felt any differently. "Fifteen years of work which no unprejudiced eye could look at without exhilaration have been ruined in a forty-eight-hour nightmare," John concluded in the *Daily News*. "It cannot be too strongly emphasized that the socialist workers are the defenders in this war and the government the attacker."

That took some gumption, Bill Shirer applauded from Paris. It was with trepidation, Shirer admitted, that he'd gone down to the *Daily News*'s bureau to read John's dispatches. He'd been worried that John had been getting entirely too fond of Dollfuss, that he'd feel the need to maintain impartiality in the conflict: "But you were grand, just as I knew you would be when a final showdown came."

Writing the truth was well enough but what was John supposed to *do*? For centuries, people had campaigned for more liberty, petitioning their leaders for equality and peace. And now? Here they were, the people themselves, putting that all in reverse, clamoring for fascism. John knew how the hero of his Credit-Anstalt novel, an able American newspaperman, an affable type but no deep thinker, would react. He'd join the Socialist Schutzbund and learn how to fire a machine gun so that he could defend Red Vienna.

John wasn't going to do that.

Dr. Stekel had an answer to John's uncertainty. Herr Gunther's authority complex had been shattered. There was nothing unusual about that. It had happened to millions of young people amid the First World War. What right had their elders to lord it over them? The breakdown of the family, the church, the institutions of government had prepared fertile soil for the rise of the dictators. Hitler, Mussolini, Dollfuss—they were all neurotics of course. But they'd also become father substitutes for the masses.

But why, John wondered, would people who distrust authority

choose to subsume themselves in a strongman? Why—of all things—did they view Hitler as God?

"People like to be afraid," said Stekel. They tell themselves that they are defiant, that they are independent. They poke their fingers in the eyes of the Jews. They roar in a crowd. The ectoplasm of the dictator envelops them. They believe they are now part of the leadership. "Obedience and defiance finally merge and the leader becomes the new savior."

STEKEL SEEMED ALMOST ABSENTMINDED as he probed, a mesmerist operating by intuition. Sometimes they sat together in the consulting rooms, but Stekel also liked to stroll in the Vienna woods with his patients. When he worked loose an interpretation, he'd stop on the path and then speak.

John related a dream he had—about a cat. "I am awakened (in my dream) by the mewing of a cat. The sound is faint, as if coming from a great distance. I shudder, and think: 'The cat is a herald of death.' Then I really awake and am appeased by finding that it is no more than a silly dream. But my heart goes on thumping for a long time."

Did John know Edgar Allan Poe's wonderful story, "The Black Cat"? Stekel asked.

He'd read quite a lot of Poe as a boy. But funny, no, he hadn't read that story.

Ah, that's a surprise, replied the analyst. Let me tell you, then, about "The Black Cat." In Poe's story, a man murders his wife. To hide the body, he removes the bricks from the wall where there had once been a chimney, props up the corpse against the inner wall, and sets about plastering so that no disturbance to the wall is visible.

Four days later, the police appear at his door. Where is his wife? She's off on a visit out of town, he replies. He bids them to search the premises, conducting them through the house himself. Hands crossed over his chest, he leads the police into the cellar. Two times, three times, four, they investigate it. Just as the officers are on the verge of leaving, the man—swept away by bravado—taps with his cane on the exact place where he'd immured his wife. Solidly built, these walls! he exclaims.

Just then, from behind the walls, comes the mewling of a cat. The detectives set about tearing down the wall, and out falls the body of his wife, and standing on her head, the black cat!

The day after Stekel told him the plot of "The Black Cat," John rummaged in the reading journals he'd kept since adolescence. Aha! He *had* read "The Black Cat," after all, when he was fourteen. Not only that, he'd made notes on Poe's story, observing that its theme was remorse.

At his next sitting, John bubbled with his discovery. He had an excellent memory and never forgot a thing that he read. He remembered the plot of books he didn't even care about, *Tess of the d'Urbervilles* and *Kenilworth*. Whatever could it mean that he'd forgotten "The Black Cat"?

Let me interpret it for you, said Stekel. The asthma is plainly connected to a murderous impulse about your wife. The cat is an association to your homicidal thoughts. Between the negative and positive emotions runs a current of electricity: desire is paired with disgust, love with hatred, a will to power with a will to submission. We do not always have to dig deep into the unconscious, as the orthodox Freudians claim. Some people's central conflicts lie there, right on the surface.

THE TWENTY-FIFTH OF JULY, 1934, was a warm, fine day. The analysis with Stekel had finished a few weeks before, and it was damn near a miracle, John wrote in his diary. "I am strong: more self-reliant: no more asthma: tremendously more potent sexually: free of most of my old inhibitions, puritanism, evasions, cowardices." Frances had started analysis with Stekel's wife; her treatment was still in process but she was better, too, he was certain. No more of her monsoons and she was making a success of her job as the Vienna correspondent of the London *News Chronicle*, circulation 1.3 million daily.

The telephone rang just as he was walking out the door. He'd put

in a good morning's work and was off to have a swim. It was 1:07 P.M.
On the line was one of his tipsters: "Have you heard the radio? The
Vienna radio has just given this announcement: 'The government of
Dr. Dollfuss has resigned.'"

Was it true or just the churning of the Austrian rumor mill? John
put in a call to the Paris office of the *Daily News,* alerting them to a
story. Then, in turn, he called Fodor, who promised to hurry over to
the Chancellery; the switchboard of the Chancellery (no answer—
curious); and finally a local Austrian wire service, which announced
a Nazi coup in the making. He phoned in the story to Paris at 1:19,
his hat pushed back on his head. He ran to get the Ford.

Before he could get down the block, though, a policeman pulled
him over. Drive me to headquarters, he commanded John. There's
been a general alarm raised, about what the officer didn't know. By
one-thirty, when John arrived at the Chancellery, Fodor was already
there. Outside was a row of Heimwehr men in apple-green uniforms standing in the shade cast by the building's wall. The gates to
the Chancellery were locked up tight, the blinds drawn.

At least Dollfuss is safe inside, John and Fodor reassured each
other. When another armored car rolled by, they tailed behind it, all
the way to the headquarters of the Austrian broadcasting company,
the Ravag. There, on a normally bustling city street, were police
trucks, bristling with rifles and bayonets, and a mêlée, the *pfffttt* of
machine guns, and blasts of hand grenades. They'd arrived just in
time. Shortly before one P.M., a pack of Nazis, fourteen strong, had
shot their way into the building in a bid to command the radio.

The conspirators had killed the guard on duty, rushed into the
studio, and taken the radio announcer hostage. With a gun stuck up
under his ribs, he'd read the Nazi message about the resignation of
Dollfuss's government. Were it not for a quick-witted girl telephone
operator, who called the police, and an official at the radio station,
who cut the wires between the headquarters and the provincial stations, the Nazis would be in charge of the airwaves. Before long, the
police arrived and stormed the building, shelling it with gas and
capturing the plotters. For the rest of the day, through a telephone

line from Linz piped into the radio transmitter at Bamberg, radio audiences across Austria would listen to waltzes.

"Well, it seems to be all over," John said at three forty-five to another correspondent on the scene, as the dead and wounded were carried out of the Ravag on stretchers. But, he continued, isn't it strange that the government would have locked themselves in the Chancellery in a crisis?

A handful of reporters had stuck around the Chancellery, loitering on the Ballhausplatz, waiting for the government to make a statement about the coup attempt. But the only word they had from inside the building was that a new police chief was coming from Berlin. What on earth did that mean? Was that Major Fey at the window? And who was inside?

At two-thirty, a Heimwehr officer, fearing for Fey's safety, had pounded on the Chancellery door: "We give you twenty minutes and then we blow up the building." From inside came a voice: "Go away or we shoot." At three fifty-seven, Fey appeared on the balcony, summoning two policemen to meet him at the back door of the Chancellery. Without their weapons, he added.

Ten minutes later, one of the officers left the Chancellery and ran to the telephone in the Imperial Palace just across the square. He spoke so loudly that the reporters could hear him. "I've been inside, I've spoken with Fey," the policeman panted down the line. "Dollfuss is apparently badly wounded. He has resigned."

By the time John tried to return to the Chancellery, at four P.M., the police had blocked off access to the surrounding streets and were turning away everyone, reporters included. Why wouldn't they permit him to proceed to the Chancellery? John asked an officer. "The building is occupied," the man barked at him. "By Nazis, Nazis disguised as army and police."

SHORTLY BEFORE ONE P.M., 150 or so Nazi plotters, taking advantage of the changing of the Chancellery guard, had swung their trucks (the sides of which were lettered MILK and MEAT) into the courtyard of the building. They were members of a secret SS regiment in Austria; most were former Austrian Army men, officers and privates, who'd been dismissed because of their Nazi sympathies. Some of the conspirators were active duty police officers; the police force was riddled with Nazis.

Once inside, they locked the gates of the Chancellery and poured out of the trucks, armed with rifles. Dividing into groups, the rebels herded civil servants and government officials into the courtyard. They'd be shot, the hostages were warned, if they made a move.

Upstairs, in the state rooms, the cabinet was meeting. Dollfuss received the alarm just before the trucks pulled into the courtyard. Why it took so long for the warning to reach him, no one could explain. Was it a conspiracy or just *Schlamperei*, Austria's notorious inefficiency? The police had been tipped off nearly an hour earlier. Quickly dismissing the cabinet, Dollfuss insisted that the ministers leave the building immediately and return to their offices. At that point, he withdrew to his private study. Hurry! said his secretary. They're in the courtyard now.

Up the main staircase ran a group of plotters. His secretary wanted Dollfuss to hide upstairs in the Chancellery, in a warren of archive rooms. Maybe there he could lock a door and they wouldn't find him. But the conspirators caught Dollfuss in a room just off the staircase. He turned, one hand on the high golden door handle, and half-raised his arms. The ex-sergeant Otto Planetta, thrown out of the Austrian Army two years earlier because of his Nazi activities, was barely two feet away. Without a word, Planetta shot the little chancellor in the shoulder. Then he fired again, from eight inches, and hit Dollfuss in the throat. "How his head cracked the floor!" Dollfuss's secretary later told the reporters.

"Stand up," commanded Planetta.

"I cannot," Dollfuss whispered.

The Nazis picked him up, depositing him on the Louis XIV divan. The pink-and-gold tapestry was soon soaked through with blood and there Dollfuss lay for another hour and a half. The plotters refused to fetch a doctor. At two-thirty, they allowed Fey to see Dollfuss.

"I wanted only peace," Dollfuss murmured to Fey. "May God forgive the others. Love to my wife and children."

Get him a doctor, Fey pleaded. At least allow him to see a priest. This, too, was refused. That Dollfuss died in agony, wrote John, was something that no one who saw that shrunken body and that crumpled face could possibly doubt.

That evening, at six P.M., the phone lines across Austria went dead. Later the same night, the border between Germany and Austria swung shut. With the help of loyal Heimwehr units, the Austrian government regained control in Vienna; the police rounded up the plotters. Mussolini rushed Italian troops to the Brenner Pass, the border between Austria and Italy, a shot across Hitler's bow: the Duce wouldn't stand for a Nazi invasion of Austria. To report the story of Dollfuss's assassination without kowtowing to the Austrian censors, John and Frances would have to drive to Bratislava, just across the Czech frontier.

AFTER IT WAS ALL over, John closeted himself away in the tiny servant's room in the apartment that he used as an office, trying to make some larger sense of what had happened. *Harper's* wanted a piece from him. Every night, once the day's work was done, he went back to work in his office. Writing out his own eyewitness account was easy enough, but the meaning of the story kept frustrating him. It took him a dozen tries before he was satisfied with his lead.

One way of reporting the Dollfuss murder was simply as a failed Putsch: a coup attempt that missed the mark badly. That was the way that John told the story in the immediate aftermath. What the Nazi conspirators hadn't anticipated was that Anton Rintelen, the former governor of Styria, who was to have taken over as chancellor after Dollfuss was shot, had been apprehended the afternoon of the coup outside the Hotel Imperial. The plotters inside the Chancellery folded once it became clear that Rintelen wasn't coming.

As a shriveled corpse—as a martyr to Austrian independence—

Dollfuss was stronger dead than he was alive, wrote John in the *Daily News* the day after the assassination. The brutality of the attack had backfired. Shocked by the violence, Austrians were rallying to their government. As hundreds of thousands of mourners lined up outside the Rathaus to file past Dollfuss's coffin, it seemed to John that the assassination marked the "death spasm for the Hitler movement" in Austria.

The other way to interpret Dollfuss's assassination—the way that John began to tell it in his long article for *Harper's*—was as an act of Hitler's personal vengeance and of international gangsterism. "It is the story of an organized conspiracy to murder," John wrote in *Harper's,* outlining the evidence he'd gathered about the millions of marks the Germans had spent on propaganda in Austria, the Nazi preparations to smuggle the Putschists over the border to safety in Germany, the pre-written German press releases heralding the change of leadership.

Viewed in that light, the Dollfuss assassination in July 1934 wasn't, in fact, a failure, but a roaring triumph. For the first time, Hitlerism was mushrooming beyond Germany's borders. For the moment, John wrote, Austria was still safe. Dollfuss's murder had bought the country "temporary security," but how long would that last?

The news agencies had beaten John on the first day's stories because he couldn't get a phone line in time. But in the weeks to come, he made up for it with a series of front-pagers—honest to God circulation-boosters, "amazingly fine" articles, praised his editor. He'd outdone all the other correspondents; he was making "distinct contributions to American thought." From Switzerland, where he was in hiding, his *Arbeiter-Zeitung* banned after February, Oskar Pollak applauded John's efforts. Even Rebecca West took note. She'd never thought much of John's reporting before. But his stuff on the Dollfuss assassination? That was quite good.

John would later say that Stekel had given him eyes to see and wings to fly. He now knew what was so important about the trip to Spital and the details of Hitler's childhood. He understood why the hatred between Stalin and Trotsky or Hitler and Dollfuss mattered so much, why dictators were rising everywhere, and why, of all things, people seemed to prefer it that way. You couldn't explain what was happening just by reporting about economics (he'd never been interested in that, anyway) or the weaknesses of political parties or the failings of the international system. There was something deeper, something more personal at work. "These monsters," he wrote, "were making our *lives*."

IS HE HITLER?

—

C HOKING OFF THE GERMAN PRESS WAS CHILD'S PLAY, JOSEPH Goebbels had crowed to his diary in 1933. He and Hermann Göring, the new Prussian minister of the interior, had managed it all within the space of a few months after the Nazis came to power. The entire left-wing press, amounting to 130-plus socialist and communist papers: the whole Jewish Bolshevik lot, gone, locked up, shot, driven into exile, swept away as if it had never existed. As for the rest of Germany's reporters: they were, per his decree of October 1933, now categorized as holders of a "public office," duty bound to protect the regime from insults.

What he hadn't anticipated was just how docile the German press would become, publishing, sheeplike, whatever stories he gave them. He'd been a journalist himself, as well an editor, writing more than seven hundred editorials in *Der Angriff,* the Nazi paper he'd founded. The reporters needed managing, he decided; they required a swift kick in the pants. He called them in to upbraid them. It wasn't enough to print the Ministry of Public Enlightenment and Propaganda's press releases verbatim! How dare they be so lazy? They needed to freshen up the news he distributed with their own words.

The foreign press, by contrast, caused him no end of aggravation.

No matter how many agents the Hitler regime sent to London or Paris or New York to propagandize, the Third Reich's standing abroad was as dismal as ever. Goebbels was sick of reading lies about attacks on Jews. "Seen any bodies in the streets?" he'd inquire of newly arrived foreign reporters.

Stymied, he turned to Ivy Lee, the master of American public relations, who'd traveled to Germany to help the chemical manufacturer I. G. Farben sell to clients in the United States. Before the First World War, Lee, a onetime reporter, had invented the press release and rehabilitated the reputation of the tycoon John D. Rockefeller. With Lee's ministrations, Rockefeller, once the most hated man in America, had risen afresh as a tenderhearted philanthropist.

You need to cultivate the American correspondents in Berlin, Lee instructed Goebbels.

Goebbels had tried. Starting in the early 1930s, as he helped to steer Hitler's bid for power, he'd met one foreign reporter after another. Putzi Hanfstaengl had served as the intermediary, arranging interviews at the Kaiserhof Hotel, where the Nazis had set up their headquarters; dinners at Horcher's restaurant; and, eventually, briefings at the Chancellery. Goebbels had a ready smile and fancied himself a charmer. Some of the reporters were dolts and hacks, but others were worth talking to. Knickerbocker, for instance. He'd whiled away a whole afternoon with him, chewing the fat.

The Nazis, Knick told him in 1932, were much respected in the United States. It was said (most vociferously by Knick himself) that Hitler had a real chance at seizing the state. But even as Knickerbocker buttered him up, Goebbels knew to be on his guard. The reporter, he recognized, was a calculating type, smart and "ice-cold"—in other words, not unlike the way Goebbels saw himself. They dined together one night at Horcher's, which had the best wine cellar in Berlin. At the end of the evening, Goebbels wrote in his diary, he felt "squeezed dry like a lemon."

Ivy Lee suggested regular press briefings and proposed that Goebbels provide foreign reporters with conveniences such as soundproof telephone boxes. But nothing Goebbels did, neither threats nor amenities, kept the foreign press in line. Still worse, he had to fend off others—like Alfred Rosenberg, the foreign minister—who wanted a crack at the problem. Rosenberg was jealous of Goebbels, envious of his close relationship with Hitler and the fact that the Führer spent evenings with Goebbels and his wife, Magda. So when Rosenberg tried to force the *Public Ledger* to recall Knick, on the grounds that the man was "spreading insidious lies," Goebbels had stepped in forcefully to countermand the order. Whatever the propaganda minister might have wanted personally, he surely couldn't tolerate Rosenberg's interference.

The fact that Knick now owed his job to Goebbels didn't make him any the more respectful. He continued on, impudent as ever. There was the afternoon that the minister of agriculture convened a meeting of the foreign press to explain the four classifications of women the government was preparing to announce. At the top of the hierarchy were the Class One women, Aryans, blond and blue-eyed, who'd be reserved to breed with the leading Nazis. At the bottom were the Class Four women, Jews and Slavs unfit for either marriage or reproduction.

Knickerbocker shot up to ask the first question: "Herr Minister, would you tell us why you wish to give *all* the advantages to Class Four women?" The reporters laughed so raucously that the minister was obliged to shut down the meeting.

GEORGE MESSERSMITH, THE AMERICAN consul general in Berlin, interpreted the tussle between Rosenberg and Goebbels over Knickerbocker as a sign that the top Nazis were finally coming to terms with the fact that they couldn't control public opinion abroad. But Hitler never stopped complaining about the Third Reich's poor publicity in America and other countries. Then came the Night of the Long Knives and the problem of the foreign press was once again, urgently, on the table.

On the evening of the thirtieth of July, 1934, the SS and Gestapo embarked on a killing spree that lasted three days and nights. Two sorts of people were targeted in the massacre. First, the mavericks in the Nazi Party, the old-timers who had their own opinions as to what National Socialism should mean. Second, the regime's critics, such as the Catholic politician Dr. Erich Klausener, who the previous week had spoken against political oppression at a mass meeting in Berlin. Most prominent among the dead was Hitler's old comrade, Ernst Röhm, the leader of the storm troopers and a notorious homosexual.

Goebbels wanted the executions to be reported as a simple police action. The Führer had defanged a plot against him by a small nest of plotters around Röhm, saboteurs whose "abnormal tendencies" threatened the integrity of the Nazi order. Instead, the foreign correspondents described the killings as bloody vigilantism, a gangster purge. They sowed doubts about whether there had been a plot at all. More than a thousand had been arrested and several hundred shot without trials, including the last chancellor of Germany, General von Schleicher, along with his wife, who was murdered so that she wouldn't talk.

"Hitler whom the world called a 'softie,' whom outsiders thought a 'sissy' has become overnight the Robespierre of the Nazi Revolution," wired Knickerbocker. He now predicted a Terror to come that would equal the French Revolution's years of bloodletting. He used the opportunity to expound on the rumors about Hitler's sexuality. Although Röhm's youthful letters to Hitler "sounded like the farewell of a sweetheart," Knick doubted that Hitler was himself a homosexual.

Later that week, Goebbels took to the radio to harangue the foreign correspondents. He wouldn't stand for this "orgy of malicious agitation and libel." He spoke in the name of the entire German people. "One's heart stops beating when one takes a glance at the entire foreign press," he mocked. Freedom of opinion had nothing to do with it. The reporters were lying scum, practitioners of "revolver journalism." Their papers were "professional lie factories" that set out to poison world opinion against the Reich. If they persisted with their atrocity stories, foreign reporters would no longer be tolerated in Germany.

The Führer's response to his speech was exactly what Goebbels had hoped for. He was "very impressed." Goebbels always noted in his diary when the Führer praised him.

WHEN THE EXECUTIONS OF the Nazi old guard started, Dorothy was already Europe-bound. By the time she arrived in Vienna, Dollfuss had been murdered. From Austria, she reported on Dollfuss's funeral, then made her way, via car, through Bavaria, en route to Berlin. She'd wanted Jimmy to accompany her, but he was in Italy and broke, and in any case, behind on the book he was supposed to be writing. She'd have to travel on her own.

Dorothy knew she'd crossed over into Germany when the towns were draped in Nazi banners. The roads were full of young men in shorts, pedaling furiously on their bikes, or gunning their motorbikes, with the occasional girl riding pillion. Where were they going? she wondered. At a summer Hitler Youth camp in the town of Murnau, she saw one answer. YOU WERE BORN TO DIE FOR GERMANY! read the gigantic banner hanging on the hillside, bold black letters against a white background. When she got back on the road, she looked down at the speedometer on her car. She was driving at top speed, sixty-five miles per hour. "I wanted to get away from there."

In Berlin, she settled into her usual digs at the Hotel Adlon, and started to make her rounds. In *Harper's*, she would convey what it was like in Germany by reporting a series of one-sided conversations, long swathes of monologue in which her interview subjects tried to explain themselves to her. A woman stenographer, the very model of probity, no Nazi originally but glad about the peace that now prevailed: "It is quieter in Germany than I can ever remember it." A mechanic who grumbled about the high cost of living, before looking around and saying in a low voice: "This country's a prison. This won't last. It will collapse." The hale young storm trooper devastated by the killing of Röhm and his comrades: "The heart's gone out of the revolution." A journalist she knew, once a liberal, now settling into accommodation with the new regime: "The clean-up was not pretty, but it has consolidated Germany."

Dorothy figured in these exchanges as the near-silent listener trying, like her readers would, to make some sense of what was happening. Meanwhile, her subjects peppered her with their own questions, none of which she answered. "Is the whole world really preparing to make war on us?" "Do you find it's so bad here as the outside world seems to think?" As they talked, she couldn't help but think of the contrast laid out before her: the pride in Germany's orderliness and the reality of a lawless killing binge. It was admirable, Dorothy said to her reporter friend, how the mail in Germany never went astray. She imagined for her readers the scene, as the cremated remains of the Catholic leader Dr. Erich Klausener, murdered in the Night of the Long Knives, were delivered in a box to the widow's doorstep. The postman was courteous. He'd ring the doorbell (twice if necessary) and ask for a signature as proof of delivery.

Dorothy had only been in Germany for a few weeks when the hotel's porter called up one morning to her room. There was a man from the secret police to see her downstairs. "Send him up," she said.

The man was young and polite, dressed in a trench coat like the one that Hitler favored. He had a letter for her and wanted a signature to confirm the delivery. Inside the envelope was an order to leave Germany within twenty-four hours. On grounds of "national self-respect," she wouldn't be permitted to remain after the damage she'd done to the country's reputation.

What exactly was her crime? Dorothy inquired. Her visa was in order; she'd hardly written a word about Germany lately. The answer came via the American consul. She'd made insulting remarks about Hitler after interviewing him three years earlier. Her series on the Nazi persecution of the Jews, she'd also wager, had stirred up the hornets.

Another laurel—or that was the way that Dorothy treated the expulsion, giving interviews even as she stuffed her clothes into her suitcases. Surely Goebbels was behind it, she said. Dorothy's colleagues in the foreign press brought bouquets of yellow roses to the railway station to send her off. By the time the express train from Berlin pulled into the station in Paris, she had a quip ready for the reporters who thronged her. Germany, she told them, "is becoming the most comfortable and most hygienic prison in the world." On the train journey, she'd memorized the order of expulsion, which she recited for her audience.

"Apparently, the Germans felt they could not keep both me and their self-respect, so I had to go." Sitting out on the café terrace at the Gare du Nord, she resumed: "I hurt their sensitive souls and delivered a blow to their amour propre." Shut down one foreign correspondent, she warned Goebbels, and another three will appear to broadcast the truth. (She knew perfectly well that sufficiently draconian measures would crush the foreign press as they had the domestic one.) Later on, in Paris, she learned that Hitler himself had ordered her to be expelled.

Dorothy made front-page news as the first American reporter to be kicked out of Germany. It proved a turning point, catapulting her to fame: she herself, not just her reporting, had become the story. While she'd make light of the expulsion as a personal matter, it was a sign of the regime's increasingly overt campaign against foreign correspondents.

The expulsions came fast and publicly. After Knick published his series on the Nuremberg Party conference in September 1934, he was denied permission to return to Germany or even to pass through its borders. Hitler had read his articles and demanded that "unreliable and hostile" correspondents be banned from Germany, even if they worked for Hearst papers. The dictators, Knick wrote his editor, "are all very sensitive people, sensitive about what happens to them but not sensitive about what they do to others, particularly foreign correspondents." Between 1933 and 1939, as many as twenty-five foreign correspondents were expelled from Germany, while another thirty or so departed when their "safety could not be guaranteed."

If he were shut out of Italy and the Soviet Union as well, Knick wrote his editor, he'd be in a "fine mess" as a reporter. Dorothy wasn't all that bothered, not least because her career was heading in a different direction. She was becoming a commentator rather than a reporter. The interview-bagging form of foreign correspondence, she'd decided, was "meretricious." What Americans needed now was sound analysis, an account of Europe's prospects in light of its historical and political dynamics.

Her change of heart was evident in a review she wrote of Knick's new book, *The Boiling Point.* The book was a hasty production, a collection of his newspaper pieces, including interviews with Mussolini, Hungary's Horthy, and Yugoslavia's King Alexander. The question he purported to answer was Will war come? (Answer: likely, yes.) It was less his answer than his method that Dorothy objected to. She began with Mr. Knickerbocker's "irritatingly straight face" in relating the substance of his interviews. She didn't call him a "journalistic whore," as John had, but she came uncomfortably close. In his dash from chancellery to chancellery, Mr. Knickerbocker had reported what he'd been told—as if he were taking dictation, unctuously, rather than rendering judgment.

Like many a mean but not unfair review, Dorothy's roast said as much about its author as its subject. Self-conscious that a writer of "special" correspondence like herself was a "parasite on honest newspaper men," she justified her own turn by denigrating Knick's reporting. His writing had turned Hearstian, "constantly he is straining to attract the reader's attention" with his "Who approaches? Lo!" technique. He was substituting flashy style and travel for thought. The most important "equipment" of the journalist, Dorothy lectured, were brains, not feet. Mr. Knickerbocker had no shortage of brains, but regrettably, he'd given in to the temptation not to think.

It was the sort of showdown that everyone had an opinion about. "An unreasonably vivid attack," opined John. What a bitch, said other newspapermen. Knick told their mutual friends he didn't object to Dorothy's criticisms—but he was more hurt than he let on. She'd been his boss in Berlin and, according to the rumors, his lover. He dodged her phone calls and her unapologetic letter of apology, which alternated between self-justification ("The book made me furious") and expressions of "very deep warm and devoted" feeling. They didn't break with each other permanently and one could still invite the two of them to a party together. However, the once affectionate correspondence between them ceased.

Back at Twin Farms in the fall of 1934, Dorothy framed her order of expulsion from Germany and hung it on the wall of her office. The next year, the *New York Herald Tribune* offered her a syndicated opinion column, "On the Record," to alternate with Walter Lippmann's three times a week.

THAT FALL OF 1934, when John left for a stint of reporting in the United States, Frances telephoned Stekel. Now that the doctor had finished John's analysis, she hoped that he would take her on as a patient. All those good paragraphs she was writing, but they didn't come together. She found herself making lists in the morning, leafing through magazines, window-shopping: anything to avoid getting down to work. She really needed to get that cleared up.

As an intellectual matter, Frances knew all about the unconscious mind: the idea that powerful forces acted on people beyond their control or even awareness. But when it came to tackling her own psyche, she—like John—proceeded with all the confidence of a nineteenth-century logician, as if she could explain herself in conscious terms. They were both exceedingly rational about irrational things. And yet, the more they sought to understand their inner life, the more it slipped from their grasp. That was the dilemma to which psychoanalysis seemed to promise a solution.

Stekel agreed to treat Frances, though he preferred patients—like John—who'd never before been analyzed. He was suspicious of people who roamed from analyst to analyst. Either they complained bitterly of their previous treatment or they extolled to the high heavens the skill of their past analysts, without of course showing the least sign of improvement. They displayed strong exhibitionist tendencies and could be remarkably crafty.

Trouble in writing, moreover, was something Stekel hadn't personally known. He just sat down at his typewriter and the books clattered out. *Frigidity in Women* and *Impotence in the Male* required two thick volumes to say what was necessary. He didn't see what was so mysterious about writing. "Sit down and write!" he'd told another analysand who was fretting about a book. "It is never too late. Write it in gold," he instructed Frances.

She often spoke a second language in her dreams, she told him. Not French or German or Russian, but a language she didn't even know.

Frances didn't understand herself, Stekel interpreted. She was searching for a path through the labyrinth of her own mind. This use of a second language could be termed the mind's "bookkeeping by double entry."

Were there other ways that she frustrated herself? Stekel wondered.

Oh, yes: she was always getting ready to do something, but then didn't. She took letters that she'd written out of drawers and hastily stuffed them back again, afraid to read what she had said. She couldn't make decisions about clothes. Day after day she went around staring at shop windows. It took her weeks to work up the courage to buy a summer dress or a winter coat or a new hat. And then she often felt that she had chosen the wrong things, umber culottes and a blouse with a Peter Pan collar when what she'd really wanted was a checked dress. The orchestra tuned and tuned but never started to play.

Did she find satisfaction in her sexual life with her husband?

No, she wanted orgasms but couldn't have them. At the critical moment, she felt an overpowering anxiety, as if she were sitting, numb, in the electric chair. She didn't know why.

In the dream notebook she was keeping, Frances recorded the associations she was making. Hitler and Franz von Papen: each of them, she noted, thought that they could use the other. Von Papen, the wily old politician—white-haired, elegant—who believed he could bend the little Austrian corporal to his own purposes. Make

Hitler chancellor, von Papen had said in January 1933: we will box him in. For his part, Hitler legitimated his bid for power with von Papen at his side. The very presence of the man announced that this was a government that big business and the generals could trust.

If John was like Hitler, did that make her von Papen? Who was really using whom? Frances would wonder. Was she using John to get her ideas out in the world? Or was he using her?

"Danger—you symbolize everything," she wrote in her dream diary. "International conflicts become your personal conflict." What were intimate relationships but geopolitics writ small? That was the question she kept asking herself.

IF ONLY SHE WERE here, John exulted from New York. The very air in America seemed charged up with possibilities. It was true that a person needed an hour less sleep in New York. An editor at Simon & Schuster was begging him to write a book, the magazine *Vanity Fair* had offered him a job. In Chicago, four hundred people crowded into a lecture he gave at the Council on Foreign Relations. Did he want to be the ambassador to Austria? he'd been asked.

The country had changed so much in six years: the end of Prohibition and the soaring buildings, the polish and sweep of the streets, the nude performances. "We have grown up over here!" There were cabs that played music—can you imagine? And not a policeman to be seen, what a contrast with Vienna. Open a tap in the bathtub and it filled instantly, a thundering Niagara of water. The hotels had immense closets, as if every guest arrived with a prince's wardrobe, and everywhere books of matches piled in bowls, just there for the taking.

No one in America had read anything he'd written in *Harper's* or *Vanity Fair* or the *Nation*. They were all much too busy for that. So busy, in fact, that they ordered their food now by the numbers: B4 for a sirloin steak, F6 for an ice-cream sundae. "Okay," agreed the Americans in practically every sentence, so cheerful the people seemed after all his years in Europe. Or "Nuts," if they didn't agree, as if a finely tuned common sense enabled them to sniff out (and reject) extremism. Just to hear President Roosevelt on the radio—that well-burnished, buoyant voice—was enough to raise your spirits.

And not a wheeze of asthma the whole trip, not even when he was in houses full of cats and dogs. He couldn't stop thinking about Frances. "It isn't twenty or forty or a hundred times a day that I think of you and want you; it is always, a perpetual stream in my subconscious." It was a miracle, he was telling people, what Stekel had done for him. Maybe Dorothy should bring Stekel to the United States to see Red, John suggested; perhaps Stekel could stop Red from drinking. The New Dealers, he learned from his old Chicago friend Jerry Frank, had their own analyst, a Dr. Glueck, who'd analyzed the brainiest of FDR's Brain Trusters, Jerry included. According to Dr. Glueck, the Germans put up with Hitler because they had a guilt complex: they were atoning for their sins.

At the Anglo-American Press Association's luncheon, Frances wrote John, she'd seen von Papen, whom Hitler had appointed the new ambassador to Austria after the murder of Dollfuss. He was a debonair liar, and when she asked him about German plans for the annexation of Austria, his eyes had just twinkled. She was filing stories for the *News Chronicle* and to cover while John was away, writing pieces for the *Daily News,* too. She'd had a party for forty people (called them all herself on the telephone). In fact, she was doing all of the things that John usually did: devouring a ham sandwich before bedtime, taking no exercise, staying in bed on Sunday mornings, buying things in shops, cultivating Nazi sources. The Central European situation was as dismal as ever. "I'm so fed up with it I could chew nails," Frances concluded. "Let's work on the New Deal too."

It was nearly time for them to come home, he agreed, to put down some roots and acquaint their son with his native soil. He hoped that Johnny was learning some English. "Europe seems extremely small & unimportant & remote." He was bursting with pride about her stories in the *Daily News.* She was his "brain trust," he wrote. "Please come and do my thinking for me!"

He'd be back to Vienna in December. "I want some more children, darling. Let us tend to this immediately." It was his way of making amends, giving back what he thought he'd taken from her.

ON THE SUBJECT OF childhood sexual trauma, as on so much else, Stekel and Freud had parted ways. Early in his career, Freud had been shocked by the numbers of cases of incest he'd discovered in treating his female patients. This, he suspected, was the basis for much of the hysteria women were suffering. It was all too incredible, his colleagues had objected. Did Freud really expect them to believe that so many fathers were interfering with their daughters? A few years later, Freud changed his mind. In a marked repudiation of his previous ideas, he now decided that the sexual scenes his patients brought forth during analysis reflected not reality but fantasy. They were reflections of a child's longing. On this basis, he generated his famous theories of the Oedipus and Electra complexes.

Unlike Freud, Stekel continued to give credence to his patients' reports, detailing in his many volumes of case studies the sexual abuse that his patients, mostly girls, but on occasion, boys, too, had suffered at the hands of their fathers, uncles, cousins, brothers, and sometimes mothers. These are "everyday tragedies," Stekel maintained: real experiences, not fantasies. He knew the disbelief people felt on this subject. That is a Viennese problem, they told him, a product of the city's peculiarly overcharged atmosphere. No, he always insisted, his patients were drawn from all over the world.

There were secret drawers in a patient's mind, Stekel liked to say, incidents into which a person did not intend to allow the analyst to pry. I don't need to discuss that with the doctor, they told themselves. How will it help me? Either they saw the subject as a diversion from the matter at hand or too humiliating to bring forth. The task of the analyst, then, was to spring open those drawers. It was best when the patient came upon the necessity himself. More often, though, it required what Stekel termed an "analytical shock": a confrontation with the facts, a concussion that produced self-awareness. The analyst had to proceed warily and choose his moment carefully: too early in the analysis and the course of treatment could be irreparably damaged, too late and valuable time would be wasted.

When Frances was thirteen, and her mother was out of town, her stepfather had persuaded her to sleep in the big double bed with him. That first night, she told Stekel, she had pretended to be asleep when he touched her.

And the next night?

The next night, she said, was different.

Had she touched his penis?

No, Frances answered quickly.

That night after her session with Stekel, she dreamed about Johnny reaching out for a curling iron. That's hot! Don't touch it. She put the curling iron away.

The time had come, Stekel decided, to administer the analytical shock. Yesterday you didn't want to admit you touched your stepfather's penis, he told her. But she had, hadn't she?

It was a delicate business, the analytical shock, Stekel advised. Some patients pretended indifference, others—nearly inconsolable—gave way to floods of tears. A minority took gross affront and broke off the analysis. Others, like Frances, persevered with the treatment.

Her stepfather had put her hand there, yes, but had she taken it away? The truth was that she couldn't stand to think about it. She felt full of evil: it bloomed inside of her. What she'd done. She hated him for what he'd done to her.

Was her stepfather her destiny? Frances wondered, writing notes in her dream diary and on loose pieces of paper. She couldn't abide the sight of him, but she'd worried, too, that he was her fate. Her mother had divorced him after they'd moved to Galveston. He had been madly jealous, accusing Sonia of having been unfaithful. Frances had egged her mother on to leave him. Back in New York, Sonia had reconciled with Frances's father. When Frances was twenty-one, she had officiated at her parents' second wedding, and then left for Europe. Her father was dead before she returned home.

Her stepfather had proposed marriage to her, Frances told Stekel.

She'd written him in 1927 to ask for money so that she could go to John, in Rome, to be married. "No, marry me," he'd said. She'd refused indignantly, of course, but there was the fact that she'd written him at all. Why had she done that? After her daughter died, she'd again been tormented by thoughts of him. Was her baby's death a punishment for what she'd done? Perhaps she should divorce John and marry him. He'd be very old now. When she was thirteen, he'd been forty-five.

The analytical shock had necessarily unsettled her, Stekel said. She was depressed because of it. But now that they'd uncovered her fixation on her stepfather, she could start to face reality. He'd observed a curious phenomenon in cases such as hers. What had happened to her was very damaging, perhaps even more so than if her stepfather had in fact raped her. The unconsummated act was an unfinished trauma, he suggested. Her imagination could not rest, and she continued to picture the scene played out to its logical conclusion. As a consequence, she reproached herself, unceasingly.

She avoided orgasms, Stekel suggested, because she didn't wish her memory to be revived. That would account for the way that she frustrated herself. It was time for her to leave her past and follow her husband.

You will find Frances much changed, Stekel informed John. Shortly after returning from the United States, John had carried off the prize—the London job, the plum post for foreign correspondents. He was settling into his new office at Bush House, where the *Daily News* rented quarters, and looking for a flat in London for the family. He'd be back to Vienna to fetch Frances and Johnny and would play a set or two of tennis with Stekel.

"She faces now reality and is longing to see you and willing to have a second child," Stekel told him. He had explained to Frances that "she loves you too much and is afraid completely to surrender." Stekel's preferred solution was another baby, and Frances had accepted that interpretation. "I hope the fight of sexes will be finished— let's hope for ever," Stekel concluded. He was making preparations to open a Jealousy Clinic in Vienna to treat married couples. Ever since the start of the world economic crisis, he'd noticed that pathological jealousy was on the rise.

"Afraid to write because afraid to confess," Frances wrote in her diary.

NO, HE WASN'T WRITING his autobiography, Jimmy said for the millionth time. The title of the book was *Personal History*, which perfectly summed up what he meant to convey—"one person's relationship to the history of the time (1918–1929)," as he put it to John. It wasn't purely historical, which was the reason that he'd objected so strongly to *In Search of History*, the "odious" title his British publisher, Jamie Hamilton, had insisted on. Nor was it purely personal, he informed Eddy Sackville-West. At least not "as the Confessions of Rousseau are personal!" He'd call the section in which Eddy appeared the "Cities of the Plain," after Sodom and Gomorrah, he teased. "'The pale, romantic figure of—' and so on. You will blush to see yourself."

Jimmy had taken a little house in the Italian village of Arolo, on the unfashionable side of Lake Maggiore. He started the book with an account of himself at the University of Chicago, one of the "couple of thousand young nincompoops whose ambition in life was to get into the right fraternity or club, go to the right parties, and get elected to something or other." He told the ignominious story of pledging the Jewish fraternity unknowingly, and then deserting it in the middle of the night. He meant to "situate" himself, he explained to Eddy, "to make the reader understand who and what he is." From there he was off—bridling against the "beatific, happy drowsiness" of the League of Nations, "the perfect dream flower" of nineteenth-century middle-class idealism; roaming across the Rif territories in search of Abd el-Krim; to China amid the Hankou Revolution; with Rayna in Moscow; ending with his disillusionment in Palestine and his conversion to the Arab cause.

It was a coming-of-age story, his own and the world's, brought together. He was mapping his own development as an individual onto the world crisis. The young American sheds the insularity of his station and upbringing to experience events for himself. He arrives in an Old World where the Victorian certainties—about the legitimacy of European empires, the beneficence of capitalism and free trade, the inevitability of progress—are in tatters. Through his reporting, he takes the measure of the new forces rising: the power of collectivism, especially Communism, and the strivings of colonial nationalism. Eyewitness to violent battles on the periphery, he sees that the twentieth-century movements are uncontainable and that the old order of class inequality and imperial exploitation cannot and should not be restored. More than that, he comes to understand, under Rayna's influence, that the struggle to right the world's wrongs is his own. He had to find his "place with relation to it," he wrote on the final page, "in the hope that whatever I did (if indeed I could do anything) would at last integrate the one existence I possessed into the many in which it had been cast."

If it wasn't an autobiography, then what sort of book was it? That was a question that would perplex Jimmy's editors and later the reviewers, for it didn't fit tidily in the established categories. Unlike the spate of war memoirs, it was much more than a tale of a young man's disillusionment. The autobiographies of writers that came to mind—*The Education of Henry Adams* (1918), *The Autobiography of Lincoln Steffens* (1931)—didn't exactly fit the bill, either. Both Steffens, the muckraker, and Adams, the Washington blue-blood, bore witness to the journalist's maturation and told stories of the great and good they had encountered. But they were old men when they wrote, and neither had done what Jimmy did, joining the global story with his own. If the hubris of the enterprise prompted some disapproving clucks (an autobiography at age thirty-four!), it was the immediacy of Jimmy's quest, the freshness of his struggle, that made the book so relevant. *Personal History* was nothing short of a modern *Odyssey*, declared one critic.

Jimmy hadn't intended to devise a new genre, but ever short on funds, he had been paying attention to what sold. "It must succeed, it must make money," he wrote Eddy. Harold Nicolson had been the one to suggest the idea to him; Harold was in the midst of writing his own book of memoirs about the Versailles conference. Jimmy knew that people liked autobiographies, even halfway decent ones, and on his lecture tour through America, he'd seen that what stirred audiences was people, not subjects. In 1933, the year he started his book, Gertrude Stein's *The Autobiography of Alice B. Toklas,* with its vivid depiction of Parisian artistic and expatriate circles and its playful glimpse into the domestic life of Stein and Toklas, became a popular hit. Like John and Dorothy, Jimmy had turned his life into fiction, but neither of his novels had yielded much in the way of either sales or critical success. What if he instead stitched together a Bildungsroman, a tale of the hero's formative years, out of reality?

Don't worry, he wrote Eddy after his letter with the joke about Sodom and Gomorrah went unanswered. The book wasn't going to be *that* revealing.

From the moment it was published in America, in February 1935, *Personal History* was a sensation, inciting a competition among publishers for books by foreign correspondents. The Literary Guild chose it as the book of the month and Jimmy's picture, handsome and serious in three-quarters profile, his tie neatly tucked into a sweater, was all over the papers. The middlebrow reviewers, like the *Chicago Tribune*'s Fanny Butcher, whose recommendations, it was said, directed what shopgirls were reading, loved it. So, too, did the most waspishly literary of critics, among them Malcolm Cowley in the *New Republic* and Mary McCarthy in the *Nation*. Sheean, Butcher had observed, was like "the hero of a well-planned novel." Cowley agreed. Were *Personal History* a novel, it would compare favorably with the best of the decade. What Sheean showed was how life had gotten ahead of fiction.

The contest between fiction and nonfiction was heating up in the 1930s, as novels ceded some territory to memoirs, biographies, and reportage. This was a long trajectory that would eventually lead, later in the twentieth century, to the rise of a hybrid category of "autofiction" and gloomy prognostications about the death of the novel and the triumph of narcissism as the dominant literary form. Cowley faulted the novelists, who, lacking the courage of Sheean's "long view," dillydallied instead with the "trivial, the formless, the typical." This was much the same point as the *Partisan Review*'s Philip Rahv would make a few years later, criticizing the "primacy of experience" in American literature, which he contrasted unfavorably with the European penchant for novels organized around ideas.

To blame the novelists, though, is to ignore the readers, for powering *Personal History*'s success was the American public's own appetite for personalities and real-life tales of spiritual striving. The book had become an "epidemic," Jimmy wrote Raymond Mortimer. He was besieged with mailbags of letters from people petitioning him for advice as to how to make their lives meaningful. All the "hysterical yearners in America" were yapping about World Ideas and the Long View. He'd caught the leftward shift in American popular opinion, the growing number of fellow travelers. "The worst is the dreadful dialect I seem to have invented, without meaning to," Jimmy repeated to Eddy. "Half the letters are couched in a language lifted straight out of the book, and converted to uses so petty that I squirm with shame." If he were in America, he'd have to be drunk all day long to deal with it. "You know how the success (the ultra-personal and peculiar success) of this book makes me feel? Exactly like a dog that's made a mess in the middle of the drawing room. I couldn't help making the mess, but now I feel very guilty and very conspicuous."

What made Jimmy so conspicuous was the fact that he'd attached not only his own name, but everyone else's to his story. Confessing the tensions of your inner life in public was becoming routine enough in the 1930s. It was a great decade for egotism, Virginia Woolf observed, surveying the mountain of autobiographies, replete with "unpleasant" truths, produced between 1930 and 1940. Still, publication was treacherous terrain. Any sort of disclosure about other people could provoke resentment or hurt feelings. Putting the words "Hell" and "Damn" in Rayna's mouth, wrote her sister reprovingly from Chicago, was "cheapening." That one he could laugh off; the newspaperman was inured to those sorts of complaints. Not so Bill

Prohme's four-page denunciation, mailed from the sanatorium in Hawaii where he was dying of tuberculosis. Bill's letter sent him straight to the bottle.

Jimmy had to have anticipated that Bill would object to his depiction of a love affair (however platonic) with Rayna. But what arrived was much worse. Of course Bill took issue with Jimmy's portrait of Rayna: it was demeaning, and made her look silly, and was proof that Jimmy had never, despite all he professed, understood her or the Bolshevik cause.

But Bill didn't stop there. Jimmy's "sexual disavowal" in relation to Rayna smacked of "exhibitionism." And couldn't Jimmy see that in every line he wrote about Rayna's last week, he showed himself a cad, or worse. He'd taken her in open cabs, himself dressed in thick wools, she in thin evening clothes; insisted on arguing with her— "merely because you were in the mood for it"—when she was already so sick. Even the casual reader would be justified in concluding that Jimmy had hastened Rayna's death. To prove his point, Bill quoted from a letter that Rayna had written him from Moscow: "Jimmy is probably the most completely selfish person I have ever encountered." It was devastating.

Though Eddy didn't say so directly, he also regarded Jimmy as the dog who'd made a mess on the floor. Through an argument that was ostensibly about Rousseau's *Confessions,* he and Jimmy conducted a proxy feud about *Personal History.* To Jimmy's exultant reading of Rousseau as a genius, Eddy replied with disdain. Rousseau, said Eddy, was the progenitor of the tell-all wave sweeping the press. Look at the blaring headlines in the tabloids: "I CONFESS!" "Tell Us Your Secrets!" It was all too vulgar for words, lurid, tasteless. Eddy, it turned out, objected to Jimmy's account in the book of a dinner party conversation about Knole.

"Eddy dear, don't get into such a stew! I don't really care enough about Jean-Jacques to become acrimonious with an old friend about him." Anyway, what did the issue of "taste" have to do with anything? There was literary taste and there was aristocratic taste, and Eddy was getting them mixed up. As an American, Jimmy didn't care much himself whether someone was a gentleman—or not. "I don't have to, not being much of one myself."

Jimmy asked Raymond Mortimer whether he'd heard about his set-to with Eddy on the subject of Rousseau. It had to do with taste. "I had to go and take several baths to be sure I didn't stink."

WHILE SOME OF JIMMY's friends bristled at his disclosures, Frances thought *Personal History* a marvel of discretion. "400 pages—not a single dirty story—not a single lay!" she wrote to John. He had read it when they were on the Semmering one weekend, and a nasty bronchitis kept him indoors for five days. Knick was very jealous of Jimmy's success, John reported, whereas he himself was merely envious. He'd have given a leg to have written it. And according to Frances, Jimmy had upped the ante for any book he might write.

John had returned from his trip to America committed to writing a book for Harper & Brothers. What the publishers wanted was a version of the idea Frances had urged on John in 1927: a behind-the-scenes account of European politics. For a few years, Cass Canfield, the dynamic young president of Harper's, had been looking for someone to take on such a project. Canfield had already considered Gunther and rejected him: he was too young and too inexperienced. Knick, Canfield thought, was the man for the job, and he proposed the book idea to him one night in London. But Knick wasn't interested. John Gunther, Knick added, was the only reporter who had the nerves and the ability for such a venture.

After saying no a few times, John changed tack. Sure, he'd write it, John told his agent, naming the ridiculous figure of $5,000 for an advance, the largest sum he'd heard of anyone getting. He was taken aback when Harper's agreed—what had he gotten himself into?—and even more surprised when Canfield showed up at his hotel, the morning before he was to sail back from New York to Europe. He'd had a late night, he wasn't packed, and there was Canfield, insisting that he sign the contract. Fine, he'd do the book, he told Canfield, just leave and let me pack so I don't miss the boat.

It went without saying that such a book would have to be published anonymously. What Harper's wanted was a bean-spilling account, the lowdown on the inner operations of European politics. If John were going to tell tales out of school, he couldn't possibly put his signature on it, at least not if he ever wanted to work as a correspondent again. Unloading gossip of that kind wasn't done. According to his editor, the book would need to be "as personal as possible in its revelation without involving libel." John's standpoint would be that of "a simple and good-hearted Uncle Sam, who is looking out upon a rather wicked and generally double-crossing world."

A Continent-hopping book would have been daunting in any case, but once John had taken up his London post, it seemed damn near impossible. London was a more taxing job than Vienna—many more newspapers scrambling for scoops, new bureaucracies to master. The only way he'd be able to write the book was to pick his friends' brains. He petitioned them for memos on the places they knew best: Duranty on the Soviet Union, Jay Allen on Spain, Fodor on the Balkans and Atatürk. Knick was in London, and over several long afternoons, John scribbled notes furiously as Knick told him everything he'd known—or suspected—about Hitler, Stalin, Mussolini, and Piłsudski.

Knick talked in full paragraphs, you could see his mind working, points and sub-points all logically organized. The secret of Hitler's power? It was his ability to figure out what the Germans were feeling before they knew it themselves. He saw the sick soul of the nation and was able to identify with it, to make use of it. He told the people: You have pretended to be reconciled to the terrible aftermath of the war. But are you? No, wake up! You're miserable. You've been kidding yourselves. Admit it. You didn't lose the war. In fact, you won it. You're sick, but I can heal you.

Hitler was more of a mesmerist and less of a realist than either Mussolini or Stalin, Knick said. He lacked their hard rationality. He was both completely sincere and capable of changing his mind. One day he said one thing, the next day, something else. It was a mark of his power that his followers trailed along behind him, shifting their beliefs to keep pace with his, as if they had never thought anything different.

IN LONDON THAT SPRING of 1935, John was seeing a lot of Knick and his girlfriend, Agnes. Frances was still in Vienna with Johnny, winding down their household in preparation for the move to England. It wasn't easy to spend time with Agnes and Knick, he reported to her. They were always squabbling. Or worse, they were making up theatrically, John supposed for his benefit.

Knick had met Agnes in Berlin in 1931, just before his wife Laura left for Topeka to be analyzed. Agnes was eighteen. She had come to Germany from Montana, her elder sister as chaperone, to study piano. One afternoon Agnes appeared in Knick's office, comely, with dark brown eyes and olive skin, her hair tucked under a broad-brimmed picture hat. She was selling newspaper subscriptions door-to-door. "I want you to subscribe to the world's greatest newspaper," she told Knick. He took her out, gave her a lunch of vodka and caviar, and had her in bed within twenty-four hours.

You don't *really* believe Agnes was a virgin when she met you? inquired Frances, to Knick's fury.

Knick's marriage to the unfaithful Laura had left him with a vehement, unreasonable jealousy. It didn't diminish after Agnes moved into the house Knick was renting in the Berlin suburbs. "Why did you make passes at Agnes?" Knick had accused John one day, as they embarked on a trip to Bucharest. John denied it, strenuously, but that hardly settled his friend down. You couldn't trust any woman, he told John. Of course, he'd like very much to sleep with Frances, he pointed out, but he'd never make any effort in that direction because he loved John too much.

Two days after Laura finally consented to a divorce, Knick married Agnes at the Caxton Hall registry office, with Frances and John in attendance. It was July 1935, and Italian troops were massing on the border of the kingdom of Abyssinia. Knick was in a hurry. He'd developed a fair idea of the horrors to come in the next war. It would be a "total war," he wrote: all-out attacks on civilians, poison gas and incendiaries, mass panic. In a series of articles published that summer, he warned that the coming war's "destruction will be on a scale so colossal that in the end Europe will be left with remnants of its population starving among the fragments of its civilization."

There was another wedding in their circle that summer as well. Jimmy was thirty-five, the age at which a man could be considered a confirmed bachelor. His bride—Diana Forbes-Robertson—had just turned twenty, not yet an adult according to Austrian law. She was obliged to wire her parents for permission to marry. The marriage ceremony took place in a black-draped room in Vienna's Rathaus.

Diana, known as Dinah, came from a famous theatrical family. Her father, Sir Johnston, was the most celebrated Shakespearean actor of his day, and her American-born mother, Gertrude, his leading lady; her aunt, Maxine Elliott, was a star of the stage who before the First World War had her own eponymous New York theater. A savvy investor, Aunt Maxine had turned her theatrical earnings into a fortune.

Jimmy had met Dinah through his British editor, Jamie Hamilton. Jamie had been married to Dinah's sister, and was still—even after his wife left him—a favorite of the Forbes-Robertsons. When Jamie heard that Dinah was on the verge of making an unsuitable match with a racehorse-mad dilettante, he went to work. He invited Jimmy to a dinner at the fashionable London restaurant Quaglino's where Dinah would be present, and then sent Dinah off to Naples with Jimmy's address in hand.

"I can't see what on earth made them pick on me," Jimmy wrote Eddy, "it seems to me simply inconceivable that anybody would consider me, at my age and with my hideous vices, a fit match for a girl of nineteen. Isn't it odd?"

He had no money, Jimmy protested to Jamie. Never mind, his editor replied, Dinah is Aunt Maxine's heiress.

Jimmy liked the girl more than he let on. Dinah was beautiful. Her eyes were a clear blue and her black hair tended to go wild. She was winsome and intelligent. If Aunt Maxine made any trouble,

Jimmy announced, he'd gladly relinquish Diana's trust fund. When he wrote Eddy later that year, he was, he said, "trembling on the brink of matrimony." He'd asked Dinah to meet him in Salzburg, for the music.

"Of course I have to have a tremendous session, telling her All (without details or names, but anyhow All), but I think she's already got a very good idea of All and doesn't seem to be frightened off by it," he confided to Eddy. Jimmy proposed to Dinah the very day she arrived in Salzburg, in an open taxicab on a bridge over the Salzach River.

To Duncan Grant, Jimmy wrote, "You will like Dinah, I feel sure—once you get over the shock of her youth." And to the rest of his friends, he sent some variant of the following: "I approve highly of the marriage state; why didn't somebody tell me how perfect it was?"

He knew full well, he told Eddy, that there would be a number of barbed, even mean comments about his marriage. But he didn't mind, really, and neither did Dinah.

FEEDING THE TIGER

—

F IT HAD BEEN UP TO FRANCES, SHE AND JOHN WOULDN'T HAVE moved to England in 1935. Among other things, it meant giving up her job as the *News Chronicle*'s Vienna correspondent at a moment when she'd finally established herself. Once she knew she was leaving, she resolved to confront the Austrian press minister, Eduard Ludwig, with a question no other reporter dared to ask. Dour and conservative, Ludwig made it his business to distribute as little information to the reporters as possible. During the February Civil War the year before, he'd hectored the foreign press, accusing them of spreading "atrocity stories." The reporters loathed him.

With little to lose, Frances challenged the fearsome Ludwig in his own office. Why was he so determined to wreck the foreign press? Frances demanded. Why not try to make friends with the correspondents? She tried a humorous tack. All the reporters really wanted, she teased, was to be patted on the head and told secrets every so often.

"As I suspected, this frontal attack made him crawl at once," she wrote John. Ludwig apologized, blaming the pressures of his job. The only secret he could come up with, though, were the plans to put an officer of his department on call daily to answer the foreign journalists' questions—"i.e. spy," as Frances put it. Short on secrets, he promised her an interview with Kurt Schuschnigg, Dollfuss's successor.

Frances's editor at the *News Chronicle* was sorry to see her go: "If every foreign correspondent were of your caliber," he wrote her, "my life would be a bed of roses."

In England, she'd be starting over, and without any fondness for the place. Unlike John, she hadn't grown up an Anglophile, and what she'd seen of British diplomats and British foreign policy amounted to little more than hypocrisy. They yammered on about liberalism and the rule of law, yet it was all power politics for the British. Why hadn't the Foreign Office uttered a peep ("something besides Hmmmm," she wrote) as Dollfuss slaughtered the Socialists? Though the official line was that Britain supported Austrian independence, it was clear to her that the British would feed the country to the Nazi tigers if it meant the continuation of business as usual.

She'd barely been in England a month when in August 1935 she entered into a very public spat with the aristocratic controversialist Osbert Sitwell. Osbert was among a trio of literary, headline-grabbing Sitwell siblings who had, in the 1920s, according to the British novelist Evelyn Waugh, taken "the dullness out of literature." The target of Frances's ire was a tongue-in-cheek article Osbert Sitwell had just published in the *Sunday Referee,* a stylish weekend broadsheet, about his pride in England. "Our conquests have been carried out with an exquisite air of amateurishness," he had drawled, world-wearily.

The next week in the *Referee,* Frances took Sitwell on. The subject of her polemic was capitalism. Had he ever looked around England? *Really* looked? "England is the richest country in the world but what a price in flesh and blood she has paid for her sterling!" Neither the slums of America nor those of the Balkans could prepare you for the appalling state of the British people. They were undernourished, their teeth were terrible, their skin blotchy: "nowhere I have seen such poor ugly wretched miserable deformed decrepit lowgrade physical specimens of humanity."

The feudal lords of England—like Sitwell himself—were canny,

Frances conceded. They threw just enough bones to the workers ("dumb sheep," she called them) to keep the populace pacified. At the root of England's troubles was the ruling gospel of trade and profit and it went far deeper than the charge that the English were a "nation of shopkeepers." The rot was manifest in relations between husbands and wives, between parents and children: "Trade—trade-spirit translated into all human relationships."

This was the sort of feud that Sitwell relished. He wasn't, he assured her, unaware of England's "nauseating deficiencies." But critical as he was of his own country, hers—abandoning the League of Nations, sending Sacco and Vanzetti to the electric chair, teetotaling—had still more to answer for. The *Referee*'s readers took up where Sitwell left off, pillorying Frances for every conceivable American failing from the Lindbergh kidnapping to the easy availability of divorce in Reno. According to one, "American culture is expressed by jazz, crooning, and the black bottom."

Frances hadn't attacked England in order to defend the United States. "The fact that America is selfish, corrupt, stupid, puritanical, unjust, intolerant, gangsteric, goldhoarding, lynching, and poignantly incapable of talk is No Excuse for the fact that England is a lot of other unpleasant things." Rather, she meant to issue a warning: the English ought to come out from their "dark counting house" before it was too late. "No man lives forever, and no empire."

"Atta girl!" declared their correspondent friends. "I haven't read anything for a long time that conveyed indignation as well as did your story. No foolin'," wrote the head of the United Press wire service in Europe. Frances had arrived, brawling.

In London, she and John took a lease on a flat in Bloomsbury above the headquarters of the Women's Total Abstinence Union. They had a maisonette on the second and third floors of the building, plenty of room for the three of them as well as Johnny's nanny, Milla, who had accompanied the family from Vienna. The only catch was a proviso written into the lease that no alcohol of any kind, not even beer, could be brought onto the premises until after six P.M., when the ladies downstairs left for the day. The lease didn't say anything about bringing out the empty bottles the next morning, Frances noted.

They set about the serious business, for the correspondent, of having parties. Few of their guests could resist a smart remark about the posters adorning the first-floor hallway: BEER IS DEADLY, ALCOHOL THE GREATEST ENEMY OF THE HUMAN RACE. No way Jimmy Sheean's at a party *here* was the joke in their crowd. He was already an infamous drunk.

WHEN WOULD THE NEXT war start? In the summer of 1935, that was a topic at the Gunthers' parties and everywhere else. The Czech foreign minister, Jan Masaryk, who visited London to shore up British commitments to an independent Czechoslovakia, said that the real trouble would begin at the end of the following year. Knick called him an end-of-36er. There were also start-of-38ers and middle-of-39ers. The only person in their circle able to muster any optimism about the future was Fodor, who—Hungarian and Jewish in Vienna—had the most to lose. It seemed possible, he told his editors, that dictatorships would be wound down in the next few years; after all, look what had happened in Spain, in 1931, when the authoritarian regime of Primo de Rivera ceded to a new democratic republic. He pitched a series on the reestablishment of parliamentary government, to focus on Yugoslavia, Greece, and Bulgaria.

If Fodor was an optimist, Britain's leaders, John thought, were delusional. He went to the House of Commons to listen to the foreign policy debates, but all the talk of fair play and free trade seemed topsy-turvy, Alice in Wonderland stuff. With the exception of a few Tory MPs, the British had no clue about the danger Hitler posed. They still didn't understand that the only way to manage the Führer was to "step on his neck and keep stepping on it," he wrote Frances. The Foreign Office's press officer agreed with John. He was despondent. Not only would there be a war, and soon, he told John, but Britain would surely be trounced.

It was in this atmosphere of dread of the coming war, on the one hand, and ostrichism, on the other, that the Abyssinian crisis erupted that summer. Abyssinia, today Ethiopia, was one of two independent Black states in sub-Saharan Africa. In 1896, Emperor Menelik II had led his troops to victory against an attempted Italian invasion of the kingdom. Starting in the spring of 1935, Italy began moving soldiers, hundreds of thousands of them, along with ship holds full of ammunition, through the Suez Canal into the territories of Eritrea and Italian Somaliland on Abyssinia's borders. Singing the fascist anthem, cheering, the soldiers arrived on ships bearing giant portraits of Mussolini, with the banner, DUCE, DUCE, WE WILL DIE FOR YOU!

Abyssinia was a member of the League of Nations, its territorial integrity guaranteed by the League's founding covenant and successive security pacts. Still, Mussolini made no secret of his intentions: the Italians would take Abyssinia to expand their African empire. Fair was fair: the British had their empire, so did the French, and a great nation like Italy could hardly expect less. What the Duce was counting on wasn't so much a sense of fair play on the part of Britain and France as fear and national self-interest. The League's covenant spelled out a process for dealing with an act of unprovoked aggression: first economic sanctions levied by the fifty-one member states, then military action. Sanctions would damage the export-oriented Italian economy, but unless the British and the French governments joined together to cut off the flow of coal and oil to Italy, the measures wouldn't be crippling. Would France's leaders, who saw Italy as their ally against German aggression, dare to punish Mussolini for an invasion of Abyssinia? Would the British? And if Mussolini were permitted to overrun Abyssinia, what, if anything, would remain of the League?

It was the gravest international crisis for the British since 1914, reported John. The prime minister returned early from his summer holiday in the spa town of Aix, as British warships massed in the Mediterranean on high alert. Newly married Knick also put his plans on hold. In Texas with Agnes for a family reunion, he got the summons from his editors: he was off to Addis Ababa. It was the rainy season in Abyssinia, downpours every day, the alleys of the city turned to rushing streams. But if the correspondents were to be there for the beginning of the "show," they had to get to Addis early. Scores of foreign correspondents, 170 in total, among them Evelyn Waugh, reporting for the *Daily Mail,* made their way to the docks at Marseilles, and from there, to Port Said, through the Suez Canal to Djibouti, and then, by rail, across the Ethiopian frontier.

Mussolini's forces had new-model bombers, poison gas, the latest in machine guns, and troops to squander. The Abyssinians, subject to an arms embargo and lacking a domestic munitions industry, had rusty old guns, guerrilla warfare, two hundred thousand–odd soldiers, many of them barefoot, armed with spears or swords—and the sympathy of liberal internationalist world opinion. Keeping the correspondents on his side, the Abyssinian emperor Haile Selassie figured, was paramount, for Mussolini's willingness to slaughter innocents might yet move the League's powers. With the invasion expected any day, he laid on a banquet at his new palace to welcome the world press. The dinner was a self-consciously Westernized affair, intended to convey the sort of "civilization" that many Europeans and Americans doubted the "natives" possessed. Presiding over the ninety-foot-long table, set with gold-engraved place cards, the emperor treated his guests to aperitifs and pâté de foie gras, fricasseed chicken and ham with Madeira sauce, a top-quality sauterne (Knick was picky about such things), and ice cream.

As soon as the rains stopped, the bombs started. Like the other reporters, Knick had imagined that Addis would be the target, but as it turned out, the Italian invasion was happening far away, in the north of the country. You can't travel there, said Selassie's government, fearing the terrible publicity that would result if the reporters were mistaken for Italians and killed en route to the north. Bored, obliged to justify their presence by sending wires every day, the newspapermen carped. They got drunk. The altitude of Addis, nearly eight thousand feet above sea level, made their hangovers even worse. They fought with each other. You're England's second-best living novelist, right behind Aldous Huxley, Knick told Waugh one night, after a game of poker. "I'll have to knock you down for that," Waugh replied, and did, and then Knick punched him back. It wasn't really a serious knockabout, said a young British reporter called upon to hold Knick's glasses.

The American correspondents, Waugh would later write, were lucky. Their public had developed such an insatiable taste for "impertinent personal details" that they—unlike the Europeans, stuck hunting for nonexistent news—could simply cable back the details of how they were passing their days, waiting for the war to reach them. Knick sent plenty of that sort of thing, including an explanation of his expense account, duly printed. Two months in Abyssinia, and he'd spent nearly $5000 on "incidentals," an astounding sum, equivalent to $90,000 in today's money. To the man in Addis, he explained, it was as necessary to have a boy servant armed with a gun as it was to have trousers in Manhattan.

Knick's access to Hearst's nearly unlimited funds, together with his own derring-do, produced the first scoop from the Ethiopian side of the war. One morning early, he flew off in a plane piloted by a French explorer. They'd secured the emperor's permission to travel to the north of the country, to the town of Dessye and beyond, photographing anything they wanted. He was the first reporter to reach the battlefields, getting the bragging rights—"How Knickerbocker Scooped World by Secret War Hop Told"—though because of the nature of guerrilla warfare, there wasn't much he could see. The story became the journey itself, made exciting (in retrospect) by the discovery, on landing back in Addis, that the plane had taken a bullet from Italian machine-gunners on the ground.

When Waugh came to write *Scoop*, his satire of foreign correspondence set in the Italo-Abyssinian war, it was this sort of adventure he meant to mock. Waugh's novel is populated by characters who gin up stories to satisfy the appetite of the wire service, concocting the news, not reporting it. Wenlock Jakes—the braggart American with the extravagant expense account, busily fabricating scoops—is part Knick, part John. After a few months in Abyssinia with his *Daily Mail* bosses hounding him for stories, Waugh was fed up. "I am a very bad journalist, well only a shit could be good at this particular job," Waugh wrote an old girlfriend.

Waugh had already started home for England by the time that Knick reached Dessye for the second time. He'd traveled there in a caravan with the other correspondents, fifteen trucks full of reporters lurching and bumping through the mountains for five days. There was no road to speak of between Addis and Dessye, 150 miles apart, just a track with hairpin turns and stomach-churning drop-offs down the canyons below. They slept out in tents, the weather in the mountains frigid. As they approached Dessye, the vegetation turned tropical. The spiderwebs were so dense and rubbery, they could knock your hat off.

Haile Selassie had given the reporters permission to travel, saying he would meet them in Dessye. He was mobilizing his troops in the north, preparing for an Italian ground invasion. Knick had been there little more than a week when the Italian bombers arrived.

It was early in the morning. Hearing the noise of the planes overhead, they ran out of the tents they'd pitched in the compound of the American Adventist hospital and stared at the silvery planes in the sky. Knick was lucky: it was a small incendiary bomb, not an explosive, that fell ten feet from him. Across the city, debris shot up in hundred-foot geysers, as the Italians bombed the hospital (its red cross, Knick could attest, visible from the sky), Selassie's palace, and the thatched-roof, round dwelling houses. By the end of the raid, Dessye was a ruin. Seven surgeons worked all night, amputating limbs, with a line of patients, holding their wounds, waiting for treatment. It was the Italians' "gift of civilization," wrote Knick, detailing the injuries he'd seen, counting up the bodies. "Two more women died of gaping wounds before my eyes."

Half the world proclaimed very confidently that the Ethiopian war was already over, Knick observed. The other half thought it had yet to begin.

———

JOHN WAS IN THE half who thought the Ethiopian war hadn't started. The British, he felt certain, would not abandon the League. Hadn't the foreign secretary, Samuel Hoare, said so himself in Geneva, when he promised the League's assembly that Britain would uphold the covenant? Besides, as John pointed out in the *Daily News,* the moral posture—defending Abyssinia and the League— almost perfectly aligned with Britain's imperial interests.

He and Frances were entertaining friends the evening after news of a pact between Hoare and the French prime minister, Pierre Laval, broke. The Italians had just bombed Dessye when Hoare, en route to an ice-skating holiday in Switzerland, met Laval in Paris. The two men worked out a deal to hand more than half of Haile Selassie's kingdom over to Mussolini in exchange for an end to the war. Before they could carve up Abyssinia, though, their secret pact leaked to the press.

That evening, all the talk at the Gunthers was about what should be done. Claud Cockburn, a communist journalist and Evelyn Waugh's cousin, was over for drinks. The Labour politicians Aneurin Bevan and Jennie Lee were there, and so was the screenwriter Herman J. Mankiewicz, who'd arrived from Hollywood three days earlier.

The debate was raucous and angry, but none of John's friends shared his shocked outrage about the deal. How could he have been so naïve as to believe Hoare's promises? True, neither Bevan nor Cockburn had imagined that the Abyssinians would be betrayed so thoroughly. But the idea that Britain would go to war for Haile Selassie's kingdom—that was unthinkable! To Mankiewicz, it was just Realpolitik. Like the good screenwriter he was (he'd later write *Citizen Kane*), Mankiewicz could already see the end of the story. Within the year, he said, Selassie would wash up in a pension in the French Riviera, a pitiful exile whose name no one could remember.

Frances had been saying for months that something like the Hoare-Laval plan was in the works. She hadn't much sympathy for the Abyssinians. Like George Bernard Shaw, she took the part of the modernizers, the road-builders—even if that meant endorsing imperialism. According to Frances, the Abyssinians really didn't belong in the League. And they certainly weren't worth either risking a war over or pushing Mussolini into bed with Hitler. That night, she and John went to bed late. She knew how hurt he was about Hoare's betrayal of the Abyssinians. They could barely speak to each other.

It isn't over yet, John had said to his friends that night. And he turned out to be right, at least so far as the Hoare-Laval pact went. At the Waldorf bar, striking up a conversation with an engineer and a few other businessmen who, hearing the exchange, joined in, he caught a whiff of public opinion. The men, well-dressed and conservative, were indignant: they felt betrayed by the prime minister and the government. By the end of the month, such sentiments—from socialists as from conservatives, from pacifists and militarists—would force the British government to repudiate the deal, and lead to Hoare's resignation, weeping, as he exited the House of Commons.

What next, then? That was the question that John asked all of the people he was seeing: Margot Asquith—widow of the Liberal prime minister H. H. Asquith—who liked knowing the bright young American correspondents; Lord Cecil, an architect of the League's covenant; H. G. Wells, Rebecca West, Lady Violet Bonham Carter, Harold Laski, Aldous Huxley. Lord Cecil pointed out that fascists wanted colonies to advance their political, not just economic, aims. H. G. Wells wasn't sure where he stood but hoped that Hitler and Mussolini were the "last eruption" of tyranny. Harold Laski was horrified by the government's sellout but nonetheless thought Abyssinian independence a lost cause; all that would be left for Haile Selassie, as Laski put it, were the "film-rights."

Among the English public, the sympathy for Selassie's kingdom was "deep, cordial, altruistic and absolutely ineffective," as Waugh (who sided with the Italians) put it. It didn't override the fear of war. Any attempt to punish Italy by cutting off its oil imports, Mussolini warned, would be taken as a provocation.

It's a test case for the League, John said to Frances. The defeat of the Italians will be a setback for fascism. Maybe Hitler will even be deterred from a similar stunt if he thinks sanctions have teeth.

Do you really think Hitler will be deterred by *precedents*? she countered.

Knick, back from Abyssinia, agreed with Frances. The Italians were going to win the war: that was a foregone conclusion. What chance did even a thousand natives with rifles have against a single Italian finger on a machine gun? The League ought to dispense with the charade of sanctions, he insisted. Britain and France had to keep the Italians in their corner—that was the most important thing. He was dead tired, sick of war.

I'm on the side of the Abyssinians, announced six-year-old Johnny out of the blue one day. He'd started kindergarten that fall. He had dreamed up an imaginary machine called Smoky, part steamship, part plane, part train, which whisked him all around the world. In just a night, he zipped to Australia, he informed his parents, tracing his finger over the globe. He could get to Vienna in a matter of hours. During the day, he parked Smoky on Mount Everest, which was a lofty enough perch to take in the universe.

THE HOARE-LAVAL PACT HAD so enraged John that he rewrote the British section of his book. He cut much of what he'd previously said about the English ruling classes' humanitarianism and idealism. In its place, he stressed Frances's theme: "For six days a week the Englishman worships at the Bank of England, and on the seventh day at the Church of England." For all the lip service the British elite paid to international morality, unless it fit in the calculus of national profit, out the window it went. He had to be quick about the changes because his book was already in proofs, and the mail boy was standing by to take the copy to the boat.

He'd written the book, more than five hundred closely spaced pages, in just under five months. Every evening after dinner he trudged back to the *Daily News*'s bureau in Bush House, the Art

Deco office block on the semicircular Aldwych, passing under the statues celebrating Anglo-American friendship at its entrance, then down the dark corridors. There were four thousand offices in Bush House but his, it seemed, was the only light burning.

Much of the book relied on John's own reporting, but he'd also drawn on the memos his friends sent. Forwarding the "dirt" on Turkey's leader, Fodor reported that Atatürk's first experiences of sex had been with his fellow students at the military academy. He also nursed a secret love for his mother, drank heavily, and suffered from kidney pain as a result of untreated gonorrhea, which he'd contracted at a Salonika brothel. The worse the pain, the more zealous Atatürk's reforms of Turkish society became: abolishing the fez amid one attack, the dervishes and polygamy during another.

Sensational stuff, but could John publish it? Knick kept telling him that he had to write *everything*, but he had to keep it dignified, not stoop to tabloid-ese. Frances agreed and insisted there had to be a point behind the juicy tidbits. So, the fact that both Dollfuss and the British prime minister, Ramsay MacDonald, were of illegitimate birth mattered because it made them outsiders, desperate to elbow their way in. On the other hand, Atatürk's dalliances with boys, an artifact of the military academy, weren't pertinent; moreover, they'd be difficult to prove and thus probably libelous. Atatürk's mother fixation, by contrast, went into the book; so did the relationship between his kidney pain (attributed, euphemistically, to his "own early sins") and his transformation of Turkish society. He "purifies a nation as a surrogate for purification of his own painful blood."

The relationship between the personal and the political became the central point of John's book. He put it right on the first page: "The fact may be an outrage to reason, but it cannot be denied: unresolved personal conflicts in the lives of various European politicians may contribute to the collapse of our civilization." It was a *personal* book, he stressed to his editors: that was the angle to play up, not its muckraking or debunking qualities. If he was catering to the same taste for personalities as Jimmy, it wasn't in any way personal about John himself, save for one important fact. He had decided to forgo anonymity. Unlike the pseudonymous author of *Our Lord and Masters,* a rival title about world leaders published as John was finishing his own manuscript, he would sign the book. He figured in its pages—hunting down Hitler's relatives in Spital, attending the Reichstag arson trial, interviewing Masaryk, Dollfuss, King Carol—but it was the personal development of Europe's leaders, not his own, that he was unmasking.

The title John finally settled on, *Inside Europe,* perfectly expressed both the perspective of the outsider, looking in, and the deeper, psychological, and personal inside he meant to convey. He organized the book as the novelist or the screenwriter would, introducing first the dominant character—Hitler—and the "little" Hitlers, the Nazi supporting cast. He then swooped in plot arcs to France and Italy, as Hitlerism drove outward to a confrontation with Mussolini; from the invasion of Abyssinia to England, the country most implicated in the crisis; then to Austria, the battleground between socialism and fascism; and finally—via the Balkans and Poland—to the Soviet Union and Stalin.

His perspective was that of the eyewitness, distilling thousands of nights of conversation at the Café Louvre or the Hotel Adlon. What it was like to ride with Hitler in an airplane: not a word did he say to any soul. The inside story about Mussolini's claustrophobia and superstitions: he took fright at an Egyptian mummy that had been given him. The hypnotic impression Stalin made when he walked into a room: "you feel his antennae." He depicted senile old men, like Ramsay MacDonald, unable to finish a coherent sentence, arrayed, helplessly, against megalomaniacs like Mussolini.

It was very much a book about the rulers, not the ruled. Stekel's ideas about the "authority complex" made a brief appearance to explain the appeal of dictatorship, but John's attention stayed firmly fixed on the leaders and on high politics. The contrast with the work of contemporary social scientists, notably the anthropologist Margaret Mead, is striking. Mead and her colleagues were trying to understand the workings of national character: why—say—the Germans submitted willingly to dictatorship or the Americans demonstrated a stubborn, wary independence. Such "culture-cracking," they believed, could be marshaled to defuse international rivalries or to win a war. Their analysis, like John's, was indebted to a sort of Freudianism, requiring the investigation of child-rearing practices and generational friction. However, the sense of what mattered most was very different. As John saw it, individual personality had jolted history into a new gear. He was making an argument about accidents and contingency rather than deeply ingrained patterns of culture.

A FEW DAYS AFTER *Inside Europe* was published in January 1936, Frances dashed into their bedroom. She was brandishing the *Daily Telegraph:* Harold Nicolson had reviewed the book! John was still in bed and he couldn't stand to look at the paper himself, so she read the review aloud while he was in his pajamas, and again at breakfast, triumphantly.

America, Nicolson began, had contributed a set of improvements to modern life that the British would do well to "slavishly" imitate. Air-conditioning, thermostat heating, orange juice for breakfast— and "the American type of wandering or perambulatory foreign correspondent," naming Sheean, Knickerbocker, Thompson, the Mowrer brothers, Walter Duranty, and Gunther as leading specimens of the type. According to Nicolson, the virtue of *Inside Europe* was that it was exciting—"so personal that it may seem dramatic"— and at the same time "educative," an evenhanded, trustworthy guidebook to foreign affairs with only the occasional detour to Hollywood sensationalism. Most important, he endorsed John's thesis about the significance of personality to the events playing out in Europe. *Inside Europe* was "a serious contribution to contemporary knowledge," Nicolson pronounced.

How *did* you uncover all that dirt? wondered the journalist Martha Gellhorn. She'd read and reread the book but couldn't figure out how John had done it. It's as if "you had at least slept with all the crowned heads of Europe and been Ministre des Finances in everybody's government," she marveled. John had managed to make the dictators familiar—to transform them from the remote, mythical personages of the newsreels to individuals as peculiar and vivid as one's own relations. It was that sense of immediacy, the telling and pungent descriptions, that reviewers—among them his fellow correspondents—admired. "I would have given a good deal to have thought of calling Adolf Hitler 'a blob of ectoplasm,'" Dorothy exclaimed in her review. In its "vigor and almost impudent candor," *Inside Europe* was an unabashedly American book, thought the veteran reporter Raymond Swing: "I cannot imagine a man of any other nationality writing it."

Harper's was printing another twenty thousand copies on the strength of the British reviews, Canfield wired John. The Book-of-the-Month Club had chosen *Inside Europe* as their pick for February. Even the inevitable criticism stoked the book's sales. John's lack of attention to economics came in for critique, especially from reviewers on the Left, as did his invocation of Stekel. The ax fell sharper in the United States than it did in Britain, where psychoanalysis was more of a novelty. Stekel was Gunther's "black angel," wrote Malcolm Cowley: "whenever his name appears in the text, the author begins talking elaborate nonsense." According to the *New York Times*'s reviewer, *Inside Europe* was "amusing" but hardly authoritative, of literary not "scientific" value. Surely Hitler's rise wasn't an "accident of personality" but a reflection of Germany's postwar ills. Leaders, after all, required followers. If you want your history with a "chocolate coating of personalities, you can't do better than read Mr. Gunther," judged the *New Yorker*.

That chocolate coating was precisely what readers did want, and in marketing the book, John and his publishers ballyhooed it. How about if you advertise the fact that the British publishers had to cut 157 passages to avoid being sued for libel? John suggested to Canfield. "He risked his career to provide you with the startling facts behind Europe's political chaos," trumpeted the ad in the American papers. It was a book to pack in your luggage when you set off for the Continent, a "political Baedeker" that permitted you to travel across Europe in the company of a man "to whom no doors are closed."

Anthony Eden, the British foreign secretary who succeeded Hoare, was seen reading it. FDR's son Frank Jr. took it on his honeymoon. The young John F. Kennedy traveled through Europe in the summer of 1937 with *Inside Europe* in hand, tempering his enthusiasm for a fascist victory in Spain after consulting what Gunther had to say.

Most important, *Inside Europe* served as a warning. Hitler wouldn't disappear on his own; he'd have to be beaten. John's book was a powerful weapon in the "successful fight for democracy and decency," observed the diplomat George Messersmith from Vienna. To keep the book up-to-date, John revised each edition afresh, and Harper's arranged for readers to get a fifty-cent rebate when they traded in their old copies for the new version. Within a couple of years, the book, banned in Germany and Hungary, was already in its thirty-ninth printing. *Inside Europe,* it was often said, did more to jolt Americans and Britons out of their complacency than any other book of the 1930s.

THERE WAS A LOT of *Inside Europe* that Jimmy thought pure nonsense and when Canfield asked him for a quotation to use in advertising the book, he delayed and delayed writing it. Finally, when he and Dinah were aboard the SS *Orion,* en route to Toulon for a belated honeymoon in Egypt, he started a sentence. "You may not agree with Gunther's central thesis on the historic role of the accidents of personality (I don't, for instance) . . ." He crossed that out and began again.

"Gunther's book amasses and arranges detail with a precision, brilliance and solidity seldom encountered in informative writing. You may not agree with his central thesis (that the accidents of personality play a very great role in history) but the book he has built round it constitutes an invaluable addition to our knowledge of the present monstrous age in European politics. Nobody has written of the characteristic monsters with greater effect."

He knew it wouldn't be all that useful. Feel free to dispense with everything but the first sentence, he cabled Canfield.

For all that Jimmy had himself written of personalities, like Abd el-Krim, the Grand Mufti, or Borodin, he didn't like John's approach, not least because it begged the question of Hitler's followers. Abd el-Krim was an exceptional character, but inasmuch as he shaped events, it was because he distilled in a single individual the historical experiences of his people. The same was true of Hitler. He represented not an accident of history, still less an aberration of child-rearing, but the recent history of Central Europe: the insult of defeat, the economic upheaval, the angry nationalism of the Germans. Had Hitler not existed, he would have had to be invented, Jimmy said.

To his credit, he told John what he thought of the book directly. That stuff he'd derived from Stekel was plain silly: "Kemal swept the Greeks into the sea because some Greeks had ill-treated his mother or that Mussolini's political career is due to a 'father bipolarity.'" Psychoanalysis was bunk, Jimmy had decided: "a symptom of disease rather than of intellectual activity" was the way he put it.

"There are much sounder reasons than these for the things that happen. Or so I think," he continued. "You think otherwise—o.k. Anyhow the book is very fine stuff and I hope it goes with a great bang."

He was sorry, he added, for how he'd behaved in London. He and Dinah had spent New Year's Eve in London with Frances and John. He'd been drinking too much and was "nervous as a witch." As was Dinah, though for reasons of her own. She was pregnant, a fact that was obvious to Agnes Knickerbocker when she saw the girl in Cairo the next month. Dinah was dressed in a Grecian-style, spring-green chiffon evening gown and was ravishing.

"For God's sake, Jimmy, she's only nineteen," objected his literary agent, Carol Hill, when she heard about the pregnancy. "Carol, what do you do when you marry a girl who knows all the words and none of the meanings?" Jimmy had replied.

His child, Jimmy decided, would be born in Ireland. He and Dinah rented a Georgian house in the northern suburbs of Dublin and settled in to await the baby.

AS *INSIDE EUROPE* BECAME a phenomenon—big displays of the book in Selfridge's windows, sold out in the shops, rushed for reprinting—Frances chided herself for being jealous of her own husband. She listed out in her mind the ideas John had got from her. Sure, he'd acknowledged "the generous and patient collaboration of my wife." On six pages, she got actual credit: "as Frances Gunther pointed out" or "as Frances Gunther wrote." But that was a tiny portion of the hundreds and hundreds of her observations that he'd appropriated for the book. He hadn't even attributed the best ones to her. Her crack about Englishmen worshipping six days at the Bank of England and then on Sunday at the Church of England? For all the reader knew, that was John's own.

When they moved to London, she'd been intending to work on her play, "Mothers and Lovers." But she was too tired for that. She told a friend that she was too busy as a wife and mother and housekeeper to do any real work. Rebecca West wanted a recipe for *Zwetchenknoedel*. Lady Asquith was owed an invitation to dinner. Miss Russell of the Society & Celebrity Press called on the phone to arrange a time to take John's photograph. Frances's mother and her brother were visiting. She had to take Johnny to the park. It was all too much for her: she couldn't write anything but titles for her stories. And the horrible London fog every morning. She woke up, looked out the window, and then pulled the covers over her head to blot it out.

She was in the blackest possible mood. John's solicitude in particular was unbearable. Are your feet warm enough? he asked her one night when she was in bed.

"My God can't you leave me alone?" she snapped.

At breakfast, he asked her to help him with an article *Cosmopolitan* wanted from him on the future of fascism. I won't think about any of his articles again, she'd promised herself. But then she did, talking on and on as if she were in a trance. She was like an Automat: feed her a coin, and she'll deliver the goods.

It's like putting a nickel in a slot, he exclaimed. "I always feel marvelous when I let myself go & think for him," she wrote in her diary.

"Didn't even put a nickel in the slot," she wisecracked. But when he tried to make love to her, she found she couldn't bear his touch.

THE ITALIANS CONQUERED ADDIS in May 1936, and in July, the League lifted its sanctions. Mussolini had taken Abyssinia and paid no price for it. It was the end of the League Covenant as a security arrangement. "The appearance of Italy back in Geneva like the cat who swallowed the canary loudly purring its fondness for all feathered things and fidelity to a vegetarian diet—meaning the League of Nations—will shock the hardest boiled of diplomats," Edgar Mowrer cabled.

In Rome, Knick arranged to interview the thirty-three-year-old Count Ciano, Italy's foreign minister and Mussolini's son-in-law. Come to the beach with me, Ciano said, and we can have lunch. Ciano liked Americans. Tanned and charismatic, he'd been the head of the state press office and had known Knick for years. As they charged down the motorway to the coast, Ciano pushing eighty-five miles per hour in his Alfa Romeo, Knick got the foreign minister talking about the bombing raids he'd led at the start of the Abyssinian invasion and reminiscing about his student days as a reporter for Rome's first fascist paper. After a lunch of fried red mullet and squid ("delectable," Knick noted), Ciano introduced him to a muscular young man in swimming trunks. "One of our pilots, he helped bomb Dessye." Knick had been there, too, Ciano told the pilot. "On the receiving end," Knick laughed and the two shook hands, amicably.

The Ethiopian campaign had been a massive publicity coup for Mussolini, Knick acknowledged. "Now not even the most skeptical can deny that Italy is a great power." When Knick interviewed Mussolini a week later, the Duce was talking of peace, of the opening of Abyssinia to foreign capital, declaring an end to his hostilities with England. Knick's sympathetic depiction of the Italian dictator fit with the hope he'd expressed to Frances and John; England and France had to keep Italy on their side. But the article was sure to raise the hackles of Knick's friends: Mussolini humanized, portrayed as triumphant but not gloating, his hair graying because of the long nights spent at the bedside of his ill little daughter. John thought Knick was dead wrong. Mussolini's victory in Abyssinia propelled fascism forward since he and Hitler represented "almost identical dynamic forces."

By then, the talk in John's London circles had moved on to the situation in Spain. The Spanish Republic was five years old, the successor state to an unpopular monarchy and Primo de Rivera's authoritarian regime. The Spanish went to the polls in February 1936 and elected a new government, a Popular Front coalition of democrats, Socialists, and Communists to battle fascism. The Republic's prime minister, Manuel Azaña, was staring down the forces of reaction: the Church, the aristocracy, and Spain's senior army officers, among them General Francisco Franco, chief of the army staff.

The magazine publisher Lady Rhondda invited John to lunch a few days after Azaña banished Franco to the Canary Islands. She was an ardent feminist and patron of radical causes. Aldous Huxley was there, too, which made John want to clam up since Huxley—of all the British novelists—was the one he, like Knick, most admired. Huxley was shy himself, and tall and gangling. He looked, John thought, like an ungainly, if oddly wise, rabbit.

What would John do if he were in Azaña's shoes? Lady Rhondda wanted to know. How far could a democracy go in using undemocratic means to suppress its enemies? Fascism called for extraordinary measures, John replied. He wouldn't permit free speech for those who'd use it to destroy the Republic; he'd outlaw fascist uniforms, try to deliver on his promises, promote education, and, if necessary, after a fair trial, shoot a few plotters if that would avoid a civil war later on.

Lady Rhondda disagreed about shooting one's enemies, even with the benefit of a trial. She was a committed anti-fascist herself, a survivor of the *Lusitania* torpedoing in 1915, but drew the line at summary justice. And Huxley, it turned out, was committed to absolute nonviolence, even if that meant the death of the Spanish Republic. He still believed in the natural goodness of man.

As usual, John felt overmatched in these conversations. Why can't we Americans converse like the English, with allusions to Spinoza and Rousseau at the ready? he'd wondered to Frances. "We lack grandfathers," she replied.

The discussion about Azaña's options turned very quickly from theoretical debate to international crisis. In July 1936, Franco departed the Canary Islands by airplane, landing in Morocco to plot the invasion of the Spanish Republic. Within a few weeks, Franco's troops, with the aid of transport planes lent by Mussolini, had arrived on the peninsula and were fighting their way across Spain to the capital city of Madrid.

That month, devastated by the events in Spain, Jimmy collapsed in Ireland. He and Dinah and their two-month-old baby were staying at a friend's country house in County Meath. Years later, when Jimmy told the story, he readily acknowledged he'd been on a drinking binge. But that didn't even begin to explain the whole thing, he insisted. To account for what happened to him, you had to understand about Spain.

The nervous breakdown came first. The night that Franco launched his coup attempt, Jimmy was off his head, delusional, bellowing at the top of his voice. The Irish doctors had him sedated and when that wasn't enough, they bundled him into a straitjacket. Next came his physical collapse. He frothed thick yellow at the mouth for days; he was burning up with a fever. In succession, his lungs, liver, and kidneys failed, and in a Dublin hospital, he slipped into a coma.

Jimmy is dying, his editor Jamie Hamilton was told. Jamie called John with the terrible news and asked him to write an obituary for *The Times*.

John stayed up late that night to do it. "There is hardly a coffee house in the Near East or a university campus in the United States where Sheean's name does not represent something," John began.

He catalogued Jimmy's daring reporting and exuberant partisanship as well as his storied charm. Jimmy humming Mozart and wearing green pants; lying on the stone floor of the Temple Mount in Jerusalem tracing out the mosaic patterns in the ceiling above; tearing a chunk out of his novel, mortified to discover a cliché. Jimmy all the time searching, searching for the relation between his one life and the many of which it was a part. Young people everywhere, added John in a scribbled note at the end, recognized that "his problem was theirs—the relation of individual lives to the world of history around them."

Looking back on the episode a year later, Jimmy asked John: "What is dying? Do you know? This has puzzled me a good deal of late." Six whole weeks had gone black for him. He had no memory of the Dublin hospital. No memory of being flown in an air ambulance from Dublin to Dijon, the nearest airport to the Swiss sanatorium Dinah had arranged. (That event was covered in the papers: "American Author, Suffering from Nervous Breakdown, Reaches Dijon by Plane.")

What he had, instead, were the sensory impressions—he didn't like to call them "hallucinations"—that had accompanied him through the darkness. Planes, on fire, falling out of the sky. He was at the Cathedral of Segovia, its dome rising from a forest of Gothic spires. His body was laid out on a slab behind an iron grille, the catafalque guarded by black-uniformed Italian policemen, the monks chanting in preparation for his burial. He'd never been to Segovia but he could see it so clearly.

The last impression he had before regaining consciousness was of floating in an icy sea, his body chopped into pieces. That was when he felt Dinah's hands holding his and heard her calling his name. Without Dinah—"her constant presence, the pull of it, which I could actually feel, physically, I mean, as a sort of tugging sensation"—he surely would have died, he wrote Raymond Mortimer.

The doctors at the sanatorium couldn't agree on what was wrong with him. He was jealous of his daughter, announced one psychoanalyst, to whom Jimmy had confided something of his past. No—it was his mother, proclaimed another doctor, a follower of Stekel. "These two quite get my goat; they both seem to believe that external experience, the whole business of observing and thinking about the world, counts for nothing at all," he complained to Raymond. Then there was the deaf Dutch psychiatrist who spoke neither French nor English: "you can imagine what brilliant results he had with me."

Jimmy's own explanation of his breakdown had nothing to do with repressed childhood trauma or the upsets of marriage or fatherhood. Rather, this was the conscience of humanity he'd prescribed in *Personal History*, taken to a radical and involuntary extreme. It was as if he'd become a sort of human seismograph for the universe's political ills. Whether that was a self-aggrandizing delusion or his comparative advantage as a reporter was something that he and John would later debate.

"Everything is autobiography, from the larger point of view," Jimmy said to John. "What I am interested in is how the individual person enmeshes with society, with the historical process of which he is a part."

"But with that as your major theme," John objected, "how do you avoid being messianic, which is something that the really serious artist should never be."

Jimmy glared at him: "I *am* messianic."

While Jimmy was convalescing in Switzerland, he wasn't permitted any newspapers, nor was anyone allowed to talk about Spain in front of him. When he eventually saw the headlines about the siege of the Alcázar, he thought he'd relapsed into insanity.

No, it's real, Dinah told him. It's actually happening. He'd woken up from one nightmare and there he was, in another. Hitler and Mussolini, once at odds over Austria, were now, after Abyssinia, banding together. As Franco's troops ringed Madrid in November 1936, Mussolini took to a stage in front of the Milan Cathedral to announce a new international order. The axis of global power, the Duce declared, ran from Rome to Berlin.

PART
THREE

THE REVOLUTION INSIDE

—

DOROTHY HAD A GREAT DEAL MORE PATIENCE WITH JIMMY'S "shemozzles" than any of their friends might have predicted. She was ferociously busy and not given to nonsense herself. After her expulsion from Nazi Germany, she was in constant demand as a lecturer and, starting in the spring of 1936, had a syndicated opinion column of her own. She was not just America's first woman political columnist but one of a small handful of opinion columnists in the entire country. The op-ed page didn't yet exist; if a paper had a political column, it was the publisher's own. But beginning in the 1930s, in recognition that the news needed interpreting, not just reporting, the political columnist—writing as she pleased—was born.

On the right-hand column of the front page of the *New York Herald Tribune*'s second section on Mondays, Wednesdays, and Fridays, alternating with Walter Lippmann's columns, which ran on Tuesdays, Thursdays, and Saturdays, Dorothy found her perch. The paper's original idea was that she'd address women readers. Before too long, though, she had an audience of millions, men and women, as she cast her eye over every subject from Hitler to FDR's Farm Bill to the state of the American soul. The beat she assigned herself, as the *New York Times* later put it, "was no less than the whole human situation." She was refining her trademark "liberal conservatism," as

John called it—by which he meant a fierce opposition to fascism, combined with a skepticism about the New Deal. Warning of "totalitarian" states that laid "claim upon every phase of life," she objected to the power FDR was arrogating to himself as well as to government programs that, if carried too far, would, she feared, sap individual American initiative.

To her chockablock schedule of speaking and writing, she added regular radio commentary on NBC, thirteen minutes every Monday night and, starting in 1937, a monthly column in the *Ladies' Home Journal*, circulation more than three million, for which she was paid a princely $1,000 each. She employed three secretaries, two of them to staff her office at the *Herald Tribune*, the other at home. On "column mornings," Dorothy, clad in a negligée, sat up in bed, surrounded by cablegrams and newspapers and books, writing her column out by hand, or if she was in a particular hurry, dictating it to the waiting secretary, black coffee and Camels at the ready. Her columns provoked such a vast correspondence that her mailbags required delivery on special trucks.

But as busy as she was, Dorothy took a real interest in Jimmy's "unreasonable perceptions," as he called them. When the Sheeans came to live at the small house at Twin Farms the summer before the war—their daughter three, another baby on the way—Jimmy often went over to Dorothy's in the evening for whiskey and political debate lasting into the small hours. Ever more in those days, the world was vibrating inside him: he couldn't rid himself of its echoes. Dorothy understood that state perfectly well. The good reporter, she would say later, had instincts that extended beyond what was provable. It was a matter of feeling, of intuition. She'd often had the sensation herself of "talking with ghosts."

In the 1920s, asked by the *Atlantic Monthly* to write about the experiences of a woman correspondent, she had protested she wasn't interested in analyzing herself: "A good newspaper man, you know, looks out, and not in," she reproached the editor. A decade later, though, her own reactions—rarely dispassionate—became the staple of her column, as she scolded FDR, dissected the revolutionary qualities of fascism, vilified appeasers, invoked mothers and babies, and prophesied a crisis of civilization. *"What is coming to a head in Europe is not a decision about Europe. It is a decision about this planet."*

This "emotionalism" was one of the signal characteristics of Dorothy's work. "She ingests the cosmos and personalizes its pains," observed the *Saturday Evening Post*. It made for a very different experience from reading Lippmann's columns. Even when he and Dorothy sounded a similar alarm, as on the New Deal, which Lippmann, a onetime radical, thought a disturbing overreach of state authority, his perspective was Olympian and detached. He appealed to the enlightened man of affairs, who he presumed would, on balance, be persuaded by logic. He liked nothing better than to criticize Republicans and Democrats alike, evidence of his own impartiality.

In the face of dictatorship, Lippmann turned philosophical. It was a mass delusion inimical to reason, that would have to burn out. Shouting at the "pitch of a Wagnerian demigod" was futile, wrote Lippmann, a barely veiled criticism of his fellow columnist. Dorothy, meanwhile, issued calls to arms. The world hung on the edge of a terrible crisis. Civilization, she wrote, would have to take a "last stand." To some of her critics, her resort to "trembly emotion" was an indication that she wasn't thinking clearly. She got in a "tizzy," they said; she wrote hysterically, she betrayed a "simple, girlish faith" in her own intuition. Her analysis was partial, illogical: the opposite of objective.

A comment by Dorothy's friend Alice Roosevelt Longworth made the rounds. "Dorothy is the only woman in history who has had her menopause in public and made it pay."

By the way, had she heard that remark? Jimmy asked Dorothy one day.

Of course she had, Dorothy said, laughing: "Alice is so funny."

Far from denying the charge of emotionalism, Dorothy was making use of it. Objectivity built trust and established a loyal clientele of readers. It was good business—which was the cynical way of explaining why press barons elevated impartial reporting to the cardinal virtue of the newsroom after the First World War. But subjectivity, especially when delivered with fervor and conviction, sold just as well, if not better. Like Jimmy, she was creating a different sort of bond with readers. By mining how she *felt*, she was giving voice to the inchoate sentiments of many, many others. The world events around them, she felt certain, were causing a sea change in the way that ordinary people, even those seemingly removed from the action, lived.

What had taken place since the Great War, Dorothy said, was a drastic transformation of private life. She offered her most thorough explication of this idea in a 1937 essay entitled "The Dilemma of the Liberal." The problem she took up was one of liberalism's fundamental tenets: the idea that a person could live a private life that was truly private—free from state interference and free, too, to nourish a self that could develop independently according to its own lights, with the prerogative to participate in civic affairs. Her parents had taken this freedom for granted. Further, they assumed a harmony between their domestic and familial lives and the nation. Theirs was an integrated existence, coherent between private and public, confident in its precepts.

By contrast, she had no personal life any longer, at least not as she would once have understood the concept. "My whole personal life has become in a profound sense of secondary importance, and indeed it, so immediate and so practical, is the part which is dream-like and unreal, and the other, more remote, touching me personally so little, is the imminent, the overwhelming reality." She loved her husband and her son, she wrote. "Yet something comes between us. What comes between us is the whole of society." Lacking a sense of common purpose, appalled by both communism and fascism, she was never free of the world. She went to sleep worrying about it and woke up in the same state: "I cannot *bear* this world!"

DOROTHY WAS IDENTIFYING WHAT would become a leitmotif of the later 1930s and 1940s. "That was our modern dilemma, receiving the many into the one, having the world thrust with such violence into one's breast," wrote the novelist Isabel Bolton after the Second World War, parroting Jimmy's phrasing from a decade earlier. Some people drew a direct line between world events and their own troubles. Reflecting in her diary on the fall of France, the writer Marjorie Worthington linked the French surrender in June 1940 to the collapse of her marriage: "The Germans seem to be on the incredible way to wiping out England and France and I, in my personal little life, have almost wiped out everything or to put it more exactly, have almost been wiped out."

F. Scott Fitzgerald saw the same phenomenon. He viewed his wife Zelda's nervous breakdown, which started a few months after the Wall Street crash, as the societal collapse in miniature. There were, as Virginia Woolf put it in *Three Guineas* (1938), inseparable interconnections between the "tyrannies and servilities" of the public and private worlds. Those interconnections became Rebecca West's obsession: "It's the poisoning of the whole life by the spread of the Nazi spirit, which is something you encounter every day in every department of your life," she wrote a friend. She was off to the Balkans to write a book that will "relieve my feelings." She intended that book—*Black Lamb and Grey Falcon*—as an investigation of the relationship between the state of the soul (her own, her husband's, that of the people they encountered on their travels) and geopolitics.

According to Rebecca West, there were patterns of thinking that distinguished men from women. Occupied by their children and their homes, women were steeped in private life. As a consequence, it was rare that they could think beyond the call of the domestic, the familial, the practical, and the personal. They were—as the ancient Greeks had termed them—"idiots," meaning a private person disengaged from public life. But were men any better? Rebecca asked. They thought only in terms of public affairs; they charged, headlong, into violence; they favored abstraction and tipped too easily into unreality. They saw "the outlines of every object but not the details indicative of their nature." If women were idiots, then men were lunatics.

How *can* nations behave so selfishly? Rebecca demanded of her banker husband as they traveled through Herzegovina. They were talking about alliance politics and the outbreak of the Great War. If she rushed around, insisting that her friends join her in a pact without ascertaining the dangers around them, wouldn't she look foolish?

But individuals are not nations, my dear, and the rules that govern them are naturally very different, her husband objected impatiently.

Yes, I understand that, Rebecca relented, for her husband would never see her point. She was being an idiot, but he was a lunatic.

Rebecca, of course, was no idiot in the Greek sense or any other, and neither was Dorothy. Both were learned, according to the conventional definition of the term, and analytically minded. Their opinions on foreign affairs were solicited by establishment organs, such as *Foreign Affairs*, where few women appeared; in the newspapers, they were quoted as experts on the international crisis. At the same time, they insisted upon the salience of a woman's perspective— of feeling *and* knowledge, of the emotions *and* the mind—in a realm where such considerations were (and are) uncommon. They went further still. The world arena, they argued, was incomprehensible without some understanding of the private heart.

The struggle against fascism engulfed every aspect of Dorothy's life. Her "whole existence," as Jimmy would put it, became "bound up" with that fight; she could talk and think of nothing else. After eight months together in the United States, she and Christa Winsloe had parted in 1934. Dorothy and Red lived together, off and on, either at Twin Farms or at the house he'd bought in Bronxville, but he felt, he complained, like the tail on the end of her comet. Even his biggest hit in years—*It Can't Happen Here* (1935), the story of a homegrown American dictator—seemed to owe something to her. She hadn't done anything but read the proofs, she insisted to the reporters who asked her for a comment. However, the fact that he'd written a novel about the very scenario she was constantly warning about seemed to place him in her shadow.

"You will have to choose," Red told her one night after hearing her on the radio. "I can't stand this. You live and move in another world than mine. I haven't a wife."

To his friends he told the story of the morning when he and Dorothy were still in bed, and FDR called. Red handed the phone over to her, the cord stretched tight across his throat, and there he lay for a half hour. Poor Mr. Dorothy Thompson pinned to the bed, while his wife (the "Talking Woman," he called her) gabbed on with the president, making the country's foreign policy.

He still appeared in her column from time to time in the personage of The Grouse, the man whose hard-bitten apathy toward politics didn't get in the way of his brilliant monologues about human nature. But after 1937, they never again lived together. A few years later, she told a reporter that her son, Michael, then eleven, was the only man from whom she willingly took orders. In the late 1930s, her annual income—from columns, syndication fees, lecture tours, and broadcasts—was reportedly $103,000, or more than $1.8 million today.

COUNTERINTUITIVE AS IT WAS, the world crisis raging around them made the dynamics of private life seem all the more exigent. But how close could you get to the truth of what had happened between people? In September 1936, John and Frances left London for America, each of them determined to offer an account of what had befallen them in Europe. They'd spend most of the following year mulling over their marriage, offering rival versions of their intimate lives, pushing up against the boundaries of what could—and couldn't—be said in public.

At the going-away party that Jamie Hamilton threw for them at the London Ritz, Aldous Huxley drank what was said to be his first cocktail and the salonnière Lady Ottoline Morrell appeared in a dress of the 1890s, draped in ropes of pearls. The fifty thousandth copy of the British edition of *Inside Europe* had just rolled off the presses and the next day, John, Frances, Johnny, and his nursemaid,

Milla, were sailing for New York. Maybe they should stay, Frances had volunteered at the last minute. They didn't really understand the British Empire yet. It would be a shame to leave too soon.

John was determined to go home. The success of *Inside Europe* meant that he could finally quit his job. There really were forty-eight stars in the American flag, observed Johnny, who insisted on counting them on board the ship; he started to say "okeydoke" like an American kid. They stayed with Dorothy in Bronxville until they rented a place of their own: a house in Norwalk, Connecticut, on Long Island Sound, with a refrigerator practically the size of their London apartment and four bathrooms. They were close enough to New York to go in for the day but far enough to avoid distractions.

It was the house John had long ago promised Frances by the sea. There, he hoped, she would finally be able to do her work. She wasn't happy being just a wife and mother, she'd told him straight out. It wasn't enough for her—not nearly enough—that he quoted her in *Inside Europe*. "I find there's a definite vacancy that can be filled only by my writing something myself." He would help her, John promised. She could write a better book than he could, he was certain: "your insight, political & human, & gift of phrase amount to genius." All she was lacking was stick-to-it-iveness. "We make a good team, (everything I do is jointly yours & I know & appreciate it) but I'll be glad to give up my half of you." If she got on with her writing, he'd be so relieved. "I feel such a pig, sponging on your mind."

John was intent on some personal history of his own. He was going through the diary he'd kept in London, with the idea of a book about the "inner and outside" life of a foreign correspondent. His luncheon with Lady Rhondda and Aldous Huxley would go in it, as would the arguments about Abyssinia, morsels of Johnny's conversation, his pen portraits of Margot Asquith and the other luminaries he knew. John's diary was as effervescent as a glass of good champagne, said the *Atlantic Monthly*'s editor, where the first installments appeared; *Nash's Pall Mall Magazine* published excerpts in England. Evelyn Waugh thought it too ridiculous for words. In *Scoop,* he satirized John's effort as typical American foolishness, giving it the keyhole-peeping title *Under the Ermine* and choice lines of nonsense parading as insight: "The Archbishop of Canterbury who, it is well known, is behind Imperial Chemicals."

Even beyond Waugh's ridicule, John's diary project turned into a fiasco. Margot Asquith, herself a famously indiscreet autobiographer, called him up and demanded that he remove the description of her weeping at the prospect of another war. The tidbit that the King's mistress, Mrs. Simpson, had been present at Margot's luncheon party had to go, too. In fact, why did he have to mention her at all? If it had just been English people whom he'd offended, he could have chalked it up to American bumptiousness, but Jimmy, too, was furious with him. John had thought he'd written admiringly about his friend, calling him "perhaps the most remarkable American of my generation whom I know." He related a story Jimmy had told on himself, about Lytton Strachey's reaction to one of his magazine articles. "Of course it's very, very good but I don't believe for one moment that Jimmy Sheean really wrote it," Strachey had said.

What the bloody hell? Jimmy fired off from Kent, where he was recuperating from his breakdown. "You see, the fact is that I don't give very much of a damn what anybody says of me, but it was a little surprising to find you hacking away like that. In print." Not only was the account "inaccurate as hell," but it indicated a deep-seated hostility that he didn't know John felt toward him. "Makes it seem more and more impossible to know anything about anybody, or understand anything." Oh, never mind, Jimmy added, forget he'd said anything. It wasn't worth arguing about.

John decided his next book would be a novel, informing his disappointed agent that he wouldn't publish any more of his London diary. He was returning, with vigor, to the long-abandoned Credit-Anstalt novel—his marriage novel—to see what he could make of it. And after that, he'd write the next "Inside" book, this one on Asia, a study of imperialism. Each book, he had decided, would have a different theme: *Inside U.S.A.* would be about democracy, he told Cass Canfield.

Frances, too, was excavating her life, making fitful progress on her autobiography. To deal with her childhood—to write about what her stepfather had done to her—would require washing a lot of dirty linen in public. But wasn't that better than burying it as a skeleton in the closet? she told herself. After all, if everybody washed their dirty linen in public, could there be dirty linen any longer?

The piece she published in *Story* magazine was a test of this proposition: an exposé of her marriage with John and a portrait of their milieu. One of the country's most prominent "little magazines," *Story* was an incubator of talent; among the authors it launched in the 1930s were Tennessee Williams, Richard Wright, J. D. Salinger, and Joseph Heller. Frances's story centered on a married couple, both foreign correspondents; the wife is the narrator. They have a fizzy, affectionate rapport. Newly arrived in Vienna, they decide to throw a New Year's Eve party. Forty are invited and sixty crowd into the apartment, Hungarians and Croatians and opera singers, and plenty of reporters, drinking and dancing. It's too loud to say much beyond the standard greetings—a relief. "Then nobody could talk to you about their soul. Or ask you about your soul."

As the night wears on, midnight and then long past, there are the husbands (including the narrator's own) making passes at the young dancers, the expatriate teachers, the secretaries, the women who aren't their wives. The wives (the narrator, too) dance with men who flirt with them, and muss their hair, trying to shake their composure. She would tell her husband to accompany the seventeen-year-old Russian dancer home and keep a young man for herself, the narrator decides, cutting between an internal dialogue and the events around her. Her husband would enjoy it. What could be the harm? And then, almost immediately, she talks herself out of it. "You're a fool," she chastises, "you can't go back to that sort of thing."

By the way, I almost took the Russian girl home, her husband tells her before they go to bed.

So why didn't you? she asks.

"I wanted to stay with you more."

A friend of John's wrote from Portland, Oregon, to say that the really fashionable people in town kept that issue of *Story* magazine out so that everyone could see that they'd read it. By publicizing their old private habits of sexual one-upmanship, Frances had caused a semi-scandal, which was precisely what she intended. The obvious connection to their lives was the point. Does John Gunther's wife really hustle him into bed with other gals? the ultramodern people in Portland were asking.

The novel that John was writing about their Vienna years told a very different story. The foreign correspondent's wife was beautiful, intelligent—and virtuous. Still, something was missing in the marriage: she loved him more than he loved her. At nights, John's hero prowled the streets where the city's prostitutes plied their trade. He had love affairs with princesses and opera singers.

Frances had told him she wouldn't read his novel until he had a draft, on the grounds that he was too sensitive to her criticism. But secretly, she snuck peeks at his pages, and what she read infuriated her. *She* was the one who'd had affairs. John couldn't (likely because of his impotence), and now he'd taken his revenge by making it seem otherwise. How the people who knew them would laugh about that! The parts of the novel that dealt with the Credit-Anstalt and the work of foreign reporting weren't half bad. But as a book about marriage? That was what he claimed he wanted to write. Measured that way, "it is shit," she declared.

IN THE SUMMER OF 1937, John was preparing for his trip to Asia and the book he envisioned on imperialism. Of course, he *wanted* her to accompany him, he told Frances. But maybe she should stay home in Connecticut and do her own writing. That way, they wouldn't have to make any arrangements for Johnny. He'd need as much as eight months away to do the reporting, which was an awfully long time to leave an eight-year-old boy in the company of his nanny. Think how much writing she could get done if she wasn't gallivanting around the East with him.

He started to plan his trip, plotting a course that followed the best weather eastward to take in Palestine, Iraq, Iran, India, Burma,

Siam, Indo-China, the Straits Settlement, the Dutch East Indies, the Philippines, China, Manchuria, and Japan. He would visit fourteen countries and a hundred cities, interview nearly a thousand people, stay in sixty-eight hotels, and take nineteen airplanes. "I feel like a mouse nibbling at an elephant," John said to everyone who asked him about the book.

Whenever Frances heard him talk about the book, she got in a stew. Did John actually think he could write a good book without her? As he admitted—too jovially for her taste—he didn't know the first thing about Asia. When it came to writing about Europe, countries he knew well, he'd depended heavily on her analysis. So how on earth could he possibly tackle Asia successfully on his own?

He'd pilfered her ideas and she resented that. But the thought that he'd leave her behind was even more unbearable. What was she going to do on her own in Connecticut? Knit baby sweaters for the college bazaar? Meet the girls for lunch and an Old Fashioned? That sounded like death. She didn't feel dead. She was like a moon, she wrote, "all cold-dead outside but burning up all inside the middle and no release for that fire." Of course she would come along.

Milla would live with Johnny and Frances's mother in New York while John and Frances were away. They wrote a new will to ensure that Frances's mother had no rights of permanent guardianship, just in case. At noon, on October 31, 1937, with a party of friends to see them off, they boarded the SS *Conte di Savoia* with seventeen suitcases, including a canvas bag stuffed full of newspaper clippings and articles about the East. "The Gunthers, traveling light!" someone joked.

The sleek Italian ocean liner was bound for Naples, and from there they'd steam on to Cairo for a few days with the Surrealist photographer and model Lee Miller, a friend of John's since their expatriate Paris days, who had since moved to Cairo to live with her new husband, an Egyptian railroad tycoon. Then they'd travel to India via Palestine, by train down the coast, the land spring green and the orange trees in bloom, through the Sinai desert to the Suez Canal, where they would board another boat that would take them across the calm waters of the Red Sea to Djibouti. From Djibouti it was another week, crossing the Indian Ocean, to the port of Bombay.

One of the most satisfying moments in life happens on a ship, Frances thought. You wave to a receding shoreline and there, before you, is the miracle of open sky and sea and a world of possibility.

THE MOMENT HE ARRIVED in a new city, John called up a half-dozen people—local worthies, friends of friends. And these days, hundreds more telephoned him back. Would Mr. Gunther offer his opinions on the situation in Europe in a public lecture? Might he honor the *Bombay Chronicle* by giving its editor an interview? The Gunthers' suite of rooms at the Taj Hotel in Bombay was magnificent, done up in ivory and gold, but the phone hadn't stopped ringing since they arrived in India a few days earlier. It was driving Frances nuts.

The Taj's miles of marble corridors were a place where a person could pace and think, providing that she could tune out the monotonous hum of ceiling fans overhead. Steps up, steps down, through arches, past air shafts: white-clad servants squatting or sleeping in front of every doorway. How like the East, thought Frances: full of obsolete structures and wrong ideas. She had steeled herself, before they left, not to fall for all that claptrap about Eastern spirituality, its so-called ageless wisdom.

The Gunthers arrived in India in mid-December 1937, at a crucial juncture. Under the pressure of near-perpetual campaigns of civil disobedience, the British had conceded a measure of self-rule to India two years earlier, and the Indian National Congress, or Congress Party, with Jawaharlal Nehru at its head, and Gandhi as its spiritual leader, had triumphed in the elections held in February 1937. But when it came right down to it, how much power would the British be willing to share with Congress-dominated provincial governments?

In Bombay, John made plans to see everyone: the nationalists in

Gandhi's Congress Party who wanted to knock the British back to the white cliffs of Dover and the officials who were struggling to shore up the Raj. Plus the Parsi millionaires and the American capitalists, the Standard Oil types, the toothpaste purveyors and motor tire salesmen, who'd figure out how to turn a profit, whatever happened. One afternoon they lunched with Muhammad Ali Jinnah, head of the All-India Muslim League. (Extremely shrewd, but full of himself and evasive, Frances thought.) A few evenings later, they dined at the Byculla, the oldest British club in Bombay: the men in boiled shirts and their winter black dinner jackets, the swizz of soda on the whiskey glasses. Because Frances insisted on attending, the party took place on the porticoed veranda, as ladies were not permitted inside.

But oh, the acrimony that accompanied the canapés and curries! It seemed that everyone who hosted them in Bombay, British or Indian, had a score to settle. How dare the Indians talk of the British suppressing their freedom and democracy, fumed the wife of the editor of the *Times of India*. They'd never heard of either before they learned them from the British. It took us three hundred years to teach them, and now, it was as if the backward child who'd finally learned to walk sought fit to correct his elders. A British official of the Burmah Oil Company asked the Gunthers to consider how the fascist states would proceed if faced with such obstreperous subjects. How long, he demanded, would the campaign of nonviolent resistance have lasted if Gandhi had tried it against an Italian or a German colonial government?

Each Indian the Gunthers met, meanwhile, spent a lot of time claiming to be superior to all the other sorts of Indians. "And they are all wrong," Frances wrote her mother. Could Indians really forge a functioning government despite these divisions? The Congress politicians were champions at tactics and strategy. For John's benefit, they'd happily spin out for John marathon-length theories about how they'd thwart their British overlords. But when it came to their own plans for governing, they were frustratingly vague.

You must press them, force them to brass tacks, Frances exhorted John. What will they accomplish with their independence? Where would they find the native technical experts to take control of irrigation and electricity, radio and education, industries and roads? She'd been shocked by what they'd seen of the situation in the countryside: the mud huts, the people squatting by the side of the road, unblinkingly watching their motor car roar past. The nationalists, she thought, vastly underestimated the difficulties that independence would present.

At the Willingdon Club, founded after the war by the former governor of Bombay in order that elite Indians and British could mix, the mood was corrosive. The whiskeys-and-soda didn't do much to take the edge off. "Lots of Indians all hating the English. Lots of English all hating the Indians," Frances noted after an evening there.

Amid all the squabbling, though, John was in his element. He started off by asking the most basic sort of questions: information about tax revenue and party membership and the structure of government, things that he had already extracted from books. He then thanked his informant in the most profuse terms, flattering him as if he had really contributed something. John never contradicted a source, not even if he knew the man was lying. He listened carefully and looked delighted, and the atmosphere softened, and people started to tell him things that they wouldn't confide to another soul. In his perfectly natural manner, he made the Indians feel he was absolutely on their side and the British likewise. The joke was on both. The truth, Frances thought, was that "he is on no side—he does not really care for any side—all he cares about is his book."

SHE SENT JOHNNY POSTCARDS of the boats they sailed on and a leaf from a rubber tree, airmail stamps from Egypt and Iraq and tiny rectangular, ruffle-edged snapshots of them riding on camels at the pyramids. In her letters, she described inching through the Suez Canal in the steamer, the elephant fight they'd seen in Jaipur, their luncheon with the Aga Khan, who gave them a new fruit to taste, a mango it was called. It resembled a very fragrant, dripping peach. We miss you terribly, she told him.

Wash your hands after you play with those stamps, John chimed in, sending his million, billion kisses.

Johnny had hung their picture in his bedroom so that he could say good morning and good night to them. He'd played a trick on Milla, putting marbles in her bed one night, and they'd laughed about it. He was learning how to roller-skate, he wrote, had gone to see the picture *Snow White* at Radio City Music Hall and ridden on a pony named Sassy Susie. In school, they'd watched a movie about what it was like on the moon, volcanoes eighty-five miles across. If you tried to hold a conversation on the moon, you couldn't.

Also, he had a riddle for them. How does a locomotive hear?

We have pondered and pondered and asked everyone we met, Frances replied, and still we are stumped. How DOES a locomotive hear? Please answer immediately, she instructed.

Frances was fretting about the cough he'd had. Was he better? Would he please try very hard to keep very, very well? She underlined every word, adding an additional bar for emphasis. She had a surprise for him, which she'd just whisper very quietly in his ear. Wherever they went, they were collecting little statues of elephants for him in ivory and jade and sandalwood and guess what other material?

A locomotive hears with its engine-ears! he exclaimed. Was the elephant made of crystal or glass or maybe silver? He was perfectly fine, he wrote in every letter, but he missed them, very very very much. "When will you come back to me?"

THE GUNTHERS HAD BEEN in India for three weeks and had yet to see either Nehru or Gandhi. Gandhi was ill with one of the spells of high blood pressure that afflicted him, and Nehru had been traveling on Congress business. They had the expectant, half-anxious feeling of the theater audience waiting in Act Two for the entrance onstage of the play's leads, absent from Act One but constantly discussed. Nehru especially was a mystery. The son of one of India's most prominent lawyers, he had profited from every advantage the English extended to their wellborn subjects, including an education at Harrow and Cambridge, and admittance to the English Bar. But no sooner had he returned to India than he joined the battle against British rule. Since the start of the noncooperation campaign, Nehru had served more than five years in prison on charges of sedition. Few of the British whom John interviewed in Bombay had met him, even those who knew Gandhi.

"Have you seen Nehru yet?" was practically the first question the British asked John and Frances. "What's he like—what's he doing—what's he up to now?"

John didn't like to give speeches when he was reporting, but when the Congress Party asked him to appear the evening of January 5, 1938, at the Cowasji Jehangir Hall and Nehru himself offered to chair the lecture, he agreed. He would take as his subject "Modern Fictions in Politics," John told the reporter who came to interview him at the Taj that morning. He was still in his pajamas, bathrobe pulled hastily on, eyes bloodshot from a long night, and smoking his fourth cigarette. He wouldn't have anything to say about Indian politics, he said. He didn't know enough yet to comment intelligently. The phone rang constantly. "Yep. Am lecturing this evening. Mr. Nehru is coming. Yep . . . Dine with me . . . Yep. See you tomorrow then."

By six o'clock, when John and Frances arrived at the Cowasji Jehangir Hall, the floor and the horseshoe-shaped balconies were packed to their capacity of twelve hundred and on the verandas, many more were clamoring for entry. The domed, neo-Gothic hall, with its expanses of patterned encaustic Minton tiles, was hot and noisy. Dozens of electric fans whirred overhead, the doors remained open for the crowd on the verandas, and the rattle of the streetcars and of pedestrians talking outside added to the din. Nehru took the stage and appealed to the audience to stand where they were, not to try to press forward. He had to shout to be heard.

Nehru was accustomed to addressing crowds of thousands in the open air, but not especially skilled at it, Frances would observe. He looked out of place, for one thing. He was dressed as he was always photographed: a white Gandhi cap pointed in front and back, the homespun spotlessly white dhoti and kurta, the vest buttoned over it. But he seemed remote, as if he were dressed to play a part. He was handsome—exceptionally so—an aristocratic, symmetrical face with an aquiline nose, full lips, and grave, tired eyes. His wife had died a little less than a year before of tuberculosis in a Swiss sanatorium, aged thirty-six; the British had suspended his prison sentence a few months early so that he could see her. After her death in February 1936, he returned to lead the Congress Party to victory in the elections the following year.

Though Nehru was tall, John stood at least a head higher, and that night in comparison, John seemed even heartier and more boyish than usual. Nehru welcomed John warmly, noting what an honor it was that the famous American journalist had consented to address the Bombay public. And John in turn complimented Nehru's autobiography—a remarkable book, he said. John would speak tonight about the European situation and wanted the audience to note the disturbing development of what they might term "fictions" in politics. It had become the fashion these days to call Italy, Germany, and Japan the "Have-Not" countries, as if their lack of colonies explained their rapacious desire for conquest. But were the fascist countries in fact threatened? Did they need more raw materials? And why were the dictators always pushing for more babies if their countries were already overcrowded? Mussolini and Hitler were prisoners of their own desire for prestige, and they claimed colonies for the purpose of political blackmail. It would be the job of the democracies, Britain, France, and the United States, John argued, to call their bluff.

The audience applauded John's lecture politely, but it was Nehru's closing remarks that drew the attention of the morning papers. For the critical observer, Nehru had said, there was an essential point that could no longer be ignored: that is, the "few hundred odd million people who were considered the possible property of one or the other Power." The problem was not just the "Have-Nots," but the "Haves," the British and the French. He thought a reckoning between the "Have" and "Have-Not" powers of Europe was unlikely. The real battle would be between the "Haves" of Europe and the real "Have-Nots" of the world—or, as the reporter for the nationalist paper, the *Bombay Chronicle,* put it more pointedly the next morning, between the "Haves" and the "countries which 'have been had.'" Mr. Gunther had the "open-hearted—and open-throated!—cordiality of an over-sized school boy." But his assessment of the world situation was completely blind to the role of imperialism. "Imperialism is the skeleton in the cupboard of Western 'civilisation.' Is it possible that like all 'civilised' men John Gunther too is superstitious about exposing it in public?"

John was a good sport about the criticism, bemused rather than offended: he was learning how the world looked outside the European capitals and America. The doors to the inner sanctum of the Indian National Congress swung a little wider open, the nationalists sniffing him out as an American reporter who could be cultivated. He and Frances had an invitation to the salon hosted by the imposing politician and poet Sarojini Naidu, who'd been by Gandhi's side in his campaigns of nonviolent resistance and had served a term as president of the Congress. John took to Mrs. Naidu: she liked to laugh—a rarity, he said, in an Indian politician. And she arranged for John to see Gandhi, warning him not to talk about politics. The Mahatma's doctor had forbidden it. Gandhi was at Juhu Beach to rest for the month. It was just a half hour's drive from their hotel.

Gandhi was sitting up in bed when John and Frances arrived the following day, a dozen Congress bigwigs, Nehru included, with him. He didn't look so fragile, Frances thought. His arm was plump and his naked torso gave the impression of vigor. He greeted the Gunthers delightedly with that famous toothless grin, and he and John talked about newspapermen they both knew while the Congress crowd looked on, mesmerized. Political questions foreclosed, John touched on other subjects. They'd had a mango out of season, he told Gandhi, with the Aga Khan, who said he was the only man in the world who could provide one. "Did the Aga Khan say that? Did he say that?" demanded Gandhi. The Mahatma snapped his fingers, and two servants brought a mango. An "unbelievable combination of Jesus Christ and Tammany Hall and your father," as John later described Gandhi to his readers.

Gandhi suggested that Frances take a walk on the beach with Nehru, Mrs. Naidu, and her daughter. With his hat off, Frances saw that Nehru was bald. He looked unhappy and uneasy, such a contrast to Gandhi, who was serenity itself. What, she wondered, must Nehru feel about Gandhi? The old man was practically a deity to his people. Crops will grow, the villagers believed, if the name of Gandhi was invoked. But Nehru had little truck with Gandhi's mysticism and, she had gleaned, he was also frustrated by the Mahatma's willingness to make deals with the British.

What, Frances asked Mrs. Naidu, does Gandhi like best? "Truth," Mrs. Naidu replied.

And Nehru? "A fight."

And what do they both hate most? "Lies."

THE BRITISH PRESS OFFICER who met John and Frances in New Delhi, shortly after they arrived in the new capital, urged that they be accorded the royal treatment. The Viceroy ought to invite them to lunch, and plan on private chat afterward. John, said the official, was absolutely the most important journalist who'd visited India in years—"British or Foreign." The stakes were high. If Gunther came away with the right impression of British rule, he could be the "finest pro-British propagandist in the world." He'd already met Gandhi and Nehru and hadn't been swayed by their vitriol. He wanted, he said, to hear the British side of things. Oh, yes, and don't neglect Mrs. Gunther, the press officer advised. Not only is she intelligent. She obviously wields a great deal of influence over her husband.

As the British authorities trundled out military and legal dignitaries for John to interview in Delhi and prepared (at his request) a dossier of material on what the British had done for India, Frances set out on her own line of interrogation. New questions were occurring to her, questions for which there had to be, somewhere, answers of fact.

"What is the wealth of Indians in India?" she asked.

The British had risked their capital in India, came the answer. They had blazed a trail for the "cautious" Indian businessman. India could never have developed its railroads, its industries, its irrigation systems, without British wealth.

So what is the wealth of the British in India? she pressed.

Stonewalled as she tried to establish even the basic facts about the economy of the Raj, she became livid about the barefaced lies the British told. Over cocktails at the assistant district commissioner's house, the grandson of the former governor of Bombay blathered about millions of Indian languages (this was the old argument that Indians were too fractured ever to rule themselves). He proclaimed that Gandhi had been born in South Africa, not (as was the fact) in the Indian coastal town of Porbandar. No one at the party contradicted him.

When the British finance minister assured the Gunthers there were no natives who were competent to manage the Indian economy, she challenged him: Which Indians have you tried to train to take your job?

In some sense, Frances's conversion to the cause of Indian nationalism wasn't at all unusual. The more Americans saw firsthand of British colonial rule in the 1930s and 1940s—the poverty of the country, the lack of infrastructural development—the more critical they became. What had the British actually been doing in India for hundreds of years? The country was still hopelessly backward, its people illiterate, sickly, and in rags. For British authorities, the nonstop criticism from Americans was maddening, hence the efforts they put into cultivating John. Every prominent American who comes here, the viceroy fulminated, turned into a disciple of Gandhi's or Nehru's. The Americans were obstinately ignorant about the need for a firm hand in India. They had an emotional attachment to the idea of independence.

In pinpointing emotion as the problem, the British authorities meant to be disparaging but they were not entirely wrong. As Frances proceeded from cocktail party to interview, the conflicts she saw around her implicated all the thinking she'd been doing on the subject of unequal relations. The British had exploited the Indians—this she now saw very clearly. However, both sides had been enfeebled, even ruined by their interaction with each other. It was just like her relationship to John. She'd conspired in her own effacement by feeding John her "priceless" ideas; John himself had been weakened, both intellectually and emotionally, by his dependence on her.

The British couldn't understand why the Indians wanted to be free. But we treat them so well! the Gunthers heard again and again. What the British couldn't fathom was that whether they treated the Indians badly or well was beside the point: they wanted to be free. "The moment the Indian people face self-rule without fear," Frances wrote, "that moment, the British Raj is over."

IN THEIR DELHI HOTEL ROOM, Frances took up her green fountain pen and a sheet of paper from the writing desk. She had a confession to make to John.

"My dear," she started, "This is like one of these Indian questions—in a way it isn't at all important, & in a way it is."

Everywhere they had been, centuries-old relations of domination and subordination were unraveling, and rapidly. It was as if the deepest human emotions lay there raw and sinister on the surface.

Hers, too. Six weeks in India had brought into focus what she had to do. She'd meant to talk to him about it last year and the year before last and even in 1935, but first he was writing *Inside Europe*, every night at the office, and then they were moving, and then he'd started a novel, and it never seemed the right moment.

"Anyhow, now when you're between books seems the best time to mention it. If I had T.B. or something, you'd take care of me, or if you had, I'd take care of you."

She couldn't lie to him any longer. After all they'd seen in India, he had to understand that she couldn't continue on as they had been. She should be talking to him, rather than writing a letter, Frances acknowledged. But she was ashamed of what she had to say, and afraid.

"You've been impotent, I've been impotent. We've both been, & I still am." That was her bombshell. Three years earlier, she'd started lying to John about her orgasms—"getting orgs.," as she put it. It was at Stekel's urging, she explained, that she first started to lie. According to Stekel, John's sexual troubles could only be cured if he believed that Frances had orgasms. Unless she cooperated, Stekel had told her, John wouldn't get well.

Even by the free-and-loose standards of early psychoanalysis, this was a startling prescription: an analyst seeing both husband and wife and prevailing upon the woman to fake her orgasms. It was in tune, though, with Stekel's understanding of the dynamics of sex. A woman's pleasure was necessarily subordinate to the man's: her satisfaction derived from his and, in a well-adjusted marriage, depended upon it. Stekel may also have suspected Frances of using her failure to climax as a form of dominance over John. "Sexual anaesthesia is an important weapon in the sex struggle," he'd advised in his textbook on female frigidity. "There are women who refuse to be made happy."

Stekel's admonition had left Frances in a bind. No matter how well John treated her, she was hemmed in by the weight of her lies, her frustration, the feeling of being thwarted. If only she could be at ease with him. If only he could help to cure her. There was another thing, too. When he let her help him with his work, she'd felt "a kind of intellectual org.," but now that he wanted to work on his own, that, too, was lacking.

"Why I need to tell you this—why I can't go on as I have—I suppose it's because either, if it's on your account. I must think of you as a weak child wanting coddling, & I don't. I think of you as a strong man; or, if it's on my account, I must think of myself as a liar, with no longer a sort of medical-moral obligation to lie, or a coward, afraid of losing your favor, practically an Indian gov. official, evasion begins pervade whole behavior. I'd rather stand or fall by the damned sacred facts. I'll stand if you'll help me by believing in me & in yourself & in us together."

It was partly a plea for help, partly a declaration of independence. John preserved Frances's confession among his papers, but there's no record as to how he responded to it. Only this: in all the rest of his extensive archive, which includes thousands of scrap notes—fragments of memories, things people told him, embarrassing feelings, revealing dreams—he never mentions Frances's confession. But it didn't go unnoticed. Years later, when John's second wife, Jane, organized his papers, she added a note: "Significant letter from Frances."

AS INDIAN NATIONALISTS VIED with British officials for the Gunthers' attention, Nehru sought to advance the Congress Party's case. If John and Frances wanted to understand Congress's appeal in the villages, Nehru told them, they ought to come north to the Frontier Province, where he would address a meeting in the city of Peshawar, in late January 1938. He'd speak to the crowd in Hindustani, but John and Frances would nevertheless get a sense of the proceedings.

By train the trip from Delhi to Peshawar in the North-West Frontier, the mountainous province between Afghanistan and India, took thirty-seven hours. It was an arid land of craggy shale and limestone, sparsely populated. Nehru spoke at Sharda Park, on the outskirts of Peshawar, with the Hindu Kush mountains in view. There were at least ten thousand people there, Frances judged, men of all different types: strapping and bone-thin, beards, clean-shaven, in rags, in silk, in dhotis, in trousers. She couldn't understand what Nehru said, of course, but his manner was, as in Bombay, distant and formal. He looked, she wrote, as if he were "addressing a select group of the Cambridge Union on a rather abstruse dull subject, not chosen by him, but dutifully accepted and conscientiously covered." Still, he held his audience rapt: Frances could see it in their faces.

John elected to return to Delhi after Nehru spoke. He had more people to see in the capital. That evening, Frances had dinner with Nehru—Jawahar, she started to call him, as everyone in India did. He was off the next morning on a trip with Abdul Ghaffar Khan, the great Pashtun tribal leader, known as the "Frontier Gandhi" for his commitment to nonviolent resistance and the loyalty he inspired among the Afridi villagers. They'd drive down from Peshawar to Kohat, where the Congress would be meeting.

"Why don't you come along with us?" Nehru asked her. On the way, they'd visit the Afridi tribal villages, a trip that would take two days. They'd sleep in tents both nights. Frances would of course have her own accommodations. She wired John in Delhi, telling him to expect her a few days later than they'd planned.

WHEN THE GUNTHERS CHECKED into their Hong Kong hotel a few weeks later, a letter in unfamiliar handwriting was waiting for Frances. Nehru wanted to thank her for the photos she'd sent of their trip to Kohat—especially that one of his hands, he teased. He'd studied them intently.

He was back at home, at the family estate in Allahabad, and setting off shortly for a holiday in the foothills of the Himalayas. He wouldn't have time for Mount Kailash or Lake Manasarovar, the sacred sites they had talked about visiting together, someday. That future was like a dreamland, wasn't it? Still, he would be thinking about her across the "the snowy barrier which separates us," to which he added, wistfully: "Is it always desirable to achieve one's heart's desire?"

WARPATH

—

I N THE FALL OF 1937, AS THE GUNTHERS HEADED TO INDIA, John's old crush Mickey Hahn hunkered down in Shanghai. At the end of November, the city had fallen to the Japanese after months of fighting. No, Mickey assured her mother, she was *not* staying in Shanghai "to Be Thrilled." Still less was she there "To Help (who?)." The August air raids that left Shanghai looking like a battlefield had scared the hell out of her. And she was heartsick and angry all the time. The city was surrounded by Japanese soldiers, cut off from the rest of China, an island of antiaircraft guns and sandbags, of dust and ruins and tangled iron, of terrified refugees with their lumpy bundles coming and going.

It's the start of a new world war, proclaimed the visiting newspapermen, Knick among them, who crowded into the nightclub on the ninth floor of the Cathay Hotel to watch the aerial dogfights between the Japanese and Chinese flyers. "You're all vultures," Mickey told Knick, who called her to say that the Chinese resistance was collapsing under the pressure of the Japanese onslaught. Nanjing was falling—hundreds of thousands of Chinese civilians had been massacred, girls and women were being raped. At this rate, said Knick, the Japanese would soon have all of China under their thumb.

Men liked war, Mickey realized: it made them feel important and alive. She hated it but she was sticking around, too.

She'd been in Shanghai for more than two years now. In March 1935, when her boat had docked, Mickey hadn't planned to stay longer than a weekend. She'd been on her way to the Congo, via the Far East, a reprise of a trip to Africa she'd made in 1930; she'd thought of becoming an anthropologist. But Shanghai, she found, suited her. Glamorous and disreputable, the city—the fifth-largest in the world—was built on trade and exploitation. The year Mickey arrived, the Shanghai police collected off the streets the corpses of twenty-nine thousand people who had starved to death. A few miles away, in the glittering International Settlement, Mickey was becoming a staple of the society columns: sheathed in silver and green lamé at the opening of Ciro's nightclub, addressing the American Women's Club on the subject of the short story. Her performance in Aristophanes's comedy *Lysistrata* caused a minor sensation. She'd played the heroine who organizes a sex strike of Greece's women to force an end to the Peloponnesian War.

In 1938, with more than a million refugees now crammed into the officially neutral zone of the International Settlement, Mickey remained in Shanghai, weaving her baby-blue Chevrolet coupé through the clutter of rickshaws. She was teaching English, studying Chinese, and jobbing as a reporter. The car was a present from one of the richest men in Asia, the Anglo-Jewish magnate Sir Victor Sassoon; he was rumored to be her lover. To the horror of Shanghai's white residents, Mickey had also acquired a Chinese paramour. A son of the former mayor of Shanghai, Zau Sinmay belonged to the city's intelligentsia; he had spent a couple of years at Cambridge. By the time Mickey met him, he had a wife and five children and lived in a large, genteelly decaying, brick gabled house overrun with servants.

In the stories she sent to the *New Yorker* about her time in the city, she called Sinmay "Mr. Pan," telling of his spendthrift gambler of a father, his servant troubles, the literary friends in his circle who took on the rhetorical styles of their favorite Western authors. Her sketches were gently comic, populated by silk-gowned men who stayed up all night pontificating and puffing on opium pipes. Her editors pleaded for more "Mr. Pan." And yet, Mickey disdained the conventions of the traveler's profile in exotic locales—the notion, as she put it, that "one Chinese can be all Chinese things to all men." In her telling, Sinmay and his friends, his wife even, were as individual, as idiosyncratic as Mickey's own family in Chicago.

As for the scandal of the relationship, that didn't bother her. She was an "exhibitionist," she said. She wasn't entirely sure that she liked being Sinmay's concubine—it was like "playing marbles with quicksilver," she told her sister Helen—but when he suggested marrying her as his second wife, a practical arrangement to safeguard some property, she readily agreed. She was deluged with callers: washed-up European refugees peddling fur coats and teacups, Chinese patriots who wanted to use her back bedroom to transmit revolutionary messages by radio. She was dangerously adrift.

Under the circumstances, the news that John and Frances were arriving in Shanghai from India didn't in the least please her. "The Gunthers are horribly almost here," she wrote her mother in April 1938.

The last time Mickey had seen John was in Paris, a decade earlier, when she'd needed an abortion. She'd picked up a French lieutenant, she said, maybe more than one. John and Frances had just been married. John helped Mickey find a doctor, and then propositioned her. Under other circumstances, she might have accepted, out of curiosity if nothing else. But the timing irked her and so did the abrupt way he made his approach.

"Will you sleep with me?" he asked.

Now *that* was a new one, she'd thought. No man had ever come right out and just petitioned her so plainly. Against the points he gained for candor, though, she deducted more for artlessness. Referring to his repeated efforts to woo her sister Helen, she told him: "It would be a shame for you, to be turned down twice in the same family." But then she did just that. His advances didn't even rate a mention in the book she published the following year, *Seductio Ad Absurdum: The Principles and Practices of Seduction, A Beginner's Handbook.*

WHEN JOHN ARRIVED AT Mickey's place, he was taken aback by her appearance. Her clothes hung loose and her skin was sallow from smoking too much opium. In bed with her was a white gibbon whom she'd named Mr. Mills. The simian dipped his hand in the tea.

Come and meet my husband, she said to John, leading him to the cottage next door. It was dark and crowded, a jumble of chests and tables, newspapers in piles in the corners, and children underfoot. Zau Sinmay had a long face, like Jesus, and you could count the hairs in his wispy reddish beard. He was reclining on some sort of divan, smoking opium. John took three pipes, sucking the smoke deeply into his lungs and trying not to cough. He didn't feel a thing.

Frances was back at the hotel, nursing a sore throat. It was just as well to have a few hours on his own with Mickey. He had seen that Frances and Nehru were writing letters to each other but apart from a few passages of Nehru's she had read aloud, Frances kept the content of their correspondence to herself. But when John jokingly told a fellow reporter that his wife was "a Nehru fan," she became furious with him. She'd barely spoken to him in days. It didn't help matters that his asthma, which had disappeared after Stekel's course of treatment, had returned in full force once they left India—a sign, perhaps, of the effect that Frances's confession about orgasms had on him. Shortly after arriving in China, he'd spent a week in the hospital in Hankou, panting and wheezing.

He had so many questions for Mickey. Could the Japanese and the Chinese tell each other apart? If so, how? And when someone invoked "Chinese civilization," what exactly did they mean? It was exhilarating to learn so much but daunting to know so little. Really, the book ought to be called *Outside Asia.* It wasn't a lack of material that was stymieing him. Quite the contrary. Because of the success of *Inside Europe,* he had undreamed-of access to Asia's leaders. Including Generalissimo Chiang Kai-shek, the leader of the Republic of China.

Since the Japanese invasion, Chiang had refused requests for interviews, but for John, he made an exception. He and his wife would receive Mr. and Mrs. Gunther in his pink villa for exactly an hour; tea would be served. The message Chiang wanted to convey to the West was clear enough: the Chinese wouldn't stop fighting until the last Japanese soldier left the country. But as dutifully as John gathered information about Chiang's preference for classical music and his abstemiousness, his shrewd sense of patience, and his devotion to his wife, the Wellesley-educated Mei-ling Soong, the portrait he was trying to draw of the Generalissimo didn't come to life. He fumbled for comparisons: Chiang was like Masaryk in that he was full of paradoxes, though he didn't otherwise resemble the Czech leader. The best line on Chiang came from Frances: "There is Methodism in his madness," she quipped. John used it, crediting her.

The Chinese never sweat, you know, Mickey told him. He wrote it down and added it to the miscellaneous material he was gathering. (She was pulling his leg and when the book was published with that detail included, she was gleeful.)

One afternoon in Shanghai, after Frances made it very plain to her that she wouldn't mind, Mickey finally did go to bed with John. Her moral standards were somewhat attenuated in those days, she'd say many years later. She always liked Frances much more than John, but she'd be grateful to him for one thing. He urged her to write a book about Madame Chiang Kai-shek and her sisters, the extraordinary trio of Soong siblings. Between them, as John would say, they'd managed the feat of "marrying a continent": two of China's leaders (the Generalissimo and Sun Yat-sen, father of the Chinese Republic) as well as the country's leading banker. John pestered an editor at Doubleday to offer Mickey a contract on the book. And inadvertently he helped in another way as well. His depiction of the Soongs in *Inside Asia* so aggravated the sisters that they were eager to talk to Mickey and clear their name.

———

AT HER HONG KONG hotel, Frances had a ready answer to the question Nehru had posed in his letter about achieving one's heart's desire. But first, she had to put him straight about a subject that had been preoccupying her since she left India: the serious shortcomings of the nationalist movement. She and John had *finally* received the Indian National Congress's pamphlets—the ones that they'd requested months earlier. Did he understand the sort of impression the Congress created? It was hopelessly disorganized, "an unwieldy combination of an amateur theatrical society and a county fair." How could the Indians ever hope to beat the British that way?

The fault, she was certain, was Gandhi's. He was a vain crackpot with absurd ideas about nonviolence, a preener who liked to have people, especially women, fussing around him. How on earth had he bewitched millions of people? Surely Nehru understood that he—and not that third-rate medicine man—was the future of India. Jawahar had been the prince in waiting so long that he was growing dreamy and stale, fiddling with the keys to the kingdom rather than turning them in the lock. He was entirely too passive, too comfortable in his role as the promising young man. He wasn't even that young any longer! If the freedom movement was to have a chance, it was imperative that Nehru take charge.

She had all manner of advice to offer, sending on pages and pages, without a moment of self-doubt. Dispense, for God's sake, with those absurd dhoti you wear. They look like diapers, "convenient for promiscuous amour in a mudhut." The British won't take you seriously unless you wear proper pants. You need a press officer, a cadre of bodyguards who can whisk you in and out of gatherings. Meet with the viceroy: he's not that smart and you'll outfox him. Don't let on that there's any tension between you and Gandhi or you and Jinnah and his Muslim League, for that matter: the British are hoping to divide and conquer. Stock your party with pragmatists, men who know how to build factories and electrical plants—and use force, if necessary.

And why was he going to Europe to meet with English liberals? It was high time that he shake off the remnants of Harrow and Cambridge: "England, that wily old bitch, has made of you not only economic slaves but political gentlemen." Rather than see friends in England, he should travel around Asia to make common cause with the other nationalist leaders. They needed to develop a coordinated strategy against the European bloodsuckers. "Make India free, then weekend in Sussex," she concluded.

This was the same way she'd started with John: lambasting him and then settling into the role of power-behind-the-throne. She was beginning to think she was wasting her talents on her husband. Steering Nehru would be a much more consequential enterprise. "What a swell job I could do with him my god."

She knew perfectly well the magnificent things that Gandhi and the Congress had accomplished. But they belonged to the past and he to the future. He was the best mind in Asia, maybe one of the half-dozen best minds in the world. He couldn't shirk, he couldn't loaf. He had to act.

"I wanted so very much to sleep with you," she wrote him of that night in Peshawar they spent together. "Don't write me polite drivel like 'Is it always desirable to achieve one's heart's desire?' You know damn well it is," she rebuked. "Don't be literary—address me in your simple, lucid style, as tho I were a peasant mass meeting."

It was astonishing cheek, but Frances knew her audience. Nehru liked teasing. The "Jewel of India," his wife and sisters had called him, mockingly: "Oh, Jewel of India, what time is it? Oh, Embodiment of Sacrifice, please pass the bread."

Six months before he met Frances, Nehru had engaged in an extraordinary public dissection of his own character in the Calcutta *Modern Review*. Under a pseudonym, he'd written a character sketch of himself of just the sort that John had perfected in *Inside Europe*. It was a biting self-analysis of the danger that Nehru posed to the independence movement. He was possessed of a "formidable conceit," a will to power that, in a crisis, threatened to betray his fine talk of democracy and socialism. He would never become a Hitler or a

Mussolini: he was too much of a snob and an aristocrat for that. But his character—shot through with "strange complexes and repressions" and "longings which he dare not acknowledge even to himself"—was far more equivocal than his adoring followers recognized.

As little as Frances knew about India, Nehru had to concede, she wasn't wrong about some things, himself included. He *was* impatient with Gandhi's mysticism; like her, he preferred a scientific sort of socialism. Moreover, he found Gandhi's rigorous celibacy discomfiting, even distasteful. He considered himself more of a pagan type. After his wife's death, he kept company with strong-minded women, among them Mrs. Naidu's daughter, Padmaja, a fellow freedom fighter, and after the Second World War, Edwina Mountbatten, the wife of the last viceroy of India, whom he counted on to talk "sanely and confidently" to him amid the devastation of Partition. His affection for Lady Mountbatten has generated endless speculation, but it was his relationship with Frances that set the mold.

"What delightful letters you write," he exclaimed to Frances: "vivid, vital, impertinent, aggressive and intimate." No doubt his own efforts would disappoint her. He was a Victorian—practically a mid-Victorian—hemmed in by tradition and restraints. Though he could appreciate the "raciness" of her language, "how in hell (observe the progress I am making) am I to get rid of my background of tradition and the thousands of years that cling to me?" Maybe he could learn some American slang, he suggested, "if I had the good fortune to be with you for a while."

In the next months, as she and John traveled farther east to the Philippines, to China and Japan, it seemed to her that she was going in entirely the wrong direction—away from Nehru. But she missed Johnny. In Manila, the president of the Philippine Telephone Company organized a telephone call for them home to New York, and to hear Johnny's voice at the other end of the line—so childlike, so far away—made them all the more eager to get back.

"No, we do not know how to put a match in water without getting it wet—we wish we did!—please tell us at once!" Frances wrote

Johnny. Traveling on the RMS *Empress of Japan* to Honolulu, and then on to New York, they were home by June 1938. All over the world, the matches were sparking to flame.

BY 1938, AS DOROTHY, Jimmy, and Knick saw it, the next world war had already started. Most people—especially most Americans—just didn't know it yet. Try to tell a deaf man about the avalanche rushing down the hill, said Jimmy. Not only does he not see it or hear it, but when you grab his arm to pull him out of the way, he won't believe you.

"This is the beginning of Europe's Thirty Years War," Knick had written John from Spain two years before. In the summer of 1936, at the start of General Franco's uprising, Knick had raced there, chartering a plane from Toulouse at four o'clock in the morning. The pilot had just enough fuel to get to the city of Burgos. Even from the air, crossing from the south of France to northern Spain, the line between peace and war was obvious. The beaches on the French side were crowded with holidaymakers. Over the Spanish border, the quiet was uncanny: not a car in sight, nor a person on the streets.

Burgos was Franco territory, though they hadn't known that when they took off. Not, as Knick would say a few months later, that the distinction between Franco's "Whites" and the Republican "Reds" made much difference to him any longer. In Toledo, he'd watched the survivors of the siege of the Alcázar—starved and clay-faced—crawl out of the crumbled fortress, their dead piled up in shell holes. So far as Knick was concerned, both sides were locked in a cycle of killing, reprisals, futility, and inhumanity. As for the avowals of neutrality emanating from the other European powers: they were hogwash. French planes were bombing Franco's troops and in Seville he ran into the Italian air force pilot whom he'd met on the beach in Ostia; fresh from Abyssinia, the man was instructing rebel flyers. "You ought to be here," Knick wrote John. "Get a lungfull of corpse & it dont seem so funny."

Knick's articles on Spain were awful, John thought. His sympathies were wholly on the Republican side. From his friend Jay Allen, he'd heard firsthand reports of Franco's massacre of thousands of Republicans in the town of Badajoz, near the Portuguese border. One weekend in Connecticut, before the Gunthers left for Asia, John and Knick had it out. That stuff Knick was writing about the "Reds" and their "atrocities" was straight out of Hearst's playbook. The Spanish Republicans weren't all "Reds": they included democrats, and liberals, and yes, some anarchists and Communists.

How could Knick possibly make any sort of moral equivalence between those people and Franco? Franco was a fascist, no better than Mussolini; he'd set out to topple a democratically elected government. Most Spaniards wanted a republic, the proof of which was that their forces—contrary to Knick's predictions—hadn't collapsed. After nearly a year of fighting, the Republicans were still holding strong in Madrid and Barcelona. It would be bad enough if Knick was writing to please Hearst, but this was worse. "You're like Goering," John burst out.

For Knick, though, the issue was not so much Franco as the fatuous sympathy that John (and more so Frances and Jimmy) still displayed for the Soviet Union and the whole idea of a class struggle. "Red" and "White," he said to John, no longer had any "rational content." Stalin's vicious purge of his political opponents—the show trials of the old Bolshevik leadership, the mania of denunciations that was gripping the populace—rendered null and void whatever claim to moral superiority Communism might once have had. The Reds had more in common with the fascists than ever before. In fact, it seemed to Knick entirely plausible—and in Hearst's *Cosmopolitan* he wrote an article predicting as much—that Hitler and Stalin would join in a pact to divide Europe up between them.

Still, when Knick returned to Spain in the spring of 1937, his sense of the balance between right and wrong was shifting. The aerial bombardment of Guernica's defenseless civilians in April gave the lie to any equivalences between Franco's forces and the Republicans. It was German flyers who'd destroyed Guernica; Spain was serving as a testing ground for Nazi tactics of terror bombing. Then there were the thirty hours Knick had spent imprisoned in a dungeon cell, thirty feet underground, courtesy of Franco's goons. Despite Knick's sympathetic reporting the previous year, Franco hadn't, in fact, been eager for his return; the war was going badly for the rebels, a fact he wanted to keep quiet. Barred from entering Spain, Knick had crossed the border anyway. He was arrested a couple of days later. "This is a monstrous mistake," Knick shouted through the three-inch, square opening in the cell's iron door.

The San Sebastián prison was the worst he'd ever seen, an inch of filth on the floor, blood smeared on the walls, a rank smell. That's the smell of death, said his cellmate, an anarchist. I will be shot tonight, the man told Knick. When they come, they'll bind my wrists with twine, and that will be the sign. Knick tried to distract the man from the sounds of the footsteps echoing down the prison corridors. Did he have children? Knick asked. Did his wife know he was in prison? How did he think the war would turn out? When the footfall stopped outside their cell door, and three guards appeared to lead the anarchist away, the man went stoically, his wrists bound in front of him, without turning back.

"I realized I had never known before what this war was like," Knick wrote. Later on, he figured out that it was the Gestapo that had been behind his arrest. It took dogged lobbying by his friend Randolph Churchill, a fellow newspaperman and Winston's son, to get him released. Now that he was out, he wouldn't have missed a stay in that dungeon for the world, Knick told his editor. In the aftermath of the adventure, though, he and Randolph had agreed to get on the wagon for the next eight months. Whoever fell off first, even with a drop of beer, had to pay the other $1,000. He'd been dry for two weeks already; it was the longest he'd gone without a drink in years.

Though Franco personally apologized to him about the prison, and granted him an exclusive interview as compensation, Knick nevertheless settled scores. In a piece filed from London to evade Spanish censorship, he treated his readers to a specimen of the table talk of Franco's press officer: a grandee, the seventeenth in his noble line. They'd shoot fifty thousand Reds as soon as Franco's army got to Madrid, the officer told Knick. Why should anyone mind? Spain had two races: rulers such as himself, and the rest, who deserved nothing better than slavery. The officer opposed public schools, favored the execution of trade unionists, despised FDR as a handmaiden of the Reds, and believed fervently in the international conspiracy of the Jews. So unremittingly vicious were the officer's opinions that Knick's article would be entered into the Congressional Record as evidence for the proposition that Franco's movement was the most reactionary sort of fascism.

Once his articles appeared, he wouldn't be welcome anytime soon in Franco's Spain, Knick informed his editor. As Dorothy said to Jimmy, it was all right to revise your opinion—six days later or six months later. That is, providing that the revised one was correct.

LIKE MOST OF THEIR circle, Jimmy never had any doubt as to which side he was on in the Spanish Civil War. This was the battle against fascist tyranny, and Spain was the only place in the world where it was being fought in earnest—with guns. Even Dorothy, who increasingly called herself a conservative because of her antipathy to FDR's New Deal, took the part of the Spanish Republicans, protesting the arms embargo the American Congress imposed on Spain in 1937 in the name of "neutrality." It was tantamount, she wrote, to handing a victory to international fascism.

Jimmy wanted to go to Spain in 1936, as Knick had, but his doctors wouldn't hear of it. He was still too ill, they said, and he wouldn't survive a relapse. The next year, Hemingway came to see him at the house the Sheeans were renting on the outskirts of Paris. "You stay here and be comfortable, kid," Hemingway jibed. "I'll go to Spain for you." Out-machoing Jimmy was a sport for Hemingway. If Jimmy needed a final straw, that was it. The *last* person he wanted going to Spain on his behalf was Ernest.

Was Jimmy washed up? He was barely writing at all. So far as Dinah's Aunt Maxine could tell, his function at this point was purely decorative. *You* will play the host, she told Jimmy when he and Dinah visited her on the Riviera for the Christmas holiday in 1937. Maxine's only other guest was Winston Churchill. He was out of office, never—as he said then—to return; clad in a ruby-colored bathrobe and a floppy straw hat, he was writing history books and painting pictures of the rocks below Maxine's splendid whitewashed art deco villa. One evening, Lloyd George was coming to dinner, as was the former king Edward VIII, the Duke of Windsor, and his wife, the ex-Mrs. Simpson.

"You have a strange party tonight, my dear," Churchill said to Aunt Maxine. "Ex-kings, ex-prime ministers, ex-politicians." The guests were in evening clothes, the table laden with champagne and delicacies, and the subject that Maxine's exalted company took up was the welfare of Welsh coal miners. Should showers be required at the pitheads or not? The Duke of Windsor had heard that the miners' wives didn't like the idea because it was an infringement on their prerogatives: they liked washing their husbands' backs. Jimmy understood that Maxine's guests meant well, but the conversation was preposterous. He didn't open his mouth. Maxine was also silent, hoping, Jimmy deduced, that the party would soon tire of talking about grimy miners.

It was too much gadding about, too much superannuated high society, too much drinking, too little purpose. Dorothy put it to him directly when she saw him later that year in New York. "You are at a point when you must decide," she said. "What is it?"

"It is Spain," he told her. "I want to go to Spain."

Little more than a month later, thanks to Dorothy, he got an assignment with the *New York Herald Tribune*. In March 1938, Jimmy boarded the evening train from Paris to Perpignan, on the Spanish frontier. He and Hemingway were traveling together. The third man in their party was Jim Lardner, the son of the late satirist and journalist Ring Lardner. Lanky, dressed in clothes that always seemed too big for him, and horn-rimmed spectacles, Jim was a twenty-three-year-old Harvard dropout and a zealous believer in the Republican cause. He'd been reporting for the *Herald Tribune* in Paris and was off to Spain, not knowing that Jimmy, too, had been dispatched by the same paper to cover the fighting. Together, the trio retired to Jimmy's compartment, testing the apparently bottomless limits of Hemingway's beat-up silver flask.

The Republic's position had weakened since Knick had left Spain the year before. The Italians and the Germans had sent thousands of troops, along with artillery and tanks, to bolster Franco's forces. Together, they sliced the Republic in half along the Ebro River down to the Mediterranean. Now the capital city of Madrid was cut off from Catalonia, and pretty much all the planes in the air were fascist. After the Italians bombed the coastal city of Tortosa for nearly three weeks, blasting it to ruins, it seemed just a matter of time before Barcelona, 112 miles to the north, would fall, too.

Was the Republic a lost cause? Jimmy's first dispatches—the front-page headlines blazoned with his name and his opinions ("Vincent Sheean Sees Catalonia Rally for Republic's Last Stand")—tended in that direction. Time was running out, if it wasn't already too late, for the democratic powers to intervene in Spain, Jimmy wrote. The situation seemed so desperate that when Jim Lardner declared that he was going to join the International Brigade and fight for the Republic, Jimmy tried to talk him out of it.

"What's the good of that?" Jimmy objected. "One more rifle doesn't matter a hell of a lot in the rest of the war." Sometime soon the brigades—the ones that survived, that is—would be going home. Why didn't Lardner just continue on as a newspaperman and contribute to the cause in that way?

Because he was tired of pounding a typewriter, Lardner exclaimed. What he didn't say—because Jimmy already knew it—was that his own presence in Spain made the young reporter superfluous. Lardner drew up a list of sixteen reasons he wanted to enlist, including his hatred of fascism and because "I think it will be good for my soul." He copied out the list and sent it to his mother.

Try as he might to dissuade young Lardner, the desire to play some part in events, to *do* something, was hardly alien to Jimmy. He'd felt it often enough himself. The longer Jimmy stayed in Spain, the more the dogged defiance of the populace buoyed him. The tone of his articles changed. "The very babies raise their clenched fists in the air against the foreign airplanes," he reported. For two years, "the fascist gentry" had been assuring the world that their victory was a foregone conclusion. But to break the populace, Jimmy saw now, would require a war to the death. It was a psychological struggle—for the soul.

"Obstinate fellow, your son," Jimmy wrote Lardner's mother. The boy was in the quiet part of the line just now, he told her: hardly any bombing, the food was plentiful and better in fact, than in the hotels. His mother didn't need to worry although he knew, of course, that she would. Dinah, who'd joined Jimmy in Barcelona to gather information about refugees, chimed in. She could imagine the mother's anxiety—she'd felt sick when Jimmy first went to Spain—but after having been there herself, she felt reassured. There is a feeling of "confidence and faith that Spain gives you," Dinah wrote. It made "people like Jim make these great decisions."

FROM SPAIN JIMMY AND Dinah proceeded to Vienna in June 1938. Three months earlier, the German army had marched into Austria in the Anschluss (or annexation) that Hitler had foretold in *Mein Kampf.* On the afternoon of March 14, 1938, the Führer's Mercedes-Benz convertible glided through the streets of Vienna. Hitler didn't set up his headquarters in the Chancellery. Instead, he took a first-floor suite at the Hotel Imperial, up a flight of stairs from the café where the correspondents had once gathered.

Before the First World War, Hitler—then a failed art student—had worked shoveling snow off the sidewalks in front of the hotel. He'd doffed his cap as the Habsburgs alighted from their carriage, close enough that he could smell the ladies' perfume. They'd paid no mind to the shivering laborers, certainly not to him, his beard unkempt, his hair long and dirty. As for the Hotel Imperial's management: they "did not even have the decency," he'd recollect bitterly, to send cups of hot coffee out to the men working in the cold.

Hitler had vowed then that he'd return to the Hotel Imperial, dreamed of walking on that red carpet under the chandeliers, making himself at home amid the grandeur. Where once he hadn't dared even to press his nose to the glass, now his secretaries were unloading suitcases and his toughs sent the hotel's other guests packing. At the reception desk, bouquets of costly orchids, white lilies, and roses piled up, tributes from his grateful Austrian subjects. "I waited for this day and tonight I am here," he told his entourage. The Hotel Imperial's balconies were draped in Nazi banners decorated with the heraldic eagle, in red, white, and black. Outside, ecstatic crowds—hundreds of thousands of people—cheered the Führer from the Ringstrasse. The mood was spontaneous, exultant. "Not a shot was fired, it was a war of flowers," was the way that Franz von Papen would describe the Anschluss.

By the time that Jimmy and Dinah arrived in Vienna, most of the other correspondents had already cleared out. The annexation that Dollfuss had fought was now a settled matter on the maps: Austria had become Ostmark, a southeastern province of the Greater German Reich. The "death of Austria," as Jimmy called it, involved much more than cartography. If the resistance in Spain—"the immense collective will into which the single will is poured"—could be the making of a young man like Jim Lardner, what was happening in Austria was the opposite. Nazism was snuffing out the individuality of the Viennese, the free-and-easy distinctiveness of the city's people. They even carried themselves differently, Jimmy observed. No longer did they idle and gossip on street corners or in the shops; those who wouldn't or couldn't wear the swastika hurried along, trying not to attract attention to themselves.

There were many ways to tell the story of the Anschluss: the destruction of Austrian sovereignty; Hitler's triumphant return to his homeland, saluting his countrymen from the balcony of the Hotel Imperial; the speedy acclimation of the Viennese to their new German masters. "Vienna, the eternal prostitute": that was Fodor's verdict on the rapturous crowds who lined the streets as the German soldiers marched by. How sincere were the Viennese? Not especially, thought Fodor, ever the optimist, though historians since have established substantial enthusiasm for amalgamation with Nazi Germany even in once Red Vienna.

What Jimmy chose to emphasize in his dispatches was the terror against the Jews. Anti-Semitism wasn't a peripheral, embarrassing by-product of the Nazi movement, as many observers still wished to believe: it was Nazism's essence. The persecution in Austria during the spring and summer of 1938—the scale of the violence and spoliation—was much worse than what German Jews had faced. But it was only a rehearsal, Jimmy warned. With each conquest, the Nazis were refining their techniques: "the day of mass murder may not be so far off as we now think." The time was drawing near, much nearer than anyone wanted to admit, when the Nazi regime would massacre all the Jews, "and the rest of the population—terrified, half believing, uncertain—will be glad to forget it in a week or so and say it was 'all greatly exaggerated by the foreign press.'"

You didn't need a crystal ball to see what was coming next. I'm off to Prague, Jimmy cabled his editors from Vienna. "America is no longer interested in Czechoslovakia" came the reply. Nevertheless, he and Dinah set off, an extra store of gasoline in the trunk of their car, driving along roads choked with soldiers and military trucks. Before long, Knick and a slew of other correspondents joined them. Fodor, too: he'd escaped from Vienna ahead of the German tanks.

By that point, they'd all seen too much of British and French diplomacy to trust in the guarantees those countries had made to Czechoslovakia about the sanctity of its borders. Prime Minister Chamberlain's "generosity" at Berchtesgaden, in September 1938, where he bargained away Czechoslovakia's perimeter to Hitler, hardly surprised Jimmy. Still, it seemed entirely possible that the Czechs, like the Spaniards, would decide to fight. From their window at the Hotel Ambassador, Jimmy and Dinah watched Czechs—men, women, old, young, workers, bourgeois—gather in Wenceslas Square, filling the immense area entirely. Patriotic songs, policemen weeping, flags, strangers locking arms. It was a demonstration of national mourning, but also resolve. Within a few days, Czechoslovakia had raised an army of a million.

Looking back, it was the dark blue light of Prague—too dim to read by—that Jimmy remembered. To thwart the German bombers, the authorities had distributed blue bulbs. As the Czechs mobilized, he and Dinah rented rooms in a village outside the city; they took lodgings for Knick, too, with the local baker. They paid for two months in advance, but they never spent a single night there. At Munich, on the thirtieth of September, 1938, Chamberlain and his French counterpart forced the Czech president to accept the dismemberment of his country. For the second time that year, Hitler conquered a country without needing to fire a single shot.

Jimmy and Dinah would take Fodor with them to Paris, they agreed. He couldn't possibly risk staying in Prague. Heading south they passed the retreating Czech army, Jimmy driving, reaching every so often for the bottle of whiskey he had beside him. Back in Paris, he got the news about Jim Lardner. On his battalion's last night in the lines, Lardner had been shelled or hit with machine-gun fire. He was missing, presumed dead: the last American to enlist in the Lincoln Brigade and the last to die, too. Jimmy tried to write to Lardner's mother—he knew he should—but he didn't know what to say.

The betrayal of the Czechs, Jimmy wrote to John, made him sick for days: a "purely political collapse," he called it. For the first time in his life, he was looking forward to returning to America. "Back, back, back to Pana, Illinois—to the womb, as your Dr. Stekel might say." Before leaving Europe, though, he was determined to return to Spain. The news from the Republican side was grim, the surrender of Barcelona expected any day. He'd find out what he could about the circumstances of Jim Lardner's death (not much, as it turned out). He felt responsible for Jim, at least to some degree. Maybe the boy wouldn't have enlisted if Jimmy hadn't appeared to take the *Herald Tribune* job.

In Paris, Jimmy had gotten a start on a new book, a sequel of sorts to *Personal History*. The publishers were going to call it *Not*

Peace, But a Sword, which wasn't the title he'd have chosen, but there wasn't any time to argue about it. What Jesus meant by the phrase was (and is) much debated. But the warning in the book of Matthew that the search for God's truth would pit brothers against one another expressed as well as anything what Jimmy meant to write: an account of the agonies of 1938 as he had seen them, "a wail over the ruins of Europe." He'd have a chapter about Jim Lardner.

But even as he wrote about Lardner, Jimmy worried that he was attaching undue significance—"an exaggerated value"—to the young man's existence. Was it his sense of kinship with the boy? Or his guilt about him? A million killed already in Spain, a million mobilized in Czechoslovakia, fifty thousand arrested in Vienna. How, in this context, could a single life possibly matter?

Lardner wasn't Abd el-Krim or the Grand Mufti, men who had redirected the course of history. He was an American raised with every comfort. Yet like Rayna Prohme, he'd been impelled by a combination of idealism and stubbornness to tie his fate to other people's struggles. His short life and his abrupt death had nonetheless served a purpose. In Jimmy's telling, the Lardners of the world functioned as the antithesis to the Chamberlains—they represented the moral energies of ordinary people: who stood for decency, who labored and sacrificed out of sight. "If the world has a future they have preserved it," wrote Jimmy, "for provinces and nations can be signed away, but youth and honor never."

FOR DOROTHY, THE SANCTITY of the individual—of individual life and autonomy—was precisely what was at stake in the 1930s. She had recoiled from the emphasis on the collective that she witnessed in the Soviet Union: an "ant-like civilization" she called it. Nazi Germany was still worse: at least the Soviets, she pointed out, feigned a belief in the French Revolutionary ideals of fraternity and equality. The problem with Nazism wasn't just its root and branch assault on minorities. What Hitler and his ilk aimed to do away with was individuality itself.

Even in the liberal democracies, Dorothy saw, the idea of the individual was being overwhelmed by a glorification of the masses. There was a lot of talk about humanity. But what about the actual humans? At a dinner in 1937 to honor the exiled German novelist Thomas Mann, she warned of the perils of abstraction, of discarding the notion of the human soul. Quoting Hamlet, she claimed man as "a piece of work, noble in reason." It was the duty of the intellectual to see the individual in the collective—to "dissolve the mob into men," as she put it. Thus, for Dorothy, it was the seventeen-year-old assassin Herschel Grynszpan who came to symbolize the plight of all of Europe's refugees.

In November 1938, when Grynszpan assassinated the third undersecretary to the German embassy in Paris, Dorothy was already one of the most outspoken authorities on the refugee question. That year, she'd published the first modern treatment of refugees—*Refugees: Anarchy or Organization?*—a book widely praised, including by Freud who was by that time himself in exile in London. Her proposals for an international agency to broker refugee resettlement efforts had attracted the attention of FDR and the State Department. She was widely credited with the idea of the Evian Conference, which FDR convened in July 1938 to discuss the coordination of emigration efforts from Germany and Austria.

Long on expressions of sympathy, Evian's delegates were completely lacking in solutions. Only a few of the thirty-two nations in attendance agreed to take more refugees. According to Jimmy, who traveled to Evian to report on the proceedings, the conference yielded little else than a windfall for the town's hairdressers. The remedy Dorothy had suggested—an international refugee resettlement fund endowed, in part, from blocked foreign exchange accounts and assets that refugees had been forced to leave behind—went nowhere.

Although Evian was a flop, Dorothy's diagnosis of the refugee problem proved incisive. The refugee crisis wasn't, she insisted, chiefly a humanitarian issue, which was the way that people thought about it, if they thought about refugees at all. Rather, Dorothy argued, it was a matter of international politics, which required diplomacy and coordination. Contrary to the League of Nations, which had hoped to wind down its refugee resettlement office, Dorothy anticipated that refugees would become a permanent feature of the international order. Nationalism had made the world a jungle, where citizens on the whim of a tyrant could be deprived of their rights, turned out of their homes, suffer the confiscation of their property. Refugees were the "people forced to run away from one part of the jungle to another part of it," Dorothy observed. They were "an advancing crowd shouting a great warning: The jungle is growing up, and the jungle is on fire!"

For Dorothy, as for the other correspondents, the refugee problem wasn't at all abstract. It was personal and pressing. Every day brought more desperate entreaties from friends and former colleagues in Central Europe. She sent thousands of dollars, wrote hundreds of testimonials, interceded where she could with American consuls, and called in favors with publishers and university presidents and newspaper editors. Her handbag in those years was always stuffed with visa affidavit papers. At Twin Farms, she invited so many refugees to stay that a German-speaking, leberwurst-eating "Mittel-Vermont," as Sinclair Lewis mockingly described it, sprang up in the adjoining hamlets.

It was both too much and not nearly enough. Even before the Anschluss and the Spanish Civil War added to their numbers, there were four million refugees in the world. Where would they all go? And who would help them? In the United States, like elsewhere, the Depression had sharpened sentiments against immigrants. "America for the Americans" was the cry. According to a poll conducted in the summer of 1938, two-thirds of Americans believed that refugees should be kept out of the country. Fears about competition for jobs played a part. So did anti-Semitism, stoked by the German-American Bund, the goose-stepping American branch of the Nazi movement. And increasingly also by the popular radio priest Father Coughlin, whose broadcasts attracted an audience estimated at thirty million.

Practical politics, conferences such as Evian, even tributes to democracy: none of these, Dorothy felt increasingly certain, were a match for the hatred being stirred up by the fascists. Her side lacked a rallying cry, a unifying creed that could satisfy people's emotional needs. Democracy had been cheapened to mean "the right to buy radios and refrigerators on the installment plan." What she had in mind was something more like a mass conversion. We need a "conspiracy of poets," she announced, people who could deliver civilization by rousing "exalted fanaticism on the side of love and human decency."

On the face of it, the cause of the assassin Herschel Grynszpan was an unlikely vehicle for Dorothy's "conspiracy of poets." On the seventh of November, 1938, Grynszpan, slight in a pin-striped suit, had made his way to the German embassy around the corner from the Gare d'Orsay. A so-called stateless person, Grynszpan was living in France illegally when he learned that his parents, for decades resident in Germany, had been stripped of their meager property and deported with twelve thousand other Jews to the Polish-German border. And there they sat, in the rain and cold, as the Polish authorities tried to figure out what to do with them.

"I have to protest in a way that the whole world hears my protest," was the message Grynszpan scrawled on a postcard to his mother and father. He then bought a gun, walked into the German embassy, climbed a flight of stairs, and shot two bullets into a diplomat by the name of Ernst vom Rath. Vom Rath's death two days later became the pretext for the Kristallnacht pogrom against Jews. Public whippings, rapes and mass arrests, the looting of Jewish stores and the burning of synagogues, and to top it all off, the next day, the Nazis levied a fine of $400 million against the Jewish community as punishment for the property damage. It was the acceleration of anti-Semitic violence that Jimmy, from Vienna, had foretold. To his diary, Goebbels expressed satisfaction: "For once, the Jews should feel the rage of the people."

"I want to talk about that boy," Dorothy told her radio listeners on the Sunday evening General Electric Program a few days later. "I feel as though I knew him, for in the past five years I have met so many whose story is the same—the same except for this unique desperate act."

As she went on, she referred to him as Herschel, conjuring up the despair felt by a penniless boy, stranded in a foreign land, powerless in the face of his parents' suffering. "'Why doesn't someone do something!'" she imagined him saying. "'Why must we be chased around the earth like animals!'" Perhaps Herschel knew, she added, that the murderers of Dollfuss were celebrated as heroes in Nazi Germany. "Maybe he thought that assassination is an honorable profession in these days."

Dorothy didn't condone the murder, but she refused to repudiate it. To answer the dictators' crimes with the same tactics was wrong, she conceded, though as she said privately, there was a venerable tradition of striking at tyrants. On the radio, she weighed up the crimes of the Nazis against this one, desperate act of resistance. "But is there not a higher justice in the case of Herschel Grynszpan, seventeen years old? Is there not a higher justice that says that this deed has been expiated with four hundred million dollars and half a million existences, with beatings, and burnings, and deaths, and suicides?"

What Dorothy demanded was an open trial for Grynszpan, the same as the murderers of Dollfuss had been granted. The French police had arrested the boy, but the Nazis insisted that he be extradited to Germany. As Goebbels spun the story, Grynszpan was an agent in an international Jewish conspiracy; the assassination was an attempt to provoke a war between France and Germany; the Reich had to get to the bottom of this matter. The French replied that Grynszpan, who readily confessed to the murder, would be put to the guillotine. No public trial, said the French prosecutor, was necessary.

A swift proceeding, the matter disposed of: that was quite in line with what the main French-Jewish organizations wanted. As they saw it, Grynszpan was a disaster, sure to bring down yet more trouble on the community. That was a sentiment broadly shared beyond

Jewish circles. A few days after the assassination, Dinah Sheean, who'd spent much of the year 1938 raising money for Spanish orphans, was at a London dinner party hosted by the newspaper magnate Lord Beaverbrook when the conversation turned to Grynszpan.

The French had to execute him, proclaimed Beaverbrook. Why risk a war over it? A friend of Beaverbrook's, a Canadian steel financier, went further: Grynszpan, he declared, should be handed over to the Germans. The only dissenters were Dinah and another woman, who angrily denounced the men for quivering in their boots to Hitler, making concessions to him, after which her husband good-humoredly shushed her: "Pipe down, Kitty, keep your hair on." For her part, Dinah ventured that the Grynszpan case was like what was happening in Spain: the fascists were counting on British and French complacency.

That was much as Dorothy thought, except the more relevant analogy, to her, was Munich. Chamberlain's settlement had been a catastrophe: "not peace—but the initiation of a terrific world crisis," she'd called it in her column. "Our Europe is gone!" she'd wept to a friend. Grynszpan was Czechoslovakia in the form of an individual, another sacrificial lamb the Great Powers were sending to slaughter. The Nazis were clamoring for him, but this time, she vowed, they wouldn't prevail.

On the radio, she returned to the point she'd made so many times before about refugees. "Who is on trial in this case? I say we are all on trial. I say the Christian world is on trial." The public's reaction was better than she could have imagined. More than three thousand telegrams, countless letters, donations: a "flabbergasting" response, she termed it. As the telegrams rolled in, she called John to ask him to join a committee she was putting together for Grynszpan's defense. She styled her effort as a campaign spearheaded by journalists, calling the committee the Journalists' Defense Fund and headquartering it, at her expense, on Fifth Avenue. The $40,000 she raised—from "non-Jews only," she insisted, for to take money from Jews would just fuel the Nazi fires—went to pay for the best Christian defense lawyer available. From prison, Grynszpan wrote her to express his gratitude for all she was doing on his behalf. If she had been a fellow Jew, he wouldn't have been surprised, he wrote. But since she wasn't, "I feel compelled, to send thank you doubly."

That was a satisfying letter to receive but there were plenty of others that year that she dispatched directly to the FBI: anti-Semitic screeds, unhinged diatribes about plots against the patriotic German people, and of course threats on her life. As Goebbels ginned up his propaganda machine abroad to counter Dorothy's campaign for Grynszpan, she became a prime target for homegrown Nazis. To make clear she couldn't be cowed, she decided to "drop in" on the mass meeting the German-American Bund was staging for Washington's birthday in February 1939.

She was on her way to address a Phi Beta Kappa meeting—so went the story she told later. She happened to be wearing an evening dress of black velvet with billowing, pale satin sleeves. Outside Madison Square Garden, the crowds were lined up for blocks, and thousands of brownshirts jostled with anti-fascists, while fifteen hundred policemen tried to keep a check on the brawling. In the lobby of the arena, boys were hawking the Reverend Coughlin's paper. Her press pass got her through the doors, and she settled into a seat in the press box, next to a line of newsmen behind typewriters, for the show.

The next morning, American newspapers carried two stories on the front page. One was a description of the Bund's rally: the denunciations of "Franklin Rosenfeld," the storm troopers taking orders in German and saluting in the glare of blue spotlights, the banners hung across the balconies reading STOP JEWISH DOMINATION OF CHRISTIAN AMERICA and SMASH JEWISH COMMUNISM. And the other story, right alongside, was a report of Dorothy's jeers, perfectly calculated to humiliate the swaggerers. When the Bund's leader praised white Christians as preeminent practitioners of the Golden Rule, Dorothy burst into loud hoots.

"If you don't like it, why don't you get out," shouted a man nearby.

"I've got as much a right here as you have," she retorted.

As the storm troopers rushed toward her, the police hustled her out of the arena. But she wasn't finished. They had no right to kick her out, she protested. She'd laughed softly, not loudly, and anyway, laughter was part of free speech. She marched back into the meeting. "Bunk!" she yelled after a few minutes. "Bunk, bunk, bunk! *Mein Kampf,* word for word!"

"It's not the rule of assembly in this country that a person in the audience must applaud everything," she told the pressmen as she departed. The white satin sleeves stood out magnificently in the photographs. Her ridicule was all the more devastating because it came from a woman, the *New Yorker* recognized: "We live in merry times, Dorothy. Take care of your larynx."

Putting her on its cover in June 1939, unsmiling in three-quarters profile, attired in a smart red-and-white striped jacket with the NBC microphone looming over her, *Time* magazine described her as "something between a Cassandra and a Joan of Arc." She called the collected volume of columns she published that August *Let the Record Speak*. But as the *New York Times's* reviewer observed—noting her "startling prophesies" of the previous three years—*I Told You So* would have made a fitting title.

AFTER JOHN AND FRANCES returned from Asia in June 1938, they moved with Johnny from Connecticut to a New York apartment overlooking Central Park. When Frances walked into the apartment and saw the windows filled with the view of the reservoir, she said to herself, Jawahar would like this. It was almost like being at sea.

Nehru had described to her his father's house in Allahabad, the old, porticoed mansion painted a butter yellow, the trees in the park he'd known from childhood, and now, in turn, she'd bring him into her apartment in New York. Her new bedroom, she wrote, was long and narrow, with a Swedish wallpaper in a pale turquoise and silver; every morning—she woke early—she could see the sun rise over the water. She'd put the bed on one end and the rest of the room was practically bare. Maybe he'd see it one day, but probably not.

Would he be surprised if he knew how often she took him along with her on walks? Through the park, so much lovelier this autumn than she'd remembered; up to Barnard, past the bench where she'd written poetry in her geometry textbook; down to the harbor, where they'd take a big boat or maybe a small one. She found the rose petals he'd given her on the North-West Frontier trip in the pocket of her fur coat. Her son, she added, was writing a book about the adventures of one Jerry Tigertail in the Himalayas.

Frances felt almost benevolent toward John these days. He'd given himself five months to finish *Inside Asia* and was "as frantic as a ten-months pregnant lady now, poor darling, but working away like a whole tank corps in action." He didn't want it to be entirely a personality book like *Inside Europe.* There was something in the relation between the anti-colonial leaders and the masses that needed describing, but it was hard to put his finger on it. Undoubtedly it was a sort of charismatic politics, but unlike the dictators, men like Gandhi and Nehru weren't afraid of their own people. "Politics in Asia are, by and large, more concerned with mass populations," he began.

That seemed like a paradox. How could Asian populations, largely illiterate and desperately poor, be more important to politics than their European counterparts? Part of the answer was imperialism, the hold of which was more tenuous, John saw, than he had imagined. He had started the book with the idea that imperialism would be his main theme, but there was less than met the eye. It was an extractive enterprise, thinly veneered with racial superiority. What was the British contribution to India? John boiled down the sheaf of documents the British had given him about their accomplishments to a scant page and a half, counterbalanced by the long list of the Congress's grievances and his own assessment of India's utility to Britain: "Above all, it gets booty, loot." He put his finger on "our weak spots all right," observed a rueful official in the India Office when John's articles about India started appearing.

If his judgment of the British Empire was damning, John's verdict on Japanese imperialism was still more critical. It was brutal but also imitative. The Japanese were a nation of copycats: they'd done nothing that the British hadn't done first. Here, the pronouncements on national character he'd avoided in *Inside Europe* flowed in torrents. Where the Chinese had all the "charming vices": flirting, gambling, idling away the hours in conversation, the Japanese were "men in armor." Hardworking, humorless, they displayed "an exaggerated tendency to hygiene." Perhaps, he speculated, it was the iodine in all the raw fish they ate that made them so touchy.

The Japanese were on the move, he warned, and their designs on China hardly marked the limits of their ambitions. By contrast, the British Raj was a smoke and mirrors game, thirty thousand dinner-jacketed striplings with riding crops and sticky fingers presiding over a subcontinent of three hundred million. Canny, yes, and lucky, too, at least thus far. But once the Indian masses were mobilized, the British didn't stand a chance. Which was precisely what Gandhi—"tough and rubbery"—was doing as he traveled on third-class trains and on foot from village to village, "his colossal spiritual integrity, on the one hand, his earthly command of politics on the other." Every step, every show of self-renunciation served as a reproach to the British. "He is a unique kind of dictator, one who rules by love," John judged.

With the exception of Emperor Hirohito, John's profiles weren't of the imperialists. Rather, he directed his attention to the anti-colonial nationalists: Gandhi, Chiang Kai-shek, Chaim Weizmann of Palestine, Manuel Quezon of the Philippines. When John wrote about the European dictators, he'd had to rely on bits of rumor and gossip scraped up at the Café Louvre or from his network of informants. The nationalists, by contrast, were eager to meet him and were practiced tellers of their life stories. Both Nehru and Gandhi had already published their autobiographies—Gandhi's was remarkably frank about his private life (including about sex)—and Weizmann and Quezon were working on theirs.

About Quezon John was sardonic, about Weizmann bullish, and Gandhi he called an "etherealized Houdini" for his ability to fast his way out of British jails. The most sympathetic portrait in the book was of Nehru. It was intimate and yet unrevealing: Nehru more or less as he depicted himself. The modern man yoked to India's "colos-

sal medievalism," he was diffident and lonely, beset by inner conflicts. He addressed mass meetings with all the sobriety of a scholar.
And yet, like Gandhi, he had an uncanny talent for winning the
hearts of his people. The drama of Nehru's life was a Freudian one,
the son with two fathers: his own, the Westernized lawyer Motilal,
who had followed Jawahar into the nationalist movement and then
to prison. And Gandhi, whom he both loved and disagreed with.

When *Inside Asia* was published in June 1939, John acknowledged
the "patient—perhaps I should say impatient—encouragement and
active collaboration of my wife." That December, *Life* magazine ran
an updated version of the Nehru chapter: the first mass-market profile of the nationalist leader to appear in the American press. It carried Frances's byline as well as his and was even more sympathetic to
the freedom movement than *Inside Asia*. Shifting John's analysis in
this direction, Frances reported to Nehru, had taken her "hours of
practically blood-curdling argument."

AT THE HEART OF *Inside Asia* was the relationship between the
leader and the masses. The same subject also anchored Frances's correspondence with Nehru. She peppered him with practical suggestions about the reform of the Congress structure, about technical
education, the need for a single, common Indian language. But more
than that, she urged him to remake India in his own image. You *are*
India, she told him. "You—Kashmiri Brahmin, Indian-nursed,
English-tutored, Harrow, Cambridge, prison-cells, diapers, adored
by your people, feared by and fearing your masters." If he felt like a
misfit in India, that was because he needed to change India.

Change India? he responded. She didn't understand what it was
like to have thousands of years of history weighing on you. He didn't
disagree with her about the dhoti and the mud huts, of course. But
he didn't think all that tradition could be swept away—as the Soviets
were trying to do—without a level of violence that he, as an indi-
vidualist, couldn't countenance. Anyway, he wasn't a man of destiny,
he protested. For one thing, he was far too self-conscious. "Men of

destiny do not try to look at themselves from outside as this is a disconcerting business and it shakes up their faith in the stars!"

He wanted to come to New York, he told her. He was tired of the old continents of Asia and Europe with all their vituperations, their never-ending quarrels. "How wonderfully you write, and as I read your letters I am carried away to New York and sit in your lovely flat, or wander about with you in that fascinating city along the river bank."

Instead, he was off to Bombay for a Congress meeting. "A big job trying to plan for a nation, especially when one finds even the planning of one's own life a difficult undertaking!"

I TOLD YOU SO

—

GERMANY INVADED POLAND ON THE FIRST OF SEPTEMBER, 1939, Panzer divisions racing east toward Krakow and Warsaw, dive-bombing Stuka fighter planes strafing civilians. Knick, still in Paris, hastily dismantled his household. The cook, in tears, left for Flanders. A chauffeur was dispatched to fetch his two daughters and their nursemaid from the Côte d'Azur, where they'd been holidaying. Pack only your clothes, he instructed Agnes, but when she insisted on bringing her skis, he didn't waste any time arguing about it.

There was no doubt in Knick's mind that Britain and France would respond with their own declaration of war. The coming conflict would be brutal and drawn-out; it might last as long as six years. He had to get his family out of Europe. Not just because of the war but on account of the story—a real corker—that he would break on front pages around the world in a couple of weeks' time.

Planning ahead, Knick had booked passage to the United States for the whole family on the *Nieuw Amsterdam*. Agnes and the girls would embark from the ship's port of origin, in Rotterdam. In the meantime, he would travel to London, to gather the final details he needed for his story and meet the ship at the Southampton dock. It was mayhem at the Gare du Nord, thousands of distraught people trying to leave Paris.

For years, Knick had been stockpiling evidence from bankers, some of them Jews, about the assets that top Nazis were hiding abroad. In London, the information he'd gathered was supplemented by a dossier from British authorities, part of a fledgling effort at "black" propaganda aimed at demoralizing the enemy. As Knick told the story, the leading Nazis had secretly deposited more than $34 million in the banks of foreign, neutral countries such as Switzerland, Luxembourg, and Argentina. Under Nazi law, it was a crime punishable by death for any German citizen to possess undeclared foreign currency or assets abroad, but nonetheless Goebbels, Göring, Hess, von Ribbentrop, Streicher, Ley, and Himmler had salted away their money. If the war went badly, Hitler's inner circle had their escape plans at the ready.

Knick documented the Bethlehem Steel and Pennsylvania Railways bonds that Hermann Göring, commander in chief of the Luftwaffe, had purchased through a German shipping firm and the life insurance policies he'd taken out in foreign currencies. He tracked the cash that Heinrich Himmler, head of the Gestapo, had stashed in Smyrna, Finland, and South America. Knick kept copies of the evidence in his traveling satchel. On the twentieth of September, 1939, his allegations made headlines across the world.

"A lying swine," Goebbels railed to his diary. On a Sunday morning, a few days after Knick's story ran worldwide, the propaganda minister summoned the foreign press to an urgent news conference.

Crowding into the room, the correspondents speculated about what Goebbels was so hell-bent on saying. Was he going to announce a peace settlement? Neither the French nor the British seemed all that keen on defending Poland, so perhaps the world war would be finished before it really started. Instead, Goebbels stormed in, his wan face boiling with anger, and spent the entire press conference ranting about Knickerbocker.

The story was a complete invention, a despicable lie, raged Goebbels—"snorting like a bull," in Bill Shirer's description. He invited the assembled international correspondents to disprove the allegations, telling them that he'd already issued a challenge to

Knickerbocker over the shortwave radio: "Publish the documents. Name the banks." If Knickerbocker produced his sources within twenty-four hours, Goebbels would see to it that he was paid 10 percent of the money he alleged had been deposited abroad.

Goebbels thought he had a sure bet: his spies had told him that Knick was already on the *Nieuw Amsterdam* in the middle of the Atlantic and would hear nothing of the challenge until long after the deadline had passed. What the spies didn't know was that Knick waited on board the ship until the very last minute, after the bells had clanged and the steward had shouted a couple of times for the well-wishers to disembark. Then he donned a slouchy hat to cover his cockscomb of ginger-red hair, bade goodbye to Agnes and John, and slipped down the gangway, proceeding to London to answer Goebbels's challenge.

"I am a neutral American journalist and I do not choose to engage in polemics with Dr. Goebbels," Knick announced. But the day after Goebbels's press conference, he served up what the propaganda minister had demanded and more. In an exclusive for *Paris-soir*, and then in newspapers across neutral and Allied countries, Knick detailed his proofs, publishing the names and addresses of the agents who had made the deposits, including the $1.85 million waiting for Goebbels in the safe of a German importing firm in Buenos Aires. He hadn't intended to reveal the particulars, wrote Knick, but "Goebbels is wrong if he thought I would not take up the challenge. I have now done so."

But were Knick's allegations true? His rival Hearst correspondent, Karl von Wiegand, doubted the story. In 1933, von Wiegand had charged Knick with spreading "insidious lies" about the Hitler regime and this seemed to him more of the same. Knick had "pulled off a good yarn to call attention to himself," noted von Wiegand to his editor, claiming the Dutch authorities didn't "take it seriously." Von Wiegand, accused of pro-Nazi sympathies, may not be the most reliable judge, but he wasn't the only skeptic. *The Times* of London thought the story too neat to be believable. The specificity of the charges—the "far too precise details"—aroused suspicion, *The Times* noted in its initial article, though subsequent ones conveyed Knick's reporting without comment.

When Goebbels denounced Knick's articles as British propaganda, he was, at least in part, correct. Knick and the two *Chicago Daily News* correspondents who broke a similar story—Edgar Mowrer and Bill Stoneman—had obtained a dossier on the Nazi leaders' assets abroad from the British Ministry of Information and the Foreign Office. Knick's charges about the top Nazis have never been confirmed, nor have they been disproven. But this much is certain. Thanks to decades of painstaking scholarly work, the massive scale of the Nazis' plundering and looting operation is well established. These spoils, concealed under numbered accounts all over the world, are still under investigation. Many will never be traced.

Having vigorously denied Knick's other accusations for years, Goebbels now found himself in the position of the boy who cried wolf with the rest of the foreign press. All over Europe, in the United States and other neutral countries, Knick's stories ran as fact and the fireworks with Goebbels only redounded to Knick's credit.

"Bet Knick will like the publicity immensely," Bill Shirer chuckled. He certainly wouldn't see a penny of the 10 percent Goebbels had promised. In sorties that month over northern Germany, Britain's Royal Air Force dropped more than three million copies of the leaflet outlining Knick's charges.

EUROPE IS LIKE A sealed train with 350 million people aboard, hurtling to some godforsaken destination, John had said in his broadcast from London in August 1939. "The window shades are drawn. The doors are locked. No one can see outside. Or even inside. No one can talk to the driver. No one knows who the driver is."

When Britain declared war on the third of September, John had been in Parliament, watching as the MPs remained on their benches despite the second air raid siren of the morning. At night, London was now pitch-black, not a child or a dog to be seen in the city. He was staying at the Dorchester Hotel, supposedly the safest building in London on account of its reinforced concrete structure. He spent his nights in the dugout with a gas mask on or, after the all-clear signal, visiting the Turkish baths in the basement. He got drunk nearly every night, just to take his mind off the war. When I broadcast, I am talking to you—for you, he told Frances.

She was in Lake Placid, visiting Johnny at camp. There was too much static on the radio in the Adirondacks for her to hear much of what John said, she informed him. Anyway, she couldn't stand the warmongering that he and Knick and the rest of their friends were doing. If he was as gung ho on the war as he sounded, then *he* ought to fight in it. Did he realize that the British Empire was more than sixty times as big as the German Empire, even including Austria and Czechoslovakia? She couldn't bear it. She was going out camping in the woods for a few days.

Soon after, a telegram arrived from Frances's brother. Your wife is dangerously ill, he wired John. While Frances was camping in the Adirondacks, her appendix had burst and she'd developed a bad case of peritonitis. The doctors had rushed her into surgery, and her condition was stable. Frances insisted that John wasn't to return home on her account. He booked the first passage home he could, on the *Nieuw Amsterdam*.

JOHN THOUGHT AGNES LOOKED none too pleased when he boarded the *Nieuw Amsterdam* with Knick. Maybe she'd been looking forward to a shipboard dalliance or two, he surmised. Knick was always so jealous. He didn't permit her to dance with other men, even to lunch with them alone. Nevertheless, at one point or another, most of the correspondents had tried their luck with her. They'd all heard Knick's stories about "that crazy little Agnes"—demure and aloof in public, but who could come any time she wished, or, more to the point, any time *he* wished, even dozens of times a night. Bill Shirer attempted to get in bed with her one night in Vienna. In Paris, when Knick was in Czechoslovakia during the Munich crisis, the broadcaster Raymond Swing made a pass she derisively characterized as "feeble."

John saw a lot of her on the ship. Knick had arranged for Agnes and the children to stay with his family in Texas. But when she returned to New York for a visit at Thanksgiving, she wrote John to say she was coming. They dined out and then had drinks at the fashionable "21" Club.

Didn't you know this would happen when I wrote you? she asked him later that night. They'd gone to her place.

When I want something, I *want* it, Agnes told John at the start of their affair. Strange as it may seem, I love my husband, she added.

WHILE FRANCES WAS CONVALESCING in the Lake Placid hospital, she had nightmares of being a soldier on a battlefield. The war had just started, and she was a Polish soldier or an English one or a German. It was night and there were wounded men all around her. She came to from the surgery and was disoriented. Why were the doctors treating her—"a useless woman," she called herself—when there were young men dying?

Before she got sick, she'd written Nehru a picture postcard from the Adirondacks: "We could have lunch here—lettuce sandwiches— fresh grilled trout. I hope you can make a boy-scout fire because I can't!" The British censor read the postcard, and then stamped it "censored" before forwarding it on. The world in which she'd written—peace, albeit an uneasy one, the plans for him to come to New York—had vanished before the card arrived. On the say-so of a single man, the British viceroy, the entire Indian subcontinent had been brought into the war. The viceroy hadn't consulted the Indian National Congress or, for that matter, any Indian leader.

With the outbreak of war, Nehru was under the strictest surveillance. The nationalists wouldn't dare to sabotage the war effort. Or would they? So ran the conversations between nervous British officials. On the one hand, neither Gandhi nor Nehru had any sympathy for fascism, and the Congress had declared itself "entirely on the side of democracy and freedom." On the other, the Congress was withholding its support for the war until the British explained both where imperialism fit into their war aims and what plans they'd made for Indian independence.

Nehru heard the news of Frances's illness from a visiting American reporter. Was it right of her not to tell him that she'd been so ill? he reproached her. *Of course* he could make a fire. He wasn't *that* much of a refined city-dweller. He sent her a photograph of himself at home in his study: in profile, beset by worries, a picture of his daughter, Indira, on top of the bookcase. He wrote her, elliptically, one eye on the censor, about the rivers of India, the Ganges and the Indus.

He knew Frances well enough to anticipate how she'd react to this trivia—Write me about something important, for God's sake. *Not* rivers. "There is our friend the censor, remember, and probably he will think that rivers are a safe subject for American consumption," Nehru reminded her. Besides, what counted as a worthwhile subject? he asked. "Something that one craves for and cannot reach?" Under the still surface of the waters lay "strange currents and unplumbed depths."

Unmentioned were the divisions in the Congress. Or the debates about mass civil disobedience in wartime, which Gandhi adamantly opposed. Or the bitter arguments about whether to demand independence immediately or settle for a commitment for freedom after the war was done. The British were intransigent, refusing to concede any right to self-determination; Nehru and the other Congress leaders were growing more impatient by the day.

In October 1940, Nehru was among the first to be rounded up in the mass arrests of nationalists whom the British government accused of undermining morale and military recruitment. Twenty-three thousand would be convicted that next year. The shock came at Nehru's sentencing. Previously, he'd been termed a political prisoner. This time, he was given four years' hard labor like a common criminal. As the Blitz began, Frances fumed to John: "I hope London is razed till there's not a stinking stone of it left—till it's bald—like Jawahar's poor old bald head."

Please send me letters, Nehru wrote her from the jail at Dehradun. "They manage to bring me a bit of yourself and that is a very welcome gift." She mailed him letters and postcards and books, including a volume of photographs of Kailash and Manasorovar and Thomas Mann's novella about the Indian goddess Sita. That one prompted him to a reverie about the mysteries of Woman. He'd always been a little afraid of the opposite sex and had been accused (with some justice, he acknowledged) of being blind—deliberately so. "When will this world settle down again, my dear? When one can write to one's friends and meet them and do more or less what one wants to?"

She'd made copies of his letters and tucked the originals inside a folder. Every once in a while, she took out those letters he'd touched and felt again the warmth of his hand. She also imagined a future for the two of them. She started one letter to Nehru while she was getting ready for a New Year's Eve party to usher in 1941. She was supposed to be meeting John there. In her imagination, though, she was in bed with Jawahar, laughing. She wrote that letter, and others like it, but never sent them.

The experience in Asia, she told Nehru, had done her tremendous good. She—who'd hardly considered herself Jewish—had become an ardent Zionist, a supporter of the armed struggle of Jabotinsky's paramilitary organization, the Irgun, for a Jewish state in Palestine. She was hosting meetings and appearing on platforms on behalf of her "Irgun lads." Her change of heart was Hitler's doing, of course, but it owed something, too, to her analysis of the British Empire. The British orated about liberty and freedom but the policies they pursued abroad were the rankest form of domination. "They eat other people's cake and have it too. They have democracy for themselves, and empire for other people."

Empire, *tout court,* was the problem—the American Empire as well—but the British Empire was a particularly malign and powerful instance of it. She'd started a new book entitled *Empire,* she told

Nehru, an attempt to tell a "psychiatric imperial case history." He was too much of an old Harrovian, she supposed, to agree entirely with her assessment of the British. Still, the line that her erstwhile friends and colleagues were drawing between the liberal democracies of Britain, France, and the United States on the one hand, and Germany and Russia, on the other—*We or They*, as one influential title had it—was too simplistic. If you looked at what the British were doing in India or in Palestine, didn't the distinction become much cloudier? Weren't the crimes the British had committed in empire the precedent for what the fascists were doing now?

She was writing and speaking, not just for the Zionists but for the Indians, too. She'd given an address at the New York festivities to mark Gandhi's birthday in 1940, a toast that the journalist Gobind Behari Lal—the first Indian to win the Pulitzer Prize—lauded as revelatory. "You psychoanalyzed world politics," Lal exulted. John's editor Cass Canfield wanted to see her manuscript. She was busy day and night, she told Nehru, and had added sculpting to her activities. Nonetheless, many were the days, she confided in him, when she wished she could take a hypodermic needle of veronal and wake up when the war was over and she could start to live again.

THOUGH DOROTHY HAD ALWAYS had a soft spot for Frances, she viewed her Anglophobia as flat-out insane and worse, a menace to civilization. Anti-British crusaders like Frances—or the *New Republic*'s Quincy Howe or the Gunthers' old friend Jerry Frank—were playing right into Nazi hands, Dorothy declared. Hitler wanted nothing more than to distract attention from his own crimes by ranting on about the British Empire. She spent a maddening evening arguing with Frank, an ardent New Dealer and the new head of the Securities and Exchange Commission, whose book, *Save America First* (1938), blamed the British elite for the mess in Europe.

Indictments of the perfidious English had long played well in American political life, especially in working-class German and Irish strongholds like Chicago. But in the 1920s and 1930s, opinions against the British gained traction among both urban liberals and American Establishment types. Many were still disgruntled about the last war: the British, they said, had snookered America into the conflict with their atrocity propaganda about the "barbaric Huns." Some also disliked appeasement. But increasingly, as for Frances, the heart of the matter was the British Empire, more particularly the nationalist struggle in India.

It wasn't that Dorothy was uncritically pro-British or enamored of British imperialism. India, she said, had been "Great Britain's ruin." But what she cared most about was the survival of Western Christian civilization, and in that effort, Britain—and American public opinion about Britain—was key. The publicity battle was shifting into a higher gear, she saw: opinion would need to be mass manufactured the same way that tanks or bombers were. And thus far, the Nazis with their formidable propaganda machine had the upper hand.

When Germany invaded Poland, Dorothy was on the radio day and night. She recognized that broadcasting was an even more potent means of reaching an audience than the printed page: it was both immediate and emotional. Her voice was clipped and feminine with the slight hint of a British accent that among Americans counted as a mark of good breeding. Decorous as she sounded, what she had to say was anything but polite. Contrary to his promises, Hitler had no intention of sparing noncombatants; Polish women and children had already died in his bombing raids. He was a liar and had always been one. She barely paused for breath once she got going. For one St. Louis station, it was all too much. Nervous about alienating their isolationist or pro-German listeners, they stopped Dorothy's broadcast in midstream. She was expressing her "personal opinion" in violation of FCC rules, the station claimed. "Dorothy Is Cut Off Air," read one front-page headline.

Dorothy worried about the pacifism she saw ascendant in America, a stance that anti-British sentiments bolstered. The forces that favored isolationism had always been strong in the United States. Why, asked the isolationists, should we mix into European troubles?

What had that gotten us in the last war, aside from fifty thousand of our boys killed and a slew of unpaid loans? Shortly after the start of the war, the aviator Charles Lindbergh—a bona fide national hero after his solo flight across the Atlantic—took to the radio to endorse American neutrality, insinuating that Jews stood behind critical reports of Nazi Germany. A few days later, Thompson lit into Lindbergh in her column. She offered a chronology of his dalliances with the Nazi Party, including his meetings with Göring and the distinguished service medal he'd been awarded by the Germans.

"Colonel Lindbergh's inclination toward Fascism is well known to his friends," she noted, depicting him in addition as a man lacking in human understanding, contemptuous of the weak, a mean practical joker. She'd met him, though she didn't say so, first in 1930, when he'd poured Listerine into a rare Burgundy decanting on his host's sideboard. She "peels the hide off Mr. Lindbergh," crowed Harry Truman to his wife after Dorothy's first column on the subject. She would publish thirteen more such columns before she was finished with Lindbergh. That incident with the Burgundy, she told Jimmy, was the key to the man's character.

Dorothy left for Europe in March 1940, when nearly every day brought rumors of secret peace negotiations to end a war that had barely begun. The Soviet Union had invaded Finland on November 30, 1939, but more than five months after the Nazi conquest of Poland, Britain, France, and Germany had yet to engage in a significant military campaign on land, on sea, or in the air. This was a "phony war," people called it, nervously looking at the sky, tuning in to the radio, rifling through the newspapers.

Never mind the rumors, Dorothy proclaimed in her column. There could be no peace until Hitler was defeated: this was a war "to make universal certain human rights, without which no individual is human." She set out for the neutral countries first, visiting Greece, Turkey, Hungary, Romania, Yugoslavia, and Switzerland. She was in Rome for an audience with the pope in April 1940, when Nazi forces seized Denmark in a lightning attack and advanced into Norway. The following month, as German columns steamrolled through

Holland, Belgium, and Luxembourg, Dorothy traveled from Paris to broadcast from the Maginot Line.

She saw the forts one hundred feet underground and took the elevator eleven stories high to watch the guns in action, counting off the artillery shots directed at the advancing Nazi forces: this one for the Czechs and that one for the Poles and the Dutch and the Norwegians, she said. But she could tell that the much-vaunted French defenses didn't stand a chance. She rushed to Genoa to sail for home and was back in New York by the time that France fell to Nazi armies after just six weeks of fighting. She'd known the French defenses would collapse as soon as she saw the grass in the Tuileries Garden. The lawns hadn't been mowed: it was as if the French had already given up. Shortly after German troops marched into Paris, the French police handed Herschel Grynszpan, the young assassin whose legal defense Dorothy had championed, over to the Gestapo. Extradited to Berlin that summer, he was imprisoned in preparation for the show trial that Goebbels was planning. That was the last that Grynszpan's family heard of him.

After her return from Europe, Dorothy's public defense of Britain became more avid. As the Royal Air Force battled the Luftwaffe to stave off a German invasion, Dorothy appeared at Aid-to-Britain meetings in front of crowds of ten thousand people; she rhapsodized about a union of the English-speaking world. "The master of the dyke against world chaos is you, Churchill, you gallant, portly little warrior." Churchill repaid the compliment. "She has shown what one valiant woman can do with the power of a pen" was the message the British prime minister sent to be read aloud at a May 1941 dinner in her honor. There were more than three thousand people in attendance at the Waldorf-Astoria Hotel that evening in New York. "Freedom and humanity," wrote Churchill, "are her grateful debtors."

In Dorothy's vision of Anglo-American unity, however, Britain would be reduced to a North American naval and air base where in the summer "we will go to eat Devonshire cream." The defining fight against fascism, she thought, would ultimately fall to America. Although she'd originally championed the dark-horse Republican candidate Wendell Willkie, in the fall of 1940, as the Blitz raged, she changed her mind. Now was no time to switch political leadership.

She'd criticized FDR, especially his New Deal, but she came out in support of his bid for a third term a month before the November 1940 election. The staunchly Republican *Herald Tribune* at first refused to print her column endorsing FDR, and then relented when she reminded its owners of the clause in her contract that permitted her to write as she saw fit. The column appeared in the paper alongside a sampling of the slew of angry readers' letters that her "betrayal" had prompted.

It was a painful break, one of a series she had to endure. Although Willkie didn't hold a grudge, the publishers of the *Herald Tribune* did. Her contract wasn't renewed, and her "On the Record" column moved to the *New York Post,* in those years a liberal paper with a working-class and Jewish readership. "On the Record" was still syndicated widely but the *Post* was a less influential paper than the *Herald Tribune* and an uneasy fit for Dorothy's opinions on subjects other than Hitler.

Then there was Red. He turned up at Twin Farms every once in a while, but they hadn't lived together since 1937. Still, Dorothy was reluctant to give him a divorce. "You are now the most prominent advocate in the whole country not only of Freedom but of generosity," he pleaded with her. "Are you going to deny your entire faith by holding an unwilling ex-associate?" If Dorothy advocated for war, he was going to rent out Madison Square Garden and rally Americans against it, he declared; he proceeded to join the America First Committee. Unless she consented to a divorce, Red had warned her, he would refuse to see their son. In November 1941, she finally acquiesced.

Stories began to circulate about the influence Dorothy was wielding in the Oval Office. "Dorothy, you lost your job, but I kept mine—ha, ha!" was the way that FDR greeted her after the election. From now on, though, he'd be on the receiving end of torrents of her exhortations, friendly suggestions, even draft speeches, conveyed in memoranda, letters, notes, cables, and telephone calls.

That was a great speech, Red purportedly said to Dorothy after one of FDR's Fireside chats. "I know, I wrote it," Dorothy proclaimed.

JIMMY WAS BEHAVING ERRATICALLY again. Ever since the Sheeans returned to New York from Europe in February 1939, he had been yelling in his sleep and weeping and drinking all the time. That was the same sort of behavior that had presaged his breakdown in Ireland, and Dinah was very worried about him. He was supposed to speak at the memorial gathering the Lincoln Battalion was holding for their dead, but *that,* she was certain, would put him straight into the loony bin. There were too many days that she had to make apologies for him when he couldn't manage to keep appointments. "Jimmy is awfully sorry," she'd say, "but really, you must forgive him. He just couldn't get himself organized this morning."

Then there were the disturbing things he said to her. He was abnormal, he kept insisting; there were obscene parts to him. Anyone who passed him on the street could figure it out. Even if she couldn't see it herself, it was a humiliation for her. It may have suited Jimmy to cast Dinah as the innocent party in the marriage, but she was far more sensitive and worldly than he acknowledged. He needed a doctor, probably of the Freudian type, Dinah figured, but in his present state, there wasn't the slightest chance that he'd agree.

Dinah had hoped that the move to Dorothy's spare house at Twin Farms that summer of 1939 might do him some good. He'd be gone from New York, where he always became so self-conscious. And the Vermont house was perfect: charmingly sloping ceilings and old, uneven floorboards, plus the modern conveniences, steaming hot water for the baths, and a fully outfitted kitchen. From the nearby farms, they'd have a limitless supply of fresh cream and eggs and butter. The countryside was practically Austrian in its mountainous beauty, and while they awaited the arrival of the baby, they could lounge in rocking chairs on the shaded porch.

Dinah hadn't reckoned, though, on the rigors of life in Dorothy's proximity. Dorothy was like her aunt Maxine: lordly, imperious, needing company around her all the time. She barely paid attention when Dinah opened her mouth. Dorothy and Red's son, Michael, was just as bad as everyone said: calling people "God-Damn Swine," and pranking the guests by slipping castor oil into their cocktails. Jimmy was up until all hours at Dorothy's, arguing and pounding his fist on the table. Under the circumstances, Dinah felt certain, the news of the Nazi-Soviet Pact would send him over the edge.

The truth was that Jimmy really didn't know what to think at first when the Soviets and the Nazis made a declaration of nonbelligerence and neutrality in late August 1939. It seemed to him like seven or eight different conflicts were happening at the same time. Among the sinners were some saints, but the reverse was also true. He'd signed an open letter calling for closer cooperation between the United States and Soviet Russia in the service of world peace. But news of the secret addendum to the Nazi-Soviet Pact—which divided up much of Eastern Europe into German and Soviet "spheres of influence"—made him change course completely.

In a two-part denunciation published in the *New Republic,* Jimmy repudiated the Soviet project root and branch. The Soviet Union, he charged, was a fascist state, and Stalin, a ruthless dictator, bent on militaristic expansion. Millions had been killed in the campaign for agricultural collectivization, which was not only brutal but unnecessary. "No reflective person outside the Soviet Union assumes that it is necessary to murder millions of people to produce an industrialization program." And what had the workers gained twenty years after the Revolution? They couldn't strike or choose the conditions of their work in any meaningful way. Their gains were of a "purely fascist nature, consisting in the psychological and social delusions of the mass meeting, chauvinism, competitive sacrifice and self-congratulation."

It was a demolition job, all the more complete for coming from a sometime fellow traveler. There were plenty of disillusioned New York intellectuals, Trotskyites, members of the anti-Stalin Left, important in *Partisan Review* circles, who were saying (or had said) what Jimmy did. But of the Soviet Union's Left-leaning critics in the 1930s, Jimmy was the rare household name. The editors of the *New Republic* felt compelled both to publish his articles and to make some answer to them. Unimpeachable as his credentials were, Sheean was a little unrealistic in his objections to Stalin's foreign policy, the *New Republic* replied; he saw expansionist aims where there were none; moreover, he indicted the entire Soviet system on the basis of the Pact.

The question Jimmy asked himself was why it had taken him so long to face up to the facts. In his circle, the human costs of the Five-Year Plan and the Great Purge were well known, and, as he conceded readily, were "very repellant." But it had been difficult, as he put it, to "surrender an obstinate hope": in the short term, an alliance of fascism's enemies in a Popular Front, in the distant future, Rayna's world of equal shares and fair play. So long as Soviet Russia was arrayed against Hitler, he'd hoped that the socialist experiment might be redeemed.

At the Communists' mass meeting in Madison Square Garden that fall, the assembled audience—tens of thousands of comrades—booed when Sheean's name was mentioned. Ah well, he wrote Eddy Sackville-West: there are so many things that Communists are prohibited from talking about these days that they have to make the most of what they can revile. Him, for instance. Also the movie *Gone with the Wind*, which seemed a piddling subject on which to foment a political storm.

The truth was that everyone was angry with Jimmy. The Stalinists denounced him as a British propagandist and the Anglophiles as a romantic Bolshevik. American isolationists sent him hate mail, and so did Nazis. "I think the best thing I can do is shut up for a while," he lamented to Eddy. The only bright spot was that Himmler had banned his writings. John and Dorothy and Bill Shirer were already banned in Germany, but in their respective decrees, they'd shared billing with a handful of other writers. Himmler's diktat of January 1940 specified Sheean alone.

FRANCES REMAINED AN ADAMANT isolationist. The argument she'd started with John during the summer of 1939 about America's role in the war dragged on all that year and the next. He acknowledged there was a kernel of truth in her vendetta against the British Empire, but thought she was going off the deep end. For her part, she threatened that if John and his friends didn't stop agitating for war, she'd move to Germany and declare herself a Nazi. It was intolerable to him that she, as a Jew, would even talk that way.

He felt completely at sea. He didn't agree with Frances or with H. L. Mencken, who'd written him to object to the "crusade against Adolf." The sentiment expressed at a *New Republic* dinner—that many Americans of his generation had quit Europe precisely because they were tired of its petty nationalisms and had no desire for further entanglement—rang truer with him. The news of the Nazi-Soviet Pact fortified the general feeling of a pox on both their houses.

He wasn't, then, in the least bit gung ho about the war—in fact, sometimes he was against it. What had the carnage of the previous world war achieved, after all? At the same time, he was fervently anti-fascist. To be anti-Nazi but not pro-intervention seemed a wishy-washy, if not downright disreputable, position among his close friends. On account of Hearst's isolationism, Knick quit his job with the International News Service in February 1941: "Journalists have more reason than any other type of citizen to work for the destruction of Hitler and his gang," Knick wrote in tendering his resignation.

From London, John's friends pleaded for him to do his part in swaying American public opinion for intervention. The stance of neutrality, Margot Asquith proclaimed, wasn't anything she could even remotely understand. She'd have put neutrals to death. Lee Miller was less vengeful but equally emphatic. She'd cast her lot with the English after leaving her Egyptian husband and moving to London to live with the artist Roland Penrose. She was heartily sick of hearing how terrible her friends at home felt about Great Britain's plight. What was needed were "fewer aneurisms, goiters and asthmas and more co-operation." She was, she added, waiting for John's return to London.

Good God, you're not an *isolationist,* are you? Dorothy asked John one day. He didn't feel as if he could tell anyone what he thought. Night after night, he attended events where people thoroughly convinced of their positions—diametrically opposed positions—tried to convince other people that they were right. He'd given a luncheon for the Conservative MP Ronnie Tree, who'd come over on the *Nieuw Amsterdam* to whip up favorable propaganda for the British cause. He and Frances hosted an evening of cocktails for Jabotinsky, inviting friends they suspected might be sympathetic to the militant Zionist cause; Frances did most of the talking. They attended a party for the America First Committee. The foremost isolationist organization in the country, America First was not yet the right-wing, anti-Semitic outfit it would become, but already it was adamantly opposed to any aid to the Allies.

He felt stuck, uncertain about what he should be doing with himself. He didn't want to sign up as a war correspondent. He'd never liked spot news reporting and, in addition, had no desire to find himself in Knick's proximity. John decided to stick with his formula and tackle *Inside South America,* but even so, he found himself whiling away hours, sunk in discontented ruminations. Most nights he was at "21" late into the night, drinking beer, not wanting to go home. Why was he going to go to Mexico when the real action was in Britain? Why was he so detached from the war effort?

"I have been trying to think things out," he wrote Frances in February 1940. "Thoughts about you, me, democracy, liberalism, war, Willkie & much else."

He blamed Frances for some of his indecision. "I don't believe in the war. F— destroyed my faith." Then there was his marriage: he wasn't in love with Frances any longer. But she still loved him, he felt certain, her attachment to Nehru notwithstanding. So even when she talked about divorce, he didn't think she meant it. The real question, to his mind, was Agnes, and here, too, he wasn't sure what to think.

He met up with Agnes again in February 1940, a few months after their first night together in New York. They'd talked once on the phone, New York to Dallas, and made a plan to meet in Florida. You and I *are* going to have a lot of happiness, she wrote. Just don't get all tragic, she said when John felt glum. Knick would be in Europe for a while still. They'd be able to see each other every other month or so. The next time he met her in Palm Beach, she told him she loved him. But you know, she said, I can't ever marry you.

"The source of my dissatisfaction & unhappiness is the failure of my marriage," John wrote in his diary after that trip. "This explains my lack of will & purpose, confusion about the war, lack of faith, lack of feeling & conviction, my confused misdirection & ineptness."

In the mail came comfort of a sort—a letter from Dr. Stekel. John had been corresponding with Stekel since the doctor and his wife fled Vienna just after the Anschluss. Frau Stekel wanted them to go to Hollywood, like Thomas Mann; John signed affidavits on their behalf and sent $500 to help.

They made it to London. Stekel sent his wife to the countryside because the bombing so unnerved her. Alone in the flat, he was depressed and sick but trying his best to write. He was working on his autobiography. "Shall I call it 'Inside my soul'?" he teased John. It would be a shocking book, scandalous even, because he wasn't holding anything back about his own sex life.

The old doctor was in a reflective mood, thinking back over his career and the advice he'd given. He'd tried to keep the Gunthers in their marriage, Stekel acknowledged to John. Back then, it seemed to him that John loved Frances and there was Johnny to consider, too. Even in those days, though, he'd wondered how John would manage. "You have a right to enjoy life and not be bothered by the changing moods of a neurotic woman."

It was the final note and a benediction of sorts. The day that France fell, on the twentieth of June 1940, Stekel committed suicide.

THE NEWS THAT AGNES was pregnant came at the same time as John learned about Stekel's suicide. It was John's child—it had to be, she insisted. Agnes found a doctor in Dallas who agreed to help her. Consider what a disaster it would be if there were no abortions, she told John. "You must love me less, John."

At the start of their affair, Agnes told John that Knick had always been faithful to her. John didn't contradict her, though he—like any newspaperman of their acquaintance—could have reeled off a long list of Knick's infidelities. That fall of 1940, after the abortion, Knick was in London covering the Battle of Britain. He stayed longer than he'd planned, and the night after he returned home, Agnes had a dream that he'd fallen in love with an English woman.

I had the strangest dream, she told him. But that was no dream, Knick confessed. In London, he'd been living with another woman. Of course he wouldn't hear of a divorce. I won't ever leave you, he said.

Agnes's jealousy surprised John, though maybe it shouldn't have. Her attitude about the affair with John—and the impossibility of a divorce from Knick—began to change. I am happier with you than I ever was with Knick, she told John. When he talked of marriage now, she didn't discourage him. "I want it just, just just as much as you do."

Still, she wouldn't tell Knick. She'd tried, she said. She started to say something about being unfaithful, but Knick's reaction was so extreme that she stopped mid-sentence. He'd kill you and me and then himself, she was certain.

It was John's hope that he could pry Agnes away from Knick that led him—seven months into the affair—finally to tell Frances. She'd been away in Florida by herself for the previous two months working on her empire book, leaving John in charge of Johnny. John didn't dine at home very often, but he tried to spend some time with Johnny every day, at least. They listened to the program *Quiz Kids*. The comic Jack Benny popped up one evening as a surprise contes-

tant, vying with the eleven- and fourteen-year-olds over the definition of "aquipotic" and the velocity of a rock falling from a
mountaintop. Johnny sounded so happy when he laughed.

John went to the airport to fetch Frances. She looked pretty as
she came off the plane, tanned and cheerful.

I have a long story to tell you, he began. Before he could say anything more, though, she interrupted him. She knew they had to divorce, she said. She just wanted to know the truth. If it was his
happiness at stake, she wouldn't be hurt by whatever he had to say.

I've fallen in love with someone else, John announced. He didn't
tell her who, and she didn't ask. He wanted to marry the girl but
she'd already turned him down. Love is very important, Frances said
to him. He shouldn't hang back. He ought to go *after* it, with conviction. But would this girl be nice to Johnny?

She was taking it all surprisingly well, he thought. Didn't you
know I'd be on your side? she asked him.

But three days later, Frances was furious with him. And hurt.
How could he be talking about marriage with another woman when
he was still married to *her*? She shouted at him on the telephone and
when he saw her, she refused to look at him. "Every idea you ever
had was mine," she told him. One day, she'd write a book entitled *My
Unlived Life*. She flung the charge of cowardice: he hadn't come
home from London because she was sick. He was just afraid of the
war.

John's lawyers drew up the separation agreement. Frances took
Johnny to California for the summer; they'd stay with her brother
and his family and visit John's uncle out in Carmel. She and John
had agreed not to say anything to Johnny until they'd worked out
the terms of the divorce.

By the way, I'm pregnant, she wrote him. It was a ruse, his doctor
assured him; the woman looked young, but she was forty-five years
old. Either she was lying or it was a hysterical pregnancy. John called
her brother, who dodged the question, saying that he couldn't talk
about it, but seemingly confirmed what John's doctor had suspected.
"Be of good cheer," Frances's brother said as he signed off.

That summer of 1941 brought the news of the Nazi invasion of the Soviet Union, which once again put the Russians in the Allied camp. It was the sort of thing he and Frances, in the past, would have chewed over for months, but now she wasn't talking to him. He knew she was back from California when he picked up the phone, repeatedly, only to hear silence on the other end of the line.

In the fall, they took Johnny together to Riverdale School, in the leafy part of the Bronx, where he'd be starting as a boarder. He didn't want to go away to school, but as Frances said to John, what choice was there now? They'd be living in separate apartments, both of them traveling. Besides, the independence would do their son good. Johnny was eleven years old and still occasionally wetting the bed. Please see to it that he doesn't spend too much of the day playing his fiddle, she'd repeated every summer to his camp counselors; she wanted him climbing mountains, swimming, and joining in sports with the other boys. At Riverdale, he'd come home every other weekend and for holidays. Fodor's son was there, and so was Dorothy Thompson's boy.

Frances had agreed to the separation, but divorce, she now said, was out of the question. A couple of weeks after they delivered Johnny to Riverdale, John moved his things out of the apartment on Central Park West. Frances had left for the day so she didn't have to see him but returned before he was finished moving out. She wept and he was close to tears himself. When they drove out to Riverdale to visit Johnny on the weekend, she refused to sit in the front seat of the car with him.

Knick was back in the United States for a lecture tour on which Agnes would join him. The affair was excruciating enough when Knick was away but when he returned home, John's position was intolerable. He tried to avoid seeing them but Knick wasn't the sort of person you could easily dodge. Knick was insistent: come and meet us for a drink, stay for dinner. Stop by tonight, won't you?

Knick wanted John to write the foreword for his new book, *Is Tomorrow Hitler's?* What could John say, other than yes? He cast the spell of mythology over their group: "We were buzzards in every foreign office, and kings on every wagon-lit. . . . When we did meet, the vault of heaven shook." The foreword was also an elegy to his friendship with Knick: the night in Berlin they listened to Putzi's rendition of Wagner; the rowboat trip on the icy Danube; those bad oysters in Madrid. John praised Knick's authority and his judgment. There were love affairs in life and then there were hate affairs: "The hate affair between Hitler and Knickerbocker is one of the most torrid in political history."

Not long after her abortion, Agnes was pregnant again. (It was Knick's this time.) The news was almost unbearable to John: his own baby disposed of, Knick's in its place. What was she *supposed* to do? Agnes asked him. She did want a baby.

That decided it for John: he'd return to London.

JIMMY AND KNICK HAD both been in England for the Battle of Britain, as the RAF, diving, sparring, held back the Luftwaffe invaders during the summer of 1940. They'd watched the battles from the cliffs west of Dover, camping out on the highest of them, Shakespeare Cliff. On the cliff a crowd of newsmen gathered with binoculars to watch the Spitfires and Messerschmitts duel it out above. The battle for freedom, as Jimmy put it, had finally begun. The dogfights weren't mass hurled against mass, but the "terrible beauty" of a clash between individuals, a boy in this plane up here, in a fight to the death against that one, there.

On the first night the Germans bombed London, Jimmy was broadcasting from a balcony of the Piccadilly Hotel, looking down on the streets below. Overhead the bombs screamed and, down by the river, the fires burned all night. He and Knick stayed on through the worst of the Blitz, taking in the stunned faces in the street, the British mania for understatement, and the dancing on the terrace of the Dorchester as the frame of the great hotel swayed and shook. In a bad air raid, those Luftwaffe bastards seemed to be almost in the room with you. Playing in the rubble, children bartered a Messerschmitt cannon shell for three large hunks of shrapnel. At a lunch at

Lady Sibyl Colefax's, the septuagenarian H. G. Wells refused to retreat to the bomb shelter. He wouldn't go until he'd finished his lunch, he insisted. "Why should I be disturbed by some wretched little barbarian adolescents in a machine? This thing has no surprises for me. I foresaw it long ago. Sibyl, I want my cheese."

Most nights Jimmy dined at the Dorchester with the glamorous, shrewd Lady Diana Cooper and her husband, Duff, the minister of information. He'd been taken up by the high Tory circles of the Churchill government. "Half poem and half bread," Jimmy called Diana Cooper, noting her practical good sense. Jimmy, she reported to her son, was one of her "supports." Jimmy's newspaper friends ragged him: "The Duchess of Westminster wants you to come to cocktails tomorrow. Will you please ring up the King tonight? And don't forget Lady Astor."

The British were avidly wooing the other American correspondents, too. A man like the CBS broadcaster Ed Murrow had the attention of millions of Americans. His reports alone, it was hoped, might sway the doubters at home. Even junior American pressmen—and there were 150 or so correspondents officially registered in 1940—had access to government officials unimaginable in the old days. This included an occasional audience with the Queen, whose insistence upon remaining at Buckingham Palace amid the Blitz had turned her into an emblem of British sangfroid. She was offered up as bait for the American newsmen. (It was "rather an ordeal" for Her Majesty, Jimmy thought.)

For Dorothy, who arrived in England in July 1941, the moral imperative was clear without any suggestion from on high. The British were fighting America's fight and it was long past time that the United States put its own shoulder to the wheel. She flew to England via neutral Lisbon, arriving in London after the bombing had already eased. "I'm so glad you're here, but you're a year too late, my dear," said Jimmy, linking arms with her.

Dorothy's editor at the *Sunday Chronicle* soon found himself conscripted into the job of social secretary. It was like managing a film star, he reflected with resigned bemusement. Operating out of three suites at the Savoy Hotel, staffed by a crew of secretaries supplied by the *Sunday Chronicle*'s publisher, she planned her campaign. She toured bomb sites; visited munitions works; had an afternoon tea alone with the Queen; saw the heads of all of the European governments-in-exile; addressed three hundred MPs in a private reception at the House of Commons; broadcast on the BBC; and attended a dance for the London Auxiliary Fire Service. "Oh, I must be with the firemen," she insisted when the invitation came. Much to the aggravation of British reporters, who hardly had a hope of a half-hour audience with the prime minister, she spent an entire weekend with Churchill. He appeared, late to meals, decked out in the leaden blue, zippered overall getup he'd designed for dressing quickly during air raids. He tapped his fingers on the table, absent-mindedly.

"How are you going to win the war?" she asked him.

"First we shall see that we do not lose it," he replied. "We can do it only with the help of Americans. You know that, don't you? We can't do it alone."

Dorothy was fresher in the evenings than she'd been in the mornings, invigorated by the work, by the resolve of the exiles she met and the bravery of the British. For all the physical destruction she'd witnessed, the war wasn't devastating British civilization but remaking it, for the better, from the ground up. "I've crowded months into weeks, prolonging my own life but shortening yours!" she chortled to her *Sunday Chronicle* editor. He admitted as much: "I was an exhilarated wreck when she left." He proceeded to write a 250-page book about her visit. A "feminine Churchill," he called her.

Back in New York, Dorothy continued her efforts to revitalize American democracy. Previously she'd called for Congress to repeal the Neutrality Acts, passed in the 1930s to limit involvement overseas. Now she also lobbied for new laws in the United States to protect all races and religions. In late September 1941, she made her appeal to an overflow crowd of more than seven thousand at Carnegie Hall; loudspeakers carried her voice to throngs on the sidewalks outside. Rediscover your own power! she pressed her fellow citizens. "It is not too early—it can soon be too late."

IN THE FALL OF 1941, it took John more than a week to get from New York to London. He flew on the Pan Am Clipper to Bermuda (where autograph hunters were waiting for him), then to the Azores for refueling, on to Lisbon, where, a few days later, he took another plane to Bristol. When he arrived at the Dorchester Hotel late that evening, there was a message waiting for him from Lee Miller. She'd been photographing the Blitz for British *Vogue*, producing oddly domesticated images of the destruction: a bombed-out building viewed through the dotted Swiss curtains of an apartment opposite. At one-thirty in the morning, Lee came up to his room and stayed that night, and others that followed, too. One good thing about the Blitz, Lee said, was that you never had to explain why you hadn't come home.

John, like Dorothy, saw everyone: the Spanish Republican leader, Juan Negrín, and the head of the Free French, Charles de Gaulle; Lloyd George and the powerful minister of labour, Ernest Bevin. He spent an evening with Churchill, marveling at his lucid table talk after tossing down one sherry, two stiff whiskeys, two drams of port, three brandies, and a glass of Cointreau. He met his old friends, too, Nye Bevan, Harold Nicolson, and Rebecca West, among others. Except for Churchill, they all had the same question for him. What *was* the United States going to do? Were the Americans going to be in—or out? He felt embarrassed, and didn't know how to respond. Didn't his fellow countrymen have any sense of the moral necessity of joining the fight? demanded the broadcaster J. B. Priestley.

John was on the radio nearly every night now. But what was he supposed to say to the American public about the war? As Ed Murrow put it, it was a no-win proposition. If he and John told the truth—that the British were still outmatched—people would call them pessimists and they'd strengthen the hand of the isolationists.

Why on earth should we join a losing cause? Americans would ask themselves. But even if the British *were* winning, John knew, broadcasting the fact might backfire. If the Brits are managing on their own, why should we enter the war? his fellow citizens would ask.

Murrow confessed to John that he was frightened. He'd managed to keep his sanity during the worst of the Blitz but every time he heard the *Ack Ack* guns now, he could hardly breathe.

You have to tell the truth in your broadcasts, John insisted.

After John had been in London for a month, he realized he didn't want to go home. He was happier than he'd been in years, charged up, as Dorothy had been. The sense of collective purpose was infectious, he wrote. In the theaters, British audiences cheered the Red Army louder than they did their own, and, to his surprise, Stalin got more applause than Churchill. The conservative *Times* of London was running a tribute ad to the Russians, topped by the Soviet hammer and sickle. In British factories, workers were producing at top speed, they told John, for the defense of their Russian comrades. Frances really ought to come here and see this for herself, he thought.

In England, the force of social leveling went far beyond the sky-high tax rates on the rich. Of course, some of Britain's elites had retreated to their country estates, but others—including the royal family and government ministers—had stayed in London. There were no more gloves to be seen in public, and few, if any, first-class compartments on trains. The black iron railings that once enclosed the city's private squares, locked and reserved for the exclusive use of the few, had disappeared, melted down for war matériel. Most astonishing of all, servants now had a legitimate right to object to their employers' guest lists, for the roast on the table was common household property, and company cut into everyone else's share.

The night before John was finally set to leave for Lisbon, Japanese bombers attacked Pearl Harbor and the American colony of the Philippines. Lee telephoned him. "We're at war with Japan!" she exclaimed. Japan counted among the Axis countries; in September 1940, its right-wing government had entered into a pact with Germany and Italy. After the U.S. Congress declared war on Japan, Hitler, in anticipation, made his own declaration of war on the United States, which the Americans reciprocated the next day. John felt instantly relieved. "Now that we *are* in," he wrote in his diary, "I'm all for it."

Lee Miller would become one of only a handful of women accredited as photojournalists with the U.S. Army, taking some of the first pictures of the liberated concentration camps at Buchenwald and Dachau and being photographed, herself, bathing in Hitler's tub the day of his suicide. Her affair with John more or less ended when he left London, reverting to what it had been previously—a friendship. Brainy, ambitious women were drawn to John, especially the beautiful ones like Lee; he had a wide circle of women friends who confided in him, asked his opinion about dresses, and talked with him about their work. It was in part his charm, the way he cast a veil of romance over an encounter, an easy way with flattery, his calm. More important than that, and unlike most men of the day, he also took women seriously as intellects, paying attention—and that was pleasing as well—to their advice and direction.

When John arrived back in New York a few days before Christmas 1941, Johnny and Frances met him at the docks. Johnny was home for the holidays from Riverdale and Frances seemed more reconciled to John's presence, though she avoided being alone with him. They had Christmas dinner together with old friends at the Adams Hotel, but all the antiwar talk got to John. He'd hoped he was over the business with Agnes, but as soon as he got home, he felt determined to see her, pregnant or not. Frances hadn't changed her mind: she still wouldn't hear of a divorce.

"Amusing to see that Frances is an isolationist," Agnes had written him. "What marriages do to people."

THE GLASS
COFFEE TABLE

—

WOULD THEY EVER RETURN TO ALL THE PLACES THEY'D been thrown out of? Jimmy asked Knick one night in 1943. Jimmy tended to elegize even in the best of times, but after more than four years of war, the list of forsaken places he reeled off made for particularly dreary contemplation: Paris, Prague, Shanghai, Singapore, Lake Maggiore, Barcelona, Munich, Salzburg, Rangoon, Athens. "What a tremendous part of the world we lost in such a short time," Jimmy wrote Dinah the next day. "It sometimes seems as if our particular generation ran the risk of not living long enough to do the job."

Sure, they'd be back, Knick was certain. There were already American soldiers in Capri, drinking overpriced Johnnie Walker red label Scotch in the sun. It would be a long, bloody slog, but Knick saw how the war would end. He'd made his predictions in print a few months earlier: the invasion of France by a vast Anglo-American force by way of Brittany; the collapse of Italy; and the Red Army battering their way to Berlin, though the Germans might well beg the Americans and the British to occupy the country first. By 1945, he prophesied, the Germans will have surrendered, though the Japanese could continue to fight for another couple of years.

Knick had been posted to Italy as a war correspondent, accred-

ited to the *Chicago Sun,* though as the war dragged on, he was drinking so much that he dropped out of the paper for weeks at a time.
Jimmy was in uniform. Several months after the United States entered the war, he'd joined the air force, aged forty-two. I've been a
warmonger for two decades, he told John. I can't just sit around
at home while American boys go abroad and get killed for Dinah
and me.

He found military service predictably tedious and pointless. A
boy of ten could do the job he'd been assigned, he grumbled. He
stood in front of a map with a pointer and explained Asia to the
generals; later on, he was sent to Morocco, to debrief French person-
nel in advance of the invasion of North Africa. He wanted to be
transferred to Wild Bill Donovan's Office of Strategic Services, the
wartime intelligence agency, and Donovan wanted to have him, but
in the military you never got anywhere by asking for something.

He was also distressed about Dinah. He heard a rumor that she
was planning to go on the stage (she wasn't). He sent her long, severe
letters about the loose morals of the theater and his fear that she'd
neglect the children.

It would be a better use of his time, and everyone else's, if the air
force just sent him home, Jimmy told anyone who'd listen. Instead,
he was dispatched to India, where he felt more disconsolate and useless than ever. The situation in India was almost as bad as Frances
Gunther had made it out to be: the English so pompous and
certain—still!—of their right to rule. The United States was making
a big mistake by attaching itself as the tail onto the Churchillian kite
there.

"Have no fear," he told a British official. "We are going to support
you in all your nefarious schemes of Empire." The man to whom he
said that took it as reassurance, but in fact Jimmy was poking fun.

He sent Churchill his last book, carefully marking the passages
that were sure to annoy the prime minister. "I've given up that young
man," Churchill announced. "He's too drunk."

Did Jimmy and Knick and the rest of them matter anymore?
They'd told the story they had needed so urgently to tell. Now what?

Dorothy reproached FDR: the government is doing a terrible job of making use of correspondents' talents. She was angling for an assignment to produce propaganda that would "drive Mr. Hitler into an insane asylum." Even without their persuasive wiles, the war, as Knick predicted, was proceeding to its inevitable conclusion. Where were he and his friends going?

SHORTLY AFTER JOHN RETURNED from London in 1941, Frances told Johnny about the separation. He burst into tears and cried for hours. But Johnny couldn't have been very surprised. John had already moved out of the apartment and his mother could barely stand his father's presence. He'd been seeing John on his own, on Sundays, building model airplanes, eating hamburgers at Schrafft's, and visiting the magic shops on Broadway and Eighth Avenue.

Johnny didn't like Riverdale, he told John, because of the emphasis on grades and religion. Also, the school didn't leave him any time to learn about the things he was interested in. He'd been reading all about the new class of sulfa drugs and had concocted his own remedy for poison ivy, sodium triphosphate to which he'd added sodium hydroxide. One summer, he'd smelted iron ore, producing pig iron out of the rocks that he'd chopped up. The program at Riverdale was rigid, and sometimes the discipline was unfair, and though he'd barely taken any French before, he'd caught up to the rest of the class in a term, without even *trying*, which indicated that there was something amiss. Johnny was young but he talked so reasonably, John observed.

Were they separating because Papa stayed out too late at nightclubs? Johnny asked Frances. Or was it because of the war? He'd heard them arguing about neutrality and intervention, and Frances had often talked to him about the plight of the Indians. If Papa is drafted, Johnny said to Frances, maybe he will change his mind about the war. To John he said something different. I have spent all my money on war bonds, Johnny wrote his father.

The U.S. entry into the war had relieved much of John's agonizing on the subject, but it didn't answer the question of what part he'd play. What should I *do*? he asked everyone he saw, many of whom were grappling with the same question themselves. Would it be war corresponding or military service? Government work or broadcasting? Reporting from the front was out, John decided. He wanted to be able to see Agnes. Moving to Washington, by contrast, had some appeal. An appointment as the head of the Office of War Information—the new government agency charged with the task of propaganda—was his for the asking, he'd heard. Bill Donovan and the OSS, it was said, wanted him, too.

In the end, he did none of those things. Instead, at his publisher's urging, he started to plot out *Inside U.S.A.* In the interim, he did some broadcasting for NBC's Blue Network and he filled in for his friends who had regular radio programs. At the director Frank Capra's behest, he went to Hollywood to write a few scripts for the films Capra was turning out for the army. He'd never liked Hollywood before—no one ever listened to anyone else there, he'd noticed. But now, dashing around town in his convertible, the sun shining, it didn't seem half bad, or at least no more aimless than the rest of his days.

"Hours of blank nothingness," he wrote in his diary. He was getting up, reading (not really) the papers, sitting around like a lump, waiting for Agnes. He'd flown down to Dallas to see her two weeks before she had her baby, bringing a present of a satin bedjacket. Knick wasn't there, having raced off to the Pacific after Pearl Harbor. Agnes was as angry at her husband as she'd ever been. In part, it was the girl he kept in London, in part, his drinking. Knick could have been a great man, Agnes lamented to John, but all that talent had gone down a whiskey bottle. She hadn't written him a single letter since he'd left, she said.

"Will you always be so good to me?" she asked John. After yet another trip to Texas—with Knick now in North Africa—Agnes got pregnant (John's again). He asked her to marry him. "Please stop asking me, John," she pleaded. The prospect of another abortion was "very dreary," she acknowledged, but unavoidable. John gave her an ultimatum. You must choose between me and Knick, he told her.

———

DESOLATE AND DIRECTIONLESS AS he felt, John was—to all appearances—a man writing his own ticket. In her syndicated column
in February 1942, Eleanor Roosevelt commented approvingly on the
observations he'd made, based upon his British reporting, about the
importance of equal sacrifice across classes. A couple of months later,
he was invited to the White House for a private meeting with FDR.
The president liked seeing reporters. Magnetic but mistrustful,
shrewd about public opinion, he kept close tabs on the press: "every
pore in his body was an ear," Dorothy said. But on this occasion,
FDR mostly wanted to talk. "No general knows anything about geography," he complained to John; one of them had mixed up Dutch
New Guinea, in Indonesia, with French Guinea, in west Africa. The
president predicted that the U.S. mainland would be bombed that
summer, albeit lightly, so the Axis generals could flaunt their air
power.

From royalties and his Hollywood work, John was earning plenty
of money, $45,000 in 1942, equivalent to more than $700,000 today.
He spent most of his nights in New York at "21" or the Stork, squir-
ing the sorts of women written up in the gossip columns: the actress
Miriam Hopkins, the thinking man's blonde; a red-lipsticked writer
named Bubbles Schinasi, whom the Hollywood producer Arthur
Hornblow, ex-husband of the actress Myrna Loy, was also courting;
the starlet Marianne O'Brien; the actress and journalist Clare
Boothe Luce, unhappily married to Henry Luce, the czar of the
Time and *Life* publishing empire. *House and Garden* sent a reporter
over to John's new apartment at 530 Park Avenue. It was a bachelor
pad in the latest, modern style: soft lighting and painted cabinetry
with curved edges, a striped accent wall in the bedroom, the round
glass coffee table in front of a semicircular white-upholstered sofa, a
glass dining table on a glass pedestal.

In those years, he was also a regular at Polly Adler's midtown
brothel, a few minutes' stroll away. It was the classiest establishment
of its kind in the city, open around the clock, and Polly was a straight

shooter. You could give her a blank check when you arrived and trust her to charge you exactly what you owed the next morning. She never named names but she liked to talk. It was more difficult to find girls to work because they were all doing war service, she told John. The sexual peculiarities these days! The higher the tensions got in Europe, the stranger the perversions.

"If only Rembrandt could paint my ass, think of what the picture'd be worth in 200 years!" Polly exclaimed.

John kept lists of girls and sexual ventures the way he'd once enumerated the varieties of battleships or epochal moments in history. He was past his old troubles, he noted in his diary; he'd screw every woman in New York if he wanted to. Eleven orgasms in the last eight days, he wrote down. He took one of Polly's girls out to "21." Miriam Hopkins chided him. What was he doing? Wasn't he a serious person? He had to be careful about who he was seen with; in particular, he needed to work harder to keep his name out of the gossip columns. The next day, Polly gave her "glamour boy" the same advice. Stay out of the columns, Polly reproached him.

"God made you good. Don't waste it," Miriam said.

Maybe it was *Miriam* he ought to marry, he thought. Or straight-talking Bubbles? She was obviously in love with him. Not Marianne O'Brien: she was too young and erratic. Marry a woman, not a problem, he told himself. He seemed always to be on the fence—about the war, about women. Why hadn't he seized the opening that Clare Luce had given him the year before? He was even seeing more of Frances, who aside from the occasional bitter outburst, seemed happy enough for his company. He walked in the snow one Sunday afternoon with her and Johnny. The strange thing was that he felt closer to Frances than he had in a long time, almost as if he could fall in love with her again.

Then, a letter from Agnes. She'd made up her mind, she wrote. Knick had vowed to stop drinking, and she was going to give him one final chance.

That's it, John decided in the summer of 1943. I won't miss the entire war. He obtained permission to broadcast for NBC's Blue

Network; he'd be in uniform, credentialed. He made his plans to leave for North Africa. He got vaccinated against yellow fever and tetanus and spent the night before he departed for Algeria with Miriam Hopkins.

Later on, he'd wonder whether he'd had the love affair with Agnes to escape the war.

BY THE FALL OF 1942, the British had jailed one hundred thousand Indian nationalists, and Gandhi's call for an end to British rule—his "Quit India" movement—was becoming a cause célèbre in America. The British spy sent to monitor the India League of America's annual dinner in January 1943 filed an alarming report. Only a few years earlier, the India League had been practically inert, its yearly gathering consisting of a handful of disgruntled expatriates and two or three Americans meeting at a local Indian restaurant for a "very indifferent meal" (as the spy put it). Now, the India League was throwing a gala fête, a dinner for seven hundred in the Grand Ballroom of New York's Biltmore Hotel.

At the helm of this invigorated India League was Frances Gunther. She'd joined the executive committee the previous summer as the mass arrests started and had given the League an important boost by bringing on board a group of people whom British agents called the "Literary Liberals," including Jimmy Sheean, Bill Shirer, the novelist Pearl Buck and Clare Boothe Luce. Taking dutiful notes on the meeting at the Biltmore, the spy jotted down the sentiments on offer. Why was America propping up the British Empire? demanded one speaker. India needed not just the Four Freedoms (of speech and belief, from fear and want) that FDR had promised, but a fifth—Freedom from England!

Was *this* the war against tyranny to which the Allies had committed themselves? The most scathing indictments came from American foreign correspondents, who accused the British authorities of everything from duplicitous dealings with the Congress leadership to outright brutality. The sorts of analogies that Frances had drawn between the Nazis and the British Empire appeared more and more frequently in print, even by those who had previously championed England's cause. Surveying American public opinion, the British Ministry of Information anxiously diagnosed a "new landslide of anti-British feeling." Unless the situation improved, both the Allied war effort and a possible postwar Atlantic partnership were in peril.

Frances was fast becoming one of the fiercest and most visible campaigners for Indian independence in the United States. Her friendship with Nehru was well known. While British officials were scathing on the subject—her "veneration" of Nehru was "almost hysterical"—they took careful note of her ties to his family. When Nehru's two nieces (the daughters of his sister, Vijaya Lakshmi Pandit) came to Wellesley College to study, it was Frances who met them on their arrival in New York and hosted them on vacations. The British spy was there when she brought the young women along to an India League meeting, where they were warmly greeted by an audience that had, earlier in the evening, hooted at anti-Churchill jibes.

Speaking on podiums and writing articles: it was as if the logjam had finally broken. She put aside her book on empire to write a series of articles on India and Britain for the progressive magazine *Common Sense*. Her short book, *Revolution in India*, followed in 1944. There, she sharpened the critiques she'd been making. India wasn't a boon for the British but a weakness. The possession of India had deformed the British economy as much as the Indian one. Worse, it had created a "political psycho-pathology"—of "power and pride, violence, shame, compulsion and much concealed bloodshed"—that made Britain cling to its Indian possession. "We mean to hold our own," Churchill had said of India; we cannot afford to give it up. But why, Frances asked, should Englishmen have to depend on India? "Isn't this rather a humiliating confession?"

That imperialism stripped the colonized of their liberty was self-evident. But equally devastating, she argued, was its effect on the colonizer. Anticipating ideas that the Tunisian French writer Albert

Memmi would make famous twenty years later, she theorized the dependence that linked the ruler to the ruled. The dynamic, she insisted, was both economic and psychological. What started as the imperialist's bid for invulnerability ended in his own abdication of liberty, as he abandoned one ideal after another in the cause of maintaining control. The English, as Frances put it, were "the slaves of the waves" they ostensibly ruled.

What the British needed was a new foreign policy, Frances argued, one that prioritized the interests of the masses over the elites who'd profited from empire. What evidence was there, she asked on a BBC roundtable in August 1943, that the British people supported Churchill's stubborn refusal to relinquish India? Would most of them even notice when India was gone? She envisioned a future England, much less indebted to the City and finance capitalism, more focused on the well-being of the populace at home.

At the heart of that reorientation, as Frances saw it, was Europe. For centuries, the British had encouraged fragmentation on the Continent to block French or German domination—or, for that matter, any kind of rapprochement between the European states. But given modern developments in communication, trade, and war, the unity of Europe was an "accomplished physical fact." The only remaining barrier was Britain's elite, who saw empire as the key to world hegemony and a closer rapport with Europe as its relinquishment: "they are not good Europeans—they are not Europeans at all, they do not even think as Europeans."

Revolution in India was a firebrand's book: hot, declarative, full of Frances's trademark epigrams. "By Our Own, Mr. Churchill means of course what is Not Our Own; he does not mean the white cliffs of Dover, nor even the playing fields of Harrow: he means, oddly enough when you come to think of it, India." Though her style was polemical and speculative, many of the substantive points she advanced have since been borne out in histories of British rule. The *Nation*'s reviewer judged the book "a mine of exact information primed with heavy charges of T.N.T." *Common Sense* issued reprints of her articles; the book sold out in a few days and went into a second printing. The British authorities in Bengal deemed the book "objectionable" and sought to suppress its sale.

Why hadn't she been writing this sort of stuff for years? the editor and publisher Oswald Garrison Villard wondered. Madame Chiang Kai-shek asked Frances the same question. They met at the hospital where Madame Chiang, under an assumed name, was undergoing medical treatment. She'd come to the United States at the invitation of Eleanor Roosevelt to campaign for the cause of a free China, barnstorming the country, lobbying Congress to send arms and planes to battle the Japanese occupiers. When Frances visited her, Madame Chiang was propped up in bed, wearing a pink velvet bed jacket and matching coral earrings, her makeup impeccable.

They talked of Nehru—Madame Chiang was also an admirer—and of Clare Boothe Luce, who'd been elected to Congress from Connecticut. Madame Chiang had just seen her; Clare, a Republican, was a keen advocate for the Chinese nationalist cause. Poor Clare, Madame Chiang said: she works so hard, one day she'll be laid up from exhaustion. Not likely, Frances retorted. Clare worked like a man, at her own job, rather than *through* a man, as other women had to do.

A few months later, Madame Chiang invited Frances to dinner at her suite at the Waldorf. A whiskey beforehand, a fillet of beef to follow. Canny and a charmer, Madame Chiang turned the conversation to personal matters.

Had she and John split up because of India? Madame Chiang asked Frances. Or was it too personal to say? She intimated that she knew far more than she'd said, about Frances and India and perhaps her marriage, too. Madame Chiang still held a grudge against John for what he'd written about her sisters. She and Frances shared a bond, she said: neither of them was Indian, but both fought for India. What Frances wrote had such life in it, she said. She needed to write *more*, Madame Chiang reiterated.

Frances was, in fact, writing. She'd returned to the empire manuscript and was taking courses at Yale in European history, the British Empire, and international law. Send my love to Frances, Nehru wrote his niece. "What is she doing at Yale? Is she not clever enough already?"

A consequence of Frances's newfound success was the accommodation she was reaching, slowly, with John. When she was working well, Frances didn't begrudge him anything, neither his fancy clothes nor his glass coffee table. Not even his dates with girls. But when she got hamstrung or stuck, she felt full of vitriol. "What kind of man are you to buy a glass table in a time of air raids?" she snapped at him one day. The separation dragged on and on, but she refused to give him a divorce.

"I have never known her to compromise a conviction," John wrote of Frances. She'd asked him to write something about her that her publisher could use to promote *Revolution in India*. "She has a very striking talent for penetrating to the inner heart of any problem by the shortest and most trenchant route," he observed, adding: "no matter who gets damaged while she is on her way." It had taken a psychoanalyst three entire days to make Frances utter the word "Fuck," John told Rebecca West. "If he had added the phrase 'the British,' there would have been no delay," Rebecca rejoined.

Frances dedicated *Revolution in India* to John. Not the standard "in love and gratitude." But an epigraph from the *Aenead:* "Perhaps it will please us one day to remember these things."

AS A FOREIGN CORRESPONDENT—on the outside, looking in— Frances had never had much regard for the ideal of objectivity. Too often it seemed to her a substitute for thinking a problem through. The role of a partisan suited her better. It was as a militant on behalf of other people's national causes—propelled by her own struggle for freedom but again, an outsider—that she came into her own, first on behalf of India, then campaigning for a Jewish state.

Her "Jews and Hindus," as John put it, made an odd pairing. They shared little other than the fact that both were waging a campaign against the British. Otherwise, they were at opposite ends of the conventional left-right spectrum: Jabotinsky's Irgun militaristic and right-wing, the Indian National Congress liberal, even socialistic, and pledged to Gandhian nonviolence. Both Gandhi and Nehru had eschewed the idea of a Jewish state in Palestine as a violation of Arab rights to self-determination; the Irgun, and Zionism more generally, paid little attention to the Indian subcontinent.

Frances tacked between both causes, propelled by her anti-British attitudes and, increasingly, by her sense of herself as a Jew. For all her opposition to imperialism, Frances didn't see a Jewish state as Gandhi or Nehru did—as an imperialistic land grab of Arab territory. The Arabs of Palestine, she insisted in a familiar argument of the time, could settle elsewhere: they had seven countries ready to welcome them. The Jews had only one and even that one was not yet theirs.

That was why from the moment she heard about the plan to smuggle a million Jews from Nazi-occupied Europe to Palestine, she committed herself to the effort. She helped Jabotinsky's spirited young foot soldier, Peter Bergson, get a visa to the United States in the spring of 1940, where he crisscrossed the country, raising funds. In 1941, alongside the screenwriter Ben Hecht, she joined Bergson's organizing committee to raise a "Jewish Army" to fight the Nazis on the side of the Allies. She served as treasurer. The fact that the established American Jewish organizations—wary of antagonizing the British and stirring up more anti-Semitism in the United States— loathed Bergson and his tactics didn't in the least deter her. They were so timid, she fumed. Couldn't they see the catastrophe unfolding in front of them?

After the first press reports of the systematic extermination of the Jews reached America in the summer and fall of 1942, Bergson's committee tried to rouse FDR's administration to a concerted response. It mounted dramatic bids for public attention. At Madison Square Garden in March 1943, the Committee for a Jewish Army sponsored Hecht's memorial pageant to the two million Jews already killed in Europe. Entitled "We Will Never Die," the pageant attracted a record-breaking crowd of forty thousand. The purpose, said Hecht, was to "bring a Madison Square Garden audience to the large grave of Jewry and let them stand for two hours looking into its remarkable contents." The audience for a special, invitation-only performance in Washington's Constitution Hall included seven Supreme Court justices, dozens of senators, hundreds of congressmen, and Eleanor Roosevelt.

The Committee for a Jewish Army changed its name to the Emergency Committee to Save the Jewish People of Europe in the summer of 1943. Still committed to the establishment of a Jewish state in Palestine, the committee's urgent efforts were now focused on the rescue of Europe's remaining Jews. To that end, it pursued the sort of hard-nosed, ends-justify-the-means techniques that Frances had long favored. As the mainstream Jewish organizations looked on appalled, the Emergency Committee pushed to new, showy extremes. It staged the only demonstration in support of rescue: a march in October 1943 of hundreds of black-coated rabbis from Washington's Union Station to the Capitol. The Emergency Committee's office was overwhelmed with donations and offers of help; by the end of the war, the membership was more than 125,000 strong.

For a ragtag group with hardly any funds, whose principal players were foreigners (some of whom had arrived in the United States barely speaking English), this was an astonishing organizational triumph. It was all the more notable given the hostility that the Emergency Committee encountered from established Jewish organizations at nearly every turn. As with the India League, the Emergency Committee's success depended on the well-connected Americans it recruited to its side, Frances and Ben Hecht chief among them. They knew how to work the levers of power and shared Bergson's taste for provocation.

The emergence of the seemingly retiring Frances as a charismatic mainstay of two nationalist organizations was no surprise to the person who knew her best. "Externally she seemed the shyest creature you ever met, almost painfully diffident; but she always knew exactly what she wanted, and she made a straight line to get it," John judged. She had a "talent for pertinent realism." When other people rambled on about strategies and tactics, Frances, John observed, would "flash like some bright bird directly to whatever was the deep basic fundamental point involved."

Alongside its public campaign, the Emergency Committee was lobbying hard for a new American government agency to coordinate rescue efforts. The State Department, they recognized, would have to be bypassed. Its leadership, fearing an influx of undesirable refugees, had no interest in saving Jews. Even worse, State Department officials were sabotaging other rescue efforts.

The resolution that came before the U.S. Congress in November 1943 ought, then, to have been a triumphant moment for the Emergency Committee. It pledged the American government to an effort to save the Jews of Europe from extermination—precisely what the Emergency Committee had been campaigning for. Bergson's performance before Congress, though, was a disaster. The hearing on the rescue resolution took the form of a chastisement, as one irritated congressman after another objected to Bergson's assertions that the American government was failing to aid the Jews.

Bergson was combative, sarcastic, unable to resist a fight even if it did his cause harm. His voice squeaked when he got agitated. The chairman of the House Foreign Affairs Committee—himself Jewish and allied with the mainstream Jewish organizations—treated Bergson with contempt. The hearing devolved into a back-and-forth between the chairman and Bergson about whether he was in the United States legally. Bergson refused to answer the question. Was the subject before the U.S. Congress saving the Jews or investigating *him*? Bergson protested. The accusation was taking hold (one that would be repeated in years to come) that the Emergency Committee was a front run by aliens for the Irgun's terrorist activities in Palestine.

Frances's testimony followed the next day. Her job, she knew, was to smooth the congressional feathers while at the same time pressing the House of Representatives to action. She wasn't accustomed to public speaking, she told the Congress, but she would do the best that she could. Her voice was low and soft.

It wasn't just Jews' lives that were at stake, she argued. The matter needed to be thought of more broadly, in terms of winning both the war and the peace. A commitment to save Europe's Jews would function as a form of psychological warfare in the same way that bombing Berlin would—only more effectively. For the United States in particular, the rescue of the Jews was particularly important. The prestige of America depended upon its commitment to freedom. To say in response to the Nazi campaigns of annihilation, "Awful! Awful!" and then to do nothing, had been a great boon to the Germans. See, they could say, the Americans don't care about humanitarianism at all.

She had a decade of experience living in Europe, she attested. She knew how permeable those borders could be. Rescuing Jews from Eastern Europe, transporting them across the Mediterranean, now Allied-controlled, wouldn't be simple, but it wasn't impossible, either. "We cannot sit by in the face of this catastrophe, this premeditated assassination of a whole great people, and do nothing. I believe we all want to do something," she said.

Bergson's antagonist, the chairman of the House Foreign Affairs Committee, asked Frances for clarification on a question that had come up repeatedly. Was it really necessary to single out the Jews when talking about the refugee problem? Why not just talk about Poles or Frenchmen? Didn't a lot of people in Europe these days need rescuing, after all?

To deny that Jews were being targeted uniquely for persecution, Frances knew very well, was the excuse for doing nothing. It was the State Department's standard reply to petitions on behalf of Jewish rescue. Nevertheless, she answered the question tactfully, as if she were hearing it for the first time. It was hard for Americans, she noted, to understand the particular racial animus that lay behind the persecution of Jews. Perhaps, in the United States, there were people with their "little prejudices," but in Europe now there was an "absolute line of demarcation" between Jews and non-Jews, which left Jewish refugees particularly vulnerable.

Was he to understand that Mrs. Gunther was saying that Jewish refugees, then, were being treated first of all as Jewish—not French or German? asked the chairman.

"You are expressing it perfectly, Mr. Chairman," Frances replied.

Was she the author John Gunther's wife? asked another congressman. Gunther was one of his favorite commentators, he said.

"One of mine, too," Frances answered.

Hers had been most valuable testimony, the congressmen agreed; in fact, the most illuminating they had heard. With the resolution stalled in the Congress, FDR finally took the initiative, recognizing that he would eventually be pushed to act. Created in January 1944, the War Refugee Board was the agency that the Emergency Committee had agitated for. It would save two hundred thousand Jews. Too little, Frances would always say, and too late.

JOHNNY WAS MUCH UNHAPPIER at Riverdale than he let on to his parents. Pudgy, a daydreamer—not yet twelve—he was younger than most of the other boys in his class and out of the swim of things. "You know your son lives in a world altogether his own," the school's headmaster told them.

When they had sent him off to boarding school, it was with the promise that he could spend summers at home rather than at camp. Frances rented a house for them in Amagansett, with a view of the Long Island Sound. She outfitted a workroom for him, chemistry things on one wall, model airplanes on the other, and carpentry tools just opposite. They had friends over, and at night, on the beach, broiled steaks over an open fire.

The next summer, she decided that Johnny would go fishing every Friday to catch their supper. She was always looking for opportunities to toughen him up.

He did it a few times, gamely, but didn't like it and told her so. He couldn't stop thinking about how he'd feel if he were the fish, he said. That's silly, Frances replied, don't think about how the fish feels!

Let *her* try, he decided. As soon as she had to extricate the hook from the fish's mouth, she changed her mind about the virtues of fishing. "Now we buy our fish," he wrote his father.

They were learning how to sail, mother and son, bailing a lot of water the whole time. They'd been reading *Hamlet* and *Julius Caesar* together. He was taking lessons in chemistry and in tennis. He was fooling around, trying to grow plants without soil. They'd planted a victory garden, and Nehru's two nieces had come to stay.

Johnny decided he wanted to move on to the high school at Deerfield Academy that fall of 1943. The headmaster at Riverdale wanted him to stay another year, but Frances was in favor of Deerfield, which had the reputation of being the most liberal and least disciplinarian of the East Coast boarding schools; it was the only one not modeled on the English public schools. John said the decision was the boy's to make, and he'd opted to go. He had his courses for the year all planned out.

Soon he won't need me at all, Frances thought. She'd relished his dependence, in a way, but now the task was different. She knew she was supposed to push him out of the nest and set him on the path to his own life. "That is the hardest duty," she wrote Nehru.

Johnny wrote her, teasingly, from Deerfield: "I try to be spontaneous, uninhibited, self-aware and self-controlled."

Back from Deerfield on his spring break, Frances insisted that Johnny see a psychiatrist. He still wet the bed—not that often, true, but nevertheless a sign of some disturbance they couldn't just ignore. John disagreed with her; Dorothy's son Michael had been a disaster since some child psychiatrist mucked around with his glands. But Frances wouldn't be deterred.

John was angry about it, especially after he met the doctor. The guy was an eminent psychoanalyst who derided Stekel, and occupied a full half-hour talking to him about the meaning of Johnny's Rorschach tests. Part of the problem, the doctor had explained, was Johnny's heredity, the combination of John's Germanness and Frances's Jewishness. Both the Jews and the Germans were defeated peoples. The Jews because they didn't fight and the Germans because they did.

I don't know how long of a treatment I can afford, John told him. "What do you want me to do? Cut the price?" demanded the psychiatrist.

Asked in the first session what he wanted most in the world, Johnny said happiness and to do some good. He wished he were more talkative and tidier.

And what bothered him the most? the psychiatrist probed. Bedwetting, he volunteered. And then school problems and interactions with other boys. Then there were his relations with his parents. "But I don't think this bothers me," he said, on reflection.

KNICK, SUNBURNED AND UNUSUALLY quiet, was already in Algeria in the summer of 1943, when John arrived for his stint of war reporting. They had lunch together and went to the PX. Your shoes are worse than useless, Knick informed him. You need boots and a bedroll and a tent. You *are* planning to go ashore, aren't you?

The operation would be a big one—that much they understood. The purpose of the so-called Second Front was to provide some relief for the Soviet forces, which for nearly two years had been battling the Nazis' eastern onslaught. The specifics, though, were top secret. Would it be Greece? Or France? Or Egypt? Or Italy? The location of the Second Front had been debated endlessly. In Washington, John got seven different answers from seven different people, all claiming to be in the know.

In Algiers, the correspondents ate together and drank together but didn't talk about their assignments. John had gotten the choicest one of all, partly because of his celebrity, partly due to a favor from a friend; his reputation for fair-mindedness probably helped, too. He would be reporting on behalf of the entire American press from the headquarters of the newly appointed supreme commander of the Allied Forces in North Africa: General Dwight D. Eisenhower. John could feel the real war reporters looking him over. "We can't all be great celebrities like you," one of them, a BBC reporter, chided him.

Consider yourself members of my staff, Eisenhower told John and his British counterpart. Ike was folksy, and at ease when mixing with reporters. He had decided that any copy they filed would be shared with every newspaper or radio station in Britain and the United States. This wouldn't make their editors happy, but the pool system ensured that no newspaper could score an exclusive on the breaking war news. To prevent the enemy from decoding a wire, their dispatches would be sent via courier plane to Tunis or Algiers.

Like any good city editor, Eisenhower knew the kind of story he wanted to see printed. He was at pains to emphasize that the military effort was united. Contrary to the reports of friction between the American and British forces—between Ike and the British general Bernard Montgomery—this was an *allied* command, the British, the Americans, and the Canadians all working together. The attack on Axis-occupied Europe would begin with an overnight aerial raid, to be followed by a massive amphibious operation on the Italian island of Sicily. A few days later, John was trailing behind Eisenhower when the general command stepped onto the Sicilian beach.

"So you're the only U.S. correspondent attached to my Army," General Montgomery said to John, appraisingly. *My* army, Montgomery called the Eighth Army. *My* troops. Rangy, he spoke in sharp, truncated sentences, as if "the" and "and" were a waste of his time.

I have a diary that'll knock the wind out of everyone between Alamein and London, Monty announced. Every day, he mailed the pages off to a strongbox, whose location he alone knew; no one was spared in its pages. How much would I get for my diary? he asked John.

About a hundred thousand dollars, John figured. "Guess won't die in poorhouse after all," Montgomery bantered.

So long as reporting was tightly constrained by the pool system, there would be few wartime scoops. One way of circumventing the restrictions was what the Hoosier-born Ernie Pyle, reporting for the Scripps-Howard papers, did. Champion of the little guy, Pyle told the story of the war from the perspective of the infantrymen in the foxholes and on the beachheads, chronicling the conflict not as heroic crusade but as an endless succession of exhaustion, monotony, fear—"an unalleviated misfortune," as the *New Yorker*'s A. J. Liebling would say. By contrast, John's response to the War Department's restraints was to return to a variant of his "Inside" technique, focusing on the generals. In his book on the Sicilian campaign, he emphasized the contrast between Eisenhower and Montgomery. It was less a war book about the fighting in Sicily—John had departed for Cairo before much of that happened—but about the process of observing a war and the men who commanded it.

Unlike Pyle, who saw the fighting in Sicily to its end, John stayed only a few weeks. Pyle was a "feuilletonist of genius," John judged, the best of the war correspondents and one of the few to produce a lasting account of the war. He himself wasn't cut out for following soldiers into combat, though. Moreover, he didn't want to run into Knick again. While he worried about what Agnes would think of him if he left mid-battle, he could at least try to put in a phone call to her from Egypt. The Italians couldn't hold out long, it seemed. Their air force was a catastrophe, their tanks idled for lack of parts. Their ration boxes had a layer of food on the top, and stones below. The Allied strategy was working as planned: the Germans would have to move troops to Italy if they wanted to prevent enemy forces from advancing on the Reich's southern borders.

"Finito Benito" was the cry John heard in a Sicilian town square just before he departed. Mussolini's Grand Council had turned on him. Even his son-in-law Count Ciano had turned Judas; the police had arrived to take the Duce away in handcuffs. There, in its birthplace, fascism had been dealt its first death blow.

JOHN WORRIED THAT FRANCES would never give him a divorce. In the interest of her causes—the Hindus and the Jews—she'd want to remain "Mrs. John Gunther." Before he left for North Africa, she came over to his apartment. They sat together at the glass dining table and tried to talk over the past. You make me cry, she told him. He cried, too.

He'd been in love with her at the start, he said—a declaration that took her aback. Living on her own had made her realize, she said, how difficult she was to live with. She wished she could be like Dorothy, who was always giving of herself and never defeated. Dorothy would certainly marry again. "I *went*. I went from myself," Frances told him, explaining how thoroughly she'd lost herself in their marriage. She was crazy but so logical about it, John thought. Of course, she assured him, she'd give him a divorce.

While he was away, his lawyer worked up the divorce papers. Together, they took Johnny to Deerfield that fall, and returned on separate trains. He watched as Frances's train left the station. "You bastard," she mouthed, and made a V for Victory sign. A couple of weeks later, he went to Amagansett to help her pack up the house she'd been renting. She signed the divorce agreement without any fuss, and on the way back to the city, they stopped at a roadhouse inn for dinner. A steak for two and warm, tender conversation. "I have never been fonder of her," John wrote in his diary.

The one condition for giving him the divorce was that he had to go to Reno to get it. After the new year, 1944, he set out for what the gossip columnist Walter Winchell called a "Reno-vation," a quickie divorce. It took just six weeks to establish residency in Nevada; the grounds for divorce were among the least onerous in America. In uncontested cases such as the Gunthers', Reno judges didn't insist on embarrassing and public cross-examination. Unlike in many other states, the divorcées could marry again immediately. An entire infrastructure had shot up around the Reno divorce industry, from local lawyers with connections to the white-shoe East Coast firms to luxurious nightclubs where one could while away the cool evenings, waiting for the decree to come through.

The formal cause for the Gunthers' divorce was desertion. Three years earlier, in 1941, John's complaint read, Frances had left him. Although she denied the charge, she didn't contest the divorce, a common enough, face-saving way to manage these matters in Reno.

While in the Gunthers' circle a marriage that ended in divorce was more the rule than the exception, there was nonetheless something shameful about it. A divorce was a defeat, as Frances saw it. For John, it was a source of guilt. Frances didn't want any alimony, she insisted, though what she'd live on he didn't know, so he included a monthly stipend in the divorce papers. She was livid about that.

Once Frances had agreed to the divorce, he came to a resolution about Agnes. He wouldn't make her choose between Knick and him, after all. He went to see her again in Dallas and then, a few months later, she came to New York. Knick had written her several contrite letters before going silent. He hardly had any stories in the paper, which meant he was back on the bottle. John broached the subject of marriage again, and this time she joined in. They talked about the asparagus bed they'd plant and the washing machine they'd buy. They picked out schools for the children in New York.

You're not writing this all down, she asked him. Are you?

From Reno, John sent Frances a farewell letter, accompanied by a scarf. Why was he sending her such mawkish stuff? she demanded. Hadn't he realized yet that they had been saying farewell practically from the moment they met twenty years ago? They'd never really be through with each other. "I'll always dominate the private parts of your heart," she wrote, "and you'll always dominate all the acts of my life."

"I await the Reno Decree with the same agonizing suspense I await Hitler's Surrender & the End of the War—the extension of the last excruciating moments of the bull-fight—the bull & matador mutually wounded," she continued. Who the bull was and who the matador she didn't say. She was writing on stationery with Mrs. John Gunther embossed in small blue capital letters at the top. She had a whole stack of it that she needed to use up.

PART
FOUR

LOVE YOUR ENEMY

—

NOT LONG AFTER THE UNITED STATES ENTERED THE WAR, Dorothy Thompson was already in a fight about the coming peace. Specifically, the fate of Germany and postwar Europe. Germany must be dismembered, broken up, turned into farmland, placed under international control! went the cry in some quarters in Washington, D.C., and among the resistance movements, the Free French, Free Czechs, and Free Poles in exile in London. Only if Germany were eliminated as a military threat could there be peace in Europe. In 1944, FDR approved a preliminary plan devised by his Treasury secretary, Henry Morgenthau, to forcibly deindustrialize Germany.

The idea of wrecking Germany to save Europe was dangerous nonsense, Dorothy had been insisting for two years. Nothing would make the Germans fight harder than the threat of an occupied and divided country. It was, as she put it, "Hitler's greatest psychological asset today." The way forward, rather, was a strong and democratic German nation-state in a federated Europe. She envisioned a European Continent organized around the principles of freedom and equality and unified in its diversity. No customs frontiers would impede the flow of goods. Europe's citizenry would be free to move across borders to work and to settle.

The "United States of Europe"—as an idea—had been kicking

around since Napoleon. During the 1930s, the vision of a federated, democratic Europe had been reinvigorated. Jerry Frank and Frances, like Dorothy, counted among its avid American proponents. What made Dorothy's conception different and prescient was the role she imagined for Germany as its bulwark. In a series of shortwave broadcasts to Europe in the spring of 1942, later published with a long prologue as *Listen, Hans,* she laid out her thoughts.

She styled her Friday broadcasts to Germany as an appeal to an old friend. "Hans" had refused to leave Germany when Hitler came to power. A German patriot but not a Nazi, Dorothy's imagined interlocutor was a person of means and substance, someone very like her old Berlin friend, the lawyer Helmuth James von Moltke. Part of what Dorothy had to say to Hans was standard-issue war propaganda. The military news was infinitely worse than the Nazi press let on, the regime was lying to its people, Germany's war effort was doomed, the Allies were unified. If the Nazis thought they could sow dissension in the United States and turn Americans against each other, they were woefully mistaken. The time was running out, she reiterated, for Hans to act.

But it was the "personal" element that distinguished Dorothy's broadcasts, for in drawing on her own experiences in Germany—in speaking over the shortwave in her headlong but ungrammatical German—she conjured up a lost world: dinners in a favorite little restaurant on the Französische Strasse in Berlin; the visits she and Hans had planned back and forth across the Atlantic; the friendships they had envisioned between her little son and Hans's children. That evocation of happier days made the moral disaster of the present all the keener. The guilt of the Germans was a "vast dirty brown wave," Dorothy said. "Do you associate yourself with this guilt, Hans? Do the German people who may hear me associate themselves with that guilt? And if not, how do you dissociate yourselves?"

Her broadcasts were psychological warfare of the type that she'd been urging on Roosevelt since the war started. She'd admitted as much from the first episode of *Listen, Hans.* What she didn't say as plainly was that her efforts were directed not just at the enemy, but at her fellow citizens as well. At a time when German "civilization" or "Kultur" had become a byword for hypocrisy at best, and barbarism at worst, *Listen, Hans* sought to persuade Americans that the German people and the German nation were both salvageable.

Rushed out in a cheap edition, *Listen, Hans* bore the subtitle "New and Constructive Thinking About the War." Together with her trademark focus on the individual (hence the appeal to Hans), Dorothy was also dissecting what she called the "German mind." She was partaking in the science of "culture-cracking," which the war had boosted. Both the U.S. Army and the civilian Office of War Information had established units staffed with anthropologists and political scientists to render lightning-quick analyses of national character. They assessed the repressed anger of the Japanese and the mindless order-taking (or was it paranoia?) of the Germans.

Dorothy's psychological portrait was somewhat more involved than the standard culture-cracking fare. It took in a vast sweep of history, philosophy, and literature. She depicted the Germans as riven by paradoxes: rational as well as romantic, precise but also prone to recklessness. "Such a psychological confusion, in a nation as in an individual, induces mental breakdown." The solution was to harness what was salutary in German culture: its universalism and idealism. She pooh-poohed the kind of propaganda that focused on a bloodless "three meals a day." Nor would Germans respond to reassurances about the reestablishment of private enterprise and a restoration of the prewar order. Americans might dream of a return to "normalcy," but for the Germans, little about the previous three chaotic decades promised hope for the future. What was needed was a new vision, both spiritual and economic. That was where a federated, democratic Europe organized around the common good came in.

These were Dorothy's old themes—the need for moral renewal, the inevitable interdependence of nations—welded to the then-fashionable anatomizing of peoples. Even as she wrote of the German mind, her preface ballooning to 130 pages, her analysis returned to the individual. "To believe that Nazism is an exclusively German phenomenon is to disregard the evidence all about ourselves," she maintained. It *could* happen here or anywhere. In a much-quoted *Harper's* essay of the year before, "Who Goes Nazi?," she'd spelled out, in the most quotidian sense, how.

Look around the next big party of your acquaintances, and try to guess who would become a Nazi, Dorothy challenged her readers. It was a "somewhat macabre parlor game," but an instructive one. How about the bluff bank vice president in the corner? He was always in the right place at the right time: clubbable, married to a rich woman. He'd join the Nazis in a second—that is, when it was personally expedient to do so. What about the demure, clinging wife of the brilliant scientist? She's so inoffensive, so weak, perpetually subject to her husband's desires. Surely not *her*? Count on it, Dorothy admonished. She's an easy mark for any jackbooted thug who bellows that a woman's place is in the kitchen: "she is looking for someone else before whom to pour her ecstatic self-abasement."

"Believe me, nice people don't go Nazi," Dorothy declared. "Their race, color, creed, or social condition is not the criterion. It is something in them." Whatever else lay at its root—economic turmoil, a lost war, national resentments—Nazism, she argued, was a matter of personality. People who knew their own mind, unostentatiously original folk, those with principles and common sense were insulated from the lures of fascism. "But the frustrated and humiliated intellectual, the rich and scared speculator, the spoiled son, the labor tyrant, the fellow who has achieved success by smelling out the wind of success—they would all go Nazi in a crisis."

In insisting on individual character, Dorothy offered an old-fashioned diagnosis to go with her analysis of national "minds" and her prescription for a new world order. Put together and delivered with panache in *Listen, Hans,* the combination garnered excellent reviews. Don't start this book at bedtime, opined the *Atlanta Constitution's* critic; you won't sleep until you've finished it. The marquee reviewers—Malcolm Cowley in the *New Republic,* John Chamberlain in the *New York Times,* the Harvard political theorist Carl Friedrich—pronounced the book a major contribution to American thought. It was "one of the most remarkable books to have come out of the war," wrote Friedrich in the *Atlantic*.

As disturbed as Dorothy was about the Allied demand for the "unconditional surrender" of Germany and Japan—a "barbarity," she called it—the failure of the Morgenthau deindustrialization plan was a satisfaction. It had fallen victim to a public outcry as soon as the outline leaked. Morgenthau was an "amorphous ass," she judged, and the notion of reducing Germany to a land of peasants was nothing more than propaganda tailor-made for Goebbels. The fact that Americans rejected it indicated that her message about the self-defeating inanity of a vengeful, Carthaginian peace was getting through.

As vehemently as she had raised the alarm a decade earlier, now Dorothy sought to map out a path back to peace. While Jimmy and John floundered, each sunk into their particular sort of wartime misery, and Knick drank too much and stopped writing for months at a time, Dorothy remained as productive and influential during the war as she'd ever been. One advantage of being a woman was that she didn't feel inadequate merely opining about the war, rather than fighting in it. Writing, lecturing, and organizing a Volunteer Land Corps to fill in for the Vermonters who'd enlisted, she seemed at forty-nine nearly tireless. "Neither your personal life nor your social existence is a series of episodes," she told the college students who'd come to Vermont for the summer from Dartmouth or Wellesley to bale hay and tend chickens. "The creation of a personality and the creation of a nation depend upon the maintenance of continuity."

That summer of 1942, as she started the prologue for *Listen, Hans* and delivered homilies about continuity in life, a refugee painter named Maxim Kopf showed up at Twin Farms. A big, exuberant man, Max was a Czech born in Vienna but raised in Prague, and a veteran of the last war. When Hitler's troops arrived in Prague, Max had rolled up his canvases and left for Paris. "I was not going to live in a country ruled by a maniac who thought he was an artist, surrounded by thugs who thought themselves Teutonic knights," he said.

In Paris, Max was arrested and interned first because he kept company with Communists. Then when he got out of prison, he fled to Morocco, where he was again imprisoned because he was suspected of having traitorous Free French allegiances. By 1941, courtesy of Jan Masaryk, who intervened on his behalf, he had made his way to the United States carrying all he had in the world: a straw suitcase with three pairs of socks and a handful of watercolor pictures.

Max arrived, unbidden, at Twin Farms, to paint Dorothy's picture. He was the friend of a friend. Really, she said, she was much too busy to sit for a portrait. The painting part of things lasted only a day. That same night, his shoes in hand, he climbed the stairs to her room, as quietly as a burly man of six feet–plus could. He kissed her right on the mouth.

She fell for him immediately. Nevertheless, she tried, half-heartedly, to warn him off. "The world crowds in on me so terribly— I hate it; I suffer terribly from it," she told him. "I have nightmares sometimes of masses of faces and hands; all staring and grabbing." They all wanted her to *do* something.

"My Great Woman," Max called her. "I kiss every spot on you." He was heard to say: "What you need a cock for if you have a tongue."

He was the man she had "always tried to marry," she told John. Self-assured, full of mirth, unafraid of anything, a good cook, not literary but able to talk about the Psalms or Heinrich Heine. In his paintings, he came back again and again to the theme of Jacob wrestling with God and Christ's body after the Crucifixion. He knew how to describe the world precisely. He could take care of Dorothy and understood that contrary to appearances, she needed that. He was very, very good to her, pronounced Rebecca West, who was a Max partisan. When people called him "Mr. Thompson," he didn't mind.

I'm so happy, Dorothy told John on the phone. It used to be that the world had been her problem, but now she had something else to fix herself to. In the summer of 1943, she and Max married at the austere, white clapboard Universalist Church in Barnard, Vermont.

John and Knick were on their way to North Africa but Jimmy, back on a short stay from his tour of duty, was there. The FBI spent a few weeks investigating whether Max Kopf was a Nazi agent, sent to the United States to soften Dorothy Thompson's attitudes toward Germany, before abandoning the inquiry.

The hands didn't stop grabbing at Dorothy, and she still conducted one-sided conversations. "I'm just the janitor here," Max would joke before retiring when the dinner party conversation no longer interested him. The early light was best for painting, he said as he excused himself.

Dorothy, it turned out, was good at marital happiness, which wasn't exactly what she would have thought based on her experiences with Joseph and Red. And amid the many losses of the war, one after another, that was a consolation. Christa Winsloe was killed in 1944, shot by a gang of mercenaries in the chaos that followed D-Day. Dorothy's stepson, Wells Lewis, who'd been a little boy when she married Red, died in France, aged twenty-seven, caught by sniper fire. "I make myself recriminations that I did not do more," she mourned. "My grief is in every cell and I do not want it assuaged. It is part of me forever and it is what remains to me of him. . . ."

Her friend Helmuth James von Moltke was dead, too. As Dorothy well knew, von Moltke had never required the spine-stiffening she administered to Hans. "How can anyone know these things and walk around free?" he asked his wife after the roundup of Berlin's Jews. By the spring of 1942, he was already leaguing against the Nazis, planning for the world to come; his estate in the Silesian countryside gave the name to the Kreisau Circle of determined, well-placed anti-Nazis. He was arrested in 1944 on the charge of treason and hanged the following year. He never knew anything of Dorothy's broadcasts.

AS PROUD AS HE was of his son, the Reverend H. D. Knickerbocker suspected that Knick was an exemplar of precisely the sort of modern mindset he had long decried from the pulpit. He was chagrined that Knick had used "hell" as a curse word when the *New Yorker* profiled him. He disapproved of his daughter-in-law's course of "Psycsyatry," a word so unfamiliar to him that he rendered it phonetically. But most of all, he, a fervent teetotaler, was distraught about Knick's drinking. The mania for personal freedom—the eschewal of "discipline and restraint"—led to "anarchy and hell," the Reverend Knickerbocker thundered. It began in the home and ended in the state.

Before Knick broke his promise to Agnes and started drinking again, he returned to the connection his father had made between morality and temperance. "I am rid of that incubus," Knick wrote her from North Africa. "I am reacquiring a moral sense, about the war, about my work, about life. This, darling Agnes is a revolution in my soul." The fact that she wasn't writing back scared him. Of course, she was mad at him, and she had a right to be. He was lying on his bedroll, out under the Algerian stars, and trying to imagine himself back home, with Agnes and the babies. He couldn't—and that scared him, too. He'd been afraid and unhappy when he was boozing, but he wasn't anymore. She was the only woman he loved, he vowed.

Agnes copied out Knick's remorseful letters and sent them to John. Though John didn't say so, he doubted that Knick's resolutions would last long. Knick had relocated to northern France for D-Day and accompanied the American army to Paris. Parisians were willing to see their city destroyed, Knick reported, to rid it of Germans. "At least, they say they are and that's more than they used to say." He'd gone to his old apartment on the Île Saint-Louis, expecting the worst after four years' absence, only to find it immaculate, every stick of furniture in place. The Norwegian maid he'd left in charge of the apartment was bald, her hair shaved off as a punishment for collaborating with the Germans.

It wasn't long before he was on another bender. He went to London and took up again with the woman he'd been seeing there. They holidayed together, and he ignored the *Sun*'s demands that he return to the front. All that freezing cold fall, as the German defenses stiffened, and the Allied advances halted, he hardly published a thing.

By the time he returned to the United States in January 1945, he was foul-tempered, constantly soused, his arrangement with the *Sun* terminated. To pay the bills he'd arranged a lecture tour across the United States, which would have been trying in the best of times.

He'd only been back in Dallas a few days when he put on an old jacket to go out to the garden. Inside the pocket he discovered a letter from John addressed to his wife. The fact that Agnes had "accidentally" left a love letter in Knick's jacket seemed to John to indicate a desire to be found out. But she denied doing it on purpose. God, the Knickerbockers wallow in their emotional messes, was the verdict of John's ex-girlfriend Bubbles.

Agnes called John to tell him that Knick was drunk and in a rage. They'd had terrible fights. To mollify him, she had said the affair started in 1942, only after she found out about his London woman. John hung up the phone and couldn't help laughing out of exhaustion and relief. At long last it was all out in the open—or almost all out. Whatever remorse John had felt about Knick at the start of the affair had been superseded by a conviction that he, and not Knick, could make Agnes happy. They'd marry soon. The only serious issue, he figured, was working out a custody arrangement. Knick was on a plane to Baltimore, en route to Johns Hopkins, where he'd dry out under the care of a doctor friend whom he'd known since his Russian days.

When Agnes told him on the phone that she was going to Baltimore, too, John was dumbfounded. Why would she do that? She couldn't leave Knick now, she replied. "We've got a human *soul* to save."

To the Johns Hopkins doctor, an acquaintance of his, John wrote long letters setting out the facts of the affair and protesting his love for Agnes. She doesn't want to see you, the doctor wired. Don't even think of coming here. "You're well out of it," he advised.

The entire episode was memorialized by John in one last work of personal fiction, published posthumously as *The Indian Sign* in 1970. In the book, the hero's entanglement with his best friend's wife has a double function. It keeps him on the home front, out of the war, about which he was ambivalent. It also represents the culmination of his frustrated, envious love for his friend ("Mac" in the story). When it's all over, he's unsure whom he will miss more, his lover or Mac. Incorporated into the novel were the real-life documents and events of the affair: barely edited pillow talk with Agnes, Frances's conversations with John, a telegram that Knick wrote denouncing John. All "capital," as he put it, that he'd accumulated in his archive.

At the end of *The Indian Sign,* the John character remarries his first wife. She's sharp, neurotic, and vulnerable, but "a large part of me belonged to her." After he sees the Agnes character for the last time, his wife turns to him and utters one of the things Frances said to him: "You don't look like a young man any longer."

THE WAR HAD BEEN over a few months when John and Jimmy met up at "21" for dinner, proceeding afterward to the Stork for a nightcap. Jimmy was back from a stint in Europe. He'd gotten himself discharged from the air force in the fall of 1944 and accredited as a war correspondent with Patton's Third Army, which was fighting its way across Central Europe. He'd arrived in Europe just as Knick was leaving, and was there for the bloody, unnecessary finale, as the German armies—without any hope of victory—nonetheless fought on.

Jimmy's view of Germany was much gloomier than Dorothy's, not least because he'd spent months talking to German prisoners. He hadn't met a single one who acknowledged even an iota of responsibility for the "vast historical crime of Hitlerism." Germany, he'd concluded, would have to be resurrected from the ground up, one individual at a time. And the United States couldn't hope to tackle such a project of human engineering without coming to some sort of agreement with the Soviet Union. It surely wasn't feasible to create one sort of Germany in the Allied zones and quite another in the territory the Red Army occupied, Jimmy opined.

And it wasn't just the Germans and the Japanese who needed reconstruction. Here, Jimmy agreed with Dorothy, whose columns were turning into lamentations over the collapse of standards and the low state of public morality. At the Stork Club, John and Jimmy met four men, pilots and bombardiers who had from their B-29s dropped the atomic bombs on Hiroshima and Nagasaki. The men were shorter than John expected. One of them was going into the leather business. Tired as they were, they also appeared carefree.

Do you think they realize they've killed more humans than anyone else in history? John asked Jimmy.

No chance of it, Jimmy answered. "Look at their faces."

Jimmy was discouraged about humanity, not just abroad but at home. The trouble with Dinah, which began with him raising hell about the idea that she'd appear on the stage, hadn't subsided. Now she was in Reno, getting a divorce on grounds of "mental cruelty." He could hardly believe it. He blamed her for the whole mess of their marriage and ranted on about a gigolo taking his place and raising his children. Not a word, John noted disapprovingly, about his own drinking or bad behavior.

Our time is done, Jimmy announced to John. They'd been the Zeitgeist for a decade. But now the game belonged to the broadcasters like Ed Murrow and the young folk like Roger Mudd and Eric Sevareid.

The good news? Their style of reporting—Jimmy called it a "school"—would endure.

John suspected Jimmy of succumbing to the boozer's nostalgia. He was certain that his own best work still lay ahead of him. I am "reconstructing myself," John had announced to Bubbles a few months after the end of his affair with Agnes. He'd finally turned to *Inside U.S.A.,* the book he'd told Cass Canfield would be about democracy. That was a subject about which Americans were thinking more—and more self-consciously—at the end of the war. Of the three great ideological systems that had battled it out in the 1920s and 1930s, only two were still standing: democracy and communism. The fact that democracy had triumphed over fascism only threw the issue of its essential qualities in starker relief. If it was indeed going to be an "American century," as the publisher Henry Luce had urged, what sort of democracy were Americans living in? What kind did they want?

John still cared, of course, about leaders and their personalities. But *Inside U.S.A.* was aiming for something different and more ambitious: an account of the people. Who *really* runs your state? was the question John started his interviews with. Then, when he had people talking, he asked: "What do you believe in most?" He was putting his questions to rubber executives and union leaders, electrical engineers, textile manufacturers, playwrights, farmers, housewives, the editors of Black newspapers, judges, professors of animal husbandry, and warehousemen. Lawyers in one town sent him to talk to lawyers in another. Through a local judge he met the archbishop and a host of bankers. He saw state senators and congressmen, and plenty of reporters. Everywhere he went, there were stories in the paper about his forthcoming book.

To Sinclair Lewis, whom John visited on one of his trips, the entire enterprise seemed unimaginable hubris. Why didn't John try writing about a single town? Just to say something meaningful about the state of Minnesota, never mind an entire country, struck Red as a stretch; it would take a person ten whole years to understand the difference between St. Paul and Minneapolis. And as blithely as John had embarked on his *Inside Asia,* he had to admit that writing about America was daunting. He'd traveled from Dublin to Damascus but he knew nothing about vast portions of his own country. Kentucky, for instance. Hadn't ever been there. Or Delaware and Oklahoma, Salt Lake City and Atlanta and New Orleans. Even the logistics were difficult. At the end of the war, every road was clogged with people on their way somewhere, and no hotel would take a reservation for longer than five days.

In trying to interpret America for Americans, John was joining a host of similar efforts, either under way or just getting started. It was the era of the survey, a new phenomenon, which sought to make sense of the nation by assessing what "ordinary" or "average" people thought. Starting in the 1930s, the reporter and adman George Gallup made use of the scientific sampling techniques devised to sell engagement rings, pancake syrup, and newspaper subscriptions to debut the first running public opinion poll. In Bloomington, Indiana, the entomologist Alfred Kinsey was interviewing volunteers about their sex lives, asking coeds how many times they'd masturbated the previous month and soliciting details from men about the angle of their penis shaft.

John didn't aspire to the sort of scientific, sampling expertise of either a Gallup or a Kinsey. He wasn't trying to map out what was normal. What interested him, rather, was America's variety: the country's raucous heterogeneity, its remarkable contrasts. Emphasizing the regional divisions that social scientists increasingly favored as a way of understanding the United States, he crammed his notebooks full of facts. Four hundred thousand Southern Californians had been born in Iowa. There were fifty million pheasants in South Dakota. Americans ate 660 million doughnuts in 1945.

What did it all add up to? That was the question John was puzzling out. On the one hand, there was the indisputable fact that America had, in a matter of months, produced the world's most formidable war machine. On the other, there was the manifest failure of national planning, evident in shortages of basics such as housing and food. Any pronouncement one wanted to make about the United States was controverted by another fact. America had the finest public education in world? What about the 37 percent of children in Kentucky who didn't even finish elementary school?

Inside U.S.A. was the first book of John's that Frances had nothing to do with. Absent her insistence on an overarching argument, he amassed more anecdotes, local chauvinisms, and witty aperçus he'd heard, creating an extravagant compendium of detail that in its form—the book would eventually stretch to 900+ closely printed pages—mirrored the American prodigality he was surveying. Ben Franklin came from "a somewhat shady family," one buttoned-up Philadelphian informed John. Don't ask a man where he's from, son, the Texan instructed his young son. "If a man's from Texas, he'll tell you. If he's not, why embarrass him by asking?"

In place of a thesis, John retreated to the play of paradoxes, what he called America's "preposterous and flamboyant contradictions." The advantage was that he avoided, by and large, stereotypes about American national character. The disadvantage was that he didn't break much below the surface.

Even mapping the surface, though, was proving eye-opening. And on no subject was that truer than the so-called "Negro problem." Attuned by his European reporting to the terrorizing effects of violence, he was gathering information about lynch mobs. But the everyday discrimination he saw seemed to him even more of an indictment. The fact that the distinguished Black sociologist he met in Atlanta couldn't come to his hotel room—that the man couldn't try on a pair of gloves or a hat in a white store, that he could never see a concert or a first-run movie—reminded John of India's caste system. Atlanta, he wrote "out-ghettoes anything I ever saw in a European ghetto, even in Warsaw."

The more John traveled and talked to people, the more racism seemed to him not an isolated Southern problem, but a pervasive American phenomenon. A "cancer," he called it, to be discussed not just in his chapters on the South but on New England and the Midwest as well. Here, John drew upon the conclusions of the Swedish economist Gunnar Myrdal in *An American Dilemma* (1944). Racial discrimination, claimed Myrdal, was founded on a completely unsupported myth of "Negro inferiority." John acknowledged that some Americans would reject Myrdal's findings. But that rejection missed the essential point. Inferiority or superiority aside, all Americans, Black or white, were entitled to equal treatment and civil liberties.

John thought about what Frances would make of what he was seeing. If she were in Atlanta with him, he wrote her, she'd have added our "Brown Brethren" to her causes alongside the Zionists and Indians. She'd be going at the problem "full blast," he suspected.

AFTER THE BUST-UP OF his affair with Agnes in February 1945, John saw more of Frances. He took her to dinner at the Colony Club and the little Italian place they liked and they went to the movies together and talked on the phone. John had other love affairs, with the Danish journalist Inga Arvad, for one. The FBI had figured Arvad, Miss Denmark of 1931, for a Germany spy. She'd hobnobbed with the Nazi top brass, conducting a series of exclusive interviews with Hitler (she was the Führer's guest at the 1936 Olympics) before pursuing a wartime romance with John F. Kennedy. As it turned out, she was just an equal opportunity enchantress.

Not long after the divorce, John had bought Frances a house in Madison, Connecticut, on the Long Island Sound. It was a cedar-shingled old summer house with its own private beach and a big stone terrace. He couldn't really afford it—the down payment amounted to half of his income for the year—but he couldn't say no to her or to Johnny, and they both loved it. It came with a boathouse and a separate studio as well as a workshop where Johnny could conduct his experiments. There was even a barn where they could put on summer theater. They called the house the "Inside Place." Sometimes it struck him that maybe he wouldn't marry again because deep down, as Frances predicted, he still thought about her as his wife.

Frances had been right about the Deerfield School. Johnny was thriving there. He was taking a fifth class, geology, rather than the standard four because he didn't want to go a year without science. Deerfield's headmaster, Frank Boyden, forty-plus years in the job and legendary for his insight into boys, had thought five classes too much, but Johnny's determination had persuaded him. Your son has a very fine mind and high IQ, Boyden wrote Frances. He was unusual, not a run-of-the-mill boy, Boyden added, even if he was maturing slowly. He was careless, always losing things; he slouched, his hands in his pockets; his coordination wasn't yet what one might expect. "Um," he said, "Um," hesitating before he spoke.

"He is a grand boy," Boyden wrote John after spring vacation. "I do hope that you will plan to see as much of him as is possible with all the pressing engagements which you have to meet."

John was aghast. Was Boyden criticizing him? Did the headmaster think he—the divorced father—was ignoring his son? I'm with him constantly when he's home from school, John replied, starchily. He stays with me, not his mother. I work at home rather than the office when he's here. On this last vacation we saw five Broadway shows together!

"SAY NICE THINGS TO MUTTI once in a while," Johnny wrote in his diary when he was fifteen. He was spending the summer with her in Madison, at the Inside House. He was gardening and playing chess, experimenting with the pressure cooker, and searching for garnets in stony outcrops. He built a rocket from a kit. He'd had headaches at school and the doctor had diagnosed eyestrain. He was doing exercises to strengthen his vision: Blink. Focus. Shift. Relax.

Frances read aloud to him an article in *Reader's Digest* about never refusing a challenge, and when he had friends over the next week, he and the other two boys took the sailboat halfway out to Faulkner's Island, the crescent in the Sound ten miles off the coast. They had to turn back because the fog was too thick, and when Mutti heard that they'd been aiming for Faulkner's, she was furious. His boat was much too small for such a long trip. Well, he was mad, too. Hadn't she been suggesting that he lacked pluck when she read him that *Reader's Digest* article? After a discussion, they patched it up.

I do remember the advice you give me, Johnny wrote her. Sometimes he arrived at resolutions on his own and then thought, Aha, *that's* what Mutti has been attempting to tell me.

After VJ Day, Frances was getting ready to leave for India. Nehru was finally out of prison. After keeping him jailed for nearly three years, the British had set him free in June 1945. The next month, he wrote Frances from Kashmir, where he was trekking with his daughter, Indira. He was on the caravan route to Tibet, an icy, sometimes treacherous passage, and he was letting his mind wander, describing mountain streams and meadows of wildflowers to her, dilating on the way that one's imagination magnified dangers. He knew even as he wrote that Frances would bring him up short. To be imaginative, he heard her saying, has certain disadvantages.

He wanted to come to New York, but could he? The situation in India was so unpredictable. He didn't know whether he'd be able to get away. He'd read her book, and liked it very much, though she did overrate his abilities. Once he returned home to Allahabad, any hope he had of visiting the United States disappeared. The Congress Party was in shambles. There would be elections to fight, an economy to try to plan. He couldn't come in a private capacity, he told Frances. Everything he did now signified something. Much as he longed to visit, it was impossible. "So many things happen too late."

He wished she'd been in Rajasthan with him to see the turreted castles and ruins. He sent her a piece of bark from a Himalayan birch tree, peeling and silver-white, and a silk scarf that suited her eyes.

If Jawahar couldn't come to her, she'd go to India, she decided. She'd travel as a member of the foreign press and accompany him on his trips around the country. She might be disillusioned, he warned her. He wasn't sure that either he or India could live up to the picture she'd built up in her mind: "But I shall take the risk for the desire to see you again is strong."

FRANCES WAS STILL IN Connecticut, planning her India trip, when John phoned her one afternoon in April 1946. She could tell that John was much more worried than he was letting on. The head of the Deerfield infirmary had just called, John said, and had put a neurologist from Springfield on the line. Johnny's eyes weren't coordinating, the pressure in his skull was abnormal; he was sick, seriously so. John had gotten hold of Dr. Tracy Putnam, professor of neurology and neurological surgery at Columbia University, and was driving him to Deerfield. They'd pick her up in New Haven on the way.

"Well, for goodness' sake!" Johnny said, as she and John came in his room. She could barely stand as she took in the scene: the infirmary bed in the small room, pushed off the wall. Johnny's right eye slack on his cheek; her sweet-faced sixteen-year-old son. Her mind was racing. Was it a blood clot? A cyst? Or something even worse? When John left the room to consult with Putnam and the local doctors, Johnny—cheerful but dazed—told her he thought he had polio. There'd been a boy at the school who'd had polio that spring. "I know it can't be really serious or they would have taken me to a hospital," Johnny told them.

Later that evening, John and the doctors, Putnam with the calm of Buddha, told her that Johnny would need surgery right away. Putnam arranged for Johnny to be transferred by ambulance early the next morning to the Neurological Institute of Columbia-Presbyterian Hospital. It was raining and cold, and Frances helped the nurse to cover Johnny's face with a gray blanket before he was lifted into the ambulance. She didn't let go of his hand.

He wouldn't know much until he operated, Putnam told them. Even if it were the worst case—a brain tumor—it could well be a benign sort: encapsulated, a relatively straightforward procedure to remove it, and, depending upon where it was located, little risk of damage from the surgery. The doctors did X-rays and an electroencephalogram, putting electrodes on Johnny's skull to measure his brain activity. They asked questions about Johnny's gait and his eyesight. Had he fallen recently or had a head injury when he was young? Had he been suffering from double vision or dizziness? No, they responded. No and no and no.

The operation lasted six impossible hours, John dozing every so often, turning the pages of the *The Snake Pit* when he was awake. Frances held herself rigidly alert, mumbling prayers. When the second nurse in a row asked them, "Is he your only child?" there didn't seem any point in telling her about Judy.

"Where are the parents?" Putnam called as he came down from the surgery floor. Johnny had done fine, he reassured her, smiling. She didn't need to stay at the hospital any longer, another doctor offered. Johnny would be unconscious all night.

Putnam took John for a walk down the corridor. The tumor was the size of an orange, Putnam said. He'd been able to remove only half of it. The rest had fingered its way deep in the brain.

Was he blind? Johnny asked them when he came to. His head was wrapped up in a turban of bandages. His eyes were swollen shut, his mouth parched. Will you bring me my physics book? he petitioned. Read me the questions from the end of the chapter. He was testing himself, trying to figure out if he'd lost his memory.

When the nurse prodded him to eat his breakfast, he quipped: "You are truly Machiavellian, like the British in India."

It would be best to tell Johnny what he had, Putnam counseled. He was so bright and avid for knowledge. They wouldn't be able to keep it from him. Already he was asking questions about everything the doctors did. When Johnny had recovered sufficiently so that he could see again and was sitting up in bed, Putnam talked to him. They were alone in the room.

"Johnny, what we operated for was a brain tumor," Putnam said.

"Do my parents know this?" was the first question Johnny asked. "How shall we break it to them?"

Before John and Frances brought him home from the hospital, they hid the volume of the *Encyclopaedia Britannica* that discussed brain tumors. Such tumors were often fatal, the volume noted, and almost always ended in blindness.

Johnny asked where volume four of the *Britannica* had gone, but after John and Frances made something up, he said nothing more about it.

CHAPTER SIXTEEN

HIS TERRIBLE
COURAGE

—

TAKE JOHNNY TO THE COUNTRY. THAT'S WHAT DR. PUTNAM advised John and Frances after the post-surgery course of radiation. Keep him as happy and comfortable as possible. Putnam could see from the sort of plans the Gunthers were making that they hadn't come to terms with the situation. They'd been thinking of a trip down to Hot Springs, in Virginia, staying in a hotel there, so that Johnny could recuperate. It would be better, Putnam said gently, if they remained close by the hospital.

Putnam tried to break the news to them slowly. Unlike many of his colleagues, he believed that patients and their families should know the truth about the prognosis. But it couldn't be sprung on them abruptly. The situation wasn't hopeless, but it wasn't good, Putnam told John after the operation.

Johnny's tumor was a glioblastoma, the deadliest kind of brain cancer. Even before the pathology report came back, Putnam could see from the way it had invaded the brain that the tumor was malignant and aggressive. He'd left the skull open so that the tumor could push outward. The open area was big as a man's hand; it was covered by a flap of scalp, nothing more. That, together with the radiation treatment, might give Johnny a few months more.

Patients with brain tumors often lose their sight, Putnam told

John and Frances. Sometimes they become vegetables, unable to move their limbs, confined to bed. Johnny's left side was already weakening.

Did Putnam get *all* of the tumor? Johnny asked Frances. Yes, of course, she said. And John replied the same way when Johnny repeated the question to him.

Johnny's room in Madison was painted a pale blue, the color of a robin's egg. Frances put his chemistry table on the porch. The rest of his workshop was still in the garage, and though he walked haltingly, he insisted on working there. He couldn't swim or go out in the boat because of the soft spot in his skull. Every day, the dressing had to be changed, his head rewrapped in a fresh, lopsided swath of bandages. She bought him colorful scarves to wrap around his head like a turban. He was much taller now than she was.

John was in New York on the weekdays, trying to finish *Inside U.S.A.* The book was due in October, and he was still many chapters short. He was nearly broke, paying for doctor after doctor, plus every test that anyone suggested; Putnam's bill alone was $4,000, which was less than John had feared but much more than he could pay. Each hospital stay cost thousands. John had to continue writing, he had to finish the book. On the weekends, he came out to Madison and lay on the beach, exhausted, with Frances and Johnny.

Johnny was determined to keep up with his schoolwork so that when he returned to Deerfield in September for his senior year, he wouldn't have fallen too far behind. His parents sent for his books and assignments; Mr. Boyden, Deerfield's headmaster, and Johnny's favorite science teacher, drove down to Madison to visit for the afternoon. Johnny had his heart set on Harvard. His subject would be physical chemistry, he noted in his application. He got up early to work on math, and when Frances protested, saying he needed his rest, he replied: "You don't understand. I have so much to do."

Did he understand the prognosis? To his childhood friend Edgar, Johnny confided his worries about the tumor. It was growing again; six weeks after the operation, the bump protruding from his skull was the size of an apple. His eyes were affected; his peripheral vision was practically gone. Edgar's mother phoned Frances to say that Johnny was frightened. She'd heard that the tumor was benign and was puzzled. John and Frances really needed to reassure Johnny.

There was nothing that Frances could say. To lie to Johnny was wrong. But to leave him utterly without hope seemed a greater cruelty, she and John had reasoned. Besides, they themselves hadn't—couldn't—give up. John wrote or telephoned every scientist he'd ever met, every doctor, university president, and research institute in America and Europe, asking about new treatments for brain tumors. Maybe physicists or atomic scientists had discovered something, Frances suggested. She scanned the papers, looking for any mention of promising directions in cancer research.

That was the way that they learned about mustard gas. According to a short article in the Sunday *Times*, intravenous injections of the deadly gas had shown some promise in the treatment of cancer. They managed to locate a supply and when Johnny once again landed in the hospital—the tumor had burst through the flap of scalp—John delivered the canister to the doctors himself. From a friend, they heard about the German Jewish refugee scientist, Max Gerson. A stringent diet that altered the body's metabolism, Gerson insisted, could arrest the progress of a tumor.

"If I could die for him," Frances thought. They had to see it through, to help him face what was coming. "All the things I want to do!" he said to her. In August, she saw him cry for the first time since the ordeal started. A few days later, he rose early and went out to his workshop. He'd asked John to bring him supplies from the city. He'd had the idea that he could liquefy ammonia with dry ice and acetone, an entirely new process. A neighbor in Madison, a chemistry teacher, helped him with the experiment. He put a leaf in his solution and froze it rigid. "Another fine day, Mother," he pronounced with contentment.

He depended on her to cut up his steak and to take off his shoes and socks so that he could walk barefoot in the grass. It showed astounding restraint, he teased her one night, that she hadn't barged in to give him his bath. "Feeling wonderful," he said after the second dose of mustard gas, when he spent the afternoon vomiting. He was pale and exhausted, consenting to lie on the daybed, which he normally resisted. She and Johnny talked—in the abstract—about death, a subject that he didn't discuss with John.

He was shielding them from the worst of it and they were trying, in turn, to protect him. They watched him die all summer. "Ask parents what you can do to make them happy," wrote Johnny in his diary.

"PRAY FOR A MIRACLE for Johnny," Frances wrote Dorothy that summer of 1946. John had already told Dorothy the prognosis, and she couldn't stop thinking of Frances, whom she doubted had the fortitude to withstand the loss of yet another child. The situation was as awful as could be, Jimmy, who'd just returned from New York, reiterated. They'd tried to persuade John to come up to Twin Farms for a rest, but there was no chance of him getting away. They were praying, of course, Dorothy wrote John. "God and nature do not waste their gifts nor concentrate so disproportionate a share of them upon so beautiful a mind and soul as Johnny's in order whimsically to destroy them."

Jimmy tried to cheer John up with a description of the doings at Twin Farms. Dorothy had surrounded herself entirely with Central European exiles, fierce anti-Communists who also assumed that all Americans were dodos. One of them, taking pity on Jimmy, had explained to him that Molière was a French comic writer. "I feel rather like the American Ambassador, except that my credentials are not honored," Jimmy complained. He was as clear-eyed about the Soviet Union as anyone, he thought. But to divide the Allies up into postwar friend and foe, as Dorothy and her émigré friends were doing, was madness. Jimmy was a "One Worlder," which meant that he believed in the possibility of peaceful cooperation between nations. After two world wars in thirty years, what other choice was there?

When Walter White, the head of the National Association for

the Advancement of Colored People (NAACP), called Jimmy on the phone in the summer of 1946, he was intrigued. White wanted Jimmy to come down to Tennessee; there was a trial there he should see. White had known Jimmy for years and knew that he could be counted on to take the side of the underdog. During the war, the NAACP had monitored with alarm the stockpiling of military equipment—machine guns, tear gas, and armored trucks—in American cities. Fearing that Black GIs would return from the front with "uppity ideas" about freedom and equality, police chiefs, mayors, and governors in the South and elsewhere were making their plans.

When a young Black navy veteran in Columbia, Tennessee, got into a scuffle with a white army man in February 1946, the stage was set for the confrontation the NAACP had feared. The First World War had been followed by an explosion of lynching and pogroms against Black veterans and Black neighborhoods, and the same sort of violence looked likely now. The white man (who'd thrown the first punch) was injured, but only slightly. In the fracas that followed, gangs of vigilante whites made forays into Columbia's Black neighborhood, only to find its residents armed and willing to fire. After four policemen were shot at, the chief of Tennessee's Highway Patrol intervened.

The chief was a former all-American football star and hothead. He deployed his forces to the neighborhood, where they presided over a night of looting and beatings. That morning, practically every Black-owned business in town was in ruins. The state patrolmen hauled more than a hundred of Columbia's Black residents to the town jail, the vast majority of them men. By the time that Thurgood Marshall, the NAACP's lawyer, arrived in Columbia a couple of days later, the police had terrorized their prisoners, shooting to death two whom they claimed were "trying to escape."

"While trying to escape." It was, as Jimmy noted in his first article on the case in the *Herald Tribune,* the classic phrase of Nazi Germany and apparently in America, too. He knew plenty about travesties of justice, but what was happening in Tennessee surpassed all imagining. Twenty-five men were being tried, ten of them army or navy veterans, by a prosecution that didn't even bother to connect them to the crime. Every bit of exculpatory evidence was suppressed; every rule of procedure set aside. "They would appear to be, quite simply, hostages for the whole Negro community, on the well known Nazi principle, happily not yet admitted in American criminal practice as a whole, of collective responsibility," Jimmy wrote.

The person Jimmy rendered most vividly in his reports was the chief of the highway patrol who'd launched the raid on the Black neighborhood. Bald, red in the face, the chief delivered his testimony with bluster. He'd tossed all the rules of the American legal system (search warrants, the doctrine of habeas corpus) out the window and expected to be congratulated for it. He recounted how he'd put his foot on the neck of a young Black boy—not a defendant in the case, just a kid in the neighborhood whom he'd knocked down the night of the raid. If the boy didn't "lay" still, the chief threatened, he'd kill him right then and there.

The chief was incensed when he read Jimmy's article.

"Did you write this article?" the chief demanded during a recess in the trial. Jimmy was a "lying, Communistic———" he fulminated, unprintably.

"Any good word from you would be the worst possible condemnation," Jimmy retorted. At the hotel, Jimmy had been getting death threats. An anonymous phone-caller laid into him, obscenely. He couldn't cash a check in town and when he tried going to a restaurant, none of the waitresses would serve him.

When a jury of twelve white men acquitted all but two of the accused, Jimmy took it as a victory for American decency. It was an astonishing turn of events. Before he read out the verdict, the judge paused for a moment and glared at the jury. They'd delivered a sharp rebuke both to the police and to the district attorney, who in his closing remarks had excoriated those "lousy pinks and pimps and punks" who had "poured out upon the American public a flood of sewage that would nauseate even a skunk." He was referring to Jimmy and the other reporters. For Walter White, the verdict was proof that publicity, providing the glare was sufficiently harsh, could have a chastening effect in even the most obdurate bastions of white supremacy.

"For once I have done something useful by writing," Jimmy recorded in his diary.

JOHNNY'S DOCTORS WERE AVOIDING them, John could tell. The doctors had objected, some of them very adamantly, to the idea of putting Johnny on the Gerson diet. The man is a crackpot, John heard again and again. He didn't disagree—he found Gerson touchy and dictatorial—but what other choice was there? Nothing else was working. Johnny was severely anemic, covered in bruises and listless. Sometimes he couldn't remember where he was. How did I get here? he asked.

No salt or fats, Gerson commanded. His patients were to survive on as little protein as possible. At the start of the regimen, there were four or five enemas a day to purge the body. The preparation of the meals, mostly fruit and vegetables, was exacting: the vegetables cooked with as little water as possible, the carrots washed but not peeled, aluminum pots and pans strictly forbidden. Plus a pile of pills every morning, and daily injections of crude liver extract.

The diet was so rigorous that many patients moved to Gerson's sanatorium in Manhattan to start their treatment. Frances left it to John to break the bad news to Johnny: he couldn't return to Deerfield for the fall semester but would instead be going to Gerson's. John dreaded telling him but Johnny took it stoically, and concentrated on the tutoring that Frances arranged. I'll be back to school later in the year, he said, and I can continue the Gerson diet there. They developed a routine. Frances stayed with him from lunchtime to bedtime. John came to see him at noon and again, later in the evening.

That fall, John went to the bank to cash in Johnny's bonds, but he didn't have the heart to do it. Instead, he sold off his own stocks at a loss. He had to borrow money from Frances and from Miriam Hopkins to pay his bills. Every evening he came home from the sanato-

rium and worked late into the night. Thank God for the end of
Daylight Saving Time, he noted in his diary: it gave him an extra
hour for writing. The day the book was due, he staggered into the
Harper's offices with a sheaf of six chapters in draft. I have to have
another advance, he told Cass Canfield. Canfield looked worried,
though he tried to hide it; John was already in debt to Harper's for
$35,000, $400,000 or so in today's dollars.

When Johnny started looking better in October 1946, John
thought he was imagining it. He'd been on the Gerson diet just a
few weeks. But the bulge on his skull seemed to be shrinking and his
blood count was returning to normal. He seemed to have more
stamina. For months, he hadn't felt up to playing chess, but now they
took out the board. He beat John handily. He was slow in maneuver-
ing the pieces but his game was as good as ever. Dorothy's husband
Max came to play chess with him, too.

Will you teach me to dance? Johnny asked Frances. In the spring,
there'd be the Deerfield senior prom. She rolled up the rug and
pushed back the chairs, and taught him how to waltz and fox-trot.
His doctors paid their visits and were dumbfounded. The tumor
wasn't rigid any longer. It had turned pulpy and soft, as if it were
dead and sloughing itself off, which was what Gerson had predicted.
"Maybe I will be a historic case after all," Johnny declared.

Frances had moved into John's apartment at 530 Park Avenue to
be closer to Johnny, while John was living around the corner at the
Hotel Alrae on East Sixty-fourth. Can't you both stay in the apartment together? Johnny asked Frances and was disappointed when
she demurred. John would stay there sometimes, she promised him.
"Got Father's and Mother's sides of divorce all straightened out," he
wrote in his diary. "What wonderful parents."

Frances has been bearing up magnificently, John wrote their
friends. She's been simply wonderful. For her part, though, she hadn't
forgiven him. When he called her up and talked on and on, she
imagined interrupting him and saying Shut Up Mr. Agnes Knickerbocker. For Johnny's sake, she'd gone along with John's "Unity line."
But as usual, he'd confused expediency with absolution. She wrote

the most vengeful thing possible to him. He, with his "disorderly life," was to blame for Johnny's illness. But she apparently didn't send that letter. She was praying all the time now. "God deliver me from evil. My own evil."

The news that the Book-of-the-Month Club's judges had selected *Inside U.S.A.* as their June 1947 title came as a deliverance. It guaranteed millions in sales. A "godsend," observed Jimmy, who knew how desperate the situation was with "every doctor in the western hemisphere gathering around to share in the spoils." The *New Yorker* sent a journalist over to profile John. The only catch was that the final book manuscript was due—absolutely due— on March 15. He still had a hundred thousand words to write.

"Tell Pop you're proud of him," Frances exhorted Johnny after the Book-of-the-Month Club news. Johnny felt shy about it but then he blurted it straight out to John. He was reading John's chapters. "It'll sell a million copies!" he declared after reading the one on Montana. For Christmas that year, John gave Frances handkerchiefs with "Mother" embroidered on them in Johnny's handwriting.

WHEN REBECCA WEST ARRIVED in New York a few months later, in March 1947, John and Dorothy Thompson were at the pier to meet her. Rebecca had been reporting for the *Daily Telegraph* and the *New Yorker* from Nuremberg, where the Allies had put twenty-four high-ranking Nazis on trial. Nuremberg was the first of the war crimes trials and for the entire ten months the court was sitting, from late November 1945 to October 1946, it was mired in controversy. Was the court "a high-grade lynching party"? That was the view of the chief justice of the U.S. Supreme Court. He didn't object to hanging Nazis, but the newfangled court was making a travesty of the judicial process.

At Nuremberg, innovative legal principles were being laid down in international law. Chief among them was the idea of a "crime against humanity." Every individual—or so argued the Allied prosecutors—had inalienable rights that transcended the long-held prerogatives of states. Sovereign powers couldn't any longer dispose of the people who lived inside their borders however they wished. The notion of a "crime against humanity" thus represented a dramatic reconfiguration of international law. It put the individual at the heart of a new legal order. It became the linchpin of what was increasingly referred to as "human rights."

Rebecca went to Nuremberg because she sensed British public opinion turning lily-livered. Some in Britain likened the war crimes trial to the Treaty of Versailles: a punitive maneuver that stored up trouble for the future. Rebecca intended to stiffen some spines. "I have never been able to write with anything more than the left hand of my mind; the right hand has always been engaged in something to do with personal relationships," she reflected after Nuremberg. That preoccupation had turned out to be not an infirmity but a strength, she thought. "My left hand's power, as much as it has, is due to its knowledge of what my right hand is doing."

At Nuremberg, her right hand was occupied by an affair with the chief American judge of the Court, Francis Biddle. He was an old friend of FDR's: well-bred, cultivated, committed to the cause of freedom, very much married. They'd met each other years before in America and when she appeared in Nuremberg, Biddle invited her to come to stay at the requisitioned villa he was occupying. He put her in the bedroom with an erotic picture painted on the ceiling. Rebecca's marriage had been sexless for a decade—her husband's doing, not hers. The affair with Biddle felt like ten glorious days of raising the shutters, only to smash them down again.

With her left hand, Rebecca was mapping out the boundaries of individual and collective responsibility. Who was to blame for the disaster of the Nazi regime? The men on trial—"abscesses of cruelty," she called them—most self-evidently. In the dock, they collapsed into a deflated, sallow group, indistinguishable one from the other, an irony in a trial that hinged on the concept of the individual. Her first job, then, was to make them vivid. Julius Streicher, the publisher of the viciously anti-Semitic weekly *Der Stürmer*, was "a dirty old man of the sort that gives trouble in parks." The number two of the

Nazi regime, Hermann Göring, possessed of unquenchable appetites, looked like "the head of a ventriloquist's dummy." The former head of the Reichsbank, Hjalmar Schacht, sat sideways in the dock, pretending to be above it all, as if he'd had nothing to do with Hitler and his gang—though he'd been the moneyman from the start.

The fault wasn't theirs alone, of course. West took note of the "call for punishment" among Germans at large, the Nurembergers who eagerly stopped reporters to express their hope that this or the other Nazi leader should hang. Beyond the transparent attempt to pin the regime's crimes on a few individuals, Rebecca detected a renascent Germany, not yet reformed but straining to return to life's pleasant things. As in *Black Lamb and Grey Falcon,* she made artful use of her conversations, quoting directly when she wanted to indict the speaker, describing a scene when she didn't. German contrition was sincere, and it was also put on; and it often was difficult to tell the difference.

What carried over from her left to her right hand was the knowledge of how good and bad could coexist in a person. Following H. G. Wells's death, which happened shortly after she returned from Nuremberg, she delivered a typical judgment: "he was a devil, he ruined my life, he starved me, he was an inexhaustible source of love and friendship to me for thirty-four years." Her sense of moral ambiguity was dualistic, Manichaean. It proceeded from the blackest of blacks and the whitest of whites; if they mixed to shades of gray at all, it was in the mind of her reader.

At Nuremberg, she didn't feel any queasiness about the Allies' right to pursue a victor's justice. The monsters in the dock, she was certain, deserved what was coming to them. At the same time, she found nothing in the proceedings to celebrate. It was distasteful to exult over hangings, even righteous ones. The improvisational nature of the proceedings she found suspect. The trial certainly wasn't the "small Allied island of hope, sanity and justice" that Janet Flanner had described in the *New Yorker.* The problem was exactly the opposite. The trial was part and parcel of the "oddity of the world," Rebecca decided. "A man's world, a man's world" was the refrain of her *New Yorker* piece. In case anyone had any doubts, she made clear she meant that in the pejorative sense.

REBECCA FOUND HERSELF IN New York in the spring of 1947 because after the affair with Biddle and H.G.'s death, she couldn't really stand to live with her banker husband. She'd asked Dorothy—who was even more skeptical about the Nuremberg tribunal than she was—to fix up something for her in America. Rebecca wanted the pretext for a long trip. Her American visit had started off well enough, despite Dorothy's tedious anti-Soviet tirades. But then the New York hotel where she was supposed to stay was insupportably filthy and the food poisonous; she tried to move but all the hotels in Manhattan were overrun. She knew the trip was cursed when she came down with pneumonia.

By some miracle John managed to get her a room at the Alrae, where he was living while Frances stayed in his apartment. It was a comfortable European sort of place, with an Alsatian manager, a mustachioed Italian bartender, and an Albanian busboy who'd been a wrestler. The first course on the breakfast menu was the choice of a Scotch sour or a dry martini. In the evenings, John came up to see her. He talked and talked. He told her about Agnes Knickerbocker, who sounded as awful as Frances, maybe worse, Rebecca suspected. But mostly he talked about Johnny. John is going through hell with his son, Rebecca wrote her husband. "The boy had seemed to be on the way to a perfect cure, it now seems the tumour may have started again."

After a few months in which the tumor had seemed to be in retreat, there wasn't any doubt about its return: the growth was getting bigger. Johnny's left-side coordination had worsened. He was talking all the time about Harvard, asking when there would be a decision about his application, and whether he could return to Deerfield to graduate with the rest of his class. John bought him a Harris tweed suit in anticipation of the ceremony.

The doctors argued about whether a second operation might give the boy more time. Putnam had left New York for California, and it was his deputy who took over the case. They'd tried to extract fluid from the tumor but it had turned rock-hard. The only thing left was another surgery. John drove Johnny up to the hospital. He just needed a few more tests, his parents assured him. The minute the nurse arrived to give him the enema, Johnny knew that the situation was more serious. When the hospital's barber arrived to shave his skull, he cried and protested.

This time, the operation lasted nearly seven hours. The surgeon came out, looking drained and pale. "I got two handfuls," he told John.

That next afternoon, Rebecca West, Clare Boothe Luce, and John's old friend Jerry Frank came to his room at the Alrae to try to take his mind off the situation. Clare understood something of what John was facing: her only child, Ann, a senior at Stanford, had died in a car crash during the war. Rebecca and Jerry carried on animatedly about the history of trial by ordeal. Clare made a valiant attempt to convert Jerry, a Jew, to Catholicism. She cut up, doing impersonation after impersonation. Bill Shirer reporting the crucifixion! Eleanor Roosevelt describing the Last Supper! It was an antic performance.

On and on they talked, three hours of it. It was "one of the most remarkable experiences I have ever had," Rebecca reported to her husband. They were running from ghosts.

AFTER JOHNNY'S SECOND OPERATION, Frances left for a trip to Florida, and John took a few days in Hot Springs by himself. Mr. Boynton had decided that Johnny could graduate with his class. He would come up to school for a week before the graduation, to take a chemistry exam and see his friends. He'd sleep in the infirmary. Please help him cut his meat at dinner, Frances instructed Johnny's friends. The night before they drove up to Deerfield, John met Jimmy for a drink at the Stork. His son is dying, Jimmy drunkenly announced to a group of young women at the bar.

Johnny was dragging his left foot badly. Neither Frances nor John was certain he'd be able to march, as was the Deerfield custom, down the center aisle of the church to the pulpit to receive his diploma. When his name was finally called, they felt scarcely able to breathe. What if he fell? Johnny had insisted on marching alone. The church was silent as he rose. But as he made his way, a tall, thin boy in a white turban, walking unsteadily but with determination, the applause broke out. The thunderous clapping didn't stop until he'd taken his place, seated, diploma in hand, back with his friends. "Nobody who saw it will ever forget it," John wrote.

After the second operation, they'd told Johnny he could eat whatever he wanted. There was no point in continuing the Gerson diet. Maybe it was the mustard gas that had stopped the tumor, the doctors hypothesized; maybe they should try it again. This was a very peculiar tumor, one said. John drove him back to the hospital. After the first mustard shot, Johnny called Frances to say he didn't want any more. He felt too sick. He could hardly walk or stand. If only she could take the tumor for him, Frances wrote. "I can't bear to see him go."

She'd gone to Madison to get his room ready, but John called to tell her to come back to town immediately. Johnny had slept much of the day and was listless and depressed when he was awake. "Father, I hope you don't mind my being somewhat glum," Johnny had told him. Frances was there in New York when the headache started. Johnny was lying in John's bed. They rushed him to the hospital.

He died there, on the last day of June 1947, of a cerebral hemorrhage. When it was all over, when the doctors had disconnected the tubes, Frances pushed aside the cellophane curtains of the oxygen tent and took his body in her arms.

"I sure will miss him. I sure will miss you both. Thank you for giving him to me," she said to John.

THE FUNERAL WAS AT Frank E. Campbell's on Madison and Eighty-first. The sunlight spilled through the chapel door as the pallbearers carried Johnny away. After the service, Frances and John went to the crematorium alone. Later that week, he came to Madison to stay with her. They swam and talked. She'd been reading Schrödinger's *What Is Life?*, and wanted to discuss cells and the mysteries of human consciousness. There was so much they could have done to make Johnny happier, she said to John.

It was all my fault, she told him.

It's nobody's fault, he replied.

It was a comfort to have John there with her. He shouldn't continue a bachelor, she told him. He needed to marry again and have more children and grandchildren. John looked so relieved when she said that. In turn, he encouraged her to write her book on the Jews.

After he drove off, Frances cried. Her maid, Eddy, comforted her. For dinner, she had calf's livers, the last thing that Johnny had eaten. "Remember your destiny, Mother," he had said to her. When she was stuck and couldn't write, he'd urged her on, impatiently. "Of course, Mother, do it!"

She hung up the watercolors he'd painted. Sailboats on the water, pictures of animals. They'd been rolled up on top of the closet. Why hadn't she put them up before? She was reviewing in her mind all of the times they'd sent him away—to walk alone to the school bus in Connecticut when he was eight, to camp in the Adirondacks, to Riverdale when she and John separated. Each time, she'd justified it to herself as the prelude to independence. Now it just seemed like selfish cruelty.

There was a dead look in her eyes when she looked in the mirror now. She saw it in the other mothers whose children had died. There were plenty of such mothers around the world. Not that many fathers had it, though. John was devastated, she didn't doubt that, but he didn't look dead inside.

God help me, God help me, she prayed. "How can I speak of peace to the world when there is war inside of me?"

CHAPTER SEVENTEEN

THE WEEK OF
SAYING EVERYTHING

—

I N THE MONTH BEFORE JOHNNY DIED, HE AND FRANCES HAD been reading Joshua Liebman's surprise bestseller, *Peace of Mind*. Mixing psychoanalytic ideas with can-do Americanism and the teachings of Reform Judaism, Liebman—the thirty-nine-year-old rabbi of Boston's Temple Israel—sought a solution to the repressions he blamed for the previous half-century of war, revolution, and social turmoil. A lasting peace required individuals who could reckon openly with the powerful emotions that Christianity had for centuries stigmatized, including sensuality, anger, and grief. And Americans, Liebman argued, were poised to usher in this psychically well-adjusted future: because of the country's traditions of democracy, a more "psychologically mature God idea" lay in their grasp.

Liebman's was an early mass-market formulation of what would become a commonsensical idea. Rebuilding the world would require more than clearing bomb rubble, demobilizing soldiers, and retooling factories for domestic production. Equally imperative was a psychological reconstruction: the creation of a healthy, self-aware citizenry able to control their emotions rather than conceal them. These were boon years for psychoanalysts, whose ambit expanded from the individual patient to the collective psyche. The threat of atomic warfare only heightened the urgency of the quest. "The greatest prerequisite for peace," the American president Harry Truman insisted in 1948, "must be sanity—sanity in its broadest sense, which permits clear thinking on the part of all citizens."

Throughout 1947, John's *Inside U.S.A.*—published in May, shortly before Johnny's Deerfield graduation—dueled with Liebman's *Peace of Mind* for the top spot on the bestseller lists. *Inside U.S.A.*, too, partook of the ambient Freudianism. Freud's apparatus lent itself especially well to the South, John found: "the whole region is a land of paranoia, full of the mentally sick; most Southerners feel a deep necessity to hate something, if necessary even themselves." But *Inside U.S.A.* and *Peace of Mind* shared something more profound: their confidence in the future of America. It was, as John put it, "a lucky country with an almost obsessive belief in the happy ending."

Harper & Brothers printed half a million copies of *Inside U.S.A.* That was the largest print run in the history of American publishing, but it was, as it turned out, just a start. *Inside U.S.A.* was a self-generating publicity machine. John's portrait of America inevitably provoked Americans to answer back. His characterizations of Houston as a city whose inhabitants thought only of money or of Californians as faddish and cult-ridden incited rafts of articles in the local papers disputing or agreeing with those propositions. Was Indianapolis in fact the dirtiest city in the country, as he'd claimed? He received reams of incensed correspondence on the subject. By the end of the year, the presses were rolling again for a second printing.

Apart from the matter of injured local pride, the reviews of *Inside U.S.A.* were the best he'd gotten—thousands of them, in nearly every paper in the country. Heavy hitters such as the American historians Arthur Schlesinger and Henry Steele Commager pronounced the book a tour de force, praising Gunther's gargantuan appetite for facts and personalities, his indefatigable interviewing and jaunty wordsmithing. They relished his optimism about America (which matched their own) and shared his assessment of the nation's failings (which neither they nor he thought fatal).

Inside U.S.A. wasn't, Commager conceded, a "three dimensional" book, by which he meant that it didn't strive, as Tocqueville's classic *Democracy in America* had, for a larger philosophical point. The book's critics, few enough but well placed, made the same point less politely. According to *Time* magazine, *Inside U.S.A.* was nine hundred–plus pages of fluff, hastily tossed off, "full of impressions passing as insights and facts palmed off as truths." The *New Yorker*'s reviewer was more jocular, but the criticism was similar. Gunther wrote without discernment, displayed an "ingenuous amazement at the discovery of commonplaces." He was like a man bolting a blue-plate special at a railway café, gobbling up impressions without pausing for breath, regurgitating them undigested.

Richard Rovere, the young reporter the *New Yorker* had sent over to profile John as he was writing *Inside U.S.A.*, had intended to assail him along those lines. But when Rovere took stock of the situation with Johnny, he couldn't do it. "So you're the hatchet man," Johnny had said to him. The more time Rovere spent with John, the more he liked him. Rather than abandoning the profile (which would have hurt John's feelings), he turned a wry eye on the Gunther phenomenon: his elbow-rubbing with the great and good, his formidable productivity and success, his self-confessed superficiality. "But of course I *am* an ignoramus," John told Rovere.

The profile that emerged was gently comical, a portrait of corn-fed, globe-trotting American hubris, the "American century" in book form. "The entire planet is his beat," Rovere remarked, calling Gunther "one of the half-dozen or so authentic international celebrities." Slyly riding the line between compliment and mockery, Rovere continued: "he is perhaps the world's foremost journalist. He is certainly the foremost world journalist."

How did you get off so easy at the *New Yorker*? John's friends ribbed him. For the veteran foreign correspondent Leigh White, an ex-colleague of John's at the *Chicago Daily News*, the *New Yorker* profile was galling. He wrote Rovere an angry letter. "Gunther, to me, is the prototype of The Rewards of Mediocrity, a phenomenon which I think menaces the survival of American society in almost every field." White continued: "I was pained to find you, of all people, in the *New Yorker,* of all publications, handling with gloves a subject whose skin is at least as thick as that of a rhinoceros."

Previously, John had been insulated from the charge of middlebrow mediocrity. His luster had been burnished by his exotic travels, his status as an eyewitness, the interviews he'd bagged, his warnings about the rise of fascism, and the audacity of his analysis (or, at least, of Frances's analysis). But after the war, middlebrow was a label that increasingly stuck to him, not least because of his success with the two engines of mass-market reading culture in America: the Book-of-the-Month Club (a subscription service that provided a vetted selection of books) and the *Reader's Digest* (the largest-circulation periodical in the world). Henceforth, the *Reader's Digest* would help to fund John's research and publish many of his articles. Ten of John's books were Book-of-the-Month Club selections, a record for an American author. Only Winston Churchill had more.

For people who fancied themselves serious thinkers, both the Book-of-the-Month Club and the *Reader's Digest* stood for conventional thinking and dumbed-down sentimentalism. These were charges that John, after years of similar criticism from Frances, shrugged off. The waspish reviews in *Time* and the *New Yorker* annoyed him, but he'd come to terms, more or less, with his lack of "profundity." What mattered was influence, not the admiration of the bien-pensants, though if one could have both, all the better.

John took pride in the fact that all across America restless high schoolers and housewives—autodidacts as John had been—were cracking open *Inside U.S.A.* or the revised edition of *Inside Europe,* learning about the inner workings of the Tennessee Valley Authority or Stalin's childhood. Courtesy of the Book-of-the-Month Club sales, he could finally pay Johnny's doctors.

"AGNES, WHO?" JOHN NEARLY said when she called him in May 1947, shortly after *Inside U.S.A.* was published. During those months when Johnny seemed to be getting better, he'd started dating Jane

Perry, the ex-wife of the reporter Jack Vandercook. She was an editor at the publishing company Duell, Sloan and Pearce. "This is the finest girl I ever met, delicately bred, style, brains, marvelous to look at," John wrote in his diary. "Of course we will marry, but it may be long delayed."

It had been more than two years since John had seen either of the Knickerbockers. After Agnes flew to Baltimore to take care of Knick during his treatment at Johns Hopkins, they'd taken their daughters to a ranch in Montana for the summer. Knick had returned to broadcasting, and lecturing, and they'd moved from Dallas to Nyack, New York. It was a full reconciliation.

Knick went to Alcoholics Anonymous and quit drinking. Shortly after Churchill decried the lowering of the "Iron Curtain" across Eastern Europe, Knick and Walter Duranty toured the United States debating the question: "Can Russia Be Part of One World?" Knick was arguing the anti-Communist position, as he always had. Walter was taking Stalin's side, "full of classical erudition and Bolshevik duplicity," as Knick put it. It turned out his life really wasn't over, Knick exclaimed to the Hopkins doctor who'd helped him get sober. To his astonishment, Dorothy had asked him to appear on a television program with her. He'd started writing again; he was lecturing and broadcasting on the radio.

Agnes told John on the phone that she'd read all the reviews of *Inside U.S.A.* "Oh, if only I hadn't gone to Baltimore," she said regretfully when they met for lunch.

THE MONTH AFTER JOHNNY DIED, John drew up a new will and helped Frances box up Johnny's things. His girlfriend Jane said he looked terrible. He was drinking too much and plagued by nightmares. He cried whenever he talked about Johnny. He spent a day reading through his and Frances's correspondence with Johnny, but that hadn't made him feel any better. His own letters were so brief, so businesslike: he'd arrived in Mexico, the food was peppery, off to

Guatemala tomorrow, here are some stamps from Brazil, All my love. By contrast, each one of Frances's letters to Johnny seemed to him a treasure.

He took the car north, first to Connecticut to see Clare Boothe Luce. Her husband Henry, Clare told him, had never once mentioned Ann's name after her death; she was only his stepdaughter, but still, she was Clare's child. At one forty-five A.M., Clare came to John's room, dressed in a negligé, and woke him up with a knock on the door. They talked for three hours about Johnny and Ann. She'd nearly lost her mind after Ann died, Clare said. Maybe Johnny had died to make John a better person, she hazarded.

That habit—of looking for the compensation in every loss—wasn't doing John any good. Makes God a son of a bitch, said Red Lewis, when John mentioned Clare's remark to him. John had stopped to see Red in Williamstown before driving on to Deerfield. He wandered through the empty campus, wondering whether they'd been right to send Johnny there. He proposed to Boyden the idea Frances had about endowing a prize in math or physics in honor of Johnny—she'd wanted something more "alive" than the usual memorial chimes or hospital bed. It was unconventional, Boyden replied. He'd have to think about it.

It was a hot night, and John could have driven directly to Twin Farms, but instead, he went to the little inn at the county seat, in Greenfield. He didn't feel like talking to anybody. Johnny had been dead exactly a month. He ate a steak and drank three Planter's Punches. He'd brought Johnny's papers along with him and spent the night putting them in order.

When John got to Twin Farms the next evening, Jimmy was in one of his moods, talking a blue streak. He'd gotten the harebrained idea that Dorothy should run for the presidency in 1948. It was a question of America's position in the world, Jimmy said. Think of the humane ideals the country could embody! A woman president at this moment was an absolute necessity. Clare Luce could nominate her. She'd introduce Dorothy as a wife and a mother who'd sacrificed one son to war, and who believed in peace. A wife—indeed, three times over, Dinah remarked when Jimmy wrote her on the subject. Dorothy's acceptance speech would be so grand that she'd sail right into office.

"Very well," said Dorothy's husband Max the next day. "I go to Reno and not be in the way!"

I've been having trouble with my three Jewish doctors, Jimmy told John. Where in Vermont had Jimmy managed to find three Jewish doctors? John wondered. Did Jimmy have his doctors coming up from New York?

No! Jimmy exclaimed. Freud, Einstein, and Marx.

Jimmy had lost his faith in materialism, once and for all. There were mysteries beyond the physical universe. Think, he said, blue eyes glittering, what the war had shown about the power of electronics! Jimmy's hair had gone white and he'd gotten thin. He was up at all hours of the night. Dorothy cabled Dinah in London to get the prescription for Jimmy's sleeping pills.

THOSE AUGUST 1947 DAYS in Vermont took on a languorous shape. John stayed over at Jimmy's house. They woke up late and talked until it was time for lunch. Then they went over to Dorothy's. Her house was only four hundred feet away from Jimmy's, but John insisted on driving the distance. During the afternoon, they walked in Dorothy's garden or meandered through town or played with the children—Jimmy's two daughters were there, and so was Dorothy's Michael, seventeen now and more obstreperous than ever. "I won't have foreigners fucking my mother," Michael shouted one night after a dispute with Max.

In the evenings, John played chess with Max while Jimmy and Dorothy debated. "Slugging talkfests" John called them, marveling at how they kept at it night after night. Dorothy was horrified that the Soviets were extending their tentacles across Eastern Europe and thought no one was taking it seriously enough. Jimmy objected to the way she talked, as if she were addressing a mass meeting of twenty thousand nincompoops. Jimmy's conversation was impossibly erudite. "*Was* Plato the first Fascist?" he asked. He burst into song, delivering an aria from *Tristan* first in Italian, then English. He wanted to talk about the time-space continuum.

How much do you believe in free will? John asked Dorothy and Jimmy. Put a percentage on it, he challenged them.

Fifty-fifty said Jimmy. Half free will, half determinism. Dorothy demurred.

There were questions that John couldn't rid himself of. Why was it so often a person's essential organ that failed them? Say, Beethoven's ears or Milton's eyes. Or Johnny's brain.

Why had Johnny died? he asked.

"He's still alive," Dorothy chimed in. She'd already written John with that idea. The only thing that comforted her when her stepson died was the idea that "life is transitional between lives." She quoted Whitman's lines about immortality: "Has any one supposed it lucky to be born? I hasten to inform him or her it is just as lucky to die, and I know it."

That wasn't much consolation, John thought. Not for him or Frances, and certainly not for Johnny.

Jimmy didn't have an answer as to why Johnny had died, but he was certain it had nothing to do with punishing John or Frances. "To think that is to become insane," he declared. Besides, he added, you can't measure a life by its duration.

As to Clare's idea about Johnny's death making John a better person, Max had a thought. "Maybe you don't want it to make you better, but it will," he offered.

John stayed for a week, and then proceeded up through the White Mountains to meet Jane at her family's summer place. After he'd gone, Jimmy wrote Frances. John had talked about her plans to go to India and Palestine, and her ideas about making peace between Jews and Arabs. Jimmy suggested that she call on the Egyptian diplomat Azzam Pasha, the secretary-general of the newly formed Arab League, who was staying at the Plaza Hotel. He promised her a letter of introduction to the Grand Mufti when she went to Jerusalem.

John's visit had been a solace for them all, Jimmy told Frances. "I need hardly tell you that we talked out some trillions of words be-

tween us, and explored the unfathomable mysteries of all our con-
catenated existences for the first time in our lives without evasion."

ON THE FIFTEENTH OF August 1947, a few days after John left Twin
Farms, Nehru raised the tricolor flag of an independent India—
saffron, white, and green—above the battlements of the Red Fort in
Delhi. The "man of destiny," as Frances had teasingly called him, was
India's first prime minister. Frances didn't attend the celebration that
the India League of America hosted in New York for the occasion.
Nor did Jimmy. Instead, he sent a message, which, despite its gloomy
tenor, was read out at the banquet. Pray for India, he admonished:
"the religions, separately, and together, should pray, for the dangers
ahead are many."

Jimmy had cut back on his drinking and he resolved to stop
smoking, too. He couldn't say that he was feeling normal, though. At
night, he stared at his illuminated globe until it became almost real.
It was as if his consciousness had broken free of his body and was
roaming the world. He could see things he hadn't consciously known
before, he told Dorothy.

He was having terrible premonitions about India. The British
were cutting and running, on their way out executing a hasty political partition of the subcontinent into two independent nations:
India and Pakistan, conceived as a new Muslim state. But how could
that possibly work? There were Muslims whose families had lived
for generations within the new boundaries of India and Hindus and
Sikhs similarly situated within the borders of Pakistan. Jimmy followed the news with dread, tuning in to the BBC, which came in via
Toronto. However bad he'd thought the violence was going to be,
the reality was still worse. Stabbings in the streets of Delhi, Bombay,
and Calcutta and retaliations in Punjab, where tin-helmeted gangs
of men were setting houses and shops ablaze. Everywhere, millions
of refugees fled for their lives, east to west, west to east. Whole districts burned and looted. The bodies of children, men, and women
stacked up on the sides of the roads.

It was imperative he go to India, Jimmy decided. "Gandhi is going to be assassinated within six months and by a Hindu," he told Dorothy.

He'd made another decision, too. He wanted Dinah back. Without her, he was a "cave of winds." He wrote Dinah to ask if he could visit her in London. Then he turned up at her flat—hours late as usual—with the proposition that they reconcile. She'd been too young when they married and he'd expected far too much from her, he acknowledged. He'd either be celibate or remarry her: those were his two options. Think it over while I'm away, he said, before she had a chance to reply.

The truth, Dinah wrote a friend, was that another man was in love with her and she wasn't sure she could endure the "Wagnerian mists" of life with Jimmy. Maybe it was just that she didn't have the strength to withstand his delusions. When he went on and on about how the "forces of history" were gusting through the living room, she couldn't help but feel the draft.

En route to Delhi, Jimmy stopped in Karachi, in the new state of Pakistan. His sympathies had been with those—like Gandhi and Nehru—who favored the preservation of the Indian subcontinent as a single independent nation. Now, as the struggle over Kashmir raged, he saw the other side. It was a reprise of what had happened in Jerusalem two decades earlier. In the *Herald Tribune*, Jimmy detailed the "Pakistan case" as its officials presented it: their fear that India wanted to "strangle" Pakistan at its birth, evidenced by Nehru's bid to hold hostage the entirety of the Raj's military stores and the funds owed Pakistan from the Reserve Bank of India until Kashmir was restored to India.

Though Jimmy hedged his reports with disclaimers about not taking the Pakistani version of the case as "gospel," his conclusion in the *Herald Tribune* was unsparing. "India wishes to destroy Pakistan as rapidly as possible," he wrote. It was an explosive assessment, all the more troubling given his well-known sympathies for the Indian freedom movement. With the matter of Kashmir pending before the newly organized United Nations, the Indian government was anxiously monitoring international opinion. When Jimmy got to Delhi, Nehru summoned him.

Jimmy was to appear at the prime minister's house on the York Road at seven o'clock in the evening. Nehru was living in a large bungalow, its grounds crowded with refugee tents. The prime minister looked tired and agitated. Point by point, he rebutted Jimmy's article, getting angrier as he proceeded. Nehru was red-faced, the tendons of his neck protruding. After two hours of dressing Jimmy down, Nehru proffered the carrot that accompanied the stick. He'd arranged for Jimmy to see Gandhi.

Gandhi was staying at Birla House, a sandstone mansion that belonged to an admirer. It was there, in the walled, arbored garden where Gandhi held his evening prayers, that Jimmy first saw him. The Mahatma was seated on a red sandstone pavilion. Wrapped in homespun, his fast for Hindu-Muslim unity just ended, he looked frail.

They held the interview in a high-ceilinged and rectangular room that gave onto the garden through French doors. In the corner was Gandhi's simple cot with white sheets. As Jimmy entered, Gandhi's secretary instructed him to take off his shoes. The photographer Henri Cartier-Bresson and his wife were there. Chagrined, Jimmy muttered about the hole in his sock.

There were questions he needed to ask Gandhi—fundamental questions about the future of the world. "How can a righteous battle produce a catastrophic result?" Jimmy wanted to know. He was thinking of the war against fascism that had ended in the threat of atomic annihilation. Fretting about the hole in his sock, he paced up and down the blue carpet with Gandhi and then sat cross-legged on the floor beside him, talking of the congruence of ends and means. People wandered past the windows, peering in.

"Renunciation is itself the law of life," Gandhi told Jimmy. After an hour of talking—about Gandhi's edition of the Bhagavad Gita, the nature of power, the superiority of religion over science, the failure of the United Nations—Jimmy realized he'd already stayed too long. "Well, this is more than I had bargained for," Gandhi said. "Do you want to come back again tomorrow?" They continued the conversation the following day.

When Jimmy next saw Gandhi a few days later, the Mahatma was in the garden of Birla House, walking toward him across the grass. The evening was brisk, and Gandhi, draped in white shawls, was on his way to the prayer meeting. Jimmy didn't see the khaki-clad man pushing his way through the crowd. The assassin—a Hindu enraged by the Partition, as Jimmy had foreseen—fired three shots into Gandhi's belly. The gunshots were quieter and duller than one might have expected.

A couple of yards away from the dying Gandhi, Jimmy, horror-struck, bent double against the brick wall of the garden. In his nightmares about an assassination, he'd thrust an arm or his whole body in front of Gandhi to avert the murder. In fact, he'd failed to save the Mahatma though he would have given his own life to do so. In the Birla House garden, Jimmy's fingers were burning and, like a child, he put them in his mouth. Later, he'd realize there were blisters on his fingers, as if his own hands bore the shame of his failure to act.

He didn't go to view Gandhi's body. It would have been unbearable to see him covered in blood. "*How can such things be?*" Jimmy asked himself, over and over.

AFTER JOHNNY'S DEATH, LETTERS came in by the hundreds: grief-stricken notes from John and Frances's friends; memories of Johnny as a child from the camp nurse; awkward, tardy missives from boys he'd known. Even people who were never at a loss for words confessed they didn't know what to write. "In the presence of such grief silence is best," wrote the Supreme Court justice Felix Frankfurter. It was no different from the situation when Judy had died two decades earlier. "I'm terrified of what life can do to us, and will," Mickey Hahn wrote Frances, "the only thing to say is the rest of what I feel, which is only that I love you."

After his week at Twin Farms, John returned to New York intending to write something about Johnny. He and Frances had discussed the idea of a memoir when he visited her in Madison. John's thought was to produce something for relatives and friends, the sort of memorial tract that circulated privately. But as he outlined the book, he abandoned the conventions of the traditional "in memoriam" volume. Rather, he would relate, in clinical detail, the story of Johnny's illness and death. The relentless advance of the tumor, the short period of remission, Johnny's undiminished personhood, the fact that he hadn't become a "vegetable" as the doctors once predicted. His bravery in the face of suffering.

It became the story of how an individual—a boy—confronted death. John started the book just after Christmas 1947. By February, he'd sent the manuscript to a few friends: Dorothy; Bill Shirer; the editor Lewis Gannett; and their family physician, Cornelius Traeger, who'd helped them manage Johnny's illness. Was it something he should publish? he asked them. Dr. Traeger thought it was a mistake—he disapproved of all the medical stuff, it was too personal—but everyone else who read it urged him to go ahead. According to Dorothy, it had the "purging quality of genuine tragedy."

Frances gave John her notes about Johnny's sickness, corrected his typescript, and registered her objections about several details, including John's description of his visits with Johnny after the divorce. They'd made the decision to include extracts from Johnny's diaries and letters, lightly edited. Somewhere along the way, she decided to write her own chapter, too. It took the form of an afterword. John recounted the events in a spare style, anguished and dignified; Johnny's own words gave readers a measure of his character; and Frances's afterword tried to make sense of what had happened to them all.

People tried to tell her that it was God's will, or meant to be, that there was a compensation for the loss. Maybe Johnny would have put his scientific talents to bad use. She'd prayed to God constantly during his illness but didn't believe that God had anything to do with it. What had gone wrong was a single cell, mutating out of control. That was nothing she could grieve about. Her grief, rather, focused on the fact that Johnny wasn't there to sail his boat or lie on the beach or talk about Freud and the Oedipus complex. That he wouldn't go to Harvard as he'd planned or marry or have a child of his own. That he wouldn't finish out the experiment she'd started and he'd picked up: to create a new sort of human being, "an aware person," as she put it, "a sound individual, adequate to life anywhere on earth." Most of all, her regret was that she—they—hadn't loved him enough.

Just to say that she'd failed him, as she did, needed explaining. Of course, Johnny knew they loved him. Still, they'd sent him away to boarding school when he didn't want to go. They'd divorced. They'd lived while he died. If only other parents could take a lesson from their story. Not to be so impatient with their children. Not to be bored. "I wish I could say to them, But they are alive, think of the wonder of that!"

How to carry on after the death of a child was a question, Frances recognized, that the war had forced on many parents. Her answer was a counterintuitive one: not to turn away from life, but to love it more. That meant, she wrote, "obliterating, in a curious but real way, the ideas of evil and hate and the enemy." It was a prescription for a kind of world citizenship—"caring more and more about people, at home and abroad, all over the earth."

You told a story, but Frances has written the inside of her heart, Jane commented to John when she read the typescript. The afterword was marvelous, emotional, real. Only a woman could have written it. John had been searching for meaning, Jane said; but Frances knew what she thought.

FRANCES AND JOHN CALLED it "Johnny's book," which was how Cass Canfield and their friends started to refer to it, too. Given the contention in their marriage about the ownership of ideas, "Johnny's book" marked a sort of truce. Under the title *Death Be Not Proud*, the opening line of John Donne's Sonnet X, Harper & Brothers in February 1949 published all three pieces—John's, Johnny's, and Frances's. For Donne, the phrase "Death Be Not Proud" had conveyed a religious belief in immortality. The memoir, by contrast, represented a bid for a secular afterlife. The volume was slim with a plain cream cover, unornamented except for a small design of a dove amid branches. Inside was a frontispiece of Johnny aged fifteen in three-quarters profile, sober, his blond hair parted on the side. He was wearing a tweed jacket and necktie, off for his first year at Deerfield. On the book's jacket and in all the advertisements was a notice that both John and Harper's felt necessary. Profits from the sale of the book would go to cancer research for children; neither the author nor the publisher would benefit.

To air publicly such an intimate story of sickness and suffering was unheard of. There were Victorian autobiographical tracts, often privately printed, that dealt with the death of a child as God's un-fathomable will. People who'd had polio or gone blind or deaf oc-casionally wrote their reminiscences for publication, accounts of triumphs against adversity such as Helen Keller's *The Story of My Life* (1903). There were few enough of these kinds of books, a couple dozen. Narratives of illness were still rarer. As Virginia Woolf had lamented a few decades earlier, there was hardly any secular writing about illness. It "has not taken its place with love and battle and jealousy among the prime themes of literature," she noted. The stan-dard source on American autobiography counts only fourteen titles dealing with illness out of the more than six thousand memoirs pub-lished before 1945. None of those are chronicles of cancer, of the twists and turns of treatment; none of them end in death; none are by a parent and about a child.

Was the book too revealing? Was it in fact indecent? The *Ladies' Home Journal* ran a long preview of *Death Be Not Proud,* accompa-nied by a full-page gouache illustration of a boy with a bandaged head and a snapshot of Johnny and Frances on the beach before he got sick. The magazine was deluged with correspondence; one in every five letters objected to the baring of such a story. What good could possibly come from relating these ghoulish details? protested one woman whose husband had a brain tumor. Some of the book's reviewers felt similarly. The fact that the proceeds of the book were donated to cancer research helped to diffuse the whiff of bad taste. Nevertheless, it was like eavesdropping on a family tragedy—embarrassing as well as painful for all concerned. "The book is just as breathtaking and shocking as would be a similar confession from a new neighbor, a complete stranger, who suddenly told you his family's most secret tragedy," judged the *Hartford Times*'s critic.

Then the readers' letters started to arrive. They came by the thousands, telling their stories in the spare, anguished manner of John's account. It was as if he'd given them not just permission but a template for how to write about their experiences. They sent photos of their dead children, the backs of the pictures a fuzzy black where they were peeled out of scrapbooks.

DEAR MR. GUNTHER, WROTE the mother.

My little girl was a clever child, affectionate, and uncomplaining. For months, we made the trip from New Bedford to Boston, sixty miles each way, every day, for treatment. Margaret had a dimple in her left cheek and gray-blue eyes. She would have been eight on her next birthday.

At the Children's Hospital in Boston, Dr. Sidney Farber was accomplishing miracles with leukemia, we'd been told. My husband and I took Margaret there, to the new clinic. There were two doctors, a nurse and a technician. They were using new medicines, among them aminopterin, and new techniques in transfusion. Margaret's spleen was enlarged and her liver, too.

The drugs reduced white blood cells and the swellings in the glands and for the first few weeks we could hardly believe our luck. Margaret was one of the fortunate ones! She was almost back to normal, smiling and playing. But the drugs proved toxic, and she felt nauseous all the time. She stopping eating. She'd had two pigtails, but her hair started to fall out—it was the drugs, the doctors said—so I just combed it straight back.

The doctors had warned us about hemorrhaging. It started by epistaxis, and then, she was bleeding from the mouth and nostrils.

Carefully, with tweezers, I used Oxycel gauze to pack my daughter's nose two or three times a week, which kept the nose bleeds in check. Her entire body was covered in reddish purple blemishes. On her left cheek bone there was a spot. Your little girl is the worst bleeder we've ever seen, the doctors told us.

After four months of treatment, the skin hung in dry folds on her buttocks and when the nurse appeared with the needle, she screamed and cried. I came to dread those injections almost as much as she did.

Margaret realized she was sick with leukemia, like the other children in the clinic. Some of them had lymphosarcoma and there was a little girl there, three years old, whose head had swollen to the size of a balloon; her eyes were bruised black and she couldn't open them any longer. The children died in little bunches, more and more of them as the winter came closer. Eddie is better, he's gone home, and doesn't need any more treatment, I told Margaret. But I knew that she saw through me. She realized she might also die.

All those mothers in the clinic tending their doomed children: sometimes it seemed too much. Margaret was too weak to walk but she tried, especially when she knew people were watching her. I carried her whenever I could.

The trips to Boston took up a whole day, and I hardly had time for my other children. The older two read to Margaret when they came home from school. They sat by her bedside. She loved stories and presents. We would have bought her anything. When we said, Margaret, what would you like? she tried to reassure us by asking for toys. But she didn't have the strength to play with them.

We took her back to the hospital just after New Year's because her hemoglobin was so low. The doctors put an IV in a superficial ankle vein that evening. The next morning, they'd do the transfusion. My husband was donating the blood. It would be best to do a full transfusion, the doctors said, removing all of her blood and putting in 5000 cc's of his, but she likely won't survive it, so we'll do only a partial one.

She surprised the doctors by dying that night. I am sorry for writing you such a long letter, Margaret's mother told John. I hadn't intended to. There is so much I haven't said, but you see that when I read about your Johnny, I had to write.

MOSTLY MOTHERS WROTE, BUT occasionally fathers. Their children were almost exactly like Johnny, they said. Frances and John put into words what they'd suffered. They'd been sitting by their children's hospital beds, too shocked to cry until they read *Death Be Not Proud,* and now the tears had come. "You see, your story was mine." A mother's sorrow had an apparently universal, essential quality: the Pietà, Mary cradling the dead body of Jesus. And yet, they hadn't been able to talk about their grief before. My minister has told me that it is time to put it behind me. Or: Don't you ever feel bitter? they asked. "I expect you did, but I suppose that doesn't help does it?"

A mother whose baby died of pneumonia cut "A Word from Frances" out of the book and put it in her Bible with her baby's footprints. One father ordered twenty copies of *Death Be Not Proud* to send to his relatives; his son had polio. Parents felt guilty that they couldn't afford more treatments and private doctors, or they regretted they had subjected their children to painful operations. Their sons had died in Japanese P.O.W. camps or in the fighting at Guadalcanal and if only they could have been there to comfort them at the end.

It wasn't just bereaved parents who wrote. Mothers sent letters to say that they'd taken Frances's advice to heart, enlisting her in the ever-higher set of expectations of motherhood created in the postwar world. They were trying not to be so short-tempered or critical. It wasn't enough to feed and clothe their children, they'd realized. They had to attend to their sons' and daughters' psychological needs, so that their children could grow up to be sound and happy individuals. I am going to see a psychiatrist so I don't fail my son, reported one woman.

For years, the letters continued to come. Deerfield got mailbags full, too. Visitors arrived asking to see the church where the commencement was held so that they could imagine the scene of Johnny's graduation for themselves. John tried to acknowledge all the letters, though after a while, it was Jane who read them because he couldn't face it. They were too sad. Or impertinent. Why don't you and Frances reconcile? readers inquired. Tune in to the International Lutheran Hour "Bringing Christ to the Nations" on Sunday. Cancer is caused by reheated vegetable oil. Or by divorce. The "separation of his procreators," judged one California woman, would certainly have caused a brain lesion in a "spirit so marvellous and rare as was Johnny's."

Above all else, though, readers wrote to thank them for sharing Johnny—for bringing him to life, for explaining the value of an existence, even one cut so short. It was John's best book, Dorothy felt certain, for it demonstrated what "a human life could be." *Death Be Not Proud* could have been "one more bleat in a slaughterhouse," as another reporter friend of John's put it. But it wasn't, because it transcended one family's private misery to become a public chronicle, much the way that Anne Frank's *Diary of a Young Girl*, published in English in 1952, would do. "Thank God there are people like you who still realize the infinite value of one soul when the world is devising new means of mass killing," one woman wrote Frances.

After a half-century that had claimed, by conservative estimates, more than seventy million lives through war and genocide, the idea that the dignity of the individual needed protecting was a common enough preoccupation. At the newly founded United Nations, delegates were debating the Universal Declaration of Human Rights. That document, adopted by the U.N. in 1948, proclaimed an inalienable right to live free from want and oppression, and—still more novel—to develop fully one's own personality.

It was this aim that the Gunthers and their friends had in their sights. For decades, they'd been scrutinizing themselves and each other. Subjects that more orthodox Freudians would have seen as the terrain of the unconscious they treated as problems to be solved through frank talk and rational analysis. Among their legacies, then, was a democratic language of plain speaking about taboo subjects.

"Little that was human," as Dorothy put it, "was alien to us." Defending the dignity of the individual, to them, meant providing a full accounting of experiences that had previously been thought beyond words. Together, they would help to bring new realms of private life into public view.

JOHN MARRIED JANE IN Chicago in March 1948, and when they returned to New York, he brought her to meet Frances, as he'd promised he would. Jane was beautiful and kind, Frances thought, and very much like the sort of girl she'd hoped John would marry. Jane would have been a very good stepmother to Johnny. She made Jane a present of a silk faille evening coat she'd once treasured and a large silver serving dish she'd always imagined giving to Johnny's bride. Jane and John were off to Europe for their honeymoon.

Seeing John happily married to Jane was like giving up a possession one had long ago prized very much, Frances told Jimmy. She was preparing to leave America herself and contemplating, she said, a life without possessions. Maybe she'd even get to India at last; after Johnny got sick, she'd barely communicated with Jawahar. Jimmy had seen Nehru, he reported, and mentioned Frances's name. Nehru "glowed at me for a moment like a live coal," he wrote.

Frances wanted to move to Palestine, but because of her work with the Bergson Boys, she was refused permission. In Madison, she tried to get to work on a book about Arab-Hebrew relations, but her old troubles with writing returned worse than ever. She read and read. You read like other people drink, she lectured herself. Her reporter friends had all had their say. "You must say yours." She considered electroshock therapy or hypnosis to jolt her out of her frozen state.

After the founding of Israel in the summer of 1948, she sold the Inside House and packed her things, putting aside her old black suitcase with its papers from Barnard—her college essays in anthropology, her little pocket diaries, her masses of notes for unfinished stories and plays—and a packet marked JUDY. In Jerusalem, she settled into a flat on Ramban Street in the Old City with a terrace that overlooked the hills.

Jimmy's letter about *Death Be Not Proud* reached her there. He could hardly read the pages of Johnny's book through his tears. "You are the mother of a hero, and I think that it makes a difference in the world," he told her. "Many people will be strengthened because of your brave boy."

IN THE SUMMER OF 1949, Knick left for Indonesia. Dutch colonial rule, interrupted during the war by the Japanese occupation, was finally limping to an end. In a belated bid for favorable publicity, the Dutch government invited a party of eleven American correspondents to tour the archipelago. They were promised "complete freedom of action" as well as an interview with the nationalist leader, Sukarno.

En route to Indonesia from Amsterdam, the correspondents traveled a roundabout itinerary, made necessary because Nehru—expressing solidarity with Indonesian nationalists—had forbidden the Dutch national airline, KLM, from landing in India. From Amsterdam, they flew to Cairo, Aden, and the Indian Ocean island of Mauritius, then a British colony. Mauritius to Java was another fifteen to seventeen hours, the longest flight any commercial airliner undertook at that time. The plane would arrive in Batavia with fuel enough for only a few more hours in the air.

It seemed to Knick that he was the only journalist aboard who was actually intent upon work. The others were drunk most of the time on cheap native rum, lollygagging in bed, and nursing their hangovers. If only he hadn't wasted his time with drink all those years! He might have been able to retire by now. But at least he'd gotten the chance to redeem himself, both as a journalist and as a husband. He and Agnes were finally happy again. "I need to beg you to forgive the brutal way I treated you," he wrote her from Cairo. "I treasure every tiny glimpse you give me of yourself."

He was back in the headlines, warning about the Soviet Union's expansionism, opining about Sukarno whom he thought wasn't a strong enough leader to forestall the advance of Communism through Indonesia. In his broadcasts, he was sharply critical of both the Dutch (as feeble) and the Indonesian nationalists (as Red). To Agnes he exclaimed: "It is fun to be back in the fore."

On the way home, the correspondents telegraphed Nehru for special permission to fly over India so that the return journey wouldn't be so arduous. Nehru agreed to make an exception for them. The correspondents' plane was fifteen miles north of Bombay when it crashed on Ghatkopar Hill. The rain had been ferocious— a monsoon—and the KLM "Constellation," a big plane with a rounded belly and a high nose, was circling the airfield for an hour and a half attempting to land. The wingtip of the plane, said witnesses, hit a rock on the hilltop. After that, the plane went down in a shower of sparks. Knick was dead at the age of fifty-one.

Before he boarded the plane in Batavia, Knick had been joking around. He'd recorded his weekly broadcast for the New York station WOR and sent it on an earlier flight.

I've provided the world with an unparalleled opportunity for posthumous correspondence, he remarked.

EPILOGUE
Enter the Obituarians

AROLO, ITALY

SEPTEMBER 1971

JIMMY HAD DRIVEN AN HOUR TO MEET THAT AWFUL WOMAN at the Milan airport, though in retrospect, why he had bothered with that particular act of chivalry, he didn't know. He'd risen in the morning to get to the airfield on time. He'd even put on a tie, which in 1971 counted as a declaration of old-fashioned gallantry. While he and Dinah waited for Mrs. Marion Sanders's plane to arrive, he'd had some brandies at the airport bar, it was true, but he wasn't the slightest bit foggy or out of sorts. At least not until Mrs. Sanders opened her mouth.

Yes, yes, Jimmy conceded, the woman had done plenty of research about Dorothy Thompson for her so-called authorized biography and god knows, Dorothy left masses of eye-popping papers for an impertinent idiot like Mrs. Sanders to paw through. She could tell you who Dorothy had an affair with in 1923, as if *that* mattered, and she had spotted every piddling flaw in her subject's character. But as for the truth about Dorothy? Mrs. Sanders hadn't the beginning of a clue.

The day after she left, Jimmy shot off a letter to Houghton Mifflin, Mrs. Sanders's publisher and his own as well. This is going to be the worst book Houghton ever published, he warned. How could someone like Mrs. Sanders—a "Manhattanese coolie," he called her—possibly fathom the nobility of Dorothy? She didn't understand the first thing about Dorothy's Christianity, had called her beloved father "a nothing, a nebbish," and couldn't imagine anyone doing anything except for profit or ambition. Mrs. Sanders would never understand that what Dorothy had wanted—the only thing Dorothy had ever wanted—was to save the world.

In a scrawled postscript, Jimmy fumed that Mrs. Sanders had broken the needle on their gramophone. "She's a meddler as well as a clown, dolt and imposter."

Mrs. Sanders reported to her editor that the stay with the Sheeans had been a total disaster. Jimmy never stopped drinking, not for a moment. Either he was gibberingly incoherent or he clammed up entirely. Sheean had been Dorothy Thompson's friend for decades and lived with her for years at Twin Farms. He had even written his own book about her. Why then, Mrs. Sanders wondered, was he completely incapable of offering up any information? To make matters worse, they were trapped for three days in the Italian sticks because Jimmy's dog was sick. Imagine living without a telephone! And you should have seen how small their icebox was.

"Poor Jimmy—he's finished, I'm afraid" was the talk at Houghton Mifflin, to whom he owed a long-planned sequel to *Personal History*.

Dinah set about trying to repair the damage. Mrs. Sanders's visit was the "misfire of the century," she acknowledged in a letter to the Houghton editors. Jimmy *had* wanted to be helpful. But almost immediately Mrs. Sanders and Jimmy had gotten off on the wrong foot. Based on a comment Mrs. Sanders made, Jimmy suspected she was a Zionist and hated him for his well-known sympathies for the Arabs. And then he held it against her that she hadn't suggested a trip to Milan to see the Poldi Pezzoli Museum or the Last Supper or the Cathedral. And when Mrs. Sanders suggested that Dorothy had taken the part of the Palestinian Arabs after the war because she was bought off by American oil companies, well, that was the final straw. Imagine anyone believing that Dorothy could be bribed!

Jimmy was not, Dinah insisted to Houghton, "a lost cause." His book was coming slowly but she was certain it would be his best yet. Yes, he'd been drunk much of the time Mrs. Sanders was there, but that wasn't so very hard to understand, was it? He really dreaded talking about Dorothy and he was terribly shy and self-conscious, which was why he drank in the first place. Plus, he suspected that Mrs. Sanders was trying to egg Dinah on to leave him. Jimmy was "expendable" but Dinah could still save herself was the unwelcome message of liberation that Mrs. Sanders came bearing.

All that fall of 1971, Jimmy walked around the house, lamenting: "My poor Dorothy, my poor Dorothy, your bones will be desecrated."

THE BIGGEST IRONY, OF course, was that *he* was the one still alive to receive the sorry parade of biographers. Who'd have imagined that Sheean would survive them all? John Gunther, with his astounding vitality, and Frances, brighter than hell, both dead now. Knick dying an honest-to-god foreign correspondent's death. Hemingway a suicide, without in fact bequeathing Jimmy the manuscripts of the thirty-seven different drafts of the last page and a half of *A Farewell to Arms* he'd once promised. (Jimmy should take more pains revising, Hemingway jibed.) And Dorothy. Despite two big coronaries, she drank like a fish and smoked fifty cigarettes a day, so apparently she'd had a death wish, too.

Jimmy had always assumed he'd die young. But when he reached the biblical age of seventy, he had to admit that perhaps he'd in fact wanted to live. Out in the evening on Lake Maggiore in a boat, belting out arias with the local fishermen, drinking red wine, and throwing the bottles (always empties, Dinah noted) in the lake, he was content enough. But back at his desk, working late into the night as he'd always done, he felt superannuated. He'd written a book on King Faisal of Saudi Arabia that his publishers had rejected and *Holiday* magazine said his article on the Iranian city of Isfahan wasn't the sort of thing that tourists would want. "I'm so old! I no longer can write for the American market!" he wailed to Dinah.

Of course Jimmy is discouraged, the playwright Thornton Wilder, an old friend, advised Dinah. Like Scott Fitzgerald or "much less sympathetically" Ernest Hemingway, Jimmy had been the very incarnation of Youth for an awestruck world. "He lived it; he shone it; he bestrode it," judged Wilder. To represent the spirit of an age and then to be irrelevantly carrying on decades later—that was the sort of thing that finished people off.

Too bad you didn't in fact die young and earn yourself a small part in the memories of Americans who can read, Rebecca West had told Jimmy.

AS DOROTHY SAW IT, journalism was their era's "most representative form of letters." What the play was to the Renaissance or the novel to the nineteenth century, reporting was to the 1920s and 1930s, she'd claimed in 1939. Novelists such as John Steinbeck, whose Pulitzer-winning *Grapes of Wrath* was published that year, drew on the techniques of reportage. The influence was mutual, for facts needed interpretation if they were to mean anything. Having an imagination, Dorothy noted, had become as important to reporters as it was to novelists. Dorothy and her friends had abandoned what she called "the field of pure reporting" for the sort of subjective analysis—the interrogation of personality, the interpretation of causation—necessary to understand the truth.

By the mid-1950s, their breed of foreign correspondents— "congeries of eccentrics and prima donnas," the *New Yorker* called them—seemed nearly extinct. The sort of freewheeling go-where-I-please attitude wasn't possible any longer once foreign correspondence became a professional job for corporate men who'd put in their time in the home office. The advent of the jet made it possible to drop in on hot spots around the world, then depart just as swiftly. As the United States sought to exert its dominance globally, remaking the world to suit, foreign correspondents became more entangled in that project, either as critics or as sympathizers. Drawing bright lines—deciding what the "truth" was—became a much more difficult enterprise absent Hitler and his lot. And so, the ideal of objectivity was re-enshrined.

In his debate with John that evening at the Stork Club in 1946, Jimmy had been right: their heyday was over. The generation of newsmen who directly followed them would recognize their influence. It was because of *Personal History,* said Walter Cronkite, that he'd become a reporter. By contrast, the New Journalists of the 1960s, who followed their lead in disdaining the notion of impartiality and putting themselves in their stories, didn't acknowledge the paternity. If Hunter S. Thompson or Tom Wolfe read Sheean, Thompson, and the rest, they didn't credit them. In all the hoopla that surrounded so-called Gonzo journalism, it was as if they'd created the genre from whole cloth.

Dorothy for one had never been under any illusion that her influence would endure. There was the ephemeral stuff she wrote and then there was Art: Red's novels or Edna St. Vincent Millay's totemic verses, which came to stand for the twenties in the way that Dos Passos's *U.S.A.* (rather than John's *Inside Europe*) did the thirties. Eight publishers vied for Dorothy's memoirs. She started gathering materials: interviewing Fodor, writing old friends from the women's suffrage campaign. Soon enough, though, her "me and the twentieth century" book bogged down in ill health and the daunting scale of the undertaking. She didn't get much further than 1903, the year she turned ten. "Mighty pretty country and centuries removed from today," she explained to a friend.

It wasn't just Dorothy. None of them found it possible to sum up what their lives had meant. Jimmy stewed over his memoirs fruitlessly—his "terminal" book, he insisted on calling it. In Jerusalem, Frances began a new project that she entitled "Theopolitics," trying to work out the balance between the political, the theological, and the personal in global affairs. It was in part a treatise on international relations, in part an autobiography. For years she labored on the manuscript, writing a little, revising a lot. Even John, rarely stymied, hardly made a start on the autobiography he'd planned since he was twenty. When he wrote fiction, he made free use of his life, but his autobiographical venture didn't extend beyond a few pieces in *Harper's* magazine about the writing of the "Inside" series. He accumulated piles and piles of notes in folders marked "Save for Autobiography" but that was as far as it went.

I'll "do" you, John joked to Jimmy. John had been amassing materials for a book on Dorothy, Jimmy, and Mickey. We'll see about that, Jimmy retorted. It depends on who kicks the bucket first.

The first to go was Red Lewis, in 1951, either from alcoholism or a heart attack, depending upon whether one took the long or the short view. When the biographers started to appear at Twin Farms, Dorothy was pragmatic as ever. What was the "essential conflict" in Red that produced his work? That was the question that the biographer authorized by the Lewis estate asked her. There wasn't one conflict, she maintained, but many. And some of them worked at violent cross-purposes.

Dorothy's ability to separate herself from the events of her life, to reflect upon them with detachment, struck Red's biographer as nothing short of astounding. She'd been emotional about the things other people approached analytically and was analytical about her own emotions. Red's biographer gave over large sections of his book to her analysis. If his book had a heroine, he said, it would be Dorothy herself, not least for the Olympian perspective she'd provided on her marriage.

The truth, Dorothy confided in Rebecca, was that their union was such a catastrophe that she had blocked it all out. She wasn't about to undertake a psychoanalysis just so she could interpret Sinclair Lewis's neuroses. Nevertheless, in a long *Atlantic* article published nearly a decade after Red's death, she made a start on it, puzzling out the familial dynamics that had made the man, airing stories of his own disastrous relations with his sons. To a reader who wrote her, incensed about the revelations, she replied simply: "Lewis was an American genius and a personal tragedy."

"I hope I can get through this without having a bloody big statue of Red stuck up on my lawn," Jimmy told John before he met Red's biographer. To talk of a "central conflict" was inanity, Jimmy said. Rebecca, it turned out, had already volunteered that Red's central conflict was "suppressed homosexuality," which Jimmy thought damn cheek given that she raised hell if anyone so much as breathed a word about her liaison with H. G. Wells. That was the start of the plague of "obituarians." Mrs. Sanders was followed by a young man writing about John Gunther and a still younger man who wanted to take Jimmy himself as the subject of his Ph.D. thesis. The "Tormentor," Jimmy nicknamed him when he turned up in Arolo and trailed behind Jimmy, room after room, tape recorder in hand.

They would "do" themselves or other people would "do" them. When Dorothy died in 1961—"like saying goodbye to a lifetime," Jimmy said—he and John talked about a book about the Lewis-Thompson marriage. John had been thinking about it since Red's death. He didn't talk to Red's official biographer because he intended to save his stories for his own book. In the end, though, Jimmy got there first. The title of the book would be *Dorothy and Red,* he told John. It would be a personal history, he acknowledged, because that was the only kind he knew how to do.

MOST OF DOROTHY'S PAPERS had ended up in the vaults of the "House of Morgan," the old limestone corner building on Wall Street belonging to the Morgan Guaranty Trust Company. Three big filing cabinets at Morgan, boxes and boxes more at Twin Farms: Dorothy seemed to have saved everything. Houghton Mifflin's first choice to write Dorothy's biography was Rebecca West, but after expressing interest, she turned the project down. She wasn't even writing her own autobiography, Rebecca explained. She was so cutting about her old friend Dorothy and everyone else that the editors at Houghton felt relieved they hadn't entrusted her with the papers.

Jimmy was Houghton's second, maybe even third choice. By the early 1960s, he'd built up something of a sideline in "necrology," as he referred to it; he'd published a short, perceptive memoir of Edna St. Vincent Millay, and had books about his friends Marian Anderson and Ethel Barrymore in the works. But do Dorothy? He didn't have enough of his own life left to write her biography, Jimmy declared. That would take another two full existences. Moreover, he didn't give a damn what the Polish assistant minister for commerce had once told Dorothy about the trade balance. The book he instead proposed to Houghton—an insider's account of Dorothy and Red's relationship—was, to say the least, unorthodox. Writing about one's own marriage (or marriages) was daring enough, the sort of things that the occasional actress or chorus girl might venture. But to dissect in print the marriage of one's friends? Jimmy was practically inviting the charge of vulgarity and disloyal opportunism.

At Houghton, Jimmy's insistence that he'd write exactly what was in Dorothy's papers—holding nothing back—caused a certain amount of consternation, especially when they saw what he'd produced. Red's impotence, his alcoholism as a cover for sexual puzzlement, Dorothy's lesbianism, the tortured back-and-forth in their letters, Red's mistreatment of their son: it was all there, unexpurgated. Dorothy's affair with Christa Winsloe, Jimmy admitted, had come as a shock to him. Red apparently knew about it, and so did Dorothy's sister, but he learned about it for the first time in Dorothy's diaries. Nevertheless, it had to go in—Christa's smooth cheek, the kisses. That was what Dorothy would have wanted. Her sister, her executors, and John Gunther all agreed. Had she managed to write her autobiography, it would have been just as forthcoming.

Whatever hesitation Houghton had about the seemliness of the endeavor was put to rest by publication day. "It may well be the frankest revelation of a marriage ever published," the press touted, its editors' unease transformed into a selling point. Some reviewers, predictably, condemned it as the worst sort of tattle. Sheean, rebuked *Time,* had done an "extraordinary thing" by invading the privacy of two well-known, recently deceased people; one read the book with "awful fascination." Just as many, if not more, praised Sheean's forthright handling of subjects that had been swept under the carpet. It was the real-life version of *Who's Afraid of Virginia Woolf?,* the play by Edward Albee then running on Broadway.

The point that Jimmy made again and again in interviews was that Dorothy and Red's marriage wasn't at all unusual. "It is the story of virtually every marriage," he maintained. Granted, the two of them were extraordinary people. However, the experiences that had riven their marriage—impotence, jealousy, affairs, drinking—were normal enough. Why, then, shouldn't such subjects be talked about? It was the same question that John had broached in writing about Johnny's illness and death. Nothing that was human should be off-limits.

Jimmy acknowledged that there was some pathos in the fact that he was cashing in on his friendship with Dorothy and Red. He soothed his conscience, though, with the idea they'd have heartily approved. Sometimes he wondered if they hadn't been writing those diaries and letters not simply for posterity, but for him in particular to read. As *Dorothy and Red* went into a second, third, and fourth printing, friends and acquaintances leapt in with corrections. No, the weather was not rainy on the Semmering, John insisted, and Helmuth James von Moltke had been among the party; Laura Knickerbocker's hair was black, not red. Knickerbocker was a much more important journalist than Dorothy, contended "A Mrs. Joseph Something of Nyack, N.Y., who turns out to be Agnes," Jimmy hooted to John. From London, Dorothy's first husband, Joseph Bard, threatened to sue *Time* for describing him in its review of the book as "a sponging Hungarian cad."

The big surprise was Rebecca's reaction. She liked the book immensely, she wrote Jimmy. She'd frightened him for nearly forty years, and finally, at a word of praise, he was wagging his behind "like a surprised spaniel." When *Dorothy and Red* made the bestseller lists, Jimmy felt vindicated. "A little late for my vices, just in time for my virtues perhaps if I can remember them, but at any rate perfectly accommodated to my comforts," he pronounced with satisfaction.

ON HIS WAY TO see Gandhi in 1947, Jimmy had stopped in Rome. He went to have cocktails with the American ambassador there.

Jimmy was going on in his usual way in those days—talking of the necessity of peace, One Worldism—when the ambassador interrupted him. "When are you going to abdicate?" the ambassador demanded.

What on earth could the man possibly mean? Jimmy wondered. "This is a question I have not been called upon to consider," he replied.

"You must abdicate. You cannot rule the world. You cannot improve it. You cannot do anything whatsoever to it. It will remain just as it is," the ambassador persisted. "Why do you have to have treaties, especially peace treaties? You and Dorothy Thompson!"

It was, as Jimmy saw, only half a joke. Through the 1950s and 1960s, he went on renouncing public life and then, when American foreign policy seemed too much to tolerate from the sidelines, charging back into the fray. It didn't escape him that the global view he'd urged on his readers had helped to justify American expansionism. An anti-imperialist to the last, he reported sympathetically from the Bandung Conference, barraged Nehru and successive American administrations with letters, appointed himself Adlai Stevenson's foreign policy expert, converted to Hinduism, became a vegetarian, and refused to kill flies. He wrote a biography of Nehru and planned for his ashes to be shipped to the prime minister, to be deposited in the Ganges. He wore a white Nehru cap and homespun dhoti. His neighbors in Vermont pretended not to notice. He half-believed in UFOs. "People never do look up," he pointed out.

There was no *Personal History II,* though he inevitably threw his own shadow over *Dorothy and Red,* not least in what he had to say about the dynamics of love and booze and sex in a marriage. He and Dinah remarried in 1949, only to separate again in a conflagration of mutual recriminations a few years later. In 1970, she returned to him, and they moved, for good, to Arolo. In those last years, they traveled to India and China, they went to the opera, and they talked and talked. "Jimmy is a hazard in my life but a necessary one," was the way Dinah explained it.

They came to New York a final time in the fall of 1974 after Jimmy was diagnosed with lung cancer. After a few months of treatment, he returned to Italy to die, as he'd always said he would. His last weeks passed in a semiconscious reverie, no pain, his mind full of fun. He composed music through the night, talking all the while. The remarkable thing, Dinah wrote their friends, was that he was finally free. Not one single word about the "state of the world." Instead, he heard an orchestra in his head and imagined a Chardin still life of a bowl sitting on a windowsill and a satchel hanging nearby. He and Dinah laughed together about all the funny things in life.

POSTSCRIPT

FRANCES GUNTHER TRAVELED TO INDIA IN 1950, STAYING with Nehru in the prime minister's official residence. His coolness toward her, and the picture of Edwina Mountbatten in his study, put an end to her thoughts of a future together. Back in Jerusalem, she struggled with her memoir and wrote articles about Arab-Israeli relations that she kept to herself, fearful (as she put it to Dorothy) of the "wrath of the Israeli fathers." In her Jerusalem apartment, she held a salon to try to reconcile her Israeli and Palestinian friends. She died in 1964 of cancer, leaving her papers to a childhood friend of Johnny's.

MARCEL FODOR made it out of Europe after the collapse of France, arriving in the United States in June 1940. He, his wife Martha, and their young son stayed for the summer with Dorothy at Twin Farms, then moved to Chicago, where Fodor—thanks to the intervention of John and Dorothy—taught at the Illinois Institute of Technology, and wrote a column for the *Sun*. After the war, Fodor worked for the American Occupation forces in Berlin, editing the U.S. military-sponsored paper, *Die Neue Zeitung*.

JIMMY SHEEAN insisted to the end of his days that his watch had stopped permanently the moment Gandhi was assassinated. "What you need are new watches," JAWAHARLAL NEHRU remarked. Jimmy and Nehru continued to correspond, contentiously, about every subject from Kashmir to the nature of happiness. Of course,

Nehru believes he's been happy, Jimmy wrote John, but he's "just got into a rut and he thinks it's the Milky Way." Be prepared to receive my ashes, Jimmy advised Nehru. Sometimes Jimmy said he didn't want a funeral, other times he planned the pallbearers who'd carry his casket: Dorothy at the head, Dinah at his foot, his friends Clare Boothe Luce and Agnes de Mille on one side and Greta Garbo and Marian Anderson on the other. Nehru died in 1964, a decade before Jimmy.

JOHN GUNTHER died in 1970 while working on his final "Inside" book about Australia. He and Frances had kept up a regular correspondence, New York to Jerusalem, affectionate and newsy on his end, alternately loving and recriminatory on hers. He married Jane in 1948, and they later adopted a son. *Death Be Not Proud* is the only one of Gunther's books still in print. It has been translated into German, Spanish, Danish, French, Arabic, Chinese, Hebrew, and Japanese.

In the fall of 1942, as the Red Army collared the Wehrmacht in Stalingrad and the Royal Air Force stepped up its bombing raids on northern Germany, JOSEPH GOEBBELS devoted his evenings to Knickerbocker's new book, *Is Tomorrow Hitler's?* It was a "typical" piece of journalism, judged the propaganda minister, brilliant in style but extraordinarily superficial. It deserved to be pitched in the trash can. As if continuing the conversation with his old adversary, Goebbels concluded his diary that night on a defiant key. "And by the way, only statesmen and military men make world history. Not journalists." Goebbels and his wife Magda murdered their six children, aged four to twelve, before committing suicide on May 1, 1945.

REBECCA WEST lived until 1983, a regal figure in a caftan issuing withering remarks about old friends and enemies alike from her South Kensington apartment. "I was never sure whether he was intelligent or stupid," she told a young man who came to interview her about John Gunther. "I've nothing good to say about Frances except that she was very pretty," West offered. "Can't think why John married her."

MICKEY HAHN outlived them all, writing for the *New Yorker* until her death, at ninety-two, in 1997. Her fifty-two books included one about D. H. Lawrence's relations with women, a volume on animal communication, and a series of memoirs politely referred to at the time as "candid." Of her startlingly frank *China to Me* (1944), her future husband admitted he wished very fervently that page 238 had never been published. "I don't care what you write about me," Mickey informed her biographer, "as long as it's the truth."

ACKNOWLEDGMENTS

—

I AM GRATEFUL, FIRST OF ALL, TO THOSE FAMILY MEMBERS AND friends of my subjects, whose assistance made this book possible. In a book that deals with all the ways that writing about people can go wrong, I am only too aware of the trust they placed in me. The late Jane Gunther offered her sharp, humane memories of her late husband and his circle. I am very grateful to Nicholas Gunther for his helpful emails as my research progressed. Miranda Knickerbocker de Kay has been a constant source of encouragement, and her curiosity and acuity about her parents' lives have sustained my work. Mary von Euler's thoughts about Frances Gunther helped me to see her afresh. The late Stephen Graubard talked with me about Sheean, Thompson, and liberalism; my thanks to Stuart Proffitt for making the introduction. Sarah Allen Wilson sent me documents from the archive of her grandfather, Jay Allen. Nayantara Sahgal provided valuable recollections of Frances Gunther and Jimmy Sheean. Ken Cuthbertson, the biographer of John Gunther, Emily Hahn, and Bill Shirer, has been a model of generosity, very kindly mailing me a precious box of interviews he conducted in the course of his own research. The late Denis Fodor—himself a consummate newspaperman—described the Café Louvre down to the style of chairs and provided a sensitive analysis of the dynamics of the *Stammtisch*. Carola Vecchio shared memories of her inimitable mother, Mickey Hahn. Linda Morton brought the warmth and fun of her grandparents, Jimmy and Dinah Sheean, to life. And Peter Kurth, whose biography of Dorothy Thompson is the standard work, has talked with me for hours about our shared interests; I am indebted to his generosity in offering me documents from his archive, his memories of Dinah Sheean, and most of all, his example.

In writing a book about a group of friends, I've drawn heavily on the patience, goodwill, and expertise of my own. A heartfelt thank-you to the friends who read this book in draft—too many drafts—and whose comments, references, grammatical interventions, and wisecracks have kept me going. Ken Alder, Leora Auslander, Deborah Baker, Daniel Immerwahr, Maya Jasanoff, Peter Mandler, Sharon Marcus, Susan Pedersen, Amy Stanley, and Tara Zahra have spent god-knows-how-many-hours talking with me about these ideas and countless others now discarded, and reading (and rereading) the manuscript: bless you all. In the later stages, a fresh regiment—Sue Grayzel, Perry Hewitt, Michael Joe, Darcy Lear, Madelyn Lugli, Sarah Maza, Bronwyn Rae, Larry Sloan, Jodi Torzewski, and Emily Tedrowe—entered the field and helped me see the book anew. Thank you to Tom Arnold-Forster for conversations about Chicago newspapers and Walter Lippmann; Nancy Cott for discussion of our shared subjects and biography more generally; Paul Preston for insights into Knickerbocker, Sheean, and Jay Allen; Vanessa Schwartz for talks about photojournalism; Benjamin Goldstein for his research into the Hearst enterprise; David Milne for a last-minute consultation about Sigrid Schultz; Judith Allen for literally opening vaults at the Kinsey Institute; and Vanessa Ogle for her expertise about Nazi assets. I'm immensely grateful to the institutions that funded this book and the people who ensured I had the resources I needed to complete it: Northwestern University (especially Annerys Cano, Laura Hein, Edward Gibson, and Adrian Randolph), the Chabraja Center for Historical Studies (especially Elzbieta Foeller-Pituch), the Newberry Library/National Endowment for the Humanities Fellowship (especially Liesl Olson, Brad Hunt, and Daniel Greene), and the Botstiber Institute for Austrian-American Studies (especially Adriana Lecuona). And my thanks to Ann Hulbert, who took a chance on me eight years ago at the *Atlantic* and is the dream editor.

Special thanks to the Special Collections Research Center at the University of Chicago (and particularly to Daniel Meyer, Eileen Ielmini, and Catherine Uecker), the Beinecke Library's exemplary staff (especially Adrienne Sharpe-Weseman), the Schlesinger Library's archivists, Syracuse University's Special Collections Research Center (especially Zoë Brown and Nicole Westerdahl), Princeton Library's Department of Special Collections (Brianna Cregle and AnnaLee Pauls), Suzy Taraba at Wesleyan's Special Collections & Archives, David Daly and Chris Wirth at the Longfellow Historic Site, Craig Wright at the Herbert Hoover Presidential Library, Fran Baker at the John Rylands Library, Kristine Krueger at the Margaret Herrick Library, Academy of Motion Pictures Arts and Sciences, Lyndsi Barnes and Isaac Gewirtz at the Berg Collection, NYPL, David Seubert at UC-Santa Barbara's Performing Arts Collection and Rebecca Bauman, Kristina Krasny, and Isabel Planton at the Lilly Library, Indiana University. I have been very lucky to work with a set of talented Leopold Fellows funded through the Chabraja Center for Historical Studies. Thank you (in chronological order) to Shira Zilberstein, Jason Mast, Claire Pak, Amanda Gordon, Martin Konstantinov, Andrew Reed, Sophia Scanlan, Meredith Ellison, Eva Herscowitz, and Sean Liu. Thank you as well to Mohammad Athar, Gil Engelstein, Elena Hoffenberg, Julie Johnson, Saskia Pedersen, Elizabeth Rickert, Cameron Sandlin, Tom Sojka, Jennie Williams, and Brenna Yellin who photographed material in archives when travel became difficult.

Without Kathy Robbins's legendary discernment and tact, I would have strayed into even more blind alleys than I did. She saw the possibilities in this book before I did and has been unstinting in her advice—and better, always right! Dorothy Thompson would have adored her. Clare Alexander's candid assessment at a crucial point early in in the writing prompted me to start over; her enthusiasm and good sense helped me to chart the way. I'm grateful to the entire Random House team: Mark Warren and Andy Ward, who signed the book, and Mark again for his encouragement and astute edits; Muriel Jorgensen for her scrupulous copyedits; Ted Allen, for running a tight production schedule; Ella Laytham and Robbin Schiff for the jacket design; and Barbara Bachman, for her inspired interior design. Jeff Miller at Faceout Studio gave the book a glamorous cover. Dr. Kelsey Rydland (Northwestern Libraries) made the maps both accurate and atmospheric. Marie Pantojan, my editor at Random House, is a master of both the cosmic and the precise edit. She's a diplomat as well as a critic and soothsayer, and her immersion in the world of the Gunthers and their friends has made for a much better book.

And to my family, "forsan et haec olim meminisse juvabit." For my mother, Helen Cohen, whose memories of *Death Be Not Proud* provided a starting point, and who is always enthusiastic about her children's strange preoccupations; my siblings, Jenny Cohen (who has discovered a talent for archive-cracking) and Joe Cohen (Stekel decoder); for Tom Silfen, who never wants an acknowledgment but deserves pages of them because as usual, he's improved every single sentence of this book; and for Alice, blazing brightly.

ARCHIVES

—

Jay Allen Papers, Private Collection

Archives of *Story* Magazine and Story Press, Manuscripts Division, Special Collections, Princeton University Library

Hamilton Fish Armstrong Papers, Seeley G. Mudd Manuscript Library, Princeton University

Carroll Binder Papers, Newberry Library

Book-of-the-Month Club Records, Yale Collection of American Literature, Beinecke Rare Book and Manuscript Library, Yale University Library

Brandt & Brandt Archives, Special Collections Research Center, Syracuse University Libraries

Louise Bryant Papers, Manuscripts and Archives, Yale University Library

William C. Bullitt Papers, Manuscripts and Archives, Yale University Library

Bundesarchiv, Lichterfelde—Sammlung Berlin Document Center, Reichskanzlei, Reichslandbund-Pressearchiv, Reichsministerium des Innern, Reichsschriftumskammer, and Reichssicherheitshauptamt

Charleston Papers, King's College Archives Centre, Cambridge University

Chicago Daily News Archive [Field Enterprises Records], Newberry Library

Henry Wadsworth Longfellow Dana Papers, Longfellow National Historic Site, Cambridge, Massachusetts

Ernestine Evans Papers, Rare Book & Manuscript Library, Columbia University

Louis Fischer Papers, Seeley G. Mudd Manuscript Library, Princeton University

Jerome New Frank Papers, Manuscripts and Archives, Yale University Library

Lewis Gannett Papers, Houghton Library, Harvard University

W. Horsley Gantt Papers, The Alan Mason Chesney Medical Archives, The Johns Hopkins Medical Institutions

G.E.R. Gedye Papers, Archive and Research Room, Imperial War Museum, London

C. Frank Glass Papers, Hoover Institute Archives

Duncan Grant Papers, Tate Archive

The *Guardian* Archive, The John Rylands Library, University of Manchester

Frances Fineman Gunther Papers, Schlesinger Library, Radcliffe Institute, Harvard University

John Gunther Papers, Special Collections Research Center [SCRC], University of Chicago:

    JG Papers I—Original deposit

    JG Papers 1972 Add.—1972 Addenda

    JG Papers II—Addenda II

Emily Hahn Papers, Lilly Library, Indiana University

Arthur and Leonora (Schinasi) Hornblow Papers, Academy of Motion Picture Arts and Sciences, Margaret Herrick Library

Houghton Mifflin Company Papers, Houghton Library, Harvard

India Office Records, British Library

John F. Kennedy Presidential Library and Museum

Kinsey Institute Library and Archives, Indiana University

Freda Kirchwey Papers, Schlesinger Library, Radcliffe Institute, Harvard University

Hubert Renfro Knickerbocker Papers, Rare Book & Manuscript Library, Columbia University

Agnes and H. R. Knickerbocker Papers, Private Collection

Frederick Kuh Papers, Special Collections Research Center, The George Washington University

Rose Wilder Lane Papers, Herbert Hoover Presidential Library and Museum

Lotte Lehmann Papers, Department of Special Collections, Davidson Library, University of California, Santa Barbara

Sinclair Lewis Papers, Beinecke Rare Book and Manuscript Library, Yale University

Louis Paul Lochner Papers, Wisconsin Historical Society

Clare Boothe Luce Papers, Manuscript Division, Library of Congress

Ken McCormick Collection of the Records of Doubleday & Company, Manuscript Division, Library of Congress

George S. Messersmith Papers, Manuscripts and Archives, University of Delaware

Fred B. Millett Papers, Special Collections and Archives, Wesleyan University

Louise Morgan and Otto Theis Papers, Beinecke Rare Book and Manuscript Library, Yale University

Raymond Mortimer Papers, Department of Rare Books and Special Collections, Princeton University

Raymond Mortimer–Eddy Sackville-West Correspondence, Department of Rare Books and Special Collections, Princeton University

Edgar Ansel Mowrer and Lilian T. Mowrer Papers, Manuscript Division, Library of Congress

Paul Scott Mowrer Papers, Newberry Library

The National Archives of Great Britain

Jawaharlal Nehru Papers, Nehru Memorial Museum and Library, New Delhi

New Yorker Records, Manuscripts and Archives Division, Humanities and Social Sciences Library, The New York Public Library

Österreichisches Staatsarchiv, Vienna

Palestine Statehood Committee "Concerning the campaigns for a Jewish Army; to save the Jewish people of Europe and the establishment of a Hebrew Republic in Palestine" Papers, MS 690, Manuscripts and Archives, Yale University Library

Reid Family Papers, Manuscript Division, Library of Congress

Franklin Delano Roosevelt Presidential Library and Museum

Richard Rovere Papers, Wisconsin Historical Society

Ellery Sedgwick Papers, Massachusetts Historical Society

Eric Sevareid Papers, Manuscript Division, Library of Congress

Vincent Sheean Papers:
>   JVS Papers, Berg—Berg Collection, New York Public Library
>   JVS Papers, Syracuse—Special Collections Research Center, Syracuse University Libraries
>   JVS Papers, WHS—Wisconsin Historical Society

William L. Shirer Papers, George T. Henry College Archives, Stewart Memorial Library, Coe College

Leland Stowe Papers, Wisconsin Historical Society

Sir Campbell Stuart Papers, Archive and Research Room, Imperial War Museum, London

Betty Gram Swing Papers, Schlesinger Library, Radcliffe Institute, Harvard University

Swiss Federal Archives, Bern, Switzerland

Dorothy Thompson Papers, Special Collections Research Center, Syracuse University Libraries

Irita Taylor Van Doren Papers, Manuscript Division, Library of Congress

Rebecca West Papers:

    RW Papers, BL [British Library]

    RW Papers, Department of Special Collections and University Archives, McFarlin Library, The University of Tulsa

    RW Papers, Yale—Beinecke Rare Book and Manuscript Library, Yale

Frances G. Wickes Papers, Library of Congress

Thornton Wilder Papers, Beinecke Rare Book and Manuscript Library, Yale University

Marjorie Worthington Papers, Special Collections and University Archives, University of Oregon Libraries, Eugene, Oregon

ABBREVIATIONS IN NOTES

—

INDIVIDUALS

AK	Agnes Knickerbocker
BS	William (Bill) Shirer
DG	Duncan Grant
DT	Dorothy Thompson
EH	Emily (Mickey) Hahn
ESW	Eddy Sackville-West
FF/FFG	Frances Fineman, Frances Gunther
HN	Harold Nicolson
HRK	Hubert Renfro Knickerbocker (Knick)
JG	John Gunther
JN	Jawaharlal Nehru
JVS	James Vincent (Jimmy) Sheean
RM	Raymond Mortimer
RW	Rebecca West
SL	Sinclair Lewis
VSW	Vita Sackville-West

ARCHIVES

BL	British Library
NMML	Nehru Memorial Museum and Library
NYPL	New York Public Library
OESt-A	Archiv der Republik, Österreichisches Staatsarchiv, Vienna
SCRC	Special Collections Research Center, University of Chicago
WHS	Wisconsin Historical Society

NEWSPAPERS/MAGAZINES

CDN	*Chicago Daily News*
LHJ	*Ladies' Home Journal*
NYHT	*New York Herald Tribune*
NYT	*New York Times*
OTR	"On the Record"

BOOKS

DBNP	*Death Be Not Proud*
IAsia	*Inside Asia*
IE	*Inside Europe*
IUSA	*Inside U.S.A.*
PH	*Personal History*
SWJN	*Selected Works of Jawaharlal Nehru*

NOTES

—

PROLOGUE

xvii **Nazi spies** *Birmingham Post,* 25 Sept. 1939, 1939 Scrapbook [#30], H. R. Knicker-bocker Papers, MS#0719, Rare Book & Mss. Library, Columbia University [HRK Papers]. Also see the sequence of files about Knickerbocker in the Bundesarchiv (Lichterfelde), including NS 18/324, R 1501/125954, R 58/9685, and R 901/59054. The boat docked in Hoboken, New Jersey.

xvii **Prepare for poison gas** Susan Grayzel, *The Age of the Gas Mask* (Cambridge: Cambridge University Press, forthcoming [2022]).

xvii **To accommodate the crowds** Ronald Tree, *When the Moon Was High: Memoirs of Peace and War, 1897–1942* (London: Macmillan, 1975), p. 94.

xvii ***Overzealous,* judged some** Tree, *When the Moon,* p. 93.

xvii **The name of the boat** On the *Nieuw Amsterdam*'s conversion to wartime use and its prewar appointments, earlofcruise.blogspot.com/2017/04/ships-of-state-nieuw-amsterdam-1938.html; Andrew Britton, *SS Nieuw Amsterdam: Classic Liners* (Cheltenham, UK: The History Press, 2015).

xvii **That was the subject** Tree, *When the Moon,* p. 94; John Gunther, *The Indian Sign* (New York: Harper & Row, 1970), p. 2.

xviii **That included many of the ship's** See, for example, "Paterson Couple Home from Europe on Holland Liner," *Morning Call* (Paterson, N.J.), 30 Sept. 1939, p. 1; "County Tourists Home from Europe," *Delaware County Daily Times,* 30 Sept. 1939, p. 1; "Robert Reiner Returns Home," *Record* (Hackensack, N.J.), 30 Sept. 1939, p. 2; "Kiwanis Hear Miss Geise," *Daily Item* (Sunbury, Pa.), 3 Oct. 1939, p. 7; "Former Shore Couple Flees from War Zone," *Asbury Park Press,* 6 Oct. 1939, p. 1.

xviii **The shabby ones** Among the refugees on board was the co-founder of Frankfurt's Institute for Social Research, Felix Weil.

xviii **Hollywood royalty** Burton J. Hendrick and Daniel Henderson, *Louise Whitfield Carnegie: The Life of Mrs. Andrew Carnegie* (New York: Hastings House, 1950), p. 290; Tree, *When the Moon,* pp. 92–95. Tree was the grandson of the Chicago department store magnate Marshall Field.

xviii **Their bylines had appeared** On the history of foreign correspondence, with a focus on Gunther, Sheean, and Thompson, Nancy Cott, *Fighting Words: The Bold American Journalists Who Brought the World Home Between the Wars* (New York: Basic Books, 2020); John Maxwell Hamilton, *Journalism's Roving Eye: A History of American Foreign Reporting* (Baton Rouge: Louisiana State University Press, 2009). See also Giovanna Dell'Orto, *American Journalism and International Relations: Foreign Correspondence from the Early Republic to the Digital Era* (New York: Cambridge University Press, 2013); Robert William Desmond, *Crisis and Conflict:*

World News Reporting Between Two Wars, 1920–1940 (Iowa City: University of Iowa Press, 1982); Morrell Heald, *Transatlantic Vistas: American Journalists in Europe, 1900–1940* (Kent, Ohio: Kent State University Press, 1988); John Hohenberg, *Foreign Correspondence: The Great Reporters and Their Times* (New York: Columbia University Press, 1964); Michael Emery, *On the Front Lines: Following America's Foreign Correspondents Across the Twentieth Century* (Washington, D.C.: American University Press, 1995). On the news agencies, especially Jonathan Silberstein-Loeb, *The International Distribution of News: The Associated Press, Press Association and Reuters, 1848–1947* (New York: Cambridge University Press, 2014); Heidi J. S. Tworek, *News from Germany: The Competition to Control World Communications, 1900–1945* (Cambridge, Mass.: Harvard University Press, 2019).

xix **"Knights-errant"** Malcolm Muggeridge, *Chronicles of Wasted Time,* vol. 2 (New York: Morrow, 1973), p. 14. For a contrary evaluation—praising American correspondents as "Elder Brothers to all the world"—see Ellen Wilkinson, "Notes on the Way," *Time & Tide,* 21 Dec. 1935. By 1940, judged Malcolm Cowley, American foreign correspondents had become "political powers capable of influencing their nations and helping to determine the outcome of the war." Malcolm Cowley, "Personal History, Cont'd," *New Republic,* 5 April 1943, p. 450.

xix **The Nazis already had** R 9361-V/41562 and R 58/9681, Bundesarchiv-Lichterfelde. For Gunther's biography, Ken Cuthbertson, *Inside: The Biography of John Gunther* (Chicago: Bonus Books, 1992); also Cott, *Fighting Words.*

xix **The book was banned** Quincy Howe, "Books About the War," *New Republic,* 5 Jan. 1942, p. 25. On the bans, Gunther, *A Fragment of Autobiography* (New York: Harper & Row, 1962), pp. 19–20.

xix **It sold** Albin Krebs, "John Gunther Dead; Wrote 'Inside' Books," *New York Times* [*NYT*], 30 May 1970, pp. 1, 23.

xix **On the eve of the war** "Who Is Knickerbocker?" *Sunday Post* (Glasgow), 2 Oct. 1939, HRK Papers, 1939 Scrapbook [#30].

xx **"With the foreign press"** Geoffrey Cox, *Countdown to War: A Personal Memoir of Europe, 1938–1940* (London: Kimber, 1988), pp. 31–32.

xx **"We were scavengers"** John Gunther, *Fragment,* p. 5.

xxi **Americans were particularly enthusiastic** Nathan G. Hale, *The Rise and Crisis of Psychoanalysis in the United States: Freud and the Americans, 1917–1985* (New York: Oxford University Press, 1995), p. 7; John Burnham, ed., *After Freud Left: A Century of Psychoanalysis in America* (Chicago: University of Chicago Press, 2012).

xxi **Shouting questions** *We Cover the World by Sixteen Foreign Correspondents,* ed. Eugene Lyons (New York: Harcourt, Brace and Co., 1937), p. 15; George Slocombe, *The Tumult and the Shouting* (New York: Macmillan, 1936), pp. 70–71; Warren Susman, "Pilgrimage to Paris: The Backgrounds of American Expatriation, 1920–1934" (unpub. Ph.D. diss., University of Wisconsin, Madison, 1958), pp. 190–91. By comparison, Siân Nicholas, "American Commentaries: News, Current Affairs and the Limits of Anglo-American Exchange in Inter-war Britain," *Cultural and Social History* 4, no. 4 (2007): 461–79. For a case study, taking Edgar Snow's reporting, Julia Lovell, *Maoism: A Global History* (London: The Bodley Head, 2019), ch. 2.

xxi **However, it helps to explain** On this transformation, John A. Thompson, *A Sense of Power: The Roots of America's Global Role* (Ithaca, N.Y.: Cornell University Press, 2015); Stephen Wertheim, *Tomorrow, the World* (Cambridge, Mass.: The Belknap Press of Harvard University Press, 2020); Andrew Preston, "Monsters Everywhere: A Genealogy of National Security," *Diplomatic History* 38 (2014): 477–500.

xxi **Knickerbocker's were the only foreign** Told by Mussolini to HRK. HRK to Barry Faris, 24 Sept. 1934, HRK Papers, Catalogued Correspondence, Box 1.

xxi **On the eve** "Cartwheel Girl," *Time,* 12 June 1939, p. 47.

xxii **From the mid-1930s** See Daniel Immerwahr's compilation in "Books of the Century," booksofthecentury.com/.

xxii **They had come** Adam Tooze, *The Deluge: The Great War, America and the Remaking of the Global Order, 1916–1931* (New York: Viking, 2014).

xxii **By 1939, the dispute** Wertheim, *Tomorrow, the World,* pp. 32–35.

xxii **Knick was all for** William Shirer, *Berlin Diary: The Journal of a Foreign Correspondent, 1934–1941* (New York: Knopf, 1941), p. 221 [diary entry, 24 Sept. 1939].

xxii **And it seemed entirely possible** JG, Envelope—Europe, General, 1939, Scrap Form—Notes on Europe, 1939, JG Papers II, Box 2, Special Collections Research Center [henceforth SCRC], University of Chicago.

xxii **Jimmy had been lecturing** William A. Caldwell, "Simeon Stylites," *The Record* (Hackensack, N.J.), 18 Oct. 1939, p. 10.

xxii **The first American correspondent** The authoritative source on Thompson is Peter Kurth, *American Cassandra: The Life of Dorothy Thompson* (Boston: Little, Brown, 1990). For her audience in "On the Record," Kurth, p. 232; also Karina von Tippelskirch, *Dorothy Thompson and German Writers in Defense of Democracy* (Berlin: Peter Lang, 2017); Marion Sanders, *Dorothy Thompson: A Legend in Her Time* (Boston: Houghton Mifflin, 1973); Susan Ware, *Letter to the World: Seven Women Who Shaped the American Century* (New York: Norton, 1998), pp. 45–83.

xxiii **"What right"** Goebbels, diary entry, 5 April 1942, part II: Diktate 1941–1945; vol. 4: April–June 1942.

xxiii **There was something shameful** JG, diary entry, 31 Oct. 1939, JG Papers II, Box 19.

xxiii **According to Dorothy** Kurth, *American Cassandra,* p. 309.

xxiii **They'd debated** Malcolm Cowley, *Exile's Return* (New York: Penguin Books, 1969 [1934, 1951]), p. 302.

xxiii **Above all else, they shared** Michael Schudson, *Discovering the News: A Social History of American Newspapers* (New York: Basic Books, 1978), chs. 2 and 3.

xxiii **They wrote what they thought** Here, my analysis differs from Daniel Schneidermann, *Berlin, 1933: La presse internationale face à Hitler* (Paris: Éditions du Seuil, 2018) in pointing to the new style of reportage that Gunther, Sheean, and Thompson helped to create.

xxiv **"Cry peace"** FFG, Telegram, 24 Aug. 1939, JG Papers II, Box 23.

xxiv **What the hell** FFG to JG, 28 Aug. 1939 and FFG to JG, 4 Sept. 1939, JG Papers II, Box 23.

xxiv **When she met** Martha Foley, *The Story of Story Magazine: A Memoir* (New York: Norton, 1980), p. 102.

xxiv **The trouble with the British** Summed up in her *Revolution in India* (New York: Island Press, 1944), discussed in chs. 13 and 14.

xxiv **"time to hold up"** FFG to Jawaharlal Nehru, June 1938, file 315, Frances Fineman Gunther Papers [FFG Papers], 87-M176–88-M130, Schlesinger Library.

xxiv **"If I ever divorce"** Don Wharton, "Dorothy Thompson," *Scribner's,* May 1937, p. 14; Kurth, *American Cassandra,* p. 167.

xxv **"Do you feel"** DT, "On the Record—Ecrasez L'Infame!" *Harrisburg Telegraph,* 30 Aug. 1939, p. 6.

CHAPTER ONE

3 **"Young-Man-Going-Somewhere"** For a description of a similar scene, H. J. Smith, *Deadlines* (Chicago: Covici McGee, 1922), p. 32. For a jaundiced view of American journalism, focusing specifically on anonymous toiling (and the lack of scope for personality), as well as conservative bias, John Macy, "Journalism," in

Harold Stearns, ed., *Civilization in the United States: An Inquiry by Thirty Americans* (New York: Harcourt, Brace and Co., 1922), pp. 35–51.

3 **He made small talk** On the dating dramas of the Hahns, Helen's practices, and John's visits to the family home, Emily Hahn, *No Hurry to Get Home* (Seattle: Seal Press, 2000 [1970]), pp. 37–40, 49–50, 54–55.

3 **He'd paid for one** Helen & Mickey Hahn for a Story, JG Papers II, Box 2.

4 **West was Britain's** On West, Victoria Glendinning, *Rebecca West: A Life* (New York: Knopf, 1987); Carl Rollyson, *Rebecca West: A Life* (New York: Scribner, 1996); Susan Hertog, *Dangerous Ambition: Rebecca West and Dorothy Thompson: New Women in Search of Love and Power* (New York: Ballantine, 2011); Lorna Gibb, *The Extraordinary Life of Rebecca West: A Biography* (New York: Counterpoint, 2014). On "ultra modern," "Novelist Will Give Sex Talk," *San Francisco Examiner*, 6 April 1924, p. N3.

4 **"There are many men"** "No Man Can Make a Harem Happy, Novelist Opines," *Chicago Tribune*, 6 Nov. 1923, p. 3.

4 **"This whole place"** RW to Lettie, 8 Feb. 1924. Copies of Rebecca West's letters to Lettie, RP 6367, Rebecca West Papers, British Library [RW Papers, BL].

4 **The skyscrapers** The image of gasoline cans is West's. Rebecca West, "Introduction," *Selected Poems of Carl Sandburg* (New York: Harcourt, Brace and Co., 1926), pp. 15–16.

4 **And the people** RW, "Introduction," p. 18; on the businessman, Rebecca West, "These American Men," *Harper's*, June 1925, pp. 450–51.

4 **Rebecca nicknamed** Letters to Helen, p. 161—note re. "John Silence" in Jane Gunther's hand, JG Papers II, Box 5.

4 **"Gothic angel"** RW to Harold Ross, 25 Aug. 1947, *New Yorker* Records, Box 66, File 9, folder 1 of 3.

5 **"This is John Gunther"** JG to FF, 19 June 1925, JG Papers II, Box 22.

5 **He was much too green** JG to John Hohenberg, 14 Dec. 1964, JG Papers II, Box 30.

5 **It was a lucky break** On the celebrity of the Prince of Wales, Laura Mayhall, "The Prince of Wales versus Clark Gable: Anglophone Celebrity and Citizenship Between the Wars," *Cultural and Social History* 4, no. 4 (2007): 520–44.

5 **With a $100 advance** JG to Helen Hahn, Oct. 1924, Letters to Helen, JG Papers II, Box 5.

5 **"like a Hindu virgin"** JG to Helen Hahn, On Board the SS *Olympic*, late Oct. 1924, JG Papers II, Box 5.

5 **Who was that** John Gunther, "England's Heir Is Not Anxious to Become King," *Akron Beacon Journal*, 1 Nov. 1924, p. 1.

6 **"Mauve spats"** JG to Helen Hahn, On Board the SS *Olympic*.

6 **In those years** Nancy Green, *The Other Americans in Paris: Businessmen, Countesses, Wayward Youth, 1880–1941* (Chicago: University of Chicago Press, 2014) notes an American colony of forty thousand in Paris in 1926 (the estimate from the *Chicago Tribune*), and hundreds of thousands of visitors each year. Also Brooke L. Blower, *Becoming Americans in Paris: Transatlantic Politics and Culture Between the World Wars* (New York: Oxford University Press, 2011); Susman, "Pilgrimage to Paris," pp. 19–20, 176; Tyler Stovall, *Paris Noir: African Americans in the City of Light* (Boston: Houghton Mifflin, 1996).

6 **American entrepreneurs** Green, *Other Americans*, chs. 4 and 5.

6 **American engineers** Joshua Freeman, *Behemoth: A History of the Factory and the Making of the Modern World* (New York: Norton, 2018), ch. 5.

6 **In Europe's leading cabarets** Stovall, *Paris Noir*, esp. pp. 25–82.

6 **Everywhere there were American dentists** Green, *Other Americans*, pp. 124–26.

7 **They'd sell the experience** See Green, *Other Americans,* p. 114; Michael Goebel, *Anti-Imperial Metropolis: Interwar Paris and the Seeds of Third World Nationalism* (New York: Cambridge University Press, 2015); Ronald Weber, *News of Paris: American Journalists in the City of Light Between the Wars* (Chicago: Ivan R. Dee, 2006).

7 **"Always I had dreams"** JG, "Autobiography in Brief," *Story* magazine, May 1938, p. 93.

7 **In the roomy kitchen** Notes on Family Background, JG Papers II, Box 2.

7 **For Christmas** "Autobiography in Brief," p. 89.

7 **John supposed** Details from Diary Scraps—Adolescence and Childhood, JG Papers II, Box 1; Notes on Family Background.

7 **He was a cheat in poker** Brock Baker's interview with Jean Gunther, nd, JG Papers II, Box 2; Ken Cuthbertson's interview with Gretchen Schoeninger, 19 June 1986, Private Collection.

7 **Crooked through** Notes on Family Background.

8 **She read the *Iliad*** Lizette Gunther to JG, 11 June 1926, JG Papers II, Box 6.

8 **There was never enough fresh air** JG, Composition on his upbringing, 1920—Nov. 2.

8 **When his mother finally** Notes on Family Background.

8 **"Papa, do you like me?"** JG to Eugene Guenther, 3 Feb. 1907, John's Childhood Letters, JG Papers II, Box 5.

8 **He sent samples** Crayolas—JG to Eugene, undated; birthday party—JG to Eugene, 23 March 1909, JG Papers II, Box 5.

8 **He got heavy and ill** Misc. Scraps for Autobiography, Various Dates, JG Papers II, Box 1; Interview with Jean Gunther.

8 **His father stormed away** Interview with Jean Gunther.

9 **During the First World War** Cuthbertson, *Inside,* p. 12.

9 **"You must be a success"** Quoted in Jane Gunther, "Early Version of My Book," JG Papers II, Box 4.

9 **By high school** On American autodidacticism in the 1920s, Warren I. Susman, *Culture as History: The Transformation of American Society in the Twentieth Century* (New York: Pantheon, 1984), pp. 107–8; Johan Huizinga, *America: A Dutch Historian's Vision, From Afar and Near,* trans. Herbert H. Rowen (New York: Harper & Row, 1972), p. 239.

9 **Arthur Conan Doyle's** Books I Have Read, p. 190 (*Ivanhoe*), JG Papers II, Box 3.

9 ***Tom Sawyer*** Books I Have Read, p. 93 (*Sign of the Four*) and p. 99 (*Tom Sawyer*), vol. 1, beginning 25 Dec. 1915.

9 **George Eliot's** Books I Have Read, p. 143 (*Silas Marner*), p. 107 (*David Copperfield*), vol. 1.

9 **"Shaw may be pessimistic"** Books I Have Read, p. 123, vol. 4, beginning 15 May 1918.

9 **"Conrad at last!"** Books I Have Read, p. 43, vol. 5, beginning 25 Feb. 1919.

9 **To the young literary** See Hemingway's *Sun Also Rises* on men getting "their likes and dislikes from Mencken."

10 **"triune"** Childhood Notes & Blackfriars a Musical Comedy (with Leonard Dankmar Weil), JG Papers II, Box 3.

10 **"Growing realization"** File Cards kept to remember past, written 1919–21, JG Papers II, Box 3.

10 **It would have to be** File Card, "Ideas for Books."

10 **"that mountain range"** Vincent Sheean, *Personal History* (Garden City, N.Y.: Doubleday, Doran & Co., 1935), p. 1 [henceforth *PH*].

10 **From its founding** On the history of the University of Chicago, Gunther, *Chicago*

Revisited (Chicago: University of Chicago Press, 1967); John Boyer, *The University of Chicago: A History* (Chicago: University of Chicago Press, 2015); John Boyer, *"We Are All Islanders to Begin With": The University of Chicago and the World in the Late Nineteenth and Twentieth Centuries* (Chicago: University of Chicago Press, 2008).

11 **His father disapproved** "Autobiography in Brief," p. 90.

11 **John was living at home** Frances Gunther, "Inside Gunther," *Fashion,* Sept. 1939, Pertaining to Frances Gunther, JG Papers II, Box 6.

11 **"barbarian"** JG, "Original Portrait of a Young Man," spring 1920, JG Papers II, Box 7.

11 **"a real barb in those days"** Brock Baker's interview with James Vincent Sheean, Dec. 1974, JG Papers II, Box 2.

11 **"I was inflamed"** "Autobiography in Brief," p. 91.

11 **"He likes to talk"** "Original Portrait of a Young Man." The format of his sketch riffed on Mencken and Nathan's *Pistols for Two.*

12 **That fear—of gonorrhea** FFG, "Graven Image of False Gods," FFG Papers, file 103.

12 **"big handicap"** "Marj" File Card, JG Papers II, Box 3.

12 **"Girls in halls"** "Lucile" File Card, JG Papers II, Box 3.

12 **What originality** JG, "The Higher Learning in America, VI: The University of Chicago," *Smart Set,* April 1922, pp. 67–77, description at p. 73.

13 **"clothes that fit tightly"** JG, "Higher Learning," p. 75.

13 **"unfair"** "News of the Quadrangles," *University of Chicago Magazine* 14, no. 6 (April 1922): 216.

13 **Three papers** JG to Hohenberg, 14 Dec. 1964.

13 **"I AM"** JG, diary entry, 13 April 1922, 1922 Diary, JG Papers II, Box 3.

13 **"Literary Capital"** H. L. Mencken, "The Literary Capital of the United States," *Nation* [London], 17 April 1920, 90–92.

14 **What was known** Liesl Olson, *Chicago Renaissance: Literature and Art in the Midwest* (New Haven: Yale University Press, 2017).

14 **"You know my city"** Sherwood Anderson, "Song of Industrial America" in *Mid-American Chants* (New York: John Lane Company, 1918), pp. 16–17.

14 **"was that it had made fucking"** JG USA Log 8—dated Nov. 25 [Nov. 19], JG Papers II, Box 2—USA Logs, 1934.

14 **Squeezed between the limestone** Emily Hahn, *Romantic Rebels: An Informal History of Bohemianism in America* (Boston: Houghton Mifflin, 1967), p. 226.

15 **If you took the flight** Alson J. Smith, "Chicago's Left Bank," *Tomorrow,* Sept. 1949; Hahn, *Romantic Rebels,* pp. 197–98.

15 **The catalyst** On Chicago's newspapers, David Paul Nord, *Communities of Journalism: A History of American Newspapers and Their Readers* (Urbana: University of Illinois Press, 2001), esp. pp. 108–32, 246–77; Julia Guarneri, *Newsprint Metropolis: City Papers and the Making of Modern Americans* (Chicago: University of Chicago Press, 2017), pp. 149–68; Michael Stamm, *Dead Tree Media: Manufacturing the Newspaper in Twentieth-Century North America* (Baltimore: Johns Hopkins University Press, 2018); Norman Howard Sims, "The Chicago Style of Journalism" (unpub. Ph.D. thesis, University of Illinois, 1979). On the place of Chicago in the wire services, Richard Schwarzlose, *The Nation's Newsbrokers.*

15 **The newspaper was the place** Smith, *Deadlines,* p. 22.

15 **Among Chicago's dozens of papers** "On the Selling of Groceries in Chicago," *Advertising & Selling,* vol. 30, no. 10, 2 April 1921, p. 33. Lloyd Wendt, *Chicago Tribune: The Rise of a Great American Newspaper* (Chicago: Rand McNally, 1979)

has similar figures: 424,026 daily and 693,895 on Sundays (p. 458); on the circulation battle between Hearst and McCormick, pp. 485–86. Mark R. Wilson, "Chicago Tribune," *The Encyclopedia of Chicago* notes a daily circulation of 650,000 by 1925. Only a handful (though the largest-circulation papers) were English-language newspapers. Chicago's dailies were published in dozens of languages, including four German papers, four Yiddish papers, and four Czech papers. On the foreign-language press in Chicago, see the Chicago Foreign Language Press Survey, flps.newberry.org/. For an overview, Jon Bekken, "The Chicago Newspaper Scene: An Ecological Perspective," *J&MC Quarterly* 74, no. 3 (Autumn 1997): 490–500; also the contemporary listings in N. W. Ayer and Son's *American Newspaper Annual and Directory*.

15 **For the *Tribune*'s** Richard Norton Smith, *The Colonel: The Life and Legend of Robert R. McCormick, 1880–1955* (Evanston: Northwestern University Press, 2003 [1997]).

15 **Then there were the weeklies** Ethan Michaeli, *The Defender: How the Legendary Black Newspaper Changed America* (Boston: Houghton Mifflin Harcourt, 2016).

15 **Its old building** Hansen, *Midwest Portraits: A Book of Memories and Friendships* (New York: Harcourt, Brace and Co., 1923), pp. 193–94.

16 **Starting at seven** Described in Smith, "The Day," *Deadlines*.

16 **On his first day** "Autobiography in Brief," p. 92.

16 **Yet they slapped** JG, "The Return of Joe Vesley," *The Best News Stories of 1923,* ed. Joseph Anthony (Boston: Small, Maynard & Co., 1924).

16 **No one ever ordered** John Drury, *Dining in Chicago* (New York: John Day Co., 1931), pp. 26–31; also Hansen, *Midwest Portraits,* pp. 3–5.

16 **"chewing gum center"** "Our First Issue," *Chicago Literary Times,* 1 March 1923, p. 1. On Hecht, Adina Hoffman, *Ben Hecht: Fighting Words, Moving Pictures* (New Haven: Yale University Press, 2019); Julien Gorbach, *The Notorious Ben Hecht: Iconoclastic Writer and Militant Zionist* (West Lafayette, Ind.: Purdue University Press, 2019).

16 **"National Cemetery"** "Concerning the Natl. Cemetery of Arts and Letters," *Chicago Literary Times,* 1 March 1923, p. 1.

17 **They'd arrived** Hansen, *Midwest Portraits,* p. 187.

17 **"purely lyrical strain"** JG, "The Collapse of Chicago," JG Papers 1972, Box 46, folder 1.

17 **By "blabbing"** H. L. Mencken to JG, 17 Oct. nd, JG Papers II, Box 35.

17 **Nineteen white men** For this picture, see fig. 1 in the insert.

17 **Which Henry James** Lizette Gunther to JG, Friday Eve, 1922, JG Papers II, Box 6.

18 **"All the things"** Lizette Gunther to JG, 25 April 1926, JG Papers II, Box 6.

18 **"You are the dearest"** Lizette Gunther to JG, nd, JG Papers II, Box 6.

18 **Weigh himself** Lizette Gunther to JG, 4 Dec. 1927, JG Papers II, Box 6.

18 **"What a store"** Lizette Gunther to John, 15 June 1926, JG Papers II, Box 6.

18 **"Biggest infl."** "Early Memories" File Card, JG Papers II, Box 3.

18 **By the first year** Carl Johnson, "Twentieth-Century Seeker: A Biography of James Vincent Sheean," Ph.D. thesis, University of Wisconsin, 1974, p. 1; on Sheean, see also Cott, *Fighting Words.*

18 **Enough books** Handwritten Notebook, undated but 1920s, Box 3, folder 6, Sheean Papers, Wisconsin Historical Society [WHS].

18 **"gang of midwestern"** "The Voice of the Turtle," 8 Dec. 1920, File 6, Sheean–Falkenau correspondence, SCRC, University of Chicago.

18 **Walking backward** For Jimmy's childhood, Johnson, "Twentieth-Century

Seeker"; Cott, *Fighting Words,* pp. 7-15; "The Voice of the Turtle"; the handwritten notebook at the WHS; and his autobiographical novel, *Bird of the Wilderness* (New York: Random House, 1941).

19 **One Christmas** Johnson, "Twentieth-Century Seeker," p. 7.

19 **There, she had everything** Johnson, "Twentieth-Century Seeker," p. 8.

19 **"Something of the flat disaster"** "The Voice of the Turtle."

19 **Father Fox** Johnson, "Twentieth-Century Seeker," p. 19.

20 **"Your second-hand information"** "The Voice of the Turtle."

20 **When Jimmy left Pana** Johnson, "Twentieth-Century Seeker," p. 19.

20 **The revolutionary changes** Josephine Herbst, *The Starched Blue Sky of Spain* (New York: HarperCollins, 1991), p. 74.

20 **The Mowrer brothers** On Bloomington and the family's move to Chicago, Paul Scott Mowrer, *The House of Europe* (Boston: Houghton Mifflin Co., 1945), chs. 3–5; Edgar Ansel Mowrer, *Triumph and Turmoil: A Personal History of Our Time* (New York: Weybright and Talley, 1968), ch. 1.

21 **Junius Wood** E. C. Alft, *Elgin: Days Gone By,* elginhistory.com/dgb/cho6.htm.

21 **Bill Shirer** William L. Shirer, *Twentieth-Century Journey: A Memoir of a Life and the Times,* vol. 1, *The Start: 1904–1930* (New York: Simon & Schuster, 1976), pp. 128–215.

21 **When Jimmy arrived** JVS to Fred Millett, postmarked 29 Nov. 1919, Fred B. Millett Papers, Special Collections & Archives, Wesleyan University.

21 **That was how he came** The fraternity (Delta Sigma Phi) was referred to on campus as "Jewish" though it in fact accepted both Jews and Christians; *PH,* pp. 13, fn. 1; 16.

21 **When a girl he knew** *PH,* pp. 10–19.

21 **Next he tried** *PH,* pp. 19–21 (re. Glenway Westcott). When you graduated from the University of Chicago, you could talk in any sort of accent you chose, sneered Hemingway on the subject of Westcott. Quoted in Roy Morris, Jr., *Gertrude Stein Has Arrived* (Baltimore: Johns Hopkins University Press, 2019), p. 50.

21 **By his junior year** JVS to Millett, postmarked 22 Dec. 1919, Millett Papers.

21 **An invitation to join** "Announce Pledging of Sheean," *Daily Maroon,* 14 May 1918, p. 4.

21 **His opinions figured** "Phoenix Deserving of Attention Says J. Vincent Sheean," *Daily Maroon,* 4 March 1920, p. 1.

21 **He'd come up to college** "The Blackfriars: 'Barbara, Behave!'" *The University of Chicago Magazine,* May 1920, vol. 12, no. 7, p. 256.

21 **He was *just*** JVS to Fred Millett, postmarked 2 May 1920, Millett Papers.

21 **That was the sound** 4 Feb. 1920, *Daily Maroon,* p. 3.

22 **"Should I be sorry?"** Handwritten Notebook, nd [1920s].

22 **"went in for the masculine stuff"** JVS to Fred Millett, "Sunday," postmarked 12 Oct. 1919; JVS to Millett, postmarked 29 Nov. 1919 [re. Harold Stansbury], Millett Papers.

22 **"but the fact is that Fred"** JVS to Raymond Mortimer, 9 March ny [1930], Raymond Mortimer Papers [RM Papers], Box 3, folder 35, Department of Rare Books and Special Collections, Princeton University.

22 **"emotionally, he has the fluidity"** Fred Millett, *Graduate Student II* (Whitman, Mass.: Washington Street Press, 1957), p. 16.

22 **Jimmy squired around** Among them, the debutante (and later singer) Janet Fairbank: see Johnson, "Twentieth-Century Seeker," p. 515, fn. 106.

22 **Intellectual developments on campus** William Isaac Thomas and Florian Znaniecki, *The Polish Peasant in Europe and America* (New York: Knopf, 1927 [1918]), vol. 1, pp. 149–50; Robert E. Park, "The Natural History of the News-

paper," *American Journal of Sociology* 29 (1923): 273–89; Robert E. Park, "News and the Power of the Press," *American Journal of Sociology* 47 (1941): 1–11. More broadly, Daniel J. Czitrom, *Media and the American Mind* (Chapel Hill: University of North Carolina Press, 1982), ch. 4; J. Michael Sproule, *Propaganda and Democracy: The American Experience of Media and Mass Persuasion* (Cambridge, UK: Cambridge University Press, 1997).

23 **"Snaps," they were** *PH,* p. 3.

23 **It was still alarmingly easy** *PH,* pp. 23–24.

23 **In 1920, Jimmy considered breaking off** JVS to Fred Millett, postmarked 30 Sept. 1920, Wesleyan.

23 **"the novel of youth"** JVS to Dear Folks, 11 July 1920, file 1, Sheean/Falkenau correspondence, Special Collections Research Center, University of Chicago.

23 **At her funeral** Fictionalized in JVS, *Gog and Magog* (New York: Harcourt, Brace and Co., 1930), pp. 319–20; see Johnson, *Twentieth-Century,* pp. 47–49.

23 **Years later, whenever he heard** Dinah Sheean to Lee Stowe, 3 Nov. 1976, Box 23, Leland Stowe Papers, WHS.

24 **Spice up the look** On the New York *Daily News,* Stamm, *Dead Tree,* pp. 132–34; Simon Michael Bessie, *Jazz Journalism: The Story of the Tabloid Newspapers* (New York: Russell & Russell, 1969 [1938]), pp. 79–134; Guarneri, *Newsprint Metropolis.*

24 **For those theorists** On the notion of the newspaper as the "bible of democracy," Lippmann, *Liberty and the News* (New York: Harcourt, Brace and Howe, 1920), p. 47.

24 **Part brothel** Stearns, ed., *Civilization,* p. 44—a criticism that lumped together the respectable press (increasingly sensationalized) and the outright tabloids.

24 **By 1926** Bessie, *Jazz Journalism,* p. 86; Edwin Emery, *The Press and America: An Interpretative History of Journalism* (Englewood Cliffs, N.J.: Prentice-Hall, 1962), pp. 622–32.

24 **Personalities were the thing** Helen M. Hughes, *News and the Human Interest Story* (Chicago: University of Chicago Press, 1940). On the "trashiness" and cultural centrality of the American newspapers, Huizinga, *America,* pp. 242–44.

25 **Mrs. Stillman was** "Mrs. Stillman Holds Whip Hand in Fight," *Sunday News,* 15 May 1921, p. 5; "Mrs. Stillman Feels Like a Hunted Animal," *Daily News,* 17 March 1921, p. 3.

25 **Mrs. Stillman countersued** "Daring Leap Foiled Mrs. Leeds' Shadows," *Daily News,* 22 March 1921, p. 3.

25 **Her pictures** "Mrs. Stillman's Life Story," *Daily News,* 18 June 1921, p. 3.

25 **Just look at the damage** "Stillman Must Face Wife in Court on June 28," *Daily News,* 16 June 1921, p. 3.

25 **"purely personal capacity"** "Beauvais Denies Selling Letters," *NYT,* 14 May 1922, p. 3.

26 **Every time, including in America** FFG, diary entry, 2 Jan. 1937, folder 7, FFG Papers.

26 **Frances was born** FFG, diary entry, 6 Dec. 1936, folder 7. Details of her childhood from these 6 Dec. 1936 and 2 Jan. 1937 entries. FFG refers to her mother as Sonia, but in the census, she's listed as Sophia Fineman.

27 **"I like the cow"** FFG, diary entry, 2 Jan. 1937.

27 **What did those careworn** FFG, "The Influence of the Rise and Fall of the Penis on International Relations," file 253, FFG Papers.

28 **Was there a woman** FFG, diary entry, 6 Dec. 1936.

28 **She enrolled** For an outline of Frances's collegiate career and travels, folder 1, FFG Papers.

28 **The college's first class** Alice Duer Miller, *Barnard College: The First Fifty Years*

(New York: Columbia University Press, 1939), p. 18—twenty students, though only that few working to a degree.

28 **taking their lessons** Miller, *Barnard College,* p. 49.

28 **By 1920, nearly half** Barbara Miller Solomon, *In the Company of Educated Women,* p. 62. Percentage declines after World War II because of the GI Bill. Most women getting educated were doing so at normal schools (teacher training) or at big state universities.

29 **A few months after arriving** As the *Columbia Daily Spectator* reported the event, Fineman used the example of Tagore to urge her fellow students to improve the quality of their work. "Barnard Scribes Are to Have Open Meeting," *Columbia Daily Spectator,* vol. LIX, no. 149, 14 April 1916, p. 6.

29 **Compared to the other women's** See, for instance, Patrick Dilley, *Transformation of Women's Collegiate Education: The Legacy of Virginia Gildersleeve* (Cham, Switzerland: Palgrave Macmillan, 2017), p. 31.

29 **"had been taught to think"** Miller, *Barnard College,* p. 97.

29 **Once the United States entered** Miller, *Barnard College,* p. 98.

29 **By now the secretary-treasurer** She was among the deputation organized by the Collegiate Anti-Militarism League to travel to Washington, D.C., to meet congressmen and senators. See "Columbia Pacifists at Washington," *Columbia Daily Spectator,* vol. LX, no. 106, 24 Feb. 1917, p. 5.

29 **In the spring and summer of 1917** On this episode, Richard Hofstadter and Walter P. Metzger, *The Development of Academic Freedom in the United States* (New York: Columbia University Press, 1955), pp. 498–502, quote at 502.

29 **"What had been folly"** Quoted in Hofstadter and Metzger, *Development of Academic Freedom,* p. 499. One of Butler's targets was a friend of Frances's: the socialist Harry Dana, an assistant professor of comparative literature at Columbia and the grandson of the poet Henry Wadsworth Longfellow. They likely met while campaigning against conscription. She went on walks with him and to a dance, referred to in 1917 as "Dr. Dana." FF diary entries, 18 and 20 April 1917, 8 and 15 May 1917, 1916/1917 Diary, folder 2, FFG Papers. See also Harry Dana's appointment books, H.W.L. Dana Papers, Series 1, Box 2, Longfellow National Historic Site.

30 **"reactionary and visionless"** Quoted in Hofstadter and Metzger, *Development of Academic Freedom,* p. 502.

30 **That June** Nicholas Butler to Virginia Gildersleeve, 25 June 1917, folder 6 of BC 5.1 (Dean's Office Correspondence 1916–1917, Box Number 29), Barnard Archives.

30 **"guilty of any overt act"** Virginia Gildersleeve to Nicholas Butler, 21 June 1917, folder 6 of BC 5.1 (Dean's Office Correspondence 1916–1917, Box Number 29), Barnard Archives.

30 **She was tossed out** Secretary to the President to Dean Gildersleeve, 23 July 1918, Frances Fineman (Gunther) student file, RGXXI, Series 1, Box 38 (Radcliffe College student files, 1890–1985).

30 **"Tennis shoes"** From Barnard 1916–1917 Diary, p. 37, FFG Papers.

30 **It was as if they'd admitted** FF, diary entry, 4 Nov. 1916, folder 2.

30 **Still, Frances wanted an education** Dean Bertha Boody to FF, 24 Sept. 1918; also FF to Dean Bertha Boody, 7 June 1919, FF Radcliffe student file.

30 **"You will enjoy talking"** Dean Gildersleeve to Dean Boody, 19 Sept. 1918, FF Radcliffe student file.

30 **At Barnard in 1916** FF, diary entry, 3 Oct. 1916, folder 2.

30 **Three years later, there was** FF, diary entry, 15 Jan. 1919, folder 2.

31 **"Perhaps—I don't care to?"** FF, diary entry, 25 June 1920, folder 2.

31 **"Frances, whom I've never seen"** M.E.R. [Mary Ross], "To Frances Considerably

After Her Nineteenth Birthday," Sept. 19, afternoon, Lewis Gannett Papers, bMS Am 1888.2 (104), Houghton Library, Harvard.

31 **She needed to acquire** Memoranda and Addresses, Jan. 1919 diary, folder 2.

31 **A night with the socialist** See Barnard, 1916–17 Diary, folder 2. As chair of the Journalism Club, Frances brought Mrs. Hurst to campus to talk. "Barnard Meets Fanny Hurst," *Barnard Bulletin,* 23 Feb. 1917, p. 1. Her introduction of Mrs. Hurst drew the objections of the *Barnard Bulletin*'s reporter, who complained that Frances's introduction was "somewhat too lengthy and stilted. . . . If one might suggest it—why try and tell us what Miss Hurst typifies, when she can do it so much better herself!"

31 **"all very stiff and formal"** FF, diary entry, 2 Nov. 1919, Radcliffe diary, 1919–20, folder 2.

31 **The *Radcliffe Magazine*** FF, diary entry, 17 Oct. 1919, Radcliffe diary, 1919–20, folder 2.

31 **Working on a play** FF, diary entry, 19 Oct. 1916, Barnard diary, 1916–17, folder 2; see also FFG chronology, folder 1 for full title.

31 **"If I could only turn out"** FF, diary entry, 27 April 1920, Radcliffe diary, 1919–20, folder 2.

31 **"I've been evading"** FF, diary entry, 4 Oct. 1919, Radcliffe diary, 1919–20, folder 2.

32 **Frances would later claim** "Note on Frances Fineman," folder 1.

32 **Dean Gildersleeve** Miller, *Barnard College,* p. 57.

32 **A formidable advocate** Dilley, *Transformation of Women's Collegiate Education,* p. 40.

32 **Theirs was the first** On this generation of women and failure, Lisa Cohen, *All We Know: Three Lives* (New York: Farrar, Straus and Giroux, 2012).

32 **"Muddle-headedness"** "Note on Frances Fineman."

CHAPTER TWO

33 **She'd done publicity** "Note on Frances Fineman" and chronologies in folder 1, FFG Papers.

33 **But until she left** Frances Powell Fineman, "Robert Edmond Jones: Non-Uplifter," *Columbia Daily Spectator,* vol. LX, no. 135, 30 March 1917, p. 7.

34 **"I love the people"** FF, diary entry, Oct. 1924 [first interview with Duncan], FF 1924/5 diary, folder 4.

35 **"You will be our Joan of Arc"** FF, diary entry, 23 Oct. 1924. Duncan's judgment here refers not just to the Soviet Union but to her own dancing school in Moscow.

35 **"Take it"** FF, diary entry, 23 Oct. 1924 [second interview with Duncan], FF 1924/5 diary.

35 **Frances's first glimpse** FF, "Leningrad," FF 1924/5 diary.

35 **"Stop Fascism!"** On the 1924 Leningrad flood, see the historian Rob Dale's website, sept1924leningradflood.wordpress.com/.

35 **And she only had** FF, "Leningrad."

35 **Although Frances looked frail** Ernestine Evans, quoted in JG, diary entry, 25 Feb. 1946, JG Papers II, Box 20.

35 **Come to the rehearsal** Untitled TS on Meyerhold, folder 128, FFG Papers.

35 **Fired by revolutionary ideals** On Meyerhold, Aleksandr Konstantinovich Gladkov, *Meyerhold Speaks, Meyerhold Rehearses* (Amsterdam: Harwood Academic, 1997); Edward Braun, *Meyerhold: A Revolution in Theatre* (London: Methuen, 1995, 2nd ed.); Robert Leach, *Vsevolod Meyerhold* (New York: Cambridge University Press, 1989).

36 **In a country where the theater** "Moscow Opera Ideals Won Through Audience," *NYT*, 22 Nov. 1925, Section X (Amusements), p. 8.

36 **"Besides, everything in Russia"** FF to unnamed friend, undated [1924], folder 103, FFG Papers.

36 **"child's play"** Francis Fineman to Meyerhold, 15 April 1925, folder 128, FFG Papers.

36 **After four months** Louis Fischer re. FFG, JG, Russian Log, 8 June 1928, JG Papers II, Box 2; JG to FFG, 8 June 1928, Russian Log, JG Papers II, Box 2. On foreign correspondents in Russia, James Rodgers, *Assignment Moscow: Reporting on Russia from Lenin to Putin* (London: I. B. Tauris, 2020), esp. chs. 2–4.

37 **The correspondents comprised** Unless you counted the wife of the *Christian Science Monitor*'s William Henry Chamberlin, a Russian émigrée who translated for her husband. See Whitman Bassow, *The Moscow Correspondents: Reporting on Russia from the Revolution to Glasnost* (New York: W. Morrow, 1988). More broadly, on the attraction of the USSR to liberated young American women, Julia L. Mickenberg, *American Girls in Red Russia: Chasing the Soviet Dream* (Chicago: University of Chicago Press, 2017), specifically ch. 4 on Anna Louise Strong's *Moscow News* in the 1930s and the presence of women stringers in the preceding decade. On the poker party, Louis Fischer, *Men and Politics: Europe Between the Two World Wars* (New York: Harper & Row, 1966 [1941]), p. 60.

37 **Dorothy Thompson had** FF, diary entry, 11 Oct. 1924, 1924/5 diary, folder 4, Frances Gunther Papers.

37 **"A young girl like that"** Dorothy Thompson, Railway Diary, 1935, Box 59, folder 3, Dorothy Thompson Papers [DT Papers], Special Collections Research Center, Syracuse University.

37 **"I have been"** Dorothy Thompson to Rose Wilder Lane, 15 July [1921], Box 11, Rose Wilder Lane Papers, Herbert Hoover Presidential Library and Museum.

37 **When Dorothy was seven** The cause was apparently a potion that DT's grandmother had administered, without her daughter's knowledge, to bring on a miscarriage. Kurth, *American Cassandra*, p. 19.

38 **According to a classmate** Jack Alexander, "Rover Girl in Europe," *Saturday Evening Post*, 25 May 1940, p. 21.

38 **"Outgrowing Things"** Kurth, *American Cassandra*, p. 33.

38 **"I used to feel"** Kurth, *American Cassandra*, p. 43.

38 **when Dorothy fell in love** Kurth, *American Cassandra*, pp. 44–47.

39 **There had long been star** Arthur Lubow, *The Reporter Who Would Be King: A Biography of Richard Harding Davis* (New York: Scribner, 1992); John Seelye, *War Games: Richard Harding Davis and the New Imperialism* (Amherst: University of Massachusetts Press, 2003); Joyce Milton, *The Yellow Kids: Foreign Correspondents in the Heyday of Yellow Journalism* (New York: Harper & Row, 1989).

39 **But for regular dispatches** Hamilton, *Journalism's Roving Eye*, ch. 12.

39 **Now Americans required** Hamilton, *Journalism's Roving Eye*, p. 157; Chris Dubbs, *American Journalists in the Great War: Rewriting the Rules of Reporting* (Lincoln: University of Nebraska Press, 2017).

39 **Seven papers** See JG, "Funneling the European News," *Harper's*, April 1930, p. 636.

39 **"long" and "exclusive"** Dorothy Thompson, "Last Interview with Cork Mayor Before He Was Arrested," *Lake County Times* (Munster, Ind.), p. 1. This story was distributed through the I.N.S., which claimed DT as a "staff correspondent."

39 **"the Goddess Minerva"** JG to Fodor, 18 Oct. 1938, JG Papers II, Box 34.

39 **"You ought to send"** Kurth, *American Cassandra*, p. 43.

40 **But together with publicity** Sanders, *Dorothy Thompson*, p. 60. On humanitarian work as an avenue for women's internationalism, Maureen Healy, *Vienna and the Fall of the Habsburg Empire: Total War and Everyday Life in World War I* (Cambridge, UK: Cambridge University Press, 2004), ch. 4; Glenda Sluga, "Women, Feminisms and Twentieth-Century Internationalisms," in Sluga and Patricia Clavin, eds., *Internationalisms: A Twentieth-Century History* (Cambridge, UK: Cambridge University Press, 2016), pp. 61–84; Mona Siegel, *Peace on Our Terms: The Global Battle for Women's Rights After the First World War* (New York: Columbia University Press, 2020).

40 **"the London of an empire"** DT, "Oh, Thou My Austria," DT Papers, Box 100.

40 **For more than a half-millennium** Pieter M. Judson, *The Habsburg Empire: A New History* (Cambridge, Mass.: Harvard University Press, 2016).

40 **At the start of the war** Martyn Rady, *The Habsburg Empire: A Very Short Introduction* (Oxford: Oxford University Press, 2017), p. 98.

40 **The collapse of the empire** Judson, *Habsburg*, pp. 439–41.

40 **In November, Emperor** Rady, *Habsburg*, p. 104.

41 **"Wolves had gotten into"** Dorothy/Fodor Conversations, 1960, DT Papers, Box 126.

41 **Much of the knowledge** On Fodor, Fabienne Gouverneur, *Personal, Confidential: Mike W. Fodor als Netzwerker und Kulturmittler* (Vienna: New Academic Press, 2019); Dan Durning, "Marcel W. Fodor, Correspondent," 2011, scribd.com/document/65502558/Marcel-W-Fodor-Foreign-Correspondent, and my interviews with Denis Fodor, 20 and 21 March 2017, Munich.

41 **"Let me explain you"** For specimens of Fodor's talk, JG, Early Draft, Ring Round, JG Papers 1972 Add., Box 29, folder 7.

42 **With little in the way of training** On the yacht, Fodor to W. P. Crozier, 7 Jan. 1933, 207/6a-g, The *Guardian* Archive, John Rylands Library, Manchester University.

42 **"Oh, the little dumplings"** Dale Warren to JG, 15 April 1958, JG Papers II, Box 35.

42 **On a jaunt to Prague** She also interviewed Dr. Edvard Beneš for six hours.

42 **"to make a country"** "Europe's Youngest Queen, Mariora of Jugo-Slavia, Just Loves Her New Tasks," *Public Ledger*, 24 Dec. 1922.

42 **"old militaristic, autocratic"** DT, "All Central Europe Is Turning Toward Reaction," Box 98, nd [1921].

42 **His great-nephew** During the war, Karl ended military dictatorship in Austria, reestablishing a constitutional monarchy; issued general amnesties that freed political prisoners; sought to mollify the Hungarians.

43 **An unlikely set of allies** Karl's first coup attempt in March 1921 was a flop: an "opéra bouffe," DT called it. "Opera Bouffe in Budapest," DT Papers, Box 102.

44 **But the next day** Recounted in Jack Alexander, "Rover Girl in Europe: The Story of Problem Child Dorothy Thompson," *Saturday Evening Post*, 25 May 1940, pp. 112–13. She reportedly avoided censorship by sending the story on to Fodor in Vienna via a wagon-lit attendant. Margaret Case Harriman, "The It Girl—I," *New Yorker*, 20 April 1940, p. 27.

44 **Her own trepidation** DT, "Not for Thousand Thrones Would He Spill Hungarian Blood, Says Captured King," Philadelphia *Public Ledger*, 29 Oct. 1921, p. 1; later discussed in DT, "Water Under Bridges," *Saturday Evening Post*, 9 April 1932; "The Last Days of the Habsburgs," DT Papers, Box 99, folder 6.

44 **"puffy-eyed, heavy man"** DT, "Last Days."

44 **"Steady old boy"** DT, "Last Days."

44 **"I would not spill"** DT, "Not for Thousand Thrones," p. 13.

44 **"If I could scoop"** The friend was Rose Wilder Lane, the writer who would later

shepherd her mother's Little House series into print. Kurth, *American Cassandra*, p. 70.

45 **"a most intimately affectionate"** DT, "The Old Outcasts," Box 100. Told differently (or perhaps just a different story) in the *New Yorker*, where she's run out of money and wires Beneš to fire the post office attendants who are refusing to send her story collect. "It Girl," p. 29.

45 **"She was a Richard Harding Davis"** Wharton, "Dorothy Thompson," p. 12.

45 **Late one night** See Karina von Tippelskirch's lucid commentary on Thompson and the May Coup, *Dorothy Thompson and German Writers*, pp. 118–19.

45 **Proceeding with a crisp** Kurth, *American Cassandra*, p. 65.

45 **Dorothy's, chimed** Harriman, "The It Girl—I," *New Yorker*, 20 April 1940, p. 28.

45 **"if any"** DT, "On Women Correspondents and Other New Ideas," *Nation*, 6 Jan. 1926, pp. 11–12.

45 **"see-what-the-little"** DT, "On Women Correspondents," p. 11.

45 **It helped, too** DT to Ellery Sedgwick, 24 Oct. nd [1925?], Carton 12, Ellery Sedgwick Papers, Massachusetts Historical Society.

46 **"That's only a man's badge"** DT, "Outline for a Talk Before the Ohio Newspaper Women's Assn," cited in Kurth, *American Cassandra*, p. 88.

46 **"which seem likely"** Paul Scott Mowrer, "The *Chicago Daily News*' Foreign Service: Principles and Instructions," 21 Nov. 1927, JG Papers II, Box 24.

47 **To that end, the *Daily News*'s** Mowrer, *House of Europe*, p. 135. See, too, Raymond Swing's memory of the Berlin bureau of the *CDN* in "Big News in Europe," *Problems of Journalism* (American Society of Newspaper Editors, 1935), pp. 91–92.

47 **He had to talk** JG to family, 7 Nov. 1924, Letters to His Family from London and Porquerolles, JG Papers II, Box 5; also 8 Dec. 1924 re. UP.

47 **"appallingly brilliant"** JG to Helen Hahn, 7 Nov. 1924, JG Papers II, Box 5.

48 **"I am most extraordinarily"** JG to Helen Hahn, 5 Dec. 1924, JG Papers II, Box 5.

48 **"Please consider me"** JG, "Introducing—In Person: 20—A Woman with Brilliant Wit," 1926 Clippings, JG Papers 1972 Add., Box 41.

48 **In the white-paneled** JG to Helen Hahn, 21 Dec. 1924, JG Papers II, Box 5.

48 **He was taking** MS of White Helen, JG Papers II, Box 7.

48 **As John embarked** "Introducing—In Person: 20—A Woman with Brilliant Wit"; JG to Helen Hahn, 23–30 Dec. 1924, JG Papers II, Box 5.

48 **Whereupon John returned** JG to Helen Hahn, 24 March 1925, JG Papers II, Box 5—Letters to Helen.

48 **"I like her"** JG to Helen Hahn, 21 Dec. 1924, JG Papers II, Box 5—Letters to Helen.

49 **"curious mixture"** H. G. Wells, *H. G. Wells in Love: Postscript to an Experiment in Autobiography* (Boston: Little, Brown, 1984), p. 94.

49 **For nearly a decade** RW to S.K. Ratcliffe, 21 March 1923 in *Selected Letters of Rebecca West*, ed. Bonnie Kime Scott (New Haven: Yale University Press, 2000), pp. 55–56.

49 **"Have I ever got"** Rollyson, *Rebecca West*, p. 76.

49 **They'd all nearly** *Selected Letters*, pp. 52–59; also RW to JG, Summer 1926, JG Papers II, Box 35.

49 **"skin of her victims"** Rollyson, *Rebecca West*, p. 73. From April 1920 to Dec. 1922, she reviewed 136 novels in 55 reviews of 2,000 words a piece.

49 **None of her contemporaries** RW to S. K. Ratcliffe [1917], in *Selected Letters*, p. 35.

49 **Unlike most men** On RW's habit of making her listeners into secondary characters, Sewell Stokes, *Pilloried!* (London: The Richards Press, 1928), p. 17.

49 **Rebecca is my only** JG to Helen Hahn, 28 Feb. 1925, JG Papers II, Box 5.

50 **"How I Was Raped"** JG to Helen Hahn, 8 Feb., JG Papers II, Box 5.

50 **"How It Feels"** JG to Helen Hahn, 9 Feb., JG Papers II, Box 5.

50 **"I Regard Marriage"** RW, "I Regard Marriage with Fear and Horror," *Cosmopolitan*, Nov. 1925, pp. 66–67, 207–10.

50 **On every street corner** JG to Helen Hahn, 24 March 1925.

50 **Rather unaccountably** JG, Green Notebook I, 1931, JG Papers II, Box 2; "Notes on Rebecca West," JG Papers II, Box 3.

CHAPTER THREE

51 **A big talker** JG to Helen Hahn, 24 May 1925, JG Papers II, Box 5. Frances and John first met in Paris in April, when he was there for a week before going to Porquerolles.

52 **Titled *The Red Pavilion*** The title, *The Red Pavilion,* from the poem by Frances Thompson, "An Arab Love-Song." JG to Helen Hahn, 29 May 1925, JG Papers II, Box 5.

52 **"a small corn-colored"** JG to Helen Hahn, 29 May 1925, JG Papers II, Box 5.

52 **"she tantalized him"** From draft of JG, *Indian Sign,* JG Papers II, Box 4.

52 **"England's most promising"** JG to Helen Hahn, 29 May, 30 May, 3 June 1925, JG Papers II, Box 5.

52 **"This Frances girl"** JG to Helen Hahn, 3 June 1925, JG Papers II, Box 5.

52 **"fatal Frances"** Eric Maschwitz to JG, undated [Saturday], JG Papers II, Box 5, Correspondence, 1928–1937: I–O.

52 **"Miss Fineman lived alone"** JG, "Chicagoan Tells of Soviets' 'Red Queen,'" *Chicago Daily News* [henceforth *CDN*], 10 June 1925, p. 2.

52 **"I am perhaps a little"** JG to Helen Hahn, 7 June 1925, JG Papers II, Box 5.

52 **You know, you could** FF to JG, 17 May 1926, JG Papers II, Box 22.

53 **"I think somehow"** JG to FF, 19 June 1925, JG Papers II, Box 22.

53 **"Shall we survive"** FF to JG, Tuesday morning, undated [1925], Envelope marked "Before Rye," JG Papers II, Box 6—Rye Letters.

53 **"Don't think I say"** FF to JG, Tuesday afternoon, 21 April 1925, JG Papers II, Box 22.

54 **"How to Psychoanalyze"** Hale, *Rise and Crisis of Psychoanalysis,* p. 76. On the "Little Blue Book" series, Melanie Ann Brown, "Five-Cent Culture at the 'University in Print': Radical Ideology and the Marketplace in E. Haldeman-Julius's Little Blue Books, 1919–1929," Ph.D. diss., University of Minnesota Press, 2017; R. Alton Lee, *Publisher for the Masses: Emanuel Haldeman-Julius* (Lincoln: University of Nebraska Press, 2018).

54 **"strangest summer"** JG to FF, 11 Sept. 1925, JG Papers II, Box 22.

54 **"my dear lord"** FF to JG, Tuesday morning, undated [1925].

54 **Like other young women** Laid out in FF, Unpub. Letter to the *New Statesman,* 3 Aug. ny [1925], Box 23, Regenstein; ideas echoed in Dorothy Bromley, "Feminist-New Style," *Harper's* 155 (Oct. 1927): 552–60.

54 **She was a new model** Mary K. Trigg, *Feminism as Life's Work: Four Modern American Women Through Two World Wars* (New Brunswick, N.J.: Rutgers University Press, 2014), esp. ch. 3; Christine Stansell, *American Moderns: Bohemian New York and the Creation of a New Century* (New York: Metropolitan Books, 2000); Christina Simmons, *Making Marriage Modern: Women's Sexuality from the Progressive Era to World War I* (New York: Oxford University Press, 2009); John D'Emilio and Estelle Freedman, *Intimate Matters: A History of Sexuality in America,* 3rd ed. (Chicago: University of Chicago Press, 2012).

54 **"a prod to urge"** FF, Unpub. Letter to the *New Statesman*.

54 **She composed a harsh** FF review, Letters about the Red Pavilion, JG Papers II, Box 29.

55 **"You see I can't do"** TS note to John, nd [1925], folder 18, FFG Papers.

55 **Sometime that summer** See RW to JG, undated [March 1926], JG Papers II, Box 35; FF to JG, 17 May 1926, JG Papers II, Box 22; JG, "Okay, Bliss," JG Papers 1972 Add., Box 154, folder 2.

55 **"The intermission lasts"** JG to FF, 11 Sept. 1925, JG Papers II, Box 22.

55 **Her own very small** JG to FF, 31 Dec. 1925, JG Papers II, Box 22.

55 **"Lay off the hysteria"** FF to JG, 14 Jan. 1926, JG Papers II, Box 22.

56 **"I want to work hard"** FF to JG, 22 Jan. 1926, JG Papers II, Box 22.

56 **"All I can say"** JG to FF, 4 April 1926, JG Papers II, Box 22.

56 **"Grand, isn't it?"** JG to Emily Hahn, 12 April 1926, Hahn I, Box 1–1926 folder, Jan.–April, Emily Hahn Papers, Lilly Library, Indiana University.

56 **Two publishers** *The Red Pavilion* would be reviewed with *The Sun Also Rises* by Charles W. Ferguson in "Five Rising Stars in American Fiction," *Bookman,* May 1927. For Gunther as for Sheean, Hemingway's transformation from jobbing reporter for the *Toronto Star,* filing sardonic dispatches from the Genoa conference in 1922, where the Bolshevik diplomatic corps appeared for the first time in Western Europe, to the author of *The Sun Also Rises* was the model and much envied.

56 **Hadn't she?** JG to Emily Hahn, 29 March 1926, Hahn I, Box 1.

56 **Of the five Hahn girls** On Hahn, Ken Cuthbertson, *Nobody Said Not to Go: The Life, Loves, and Adventures of Emily Hahn* (Boston and London: Faber and Faber, 1988); on Hahn in Shanghai, Taras Grescoe, *Shanghai Grand: Forbidden Love and International Intrigue in a Doomed World* (New York: St. Martin's Press, 2016).

57 **"restless spirit"** Hahn, *No Hurry,* p. 18.

57 **"female mind"** Hahn, *No Hurry,* pp. 57–58.

57 **So the summer** Hahn, *No Hurry,* pp. 72–73.

57 **They crowded the halls** Described in JG, Green Notebook II, JG Papers II, Box 2.

57 **Mickey mostly treated** Emily Hahn, "Raymond" and "That Young Man" (about JG) in *No Hurry.*

57 **"got away without listening"** EH, Diary, Hahn I, Box 15, Emily Hahn Papers.

58 **"Ask John"** Dad to Mickey, 24 Feb. 1926, Hahn 1, Box 1.

58 **Stay for several months** H. R. Knickerbocker [HRK] to Frederick Griffin, 10 April 1931, HRK Papers, Uncatalogued correspondence, Box 2; JG to FFG, 24 June 1928, Russian Logs, JG Papers II, Box 2.

58 **As such, it was among those territories** For an overview of the situation in Syria, Susan Pedersen, *The Guardians: The League of Nations and the Crisis of Empire* (Oxford and New York: Oxford University Press, 2015), ch. 5.

59 **For three days** "No Prisoners Taken in Druse Warfare," CDN Special Cable, dated 7 June 1926 [delayed], Box 41, folder 7.

59 **The Syrian Rebellion** Little of the American press coverage was based on reporting from Druze sources. As Pedersen points out, the bombing of Damascus in the fall of 1925 did cause a humanitarian outcry, leading internationalists such as the lawyer Quincy Wright to see Syria as a state in the making. Pedersen, *Guardians,* pp. 145–50.

59 **"I was amazed"** JG, "Interesting Jaunt into Druse Country," *CDN,* dateline 15 June 1926, JG Papers 1972 Add., Box 43, folder 9.

60 **"her dense black hair"** JG, "Hunt for Emir, Find Queen of the Druses," *CDN,* dateline 15 June 1926, JG Papers 1972 Add., Box 43, folder 9.

60 **"a Palm Beach suit"** JG, "Arslan, Druse Chief, A Dandified Rebel," *CDN,* dateline 15 June 1926, JG Papers 1972 Add., Box 43, folder 9.

60 **Another American journalist** See Pedersen's discussion of the report by B. F. Dawson in Pedersen, *Guardians,* pp. 165–66.

61 **"Damascus," he said later** JG, Radio talk, 1926, JG Papers 1972 Add., Box 44, folder 5.

61 **"I am as zestful"** JG to Emily Hahn, 22 June 1926, 1926 folder, May–Aug., Hahn I, Box 1.

61 **Like every cub correspondent** Heald, *Transatlantic,* pp. 178–81.

62 **In Poland** John Gunther, *Inside Europe* (New York: Harper & Bros., 1936), pp. 387–89.

62 **"Well, my idea"** JG to Emily Hahn, 22 June 1926.

62 **To put them off the scent** FF to JG, 21 March 1926, JG Papers II, Box 22.

63 **The meeting dragged** Rebecca West [RW] to JG, nd [March 1926], JG Papers II, Box 35.

63 **"shepherding instinct"** JG, entry dated Feb. 1931, Juan les Pins, Green Notebook I.

63 **"I think of you"** FF to JG, 26 May 1926, JG Papers II, Box 22.

63 **"And what's this"** FF to JG, 2 Sept. nd [1926], JG Papers II, Box 22.

64 **Frances was coming** JG to FF, 16 Sept. 1926, JG Papers II, Box 22. FF was working for the producer Archie Selwyn.

64 **Rebecca heard** RW to JG, nd [fall 1926], JG Papers II, Box 35.

64 **According to Rebecca** RW to JG, nd, and RW to JG, nd [Dec. 1926], JG Papers II, Box 35.

64 **"If I've sounded raucous"** RW to JG, nd [1927], JG Papers II, Box 35.

64 **From New York** RW to JG, nd [Dec. 1926], JG Papers II, Box 35.

64 **Rebecca feared** JG, Green Notebook I, 1931, JG Papers II, Box 2.

65 **"Marry me?"** Cuthbertson, *Inside,* pp. 71–72.

65 **"If John Gunther"** RW to Lettie, nd [1927], Copies of Rebecca West's letters to Letitia Fairchild, RP 6367, British Library.

65 **It was a peculiar** Rebecca West, *A Letter to a Grandfather* (London: Hogarth Press, 1933), p. 34.

65 **"There is nothing rarer"** Rebecca West, *Black Lamb and Grey Falcon: A Journey Through Yugoslavia* (London: Penguin, 2007 [1941]), p. 1102.

65 **Instead, Wells shunted** Glendinning, *Rebecca West,* pp. 54–55.

65 **"It is your nature"** Quoted in Rollyson, *Rebecca West,* p. 66.

66 **"Give her my dear love"** Rollyson, *Rebecca West,* p. 57.

66 **"She was, in the vulgar phrase"** Anthony West, *Heritage,* new intro. (New York: Washington Square Press, 1984), unpaginated, last page.

66 **Anyway, Helen insisted** Interview with Helen Hahn, 26 Dec. 1986, cited in Cuthbertson, *Inside,* p. 73.

66 **"I wish to God"** RW to JG, nd [1927], JG Papers II, Box 35.

66 **Lizette, John's mother** "John Gunther Is Wed After Cable Romance," JG Papers II, Box 6.

67 **Before posting the banns** JG, Green Notebook II, JG Papers II, Box 2.

67 **At the time, he was turning** JG note, Greensboro, July 31, 1952, More Diary Scraps, H. Luce, Dollfuss etc. Various Dates, JG Papers II, Box 1.

67 **"a tin-foil plow"** R.L., *New Republic,* 26 Jan. 1927, p. 283; Fanny Butcher in the *Chicago Tribune* (29 Jan. 1927) sounded many of the same notes as Frances had.

67 **He'd write six more** *Eden for One* (1927—published in Britain as *Peter Lancelot*), *Golden Fleece* (1929), *Bright Nemesis* (1932), *Troubled Midnight* (1945), *Lost City* (1964), *Indian Sign* (1970).

67 **When John found himself stuck** JG, diary entry, 7 April 1952, JG Papers II, Box 1. So faithfully did he represent his own reality that his publishers, fretting about

libel suits, called in the lawyers to scrutinize his characters. On at least one occasion, Harper & Brothers sought out contemporaries of John's who knew the scene and the relevant figures to weigh in on what alterations were needed to ensure that no one would be recognizable. The lawyers demanded pages and pages of changes. The fracas around Ring Round Vienna detailed in JG to Cass Canfield, 27 Jan. 1938, JG Papers 1972 Add., Box 150, folder 8; also Fodor to Hamish Hamilton, 2 Feb. 1938; JG to Hamilton, 21 Feb. 1938, Hamilton to JG, 1 March 1938, JG Papers 1972 Add., Box 118, folder 5.

67   **Among John's unpublished pieces** JG Papers 1972 Add., Box 154, folder 2.

68   **"It's my damn hungry"** Green Notebook I, 1931, JG Papers II, Box 2.

68   **Inside is a shriveled** The fetus appears again in *Indian Sign,* though this time in London, not Rome, the product of an inept curettage. John Gunther, *Indian Sign* (New York: Harper & Row, 1970), p. 120.

CHAPTER FOUR

69   **From their yachts** Fischer, *Men and Politics,* p. 27.

69   **A catastrophic hyperinflation** Martin Geyer, *Verkehrte Welt: Revolution, Inflation und Moderne: München 1914–1924* (Göttingen: Vandenhoeck & Ruprecht, 1998).

70   **By day, she sniffed out** Among others, DT, "Gen. von Seeckt Resigns as Head of Reichswehr," *Public Ledger,* dateline 6 Oct. 1926; "Plot to Make Hindenburg Dictator Charged in Berlin," *Public Ledger,* dateline 13 Feb. 1927; "German Theatre Celebrates Reinhardt's Anniversary," *Public Ledger,* dateline Berlin, Saturday [1926], in Microfilms of DT Public Ledger articles, DT Papers, Box 71.

70   **In 1925, she had become** See Kurth, *American Cassandra,* p. 95. This was an honor that the *Chicago Tribune*'s Sigrid Schultz later claimed for herself. My thanks to David Milne for an email exchange on this point.

70   **"hairdresser, with a naïve passion"** RW to JVS, 25 Dec. 1963, Houghton Mifflin Company Papers, bMS Am 2105 (228), Houghton Library, Harvard. She had met Dorothy in 1925; John Gunther had introduced them. On this meeting, Hertog, *Dangerous Ambition,* pp. 7–13.

70   **"great, serious, unfinishable"** Kurth, *American Cassandra,* p. 96.

70   **For a few years** Kurth, *American Cassandra,* pp. 96–97.

70   **"she could always step"** Vincent Sheean, *Dorothy and Red* (Boston: Houghton Mifflin, 1963), p. 3.

70   **Edgar was the paper's** Lilian Mowrer, *Journalist's Wife* (New York: W. Morrow, 1937), pp. 215–16.

71   **Choose an evening** On Dorothy's guests, JG, "A Blue-Eyed Tornado," *New York Herald Tribune* [*NYHT*], 13 Jan. 1935, p. 6.

71   **"very nice boy"** DT, diary entry, 30 Sept. 1927, DT Papers, Box 59, folder 2.

71   **"All come to Moscow"** Described in JVS, *Dorothy and Red,* quote on p. 36.

71   **"O you *must* come"** JVS, *Dorothy and Red,* p. 37.

72   **Then he proceeded** JVS, *PH,* p. 279.

72   **Though no one could** DT, diary entry, 30 Sept. 1927.

72   **It was then that the distinction** JVS, *Dorothy and Red,* p. 56.

72   **One day, Jimmy supposed** JVS, *PH,* p. 216.

72   **"Uplifters," Dorothy called them** Dorothy Thompson, *The New Russia* (New York: H. Holt and Co., 1928), pp. 43–44.

72   **She'd divorced one** Rayna's first husband was Samson Raphaelson, whose play *The Jazz Singer* was being made into a movie that year, 1927. On Prohme, Cott, *Fighting Words,* esp. ch. 5; Baruch Hirson and Arthur J. Knodel, ed. Gregor Benton, *Reporting the Chinese Revolution: The Letters of Rayna Prohme* (London and

Ann Arbor: Pluto Press, 2007); Peter Rand, *China Hands: The Adventures and Ordeals of the American Journalists Who Joined Forces with the Great Chinese Revolution* (New York: Simon and Schuster, 1995), pp. 35–78; Dorothy Day, *From Union Square to Rome* (Silver Spring, Md.: Preservation of the Faith Press, 1939), ch. 5. Bill Prohme was frequently referred to as Rayna's husband (as I do here). But in all likelihood, as Cott notes, they never married legally, though other people assumed that they had; Jimmy, like her other friends, referred to her as Rayna Prohme. See, for instance, the account by Milly Bennett, *On Her Own: Journalistic Adventures from San Francisco to the Chinese Revolution, 1917–1927*, ed. A. Tom Grunfeld (Armonk, N.Y.: M. E. Sharpe, 1993), pp. 49–51.

73 "How's the weather" JVS, *PH*, p. 215; for another view of JVS, Bennett, *On Her Own*, esp. pp. 197–99, 229–30.

73 "All the people who think" JVS to Raymond Mortimer, 31 April 1927, RM Papers, Box 3, folder 35.

73 One of the earliest anticolonial Pablo La Porte, "'Rien à ajouter': The League of Nations and the Rif War (1921–1926)," *European History Quarterly* 41 (2011): 66–87; more generally, C. R. Pennell, *A Country with a Government and Flag: The Rif War in Morocco, 1921–1926* (Wisbech, Cambridgeshire: Middle East and North African Studies Press, 1986); David Woolman, *Rebels in the Rif: Abd el-Krim and the Rif Rebellion* (Stanford: Stanford University Press, 1968); C. R. Pennell, "How and Why to Remember the Rif War (1921–2021)," *The Journal of North African Studies* 22 (2017): 798–820.

73 He stood accused Vincent Sheean, *An American Among the Riffi* (New York and London: The Century Co., 1926), pp. 174–75.

73 Fitted out JVS, *PH*, pp. 94, 126.

74 He was one of the few JVS, *PH*, p. 139; "War Correspondent," *El Paso Herald*, 3 Oct. 1925, p. 9. The *Chicago Daily News*'s Paul Scott Mowrer had interviewed el-Krim in October 1924, before the blockade. See Shannon E. Fleming, "The First 'American Among the Riffi': Paul Scott Mowrer's October 1924 Interview with Abd-el-Krim," *The Journal of North African Studies* 25 (2020): 594–615. Other key sources on the Rif conflict were Walter B. Harris (reporting for the London *Times*) and Ward Price (*Daily Mail*).

74 The suspicion of European imperialism John Moser, *Twisting the Lion's Tail: Anglophobia in the United States, 1921–1948* (New York: New York University Press, 1999).

74 "most persistent and heroic nationalism" JVS, *American*, p. 122.

74 "You may say for me" JVS, "Abd-el-Krim Bitterly Scores Imperialism of Two Enemies," *Great Falls Tribune*, 23 Oct. 1925, p. 2.

74 "I understood that nobody" JVS, *PH*, pp. 139, 141.

74 He could be the next JVS, *PH*, p. 246.

75 It was that curiosity For a survey of foreign reporting about China, Paul French, *Through the Looking Glass: China's Foreign Journalists from Opium Wars to Mao* (Hong Kong: Hong Kong University Press, 2009).

75 For the new Soviet regime Alexander Pantsov, *The Bolsheviks and the Chinese Revolution, 1919–1927* (London: Routledge, 2013 [2000]).

75 Its failure, conversely Steve Smith, *A Road Is Made: Communism in Shanghai, 1920–1927* (Honolulu: University of Hawaii Press, 2000); C. Martin Wilbur, *The Nationalist Revolution in China, 1923–28* (Cambridge, UK: Cambridge University Press, 1983).

76 "and many of my ideas" JVS to Raymond Mortimer, 31 April [sic] 1927. In *Personal History*, JVS puts his first meeting with Prohme in early May 1927.

76 As editor of the Hankou Bill Prohme was the head of the Nationalist News

Agency in Beijing, but because of his chronic tuberculosis, Rayna ended up often subbing for him as well as starting the *Hankow People's Tribune*, the party's English-language organ. See Hirson and Knodel, *Reporting*, pp. 42–68; Henry Francis Misselwitz, *The Dragon Stirs* (New York: Harbinger House, 1941); Kenneth E. Shewmaker, *Americans and Chinese Communists, 1927–45* (Ithaca: Cornell University Press, 1971).

76 **She felt the cruelty** JVS, *PH,* p. 270.

77 **"I knew you'd turn"** JVS, *PH,* p. 263.

77 **"a darling"** Rayna to Bill Prohme [BP], Thursday [25 Aug. 1927], Box 1, folder 10, C. Frank Glass Papers, Hoover Institution, Stanford. This run of correspondence is reprinted in Hirson and Knodel, *Reporting*.

77 **"at least, not as the phrase"** JVS, *PH,* p. 261.

77 **He would describe** JVS, *PH,* p. 217.

77 **The proper relationship between the individual** On the ubiquity of "group" talk in America, Huizinga, *America*, pp. 275–76. More broadly, Wilfred M. McClay, *The Masterless: Self & Society in Modern America* (Chapel Hill: University of North Carolina Press, 1994); William Graebner, *The Engineering of Consent: Democracy and Authority in Twentieth-Century America* (Madison: University of Wisconsin Press, 1987); Susan Hegman, *Patterns for America: Modernism and the Concept of Culture* (Princeton: Princeton University Press, 1999); Robert C. Bannister, *Sociology and Scientism: The American Quest for Objectivity, 1880–1940* (Chapel Hill: University of North Carolina Press, 1987).

77 **What duty did the individual** On Catholic social teaching in the early-twentieth-century United States, Francis L. Broderick, *Right Reverend New Dealer: John A. Ryan* (New York: Macmillan, 1963), esp. pp. 105–11; Aaron Abell, *American Catholicism and Social Action: A Search for Social Justice, 1865–1950* (Garden City, N.Y., and Notre Dame, Ind.: University of Notre Dame Press, 1960), pp. 189–263. My thanks to Madelyn Lugli for this point.

78 **He left in a flurry** Rayna to BP, 22 Sept. [1927], Box 1, folder 10, Frank C. Glass Papers.

78 **"you remember his affectionate"** Rayna to BP, 16 Sept. 1927, Box 1, folder 10, Frank C. Glass Papers.

78 **"only without a single"** Rayna to BP, 22 Sept. 1927, Box 1, folder 10, Frank C. Glass Papers.

78 **Rayna had been glad** Rayna to BP, 21 and 22 Sept. 1927, Box 1, folder 10, Frank C. Glass Papers.

78 **She'd been expected** Rayna to BP, 6/7 Sept., 25 Sept. 1927, 2 Oct. 1927, Box 1, folder 10, Frank C. Glass Papers.

78 **She'd barely learned** Rayna to BP, 2 Nov. 1927, Box 1, folder 10, Frank C. Glass Papers.

79 **"selfish beast"** Rayna to BP, 19 Oct. 1927, Box 1, folder 10, Frank C. Glass Papers.

79 **She'd heard that Jimmy** Rayna to BP, 8 Oct. 1927, Box 1, folder 10, Frank C. Glass Papers.

79 **Infinite columns of marchers** "Mammoth Parade in Moscow Marks Decade of Soviet," *Gazette* [Montreal], 8 Nov. 1927, p. 19.

79 **According to Jimmy, she'd made** On the ILS, Julia Köstenberger, "Die Internationale Lenin-Schule (1926–1938)," in Michael Buckmiller and Klaus Meschkat, eds., *Biographisches Handbuch zur Geschichte der Kommunistischen Internationale: Ein deutsch-russisches Forschungsprojekt* (Berlin: Akademie Verlag, 2007), pp. 287–309; Gidon Cohen and Kevin Morgan, "Stalin's Sausage Machine: British Students at the International Lenin School 1926–37," *Twentieth Century British History* 13, no. 4 (2002): 327–55 and discussions in *TCBH* that ensued.

79 "Don't be a damn fool" JVS, *PH*, p. 288.

80 "I can't imagine him weeping" Rayna to BP, 9 Nov. 1927, Box 1, folder 10, Frank C. Glass Papers.

80 **Dorothy had come by** Cott suggests Jimmy may have concocted this episode of the Lenin Institute and the last supper, but against that supposition is DT's own contemporaneous account, recorded in a letter to SL, Monday [21 Nov. 1927], DT Papers, Box 47, and discussed again (with reference to RP being dispatched to the "Orient") in DT, "On the Record: The Conspiratorial Mind," *NYHT*, 27 Jan. 1937, p. 21. Cott, *Fighting Words*, p. 203.

80 **the "grandiose scheme"** DT, *New Russia*, pp. 38–39.

80 **"In the matter of kitchens"** DT, *New Russia*, p. 17.

80 **"had balled up her life"** DT to SL, 21 Nov. 1927, DT Papers, Box 47.

80 **The German doctor** On Rayna's illness, JVS to Samson Raphaelson, 21 Nov. 1927 and JVS to Helen Freeland, 21 Nov. 1927, Box 1, folder 13, Frank C. Glass Papers.

80 **"Will you tell me"** JVS, *PH*, p. 297.

81 **She dictated cablegrams** Anna Louise Strong to Mrs. Simon, 22 Nov. 1927, Box 1, folder 15, Frank C. Glass Papers.

81 **That night, it snowed in Moscow** Fischer, *Men and Politics*, p. 157.

81 **Whether the cause of the abscess** Bill Prohme to JVS, nd [1935], Box 1, folder 11, Frank C. Glass Papers.

81 **The case was a rare** JVS to Helen Freeland, 3 Jan. 1928; JVS to Freeland, 21 Nov. 1927, Box 1, folder 13, Frank C. Glass Papers.

81 **Dorothy was there, too** Described in JVS, *Dorothy and Red*, p. 58; JVS, *Personal History*, pp. 300–302.

81 **"What a funny thing"** DT to SL, Thursday, Thanksgiving [1927], DT Papers, Box 47.

81 **Rayna's coffin** On flowers, Anna Louise Strong's report on Prohme's funeral, Box 1, folder 15, Frank C. Glass Papers.

82 **As the bier** Fischer, *Men and Politics*, p. 158.

82 **Earlier that same year** They were living in the apartment of Anaïs Nin's mother. See Anaïs Nin, *The Early Diary of Anaïs Nin*, vol. 4, 4 Aug. 1927 (San Diego and New York: Harcourt, Brace, 1985), p. 4.

82 **Frances opened** JG to FFG, 26 Nov. 1927.

82 **"Marriage Rome"** FF to JG, 29 Jan. 1927, JG Papers II, Box 22.

82 **Please don't say** JG to FFG, 3 Dec. 1927; also FFG to JG, 11 Dec. 1927, JG Papers II, Box 22.

82 **They'd already had plenty** For this correspondence, Charles H. Dennis to JG, 2 Aug., 16 Aug., 29 Nov. 1926, JG Papers II, Box 5, 1989-001—Correspondence *Chicago Daily News*, pre-1930 through 1932.

82 **Why that was the case** For these stories, see JG Papers 1972 Add., Box 41, folders 8 and 9 and Box 42, folder 1.

82 **Amid his 1926 coup** "Dictator Refused Proffered Crown," dateline 25 May 1928, *CDN*, JG Papers 1972 Add., Box 42, folder 1.

82 **Be glad you're not** JG to FFG, 15 Nov. [1927], JG Papers II, Box 22.

83 **"but so *dirty*!"** See also "Bratiano Is Ill: Trouble Brewing," dateline 27 Feb. 1928, *CDN*, JG Papers 1972 Add., Box 42, folder 1.

83 **Tea was on** FFG to JG, 27 Nov. 1927, JG Papers II, Box 22.

83 **All nearly identical** JG to FFG, 15 Nov. 1927, JG Papers II, Box 22.

83 **"Well, remember"** FFG to JG, 10 Nov. 1927, JG Papers II, Box 22.

83 **"Note down"** FFG to JG, 27 Nov. 1927, JG Papers II, Box 22.

83 **"yes, from what you say"** Emily Hahn to Helen, 15 Nov. 1928, Hahn 1, Box 1, 1928–1929, March, Emily Hahn Papers.

84 **She'd been working** "Tulsa an Eye-Opener to St. Louis Banker," *Fuel Oil Journal*, November 1915, p. 29.

84 **"I don't want to grow"** Emily Hahn to JG, undated, JG Papers II, Box 34.

84 **"I've dreamed of winning you"** JG to Emily Hahn, 9 Feb. 1927, Hahn I, Box 1, Emily Hahn Papers.

84 **"Lord knows it's easy enough"** Emily Hahn to JG, 14 Feb. 1928, Hahn I, Box 1, Emily Hahn Papers.

84 **"I do like states of indecision"** Emily Hahn to her parents, 19 April 1927, Hahn I, Box 1, Emily Hahn Papers.

85 **"Am I a complete bounder"** JG to RW, 2 Dec. [nd, 1927], GEN 105, Series I, Box 9, folder 335, Rebecca West Papers, GEN MSS 105, Beinecke Rare Book and Manuscript Library, Yale.

85 **Frances joined John** JG to FFG, 3 Dec. 1927, JG Papers II, Box 22.

85 **They celebrated Christmas** JG, "Turkey Captured by Santa Claus," dateline 24 Dec. 1927, JG Papers 1972 Add., Box 41, file 9.

85 **"God's victory"** JG, Green Notebook, I.

85 **"I'm prepared to argue"** JG to FFG, 21 July 1928, Russian Log, JG Papers II, Box 2.

86 **It was out of the question** JG to FFG, 11 June 1928, Russian Log, JG Papers II, Box 2.

86 **Send me pictures** JG to FFG, 28 June 1928, Russian Log, JG Papers II, Box 2.

86 **He slept with those** JG to FFG, 5 Aug. 1928, Russian Log, JG Papers II, Box 2.

86 **Drink bottles** JG to FFG, undated [early April 1928], JG Papers II, Box 22 and JG to FFG, undated [summer 1928], Russian Log, JG Papers II, Box 2.

86 **She no longer hid** FFG to JG, 18 June 1928, JG Papers II, Box 23.

86 **My belly looks** FFG to JG, 2 Aug. 1928, JG Papers II, Box 22.

86 **"Not to have taken care"** JG to FFG, nd [April 1928], JG Papers II, Box 22.

86 **Most of the Western correspondents** JG to FFG, 16 June 1928, Russian Log, JG Papers II, Box 2.

86 **All the Louis Quinze** DT, *New Russia*, p. 26.

86 **Through profligate tipping** JG to FFG, 6 June 1928, Russian Log, JG Papers II, Box 2.

87 **The Kremlin** FFG to JG, 11 July 1928, JG Papers II, Box 23.

87 **How surprising** JG to FFG, 12 June 1928, Russian Log, JG Papers II, Box 2.

87 **The absence of outdoor cafés** For these details, JG, "Animated Evenings Mark Life in Russia's Capital," *CDN*, dateline 25 July 1928, JG Papers 1972 Add., Box 42, folder 1.

87 **The complete lack** JG, "Wear Blue Shirts at Moscow Opera," *CDN*, dateline 25 July 1928, JG Papers 1972 Add., Box 42, folder 1.

87 **a "charming fellow"** JG to FFG, 6 June 1928, Russian Log, JG Papers II, Box 2.

87 **How on earth** JG to FFG, 24 June 1928, Russian Log, JG Papers II, Box 2.

87 **"I feel rather"** JG to FFG, 8 June 1928, Russian Log, JG Papers II, Box 2. On getting rid of his dinner suit before traveling to Moscow, Muggeridge, *Chronicles*, vol. 1, p. 205.

88 **At loose ends** JG to FFG, 12 and 20 June 1928, Russian Log, JG Papers II, Box 2.

88 **"I haven't an iota"** JG to FFG, 1 July 1928, Russian Log, JG Papers II, Box 2.

88 **"the perfectly extraordinary resemblance"** JG to FFG, 12 June 1928, Russian Log, JG Papers II, Box 2.

88 **And Russians had that same amiable** JG to FFG, 12 June 1928, Russian Log, JG Papers II, Box 2.

88 **"Likens Moscow"** JG, *CDN*, dateline 25 July 1928, JG Papers 1972 Add., Box 42, folder 1.

88 **Vlad had been a skeptic** FFG to JG, 2 Aug. 1928, JG Papers II, Box 22.

89 "Jesus, you've spent" FFG to JG, 11 July 1928, JG Papers II, Box 23.

89 "You seem to be leading" FFG to JG, 11 July 1928, JG Papers II, Box 23.

89 She felt contrite FFG to JG, 10 July 1928, JG Papers II, Box 23.

89 Maybe *she* would just JG to FFG, 15 July 1928, Russian Log, JG Papers II, Box 2.

89 Eisenstein, John learned JG to FFG, 5 Aug. 1928, Russian Log, JG Papers II, Box 2.

89 "Of course I'm a propagandist" JG, "Bull Takes Lead in Soviet Film," *CDN*, dateline 25 Aug. 1928, JG Papers 1972 Add., Box 42, folder 1.

90 "uttermost possible poles" JG, "Likens Moscow to Modern Rome," *CDN*, dateline 25 July 1928, JG Papers 1972 Add., Box 42, folder 1.

90 "I think that my emotions here" JG to FFG, 20 June 1928, Russian Log, JG Papers II, Box 2. The date he chose, 1793, is amid the Reign of Terror, but his reference doesn't appear to be to that violent period, but rather the French Revolution in general.

90 "On the whole, I <u>don't</u> like it" JG to FFG, 9 Sept. 1928, JG Papers II, Box 2.

90 "oh Lord!" JG to FFG, 5 Aug. 1928, Russian Log, JG Papers II, Box 2, and FFG to JG, 2 Aug. 1928, JG Papers II, Box 22.

90 "this effort to skip" JG, "Russia Land of Many Paradoxes," *CDN*, dateline 6 Oct. 1928, JG Papers 1972 Add., Box 42, file 1.

91 The fields were mucky "Oil Makes Baku a Modern Town," dateline 1 Oct. 1928, Box 42, file 1.

91 "I have great times thinking" JG to FFG, undated [summer 1928], Russian Log, JG Papers II, Box 2.

91 "You shall have 3 babies" JG to FFG, 9 Sept. 1928, JG Papers II, Box 2.

CHAPTER FIVE

92 "a wretched American" Virginia Woolf to Vanessa Bell, 23 May [1931] in *The Letters of Virginia Woolf: 1929–1931* [vol. 4], eds. Nigel Nicolson and Joanne Trautmann Banks (New York: Harcourt Brace, 1978), p. 336.

92 The Bloomsbury Group On Bloomsbury, among others, Peter Clarke, *Keynes* (London: Bloomsbury, 2009); Leon Edel, *Bloomsbury: A House of Lions* (London: Hogarth Press, 1979); Derek Ryan and Stephen Ross, eds., *The Handbook to the Bloomsbury Group* (London: Bloomsbury, 2018).

93 "lived in squares" Whether Parker originated this phrase is disputed. For the claim that the phrase is Margaret Irwin's, see Stuart N. Clarke, "squares where all the couples are triangles," *Virginia Woolf Miscellany*, fall 2017/winter 2018, no. 92, p. 49.

93 As Jimmy saw it JVS, *PH*, pp. 272–78.

93 "We discussed copulation" VW, "Old Bloomsbury" (1921/22) in *The Bloomsbury Group: A Collection of Memoirs and Commentary*, ed. Stanford Patrick Rosenbaum (Toronto: University of Toronto Press, 1995), p. 54.

93 At meetings S. P. Rosenbaum, *The Bloomsbury Group Memoir Club*, ed. James M. Haule (Basingstoke: Palgrave Macmillan, 2014).

93 Nicolson was married On Nicolson, Norman Rose, *Harold Nicolson* (London: Jonathan Cape, 2005); James Lees-Milne, *Harold Nicolson: A Biography*, 2 vols. (London: Chatto & Windus, 1980, 1981).

93 He was also in love On Nicolson and Mortimer, Rose, *Harold Nicolson*, pp. 137–41.

93 "demi-gods" JVS to Raymond Mortimer [RM], 9 March [1930], RM Papers, Box 3, folder 35.

93 "Glad you had Jimmy" Vita Sackville-West [VSW] to Harold Nicolson [HN], 7 Nov. 1927, quoted in Lees-Milne, *Harold Nicolson*, vol. 1, p. 326.

94 **Harold Nicolson's recklessness** JVS to RM, 4 Oct. 1926, RM Papers, Box 3, folder 35.

94 **"simply fatal"** JVS to RM, 3 Feb. nd [1930], RM Papers, Box 3, folder 35.

94 **"bad practices"** Robert McCormick to Joseph Patterson, 5 May 1928, Patterson Papers. Quoted in Hamilton, *Journalism's Roving Eye,* p. 198. On the controversy about JVS's reporting from the Vatican, see George Seldes, *Witness to a Century* (New York: Ballantine, 1987), ch. 24.

94 **"not one of the fils"** JVS to Edward Sackville-West [ESW], 28 June ny [1929], Vincent Sheean Papers—Berg Collection, New York Public Library; also JVS to RM, Vienna nd [1929], RM Papers, Box 3, folder 35.

94 **In the 1920s and 1930s** George Chauncey, *Gay New York: Gender, Urban Culture, and the Making of the Gay Male World, 1890–1940* (New York: Basic Books, 1994); Matt Houlbrook, *Queer London: Perils and Pleasures of the Sexual Metropolis, 1918–1957* (Chicago: University of Chicago Press, 2006).

94 **Bisexuality was a term** Steven Angelides, *A History of Bisexuality* (Chicago: University of Chicago Press, 2001).

94 **Even in circles** Brenda S. Helt and Madelyn Detloff, eds., *Queer Bloomsbury* (Edinburgh: Edinburgh University Press, 2016).

94 **"Forgive me if this question"** JVS to Duncan Grant [DG], Friday [postmarked 6 March 1931], Duncan Grant Papers 20078/1—Sheean Box 19 [H62a] [DG Papers], Tate Archive.

94 **If homosexuality** Deborah Cohen, *Family Secrets: Shame and Privacy in Modern Britain* (New York: Oxford University Press, 2013), ch. 5.

94 **"I'm no good"** Quentin Bell to Vanessa Bell, 23 March 1931, CHA/1/58/3/6, Quentin Bell to Vanessa Bell, 1931, King's College Archive Centre, Cambridge.

95 **"the most notorious bugger"** JVS to DG, 3 Sept., nd, DG Papers.

95 **Like Duncan Grant** See JVS to Louise Bryant, 19 June [1922?], Box 7, folder 97, Louise Bryant Papers, Yale Manuscripts & Archives.

95 **He couldn't handle affairs** JVS to Raymond Mortimer, 28 April nd [1935?], RM Papers, Box 3, folder 35.

95 **In the year after Rayna died** Eddy Sackville-West, Visitor Book, Knole.

95 **"rather awful"** Vita Sackville-West to Harold Nicolson, quoted in Nino Strachey, *Rooms of Their Own* (London: National Trust, 2018). On ESW, see Michael De-La-Noy, *Eddy: The Life of Edward Sackville-West* (London: Bodley Head, 1988).

95 **"tiny lap dog"** VW to Jacques Raverat, 24 Jan. 1925, in *The Letters of Virginia Woolf, 1923–1928,* vol. III, eds. Nigel Nicolson and Joanne Trautmann (New York: Harcourt Brace, 1978), p. 155. Apostrophe missing from quote.

95 **No matter how many fires** JVS to Fred Millett, 11 Jan. ny [1931], Millett Papers.

95 **"what the music"** JVS, Jerusalem to ESW, 3 Aug. [1929], JVS, Berg.

95 **"carnal desires"** JVS, Vienna to ESW, 25 Nov. 1929, JVS, Berg.

96 **"Dearest, I love you"** JVS, Jerusalem to ESW, 28 June [1929], JVS, Berg.

96 **"I adore him"** JVS, Vienna to RM, Monday, Vienna, nd [Nov. 1929], RM Papers, Box 3, folder 35.

96 **Eddy told Jimmy** JVS to ESW, 3 Aug. [1929], NYPL; JVS, Athens to ESW, 17 Nov. 1929, JVS, Berg.

96 **"My instability is not only"** JVS, Vienna to Raymond Mortimer, Monday, Vienna, nd [Nov. 1929].

96 **"I'm a constant creature"** JVS to ESW, 3 Aug. [1929], JVS, Berg.

96 **His advance** JVS, *PH,* pp. 342–43. On the subtleties of translating historic values to present-day money, see measuringworth.com.

96 **Sympathetic as he was** JVS, *PH,* p. 335.

96 **In the divvying up** On the Palestine Mandate, among many others, Bernard

Wasserstein, *The British in Palestine: The Mandatory Government and Arab-Jewish Conflict, 1917–1929* (London: Royal Historical Society, 1978); Rashid Khalidi, *Palestinian Identity: The Construction of Modern National Consciousness* (New York: Columbia University Press, 1997); Kenneth W. Stein, *The Land Question in Palestine, 1917–1939* (Chapel Hill: University of North Carolina Press, 2017); Pedersen, *Guardians,* esp. ch. 12, and Susan Pedersen, "The Impact of League Oversight on British Policy in Palestine," in *Palestine, Britain and Empire: The Mandate Years,* ed. Rory Miller (Farnham: Ashgate, 2010), pp. 39–65; Tom Segev, *One Palestine, Complete: Jews and Arabs Under the British Mandate* (New York: Metropolitan Books, 2000); Penny Sinanoglou, *Partitioning Palestine: British Imperial Policy-making at the End of Empire* (Chicago: University of Chicago Press, 2019).

97   **The situation was volatile** Great Britain, Commission on Palestine disturbances of August 1929, and Walter Sidney Shaw, *Report of the Commission on the Palestine Disturbances of August, 1929* (London: H. M. Stationery Office, 1930, Cmd. 3520) [Shaw Report], p. 152; Jacob Metzer, *The Divided Economy of Mandatory Palestine* (Cambridge, UK: Cambridge University Press, 1998), pp. 70–72. Between 1922 and 1928, the Jewish population of Palestine had nearly doubled, a rate of increase that topped even the flow of people to Australia and New Zealand.

97   **Jewish trusts** Kenneth Stein, *The Land Question in Palestine, 1917–1939* (Chapel Hill: University of North Carolina Press, 1984), esp. chs. 1–4.

97   **"distilling fact"** JG to FFG, 8 Sept. nd [1929], JG Papers II, Box 22.

97   **The streets resembled** JVS to ESW, 28 June [1929], JVS Papers, Berg.

98   **Before he arrived in Jerusalem** JVS, *PH,* pp. 337–47.

99   **Jimmy would sit** Interview with Sheean—Obituary, JG Papers II, Box 31.

99   **An Arabic paper** JVS, *PH,* pp. 342–43.

99   **"All my interest"** JVS to ESW, 8 Aug. [1929], JVS Papers, Berg.

99   **On the afternoon of August 14** As recounted in JVS's testimony to the Royal Commission, Minutes of Evidence [*Palestine Commission Evidence*], Sessions of 12 and 13 Nov. 1929, pp. 205–13.

100   **"We have to show"** Testimony, p. 212 (13 Nov. 1929).

100   **"She was inconceivably"** JVS, *PH,* pp. 355–56.

100   **His friend George Antonius** Antonius returned to Jerusalem on the twenty-first of August; see *Palestine Commission Evidence,* vol. 1, pp. 396–99. On Antonius, Susan Silsby Boyle, *Betrayal of Palestine: The Story of George Antonius* (Boulder, Colo.: Westview Press, 2001), p. 158.

100   **"Every day I expect"** JVS, *PH,* p. 360.

101   **Palestine was in the throes** Those were figures, thought Jimmy, that almost certainly understated the Arab casualties. Shaw Report, p. 65. On "racial war," see for example, "British Troops Land in Palestine," *Standard-Speaker* (Hazelton, PA), 27 Aug. 1929, p. 1.

101   **Jewish reporters could not** JVS, *PH,* p. 364. NANA pieces advertised as such. Wire service between Palestine and London was not permitted. Re. censorship— see, too, the claim made by Sir Boyd Merriman that the Government of Palestine asked *The Times* to remove Agronsky as their correspondent "on the ground that he was a Jew." Evidence, 12 Nov. 1929, p. 210. The Shaw Commission thought that censorship had been too lax and recommended more stringent measures.

101   **"Zionist fascisti"** JVS's first NANA story was printed in papers around the country. See, for instance, JVS, "Death Toll at Jerusalem," *Montana Standard,* 26 Aug. 1929, p. 2.

101   **There were irate letters** JVS, *PH,* pp. 375, 380–81.

101   **The paper backed away** *New York World* editorial, quoted in the *Wisconsin Jewish Chronicle,* 13 Sept. 1929, p. 8.

101 "cruel misrepresentations" Letter to the Editor, "The Point of View: The Palestine Tragedy," *Courier Journal* (Louisville, Kentucky), 27 Aug. 1929, p. 6.

101 **Shaken by the screams** JVS, "Witness Describes Butchery of Jews," *Spokane Chronicle*, 27 Aug. 1929, p. 1.

102 "mental derangement" JVS, *PH*, pp. 374–75.

102 "aggressive dangerous" JVS Testimony, 13 Nov. 1929, *Palestine Commission Evidence*, p. 211.

102 "best non partisan" Testimony, 13 Nov. 1929, p. 211.

102 "Do Not Annoy" Interview with Sheean—Obituary, JG Papers II, Box 31.

102 **The allegations** Among others, "Says 'World' Correspondent Turned Anti-Zionist Because of Refusal of Zionist Organization to Grant \$1500," *Jewish Daily Bulletin*, 19 Nov. 1929, with claim that JVS had turned anti-Zionist because the *New Palestine* had withheld a payment of \$1,500.

102 **In a series of mailers** See JG, *CDN* News Cuttings, 1929, JG 1972 Add., Box 42, folder 2.

102 "extreme fascist wing" JG, "Battle Waged Outside Gates of Jerusalem," dateline 5 Sept. 1929, *CDN* News Cuttings, JG 1972 Add., Box 42, folder 2.

102 "In each case" JG, "The Realities of Zionism," *Harper's*, July 1930, p. 210.

103 "all of this exactly comparable" JG, "The Realities of Zionism."

103 "remote experiment plodding" JG, "Bayonets Only Check on Hate of Holy Land," dateline 1 Oct. 1929, *CDN* News Cuttings.

103 "a question with no solution" JG, "Mandate Faces Blank Wall in Arab Hostility," dateline 7 Oct. 1929, *CDN* News Cuttings.

103 "I should like to join" JG to FFG, 18 Sept. 1929, JG Papers II, Box 22.

103 **But in 1929** After the 1929 riots, the Comintern also labeled the Zionists as "fascists," and the Communist Party of America followed suit, with the consequence that Jews in droves left the CPA. See Jacob Hen-Tov, *Communism and Zionism in Palestine During the British Mandate* (New York: Taylor and Francis, 2017 [1974]), pp. 152–53.

103 **The right-wing Zionist leader** Daniel Kupfert Heller, *Jabotinsky's Children: Polish Jews and the Rise of Right-Wing Zionism* (Princeton: Princeton University Press, 2017). Madeleine Tress, "Fascist Components in the Political Thought of Vladimir Jabotinsky," *Arab Studies Quarterly* 6, no. 4 (fall 1984): 304–24. For an emphasis on Jabotinsky's democratic leanings, Eran Kaplan, *The Jewish Radical Right: Revisionist Zionism and Its Ideological Legacy* (Madison: University of Wisconsin Press, 2005).

103 **Jabotinsky's Jewish opponents** Henry Near, *The Kibbutz Movement: A History*, vol. 1: *Origins and Growth, 1909–1939* (London: Littman Library, 1992), p. 169.

103 "Zionism," wrote John JG, "The Realities of Zionism," p. 206.

103 **The Mufti was a fervent** JVS, *PH*, p. 372. For an assessment of the Mufti's role, Philip Mattar, "The Mufti of Jerusalem and the Politics of Palestine," *Middle East Journal* 42, no. 2 (Spring 1988): 227–40.

104 "I've never seen such a thing" JVS to ESW, 22 Sept. [1929], JVS Papers, Berg.

104 **He'd been suffering** JVS, *PH*, pp. 387–89; also JVS to JG, 20 Nov. 1929, JG Papers II, Box 35.

104 "Just a journalist" JVS, *PH*, p. 388.

104 "You did not seem very surprised" *Testimony*, 12 Nov. 1929, p. 207.

105 **No, she hadn't said anything** *Testimony* [Anne Goldsmith], 13 Nov. 1929, pp. 220–23.

105 "I don't think my testimony" JVS to JG, 20 Nov. 1929, JG Papers II, Box 35.

105 "I warn you to be prepared" JVS to Eddy, 25 Nov. 1929, JVS Papers, Berg.

105 **"private vices"** JVS to RM, 17 Nov. 1929; also JVS to RM, Monday, Vienna, nd [1929], RM Papers, Box 3, folder 35.

105 **"I have (don't laugh)"** JVS to RM, 17 Nov. 1929, RM Papers, Box 3, folder 35.

105 **Doubtful as Jimmy was** JVS to RM, Good Friday, 1930, RM Papers, Box 3, folder 35: "The list of causes for the disturbance—even the order of the list— might have been prepared from my own articles."

105 **Drawing on evidence** Shaw Report, p. 4.

105 **It identified as a proximate cause** Shaw Report, p. 155. (Though characterizing the disturbances as an "unbroken" "chain of circumstances" on both sides.)

106 **The conflict's deeper roots** The recommendations of the Shaw Report found expression in the 1930 Passfield White Paper, which proposed sharply curtailing Jewish immigration and land purchases. After fierce lobbying by Chaim Weizmann, among others, who argued that a change in policy would be the end of Zionism, the British government reverted to the status quo.

106 **The Grand Mufti in particular** See, for instance, Pinhas Ofer, "The Commission on the Palestine Disturbances of August 1929: Appointment, Terms of Reference, Procedure and Report," *Middle Eastern Studies* 21, no. 3 (July 1985): 349–61; Martin Kolinsky, "Premeditation in the Palestine Disturbances of August 1929?" *Middle Eastern Studies* 26, no. 1 (Jan. 1990): 26. For a dissenting point of view about the Mufti, Philip Mattar, "The Mufti of Jerusalem and the Politics of Palestine," *Middle East Journal* 42, no. 2 (Spring 1988): 227–40.

106 **By blaming Zionism** Ofer, "The Commission," p. 353.

106 **When the Shaw report** "Vincent Sheean Gives Talk at Sheboygan Club," *Wisconsin State Journal,* 16 Feb. 1930, p. 13; "Vincent Sheean Forum Supper Speaker at Y," *Pittsburgh Press,* 30 March 1930, p. 52; "Palestine Riots Are Blamed on British Policy," *Minneapolis Daily Star,* 26 Feb. 1930, p. 17; "Hold January Meetings," *Pasadena Post,* 15 Jan. 1930, pp. 6, 11.

106 **The Commission's findings** JVS to JG, 8 April nd [1930], JG Papers II, Box 35; also JVS to RM, Good Friday [1930], RM Papers, Box 3, folder 35.

106 **"truths of the most unpleasant"** JVS, "The Palestine Report," *Commonweal,* 30 April 1930, pp. 738, 739.

107 **"Fascists in their own affairs"** JVS to George Antonius, 2 April 1930, Israel State Archives, record group 65, file 1961, quoted in Boyle, *Betrayal,* p. 160.

107 **How would the non-Jewish** JVS to Antonius, 2 April 1930.

107 **"Nearly everywhere I go"** JVS to JG, nd [1930], JG Papers II, Box 35.

107 **Jimmy was the only person** JG to FFG, 18 Sept. 1929, JG Papers II, Box 22.

107 **"amusing beggar"** JG to FFG, 15 Sept. 1929, JG Papers II, Box 22.

107 **It puzzled him** Green Notebook I, 1931, JG Papers II, Box 2.

108 **She'd arrived in time** Xmas card, 1928, folder 64, FFG Papers.

108 **"Now you will have to begin"** Cecil Sprigge to FFG, 11 Oct. 1928, folder 46, FFG Papers.

108 **"I have such a guilty conscience"** Lizette Gunther to JG, 16 Oct. 1927, JG Papers II, Box 6.

108 **Mostly he paced** Jane Gunther with Sally Taylor, TS MS Autobiography of Sorts, JG Papers II, Box 31.

108 **"invariably chosen the fine thing"** Lizette Gunther to JG, nd [1922 or 1924], JG Papers II, Box 6.

108 **His mother had been alarmed** For Lizette's reactions to JG's marriage, see Lizette to JG, 27 Feb. 1927; 7 March 1927; Lizette to Frances, 18 March 1927, JG Papers II, Box 6.

108 **"alarmingly frank"** Lizette Gunther to JG, 25 April 1926, JG Papers II, Box 6.

109 **"Did the nurse"** Green Notebook I, 1931, JG Papers II, Box 2.

109 **"You should have no fear"** Julius Miller, MD, to FFG, 28 Feb. 1929, folder 46, FFG Papers.

109 **In 1900, pneumonia** CDC. 1999. a. Achievements in Public Health, 1900–1999: Control of Infectious Diseases. Morbidity and Mortality Weekly Report. July 30, 1999 / 48(29): 621–29. (Also appeared in *Journal of the American Medical Association* 282, no. 11 (1999): 1029–32) [Online]. Available: cdc.gov/mmwr/preview/ mmwrhtml/mm4829a1.htm. See also Richard Meckel, *Save the Babies: American Public Health Reform and the Prevention of Infant Mortality, 1850–1929* (Baltimore: The Johns Hopkins University Press, 1990); Katherine Eriksson, Gregory T. Niemesh, and Melissa Thomasson, "Revising Infant Mortality Rates for the Early Twentieth Century United States," *Demography* 55, no. 6 (December 2018): 2001–24. CDC. 1999. b. Achievements in Public Health, 1900–1999: Healthier Mothers and Babies. Morbidity and Mortality Weekly Report 48(38): 849–58. [Online]. Available: cdc.gov/mmwr/preview/mmwrhtml/mm4838a2.htm.

109 **"My dear fellow"** Don [Lawder?], *New Yorker,* to JG, 4 Feb. 1929, JG Papers II, Box 6, 1989-001—Pertaining to Frances Gunther.

109 **"There's nothing"** Stephen Bénet to JG, nd [1929], JG Papers II, Box 6.

110 **"It's Judy's day"** FFG to JG, 22 Sept. nd [1929], JG Papers II, Box 22.

110 **He hadn't forgotten** JG, Geneva to FFG, nd [1931?], JG Papers II, Box 23.

110 **"Whenever you do anything grand"** FFG to JG, 22 Sept. nd [1929], JG Papers II, Box 22.

110 **I'd have been so much happier** TS, "Happy New Year," JG Papers II, Box 6.

110 **It was there, in a cottage** Journal of FFG re. JG Jr., Punch. 1929–38, FFG Papers, file 5.

110 **The term referred to the cohort** Craig Monk, *Writing the Lost Generation: Expatriate Autobiography and American Modernism* (Iowa City: University of Iowa Press, 2010).

110 **Hemingway, who made the phrase famous** This is Hemingway's version. Stein's own version was that she heard it from a hotel keeper. Alice B. Toklas, *What Is Remembered,* p. 54, cited in Morris, *Gertrude Stein Has Arrived,* p. 55.

110 **"grown up to find all Gods"** F. Scott Fitzgerald, *This Side of Paradise* (New York: A. L. Burt Co., 1920), p. 304.

111 **Cowley's 1934 memoir** As Cott demonstrates, it was the revised and reprinted 1951 edition that proved influential. See Nancy Cott, "Revisiting the Transatlantic 1920s: Vincent Sheean vs. Malcolm Cowley," *American Historical Review* 118, no. 1 (Feb. 2013): 46–75; Blower, *Becoming Americans,* ch. 6.

111 **In his roster** Included first in the 1951 ed. (Cowley, *Exile's Return,* pp. 311–16).

111 **For them, the 1930s marked** Blower, *Becoming Americans,* esp. pp. 213–16, 236–41.

111 **How an uprising against British rule** JVS, "The Japanese View of the World: How It Led to War, and How It Affects the Efforts for a Peace That Will Endure," *Redbook* 86, no. 1 (Nov. 1945): 23.

CHAPTER SIX

115 **In Italy, Mussolini** For a contemporary account, H. R. Knickerbocker, *Can Europe Recover?* (London: John Lane, 1932), esp. chs. 7–11.

116 **"the revolver muzzle"** See, for instance, 7 April 1921, *Newark Ledger,* HRK Papers, Scrapbook #3.

116 **Any errors** Knick to Maederlund [Berlin editor of the *Stockholms Dagblad*], 11 Jan. 1931, HRK Papers, Uncatalogued correspondence, Box 2, 1931 file.

116 **No movies, though** Emily Z. Friedkin to Alexander Woollcott, 21 May 1933, HRK Papers, Catalogued correspondence, Box 1.

116 **Now he wanted perspective** Friedkin to Woollcott; "A Texas Globe-Trotter," *Kansas City Times,* 22 Nov. 1938, p. 2; also HRK Papers, Box 5, "Libel Suit, 1949" folder.

116 **He wrote with a vinegary** For the police court imagery, George Seldes, "Our Journalistic Noblesse," *Nation,* 25 March 1936, pp. 375–76.

116 **Then he put in a couple** Knick to Maederlund, 11 Jan. 1931.

116 **They'd met as undergraduates** "Knickerbocker-Patrick," Wedding Announcement, *Georgetown Sun,* May 1918, HRK Papers, Scrapbook in Flat Box 307; Correspondence File, 1927, Uncatalogued correspondence, Box 1.

116 **At a briefing** Kurth, *American Cassandra,* p. 105.

117 **Knick figured** Recounted in Mowrer, *Journalist's Wife,* pp. 248–50. Mowrer doesn't name the cabaret but notes that the sign outside read HIER IST RICHTIG, which identifies it as the El Dorado.

117 **The cabaret scene** Mowrer, *Journalist's Wife,* p. 250.

117 **"He is tied up"** JG to FFG, nd [1930?], JG Papers II, Box 22.

117 **Laura had been operatically** Notes for Indian Sign, JG Papers 1972 Add., Box 5, folder 1.

117 **When Conrad was two** Passenger list, SS *Karlsruhe,* Bremen to New York, arrival 26 May 1931, ancestry.com.

117 **She went to Topeka** Rev. H.D. Knickerbocker to HRK, 26 Oct. 1932, HRK Papers, Uncatalogued correspondence, Box 3, folder 1932.

117 **After she'd gone, Knick hired** Notes for Indian Sign.

118 **He'd never let himself love** Green Notebook II, 1931–4, JG Papers II, Box 2.

118 **If he were a tribesman** Green Notebook II.

118 **The son of a Southern Methodist** "Who is Knickerbocker?" *Glasgow Sunday Post,* 2 Oct. 1939, HRK Papers, 1939 Scrapbook [#30].

118 **Knick sat in the rear** "Eine Unterredung mit Edzard," *Weser-Zeitung-Bremen,* dateline 15 Aug. 1927, HRK Papers, Scrapbook #4.

118 **In the summer of 1930** H. R. Knickerbocker, *The Soviet Five-Year Plan* (London: J. Lane, 1931), p. 8.

118 **He'd be gone for two months** HRK, *Soviet Five-Year,* p. 27.

118 **She insisted on changing** HRK, *Soviet Five-Year,* pp. 124, 134.

118 **Really, she told Knick** HRK, *Soviet Five-Year,* p. 128.

119 **"and then adopt"** HRK, *Soviet Five-Year,* p. 242.

119 **"let the worthy capitalists"** Quoted in Robert C. Tucker, *Stalin in Power: The Revolution from Above, 1928–1941* (New York: Norton, 1990), p. 92.

119 **Looking at the windows** HRK, *Soviet Five-Year,* p. 20.

119 **Three years earlier** HRK, *Soviet Five-Year,* p. 9.

119 **The wait for a government-made** HRK, *Soviet Five-Year,* p. 25.

119 **The rest had tattered** HRK, *Soviet Five-Year,* p. 11.

119 **"colossal coercive savings plan"** HRK, *Soviet Five-Year,* p. 240.

119 **In Moscow, cynics** HRK, *Soviet Five-Year,* pp. 60–61.

119 **The furnaces** HRK, *Soviet Five-Year,* p. 64.

120 **Unlike Knick, many of them** David C. Engerman, *Modernization from the Other Shore: American Intellectuals and the Romance of Russian Development* (Cambridge, Mass.: Harvard University Press, 2004), p. 155; Mickenberg, *American Girls.*

120 **As many as eight million** Engerman, *Modernization,* esp. chs. 8 and 9; Timothy Snyder, *Bloodlands: Europe Between Hitler and Stalin* (New York: Basic Books, 2010).

120 **The people were hungry** Walter Duranty, "Russians Hungry But Not Starving," *NYT,* 31 March 1933.

120 **Duranty has become known** On Duranty, Taylor, *Stalin's Apologist;* Engerman, *Modernization;* Rodgers, *Assignment,* ch. 3; James William Crowl, *Angels in Stalin's Paradise: Western Reporters in Soviet Russia, 1917 to 1937, a Case Study of Louis Fischer and Walter Duranty* (Lanham, Md.: University Press of America, 1982), esp. ch. 6.

120 **"glorifying steel and kilowatts"** Louis Fischer, Untitled essay in *The God That Failed: Six Studies in Communism,* ed. Richard Crossmann (New York: Bantam Books, 1959 [1949]), p. 189.

120 **Fischer was enchanted** Engerman, *Modernization,* ch. 9; also Fischer, *Men and Politics,* pp. 187–203.

121 **"Zeal and terror"** HRK, *Soviet Five-Year,* p. 237.

121 **"Skepticism in Bolshevik Russia"** HRK, *Soviet Five-Year,* pp. 238–39.

121 **"nothing short of horrible"** HRK to Julian Mason, 18 Nov. 1930, HRK Papers, Uncatalogued correspondence, Box 1.

121 **During the run of Knick's** Oswald Villard, "Knickerbocker's Red Menace," *Nation,* 3 June 1931, HRK Papers, Scrapbook, Flat Box 308.

121 **"Stalin's Mother Talks!"** HRK Papers, Scrapbook in Flat Box 308.

121 **"What does this mean"** HRK Papers, Scrapbook in Flat Box 308.

121 **In 1931, Knick won** Knickerbocker came close to winning the Pulitzer the following year as well (for his "Fighting the Red Trade Menace" series, but the jury recommended against selecting him since he'd won the 1931 award). Crowl, *Angels,* p. 144.

121 **But after 1930 the Press Office** On the reporting of Ralph Barnes and William Stoneman in the North Caucasus early in 1933, see Stoneman, Unpub. Autobiography, pp. 17–18, Box 1, Bentley Library.

122 **Even as Moscow-bound** On Gareth Jones, Margaret Siriol Colley, *More Than a Grain of Truth* (Newark, UK: Nigel Linsan Colley, 2005); Ray Gamache, *Gareth Jones: Eyewitness to the Holodomor* (Cardiff: Welsh Academic Press, 2013); Ray Gamache, "Breaking Eggs for a Holodomor: Walter Duranty, the *New York Times,* and the Denigration of Gareth Jones," *Journalism History* 39, no. 4 (January 2014): 208–18.

122 **"reliability and impartiality"** H. R. Knickerbocker, "Famine Grips Russia, Millions Dying, Idle on Rise, Says Briton," *New York Evening Post,* 29 March 1933, p. 1. Unlike Edgar Mowrer, who also broadcast Jones's account, Knick offered this endorsement of Jones's bona fides and quoted extensively from Jones's own statement. See Mowrer, "Russian Famine Now as Great as Starvation of 1921, Says Secretary of Lloyd George," *CDN,* 29 March 1933, p. 2.

122 **"mostly bunk"** Walter Duranty to HRK, 27 June 1933, HRK Papers, Catalogued correspondence, Box 1.

122 **"to put it brutally"** Duranty, "Russians Hungry."

122 **"I'm a reporter"** Walter Duranty, *I Write as I Please* (New York: Simon & Schuster, 1935), pp. 166–67.

122 **In May 1930** On the circle of foreign reporters in Vienna and Austria in the early 1930s, Waldemar Zacharasiewicz, *Transatlantic Networks and the Perception and Representation of Vienna and Austria Between the 1920s and 1950s* (Vienna: Austrian Academy of Sciences Press, 2018), esp. ch. 3 on Gunther and Shirer.

122 **His editors praised him** See, for instance. Hal O'Flaherty to JG, 29 Nov. 1929; Wallace R. Deuel to JG, 11 Nov. 1929, JG Papers II, Box 5—Correspondence *Chicago Daily News,* pre-1930 through 1932.

122 **"reflect human nature"** Charles H. Dennis to JG, 31 Jan. 1930, JG Papers II,

Box 5—Correspondence *Chicago Daily News,* 1930 file. On Dennis's preferences for color stories, Heald, *Transatlantic Vistas,* pp. 102–3.

123 **It was said** See, among others, JG, "Viennese Life Is Famous for Its 'Quiddities'" and "Groschen Used in Many Ways," both *CDN,* datelines 14 Jan. 1932 and 13 Jan., 1932 Clippings, JG Papers 1972 Add., Box 43, folder 1.

123 **Blame the *Föhn*** JG, "Austria—The Willing Virgin," nd [1930?], JG Papers 1972 Add., Box 44, folder 4.

123 **Where had the legendary** JG, "Where Are the Viennese Beauties," *CDN,* 7 Jan. 1931, 1931 Clippings, Box 42, folder 5.

123 **Sometimes the whole place** JG, Original draft of Lived on Earth (*Ring Round*), JG Papers 1972 Add., Box 30, folder 7.

123 **Remember, Walter Duranty told John** Quoted in JG, London Diary, 28 Dec. 1936, JG Papers II, Box 23a.

123 **John's editor chimed in** Charles H. Dennis to JG, 16 Sept. 1930, JG Papers II, Box 5, Correspondence *Chicago Daily News,* pre-1930 through 1932 and Charles H. Dennis to JG, 31 Jan. 1930, Correspondence *Chicago Daily News,* 1930.

123 **"They are free"** JG, "Hungary Tense in Demands for More Territory," *CDN,* dateline 25 Aug. 1930, JG Papers 1972 Add., Box 42.

124 **"I wish I could get over being"** JG to FFG, nd [1930?], JG Papers II, Box 22.

124 **From the start of their relationship** See, for instance, Frances's appraisal of *The Red Pavilion,* "F. Notes," JG Papers II, Box 6, Pertaining to Frances Gunther.

124 **Politics bored him stiff** Green Notebook I, 1931, JG Papers II, Box 2.

124 **If you're going to understand** FFG, diary entry, 31 Aug. 1937, FFG Papers, file 7.

124 **And then there was the fact** Her phrase was "moral feeling"—FFG to JG, Sept. 1930, JG Papers II, Box 22.

124 **"What the hell"** JG to FFG, "Sunday," [labeled 1931 but possibly 1930], JG Papers II, Box 22.

124 **Try as he might** Green Notebook I, 1931; also M. W. Fodor to Brock Baker, JG Papers II, Box 2.

124 **People, all sorts of people** For a description of JG's technique and the cushion metaphor, Brock Baker's interview with Lee Miller, 4 Jan. 1975, JG Papers II, Box 2.

124 **Most mornings** M. W. Fodor to Brock Baker, 17 Nov. 1975, JG Papers II, Box 2; Author interview with Denis Fodor, Munich, 20 March 2016.

125 **A smattering of turpentine and flax brokers** Original draft of Lived on Earth (*Ring Round*), JG Papers 1972 Add., Box 30, folder 7; TS on Viennese coffee-houses, 1930, JG Papers 1972 Add., Box 44, folder 4.

125 **There was an aroma** JG, Original draft of Lived on Earth (*Ring Round*). More generally on the Imperial, also Walther F. Ziehensack, *Hotel Imperial* (Vienna and Hamburg: Paul Zsolnay, 1979).

125 **The Austrian elections** JG, "Heimwehr Plans March on Vienna with 100,000 Men," *CDN,* dateline 20 Oct. 1930, JG Papers 1972 Add., Box 42, folder 4.

125 **Two months earlier** Volker Ullrich, *Hitler: Ascent, 1889–1939,* trans. Jefferson Chase (New York: Knopf, 2016), p. 229.

125 **"Let's give a sound thrashing"** Ullrich, *Hitler: Ascent,* pp. 231–32.

125 **When the ballots** Ullrich, *Hitler: Ascent,* p. 232.

125 **But Austria was different** See, for instance, M. W. Fodor, *South of Hitler* (Boston: Houghton Mifflin, 1939 [1937]), chs. 1, 17; M. W. Fodor to W. P. Crozier, 22 May 1933, *Guardian* Archive, 208/67a-67d. On the transnational influence of paramilitaries, Robert Gerwarth, "The Central European Counterrevolution: Paramilitary Violence in Germany, Austria and Hungary After the Great War," *Past & Present* 200 (2008): 175–209.

126 **Outside of Moscow** Fodor, *South of Hitler,* ch. 15; Helmut Gruber, *Red Vienna: Experiment in Working-Class Culture, 1919–34* (New York: Oxford University Press, 1991).

126 **Much more important was the so-called Heimwehr** Walter Wiltschegg, *Die Heimwehr: Eine unwiderstehliche Volksbewegung?* (Munich: R. Oldenbourg, 1985).

127 **"Our poor little Owstria"** JG, *Lost City,* p. 153. For this and other samples of Fodor's conversation, JG Papers 1972 Add., Box 29, folder 1.

127 **In the afternoons** Dan Durning, "Vienna's Café Louvre in the 1920s and 1930s: Meeting Place for Foreign Correspondents," Feb. 2012, scribd.com/doc/8122 3692/Vienna-s-Cafe-Louvre-in-the-1920s-1930s-Meeting-Place-for-Foreign -Correspondents.

127 **They sent the news home** Nationalist leaders such as Gandhi rightly saw the American correspondents, with their talk of freedom and hatred of territorial conquest, as natural allies against the imperialist British and French. Lyons, ed., *We Cover the World,* p. 15. On Shirer's interviews with Gandhi, see William Shirer, *Gandhi: A Memoir* (New York: Simon & Schuster, 1979), p. 26. Also Bill Shirer to Tess Shirer, 28 March 1931, Letters to Tess, William L. Shirer Papers [Shirer Papers], George T. Henry College Archives, Stewart Memorial Library, Coe College; Shirer to Spykman, 5 Feb. 1932, Correspondence, India—1930–1932. See Chandrika Kaul, *Communications, Media and the Imperial Experience: Britain and India in the Twentieth Century* (Basingstoke, UK: Palgrave Macmillan, 2014), 71–122.

127 **The British and French papers** Hohenberg, *Foreign,* pp. 164–67, 175.

127 **Bill Shirer** JG to Charles Dennis, 18 June 1930, JG Papers II, Box 24; Brock Baker's Interview with Leonora Hornblow, 10 Dec. 1975, JG Papers II, Box 2.

127 **Dorothy, of course** Sanders, *Dorothy Thompson,* pp. 175–77.

127 **It was like living amid a detective** DT, "Writing Contemporary History," *Saturday Review of Literature,* 20 May 1939, p. 13.

128 **"Yugoslavia?. . . The dictatorship"** JG, *Lost City,* p. 113. See also Junius Wood, "Do Dictators Die in Bed?," in Lyons, *We Cover the World,* pp. 181–201.

128 **"Stalin? A lump"** JG, *Lost City,* p. 234.

128 **It was a professional vice** Negley Farson, *A Mirror for Narcissus* (Garden City, N.Y.: Doubleday, 1957), p. 42.

128 **"Most of the putsch talk"** Ignaz Seipel, the Conservative politician, quoted in JG, "Austrian Vote Eyed for Gain in Fascism," *CDN,* dateline 3 Nov. 1930, JG Papers 1972 Add., Box 42, folder 4.

128 **In the spring of 1931, a little less** See Brock Baker's interview with Fodor; JG, "Vienna Announces Union; Czechs Register Protest," *CDN,* dateline 21 March 1931, JG Papers 1972 Add., Box 42, folder 6.

129 **Desperate to prevent** On the collapse of the Credit-Anstalt, Aurel Schubert, *The Credit-Anstalt Crisis of 1931* (Cambridge, UK: Cambridge University Press, 1991); for a revisionist account of international efforts to rescue the Credit-Anstalt, Nathan Marcus, *Austrian Reconstruction and the Collapse of Global Finance, 1921–1931* (Cambridge, Mass.: Harvard University Press, 2018), ch. 8.

129 **The French now had the leverage** Iago Gil Aguado, "The Creditanstalt Crisis of 1931 and the Failure of the Austro-German Customs Union Project," *Historical Journal* 44, no. 1 (March 2001): 199–221.

129 **In November, the city's leading** *Arbeiter-Zeitung,* 21 Nov. 1931. JG's first article about the bribery scandal, "Credit Anstalt Plunged into Publicity Scandal," is datelined 23 Nov. 1931, JG Papers 1972 Add., Box 42, folder 6.

129 **He and Bill Shirer** Bill Shirer to Col. McCormick, nd [1932] 1930s file, Dated Correspondence, 1920s through 1939, Shirer Papers. According to Shirer, though

Best and Miss Marion McGimsey were listed in the Credit-Anstalt's ledgers, neither turned out to be guilty. For "stink," see JG to Paul Mowrer, 21 Jan. 1932, JG Papers II, Box 5, Correspondence *Chicago Daily News,* pre-1930 through 1932. Also JG, "Austria Pushed Inquiry into Press Bribery," *CDN,* dateline 19 Dec. 1931, JG 1972 Add., Box 42, folder 6; JG to Eric Phipps, 28 Dec. 1931, JG Papers II, Box 5.

130 **He was working fifteen-hour** Green Notebook II, 1931–4.

130 **In John's fictionalized version** "Notes for Ring Around Vienna," JG Papers 1972 Add., Box 29, folder 1.

130 **"caused, personally"** JG, "Note on New Novel. Projected Title: KISS THE HAND," Brandt & Brandt Records, Box 1, Special Collections Research Center, Syracuse University Libraries.

130 **Rather, John put his hero** Printer's copy of *Ring Round Vienna,* JG Papers 1972 Add., Box 32, folder 3.

130 **Why didn't he try his luck** Green Notebook I, 1931.

131 **"Do you think we ought to miss"** FFG to JG, nd, [Sept. 1931 in pencil], JG Papers II, Box 23.

131 **When he returned, he typed up** FFG to JG, 28 Jan. 1931, JG Papers II, Box 23.

131 **"Gee, we're getting too fond"** Green Notebook I, 1931.

131 **This apartment** FFG to Tess Shirer, nd [1932], Dated Correspondence, 1920s through 1939, Shirer Papers.

131 **They turned the hallway** Journal of Frances Gunther re. JG Jr., Punch, FFG Papers, file 5.

131 **They threw parties** JG to Charles Dennis, 28 Nov. 1930, JG Papers II, Box 24; also Swing in *Problems of Journalism,* p. 93.

131 **In addition to the other reporters** JG, "Dateline Vienna," *Harper's,* July 1935; M. W. Fodor to Brock Baker, 17 Nov. 1975, JG Papers II, Box 2.

132 **While he was gone** See Aug. 31, 1937, 14 Dec. 1937 diary entries, 1937/8 Diary, FFG Papers, file 7; Cuthbertson, *Inside Gunther,* pp. 114–16.

132 **She didn't seem to mind** Green Notebook II, 1931–34.

132 **Bill was chasing** Agnes Knickerbocker, TS memoir.

132 **She'd done it in Vienna** JG to FFG, 21 Oct. 1932, JG Papers II, Box 4, Clips from Diaries—Category: Frances Gunther: Not Used.

132 **She'd been using her** FFG to JG, nd [1932], JG Papers II, Box 23.

132 **As many as a fifth** Leslie Reagan, *When Abortion Was a Crime: Women, Medicine, and Law in the United States, 1867–1973* (Berkeley: University of California Press, 1998), p. 23. Estimates ranged from 10 percent to 23 percent.

132 **During the Depression** Reagan, *When Abortion,* ch. 5.

132 **Abortion increasingly figured** See Meg Gillette, "Modern American Abortion Narratives and the Century of Silence," *Twentieth-Century Literature* 58, no. 4 (Winter 2012), esp. 665–67.

132 **"It wasn't sin"** Floyd Dell, *Janet March,* p. 213, cited in Gillette, "Modern American Abortion Narratives," p. 672.

132 **Helen Hahn made reference** Green Notebook I, 1931; "Graven Images of False Gods," FFG Papers, file 103.

132 **When Helen's sister** Helen & Mickey Hahn for a Story, JG Papers II, Box 2.

133 **"Feeling better!"** Emily Hahn to JG, Paris, nd, JG Papers II, Box 34.

133 **My darling, my darling** JG to FFG, 21 Oct. 1932; JG to FFG, 6 Nov. 1932, JG Papers II, Box 23.

133 **What an unspeakably awful** JG to Bill and Tess Shirer, 21 Oct. 1932, Dated correspondence, 1932 file, Shirer Papers. The Shirers left Vienna for Spain after the mercurial Colonel McCormick fired Bill from the *Chicago Tribune.*

133 Jimmy Sheean thought the expression JVS, *PH,* p. 304.

133 The larger problem See JVS, *PH,* pp. 280–81.

134 Where Jimmy was drawn to causes On Hemingway's annoyance with the political Johnny-come-latelies, Blower, *Becoming Americans,* pp. 236–37. On his disdain for politics, Stephen Cooper, *The Politics of Ernest Hemingway* (Ann Arbor: UMI Research Press, 1985).

134 His novel, *Gog and Magog* JVS called it a "young man's novel"—"the autobiographical outburst, ending in Byronic despair" in his own appraisal, JVS to RM, Monday, Vienna, nd [Nov. 1929], RM Papers, Box 3, folder 35.

134 "The whole thing" JVS to ESW, 2 Feb. 1930, JVS Papers, Berg. Though a "wooden, morose-looking boy named Gary Cooper" counted as consolation of sorts.

134 "Clara Bow Marshmallow" JVS, "I'll Take an Apple," *New Republic,* 2 April 1930, pp. 190–92.

134 Unlike the repentant For example, Harold Stearns, "Apologia of an Expatriate," *Scribner's Magazine,* March 1929, pp. 338–41; Waldo Frank, "I Discover the New World," *Harper's,* Jan. 1926, pp. 204–10.

134 A tour JVS to RM, 30 Sept. (Tues), ny [1931?], RM Papers, Box 3, folder 35.

135 He'd started posing JVS to DG, nd [postmarked 4 March 1931], DG Papers.

135 "you have shoved your nose" ESW to DG, Private, 26 Feb. [1931], DG Papers 20078/1—Sheean Box 19 [H62].

135 "Surely you and I can" JVS to DG, Saturday, ny [1931]; on Lovatelli, JVS to DG, Saturday morning [4 April 1931], DG Papers.

135 "'Sophie would be furious!'" JVS to DG, Thursday [postmarked 12 March 1931], DG Papers.

135 "God! How I waste my time" JVS to DG, Saturday [postmarked 15 March 1931], DG Papers.

135 "I can't stand it" JVS to DG, nd [1931], cited in Frances Spalding, *Duncan Grant: A Biography* (London: Chatto & Windus, 1997), p. 308.

135 The fact that Duncan cried JVS to DG, nd [April/May 1931], DG Papers.

135 "You know how I am" JVS to DG, nd [1932], DG Papers.

CHAPTER SEVEN

136 No amount of money See DT to SL, undated [Feb. 1931], DT Papers, Box 47; also Agnes Knickerbocker, TS memoir, Private Collection.

136 The two men nearly JG, Green Notebook II, 1931–4, JG Papers II.

136 "Has interviewed Lloyd George" *Who's Who,* vol. 18, 1934–1935, ed. Albert Nelson Marquis (Chicago: A. N. Marquis Co., 1934), p. 1035.

137 If you worked for Hearst David Nasaw, *The Chief: The Life of William Randolph Hearst* (Boston: Houghton Mifflin, 2000), pp. 387–88, 470–75.

137 But by the same token Trotsky to HRK, 6 Jan. 1939, HRK Papers, Catalogued correspondence, Box 1.

137 These figures had managed JVS, *PH,* pp. 141–42, 203–4.

137 Nor had liberals or conservatives devoted On the significance of the individual to the age of revolutions, David Bell, *Men on Horseback: The Power of Charisma in the Age of Revolution* (New York: Farrar, Straus and Giroux, 2020); also David Bell, "Donald Trump Is Making the Great Man Theory of History Great Again," *Foreign Policy,* foreignpolicy.com/2017/01/12/donald-trump-is-making-the-great-man-theory-of-history-great-again/. On the counterexample of Karl Lueger, Brigitte Hamann, *Hitler's Vienna: A Dictator's Apprenticeship,* trans. Thomas Thornton (New York: Oxford University Press, 1999), pp. 204–33.

137 In that sense, they were interchangeable When Woodrow Wilson arrived for the

Paris Peace Conference, he seemed likely to break that mold. However, the fact that Wilson so quickly disappointed the hopes vested in him, leaving a hornet's nest of nationalisms as his legacy, tended to diminish rather than enhance the idea of the individual's motive force. Erez Manela, *The Wilsonian Moment: Self-Determination and the International Origins of Anticolonial Nationalism* (New York and Oxford: Oxford University Press, 2007), esp. chs. 3 and 4; John Milton Cooper, *Breaking the Heart of the World: Woodrow Wilson and the Fight for the League of Nations* (Cambridge, UK: Cambridge University Press, 2001).

137 **"authority of personality"** Quoted in Ullrich, *Hitler: Ascent*, p. 230. More generally, on the cult of personality, Frank Dikötter, *How to Be a Dictator: The Cult of Personality in the Twentieth Century* (New York and London: Bloomsbury, 2019); Ruth Ben-Ghiat, *Strongmen: Mussolini to the Present* (New York: Norton, 2020).

137 **"nearly everything"** H. R. Knickerbocker, *Is Tomorrow Hitler's? 200 Questions on the Battle of Mankind* (New York: Reynal & Hitchcock, 1941), p. 14.

138 **He disliked interviews** Hans V. Kaltenborn, "An Interview with Hitler," 17 August 1932, *The Wisconsin Magazine of History* 50, no. 4 (Summer 1967): 283.

139 **Dorothy had been petitioning** DT, *"I Saw Hitler!"* (New York: Farrar & Rinehart, 1932), p. 3. [This booklet is a reprint of the article first published in *Cosmopolitan* in March 1932.] On Putzi, Peter Conradi, *Hitler's Piano Player: The Rise and Fall of Ernst Hanfstaengl, Confidant of Hitler, Ally of FDR* (New York: Carroll & Graf, 2004).

139 **Like "a vampire"** Quoted in Kurth, *American Cassandra*, p. 142.

139 **In the pages** SL and DT, "Is America a Paradise for Women?" *Pictorial Review*, June 1929, pp. 14, 15, 54, 56, quote at 56.

139 **Many of the people she met** DT, "Poverty De Luxe," *Saturday Evening Post*, 2 May 1931, p. 6.

140 **"startling insignificance"** DT, *I Saw*, p. 3.

140 **"I Saw Hitler!"** DT, *I Saw*, pp. 13–14.

140 **"I bet he crooks"** DT, *I Saw*, p. 14.

140 **"What will you do"** DT, *I Saw*, p. 17.

140 **"agitator of genius"** DT, *I Saw*, p. 29.

140 **"If Hitler comes into power"** DT, *I Saw*, pp. 23, 36.

140 **"comico-terrible gaffe"** JG to Miss Ford, 12 Sept. 1963, JVS Papers, WHS, Box 2, folder 9—Correspondence about Dorothy and Red. This memo setting out errors in the manuscript of Dorothy & Red was written to Ford but intended for JVS.

141 **He'd been traveling around Germany** HRK's series, "Behind the German Smoke Screen," ran in papers in January and February 1932, published as *The German Crisis* (New York: Farrar & Rinehart, 1932).

141 **Courtesy of Putzi** Address of Mr. H. R. Knickerbocker before the Palm Beach Round Table on World Affairs, 3 Feb. 1940, HRK Papers, Box 5, folder 1; for the newspaper report of the 1932 interview, HRK, "Behind the German Smoke Screen," *Green Bay Press Gazette*, 3 Feb. 1932, p. 1. Also described in *German Crisis*, ch. 22; see also Ernst Hanfstaengl, *Hitler: The Missing Years* (New York: Arcade, 1994 [1957]), p. 175.

141 **"Mr. Knickerbocker is perhaps"** "Germany's Future," *New Statesman and Nation*, HRK Papers, Scrapbook in Flat Box 308.

142 **In the years that followed** Kurth, *American Cassandra*, pp. 162, 193.

142 **So livid was the Nazi leader** Kaltenborn, "An Interview," pp. 284–85.

142 **If Hitler ever did** Michael March, "Page After Page," *Brooklyn Citizen*, 5 March 1932, p. 12.

142 **The Italian dictator liked** Kaltenborn, "An Interview," p. 283; also John T. Whittaker, *We Cannot Escape History* (New York: Macmillan, 1943), pp. 57–59. More

generally, on Mussolini's appeal to American correspondents, Mauro Canali, *La scoperta dell'Italia: Il fascismo raccontato dai corrispondenti americani* (Venice: Marsilio, 2017).

142 **He made a point of seeing** Anthony F. Ambrogi, "The Marketing of Mussolini: American Magazines and Mussolini, 1922–1935," MA thesis, University of Richmond, 2006, pp. 38–41, 50–51.

142 **"Your statements on my general thesis"** HRK to Mussolini, 29 July 1932, HRK Papers, Catalogued Correspondence, Box 1.

142 **The room on the other side** H. R. Knickerbocker, *Can Europe Recover?* (London: John Lane, 1932), p. 140.

143 **"Benevolent, agreeable"** HRK to Percy Winner, 10 Aug. 1932, HRK Papers, Uncatalogued correspondence, Box 3—folder 1932–3.

143 **"And what do you think"** HRK to Barry Faris, 24 Sept. 1934, Catalogued Correspondence [Mussolini file], Columbia.

143 **"No man has a better grasp"** HRK, "Ten Years of Peace Seen by Mussolini Who Upholds Austria," *Lancaster New Era*, 26 Feb. 1934, p. 11.

143 **"I hope nobody interprets"** HRK to Renaud, 8 Aug. 1932, HRK Papers, Uncatalogued correspondence, Box 3—folder 1932–3.

144 **Expelled by Stalin** On Trotsky's paid interviews, Jean van Heijenoort, *With Trotsky in Exile: From Prinkipo to Coyoacán* (Cambridge, Mass.: Harvard University Press, 1978), p. 34.

144 **Before John could see Trotsky** JG, "Trotsky at Elba," *Harper's*, April 1933, pp. 587–97.

145 **"the thing that made an overwhelming"** JG, "Trotsky at Elba," p. 589.

145 **"Will the capitalist system"** JG, "Japan, Backed by France, Aims at War with Russia, Says Trotsky in Interview," 1932 *CDN* Clippings, JG Papers 1972 Add., Box 43.

145 **"a packet of dynamite"** JG, "Trotsky at Elba," p. 587.

146 **When he slept** van Heijenoort, *With Trotsky,* pp. 18, 20.

146 **"A genius in the sense"** JG, "Trotsky at Elba," p. 587.

146 **"couldn't be explained by any rationalization"** JG, "Trotsky at Elba," p. 588.

146 **Most newspapermen** JG, Broadcast about Raymond Swing, 26 Sept. 1942 in JG Papers II, Box 35.

146 **Stories of reporters** On the role of newspapermen in the Kellogg-Briand Pact, see JG, "Funneling."

147 **Why wouldn't they just write** See, for instance, the Frances character in JG, *Lost City* (New York: Harper & Row, 1964), p. 41.

147 **"Why should these powerful people"** FFG to JG, 14 July 1932, JG Papers II, Box 23.

147 **She'd been working on a play** FFG, "Mothers and Lovers," FFG Papers, file 307.

147 **She helped John with his work** See, for instance, JG to Lloyd Lewis, 12 May 1932, JG Papers II, Box 24, folder labeled Some *Chicago Daily News* letters.

147 **The London *News Chronicle*** FFG apparently started work on the *News Chronicle* in the spring of 1932, though it's difficult to pinpoint for certain because her articles weren't always signed. She worked for the *News Chronicle* until 1935.

148 **Of course, there was Johnny** Journal of Frances Gunther re. JG Jr., FFG Papers, file 5.

148 **"But Mama"** Green Notebook II.

148 *Alle drei lieb haben* Journal of Frances Gunther re. JG Jr.

148 **"My Experiment in Johnny"** FFG, folder 130, FFG Papers.

149 **"I am a Penelope writer"** Green Notebook II.

149 "**premature emission**" FFG, Dream diary, Journals of FFG re. dreams and psych. case studies, ca. 1930s FFG Papers, folder 8.

149 "**I loathe it unendurably**" JG to FFG, 20 Nov. nd [1931?], FFG Papers, file 174.

149 "**The End of Bourgeois Morality**" DT to Rose Wilder Lane, 28 June 1932, Rose Wilder Lane Papers; Kurth, *American Cassandra*, p. 183.

149 **She briskly dissected** DT, "All the King's Horses," *Saturday Evening Post*, 6 Aug. 1932.

149 "**the college professor**" DT, "Why Call It Post-War—A Study in Illusion," *Saturday Evening Post*, 23 July 1932, p. 7.

150 "**The only international**" DT, "The Gray-Squirrel Complex," *Saturday Evening Post*, 20 Feb. 1932, p. 6.

150 **To point up the idiocy** DT, "Gray-Squirrel Complex," p. 97.

150 "**complicated by profound**" DT, "Will Gangs Rule the World?" *Saturday Evening Post*, 16 July 1932, p. 64.

150 "**Any group of more than six**" DT, "Why Call It Post-War," *Saturday Evening Post*, 23 July 1932, p. 56.

150 "**She always was a diligent**" Junius Wood to JG, 22 July 1934, JG Papers II, Box 35.

151 "**all the smut and slime**" JG to FFG, 23 April 1932, JG Papers II, Box 23.

151 "**a cuckoo clock in aspect**" Sinclair Lewis, quoted in Sheean, *Dorothy and Red*, p. 171.

151 **Promising tobogganing** Roosevelt's title was minister to Hungary, as the country wasn't yet deemed worthy of an ambassadorial position.

151 **The party on the Semmering** Sheean, *Dorothy and Red*, pp. 172–73; also JG to Miss Ford, 12 Sept., JVS Papers, WHS, Box 2, folder 9—Correspondence about Dorothy and Red; JG to Mark Schorer, JG Papers, Box 35.

151 **What was beyond dispute** Green Notebook II.

151 **Frances was taking notes** "Dorothy," FFG Papers, file 18; JG to DT, 16 May 1932, JG Papers II, Box 35.

151 **By that point, there were** Whit Burnett to JG, 6 June 1933, JG Papers II, Box 5; also "Aw, Run Yer Own Errands," *Reading Times*, 17 May 1933, p. 10, among many other papers.

151 "**This year, sometimes I've thought**" FFG, "Dorothy," Dreams, Diary Notes, 1930s–1950s, FFG Papers, file 18.

152 "**I must save myself**" DT to SL, 25 March 1933, Box 48, DT Papers; Kurth, *American Cassandra*, p. 183.

152 **When she was pregnant** JVS, *Dorothy and Red*, p. 146. She didn't check in, fearing that her signature on the guestbook would yield a publicity storm.

152 "**will not let men swallow**" DT Diary, 9 Sept. 1927, Sept. 1927 to Feb. 1928 Diary, DT Papers, Box 59, folder 2.

152 **Having once disdained** DT to RWL, 15 July 1921, Rose Wilder Lane Papers; on DT and intergenerational hostility, Phyllis Bottome and Dorothy Thompson, *The Depths of Prosperity* (New York: Doran, 1925).

153 "**But do you *feel* stifled?**" Quoted in Green Notebook II.

153 "**as incestuous as white mice**" JG, "Slaughter for Sale," *Harper's*, May 1934, p. 652.

153 "**Aren't you impressed**" FFG to Jerry Frank, 5 Jan. 1934, Jerome Frank Papers, Box 12, folder 95, Yale Manuscripts and Archives.

153 **Following a succession** Although the Nazis in 1932 won the largest number of votes in Germany, between the July and November elections, the party's percentage of the vote declined, from 37 percent to 33 percent.

153 **Arriving in a rush** Marcia Davenport, *Too Strong for Fantasy* (London: Collins, 1968), p. 170.

153 **"It is a shocking catastrophe"** JG to Bullitt, 7 March 1933, William C. Bullitt Papers, Group No. 112, Series No. 1, Box 34, folder 787, Yale Manuscripts and Archives.

154 **"as if they were bolts"** JG, "Hitler Opens Campaign with Stirring Talk," *CDN*, 11 Feb. 1933, 1933 cuttings, JG Papers 1972 Add., Box 43.

154 **"childish, hysterical"** JG to FFG, nd [Feb. 1933], JG Papers II, Box 23.

154 **"See all the outs"** FFG to JG, 14 Feb. 1933, Box 22.

154 **"charming fellow"** JG to FFG from Berlin, nd [Feb. 1933], JG Papers II, Box 23.

154 **More useful were the meetings** For Putzi's version, Hanfstaengl, *Hitler*, pp. 95, 99.

154 **He might even be able** JG to FFG, nd [Feb. 1933]; HRK to Barry Faris, 24 Sept. 1934, HRK Papers, Catalogued correspondence, Box 1; JG, "Notes About Hitler," JG Papers I, Box 5, folder 13; JG's Notes from conversation with Knickerbocker, Putzi Hanfstaengl, Feb. 1933, Box 6, folder 13.

155 **But, Putzi, you play** JG's Notes from conversation with Knickerbocker, Putzi Hanfstangel, Feb. 1933, JG Papers I, Box 6, folder 13.

155 **"It is a glorious victory"** Quoted in JG to Bullitt, May 11, 1933, JG Papers II, Box 34.

155 **If she hadn't seen the consequences** DT to Harriet Cohen, 18 March 1933, quoted in Kurth, *American Cassandra*, p. 187.

156 **Then they met every night** DT, "Nazi Murder-Torture Reign Leaves Bloody Hospital Trail," *Jewish Daily Bulletin*, 7 May 1933, pp. 1, 2, 11; also DT, "Our Foreign Correspondents and How They Work" and "Pall Mall Broadcast, 1 March 1938," DT Papers, Box III, folder 3.

156 **"utterly to destroy German Jewry"** DT, "Starve, Humiliate, Degrade the Jew in Every Walk, Trade, Profession, Nazi Pressure in Law and Slogan," *Jewish Daily Bulletin*, 14 May 1933, p. 1.

156 **"Most discouraging of all"** DT to SL, 13 March [1933], DT Papers, Box 48, folder 1.

156 **"pure inventions"** "German Jewry Makes Denial," *Los Angeles Times*, 25 March 1933, p. 3. The April 1, 1933, retaliatory boycott of Jewish businesses that Goebbels was planning proceeded despite the statements.

156 **"There remains, therefore, a single agency"** DT, "Nazi Murder-Torture Reign," pp. 1, 2.

157 **After Knick's blistering series** HRK, "600,000 Jews in Germany Are Classed as People Without a Country," *Pittsburgh Post-Gazette*, 13 April 1933.

157 **The purpose was to demonstrate** HRK to Morrison, 12 June 1933, HRK Papers, Uncatalogued correspondence, Box 4, folder 1933–2; also Andrew Nagorski, *Hitlerland: American Eyewitnesses to the Nazi Rise to Power* (New York: Simon & Schuster, 2012), pp. 123–25.

157 **In Memphis** JG to Bullitt, 11 May 1933, JG Papers II, Box 34.

157 **"The Nazi press"** HRK to Mr. Morrison, 7 Feb. 1933, HRK Papers, Uncatalogued correspondence, Box 3, folder 1932–3.

157 **The Nazis expelled Soviet reporters** The British correspondent was Noel Panter, the *Telegraph* correspondent.

157 **The Mowrers woke up** JG to Bullitt, 11 May 1933. On Mowrer's reporting about brutality toward Jews, Nagorski, *Hitlerland*, p. 106.

157 **What chance** Benjamin Carter Hett, *Burning the Reichstag: An Investigation into the Third Reich's Enduring Mystery* (New York and Oxford: Oxford University Press, 2014).

158 **"With dreadful pertinacity"** JG, *Inside Europe*, p. 44; JG, "Arson de Luxe: The Riddle of the Reichstag Fire," *Harper's*, Oct. 1933; Hett, *Burning the Reichstag*, pp. 140–74.

158 **In his closing statement** In 1935, Louis Fischer took JG to see Dimitrov in Russia. "I remember your face. I watched you from the prisoners' box. The sympathy on the faces of the foreign correspondents was encouraging," Dimitrov told JG. See Fischer, *Men and Politics*, p. 404.

158 **"Tell them in America"** JG, "Germany Too Controversial for Comfort," dateline 1 Nov. 1933, *CDN*, 1933 Clippings, JG Papers 1972 Add., Box 43.

158 **Unable to muster an armed challenge** JG, "Germans Tell Woes in Two Little Songs," dateline 1 Nov. 1933, *CDN*, 1933 Clippings, JG Papers 1972 Add., Box 43.

159 **Worst of all was the situation** Ullrich, *Hitler: Ascent*, pp. 329–30, 348.

159 **"more diversified"** Hal O'Flaherty to JG, 16 Sept. 1933, JG Papers II, Box 5, Correspondence the *Chicago Daily News*, 1933 file. On the *Daily News*'s coverage of the rise of the Nazis (comparing it to the *NYT* and the *Tribune*), Gary A. Klein, "The American Press and the Rise of Hitler, 1923–1933," unpub. Ph.D. thesis, London School of Economics, 1977 see esp. pp. 219–30, 241–45, 256–58, 295–307.

159 **"lost sight of our major purpose"** Hal O'Flaherty to JG, 10 Oct. 1933, JG Papers II, Box 24, folder labeled Some *Chicago Daily News* letters.

159 **It's become commonplace** Deborah E. Lipstadt, *Beyond Belief: The American Press and the Coming of the Holocaust* (New York: Free Press, 1986); Laurel Leff, *Buried by the Times: The Holocaust and America's Most Important Newspaper* (New York and Cambridge: Cambridge University Press, 2005).

159 **Having fallen for the propaganda** On the reports of the Armenian genocide, Michelle Tusan, "'Crimes Against Humanity': Human Rights, the British Empire, and the Origins of the Response to the Armenian Genocide," *American Historical Review* 119, no. 1 (Feb. 2014): 47–77.

159 **In the face of hot Nazi denials** Hal O'Flaherty to JG, 10 Oct. 1933, Gunther Papers, Addenda II, Box 24, 1989-002, folder labeled Some *Chicago Daily News* letters.

159 **New York Times, historians** Leff, *Buried*, pp. 19–48.

159 **Yet to follow the articles of Thompson** Ron Hollander, "*We Knew:* America's Newspaper Report the Holocaust," in *Why Didn't the Press Shout? American & International Journalism During the Holocaust* (Jersey City: Yeshiva University Press, 2003), pp. 41–49; Klein, "American Press," ch. 7.

160 **"There must be two sides"** A. L. Delin, "Footnotes on Headlines," *Montclair Times*, 14 April 1933, p. 10; also "Assert Nazis Made Victims of Unfairness," *Edmonton Journal*, 6 May 1933, p. 24.

160 **The reporters' dilemma** DT, "Nazi Murder-Torture Reign," pp. 1, 2, 11.

160 **"Sure, I say, so it is"** DT to JG and FFG, 3 April [1933], JG Papers II, Box 35.

160 **"I lie awake nights"** DT to SL, 1933, DT Papers, Box 48, folder 1.

160 **No, she and Red weren't divorcing** Harry Salpeter, "Dorothy Thompson, Safe from Nazis, Is Home to Find City Agog over Her," *Jewish Daily Bulletin*, 14 May 1933, p. 2. It was during this trip that Walter Winchell offered up the divorce rumor. However, as Peter Kurth notes, rumors about an impending divorce were common through the 1930s. See, for instance, Kurth, *American Cassandra*, p. 184.

160 **Just as her notebooks** See Kurth, *American Cassandra*, pp. 176, 193.

161 **In 1933, there were tens of thousands** Gerwarth, "The Central European Counterrevolution."

161 **"Did you hear the new one"** JG, Green Notebook II.

162 **"so many rumors of Putsches"** JG to Bill and Tess Shirer, 28 March 1933, Shirer Papers, John Gunther File, Named Correspondence, D–L.

162 **"One must not have any illusions"** Fodor to W. P. Crozier, 22 May 1933, *Guardian* Archive, 208/67a–67d.

162 **Dollfuss was at heart** On the tradition of seeing Dollfuss as a conservative, not a

fascist, Jill Lewis, "Conservatives and Fascists in Austria, 1918–1934," in *Fascists and Conservatives,* ed. Martin Blinkhorn (London: Unwin Hyman, 1990), pp. 98–117; for a reevaluation of the Dollfuss regime and Austrofascism more generally, Ilse Reiter-Zatloukal, Christiane Rothländer, and Pia Schölnberger, eds., *Österreich 1933–1938: interdisziplinäre Annäherungen an das Dollfuss- / Schuschnigg-Regime* (Vienna: Böhlau, 2012); Florian Wenninger and Lucille Dreidemy, eds., *Das Dollfuß/Schuschnigg-Regime 1933–1938. Vermessung Eines Forschungsfeldes* (Vienna: Böhlau, 2013); Emmerich Tálos, *Das Austrofaschistische Herrschaftssystem* (Vienna: LIT Verlag, 2013); Tim Kirk, "Dictatorship, Fascism and the Demise of Austrian Democracy" in Günter Bischof, Anton Pelinka, and Alexander Lassner, eds., *The Dollfuss/Schuschnigg Era in Austria: A Reassessment* (New Brunswick, N.J.: Transaction Publishers, 2003).

162 **The police tracked** Fodor to Crozier, 29 Sept. 1933, *Guardian* Archive, 209/228.

162 **Several months after Dollfuss** DT to JG and FFG, 14 June 1932, JG Papers II, Box 35.

162 **John looked over at Fodor** On JG's irritation, foreword to M. W. Fodor's *Plot and Counterplot in Central Europe* (Boston: Houghton Mifflin, 1937), p. xiv.

162 **But what could Fodor** JG wrote about the visit to Spital on six occasions: in two articles published in the *CDN,* datelined 30 May 1933; in the foreword to M. W. Fodor's *Plot and Counterplot,* p. xiv (where he discusses the surprise visit); in "Has Hitler a Mother Complex," *Vanity Fair,* Sept. 1934, pp. 17–18; in *Inside Europe,* pp. 20–24; and in his Vienna roman à clef, *The Lost City* (New York: Harper & Row, 1964), p. 410. Fodor's article ran in the *New-York Evening Post* on 13 June 1933.

163 **"No, we don't hear from him"** JG, "Hitler's Kinfolk in Austria Just Plain Farmers," *CDN,* dateline 30 May 1933, 1933 Clippings, Box 43.

163 **"Oh go on . . . !"** JG, "Hitler's Mother Once a Servant of His Father," *CDN,* dateline 30 May 1933.

163 **John's German wasn't good enough** Fodor to W. P. Crozier, 14 July 1933, *Guardian* Archive, 209/37a-37c.

164 **"She told Adolf he must be"** JG, "Has Hitler a Mother Complex," *Vanity Fair,* Sept. 1934, p. 18.

165 **Imagine: little Adolf** Fodor to W. P. Crozier, 14 July 1933. For a discussion of Hitler's lineage, Hamann, *Hitler's Vienna,* pp. 6–22, 34–38.

165 **"I tell you the truth"** See JG's account of his conversation with Fodor after the Spital trip, in *Lost City,* p. 410.

165 **"There are many extraordinary things"** JG, "Hitler's Mother Once a Servant of His Father."

166 **"It is simply that I have admired"** JG to Freud, 22 June 1933, JG Papers II, Box 34.

166 **"His wife spoke of him"** JG, "Charming Wife Presides over Freud's Home," *CDN,* dateline 10 Oct. 1932, 1932 Clippings, JG Papers 1972 Add., Box 43.

CHAPTER EIGHT

167 **Frances had been urging** FF to JG, 21 April 1925, JG Papers II, Box 22; on asthma, Green Notebook II.

167 **Where does the shoe** Wilhelm Stekel, *Technique of Analytical Psychotherapy,* trans. Eden and Cedar Paul (New York: Liveright, 1950 [1938]), pp. 9, 45.

167 **Just entering a room** JG Papers 1972 Add., Box 29, folder 6, Early Draft, *Ring Round.*

167 **But there were other problems** Green Notebook II. See also Stekel, *Technique,* p. 47.

167 **Here is how we shall** On Stekel's techniques, including the trial period, the dream book, and the pledge of no discussion while the analysis was ongoing, Stekel, *Technique,* pp. 26, 50, 63.

168 **"I have never heard of a crime"** Quoted in Wilhelm Stekel, MS Autobiography, p. 5, Kinsey Institute, 925.2 St8a. (Deposited by John Gunther.)

168 **That was the way Stekel told** Stekel, MS Autobiography, pp. 137, 152.

168 **"Stekel is going his own way"** Stekel, MS Autobiography, pp. 154–55; summarized in the published *Autobiography,* ed. Emil A. Gutheil (New York: Liveright, 1950), pp. 244–49. See also Philip Kuhn, "'A Pretty Piece of Treachery'": The Strange Case of Dr. Stekel and Sigmund Freud," *The International Journal of Psychoanalysis,* vol. 79, no. 6 (Jan. 1998): 1151–71.

169 **Painful as it was for him** Stekel, *Technique,* p. xvii, quote at 1166.

169 **Stekel didn't take on a patient** Stekel, MS Autobiography, pp. 145, 224.

169 **"not a kissing-game"** Stekel, MS Autobiography, pp. 213, 220, 221.

169 **Stekel's method** Stekel, *Technique,* chs. 1 and 2.

169 **John filled up his green notebooks** Gunther Papers, Addenda II, Box 4, 1989-001—Clips from Diaries—Category: Frances Gunther: Not Used.

169 **"Darling, please screw me"** Green Notebook I.

170 **"If you don't"** Green Notebook II.

170 **"Frances is certainly the most intelligent"** Green Notebook I.

170 **He'd known her for nine years** Green Notebook II.

170 **Her wit and her brightness** Green Notebook I.

170 **"So, I'm wrong!"** Notes for Novel, "Made in Heavens," 1931, JG Papers II, Box 30.

170 **When it came to choosing a dessert** Green Notebook II.

170 **She could hardly scramble** Ken Cuthbertson, Interview with Judith de Mille Donelan, 23 March 1987.

170 **She was never on time** Clips from Diaries—Category: Frances Gunther: Not Used. JG Papers II, Box 4.

170 **"A tremendous paradox"** Green Notebook I.

170 **"My diaries get nothing of F's delicacy"** Green Notebook I.

170 **He also left out the habits** See, among others, Cuthbertson, Interview with William Shirer, 10 Nov. 1986, cited in *Inside,* p. 193; Brock Baker's Interview with Lee Miller, 4 Jan. 1935, JG Papers II, Box 2.

170 **"let go"** Mickey Hahn to JG, 10 Sept. ny [1938], JG Papers II, Box 34.

170 **"was a B-I-T-C-H"** Peter Kurth interview with Lilian Mowrer, quoted in Kurth, *American Cassandra,* p. 177; Brock Baker's Interview with Anthony West, 2 May 1975, London, JG Papers II, Box 2.

170 **"You've got to feel strongly"** FFG, diary entry, 31 Aug. 1937, FFG Papers, file 7.

171 **It was one of his strengths** JG to FFG, Russian Log, 26 June 1928, JG Papers II, Box 2; *Ring Round Vienna* Galley, JG Papers 1972 Add., Box 32, folder 4.

171 **Preserving the public's trust** See Schudson, *Discovering the News,* esp. chs. 3 and 4, esp. his point about objectivity as an "ideology of the distrust of the self" (71). More generally, on objectivity: Richard L. Kaplan, *Politics and the American Press: The Rise of Objectivity, 1865–1920* (Cambridge, UK: Cambridge University Press, 2002); Dan Schiller, *Objectivity and the News: The Public and the Rise of Commercial Journalism* (Philadelphia: University of Pennsylvania Press, 1981); David T. Z. Mindich, *Just the Facts: How "Objectivity" Came to Define American Journalism* (New York: New York University Press, 1998). Before the *Times* adopted the motto, "All the News That's Fit to Print," it advertised itself with the slogan, "It Will Not Soil the Breakfast Cloth." Elmer Davis, *History of the New York Times, 1851–1921* (New York: New York Times, 1921), p. 218.

171 **But if impartiality** Schudson, *Discovering,* pp. 121–59.

171 **The rise of the syndicated political** Schudson, *Discovering,* p. 145.

171 **Reporters, argued the journalist** Lippmann, *Liberty and the News,* pp. 48–49, 77–82, 87–89; *Public Opinion,* pp. 343–44, 359–62. On the significance of psychology to Lippmann's theories, Tom Arnold-Forster, "Walter Lippmann and American Democracy" (unpub. Ph.D. thesis, Cambridge University, 2018, esp. ch. 1). See also John Chamberlain, "Personal Historian," *New Republic,* 2 Aug. 1939, pp. 367–68.

171 **According to the publisher** Alan Brinkley, *The Publisher: Henry Luce and His American Century* (New York: Knopf, 2010), chs. 4 and 5, esp. pp. 93–94; W. A. Swanberg, *Luce and His Empire* (New York: Scribner, 1972), pp. 141–43.

172 **Foreign correspondents** See, for example, Mowrer, "The *Chicago Daily News'* Foreign Service"; Raymond Gram Swing, comment, "The Big News in Europe, What It Means and How to Get It," 13th Convention of the American Society of Newspaper Editors, 18–20 April 1935, in *Problems of Journalism* (Washington, D.C.: American Society of Newspaper Editors, 1935), p. 92.

172 **They were permitted** JG, 17 Dec. 1936 Diary, London Diary, JG Papers II, Box 19, p. 23. For a contrary case, Kevin L. Stoker, "The Journalist Who Interpreted Too Much: The New York Times' Courtship, Defense, and Betrayal of John W. White," *Journalism & Communication Monographs* 19, no. 3 (2017): 177–236. See also Walter Lippmann, "The Press and Public Opinion," *Political Science Quarterly* 46 (June 1931): 161–70.

172 **With the exceptions of a few partisans** Described by JG in *Ring Round Vienna* Galley, JG Papers 1972 Add., Box 32, folder 4. Yellow press men had often mixed into the events they were covering. For instance, Richard Harding Davis had charged up San Juan Hill in aid of Teddy Roosevelt's Rough Riders. Similarly, there had always been partisans, such as John Reed, suspicious that the vaunted "detachment" was a means of inducing quiescence. *Metropolitan* had hired Reed to cover Pancho Villa's campaign but by the time he departed for Russia (where he took up arms on behalf of the Bolsheviks), only radical papers, such as the *Masses,* would hire him. Hamilton, *Foreign Correspondence,* pp. 52, 105; Robert A. Rosenstone, *Romantic Revolution: A Biography of John Reed* (New York: Knopf, 1975).

172 **Fodor had seen Dollfuss** Fodor to Crozier, 10 July 1933, *Guardian* Archive, 209/24 and 25.

173 **"greatest disappointment in my life"** Fodor to Crozier, 28 Sept. 1933, *Guardian* Archive, 209/226a–226c.

173 **"There is something terribly"** Fodor to Crozier, 29 Dec. 1933, *Guardian* Archive, 210/282a–282b. Similarly, Stefan Zweig, *Die Welt von Gestern: Erinnerungen eines Europäers* (Hamburg: Deutscher Bücherbund, 1964 [1942]), p. 33.

173 **"The Austrian does not think"** John Gunther, "Dollfuss and the Future of Austria," *Foreign Affairs* 12, no. 2 (Jan. 1934): 307.

173 **"curious innocence"** JG, "Dollfuss," pp. 306–7.

173 **"hypnotized sheep"** JG, "Dollfuss," p. 313.

173 **"political darling"** JG, "Dollfuss," p. 307.

174 **"Detectives found a mousetrap"** Knick to Alexander Woollcott, 30 Dec. 1933, Woollcott Papers, bMS Am 1449 (919), Houghton Library, Harvard.

174 **"He is pursuing a courageous"** JG to Colonel Knox, 13 Nov. 1933, JG Papers II, Box 5, Correspondence the *Chicago Daily News,* 1933 file.

174 **"Mr. John GUNTHER"** Bericht der Poldian [Poldich?] an das Bundeskanzleramt, Wien, 19 Jan. 1934: "Die politische Einstellung der anglosächsischen Korrespondenten in Wien," in G.E.R. Gedye Papers, GERG 19, IWM; see also

Anglo-American Press Association of Vienna (Anglo-Amerikanische Presse Vereinigung in Wien), BKA BKA-I BPDion Wien VB Signatur VIII-4355, Archiv der Republik, Österreichisches Staatsarchiv, Vienna [OESt-A]. See G.E.R. Gedye, "Spying on Press in Vienna Bared," *NYT,* 26 June 1934, p. 9.

174 **"One thing is certain"** JG, "Dollfuss," p. 316.

174 **The next month** JG, *Inside Europe,* p. 290; JG, *Lost City,* p. 528. On depictions of the Civil War, Zacharasiewicz, *Transatlantic Networks,* pp. 177–89.

174 **They'd become wary** G.E.R. Gedye, *Betrayal in Central Europe: Austria and Czechoslovakia: The Fallen Bastions* (New York and London: Harper Brothers, 1939), p. 92.

175 **They wouldn't be taken like cattle** JG, "Austria Gripped by Revolt," *CDN,* dateline 12 Feb. 1934, 1934 Clippings, JG Papers 1972 Add., Box 43.

175 **"Tomorrow," Fey proclaimed** JG, *Inside Europe,* p. 289; Gedye, *Betrayal,* pp. 90–91.

175 **Maybe little Dollfuss will keep** JG, *Inside Europe,* p. 325.

175 **She filled the two bathtubs** FFG, "Foreign Affairs at Home," FFG Papers, TS, folder 106.

175 **On the walls of buildings** Gedye, *Betrayal,* p. 95.

175 **Such a thing was unimaginable** Conversation reported by Gedye (possibly with Fodor), *Betrayal,* p. 96.

176 **Zigzagging through the city** Fodor, *South of Hitler,* pp. 220–21.

176 **The ground was a hard crust** Gedye, *Betrayal,* p. 95.

176 **The Socialists had orders** JG, *Inside Europe,* pp. 295–96.

176 **They'd bring in armored tanks** Charles A. Gulick, *Austria from Habsburg to Hitler,* vol. 2: *Fascism's Subversion of Democracy* (Berkeley: University of California Press, 1948), p. 1285.

176 **"John, drive on!"** Fodor, *South of Hitler,* p. 221. (It was not FFG's first experience of civil unrest, as Fodor claims. She was in Vienna in 1927 as well with DT and Sinclair Lewis.)

176 **It was said he was in hock** Gedye, *Betrayal,* p. 47.

176 **"Jewish-Marxist betrayers"** Quoted in Gedye, *Betrayal,* p. 48. See also Ernst Rüdiger Starhemberg, *Between Hitler and Mussolini: Memoirs of Ernst Rüdiger Starhemberg: Former Vice Chancellor of Austria* (London: Hodder and Stoughton, 1942).

177 **On a hot Vienna summer day** Fodor, *South of Hitler,* p. 159; Gedye, *Betrayal,* p. 49.

177 **"In 'the people'"** Gedye, *Betrayal,* p. 48.

177 **"We know that the strength"** Quoted in JG, "Austria Stirred by New Fear of Heimwehr Coup," 1930 *CDN* Clippings, JG Papers 1972 Add., Box 42, folder 4.

177 **To Frances, he seemed a nasty** FG, Notes on Starhemberg, Journal of FFG re: dreams and psych. Case studies, ca. 1930s, FFG Papers, file 8.

177 **"From my experience in fascist countries"** FFG to Mr. Vallance, 10 July 1934, FFG Papers, file 64.

178 **As an intellectual matter** For the *Arbeiter-Zeitung*'s chess editorial, cited in Gedye, *Betrayal,* pp. 97–98.

178 **But in their decency** Cited in JG, *Inside Europe,* pp. 292–93; also see FG, "A Year Ago," *News Chronicle,* 12 Feb. 1935, in BKA-Inneres—316.374/35, OESt-A.

178 **The workers' library, fifteen thousand** Eve Blau, *The Architecture of Red Vienna, 1919–1934* (Cambridge, Mass.: MIT Press, 1999).

178 **But all of that had to be defended** On debates about Austro-Marxism and accommodation to bourgeois politics, see Tim Kirk, "Ideology and Politics in the State No One Wanted: Austro-Marxism, Austrofascism, and the First Austrian Republic," in *Global Austria,* eds. Günter Bischof, Fritz Plasser, Anton Pelinka,

and Alexander Smith (New Orleans: University of New Orleans Press, 2011), pp. 81–98, esp. 84–89.

178 **Much to Fodor's relief** Fodor, *South of Hitler,* p. 221.

178 **John ran the car** JG, "Artillery Fires on Socialists," *CDN,* dateline 13 Feb. 1934, 1934 Cuttings, JG Papers II, Box 43. See also FFG's *News Chronicle* articles, FFG Papers, file 130.

178 **On the radio, there were** Gedye, *Betrayal,* p. 107; JG, *Lost City,* p. 539.

178 **"hyenas to the devil"** Gulick, *Austria,* vol. 2, p. 1291.

179 **How could anyone possibly sleep?** Gedye, *Betrayal,* p. 103.

179 **If you could only have seen** "Note from Vienna," JG Papers II, Box 10, 1926–1937 Clippings; JG, *Inside Europe,* pp. 290–91.

179 **This was the vengeance meted out** JG, "Rumors of Czech and Italian Intervention in Austria Held Unfounded; France Stays Out," dateline 14 Feb. 1934, Clippings, JG Papers II, Box 43.

179 **"Of course even the Heimwehr"** JG to Bill Shirer, 7 March 1934, Shirer Papers, Dated Correspondence, 1920s through 1939.

179 **John now knew why there had** JG, *Inside Europe,* pp. 295–96. Important, too, was the fact that Dollfuss and preceding governments confiscated the Schutzbund's weapons and tended to spare those of the Heimwehr.

179 **They'd chipped away** Gedye, *Betrayal,* p. 95.

180 **The entire thing lasted just** Gedye, *Betrayal,* p. 113. On the battle over casualty statistics, see Winfried R. Garscha, "Opferzahlen als Tabu: Totengedenken und Propaganda nach Februaraufstand und Juliputsch 1934," in Reiter-Zatloukal, Rothländer, and Schölnberger, eds., *Österreich 1933–1938,* pp. 111–28.

180 **In the sewers of Vienna** Gedye, *Betrayal,* p. 104.

180 **Inside one housing project** Fodor, *South of Hitler,* p. 224.

180 **The Socialist Party is dissolved!** JG, *Lost City,* p. 540.

180 **It was that they weren't Bolshevik** See Green Notebook II; FFG, TS "Vienna," FFG Papers, file 129. See Raimund Löw, Siegfried Mattl, and Alfred Pfabigan, *Der Austromarxismus: Eine Autopsie: Drei Studien* (Frankfurt: Isp-Verlag, 1986); Paul Dvořak, "Die Geschichte der österreichischen Sozialdemokratie 1930–1938," in Wenninger and Dreidemy, *Das Dollfuß/Schuschnigg-Regime,* pp. 17–40.

180 **It was rumored that one Schutzbund** On these stories, Gedye, *Betrayal,* p. 102; see also Friedrich Scheu, *Der Weg Ins Ungewisse: Österreichs Schicksalskurve 1929–1938* (Vienna and Munich: Molden, 1972), pp. 147–50, disputing JG's depiction of the Schutzbund.

180 **Austrian officials lodged bitter protests** The Chargé in Austria (Kliefoth) to the Secretary of State, 16 Feb. 1934, 863.00/868: Telegram, FRUS Diplomatic Papers, 1934, Europe, Near East and Africa, vol. II, p. 17.

180 **"atrocity stories"** Gulick, *Austria,* vol. 2, p. 1303.

180 **On one evening in late February** "5,000 Reds Battle with Socialists at Garden Rally," *NYT,* 17 Feb. 1934, p. 1.

181 **"You know how gentle"** JG, "Dollfuss Tells Germany Not to Make Trouble," dateline 22 Feb. 1934, 1934 Clippings, JG Papers 1972 Add., Box 43, folder 5.

181 **"Austro-Bolshevists"** Quoted in "What Lies Behind Austria's Civil War," 27 Feb. 1934, Gedye Papers, Press Cuttings, vol. 11.

181 **And yet the Nazis** FFG, "Vienna," FFG Papers, file 129.

181 **"adults cannot be happily governed"** Rebecca West, *Black Lamb and Grey Falcon,* p. 1111.

182 **After the fighting was done** See *Ring Round Vienna* typescript, JG 1972 Add., Box 29, folder 5. Gedye describes a similar phenomenon, *Betrayal,* p. 103.

182 **"It cannot be too strongly emphasized"** JG, "Rumors of Czech and Italian Intervention in Austria Held Unfounded."

182 **"But you were grand"** Bill Shirer to JG & FFG, nd [1934], Shirer Papers, Dated Correspondence, 1920s through 1939: 1934 file.

182 **John wasn't going to do that** JG, "Autobiography in Brief."

182 **But they'd also become father substitutes** JG, "World 'Authority Complex' Breaks Down, Says Stekel," *CDN,* dateline 10 June 1934, 1934 Cuttings, JG Papers II, Box 43, folder 6.

183 **"Obedience and defiance finally"** JG, "Calls Dictator Substitute for Old Family Authority," *CDN,* 10 June 1934, 1934 Cuttings, JG Papers II, Box 43, folder 6.

183 **When he worked loose an interpretation** On Stekel's methods—*Freud and the Child Woman: The Memoirs of Fritz Wittels,* ed. Edward Timms (New Haven: Yale University Press, 1995), p. 115.

183 **"I am awakened (in my dream)"** Stekel, *Technique,* pp. 242–43.

184 **Not only that, he'd made notes** In his case study, Stekel says that JG made two pages of notes on the story. In his "Books I Have Read" volume, there are brief notes on the Poe collection, and he does comment directly on "The Black Cat." JG appears as well in Stekel's *The Interpretation of Dreams,* vol. 1, trans. Eden and Cedar Paul (New York: Liveright, 1943), pp. 369–71.

184 **He remembered the plot of books** Gunther with Taylor, *Autobiography of Sorts,* p. 4.

184 **Some people's central conflicts lie** Stekel, MS Autobiography, p. 150.

184 **The telephone rang** JG's most detailed narrative of 25 July 1934 (the main points of which were repeated in *Harper's* and in *Inside Europe*) is JG, TS "The Dollfuss Murder: A Personal Narrative," JG Papers 1972 Add., Box 46, folder 3.

185 **By one-thirty, when John arrived** So was the British reporter, G.E.R. Gedye, working for the *New York Times* and the *Daily Telegraph.* On Gedye, Peter Pirker, "'Paradoxia': Wie G.E.R. Gedye Österreich den Anglo-Amerikanern Erklärte," in Joshua Parker and Ralph J. Poole, eds., *Austria and America: Cross Cultural Encounters 1865–1933* (Zürich: Lit Verlag, 2014), pp. 133–70; "Reunion in Vienna," *Time,* 10 Sept. 1945, pp. 60–61.

185 **Outside was a row** [FFG], "Day of Wild Rumours," *News Chronicle,* 28 July 1934, FFG Papers, file 130.

185 **The gates to the Chancellery** Fodor, *South of Hitler,* p. 230.

185 **For the rest of the day** Fodor, *South of Hitler,* p. 231.

186 **"Well, it seems to be all over"** For a photo of the scene, doew.at/erinnern/fotos -und-dokumente/1934-1938/ns-putsch-juli-1934/wien-ravag/doew-foto-968.

186 **A handful of reporters had stuck** Gedye, *Betrayal,* p. 122.

186 **By the time John tried to return** Fodor didn't bother arguing about it; instead, realizing that the number 9 bus line, which traversed the district, was still running, he boarded a bus and jumped off once he was inside the police cordon. Fodor, *South of Hitler,* p. 233.

187 **The ex-sergeant Otto Planetta** Gedye, *Betrayal,* p. 127.

188 **To report the story of Dollfuss's** FFG, "Five Hours of Drama," *News Chronicle,* 26 July 1934, FFG Papers, file 130.

188 **It took him a dozen tries** JG, Memo for Mr. Burnett, July 1942, Archives of *Story* Magazine and Story Press, Box 3, folder 14, Manuscripts Division, Department of Rare Books and Special Collections, Princeton University Library.

188 **As a shriveled corpse** On the effort to turn Dollfuss into a victim of German fascism rather than an architect of Austrian fascism, Lucille Dreidemy, *Der Dollfuß-Mythos: Eine Biographie des Posthumen* (Vienna: Böhlau, 2014); on the role that

Anglo-American commentators played in that process, Florian Wenninger, "Austrian Missions—Das Problem der politischen Äquidistanz der Forschung am Beispiel Austrofaschismus," in Reiter-Zatloukal, Rothländer, and Schölnberger, eds., *Österreich.*

189 **As hundreds of thousands of mourners** JG, "Dollfuss, Dead, Seen as Keeping Nazis from Power," *CDN,* dateline 26 July 1934, JG Papers 1972 Add., Box 43, folder 6. "30,000 Viennese File Past Dollfuss' Bier in Last Farewell," *CDN,* dateline 27 July 1934, JG Papers 1972 Add., Box 43, folder 6. Three hundred thousand people visited the Rathaus to pay their respects to Dollfuss. See *Bulletin of International News,* vol. 11 (1934), p. 87.

189 **"It is the story of an organized conspiracy"** JG, "Policy by Murder," *Harper's,* Nov. 1934, p. 651.

189 **"amazingly fine"** T. [*CDN,* New York Bureau] to JG, 7 Sept. 1934 reporting about the opinion of Gilligan of the *Sun,* which carried the *CDN* cable copy, JG Papers II, Box 5, Correspondence *Chicago Daily News,* 1933–1936.

189 **"distinct contributions"** T. to JG, 7 Sept. 1934.

189 **From Switzerland** Oskar Pollak to JG, 14 Aug. 1934; Oskar Pollak to JG, undated, Correspondence, 1927-1937, P-Z, JG Papers II, Box 5.

189 **She'd never thought much** RW to Harold Ross, 25 Aug. 1947. For one thing, RW wrote, he'd spent far too much time listening to the musings of that "ass" Fodor, whom she called a "propagandist for the defunct Austro-Hungarian Empire."

189 **That was quite good** West, *Black Lamb and Grey Falcon,* p. 836.

189 **John would later say that Stekel** Dedication, Notes for MS *Ring Round Vienna,* JG Papers 1972 Add., Box 29, folder 1; FFG, diary entry, 14 Dec. 1937, FFG Papers, file 7.

190 **"These monsters"** Re. *Inside Europe*—59, More Diary Scraps, H. Luce, Dollfuss etc. Various Dates, JG Papers II, Box 1.

CHAPTER NINE

191 **The entire left-wing press** Goebbels, Diary entries for 13 and 15 Feb. 1933—all diary entries refer to Die Tagebücher von Joseph Goebbels Online, ed Elke Fröhlich (translations my own); Roger Manvell and Heinrich Fraenkel, *Doctor Goebbels* (London: Heinemann, 1960), p. 114; Hale, *Captive Press in the Third Reich* (Princeton: Princeton University Press, 1964). On the Weimar press, Bernhard Fulda, *Press and Politics in the Weimar Republic* (Oxford: Oxford University Press, 2009).

191 **What he hadn't anticipated** Peter Longerich, *Goebbels: A Biography* (New York: Random House, 2015), p. 256.

191 **The reporters needed managing** On Goebbels's identity as a journalist, Simone Richter, *Joseph Goebbels—Der Journalist, Darstellung seines publizistischen Werdegangs 1923 bis 1933* (Stuttgart: Franz Steiner, 2010).

191 **It wasn't enough to print** Longerich, *Goebbels,* pp. 257–58.

192 **"Seen any bodies"** Recounted by Leland Stowe, Unpubl. autobiography entitled The Magnificent Assignment, Leland Stowe Papers Additions, Newberry Library.

192 **You need to cultivate** Manvell and Fraenkel, *Doctor Goebbels,* p. 133; On Ivy Lee's work in Germany, Scott M. Cutlip, *The Unseen Power: Public Relations. A History* (Hillsdale, N.J.: Taylor and Francis, 2013), pp. 148–50; Ray Hiebert, *Courtier to the Crowd: The Story of Ivy Lee and the Development of Public Relations* (Ames: Iowa State University Press, 1966).

192 **He'd whiled away a whole** Goebbels, diary entry, 17 Feb. 1932.

192 **smart and "ice-cold"** Goebbels, diary entry, 10 March 1932.

192 **"squeezed dry like a lemon"** Goebbels, diary entry, 12 March 1932.

193 **So when Rosenberg tried to force** Recounted in George Messersmith to Sec'y of State, Strictly Confidential, 12 May 1933, Messersmith Papers; Knick to Morrison, 15 May 1933, HRK Papers, Uncatalogued correspondence, Box 4—folder 1933 #2; on the animosity between Goebbels and Rosenberg, Viktor Reimann, *Goebbels,* trans. Stephen Wendt (Garden City, N.Y.: Doubleday, 1976), pp. 231–32.

193 **"Herr Minister, would you tell us"** Mowrer, *Triumph and Turmoil,* p. 219. Emphasis mine.

194 **Most prominent among the dead** See Andrew Wackerfuss, *Stormtrooper Families: Homosexuality and Community in the Early Nazi Movement* (New York: Harrington Park Press, 2015); Robert Beachy, *Gay Berlin: Birthplace of a Modern Identity* (New York: Knopf, 2015).

194 **"Hitler whom the world called"** HRK, "Hitler Ruthless, Kills Friend and Foe Alike," Camden *Evening Courier,* 2 July 1934, pp. 1, 4. This was an INS story and not all of the local papers printed the homosexual discussion.

194 **"orgy of malicious agitation"** "Dr. Goebbels Attacks the World's Press," *Daily Telegraph,* 9 July 1934, Gedye Papers—Press Cuttings, vol. 11, IWM.

195 **"very impressed"** Goebbels, diary entry, 11 July 1934.

195 **She'd have to travel** JVS to Ellery Sedgwick, 6 July nd [1934], Ellery Sedgwick Papers, Massachusetts Historical Society.

195 **"I wanted to get away"** DT, "Good-by to Germany," *Harper's,* Dec. 1934, p. 46; see also DT, "Dilemma of a Pacifist," in *Dorothy Thompson's Political Guide* (New York: Stackpole Sons, 1938).

195 **"It is quieter in Germany"** DT, "Good-by," pp. 48, 50.

196 **"Send him up"** DT, "Good-by," p. 51.

196 **On grounds of "national self-respect"** For DT's own account, "Dorothy Thompson Tells of Nazi Ban," *NYT,* 27 Aug. 1934, p. 8.

197 **"is becoming the most comfortable"** "Hitler Called Teuton 'Deity,'" *Salt Lake Telegram,* 27 Aug. 1934, p. 8.

197 **"Apparently, the Germans felt they"** "Woman Writer Says Germany in Prison," *Muncie Evening News,* 27 Aug. 1934, p. 1.

197 **Shut down one foreign correspondent** "Expulsions Futile, Says Miss Thompson," *NYT,* 30 Aug. 1934, p. 13.

197 **While she'd make light of the expulsion** The year before, in the summer of 1933, the threats had been more veiled. The German government could not guarantee Edgar Mowrer's physical safety, the *Chicago Daily News's* proprietors had been told. Mowrer was due to leave Germany anyway, so the paper recalled him a few days early, and the matter was dealt with "informally." At the station, Mowrer loudly announced that he'd be back to Germany when he could return with two million of his countrymen. Mowrer, *Triumph,* pp. 225–26. On British reporters expelled, Will Wainewright, *Reporting on Hitler: Rothay Reynolds and the British Press in Nazi Germany* (London: Biteback Publishing, 2017); on the American press, among other eyewitnesses, Nagorski, *Hitlerland.*

197 **"unreliable and hostile"** HRK to Barry Faris, 18 Nov. 1934, HRK Papers, Uncatalogued correspondence, Box 4, folder 1934.

197 **"are all very sensitive people"** HRK to Barry Faris, 14 Dec. 1934, HRK Papers, Uncatalogued correspondence, Box 4, folder 1934.

197 **Between 1933 and 1939, as many** Vernon McKenzie, cited in Manvell and Fraenkel, *Doctor Goebbels,* p. 137.

198 **"fine mess"** Knick to Faris, 14 Dec. 1934.

198 **"irritatingly straight face"** DT, "The European Pot," *The Saturday Review of Literature,* 16 June 1934, p. 749.

198 **"parasite on honest newspaper men"** DT, "Big News in Europe," *Problems of Journalism,* p. 105; DT, "The European Pot," p. 751.

198 **"An unreasonably vivid attack"** JG, "Blue-Eyed Tornado," p. 7.

198 **What a bitch** DT to HRK, Monday [Aug. 1934], HRK Papers, Catalogued correspondence, Box 1. More measured was Raymond Swing to HRK, 10 Sept. 1934, noting suspicion of Hearst's influence, HRK Papers, Uncatalogued correspondence, Box 4, folder 1933–2.

198 **Knick told their mutual friends** JG, "Blue-Eyed Tornado," p. 7.

198 **She'd been his boss in Berlin** Kurth, *American Cassandra,* p. 487, fn. 62.

199 **"The book made me furious"** DT to HRK, Monday [Aug. 1934].

199 **Back at Twin Farms in the fall of 1934** Sanders, *Dorothy Thompson,* p. 199.

199 **Now that the doctor had finished** FFG to JG, 3 Nov. 1934, JG Papers II, Box 23.

199 **That was the dilemma to which** Stekel, *Interpretation of Dreams,* vol. 2, pp. 369–71.

199 **He was suspicious of people who roamed** Stekel, *Interpretation of Dreams,* vol. 2, p. 317.

200 **"Sit down and write!"** Timms, ed., *Freud and the Child,* p. 117.

200 **"It is never too late"** FFG, Dream diary, FFG Papers, file 8.

200 **Not French or German** Stekel, *The Interpretation of Dreams,* vol. 1, p. 179.

200 **At the critical moment, she felt** Stekel, *Interpretation of Dreams,* vol. 1, p. 178.

201 **Or was he using her?** FFG, Dream diary.

201 **"Danger—you symbolize everything"** FFG, Dream diary.

201 **The very air in America seemed** Citing Lewisohn's "An American Comes Home," in JG, USA Logs, 12 Oct. 1934, JG Papers II, Box 2.

201 **In Chicago, four hundred people** JG, USA Logs, 7 Oct. 1934, 12 Oct. 1934.

201 **Did he want to be** JG, USA Logs, 21 Oct. 1934.

201 **The hotels had immense closets** JG, USA Logs, 14 Oct. 1934, 10 Oct. 1934.

201 **Or "Nuts"** JG, USA Logs, 10 Oct. 1934.

202 **"It isn't twenty or forty"** JG, USA Logs, 25 Oct. 1934.

202 **It was a miracle** JG, USA Logs, 24 Oct. 1934, said to Ernestine Evans.

202 **Maybe Dorothy should bring Stekel** JG, USA Logs, 18 Nov. 1934.

202 **According to Dr. Glueck** JG, USA Logs, 2 Dec. 1934.

202 **He was a debonair liar** FFG to JG, 17 Sept. 1934, JG Papers II, Box 23.

202 **In fact, she was doing all** FFG to JG, 3 Nov. 1934.

202 **"I'm so fed up with it"** FFG to JG, 14 Oct. 1934.

202 **"brain trust"** JG, 12 Oct. 1934, USA Logs.

203 **"I want some more children"** JG, 4 Nov. 1934, USA Logs.

203 **Early in his career, Freud** On the controversy over the "seduction theory," Jeffrey Masson, *The Assault on Truth: Freud's Suppression of the Seduction Theory* (New York: Farrar, Straus and Giroux, 1984) and Janet Malcolm, *In the Freud Archives* (New York: Knopf, 1984); Jean G. Schimek, "Fact and Fantasy in the Seduction Theory: A Historical Review," *Journal of the American Psychoanalytic Association* 35 (1987): 937–65; Han Israëls and Morton Schatzman, "The Seduction Theory," *History of Psychiatry* 4 (1993): 23–59; Bennett Simon, " 'Incest—See Under Oedipus Complex': The History of an Error in Psychoanalysis," *Journal of the American Psychoanalytic Association* 40, no. 4 (1992): 955–88; G. J. Makari, "The Seductions of History: Sexual Trauma in Freud's Theory and Historiography," *International Journal of Psychoanalysis* 79 (1998): 857–69.

203 **"everyday tragedies"** Stekel, *Technique,* p. 301.

203 **There were secret drawers** Stekel, *Technique,* p. 223.

204 **When Frances was thirteen** See FFG, Notes for memoir, Diary 1937, FFG Papers, file 7.

204 **But she had, hadn't she?** Recounted in FFG, Dream Diary, FFG Papers, file 8.

204 **It was a delicate business** Stekel, *Technique,* pp. 122–23.

204 **She hated him for what he'd** Recounted in Stekel, *Interpretation,* vol. 1, pp. 176–78.

204 **Her stepfather had proposed marriage** Stekel, *Interpretation,* vol. 1, pp. 176–78.

205 **The unconsummated act** FFG, diary entry, 12 Feb. 1936 [labeled Journal, 1935], FFG Papers, file 6.

205 **"She faces now reality"** Stekel to JG, 19 April 1935, JG Papers II, Box 35.

205 **"I hope the fight of sexes"** Stekel to JG, 25 May 1935, JG Papers II, Box 35.

206 **Ever since the start** Stekel, *The Autobiography of Wilhelm Stekel,* pp. 242–43; "Spital für Eifersüchtige in Wien eröffnet, Dr. Wilhelm Stekel über die neueste Klinik Wiens," *Der Morgen,* 7 Oct. 1935, p. 6.

206 **"Afraid to write because"** FFG, Dream Diary.

206 **No, he *wasn't* writing** JVS to ESW, 16 April 1934, JVS Papers, Berg; see also JVS to Jamie Hamilton, 8 April nd [1935], JVS Papers, WHS, Box 1, folder 26.

206 **"one person's relationship"** JVS, London to JG, 29 Nov. 1934, JG Papers II, Box 35.

206 **It wasn't purely historical** JVS to JG, 28 March nd [1935], JG Papers II, Box 35. For the argument about titles, JVS Papers, WHS, Box 1, folder 26—Letters to Jamie Hamilton, Jan.–April 1935.

206 **" 'The pale, romantic' "** JVS to ESW, 16 April 1934, JVS Papers, Berg.

206 **"couple of thousand young nincompoops"** JVS, *PH,* p. 9.

206 **"beatific, happy drowsiness"** JVS, *PH,* p. 78.

207 **"place with relation to it"** JVS, *PH,* p. 398.

207 **That was a question that would** See, for instance, JVS correspondence with Ellery Sedgwick, Sedgwick Papers, Carton 12.

207 **If the hubris** Dan A. Cameron, "Weekly Book Review," *The Leader-Post* (Saskatchewan), 3 May 1935, p. 14. Retrospectively, his editor Harry Maule's assessment in John Selby, "Sheean Changed Correspondents' Books," *Democrat and Chronicle,* 26 Sept. 1943, p. 74.

207 ***Personal History* was nothing short** "Business Women Hear Review of Sheean Volume," *Kenosha Evening News,* 16 April 1935, p. 4.

207 **Harold Nicolson had been the one** JVS to RM, 5 Aug. nd [1935], RM Papers, Box 3, folder 35.

208 **Don't worry, he wrote Eddy** JVS to ESW, Sunday [May? 1934], JVS Papers, Berg. Even for the assiduous reader between the lines, Sheean's love affairs with men are well hidden. A stray reference to sexual liberty comes in the discussion of the good things in life that he wouldn't surrender for revolution. There's a brief excursion into the promiscuity of the 1920s indulged in by respectable young people, and the precipitous decline of Victorianism. See *PH,* esp. pp. 310–12.

208 **From the moment it was published** A genre that included Walter Duranty's *I Write as I Please* (1935), Negley Farson's *The Way of a Transgressor* (1936), John Whitaker's *And Fear Came* (1936), and William Shirer's *Berlin Diary* (1941). Between 1932 and 1946, foreign correspondents also furnished the subject for more than forty Hollywood movies. Hamilton, *Journalism's Roving Eye,* p. 230.

208 **The middlebrow reviewers** Fanny Butcher, "Vincent Sheean Reveals Growth of a Philosophy," *Chicago Tribune,* 23 Feb. 1935, p. 8; Harry Hansen, *Midwest Portraits,* p. 199.

208 **So, too, did the most waspishly** Mary McCarthy, "One Man's Road," *Nation,* vol. 140 (1935), pp. 282–83; Malcolm Cowley, "The Long View," *New Republic,* 20 Feb. 1935, pp. 50–51.

208 **The contest between fiction and nonfiction** See, for instance, Keith Hollings-

worth, "In the First Person," *The English Journal* 24, no. 10 (Dec. 1935): 801–7; on "fictionalized biography," Frances Winwar, "Biography Today," *The English Journal* 27, no. 7 (Sept. 1938): 543–55; Stephen Spender, "Confessions and Autobiography," reprinted in James Olney, *Autobiography: Essays Theoretical and Critical* (Princeton: Princeton University Press, 1980); Walton E. Bean, "Is Clio a Muse?" *Sewanee Review* 45, no. 4 (Oct.–Dec. 1937): 419–26.

208 **This was a long trajectory** Alex Clark, "Drawn from Life: Why Have Novelists Stopped Making Things Up," *Guardian*, 23 June 2018, theguardian.com/books/2018/jun/23/drawn-from-life-why-have-novelists-stopped-making-things-up; Marjorie Worthington, *The Story of "Me": Contemporary American Autofiction* (Lincoln: University of Nebraska Press, 2018).

209 **This was much the same point** Philip Rahv, "The Cult of Experience in American Writing," *Partisan Review* 7, no. 6 (Nov.–Dec. 1940): 412–24.

209 **"hysterical yearners"** JVS to RM, 28 April nd [1935], RM Papers.

209 **He'd caught the leftward shift** Michael Denning, *The Cultural Front: The Laboring of American Culture in the Twentieth Century* (London: Verso, 2010); Susman, "The Culture of the Thirties." He'd become, as Mary McCarthy would depict him (and *PH*) in *The Company She Keeps*, the sort of reference a young man on a Pullman dangled in front of an intellectual girl, a lure to pick her up. Mary McCarthy, *The Company She Keeps* (San Diego and New York: Harcourt Brace Jovanovich, 1970 [1942]), pp. 82–83.

209 **"The worst is the dreadful dialect"** JVS to ESW, 9 May 1935, JVS Papers, Berg.

209 **Confessing the tensions of your inner life** On confessions in the 1930s, Cohen, *Family Secrets*, ch. 6.

209 **It was a great decade for egotism** Virginia Woolf, "The Leaning Tower," in *The Moment and Other Essays* (London: Hogarth Press, 1947), p. 120.

209 **Putting the words "Hell"** JVS to RM, 5 Aug. nd [1935], RM Papers, Box 3, folder 35.

209 **Not so Bill Prohme's four-page** JVS to Helen Freeland, 24 Sept. nd [1935?], Frank C. Glass Papers, Box 1, folder 13.

210 **But what arrived was much worse** Bill Prohme to JVS, nd [1935], Box 1, folder 11, Frank C. Glass Papers; from the same file, Bill Prohme to Gracie, 5 Oct. 1935 noting the "complete disagreement between Jimmy and me about what is and what is not permissible, for decent people, in writing about real people with real names."

210 **it was devastating** JVS to Lewis Gannett, 24 Feb. [1936], Lewis Gannett Papers, bMS Am 1888 (1080).

210 **"Eddy dear, don't get"** JVS to ESW, Monday [5 Aug 1935], JVS Papers, Berg.

211 **"I don't have to, not being"** JVS to ESW, 13 July 1935, JVS Papers, Berg.

211 **"I had to go and take several baths"** JVS to RM, 24 July, nd [1935], RM Papers, Box 3, folder 35.

211 **"400 pages—not a single"** FFG to JG, Friday, nd [March 1935], JG Papers II, Box 23.

211 **Knick was very jealous** JG to FFG, 9 May 1935, JG Papers II, Box 23.

211 **Canfield had already considered** Gunther Reminiscences of Cass Canfield, Oral History Research Office, Columbia, 1967, p. 206.

211 **Sure, he'd write it** JG, *Fragment*, p. 7.

211 **He was taken aback when** JG to Hamilton Fish Armstrong, 11 Feb. 1935, Hamilton Fish Armstrong Papers, Box 33, John Gunther file (1), Mudd Manuscript Library, Princeton University Archives; story about Canfield at the hotel related by JG in *Fragment*, p. 8, and in Canfield's oral history, pp. 206–7.

212 **If John were going to tell** For the publisher Ray Long, John had already taken part a few years earlier in a tell-all book, modeled on the bestseller *Washington Merry-Go-Round* about European politics, entitled *Not to Be Repeated*. In his (anonymous) chapters on Austria and the Balkans, he relayed the scandals of the Romanian crown and told tales of the foulmouthed Marshal Piłsudski. Long was a small publisher and the book didn't sell.

212 **"as personal as possible"** Eugene Saxton to JG, 19 May 1934, JG Papers II, Box 29, Harper's Correspondence about *Inside Europe*, 1935.

212 **The only way he'd be able** JG, *Fragment*, p. 9.

212 **Knick was in London** JG to FFG, 9 May 1935, JG Papers II, Box 23.

212 **Knick talked in full paragraphs** Conversation with Knick, nd [1935], JG Papers I, Box 6, folder 14.

213 **Or worse, they were making up** JG to FFG [May 1925]; also JG to FFG, 9 May 1935, JG Papers II, Box 23.

213 **Knick had met Agnes in Berlin** Agnes Knickerbocker, TS memoir, p. 18.

213 **He took her out** Green Notebook II.

213 **You don't *really* believe Agnes** Green Notebook II.

213 **"Why did you make passes"** Green Notebook II.

214 **"destruction will be on a scale"** HRK, "Non-Combatants Will Suffer Barbaric Treatment When Next War Comes," *Akron Beacon Journal*, 15 July 1935, p. 18; HRK, "Panic Declared Worst Menace of Future War," *Nashville Banner*, 17 July 1935, p. 3; HRK, "Nations Unable to See Any Way Out of Carnage," *Minneapolis Star*, 24 July 1935, p. 11.

214 **She was obliged to wire** On the courtship and marriage, Johnson, "Twentieth-Century Seeker," pp. 235–41.

214 **Her father, Sir Johnston** Diana Forbes-Robertson, *Maxine* (London: Hamish Hamilton, 1964), pp. 176–89.

214 **A savvy investor** Forbes-Robertson, *Maxine*, pp. 176–78 on the Morgan rumors and ME's investments.

214 **"I can't see what on earth"** JVS to Eddy, Naples, Thursday [Feb. 1935?], JVS Papers, Berg.

214 **Her eyes were a clear blue** Dorothea Straus, *Showcases* (Boston: Houghton Mifflin, 1974), p. 141.

214 **If Aunt Maxine made** On Dinah's trust fund, JVS to Jane Gunther, nd, early 1960s, JG Papers II, Box 35.

215 **"trembling on the brink"** JVS to ESW, 13 July 1935, JVS Papers, Berg.

215 **"Of course I have to have"** Did he tell All? If so, Dinah may not have fully understood what he was saying. "I only regret he couldn't bring himself to be frank with me (perhaps impossible at first because I was so hideously young and inexperienced)." Diana Forbes-Robertson Sheean to Marshall Best, Viking Press, no date, Private Collection.

215 **"You will like Dinah"** JVS to DG, 11 Oct. nd [1935], Duncan Grant Papers.

215 **"I approve highly of the marriage"** JVS to DG, 11 Oct.; similarly to JG (3 Oct. [1935], JG Papers II, Box 35), to Irita Van Doren (14 Oct. [1935], Irita Van Doran Papers, Box 8).

215 **But he didn't mind, really** JVS to ESW, Monday [23 Sept. 1935], JVS Papers, Berg.

CHAPTER TEN

216 **The reporters loathed** Scheu, *Der Weg*, pp. 96–97.

216 **"As I suspected, this frontal"** FFG to JG, 24 April 1935, JG Papers II, Box 23.

217 **"If every foreign correspondent"** Cecil Gabbertas to FFG, 8 April 1935, FFG Papers, file 64. The throng of unemployed reporters petitioning her to put in a good word for them at the *News Chronicle* made clear what she was losing.

217 **They yammered on** FFG, "Notes on Jugoslav Piece," re. interview with Sir Neville Henderson in Belgrade, JG Papers I, Box 7, folder 18. "He's a very sound Liberal," she wrote of Sir Walter Layton, the editorial director of the *News Chronicle*, "the British Empire comes first, the B.E. comes second, the B.E. comes third, and then comes Liberalism." FFG to JG, 4 Sept. 1934, JG Papers II, Box 23.

217 **"something besides Hmmmm"** Article re. anniversary of Feb. 1934 revolution, FFG Papers, file 129.

217 **"the dullness out of literature"** Evelyn Waugh, *Sunday Times*, 1 Dec. 1952, p. 7, quoted in G. A. Cevasco, "Dame Edith Louisa Sitwell," Oxford Dictionary of National Biography online.

217 **"England is the richest country"** FFG, "An American Flays Us for Our Shortcomings, This England," *Sunday Referee*, 18 Aug. 1935, JG Papers II, Box 6.

218 **"nation of shopkeepers"** An idea originating with Adam Smith, see Peter Mandler, *The English National Character: The History of an Idea from Edmund Burke to Tony Blair* (New Haven: Yale University Press, 2006), p. 136, and on Sitwell's postwar laments, p. 201.

218 **"nauseating deficiencies"** Osbert Sitwell, "England Has Faults, but Can America Crow About This Record?" JG Papers II, Box 6.

218 **"American culture is expressed by jazz"** T. E. Clarke, Clapham, "Home Truths," Letter to the editor, *Sunday Referee*, 25 Aug. 1935.

218 **"The fact that America is selfish, corrupt"** FFG, TS reply, JG Papers II, Box 6.

218 **"I haven't read anything"** Webb Miller to FFG, 19 Aug. 1935, FFG Papers, folder 64. Bill Shirer was similarly complimentary. BS to JG, undated [1935], JG Papers II, Box 5. Raymond Swing thought FFG's attack was unfair, a product of seeing England through Continental eyes. Raymond Swing to FFG and JG, 26 Dec. 1935, JG Papers II, Box 35.

218 **The lease didn't say anything** FFG, "Foreign Affairs at Home."

219 **No way Jimmy Sheean's** Re. Julian Huxley, mentioned in JVS to JG, 24 Jan. ny [1936?], JG Papers II, Box 35.

219 **He pitched a series** Fodor to Crozier, 6 Dec. 1935, *Guardian* Archives, 214/320.

219 **"step on his neck"** JG to FFG, 9 May 1935, JG Papers II, Box 23.

219 **It was in this atmosphere** On the dread of air war, and the summer of 1935 as the initiation of Britain's civil defense efforts, Grayzel, *Age*, ch. 3. On the Italo-Ethiopian War, the British, and the League of Nations, Susan Pedersen, "The Racial Order in Question," Lecture #4, 21 Feb. 2014, The Ford Lectures, Oxford, 2014, academiccommons.columbia.edu/doi/10.7916/d8-m672-1p02; G. Bruce Strang, ed., *Collision of Empires: Italy's Invasion of Ethiopia and Its International Impact* (Surrey, UK: Ashgate, 2013); George Baer, *Test Case: Italy, Ethiopia, and the League of Nations* (Stanford: Stanford University Press, 1976); R.A.C. Parker, "Great Britain, France and the Ethiopian Crisis, 1935–1936," *The English Historical Review* 89, no. 351 (April 1974): 293–332; Michael L. Roi, "'A Completely Immoral and Cowardly Attitude': the British Foreign Office, American Neutrality and the Hoare-Laval Plan," *Canadian Journal of History* 29, no. 2 (Aug. 1994): 331–51.

220 **DUCE, DUCE** JG, "Duce's Ethiopian Adventure Means Profit to Suez Canal," *CDN*, dateline 6 Aug. 1935, 1935 Cuttings, JG Papers II, Box 43, folder 7.

220 **It was the gravest international** JG, "British Cabinet to Meet on Gravest Crisis Since 1914," *CDN*, dateline 20 Aug. 1935, 1935 Cuttings, JG Papers II, Box 43, folder 7.

220 **The prime minister returned early** JG, "British Cabinet Meets, Studies Peace Possibilities," *CDN*, dateline 24 Sept. 1935 and "Britain at Last Seriously Fears War with Italy; 7-to-5 Chance on Start in 2 Months," 1935 Cuttings, JG Papers II, Box 43, folder 7.

221 **But if the correspondents** Baer, *Test Case*, pp. 43–45; Philip Knightley, *The First Casualty: From the Crimea to Vietnam: The War Correspondent as Hero, Propagandist, and Myth Maker* (New York: Harcourt Brace Jovanovich, 1975), pp. 173–89.

221 **The Abyssinians, subject to an arms** HRK, "Ethiopia's War Drums Ready to Sound Mobilization Call," dateline 14 Sept. 1935, HRK Papers, Scrapbook #29, flat box 310.

221 **Keeping the correspondents on his side** The emperor's "most potent ally to date," commented Knick, was the "world press." See "Correspondents Dine with Selassie at Palace Feast," dateline 20 Sept. 1935, HRK Papers, Scrapbook #29.

221 **With the invasion expected any day** On Selassie's new palace "like the villa of a retired Midland magnate," Evelyn Waugh, *Waugh in Abyssinia* (London: Longmans, 1936), p. 133.

222 **"I'll have to knock you"** Recounted in Agnes Knickerbocker, TS memoir, p. 32. See W. F. Deedes, *At War with Waugh: The Real Story of Scoop* (London: Macmillan, 2003).

222 **It wasn't really a serious knockabout** See Deedes, *At War with Waugh.*

222 **"impertinent personal details"** Waugh, *Waugh in Abyssinia*, p. 116.

222 **To the man in Addis** [main title cut off], "Knickerbocker Sends $4945 Figure to Boss for War Incidentals," dateline 21 Dec. 1935, HRK Papers, Scrapbook #29.

222 **They'd secured the emperor's permission** HRK, "Knickerbocker Makes Thrilling Flight over Ethiopian Front to Get First-Hand Report of War," dateline 11 Nov. 1935, HRK Papers, Scrapbook #29.

222 **He was the first reporter** Reporters with Italian forces had seen parts of the battlefield. "How Knickerbocker Scooped World by Secret War Hop Told," *Chicago American*, dateline 27 Dec. 1935; also "Knickerbocker Makes Thrilling Flight over Ethiopian Front to Get First-Hand Report of War," dateline 11 Nov. 1935, "Knickerbocker Gets Thrill After Flight to Find Italians Hit Plane," dateline 14 Nov. 1935, HRK Papers, Scrapbook #29.

222 **Wenlock Jakes** In broad outlines, Jakes is Knick (the highest-paid correspondent, the scoops). But the book Jakes is writing (titled *Under the Ermine*) is a send-up of John's London diary, published in *Nash's Pall Mall Magazine* in 1937 as Waugh was finishing *Scoop*. For Jakes as Knick, Douglas Lane Paley, *The Life of Evelyn Waugh: A Critical Biography* (Cambridge, Mass.: Blackwell, 1998), p. 383, n. 42. On the London diary, ch. 11.

223 **"I am a very bad journalist"** Waugh to Penelope Betjeman, quoted in Donat Gallagher, Ann Pasternak Slater, and John Howard Wilson, eds., *"A Handful of Mischief": New Essays on Evelyn Waugh* (Madison and Teaneck, N.J.: Fairleigh Dickinson University Press, 2011), p. 126.

223 **Waugh had already started home** EW, *Waugh in Abyssinia*, p. 212. He notes that he left before the bombing. Eight months later, he returned to survey the Italian occupation.

223 **He'd traveled there in a caravan** HRK, "Writers Shiver in Mountain Cold," dateline 19 Nov. 1935, HRK Papers, Scrapbook #29.

223 **The spiderwebs** HRK, "Scribes with Ethiops Find Travel About as Disagreeable as War," dateline 22 Nov. 1935, HRK Papers, Scrapbook #29.

223 **Haile Selassie had given** HRK, "Writers and Cameramen to See Trenches," dateline 2 Nov. 1935, HRK Papers, Scrapbook #29.

223 **"gift of civilization"** HRK, "200 Dead or Wounded in Dessye Raid," dateline 7 Dec. 1935, HRK Papers, Scrapbook #29.

223 **The other half thought** HRK, "Ethiopian Horde Moving to War Front as Whole People," dateline 20 Nov. 1935, HRK Papers, Scrapbook #29.

224 **Besides, as John pointed out** JG, "Baldwin Hints Great Britain Is Ready to Wage War for League in Maintaining Peace," dateline 5 Oct. 1935, 1935 Cuttings, JG Papers II, Box 43, folder 7.

224 **The Italians had just bombed** JG, *IE*, p. 210.

224 **The Labour politicians** JG, diary entry, 10 Dec. 1935, Goodbye London, JG Papers II, Box 19. [This is the unexpurgated draft TS of the diary he later published in *Nash's* and the *Atlantic Monthly*.]

224 **Like the good screenwriter** JG, diary entry, 17 Dec. 1935, Goodbye London.

225 **Like George Bernard Shaw** JG, diary entry, 14 Jan. 1936, Goodbye London; George Bernard Shaw, "Shaw Argues for Hands Off Italy," *NYT*, 30 Aug. 1935, p. 6.

225 **According to Frances, the Abyssinians** Pedersen, "The Racial Order" and Adom Getachew, *Worldmaking After Empire: The Rise and Fall of Self-Determination* (Princeton: Princeton University Press, 2019), ch. 2 on arguments about Ethiopia's "fitness" for League membership.

225 **They could barely speak** JG, diary entry, 10 Dec. 1935, Goodbye London.

225 **At the Waldorf bar, striking** JG, diary entry, 19 Dec. 1935, Goodbye London.

225 **By the end of the month** JG, "Baldwin Pays High Price in Prestige for Vote Victory," *CDN*, dateline 20 Dec. 1935, 1935 Cuttings, JG Papers II, Box 43, folder 7.

225 **That was the question that John** See Michael Arlen, "More, and Still More Memories of the Nineteen-Twenties," *New Yorker*, 2 Jan. 1960, p. 22.

225 **H.G. Wells wasn't sure** JG, diary entry, 6 March 1936, Goodbye London.

225 **"film-rights"** Quoted in M. Newman, *Harold Laski: A Political Biography* (London: Palgrave Macmillan, 1993), p. 186.

225 **"deep, cordial"** Waugh, *Waugh in Abyssinia*, p. 156.

225 **It didn't override** On this point, especially, Pedersen, "Racial Order," pp. 71, 77–78.

226 **Do you really think Hitler** JG, diary entry, 14 Jan. 1936, Goodbye London.

226 **He was dead tired** JG, diary entry, 13 March 1936, Goodbye London.

226 **I'm on the side** JG, diary entry, 16 Jan. 1936, Goodbye London.

226 **He cut much of what** JG, diary entry, 18 Dec. 1935. As an example, JG, "Baldwin Hints."

226 **"For six days a week"** JG, *IE*, p. 215.

226 **For all the lip service** FFG, "Notes on England," JG Papers I, Box 7, folder 23.

226 **Every evening after dinner** Built as a center for international and especially Anglo-American trade, Bush House (as of the Second World War) housed the BBC World Service.

227 **There were four thousand** JG, diary entry, 27 Jan. 1936, Goodbye London.

227 **He also nursed a secret** Fodor to JG, 16 May 1935, JG Papers I, Box 7, folder 17. Still unsettled questions about Atatürk: see Andrew Mango, *Atatürk: The Biography of the Founder of Modern Turkey* (Woodstock, N.Y.: Overlook Press, 1999) and George W. Gawrych, *The Young Atatürk: From Ottoman Soldier to Statesman of Turkey* (London: I. B. Tauris, 2013).

227 **"purifies a nation"** JG, *IE*, p. 382.

227 **"The fact may be an outrage"** JG, *IE*, p. ix.

227 **It was a *personal* book** JG to Eugene Saxton, 3 Dec. 1935, JG Papers II, Box 29, Harper's Correspondence about Inside Europe.

228 **He organized the book** On JG's career as a novel writer and *IEur*, Fischer, *Men and Politics*, p. 154. (On JG in Moscow in 1927: "he did not yet realize the public

would prefer books psychoanalyzing continents to novels psychoanalyzing individuals in love.")

228 **It was very much a book** Michaela Hoenicke Moore, *Know Your Enemy: The American Debate on Nazism, 1933–1945* (New York: Cambridge University Press, 2010), pp. 48–50. Gunther's comments on German national character were in the way of throwaway lines (their docility, for instance), not observations to be subjected to critical scrutiny.

228 **The contrast with the work** On Mead, especially Peter Mandler, *Return from the Natives: How Margaret Mead Won the Second World War and Lost the Cold War* (New Haven: Yale University Press, 2013), chs. 1 and 2. Not until World War II did Mead begin to refer to "national character" (p. 56). On the longer trajectory of ideas of national character, Mandler, *English National Character.*

229 **"the American type of wandering"** Harold Nicolson, "Guide Which Makes Foreign Affairs Exciting," *Daily Telegraph,* 17 Jan. 1936, JG Papers II, Box 11, *Inside Europe* Clippings.

229 **She'd read and reread** Martha Gellhorn to JG, 8 Feb. nd [1937?], JG Papers II, Box 5.

229 **"you had at least slept"** Martha Foley to JG, 6 Feb. 1936, JG Papers II, Box 5.

230 **"I would have given a good"** DT, "European Case Histories," *Saturday Review of Literature,* 15 Feb. 1936, *Inside Europe* Clippings. Given her merciless reviewing, and the fact that she'd attacked Knick for promiscuously mixing the trivial and the important (Dollfuss's short stature and the attack on Red Vienna), the review was surprisingly positive. Unlike *The Boiling Point,* a rather disconnected set of articles, *Inside Europe* had an underlying thesis. Still, she thought the sections on Germany the weakest part of the book.

230 **"vigor and almost impudent"** Raymond Swing, "Europe as Portraiture," *Nation,* 4 March 1936, p. 285.

230 **Even the inevitable criticism** Among British reviewers, Goronwy Rees, "The Inside Story," *Spectator,* 24 Jan. 1936; of the Americans, Malcolm Cowley, "The Personal Element," *New Republic,* 12 Feb. 1936, p. 22–23.

230 **"black angel"** Cowley, "The Personal Element."

230 **According to the *New York*** John Chamberlain, "Books of the Times," *NYT,* 8 Feb. 1936, *Inside Europe* Clippings.

230 **"chocolate coating of personalities"** Kip Fadiman, "John Gunther's Baedeker," *New Yorker,* 8 Feb. 1936, *Inside Europe* Clippings.

230 **How about if you advertise** JG to Cass Canfield, 25 Feb. 1936, JG Papers I, Box 118, folder 2.

230 **"He risked his career"** Ad in *Publishers Weekly,* 18 Jan. 1936, *Inside Europe* Clippings.

230 **"political Baedeker"** "Dictators and Others: An American Looks at Europe," *TLS,* 15 Feb. 1936; ad in *Publishers Weekly,* 18 Jan. 1936, *Inside Europe* Clippings.

231 **Anthony Eden** Cass Canfield to JG, 26 March 1936—"If you could ever get a photograph of him holding a copy of INSIDE EUROPE, it would be worth ten and a half times its weight in gold." JG Papers II, Box 5, Correspondence, 1927–1937 Brandt, Harper's, Schoeninger.

231 **FDR's son** JVS to JG, 1 Sept. nd [1937], JG Papers II, Box 35. According to Frank's bride, Sheean related, *Inside Europe* was "the third party, a sort of ghost, at their honeymoon."

231 **The young John F. Kennedy** John F. Kennedy, diary entry for 28 July 1937, Travel Diary, JFK Library. JFK found Gunther too enamored of socialism and communism. "What are the Evils of Fascism as opposed to communism?" he wondered.

231 **"successful fight"** George Messersmith to JG, 19 Jan. 1937, JG Papers II, Box 5.

231 **To keep the book up-to-date** JG, *Fragment*, p. 21.

231 **"You may not agree with Gunther's"** JVS to Cass Canfield, 23 Jan. [1936], JG Papers II, Box 35.

232 **Had Hitler not existed** JVS to Ellery Sedgwick, 6 July nd [1934], Sedgwick Papers.

232 **"Kemal swept the Greeks"** JVS to JG, 21 Jan. nd [1936], JG Papers II, Box 35.

232 **"a symptom of disease"** JVS, "Without Hate," p. 72.

232 **Dinah was dressed** Agnes Knickerbocker, TS Memoir, p. 32.

232 **"Carol, what do you do"** Quoted in Johnson, "Twentieth-Century Seeker," p. 263.

232 **His child, Jimmy decided** JVS to JG, 15 April 1936, JG Papers II, Box 35. JVS disputed that they'd moved to Ireland for "sentimental, racist or nationalist reasons." He was planning a book on Ireland that, according to Dinah, he found "too destroying" to write. Johnson, "Twentieth-Century Seeker," pp. 268–69.

233 **As *Inside Europe* became a phenomenon** FFG, diary entry, 13 Feb. 1936, FFG Papers, file 6. The journalist Friedrich Scheu, who knew the Gunthers in Vienna, corroborated in his memoir the importance of FFG's thought to JG's work: "During the years of John Gunther's rise, she functioned as the driving, dynamic force behind his achievements." She looked like a dainty doll, Scheu observed, but was in fact a "brilliant woman." Scheu, *Der Weg*, p. 61.

233 **"the generous and patient collaboration"** JG, *Inside Europe*, p. 580.

233 **For all the reader knew** Literary marriages are famously riven by battles over authorship. F. Scott and Zelda Fitzgerald fought constantly over literary property. He usurped her diaries and letters, incorporating them, word for word, into his fiction. When she wrote her own roman à clef, he objected that she'd gathered the "crumbs" of his dinner table and sought to block her novel's publication. Deborah Pike, *The Subversive Art of Zelda Fitzgerald* (Columbia: University of Missouri Press, 2017). FFG was familiar enough with these dynamics. At least your husband quotes you, the correspondent Edgar Snow's wife said to her, adding: "Mine never does. He uses all my lines, & I never get any credit." In her diary that day, FFG invoked the famous British Fabian duo Beatrice and Sidney Webb as a model (18 April 1938, FFG Papers, file 7). On literary partnership as the consummation of a marriage, Will and Ariel Durant, *A Dual Autobiography* (New York: Simon & Schuster, 1977), pp. 104, 109, 332, 338.

233 **She told a friend** 11 Jan. 1936, JG Papers II, Box 23a, 1989-001, London Diary 1936, Jan–May.

233 **Miss Russell of the Society** FFG, diary entry, 14 Feb. 1936, FFG Papers, file 6.

233 **She woke up** Recalled in FFG to JN, 1 June 1942, Jawaharlal Nehru Papers, vol. 29, Nehru Memorial Museum and Library [NMML].

233 **"My God can't you leave"** FFG, diary entry, 27 Feb. 1936, FFG Papers, file 6.

234 **"The appearance of Italy"** Quoted in JG, diary entry, 12 May 1936, Goodbye London.

234 **"Now not even the most skeptical"** HRK, "Ciano Most Trusted Aide of Mussolini," dateline 9 July 1936, HRK Papers, Scrapbook #29.

235 **But the article was sure to raise** H. R. Knickerbocker, "Mussolini Ends Fear of War with England," *Fort Worth Star-Telegram*, 13 July 1936, p. 4.

235 **"almost identical dynamic forces"** JG, *IE*, p. 212.

235 **What would John do** JG, diary entry, 28 Feb. 1936, Goodbye London.

236 **"We lack grandfathers"** JG, diary entry, 27 Feb. 1936, Goodbye London.

236 **The nervous breakdown** Jimmy told the story of this breakdown on many occasions: see esp. JVS to RM, 11 Oct. nd [1936] and 18 Jan. nd [1937], RM Papers, Box 3, folder 35; JVS to Dr. Rhine, 8 April 1953, DT Papers, Box 27.

237 **"What is dying"** JVS to JG, 13 June 1937, JG Papers II, Box 35.

237 **"American Author"** Among others, "Vincent Sheean on Way to Swiss Sanatorium," *Baltimore Sun,* 18 Aug. 1936, p. 11.

238 **"These two quite get my goat"** JVS to RM, 11 Oct. nd [1936], RM Papers, Box 3, folder 35.

CHAPTER ELEVEN

241 **"shemozzles"** JVS's term, JVS to JG, 15 Sept., nd [1950s], JG Papers II, Box 35.

241 **She was not just America's** Kurth, *American Cassandra,* p. 213. On the arrangements for the column, DT to Helen Reid, 20 Jan. 1936, Box I, D255 and Box I, D92, Helen Rogers Reid Papers in Reid Family Papers, Library of Congress. Anne O'Hare McCormick joined the *New York Times's* editorial board in June 1936, writing on European politics and, from 1942, the thrice-weekly "Abroad" column.

241 **The paper's original idea** On women readers as an important but underserved constituency, Mrs. Anna Steese Richardson, "What I Think Women Want in a Newspaper," *Problems of Journalism: Proceedings of the 14th Annual Convention, American Society of Newspaper Editors* (Washington, D.C., 1936), pp. 20–29. On p. 21, her observations about *NYHT* becoming a women's paper.

241 **"was no less than the whole"** "Dorothy Thompson," *NYT,* 1 Feb. 1961, p. 34. "Readers, agreeing or not, sensed that here was a go-getter who was go-getting for all."

241 **"liberal conservatism"** This phrase, derived from the headline to "Blue-Eyed Tornado," would be used to advertise "On the Record" in advertisements. See, for example, "Dorothy Thompson," *Lancaster New Era,* 9 July 1936, p. 8.

242 **"claim upon every phase"** *Dorothy Thompson's Political Guide,* p. 15. On the development of the idea of "totalitarianism" in the United States, Benjamin L. Alpers, *Dictators, Democracy, and American Public Culture: Envisioning the Totalitarian Enemy, 1920s–1950s* (Chapel Hill: University of North Carolina Press, 2003), esp. p. 11, p. 33, pp. 79–82 on DT.

242 **To her chockablock** According to Charles Fisher, *The Columnists* (New York: Howell, Soskin, 1944), p. 18. On radio and international politics, David Holbrook Culbert, *News for Everyman: Radio and Foreign Affairs in Thirties America* (Westport, Conn.: Greenwood Press, 1976). One thousand dollars in 1937 dollars equals something like seventeen thousand dollars today.

242 **On "column mornings"** Kurth, *American Cassandra,* p. 262.

242 **It was a matter of feeling** On this point, Dale Warren, "Strictly Personal: 'Off the Record' with a Columnist," *Saturday Review,* 10 June 1944, pp. 13–14.

242 **"A good newspaper man"** DT to Ellery Sedgwick, 24 Oct. ny [1926?], Sedgwick Papers, Carton 12.

243 **"What is coming to a head"** DT, "On the Record: The Summer and the President, V. American Foreign Policy," *NYHT,* 16 Aug. 1939, p. 21A.

243 **This "emotionalism"** On the use of emotionalism in international politics, Leila J. Rupp, *Worlds of Women: The Making of an International Women's Movement* (Princeton: Princeton University Press, 1997); Siegel, *Peace on Our Terms.*

243 **"She ingests the cosmos"** Jack Alexander, "The Girl from Syracuse: The Story of Problem Child Dorothy Thompson," *Saturday Evening Post,* 18 May 1940, p. 1.

243 **Even when he and Dorothy** Walter Lippmann, "Today and Tomorrow: Dark Fears," *NYHT,* 1 Nov. 1932. On Lippmann and Thompson, compared, Dwight Macdonald, "They, the People," *New International,* July 1938, pp. 209–11.

243 **He appealed to the enlightened** Readers praised Lippmann as "intensely interesting," well-informed, and logical. See Letters to the Editor, "The False Gods," *NYHT,* 21 May 1932, p. 14.

243 **He liked nothing better** WL, "Today and Tomorrow: Glass Houses," *NYHT,* 18 Oct. 1932, p. 17.

243 **"pitch of a Wagnerian"** WL, "Today and Tomorrow: Intermission," *NYHT,* 28 May 1938, p. 13. In explaining dictatorship, Lippmann also invoked economic exigency and the power of propaganda. See, for instance, WL, "Today and Tomorrow: How Liberty is Lost," *NYHT,* 16 July 1938, p. 11. Lippmann could himself occasionally play Cassandra, as on the subject of FDR's proposed Supreme Court reforms. WL, "Today and Tomorrow: Cassandra Speaking," *NYHT,* 1 April 1937, p. 21. My thanks to Tom Arnold-Forster for conversations about Lippmann.

243 **The world hung** DT, "On the Record: 'Peace'—and the Crisis Begins," *NYHT,* 1 Oct. 1938, p. 13.

243 **"last stand"** DT, "On the Record: Write It Down," *NYHT,* 18 Feb. 1938, p. 21.

243 **"trembly emotion"** John Chamberlain, "Delilah of the Ink-Pot," *New Republic,* 27 Sept. 1939, p. 220.

243 **She got in a "tizzy"** Fisher, *Columnists,* pp. 3, 31. Also John S. Kennedy, "Global Lady" in *Moulders of Opinion,* ed. David Bulman (Milwaukee: Bruce, 1945), p. 24.

243 **"Dorothy is the only woman"** JVS, *Dorothy and Red,* p. 215; see also William B. Barnes to Gentlemen, *NYHT,* 15 March 1941—"the only woman who ever had a change of life in public."

244 **But subjectivity, especially when delivered** On the recognition of subjectivity in reporting as inevitable, Schudson, *Discovering,* pp. 154–58.

244 **Like Jimmy, she was creating** See, for instance, A.F.H., Letter to the Editor— Suggests Nobel Prize, *NYHT,* 25 June 1937, p. 20.

244 **"My whole personal life"** DT, "The Dilemma of the Liberal," *Story Magazine,* Jan. 1937, p. 2. Steven Marcus (in a review of Sheean's *Dorothy and Red*) judges both Thompson and Lewis as entirely externalized people—"abstract and depersonalized," calling their marriage "more like a treaty or trade agreement between two minor nations than what is usually thought of as a marriage" (pp. 54–55). Steven Marcus, *Representations: Essays on Literature and Society* (New York: Random House, 1975).

244 **"I cannot *bear* this world!"** DT, "Dilemma," p. 4.

244 **Dorothy was identifying** For FFG's critique of this piece, especially focused on DT's Republican politics, Frances Gunther, "Dilemma of Dorothy Thompson," FFG Papers, file 103.

244 **"That was our modern dilemma"** Isabel Bolton, *Do I Wake or Sleep* (1947) in *New York Mosaic* (South Royalton, Vt.: Steerforth Press, 1997), p. 36.

245 **"The Germans seem to be"** Marjorie Worthington, diary entry, 7 June 1940, 1940 Diary—152/2/1, Marjorie Worthington Papers, Special Collections and University Archives, University of Oregon Libraries.

245 **He viewed his wife Zelda's** David S. Brown, *Paradise Lost: A Life of F. Scott Fitzgerald* (Cambridge, Mass.: Harvard University Press, 2017), esp. ch. 14.

245 **"inseparable interconnections"** Virginia Woolf, *Three Guineas* (London: Hogarth Press, 1943 [1938]), p. 258.

245 **"It's the poisoning"** RW to Irita Van Doren, nd, Irita Van Doren Papers, Box 9.

245 **"the outlines of every object"** RW, *Black Lamb and Grey Falcon,* p. 3. For a critique of RW's ideas here, Mary Ellmann, *Thinking About Women* (New York: Harcourt, Brace & World, 1968), pp. 108–9.

246 **But individuals are not** RW, *Black Lamb and Grey Falcon,* p. 281. See DT's analogy in "Dilemma of a Pacifist," p. 37.

246 **The world arena** DT to RW, 12 Oct. 1942, RW Papers, Yale, GEN 105, Series I, Box 16, folder 823. Of RW's work, DT remarked: "I might have done it myself if I had been clever enough." JVS, *Dorothy and Red,* p. 208.

246 "whole existence" JVS, *Dorothy and Red,* p. 239.

246 **She hadn't done anything** James B. Reston, "A New Yorker at Large," *Wilkes-Barre Record,* 25 Nov. 1935, p. 14.

247 **"You will have to choose"** DT, diary entry, 18 Nov. 1935, quoted in *Dorothy and Red,* p. 217.

247 **To his friends** Louis Untermeyer, *Bygones* (New York: Harcourt, Brace & World, 1965), p. 85.

247 **A few years later, she told** Avery Strakosch TS, p. 5 [published as "House of Maps of Words," *Look,* 7 April 1942], DT Papers, Box 140.

247 **In the late 1930s, her annual** Figure from 1939, Kurth, *American Cassandra,* pp. 252–53.

247 **At the going-away party** Jamie Hamilton to JVS, 25 Sept. 1936, JVS, WHS, Box 1, folder 29—Correspondence with Hamilton, July 1936–Nov. 1936.

248 **Maybe they should stay** JG, diary entry, 13 April 1936, 25 July 1936, Goodbye London.

248 **"okeydoke"** FFG to Louise Morgan, 23 Feb. 1937, Morgan-Theis Papers, Gen. Mss. 80—Series I, Box 9, Beinecke Library.

248 **"I find there's a definite vacancy"** FFG to JG, nd [labeled "Please keep"], Aug./Sept. 1936, JG Papers II, Box 23.

248 **"your insight, political & human"** JG to FFG, 6 Sept. 1936, FFG Papers, file 174.

248 **He was going through the diary** JG to Carl Brandt, 10 July 1936, JG Papers I, Box 118, folder 2.

248 **John's diary** Ted Weeks to Carl Brandt, 4 Jan. 1937, JG Papers II, Box 29, Correspondence with Ray Long about Europe's Merry Go Round.

249 **In fact, why did he have** Dick Mealand to JG, 21 Jan. 1937, JG Papers II, Box 29; Corrections for Diary, with London Diary Typescript, nd [fall 1936]; also telegram, NLT Brooks Script London.

249 **"perhaps the most remarkable"** JG, diary entry, 30 March 1936, Goodbye London.

249 **"You see, the fact is"** JVS to JG, 6 June ny [1937?], JG Papers II, Box 35.

249 **John decided his next book** Carl Brandt to JG, 17 March 1937, JG Papers II, Box 5, Correspondence, 1927–1937 Brandt, Harper's, Schoeninger.

249 **Each book, he had decided** JG, *Fragment,* p. 25; Whit Burnett, interview notes, *Story* Archive, Box 60, folder 18.

250 **After all, if everybody** FFG, diary entry, 7 Dec. 1936, Journal of Frances Gunther, 1936/7, FFG Papers, file 7.

250 **"Then nobody could talk to you"** Frances Gunther, "Another Year," *Story* magazine, January 1937, p. 78. For a version without pseudonyms, see FFG, "Happy New Year," JG Papers II, Box 6.

250 **"You're a fool"** FFG, "Another Year," p. 84.

250 **"I wanted to stay"** FFG, "Another Year," pp. 84–85.

251 **Does John Gunther's wife** Jay Allen to JG, nd [1937], JG Papers II, Box 34.

251 **The foreign correspondent's wife** Early draft of *Ring Round,* JG Papers 1972 Add., Box 32, folder 4.

251 **Still, something was missing** JG Papers 1972 Add., Box 29, folder 5, Early Draft, Ring Round; also FFG, diary entry, 31 Aug. 1937, FFG Papers, file 7.

251 **But secretly, she snuck** FFG, diary entry, 14 Dec. 1937, 1937/8 Diary, FFG Papers, file 7.

251 **But maybe she should** JG notes, JG Papers 1972 Add., Box 4, folder 8; FFG, diary entries, 26, 27, 30, 31 Aug. 1937, 1937/8 Diary, FFG Papers, file 7.

252 **He would visit** JG to Personal and Otherwise Department, *Harper's,* 17 Oct. 1938, JG Papers II, Box 24, folder labeled letters, 1938–40.

252 **"I feel like a mouse"** JG, "New Ferment in India," *Nation*, 19 Feb. 1938, p. 203; another formulation, Cass Canfield to JG, 19 Jan. 1939, JG Papers II, Box 24.

252 **Did John actually think** FFG, diary entry, 27 Aug. 1937, 1937/8 Diary, FFG Papers, file 7.

252 **"all cold-dead outside"** FFG, diary entry, 20 Aug. 1937, 1937/8 Diary, FFG Papers, file 7.

252 **They wrote a new will** JG to Carl Brandt, 29 Oct. 1937, JG Papers II, Box 5, Correspondence, 1927–1937 Brandt, Harper's, Schoeninger.

252 **"The Gunthers, traveling light!"** FFG, Asia trip notes, 30 Oct. 1937, FFG Papers, file 221. [This typescript is a reworked, in some case expanded, version of the 1937/8 diary in folder 7.]

253 **From Djibouti** FFG to Johnny, 8 Dec. 1937, FFG Papers, file 52.

253 **You wave to a receding** FFG, "Political Reporting," FFG Papers, file 221.

253 **The Taj's miles of marble** On details of Taj, Henrietta Sands Merrick, "Travel in India," *Vogue*, 15 Dec. 1932, p. 68; "The Modernised Taj Mahal Hotel," *Times of India*, 25 Nov. 1933, p. 21.

253 **She had steeled herself** FFG, diary entry, 2 Nov. 1937, 1937/8 Diary, FFG Papers, file 7.

254 **Extremely shrewd** FFG, "If India Loses, We Lose," *Common Sense*, Oct. 1942, p. 330; FFG, diary entry, 23 Dec. 1937, 1937/8 Diary, FFG Papers, file 7.

254 **Because Frances insisted on attending** Asia trip notes, 21 Dec. 1937, FFG Papers, file 221; Samuel T. Sheppard, *The Byculla Club, 1833–1916* (Bombay: Bennett, Coleman & Co, 1916).

254 **"And they are all wrong"** Referenced in diary entry, FFG to Sonia Fineman, 18 Dec. 1937, folder 7.

255 **You must press them** FFG, diary entry, 23 Dec. 1937, 1937/8 Diary.

255 **"Lots of Indians"** FFG, diary entry, 18 Dec. 1937, 1937/8 Diary.

255 **"he is on no side"** FFG, diary entry, 20 Jan. 1938, 1937/8 Diary.

255 **She sent Johnny** FFG to Johnny, 24 Feb. 1938 [labeled 1937], FFG Papers, file 52.

256 **It resembled a very fragrant** FFG to Johnny, 18 Dec. 1937, FFG Papers, file 52.

256 **Wash your hands** JG to Johnny, 28 Nov. 1937, FFG Papers, file 52.

256 **Johnny had hung** Johnny to FFG and JG, 13 Jan. 1938, JG Papers II, Box 6.

256 **He was learning** Johnny to FFG and JG, 4 April 1938; 16 May 1938, JG Papers II, Box 6.

256 **If you tried to hold** Johnny to FFG and JG, 19 Feb. 1938, JG Papers II, Box 6.

256 **Please answer immediately** FFG to Johnny, 17 Jan. 1938, FFG Papers, file 52.

256 **She underlined every word** FFG to Johnny, 6 Feb. 1938, FFG Papers, file 52.

256 **Was the elephant made** Johnny to FFG and JG, 23 Feb. 1938, JG Papers II, Box 6.

256 **"When will you come"** Johnny to FFG and JG, 11 April 1938, JG Papers II, Box 6.

257 **"Have you seen Nehru"** JG, *Inside Asia* (New York: Harper & Brothers, 1939), p. 425.

257 **John didn't like to give** Account of JG's lecture in "Tug of War Between 'Haves' and 'Have-Nots,'" *Bombay Chronicle*, 6 Jan. 1938; for a contemporary description of what it was like to speak in a packed Cowasji Jehangir Hall, Margaret Sanger, *Margaret Sanger: An Autobiography* (New York: Norton, 1938), p. 466.

257 **"Yep. Am lecturing"** K.A.A., "Novelist Maugham & Newsman Gunther," *Bombay Chronicle*, 7 Jan. 1938.

258 **Nehru was accustomed** FFG, 26 Jan. 1938, 1937/1938 Diary. [Peshawar entry is undated but preceding entry of which it is a part is dated 26 Jan.]

258 **"few hundred odd million"** "Tug of War," 6 Jan. 1938; "Fascist Threat to World Peace," *Times of India*, 6 Jan. 1938, p. 12.

259 **"open-hearted—and open-throated!"** "Novelist Maugham."

259 **The doors to the inner sanctum** See, for instance, his assessment of Nehru in the *Nation,* "New Ferment in India," 19 Feb. 1938, p. 204; opinion of Sarojini Naidu, also p. 204.

259 **He didn't look so fragile** FFG, diary entry, 6 Jan. 1938, 1937/8 Diary.

260 **"Did the Aga Khan say that?"** Leonard Lyons, "Report on Reporters," *Click* magazine, March 1944; also FFG, 6 Jan. 1938, 1937/8 Diary.

260 **"unbelievable combination"** JG, "New Ferment," p. 204.

260 **"Truth," Mrs. Naidu replied** FFG, diary entry for 6 Jan. 1938, 1937/8 Diary.

260 **The British press officer** Jossleyn Hennessy, Bureau of Public Information, to J. G. Laithwaite, Private Sec'y to the HE the Viceroy, 18 Jan. 1938, IOR: L/I/1/1388—Gunther, John, British Library. [IOR citations below from this file.]

260 **"British or Foreign"** Gunther—or so the official hoped—promised to be the second coming of Katherine Mayo, the American journalist whose vitriolic *Mother India* (1927) sought to bolster British rule. Mrinalini Sinha, *Specters of Mother India: The Global Restructuring of an Empire* (Durham and London: University of North Carolina Press, 2006).

260 **She obviously wields** See also Major Evans F. Carlson's assessment, *Twin Stars of China* (New York: Dodd, Mead & Co., 1940), p. 133.

260 **As the British authorities** A. H. Joyce to Hennessy, 10 May 1938, IOR.

261 **"What is the wealth"** FFG, undated, 1937/8 Diary.

261 **India could never have developed** "Notes on the British in India," enclosed in Jossleyn Hennessy, Principal Information Officer, Home Department, Simla [also referred to in a 1937 letter as the Director of Public Information, Gov't of India], to Joyce, India Office, Whitehall, 21 May 1938, IOR.

261 **No one at the party** FFG, diary entry, 23 Dec. 1937, 1937/8 Diary.

261 **The more Americans saw firsthand** Deborah Cohen, "The Geopolitical Is Personal: India, Anglophobia and American Foreign Correspondents in the 1930s and 1940s," the Ben Pimlott Memorial Lecture (2017), *Twentieth-Century British History* 29, no. 3 (August 2018): 388–410.

261 **Every prominent American** Cohen, "Geopolitical Is Personal," pp. 399–401; Kenton J. Clymer, *Quest for Freedom: The United States and India's Independence* (New York: Columbia University Press, 1995), pp. 102–5.

262 **"The moment the Indian people"** FFG, diary entry, 26 Jan. 1938, 1937/8 Diary.

262 **"My dear"** FFG to JG, 16 Jan. 1938, JG Papers II, Box 23.

263 **According to Stekel** See also Martha Foley's account of this episode: Foley, *Story,* p. 104. Foley loathed JG, whom she depicts as an insincere, untalented misogynist apt to blame a wife for every problem her husband suffered (105).

263 **A woman's pleasure** Wilhelm Stekel, *Frigidity in Woman in Relation to Her Love Life,* trans. James S. Van Teslaar (New York: Boni and Liveright, 1926), 2 vols., esp. I, pp. 93–94, 98–99, 209–10, and II, chs. 10 and 15; Alison Moore, "Relocating Marie Bonaparte's Clitoris," *Australian Feminist Studies* 24 (June 2009): 149–65; Katie Sutton, *Sex Between Body and Mind: Psychoanalysis and Sexology in the German-Speaking World, 1890s–1930s* (Ann Arbor: University of Michigan Press, 2019), ch. 5.

263 **"Sexual anaesthesia"** Stekel, *Frigidity,* vol. II, p. 17; also p. 276.

263 **"There are women"** Stekel, *Frigidity,* vol. II, p. 25.

263 **Stekel's admonition** Foley, *Story,* p. 104.

264 **If John and Frances wanted** Nehru to JG, undated [Dec. 1937], Gunther Papers, Addenda II, Box 24, 1989-002, folder labeled letters 1938-40, I-S.

264 **By train the trip** "The Frontier Mail," *Times of India,* 27 Feb. 1930, p. 17.

264 **"addressing a select group"** FFG, 26 Jan. 1938, 1937/8 Diary. [Peshawar entry is undated but preceding entry of which it is a part is dated 26 Jan.]

265 **"Why don't you come"** FFG, *Revolution in India*, p. 81.

265 **He was back at home** FFG to Nehru, 4 Aug. 1938, Jawaharlal Nehru Papers, Part I, no. 29. On JN's trip, JN, "Escape," *The Modern Review*, May 1938, reprinted in *Selected Works of Jawaharlal Nehru [SWJN]*, Series 1, vol. 8, p. 873.

265 **"Is it always desirable"** Nehru to FFG, 9 March 1938, FFG Papers, file 315.

CHAPTER TWELVE

266 **"to Be Thrilled"** Emily Hahn [EH] to mother, 25 March 1938, Hahn Papers I, Box 1.

266 **And she was heartsick** EH to family, 24 August 1937, Hahn Papers I, Box 1. See James Carter, *Champions Day: The End of Old Shanghai* (New York: Norton, 2020), esp. ch. 10.

266 **It's the start of a new** On the Sino-Japanese War, Rana Mitter, *China's War with Japan, 1937–1945: The Struggle for Survival* (London: Penguin, 2014).

266 **"You're all vultures"** EH, *China to Me: A Partial Autobiography* (Boston: Beacon Press, 1988 [1944]), p. 51.

267 **Men liked war** EH to mother, 8 Aug. 1937, Hahn Papers I, Box 1. A sentiment similar to that expressed by Virginia Woolf in *Three Guineas* (1938).

267 **She'd been on her way** "Mining engineer" was the profession Hahn listed on her passport when she embarked in 1930, at long last, for the Congo, carrying in her tin chests a revolver and a typewriter, a pile of dresses, shoes for the bush, and the engagement ring given her by the fiancé she'd thrown over. She was off to visit a Harvard man, an anthropologist with an untamed red beard, whom she'd met at a party in Paris. He'd invited her to stay at the Red Cross station he was running in a remote settlement two hundred miles from Stanleyville, Congo's capital city. It proved a misadventure. She learned how to give injections, gamely cleaned out wounds, even assisted in an amputation. But the cruelties that she was supposed to take for granted—the viciousness of the Belgian overlords to the Congolese, the abuse visited by men on women—were nearly unbearable. So enchantingly eccentric at the party in Paris, the Harvard anthropologist revealed himself as a sub-Conradian character, who chained up his native wives in iron collars when they misbehaved and intended to add Mickey to his ménage. Even the legendarily majestic Lake Kivu, which she reached after weeks of trekking through the swampy Ituri Forest, following elephant roads and logging trails, accompanied by a pygmy guide, a dozen porters with her tin boxes balanced on their heads, and a baby baboon, was a disappointment. Still worse, the book that she wrote about her trip, *Congo Solo,* had to be gutted of its main character when the anthropologist's rich Bostonian parents threatened to sue her. See EH, *Congo Solo: Misadventures Two Degrees North,* ed. Ken Cuthbertson (Montreal: McGill-Queen's University Press, 2011 [first pub. 1933 in truncated form]).

267 **Glamorous and disreputable** Ernest O. Hauser, *Shanghai, City for Sale* (New York: Harcourt, Brace and Company, 1940); Harriet Sergeant, *Shanghai* (London: J. Cape, 1991); Carter, *Champions Day,* esp. chs. 8 and 9.

267 **The year Mickey arrived** JG, *Inside Asia,* p. 168.

267 **A few miles away** "Here and There," *North-China Herald,* 11 Nov. 1936, p. 255; "Fashions at the Spring Races," *North China Daily News,* 7 May 1936, p. 11.

267 **She'd played the heroine** Sergeant, *Shanghai,* p. 292; even before it opened, the play (adapted by Gilbert Seldes) was the subject of rumors. See R.J.E. Price, Let-

ter to the Editor, 4 Dec. 1935, *China Press,* 5 Dec. 1935, p. 10; "Enthusiast," Letter to the Editor and esp. critic's response, *North-China Herald,* 25 Dec. 1935, p. 530.

267 **In 1938, with more than** Carter, *Champions Day,* p. 151.

267 **She was teaching English** Though Hahn wrote for the *North China Daily News,* a search of the digitized version of the paper doesn't yield any articles by her as few of the articles were bylined. She wrote regularly for *T'ien Hsia Monthly* on subjects as various as Chinese students and Aldous Huxley; she had a hilarious exchange in the correspondence columns with Gerald Durrell. The periodical that Sinmay Zau and Mickey edited together was entitled *Vox.*

267 **A son of the former mayor** On Sinmay Zau, Jonathan Hutt, "Monstre Sacré: The Decadent World of Sinmay Zau," *China Heritage Quarterly,* no. 22 (June 2010), chinaheritagequarterly.org/features.php?issue=022&searchterm=022_monstre .inc.

267 **In the stories she sent** EH, "Cathay and the Muse," *New Yorker,* 14 March 1936, pp. 80–83; EH, "Only the Chinese," *New Yorker,* 31 July 1937, pp. 18–19; "The Case of Mr. Chow," *New Yorker,* 6 Nov. 1937, pp. 19–21.

268 **"one Chinese can be all"** EH, "Heh-Ven as Sage," *New Yorker,* 17 July 1937, p. 19.

268 **She was an "exhibitionist"** EH to Helen, 27 Nov. 1935, Hahn I, Box 1.

268 **"playing marbles with quicksilver"** EH to Helen, 1 April 1937, Hahn I, Box 1.

268 **She was deluged** EH, *China to Me,* pp. 78–81.

268 **"The Gunthers are horribly"** Emily Hahn to mother, 11 April 1938, Hahn I, Box 1.

268 **She'd picked up a French lieutenant** Emily Hahn to JG, 13 Nov. [1928], JG Papers II, Box 34.

268 **"It would be a shame"** JG Papers II, Box 2—Helen & Mickey Hahn for a Story.

269 **Her clothes hung loose** EH, "The Big Smoke," in EH, *No Hurry to Get Home,* intro. by Ken Cuthbertson (Seattle: Seal Press, 2000).

269 **He didn't feel a thing** FFG, diary entry, 18 April 1938, 1937/8 Diary; Helen & Mickey Hahn for a Story.

269 **"a Nehru fan"** FFG, diary entry, 29 March 1938, 1937/8 Diary. JG's conversation was with Agnes Smedley.

269 **"Chinese civilization"** JG, *Inside Asia,* p. 153.

269 **Really, the book ought** *Inside Asia,* p. ix; on writing *Inside Asia,* JG, *Fragment,* pp. 24–34; also *Current Biography Yearbook,* 1941, p. 357.

270 **He and his wife** "Chiang Believes Myth of Japanese 'Invincibility' Successfully Challenged: Leader Tells John Gunther Will Win War," via NANA, syndicated in *Chattanooga Daily Times,* 10 April 1938, p. 4.

270 **He fumbled** *Inside Asia,* p. 180.

270 **"There is Methodism"** JG, *Inside Asia,* p. 188.

270 **She was pulling his leg** Interview with Emily Hahn, 2 May 1975, JG Papers II, Box 2—Brock Baker Interviews.

270 **Her moral standards** Brock Baker interview with Emily Hahn.

270 **"marrying a continent"** JG, *Inside Asia,* p. 201.

270 **His depiction of the Soongs** Cuthbertson, *Nobody Said Not to Go,* p. 171.

271 **"an unwieldy combination"** FFG to Nehru, March 1938, FFG Papers, file 315.

272 **"England, that wily old"** FFG to Nehru, June 1938, FFG Papers, file 315.

272 **"What a swell job"** FFG, entry for 16 March 1938, 1937/8 Diary.

272 **She knew perfectly well** FFG to Nehru, 14 April 1938, FFG Papers, file 315; copy in Jawaharlal Nehru Papers, vol. 29.

272 **"I wanted so very much"** FFG to Nehru, March 1938, Jawaharlal Nehru Papers, vol. 29.

272 **"Jewel of India"** John and Frances Gunther, "Nehru of India," *Life,* 11 Dec. 1939,

p. 98. Aruna Asaf Ali in association with G.N.S. Raghavan, *Private Face of a Public Person: A Study of Jawaharlal Nehru* (New Delhi: Radiant Publishers, 1989), p. 28.

272 **"formidable conceit"** "The Rashtrapati," *Modern Review* (Calcutta), Nov. 1937, reprinted in *SWJN*, ser. 1, vol. 8, pp. 520–23.

273 **He considered himself more** JN to Gandhi, 24 July 1941, quoted in Ali and Raghavan, *Private Face*, p. 34.

273 **"sanely and confidently"** Janet Morgan, *Edwina Mountbatten: A Life of Her Own* (New York: Scribner's, 1991), 421. Unlike Frances, Edwina apparently didn't often bring him up short (p. 462). Expressing similar restraints in writing, p. 427. Just as with FFG, he sent Edwina a piece of birch bark from Kashmir, p. 428.

273 **"What delightful letters you write"** JN to FFG, 29 April 1938, quoted in Ali and Raghavan, *Private Face*, p. 93.

274 **Try to tell a deaf man** JVS, "Without Hate, Without Love, Without Fear," *Redbook*, Aug. 1945, p. 74.

274 **"This is the beginning"** HRK to JG, nd [after August 1936], postcard, JG Papers II, Box 24, folder labeled Some letters from H. R. Knickerbocker. On the Spanish Civil War and reporters, Paul Preston, *We Saw Spain Die: Foreign Correspondents in the Spanish Civil War* (London: Constable, 2008); Knightley, *First Casualty*, ch. 9; on Hemingway/Gellhorn, Amanda Vaill, *Hotel Florida: Truth, Love and Death in the Spanish Civil War* (New York: Farrar, Straus and Giroux, 2014).

274 **In the summer of 1936** HRK, "I Saw It Happen!" *Cosmopolitan*, April 1938, p. 151.

274 **Over the Spanish border** Described by Sefton (Tom) Delmer, who was on the plane with Knick. Delmer, *Trail Sinister* (London: Secker & Warburg, 1961), p. 270.

274 **So far as Knick was concerned** HRK, "Foreword," *The Siege of Alcazar* (Philadelphia: David McKay Company, 1936); HRK to JG, nd [after Aug. 1936] postcard.

274 **French planes were bombing** HRK, *Siege*, p. 14.

275 **From his friend Jay Allen** On Jay Allen, Preston, *We Saw Spain Die*, ch. 9.

275 **That stuff Knick was writing** For criticisms of Knick's reporting from Spain, see (for the Communist point of view), Harry Gannes, "The Truth About the Fascist Plot," in *Spain Defends Democracy* (New York: Workers Library Publishers, 1936), p. 13: "Hearst's foremost foreign publicist"; George Seldes, *The Facts Are . . . A Guide to Falsehood and Propaganda in the Press and Radio* (New York: In Fact, 1942), esp. pp. 93–95; George Seldes, *The People Don't Know: The American Press and the Cold War* (New York: Gaer Associates, 1949), pp. 45–46. On the mislabel of "Reds," see JVS, "Spain Held Red Only in Views of Ill-Informed," *NYHT,* 20 June 1938, p. 7.

275 **"You're like Goering"** Chronology in X Notes—(Of Her Talk), JG Papers II, Box 22.

275 **"rational content"** HRK to JG, nd [after Aug. 1936], postcard.

275 **In fact, it seemed to Knick** HRK, "It Need Not Happen Here," *Cosmopolitan*, June 1937, p. 186.

275 **Still, when Knick returned to Spain** HRK, "Terror Is New Weapon Employed in Warfare," *Lancaster New Era*, 30 April 1937, p. 17.

276 **Then there were the thirty hours** HRK, "Reporter, Hurled into Dungeon, Finds Doomed Spaniards' Tales 10 Times Worse than Battlefields," *Press and Sun-Bulletin* (Binghamton, N.Y.), 28 April 1937, p. 8. See also Preston, *We Saw*, pp. 190–91.

276 **Despite Knick's sympathetic** The Ambassador to Spain (Bowers) to Sec'y of State, 12 April 1937, reprinted in *The Foreign Relations of the United States,* 1937, vol. 1, pp. 280–81.

276 **"This is a monstrous mistake"** HRK, "Knickerbocker's Eyes Opened by Doomed Cell Mate," *Pomona Progress Bulletin,* 29 April 1937, pp. 1–2.

276 **"I realized I had never"** HRK, "Reporter, Hurled into Dungeon," p. 8.

276 **Later on, he figured** HRK to Barry Faris, 27 May 1937, HRK Papers, Uncatalogued correspondence, Box 4—folder 1937; *Is Tomorrow,* p. 25. On the circumstances of HRK's imprisonment, see C2992/16, Archivo General Militar de Avila; also the papers of Gonzalo de Aguilera y Munro, especially folder 3/8, Servicio de Archivos, Universidad de Salamanca. My thanks to Benjamin Goldstein for these documents.

276 **In a piece filed from London** HRK, "Reds Slaves Says General of Rebels," *Orlando Reporter-Star,* 10 May 1937, p. 3; Preston, *We Saw,* p. 190 for the identification of "Sanchez" as Gonzalo de Aguilera y Munro; also Paul Preston, "'The Answer Lies in the Sewers': Captain Aguilera and the Mentality of the Francoist Officer Corps," *Science and Society* 68 (fall 2004): 277–312. HRK's article the previous year about Aguilera had depicted him favorably: HRK, "Reporters Get News Lying in War Trenches," *Evening News* (Wilkes-Barre), 15 Oct. 1936, p. 19.

277 **So unremittingly vicious** *Congressional Record,* 12 May 1937, HRK syndicated article in *Washington Times,* 10 May 1937, cited by Rep. Jerry J. O'Connell, Montana.

277 **Once his articles appeared** HRK to Barry Faris, 27 May 1937, HRK Papers, Uncatalogued correspondence, Box 4—Folder 1937.

277 **That is, providing** JG, diary entry, 16 Oct. 1939, JG Papers II, Box 19.

277 **It was tantamount** DT, "On the Record: Lessons of Spain," *NYHT,* 19 April 1937, p. 14.

277 **"You stay here"** JVS, *Dorothy and Red,* p. 234.

277 **Out-machoing Jimmy** Ernest Hemingway, *Selected Letters, 1917–1961,* ed. Carlos Baker (Toronto: Granada, 1981), pp. 540–41, 545.

277 **The *last* person he wanted** JVS, *Dorothy and Red,* p. 234.

278 ***You* will play the host** Vincent Sheean, *Between the Thunder and the Sun* (London: Macmillan & Co., 1943), p. 48.

278 **"You have a strange party"** JVS, *Between the Thunder,* p. 48.

278 **The guests were in evening** JVS, *Between the Thunder,* p. 50.

278 **"It is Spain"** JVS, *Dorothy and Red,* p. 235.

279 **"Vincent Sheean Sees"** *NYHT,* 4 April 1938, p. 1.

279 **"What's the good of that?"** Vincent Sheean, *Not Peace But a Sword* (New York: Doubleday, Doran & Co., 1939), p. 244. Also Ring Lardner, Jr., *The Lardners: My Family Remembered* (New York: Harper & Row, 1976).

279 **"I think it will be good"** Jim Lardner to Ellis Lardner, 3 May 1938, James Lardner Papers, ALBA No. 67, Tamiment Library, NYU. Jimmy says nineteen. *Not Peace,* p. 246.

279 **He copied out the list** Where Jimmy sought to dissuade him, Hemingway said of course it would be very noble for young Lardner to fight the fascists, but it was a personal decision, which only he could make.

280 **"The very babies"** JVS, "Loyalists Insist Franco Is Halted and Still Believe They Will Win," *NYHT,* 5 May 1938, p. 1.

280 **It was a psychological** JVS, "Loyalist Spain Viewed as Getting Its 'Second Wind' with Morale Up," *NYHT,* 27 May 1938, p. 6.

280 **"Obstinate fellow"** JVS to Ellis Lardner, 15 May 1938, James Lardner Papers.

280 **Dinah, who'd joined Jimmy** On the photographer Robert Capa's role in helping Dinah to get started in refugee work, see Richard Whelan, *Robert Capa: A Biography* (New York: Knopf, 1985), p. 149.

280 **"confidence and faith that Spain gives"** Diana Sheean to Ellis Lardner, 28 July 1938, James Lardner Papers.

280 **Instead, he took a first-floor** Ziehensack, *Hotel Imperial,* pp. 137–41.

280 **They'd paid no mind** Hamann, *Hitler's Vienna,* p. 379.

280 **"did not even have the decency"** Cited in John Toland, *Adolf Hitler* (Garden City, N.Y.: Doubleday, 1976), p. 455.

281 **Where once he hadn't** John Lehmann, *Down River: A Danubian Study* (London: The Cresset Press, 1939), p. 142.

281 **At the reception desk** Christa Schroeder, *He Was My Chief: The Memoirs of Adolf Hitler's Secretary,* trans. Geoffrey Brooks (Croydon: Pen & Sword, 2009 [1985]).

281 **"I waited for this day"** Toland, *Hitler,* p. 480.

281 **"Not a shot was fired"** Testimony of Franz von Papen, in Office of United States Chief Counsel for Prosecution of Axis Criminality, Nazi Conspiracy and Aggression, Supplement A (Washington, D.C.: U.S. Gov't Printing Office, 1947), p. 498.

281 **"death of Austria"** JVS, *Between the Thunder,* p. 2.

281 **"the immense collective will"** JVS, *Not Peace,* p. 259.

281 **They even carried themselves** JVS, "Good-bye Vienna," *New Republic,* 31 Aug. 1938, pp. 98–99. Also JVS, TS article, "Jews in Vienna and Life Under Fascism," JVS Papers, Berg.

281 **"Vienna, the eternal prostitute"** Fodor, *South of Hitler,* p. 311.

281 **Not especially, thought Fodor** Evan Burr Bukey, *Hitler's Austria: Popular Sentiment in the Nazi Era, 1938–1945* (Chapel Hill: University of North Carolina Press, 2000), esp. chs. 2 and 4; Gerhard Botz, "Arbeiterschaft und österreichische NSDAP-Mitglieder (1926–1945)," in *Arbeiterschaft und Nationalsozialismus in Österreich,* eds. Rudolf G. Ardelt and Hans Hautmann (Vienna: Europaverlag, 1990), pp. 29–48.

282 **What Jimmy chose to emphasize** JVS, *Not Peace,* pp. 94–120; JVS, "Austrian Jews Forced to 'Give' Wealth to Nazis," *NYHT,* 7 July 1938, p. 7; JVS, "The Persecution Is Total," *Redbook,* Feb. 1939, pp. 20–21; 113–16.

282 **The persecution in Austria** JVS, "Austrian Jews Forced to 'Give' Wealth to Nazis," *NYHT,* 7 July 1938, p. 7.

282 **"the day of mass murder"** JVS, *Not Peace,* p. 138.

282 **"and the rest of the population"** JVS, *Not Peace,* p. 108.

282 **"America is no longer interested"** JVS, *Not Peace,* pp. 211–12; JVS, "Last Days of a Nation," *Redbook,* Jan. 1939, pp. 24–25, 65–66.

282 **Prime Minister Chamberlain's** JVS, *Not Peace,* p. 218.

282 **Still, it seemed entirely possible** JVS, *Not Peace,* pp. 276–89.

283 **As the Czechs mobilized** JVS, *Not Peace,* pp. 290–94. Also discussed in Geoffrey Cox, *Countdown to War: A Personal Memoir of Europe, 1938–40* (London: Kimber, 1988), p. 73. On Knick in Czechoslovakia, Whittaker, *We Cannot,* pp. 124–53.

283 **He couldn't possibly risk staying** Fodor to JG, 28 Oct. 1938, JG Papers II, Box 34.

283 **Heading south they passed** Cox, *Countdown,* p. 79.

283 **Jimmy tried to write** JVS to John H. Wheeler, 2 Jan. ny [1939], James Lardner Papers, ALBA.

283 **"Back, back, back"** JVS to JG, 27 Oct. 1938, JG Papers II, Box 35.

284 **"an exaggerated value"** JVS, *Not Peace,* p. 248.

284 **"If the world has a future"** JVS, *Not Peace,* p. 270.

284 **"ant-like civilization"** DT, *New Russia,* pp. 108, 119, 219.

285 **At a dinner in 1937** DT, "A Toast to Thomas Mann," 20 April 1937, in Dorothy Thompson, *Let the Record Speak* (Boston: Houghton Mifflin, 1939), p. 81. On this subject, Rose Wilder Lane to DT, 3 Aug. 1932, DT Papers, Box 16. "There's been no room for the human being in it, since Humanity began taking up so much space."

285 "dissolve the mob into men" DT, *Let the Record,* p. 83.

285 That year, she'd published Dorothy Thompson, *Refugees: Anarchy or Organization?* (New York: Random House, 1938); preceded by DT, "Refugees: A World Problem," *Foreign Affairs,* April 1938, pp. 375–87.

285 Her proposals for an international Hamilton Fish Armstrong preface to *Refugees,* p. xi.

285 According to Jimmy JVS, *Not Peace,* p. 91.

285 The remedy Dorothy had suggested On DT's reluctant endorsement of the Rublee plan, David S. Wyman, *Paper Walls: America and the Refugee Crisis, 1938–1941* (Amherst: University of Massachusetts Press, 1968), p. 55.

285 Although Evian was a flop See the assessment of Lyndsey Stonebridge, "Humanitarianism Was Never Enough: Dorothy Thompson, *Sands of Sorrow,* and the Arabs of Palestine," *Humanity* 8, no. 3 (Winter 2017): 441–65.

286 Contrary to the League of Nations DT, "Refugees," *NYHT,* 11 Oct. 1938: "A defeatist attitude toward the refugee problem becomes a defeatist attitude toward democracy itself."

286 "people forced to run away" DT, "Escape in a Frozen World," *Survey Graphic,* Feb. 1939, p. 93.

286 For Dorothy, as for When the Gunthers returned home from Asia a few months after the Anschluss, a stack of letters were waiting. Among others, Hilda Stekel to FFG, 8 April [1938], JG Papers II, Box 35. For appeals from refugee friends, JG's correspondence files—esp. JG Papers II, Box 24.

286 Every day brought more von Tippelskirch, *Dorothy Thompson and German Writers,* pp. 210–16; 240–44; Kurth, *American Cassandra,* p. 275; Kerstin Feller, "Dorothy Thompson: Eine Schlüsselfigur der Welt des Exils," in *Deutschsprachige Exilliteratur seit 1933,* eds. John M. Spalek, Konrad Feilchenfeldt, and Sandra H. Hawrylchak, vol. 3, pt. 3 (Zurich: De Gruyter, 2005), pp. 364–409, esp. 375–81.

286 Her handbag in those years Sanders, *Dorothy Thompson,* p. 239.

286 At Twin Farms, she invited JVS to JG, 24 May 1963 in Houghton Mifflin Company Records, cited in Kurth, *American Cassandra,* p. 274. See also Klaus Mann, *Der Wendepunkt; Ein Lebensbericht* (Munich: Nymphenburger Verlagshandlung, 1969), p. 377.

286 According to a poll Wyman, *Paper Walls,* p. 47.

287 "the right to buy radios" DT to Robinson Jeffers, 10 Oct. 1938, Box 131, folder 1, Edna St. Vincent Millay Papers, Library of Congress.

287 "conspiracy of poets" DT to Eugene Boissevain, 18 Oct. 1938, Box 131, folder 1, Edna St. Vincent Millay Papers; an idea that she presented at the PEN conference she organized in May 1939 at the New York World's Fair; see Kurth, *American Cassandra,* pp. 307–8.

287 On the face of it On the Grynszpan case, Jonathan Kirsch, *The Short, Strange Life of Herschel Grynszpan: A Boy Avenger, a Nazi Diplomat and a Murder in Paris* (New York: Liveright, 2013); Gerald Schwab, *The Day the Holocaust Began: The Odyssey of Herschel Grynszpan* (New York: Praeger, 1990).

287 "I have to protest" Kirsch, *Short, Strange,* p. 100.

287 Public whippings On Kristallnacht, especially as an act of violence from below, Alan Steinweis, *Kristallnacht 1938* (Cambridge, Mass.: Belknap Press of Harvard University Press, 2009).

287 "For once, the Jews should feel" Goebbels, diary entry, 10 Nov. 1938.

288 "I feel as though I knew him" "Herschel Grynzspan," 14 Nov. 1938 Broadcast, in DT, *Let the Record,* p. 256.

288 As she went on, she referred DT, *Let the Record,* p. 257.

288 To answer the dictators' crimes Kurth, *American Cassandra,* pp. 283–84. Charac-

terizing the murder as an "act of counter-violence" (as DT did) was exceptional, Kirsch argues. *Short, Strange,* p. 267.

288 **"But is there not a higher justice"** DT, *Let the Record,* p. 259.

288 **As they saw it, Grynszpan** Later, the Nazi government threatened that if any Jew rallied to the assassin's cause, the reckoning for those who remained in Germany would be all the more dire.

289 **A few days after the assassination** Dinah Sheean to Louis Fischer, 15 Nov. 1938, Box 11, folder 19, Louis Fischer Papers, Mudd Manuscript Library, Princeton. [All Sheean/Fischer correspondence cited below is from this folder.]

289 **"Pipe down, Kitty"** The woman was Lady Kitty Brownlow, wife of the 6th Baron, who was credited with the revival of the theater after the First World War.

289 **"not peace—but the initiation"** DT, "Peace—And the Crisis Begins," *NYHT,* 1 Oct. 1938.

289 **"Our Europe is gone!"** Phyllis Bottome, "Dorothy Thompson," DT Papers, Box 140, folder 10. Bottome was the author (among other books) of the anti-fascist novel *The Mortal Storm* (1937). Note DT's horror at Bottome's portrayal of her private life in this article.

289 **The Nazis were clamoring** DT, "On the Record: Give a Man a Chance," *NYHT,* 16 Nov. 1938, p. 23.

289 **"Who is on trial"** DT, *Let the Record,* p. 260.

289 **More than three thousand** DT, "Give a Man a Chance."

289 **As the telegrams rolled** JG, diary entry, 15 Nov. 1938, JG Papers II, Box 19.

289 **She styled her effort** The other members of the committee included Hamilton Fish Armstrong, the editor of *Foreign Affairs;* Raymond Swing; Heywood Broun; Oswald Villard, the editor of the *Nation,* and the *New Yorker* writer Alexander Woollcott.

290 **"I feel compelled"** Herschel Grynszpan to DT, 29 July 1939, DT Papers, Box 13, folder 4, "Grynszpan Case."

290 **That was a satisfying letter** FBI file No. 9-7990. See also Kurth, *American Cassandra,* pp. 284–85.

290 **As Goebbels ginned** Kirsch, *Short, Strange,* p. 160.

290 **To make clear she couldn't** Kurth, *American Cassandra,* p. 287. On the Bund, Hart, *Hitler's,* pp. 23–48.

290 **One was a description** "Bund Talk 'Bunk' to Her," *Baltimore Sun,* 21 Feb. 1939, p. 1; *Dayton Daily News,* 21 Feb. 1939, p. 12.

290 **"If you don't like it"** "Kuhn Attacked on Stage at Nazi Rally," New York *Daily News,* 21 Feb. 1939, p. 474.

291 **"Bunk, bunk, bunk!"** Recounted in Kurth, *American Cassandra,* pp. 287–89.

291 **"It's not the rule of assembly"** "She Tests Free Speech," *Kansas City Times,* 21 Feb. 1939, p. 1.

291 **"We live in merry times"** "Notes and Comment, The Talk of the Town," *New Yorker,* 4 March 1939, p. 11.

291 **"something between a Cassandra"** "Cartwheel Girl," *Time,* 12 June 1939, p. 47. A sentiment *Time* attributed to her women readers.

291 **"startling prophesies"** Shepard Stone, "Dorothy Thompson Calls the Turn," *NYT,* 3 Sept. 1939, BR, p. 5. Similarly, Robert Gale Woolbert, Review of *Let the Record Speak, Foreign Affairs,* Jan. 1940.

291 **When Frances walked into** FFG to JN, Dec. 1938, Jawaharlal Nehru Papers, vol. 29.

292 **She found the rose petals** FFG to JN, Dec. 1938, Jawaharlal Nehru Papers, vol. 29.

292 **"as frantic as a ten-months"** FFG to JN, 5 April 1939, FFG Papers, file 315.

292 How could Asian populations JG, *Inside Asia,* pp. ix, 344.

292 "Above all, it gets booty, loot" JG, *Inside Asia,* p. 474.

292 "our weak spots all right" Handwritten note at the top of A. A. Dudley to A. H. Joyce, 11 May 1938, signed BR? or MR? L/I/1/1388, IOR.

293 "charming vices" His depiction of Chinese hedonism echoed Lin Yutang's best-seller of the year before, *The Importance of Living.*

293 "an exaggerated tendency" JG, *Inside Asia,* p. 29.

293 Perhaps, he speculated JG, *Inside Asia,* p. 33.

293 "tough and rubbery" JG, *Inside Asia,* pp. 345, 363.

293 "He is a unique kind" JG, *Inside Asia,* p. 346. See John Chamberlain, "Swing Around Asia," *New Republic,* 28 June 1939, p. 219.

293 "etherealized Houdini" JG, *Inside Asia,* p. 344.

293 It was intimate and yet On the "obliquity of the personal" in Nehru's writings, Sunil Khilnani's introduction to JN's *Autobiography* (New Delhi: Penguin, 2017), p. xvii.

294 And yet, like Gandhi JG, *Inside Asia,* p. 408.

294 And Gandhi, whom he both JG, *Inside Asia,* p. 409.

294 "patient—perhaps I should say" JG, *Inside Asia,* p. 577.

294 It carried Frances's byline Frances Gunther and John Gunther, "Nehru of India," *Life,* 11 Dec. 1939, pp. 92–101.

294 "hours of practically blood-curdling" FFG to JN, 1 Dec. 1939, file 315.

294 "You—Kashmiri Brahmin" FFG to JN, June 1938, file 315.

294 "Men of destiny" JN to FFG, 5 May 1938, *SWJN,* Series 1, vol. 14, p. 627.

295 "How wonderfully you write" JN to FFG, 1 June 1939, FFG Papers, file 315.

CHAPTER THIRTEEN

296 Pack only your clothes Agnes Knickerbocker, TS memoir, p. 29.

296 The coming conflict HRK, "Behind the War News," *Pomona Progress Bulletin,* 18 Sept. 1939, HRK Papers, 1939 Scrapbook [#30].

296 Planning ahead, Knick had booked He'd planned a lecture tour for Colson Leigh. See Agnes Knickerbocker, TS Memoir, p. 29.

297 In London, the information he'd gathered See HRK Papers, 1939 Scrapbooks [#30, #35, and #36 for British, American, French, German, and Italian coverage]; also Edgar Mowrer, *Triumph and Turmoil,* pp. 299–300; the file B.46.A.32.9 on Knick's articles, Swiss Federal Archives; Sir Campbell Stuart, "Sources of Information and Intelligence," [after Sept. 1939], Box 2, Private Papers of Sir Campbell Stuart, Imperial War Museum.

297 As Knick told the story For a representative sample, H.R.K., "Nazi Leaders Send Big Fortunes Abroad," *El Paso Herald-Post,* 20 Sept. 1939; "Nazi Chiefs' 7,000,000 Sent Abroad," *Daily Mail,* 21 Sept. 1939 and many more in HRK, 1939 Scrapbooks.

297 He tracked the cash that "Mistrustful of Germany's Future: Nazis with Fortunes Abroad," *Illustrated London News,* 30 Sept. 1939.

297 Knick kept copies of the evidence On the reverberations of HRK's findings, see Memorandum for the Secretary's Files, 18 June 1941, Diaries of Henry Morgenthau, Jr., vol. 410, FDR Library (NA 28276714) and eventually, Operation Safehaven. On Safehaven, Martin Lorenz-Meyer, *Safehaven: The Allied Pursuit of Nazi Assets Abroad* (Columbia: University of Missouri Press, 2007), p. 298 (unsubstantiated rumors of Göring's assets in Sweden) and Arthur Lee Smith, *Hitler's Gold: The Story of the Nazi War Loot* (Oxford: Berg, 1996). William Stoneman of

the *CDN* and *New York World-Telegram* reported a similar story but it was HRK's that got the bulk of the attention. See "Say Hitler Aides Deposit Millions Abroad," *Des Moines Tribune*, 20 Sept. 1939, p. 1; "The Nazi Chiselers—Including Hitler," *Montgomery Advertiser*, 24 Sept. 1939, p. 4.

297 **"A lying swine"** Goebbels, diary entry, 22 Sept. 1939.

297 **Crowding into the room** William L. Shirer, *Berlin Diary: The Journal of a Foreign Correspondent, 1934–1941* (New York: Knopf, 1941), pp. 221–22; Louis Lochner, diary entry, 30 Sept. 1939, Louis Lochner Papers, Box 11, folder 18, WHS.

298 **"Publish the documents"** "Dr. Goebbels and His Foreign Nest Egg," *South Wales Evening Post*, nd, 1939 Scrapbook [#30].

298 **What the spies didn't know** HRK, *Paris-soir*, 1939 Scrapbook [#30].

298 **"I am a neutral American journalist"** *Birmingham Post*, 25 Sept. 1939, 1939 Scrapbook [#30].

298 **"Goebbels is wrong if he thought"** HRK, *Paris-soir*, 1939 Scrapbook [#30]. See also Edgar Ansel Mowrer, "Further Proof Is Offered That Nazi Leaders Placed Rich 'Nest Eggs' Abroad," *Dayton Herald*, 27 Sept. 1939, p. 4.

298 **"insidious lies"** Telegram from Karl von Wiegand to Clinton Gilbert, 8 May 1933, NARA RG 59/811.81262/109. My thanks to Benjamin Goldstein for this reference and the one that follows. On von Wiegand, see Benjamin Goldstein, "'A Legend Somewhat Larger than Life': Karl H. von Wiegand and the Trajectory of Hearstian Sensationalist Journalism," *Historical Research*, 94, no. 265 (Aug. 2021): 629–59.

298 **"pulled off a good yarn"** Karl von Wiegand to E. D. Coblentz, 28 Sept. 1939, Edmond Coblentz Papers, Box 9, Bancroft Library, University of California, Berkeley.

298 **"far too precise details"** "Nazis' Fortunes Abroad," *The Times* [London], 22 Sept. 1939, p. 7. Subsequent stories (on 28 and 29 September) were reported without skepticism, but in HRK's obituary, *The Times* referred to his "circumstantial account"—noting "the matter has never been conclusively proved one way or the other" (13 July 1949, p. 7). Chaim Weizmann's source—the chemist Richard Willstätter—thought that Knickerbocker's figures were probably an understatement. *The Letters and Papers of Chaim Weizmann*, Series B, vol. II, ed. Barnet Litvinoff (Jerusalem: Israel Universities Press, 1984), p. 379. Claims about "Nazi nest eggs" continued to circulate. See, for instance, Stanley Ross, "Nazi Nest Eggs in Argentina," *Collier's*, 21 April 1945, pp. 13, 70, 72.

299 **Knick and the two** "Statement of Edgar Ansel Mowrer," 31 March 1965, Congressional testimony before the House Committee on Un-American Activities, 89th Congress, 1st Session, p. 21. On "black" propaganda, Ellic Howe, *The Black Game: British Subversive Operations Against the Germans During the Second World War* (London: M. Joseph, 1982), esp. illuminating on the fraction of total records represented by FO 898.

299 **Knick's charges about the top** See the discussion of the assets of Friedrich Kadgien, an adviser to Göring, in Christiane Uhlig, Petra Barthelmess, Mario König, Peter Pfaffenroth, and Bettina Zeugin, *Tarnung, Transfer, Transit: Die Schweiz als Drehscheibe verdeckter deutscher Operationen (1938–1952)*, Publications of the Independent Commission of Experts, Switzerland—Second World War, vol. 9 (Zurich: Chronos, 2001), pp. 383–434. For Robert U. Vogler, the fact that Kadgien's is one of the relatively few proven cases of assets transferred abroad suggests that the scale of this activity (at least in Swiss banks) was minimal. Vogler, *Swiss Banking Secrecy: Origins, Significance, Myth* (Zurich: Association for Financial History, 2006), pp. 61–62; 99, fn. 140. On Argentina, especially allegations about Göring's assets, Eizenstat Report, Supplement to Preliminary Study on U.S. and Allied Efforts to Recover and Restore Gold and Other Assets Stolen or Hidden by

Germany During World War II, 1998, p. 154. My thanks to Vanessa Ogle for discussion of this subject.

299 **Thanks to decades of painstaking** Uhlig et al., *Transfer, Transit,* esp. pp. 128–54, chs. 10–11; Adam LeBor, *Hitler's Secret Bankers* (London: Pocket Books, 1997). On Liechtenstein, Hanspeter Lussy et al., *Finanzbeziehungen Liechtensteins zur Zeit des Nationalsozialismus* (Zurich: Chronos, 2005).

299 **"Bet Knick will like"** William Shirer, diary entry, 25 Sept. 1939, Shirer Papers, Looseleaf Box.

299 **In sorties that month** "Das sind Euer Führer" psywar.org/product_1939EH158 .php, accessed 10 Jan. 2021; "RAF Tell Germany of Secret Nazi Cash," *Star,* 30 Sept. 1939, Knickerbocker, 1939 Scrapbook [#30]. Many of the leaflets were backfiring, the British Cabinet heard in October 1939. An exception was the one containing Knick's story. Vernon McKenzie, *Here Lies Goebbels!* (London: M. Joseph, 1940), p. 307. See also Lord Halifax's appraisal to the Cabinet, "The Effect of the Dropping of Leaflets in Germany," 9 Oct. 1939, p. 3, W.P. (39) 82.

299 **"The window shades are drawn"** JG, *The High Cost of Hitler* (London: Hamish Hamilton, 1939), pp. 65–66. Broadcast given from London, 28 Aug. 1939.

299 **When Britain declared war** JG, "Live World War Ghosts Stir House of Commons," *Boston Globe,* 4 Sept. 1939, p. 22.

299 **He was staying at the Dorchester** Matthew Sweet, *The West End Front: The Wartime Secrets of London's Grand Hotels* (London: Faber, 2012).

300 **When I broadcast** JG to FFG, 9 Sept. 1939, FFG Papers, file 173.

300 **There was too much static** JG to FFG, 9 Sept. 1939.

300 **If he was as gung ho** FFG to JG, 4 Sept. 1939, JG Papers II, Box 23.

300 **Did he realize** FFG to JG, 28 Aug. 1939; 1 Sept. 1939, JG Papers II, Box 23.

300 **Soon after, a telegram** Cablegram, 19 Sept. 1939, JG Papers II, Box 23.

300 **Maybe she'd been looking** JG, Notes for Indian Sign, JG Papers 1972 Add., Box 5, folder 1.

300 **He didn't permit her** JG, Notes for Indian Sign.

300 **Nevertheless, at one point** Ken Cuthbertson's Interview with Bubbles Hornblow, cited in Cuthbertson, *Inside,* p. 191.

300 **"that crazy little Agnes"** Green Notebook II; also JG, *Indian Sign,* p. 9.

300 **In Paris, when Knick** Agnes Knickerbocker, TS Memoir, p. 26.

301 **Strange as it may seem** "X—Notes on Her Talk," JG Papers II, Box 22; also (with slightly different wording) JG, *Indian Sign,* p. 42.

301 **"a useless woman"** FFG, Draft letter to Nehru, spring 1940 [not at NMML], FFG Papers, file 132; expressed similarly in FFG to Betty Gram Swing, 8 Oct. ny [1940], Betty Gram Swing Papers, MC 890, folder 6.1, Schlesinger Library.

301 **"We could have lunch here"** FFG to JN, dated July 1939, postmarked 20 Aug. 1939 [censored], Jawaharlal Nehru Papers, vol. 29.

302 **"entirely on the side of democracy"** Srinath Raghavan, *India's War: World War II and the Making of Modern South Asia, 1939–1945* (London: Allen Lane, 2016), ch. 1; Clymer, *Quest for Freedom,* pp. 15–17; Yasmin Khan, *The Raj at War: A People's History of India's Second World War* (London: The Bodley Head, 2015).

302 **Nehru heard the news** JN to FFG, 25 April 1940, FFG Papers, file 316.

302 **He wasn't *that* much** JN to FFG, 16 Nov. 1939, FFG Papers, file 315.

302 **He sent her a photograph** JN to FFG, 14 July 1940, FFG Papers, file 316.

302 **"Something that one craves"** JN to FFG, 7 April 1940, *SWJN,* Series 1, vol. 14, p. 633.

302 **Twenty-three thousand** Clymer, *Quest,* p. 18; Kenton J. Clymer, "Jawaharlal Nehru and the United States: The Pre-independence Years," *Diplomatic History* 14 (Spring 1990): 143–61.

302 "I hope London is razed" FFG to JG, nd [fall 1940], JG Papers II, Box 23.

303 "They manage to bring me" JN to FFG, 15 Oct. 1941, FFG Papers, file 316.

303 She mailed him letters JN to FFG, 7 Aug. 1941, FFG Papers, file 316.

303 "When will this world" JN to FFG, 15 Oct. 1941.

303 Every once in a while FFG to JN, 19 Sept. 1943, FFG Papers, file 316.

303 In her imagination, though FFG to JN, unsent draft? [not at NMML], New Year's Eve, 1941, FG Papers, file 316.

303 The experience in Asia FFG to JN, 6 July 1940, Jawaharlal Nehru Papers, vol. 29.

303 She—who'd hardly considered On support for the Irgun in the United States, Rafael Medoff, *Militant Zionism in America: The Rise and Impact of the Jabotinsky Movement in the United States, 1926–1948* (Tuscaloosa: University of Alabama Press, 2002).

303 "Irgun lads" FFG to JG, 11 July 1939, JG Papers II, Box 23. Frances's brother, the movie producer Bernard Fineman, had also become involved. He married one of Bergson's organizers, the Palestinian Miryam Hayman (or Miriam Heyman) in May 1942.

303 "They eat other people's cake" Draft MS of FFG's "Empire," FFG Papers, file 265; on the concept of "reverse tutelage," see also Priyamvada Gopal, *Insurgent Empire: Anticolonial Resistance and British Dissent* (London: Verso, 2019), esp. chs. 6–9.

303 She'd started a new book FFG, "Empire: Notes for a Study of the Theory and Practice of Empires," FFG Papers, file 253; FFG to JN, 6 July 1940.

304 He was too much of an FFG to JN, 6 July 1940.

304 Still, the line that her erstwhile *We or They* by Hamilton Fish Armstrong, the editor of *Foreign Affairs* and a friend of the Gunthers.

304 Weren't the crimes the British FFG, *Revolution in India*, p. 69.

304 "You psychoanalyzed" Gobind Behari Lal to FFG, 8 Oct. 1940, FFG Papers, file 64.

304 John's editor Cass Canfield to FFG, 5 April 1940, FFG Papers, file 64.

304 She was busy day FFG to JG, 8 Oct. 1940, FFG Papers, file 173.

304 Nonetheless, many were the days FFG to JN, 6 July 1940.

304 She spent a maddening evening Conversation described in DT to Benny, undated, DT Papers, Box 42, folder 4; see also Jerome Frank to DT, 23 Sept. 1938 and Frank to DT, 17 Oct. 1938, DT Papers, Box 11.

304 Indictments of the perfidious Moser, *Twisting the Lion's Tail.*

305 "Great Britain's ruin" DT to Mr. Dennis, draft, undated, DT Papers, Box 42, folder 4; also DT, *Listen, Hans,* pp. 40–41.

305 But what she cared JG, diary entry, 29 Nov. 1942, JG Papers II, Box 19.

305 And thus far, the Nazis On Thompson and broadcasting, Irving E. Fang, "Dorothy Thompson" in *Those Radio Commentators!* (Ames: Iowa State University Press, 1977), pp. 131–49.

305 She was expressing her "personal opinion" "KWK Explains Broadcast Cut," *St. Louis Globe-Democrat,* 2 Sept. 1939, p. 4.

305 "Dorothy Is Cut Off Air" *Marysville Journal-Tribune* (Marysville, Ohio), 2 Sept. 1939, p. 1.

306 What had that gotten us Susan Dunn, *1940: FDR, Willkie, Lindbergh, Hitler—the Election Amid the Storm* (New Haven & London: Yale University Press, 2013); Lynne Olson, *Those Angry Days: Roosevelt, Lindbergh, and America's Fight over World War II, 1939–1941* (New York: Random House, 2013); Sarah Churchwell, *Behold, America: The Entangled History of 'America First' and 'the American Dream'* (London: Bloomsbury, 2018); Justus Doenecke, *Storm on the Horizon: The Challenge to American Intervention, 1939–1941* (Lanham, Md.: Rowman & Littlefield,

2000); Wayne Cole, *America First: The Battle Against Intervention, 1940–1941* (Madison: University of Wisconsin Press, 1953).

306 **Shortly after the start** "Text of Lindbergh Speech Warning U.S. Against War," *Detroit Free Press*, 16 Sept. 1939, p. 8. See Bradley W. Hart, *Hitler's American Friends: The Third Reich's Supporters in the United States* (New York: Thomas Dunne/St. Martin's Press, 2018), pp. 168–74.

306 **She offered a chronology** DT, "On the Record—Col. Lindbergh and Propaganda," *NYHT*, 20 Sept. 1939, p. 25.

306 **"Colonel Lindbergh's inclination"** JVS, *Dorothy and Red*, p. 139.

306 **"peels the hide off"** Harry S. Truman to Bess Truman, 20 Sept. 1939, Harry S. Truman Papers—Family and Business Papers, catalog.archives.gov/id/147870078.

306 **She would publish thirteen** Kurth, *American Cassandra*, p. 314.

306 **"to make universal certain human"** DT, "On the Record: War Issue Is the Brutal, Naked, Criminal Power of the Runaway State," *Spokesman-Review* (Spokane, Wash.), 10 March 1940, p. 30.

306 **She was in Rome** DT, "On the Record: Europe at War," *South Bend Tribune*, 9 April 1940, p. 6.

307 **But she could tell that** DT, "The Maginot Line: A Fort in Action," *Current History*, June 1940, pp. 51–52.

307 **The lawns hadn't been mowed** James Drawbell, *Dorothy Thompson's English Journey* (London: Collins, 1942), p. 61.

307 **Shortly after German troops** Grynszpan's efforts to secure French protection are detailed in Stephen Koch, *The Boy Assassin and the Holocaust* (Berkeley: Counterpoint, 2019), pp. 149–59.

307 **That was the last** At the end of the war, he was declared dead.

307 **"The master of the dyke"** Text of a speech for the Canadian Broadcasting Corporation (21 July 1940), printed as DT, "Winston Churchill: He Inspires an Empire in Its Hour of Need," *Life*, 27 Jan. 1941.

307 **"Freedom and humanity"** Churchill's telegram in Wendell Willkie papers, quoted by Kurth, *American Cassandra*, p. 328.

307 **"we will go to eat Devonshire"** DT to Wendell Willkie, draft letter, undated [1940], DT Papers, Box 42, folder 5.

308 **Now was no time** A point she began to make in May 1940, see DT, "On the Record: Change Is Perilous," *Charlotte News*, 16 May 1940, p. 6.

308 **She'd criticized FDR** DT, "On the Record: The Presidency," *NYHT*, 9 Oct. 1940, p. 27; DT, "On the Record: The Axis and the Campaign," *NYHT*, 18 Oct. 1940, p. 23A.

308 **The column appeared in the paper** For a sampling: "Readers Disagree with Dorothy Thompson," *NYHT*, 10 Oct. 1940, p. 23; 11 Oct. 1940, p. 21; "Astounded and Amazed," *NYHT*, 11 Oct. 1940, p. 21; "Astonished at Column," *NYHT*, 10 Oct. 1940, p. 23.

308 **Her contract wasn't renewed** DT to the Reids, 8 Jan. 1941; DT to Helen Reid, 23 Jan. 1941, Helen Reid Papers.

308 **"You are now the most prominent"** SL to DT, 3 July 1941, Private Collection, quoted in Kurth, *American Cassandra*, p. 337.

308 **If Dorothy advocated** Mark Schorer, *Sinclair Lewis: An American Life* (New York: McGraw-Hill, 1961), pp. 661, 679. On Virginia and Leonard Woolf's dispute about the war, Francesca Wade, *Square Haunting: Five Writers in London Between the Wars* (New York: Tim Duggan Books, 2020), pp. 249–50.

308 **Unless she consented** Kurth, *American Cassandra*, p. 338.

308 **"Dorothy, you lost your job"** JG, *Roosevelt in Retrospect* (New York: Harper, 1950), p. 36.

308 **From now on, though** For DT's influence with FDR, Kurth, *American Cassandra,* pp. 331–32; 518, fn. 12; Raymond Gram Swing, *"Good Evening!" A Professional Memoir* (New York: Harcourt, Brace and World, 1964), p. 283.

309 **"I know, I wrote"** Barnaby Conrad, "Portrait of Sinclair Lewis," *Horizon,* March 1979, cited in Kurth, *American Cassandra,* pp. 331–32. Also on DT's ghostwriting for FDR, Raymond Swing, *"Good Evening!,"* p. 283.

309 **He was supposed to speak** Dinah Sheean to Louis Fischer, 17 Feb. 1939, 21 March 1939, Louis Fischer Papers.

309 **"Jimmy is awfully sorry"** Frederick van Ryn, "Dream Jobs," *Redbook* (April 1942), p. 96.

309 **Even if she couldn't** Dinah Sheean to Louis Fischer, 17 Feb. 1939, Louis Fischer Papers.

309 **He needed a doctor** Dinah Sheean to Louis Fischer, 31 March 1939, 10 April 1939, Louis Fischer Papers.

309 **Dinah had hoped** Dinah Sheean to Louis Fischer, 18 June 1939, Louis Fischer Papers.

309 **The countryside was practically** Dinah Sheean to Louis Fischer, 18 June 1939, Louis Fischer Papers.

310 **Dorothy was like her aunt** Dinah Sheean to Louis Fischer, 12 July 1939, Louis Fischer Papers.

310 **"God-Damn Swine"** Dinah Sheean to Louis Fischer, 30 June 1939; 12 July 1939; 7 Aug. 1939, Louis Fischer Papers.

310 **It seemed to him like** JVS to ESW, 22 Dec. ny [1939], JVS Papers, Berg.

310 **Among the sinners** Frederick Van Ryn, "Dream Jobs," *Redbook* (April 1942): 94.

310 **He'd signed an open** "To All Active Supporters of Democracy and Peace," *Soviet Russia Today* (Sept. 1939): 24–25, 28.

310 **The Soviet Union** JVS, "Brumaire, II: The Soviet Union as a Fascist State," *New Republic,* 15 Nov. 1939, pp. 104–6.

310 **"No reflective person outside"** JVS, "Brumaire: The Soviet Union as a Fascist State," *New Republic,* 8 Nov. 1939, p. 8.

310 **There were plenty of disillusioned** See, for instance, Alan M. Wald, *The New York Intellectuals: The Rise and Decline of the Anti-Stalinist Left from the 1930s to the 1980s* (Chapel Hill: University of North Carolina Press, 1987).

311 **But of the Soviet Union's** See for instance Herbert Agar, "Time and Tide," *Courier Journal* (Louisville), 19 Nov. 1939, p. 30; Frank N. Trager, "Bogus Friends of Freedom," *North American Review* 248, no. 2 (Winter 1939/40): 366–73, esp. 372–73.

311 **Unimpeachable as his credentials** "Common Sense About Russia," *New Republic,* 15 Nov. 1939, pp. 98–100.

311 **"very repellant"** JVS, "Mr. Sheean and His Critics," *New Republic,* 13 Dec. 1939, p. 232; on his arguments in 1940 with Communist intellectuals, JVS, *Between the Thunder,* pp. 200–202.

311 **At the Communists' mass meeting** JVS to ESW, 22 Dec. 1939, JVS Papers, Berg.

311 **Also the movie** On Communist critiques of *Gone with the Wind,* Nina Silber, *This War Ain't Over: Fighting the Civil War in New Deal America* (Chapel Hill: University of North Carolina Press, 2018), pp. 151–53.

311 **"I think the best thing"** JVS to ESW, 22 Dec. 1939, JVS Papers, Berg. For a more sympathetic account of Jimmy's volte-face, see Joseph North, *No Men Are Strangers* (New York: International Publishers, 1958), pp. 150–60.

311 **John and Dorothy** JVS, new introduction (1969) to *Personal History* (Boston: Houghton Mifflin, 1969), p. xiii.

312 **The argument she'd started** She was a sponsor of the "America First" rally on 30 Oct. 1941 in Madison Square Garden. See *America First Bulletin*, 1 Nov. 1941, p. 1.

312 **For her part, she threatened** FFG to JG, 28 Aug. 1939, 1 Sept. 1939, JG Papers II, Box 23.

312 **It was intolerable to him** JG, diary entry, 7 Nov. 1939, JG Papers II, Box 19.

312 **"crusade against Adolf"** H. L. Mencken to JG, 30 Aug. 1939, JG Papers II, Box 35.

312 **The sentiment expressed** JG, diary entry, 9 Nov. 1939, JG Papers II, Box 19.

312 **The news of the Nazi-Soviet** JG diary entry, 26 Oct. 1939, JG Papers II, Box 19.

312 **To be anti-Nazi** Kurth, *American Cassandra*, p. 309. The only thing he'd favored was, as he recognized, itself a compromise: the revised Neutrality Act that FDR had at the start of the war shepherded through Congress against the protests of Lindbergh and other isolationists.

312 **"Journalists have more reason"** Knick to J. V. Connolly, 9 Feb. 1941, HRK Papers, Uncatalogued correspondence, Box 4, folder 1941-8.

312 **She'd have put neutrals** Margot Asquith to JG, 4 Dec. 1941, JG Papers II, Box 35; Margot Asquith to HRK, 10 Oct. 1940, HRK Papers, Catalogued correspondence, Box 1.

313 **"fewer aneurisms, goiters"** Lee Miller to JG, 24 June 1940, JG Papers II, Box 35.

313 **He'd given a luncheon** JG, diary entry, 10 Nov. 1939, JG Papers II, Box 19.

313 **He and Frances hosted** JG to Joseph Barnes, 14 March 1940, Joseph Barnes Papers, Box 2, Columbia; for FFG's efforts, see also Medoff, *Militant Zionism*, pp. 34-35, 39.

313 **The foremost isolationist** JG, diary entry, 23 May 1941, JG Papers II, Box 19.

313 **John decided to stick** For instance, JG diary entries, 31 Oct. 1939, 12 July 1940, JG Papers II, Box 19.

313 **Most nights he was** FFG, "Inside Gunther," *Fashion*, Sept. 1939, JG Papers II, Box 6, Pertaining to Frances Gunther.

313 **Why was he so detached** JG, Misc. Scraps for Autobiography, Various Notes, JG Papers II, Box 1.

313 **"I have been trying"** JG to FFG, 22 Feb. ny [1940], FFG Papers, file 173.

313 **"I don't believe in the war"** Misc. Scraps for Autobiography, Various Dates, JG Papers II, Box 1.

313 **The real question** JG, diary entry dated Virginia Beach, June 1940, JG Papers II, Box 19.

314 **You and I *are* going** Agnes Knickerbocker [AK] to JG, Sunday (August) ny [1940], JG Papers II, Box 22.

314 **"The source of my dissatisfaction"** JG, diary entry dated Virginia Beach.

314 **Frau Stekel wanted them** Hilda Stekel to FFG, 8 April ny [1939?], JG Papers II, Box 35.

314 **"Shall I call it"** Wilhelm Stekel to JG, 15 June 1939, JG Papers II, Box 35.

314 **It would be a shocking** Wilhelm Stekel to JG, 18 Jan. 1940, JG Papers II, Box 35.

314 **"You have a right to enjoy"** Stekel to JG, 6 March 1940, JG Papers II, Box 4, Clips from Diaries—Category: Frances Gunther: Not Used.

315 **The news that Agnes** AK to JG, early Aug. ny [1940], JG Papers II, Box 22.

315 **Consider what a disaster** "NY and Conn, Sept. 1940," X Notes (Of Her Talk), JG Papers II, Box 22.

315 **"You must love me less"** AK to JG, Sunday (August) ny [1940], JG Papers II, Box 22.

315 **At the start of their affair** "Trip I—Feb. 1940 notes," JG Papers II, Box 22.

315 **I won't ever leave** Agnes Knickerbocker, TS memoir, p. 30.

315 **Agnes's jealousy** JG, *Indian Sign*, p. 51.

315 **I am happier with you** 3 March 1941, X Notes (Of Her Talk), JG Papers II, Box 22.

315 **"I want it just"** 10 March 1941, X Notes (Of Her Talk), JG Papers II, Box 22.

315 **He'd kill you and me** 27 Feb. 1941, 3 March 1941, X Notes (Of Her Talk), JG Papers II, Box 22.

315 **It was John's hope** Notes of this conversation in June 1941, X Notes (Of Her Talk), JG Papers II, Box 22.

315 **She'd been away in Florida** See FFG to JN, May 1941 re. length of Florida stay, Jawaharlal Nehru Papers, vol. 29, p. 292.

315 **The comic Jack Benny** Recording available on Radio Echoes site, 16 April 1941 program with Jack Benny: radioechoes.com/?page=play_download&mode=play &dl_mp3folder=Q&dl_file=quiz_kids_1941-04-16_jack_benny.mp3&dl_series= Quiz%20Kids&dl_title=Jack%20Benny&dl_date=1941.04.16&dl_size=9.93 %20MB.

316 **Johnny sounded so happy** JG, diary entry, 16 April 1941, JG Papers, Box 19.

316 **She looked pretty** Recounted in "JG on F," Phone, etc. folder, May/June 1941, JG Papers, Box 22.

316 **"Every idea you ever had"** JG, diary entry, 21 Sept. 1941. See also FFG's conversation with Agnes Smedley, summarized in Ruth Price, *The Lives of Agnes Smedley* (New York: Oxford University Press, 2005), p. 360. John's entry in the *Current Biography* for 1941 praised his "honorable restraint" in not appropriating Frances's epigrams; it credits "attractive Frances Gunther" as a writer and authority on world affairs who edited her husband's work and did much of his research (p. 351).

316 **One day, she'd write** Diary Scraps on F. Used for Indian Sign, JG Papers II, Box 1.

316 **Either she was lying** See JG diary entries, 21 July 1941, 2 Aug. 1941, JG Papers II, Box 19.

316 **"Be of good cheer"** JG, diary entry, 2 Aug. 1941, JG Papers II, Box 19.

317 **He knew she was back** JG, diary entry, 18 Sept. 1941, JG Papers II, Box 19.

317 **He didn't want to go** FFG to JN, 1 June 1942, Jawaharlal Nehru Papers, vol. 29.

317 **Please see to it that** Among others, Dick Cutler to Mrs. Gunther, 14 Sept. 1938, JG Papers I, Box 44, folder 6; Mrs. Douglas Haskell to FFG, 5 Aug. 1939, JG Papers II, Box 24, folder labeled letters 1938–40, S-Z.

317 **Fodor's son was there** JG to Billie, 17 Sept. 1941, JG Papers II, Box 24, folder labeled Family Letters.

317 **She wept and he was close** JG diary entry, 26 Sept. 1941, JG Papers II, Box 19.

317 **When they drove out** JG diary entry, 27 Sept. 1941, JG Papers II, Box 19.

317 **Stop by tonight** JG diary entries, Aug. 1941, JG Papers II, Box 19.

317 **Knick wanted John to write** JG diary entry for 22 Sept. 1941, JG Papers II, Box 19.

317 **"We were buzzards"** JG, "Foreword," *Is Tomorrow Hitler's?*, pp. xi, xiv.

318 **She did want AK to** JG, Sunday afternoon ny [1941], JG Papers II, Box 22.

318 **The dogfights** JVS, *Between the Thunder*, pp. 154, 159; see also Ben Robertson, *I Saw England* (New York: Knopf, 1941), p. 94.

318 **Overhead the bombs screamed** Peter Stansky, *The First Day of the Blitz* (New Haven and London: Yale University Press, 2007).

318 **He and Knick stayed on** JVS, *Between the Thunder*, pp. 181–92.

318 **In a bad air raid** Virginia Cowles, *Looking for Trouble* (London: Faber, 2010 [1941]), p. 440 (quoting Sheean).

318 **Playing in the rubble** JVS, *Between the Thunder*, p. 173.

319 **"Why should I be disturbed"** JVS, *Between the Thunder*, p. 194.

319 **"Half poem and half bread"** JVS, *Between the Thunder*, p. 190.

319 **Jimmy, she reported to her son** Diana Cooper, *Autobiography: The Rainbow Comes and Goes; The Lights of Common Day; Trumpets from the Steep* (New York: Carroll & Graf, 1985), p. 553. According to Diana Cooper's biographer, her assiduous

courting kept Jimmy from complaining as much about the Ministry of Information's stringent censorship as he would otherwise have done. He nevertheless criticized the British censorship regime harshly. See, for instance, JVS, "So Much to So Few," *Redbook,* Dec. 1940, pp. 15, 48–49, 106–10. Philip Ziegler, *Diana Cooper: A Biography* (New York: Knopf, 1982 [1981]), p. 198.

319 **"The Duchess of Westminster wants"** JVS, *Between the Thunder,* p. 189.

319 **His reports alone** Stanley Cloud and Lynne Olson, *The Murrow Boys: Pioneers on the Front Lines of Broadcast Journalism* (Boston and New York: Houghton Mifflin, 1996); Lynne Olson, *Citizens of London: The Americans Who Stood with Britain in Its Darkest, Finest Hour* (New York: Random House, 2010).

319 **She was offered up** Diana Cooper to John Julius Norwich, 15 July 1940, in *Darling Monster: The Letters of Lady Diana Cooper to Her Son John Julius Norwich, 1939–1952* (London: Chatto & Windus, 2013).

319 **"rather an ordeal"** JVS, *Between the Thunder,* p. 196.

319 **For Dorothy, who arrived** DT, "On the Record—By Such Small Things See England," *Knoxville Journal,* 16 Aug. 1941, p. 6.

319 **The British were fighting** DT, "On the Record—Some Geographical Reality," *Fort Worth Star-Telegram,* 7 Sept. 1941, p. 20.

319 **She flew to England** The air war was far from over, continuing through 1945, with the V-rocket campaigns. See Grayzel, *Age.*

319 **"I'm so glad you're here"** Quoted in Drawbell, *English Journey,* p. 69.

319 **It was like managing a film** Drawbell, *English Journey,* p. 73.

320 **She toured bomb sites** Drawbell, *English Journey;* James Drawbell, *An Autobiography* (New York: Pantheon, 1964 [1963]), pp. 357–64, gloves at p. 361. On British reporters, JG, diary entry, 29 Oct. 1941.

320 **"Oh, I must be"** Drawbell, *English Journey,* p. 83.

320 **He tapped his fingers** DT, "On the Record—Winston Churchill," *The Cincinnati Enquirer,* 8 Aug. 1941, p. 6.

320 **For all the physical destruction** DT, "Present War Is Recreating Civilization in Britain," *The Spokesman-Review* (Spokane, Wash.), 1 Sept. 1941, p. 4.

320 **"I've crowded months into weeks"** Drawbell, *Autobiography,* p. 362.

320 **"I was an exhilarated wreck"** Quoted in Kurth, *American Cassandra,* p. 336.

320 **"feminine Churchill"** Drawbell, *English Journey,* p. 107.

321 **"It is not too early"** "Huge N.Y. Assembly Petitions Congress to Repeal Neutrality Act," *Evening Citizen* (Ottawa), 25 Sept. 1941, p. 15. See also the Ring of Freedom Petition to Congress, 24 Sept. 1941, DT Papers, Box 24.

321 **He flew on the Pan Am** JG, London Diary, undated entry [first in the book, Oct. 1941], JG Papers II, Box 19.

321 **She'd been photographing the Blitz** See, for example, her "Dolphin Court," 1940. Becky Conekin, *Lee Miller in Fashion* (New York: Monacelli, 2013); Hilary Roberts, *Lee Miller: A Woman's War* (London: Thames & Hudson, 2015).

321 **One good thing about the Blitz** JG, diary entry, 28 Oct. 1941, London Diary.

321 **He spent an evening** JG diary Entry, 1 Nov. 1941, London Diary.

321 **He felt embarrassed** JG, diary entry for 30 Oct. 1941, London Diary.

321 **Didn't his fellow countrymen** JG, diary entry for 20 Nov. 1941, London Diary.

322 **But even if the British** See JG, diary entry for 11 Nov. 1941, London Diary.

322 **He'd managed to keep** JG, diary entry for 3 Nov. 1941, London Diary.

322 **In the theaters, British audiences** JG, "John Gunther Looks Abroad," *Arizona Daily Star,* 6 Dec. 1941, p. 11; JG, diary entry, 27 Nov. 1941, London Diary.

322 **In British factories, workers** JG, "'Our Gallant Ally': Russia Holds British Hopes," *The Daily Oklahoman,* 7 Nov. 1941, p. 10.

322 **Most astonishing of all** JG, diary entry for 30 Nov. 1941, London Diary.

323 "Now that we *are* in" JG, diary entry for 11 Dec. 1941, London Diary.

323 They had Christmas dinner JG, diary entry for 25 Dec. 1941, London Diary.

323 "Amusing to see that Frances" AK to JG, Sunday afternoon, nd, [Early autumn, 1941], JG Papers II, Box 22.

CHAPTER FOURTEEN

324 "What a tremendous part" JVS to Dinah Sheean, 5 Oct. 1943, JVS Papers, WHS, Box 1, folder 1, Letters to Dinah, 16 July 1943–9 Feb. 1944.

324 There were already American soldiers HRK, "Capri's Beauty Still Unhurt," *Austin American-Statesman*, 23 Sept. 1943, p. 17.

324 It would be a long, bloody HRK, "Next War Moves 'Plotted' by Foreign Correspondent," *Tennessean*, 25 May 1943, p. 1.

324 By 1945, he prophesied HRK, "Long and Bitter War Is Foreseen by H. R. Knickerbocker in Address Here," *Fort Worth Star-Telegram*, 9 Feb. 1943, p. 17.

325 I can't just sit around JG, diary entry, 30 Sept. 1942, JG Papers II, Box 19.

325 A boy of ten could do JG, diary entry, 30 Sept. 1942, JG Papers II, Box 19. Quentin Reynolds claims that Jimmy in fact rendered significant service as an aide to General Cannon. See Quentin Reynolds, *The Curtain Rises* (New York: Random House, 1944), p. 283. Hemingway pointedly didn't want to be a "Lt. Col like Jimmy Sheean to whom I have always previously had to point out which end of a battlefield was which . . ." (EH to Archibald MacLeish, 10 Aug. 1943, in *Ernest Hemingway, Selected Letters, 1917–1961* [New York: Scribner, 1981], p. 549). On Hemingway's deleterious effect on JVS, Dinah Sheean to Thornton Wilder, 30 Dec. 1974, Thornton Wilder Papers, YCAL MSS Box 56, folder 1540, Beinecke Library.

325 He wanted to be transferred Johnson, "Twentieth-Century Seeker," pp. 412–24.

325 He sent her long, severe letters JVS to Dinah Sheean, 5 Sept. 1943 and others, JVS Papers, WHS, Box 1, folder 2.

325 It would be a better use JVS to Dinah Sheean, 6 Oct. ny [1943?], JVS Papers, WHS, Box 1, folder 2, Letters to Dinah, 4 July 1942–22 March 1944.

325 Instead, he was dispatched JVS, diary entry, 25 May 1944, JVS Papers, WHS, Box 1, folder 38, diary, 1944–46.

325 The situation in India JVS, diary entry, 24 Aug. 1944, JVS Papers, WHS, Box 1, folder 38. See also FFG to JVS, 16 March 1942 and JVS to FFG, 4 April 1942, FFG Papers, file 229.

325 The United States was making JVS, diary entry, 9 Aug. 1944, JVS Papers, WHS, Box 1, folder 38.

325 "Have no fear" Reported in Viscount Halifax, Weekly Political Summary, Washington to Foreign Office, 1 May 1944, FO 371/38524, The National Archives.

325 "I've given up that young man" JG, diary entry, 23 May 1943, JG Papers II, Box 19.

326 "drive Mr. Hitler" DT to FDR, undated [addressed "To the President of the United States (without Protocol)"], cited in Kurth, *American Cassandra*, p. 359.

326 He burst into tears JG, diary entry, 24 Feb. 1942, JG Papers II, Box 19.

326 He'd been reading all about Johnny to JG, nd [1941], JG Papers II, Box 6.

326 One summer, he'd smelted Helen Haskell to FFG, 5 Oct. 1940, JG Papers I, Box 44, folder 6.

326 Johnny was young JG, diary entry, 18 Jan. 1942, JG Papers II, Box 19.

326 Were they separating JG, diary entry, 24 Feb. 1942, JG Papers II, Box 19.

326 I have spent all my money Johnny to JG, nd, [1941 or 1942], JG Papers II, Box 6.

327 What should I *do*? JG, diary entries for late 1941 and early 1942, esp. 27 Dec. 1941, 1–10 Jan. 1942, JG Papers II, Box 19.

327 **Reporting from the front** See Ray Moseley, *Reporting War: How Foreign Correspondents Risked Capture, Torture and Death to Cover World War II* (New Haven: Yale University Press, 2017).

327 **An appointment as the head** JG, diary entry, 16 April 1942; Cass Canfield to JG, 8 Jan. 1961, JG Papers II, Box 6. On OWI, Allan M. Winkler, *The Politics of Propaganda: The Office of War Information, 1942–1945* (New Haven: Yale University Press, 1978).

327 **At the director Frank Capra's** JG, diary entry, 13 April 1942, JG Papers II, Box 19.

327 **He'd never liked Hollywood** JG, diary entry, 30 July 1942, JG Papers II, Box 19.

327 **But now, dashing around town** JG, diary entry, 13 Aug. 1942, JG Papers II, Box 19.

327 **"Hours of blank nothingness"** JG, "Recent Diary Notes, etc.," 1942 diary, JG Papers II, Box 19.

327 **He'd flown down to Dallas** AK to JG, 18 March 1942, JG Papers II, Box 22.

327 **Knick could have been** 24 Feb. 1941 notes (Lunch, Mauds), X (Notes of Her Talk), NY Feb.–April. 1941 notes, JG Papers II, Box 22.

327 **She hadn't written** AK to JG, Friday, nd [Feb. 1943], JG Papers II, Box 22.

327 **"Will you always"** 30–31 May 1942, X (Notes of Her Talk), JG Papers II, Box 22.

327 **"very dreary"** AK to JG, Sunday, undated [Jan. 1943], JG Papers II, Box 22.

328 **In her syndicated column** Eleanor Roosevelt, "My Day," dateline 26 Feb. 1942, *Tampa Morning Tribune*, 26 Feb. 1942, p. 11.

328 **"every pore in his body"** JG, *Roosevelt in Retrospect*, p. 63. On FDR's cultivation of the press, Graham J. White, *FDR and the Press* (Chicago: University of Chicago Press, 1979); Betty Houchin Winfield, *FDR and the News Media* (New York: Columbia University Press, 1990); Steven Casey, *Cautious Crusade: Franklin D. Roosevelt, American Public Opinion, and the War Against Nazi Germany* (Oxford and New York: Oxford University Press, 2001).

328 **"No general knows"** JG, diary entry, 23 April 1942. Quote in diary is "Generals don't know anything about geography." I've used the printed version, included in JG, *Roosevelt in Retrospect*, p. 27.

328 **From royalties** Calculated in terms of real wealth value; see measuringworth .com/calculators/uscompare/relativevalue.php.

328 **He spent most of his nights** Sylvia Jukes Morris, *Price of Fame: The Honorable Clare Boothe Luce* (New York: Random House, 2014); Brinkley, *Publisher*.

328 ***House and Garden* sent a reporter** "John Gunther Prefers Modern," *House and Garden*, Nov. 1942, pp. 42–43.

328 **In those years, he was** Polly Adler, *A House Is Not a Home* (New York: Rinehart, 1953), pp. 241–44; Debby Applegate, *Madam: The Biography of Polly Adler, Icon of the Jazz Age* (New York: Doubleday, 2021).

329 **It was more difficult** JG, diary entry, 12 April 1944, JG Papers II, Box 19.

329 **The higher the tensions** Adler, *A House*, pp. 337–38.

329 **"If only Rembrandt could"** JG, diary entry, 12 April 1944, JG Papers II, Box 19.

329 **He was past** JG, note, Thurs. 3 April ny [1943], JG Papers II, Box 22.

329 **Eleven orgasms** JG, diary entry, 5–7 May 1942 diary; see also 21 Oct. 1942, JG Papers II, Box 19.

329 **He had to be careful** Diary entry, 3 Oct. 1942, JG Papers II, Box 19.

329 **"glamour boy"** Diary entry, 4 Oct. 1942, JG Papers II, Box 19.

329 **"God made you"** JG, diary entry for 7 Oct. 1942, JG Papers II, Box 19.

329 **Marry a woman** JG, diary entry for 13 Dec. 1942, June 16–18, 1943, JG Papers II, Box 19.

329 **Why hadn't he seized** JG, diary entry for 10 April 1943, JG Papers II, Box 19.

329 **He was even seeing more** JG, diary entry, 29 Jan. 1943, JG Papers II, Box 19.

329 **He walked in the snow** JG, diary entry, 31 Jan. 1943, JG Papers II, Box 19.

329 **Knick had vowed** AK to JG, 28 May ny [1943], JG Papers II, Box 22.

330 **By the fall of 1942** M. S. Venkataramani and B. K. Shrivastava, *Quit India: The American Response to the 1942 Struggle* (New Delhi: Vikas, 1979); M. S. Venkataramani and B. K. Shrivastava, *Roosevelt, Gandhi, Churchill: America and the Last Phase of India's Freedom Struggle* (New Delhi: Radiant, 1983); Clymer, *Quest;* Cohen, "The Geopolitical Is Personal."

330 **Now, the India League** "India League of America—India Day Dinner," 30 Jan. 1943, India Office Records, 262/35/L/P&J/12/487, Asia and Pacific Collections, British Library. On the India League, Venkataramani and Shrivastava, *Quit India,* pp. 290–93; Venkataramani and Shrivastava, *Roosevelt, Gandhi, Churchill,* pp. 245–56; Clymer, *Quest,* 22, 23, 100, 218.

330 **"Literary Liberals"** "India League of America—India Day Dinner," 30 Jan. 1943, f. 9, India Office Records, 262/35, L/P&J/12/487; for an estimation of FFG's importance, "India League of America—Financial Position," 7 Jan. 1943, f. 4 and "India League of America," 13 Aug. 1943, f. 49.

330 **India needed** "India League of America—India Day Dinner." The speaker was the author Dr. Lin Yutang.

330 **The most scathing indictments** Cohen, "The Geopolitical Is Personal."

330 **The sorts of analogies** FFG, "Free India First" [letter to the editor], *New Republic,* 10 Aug. 1942, pp. 175–76. See, for instance, Eric Sevareid, *Not So Wild a Dream* (New York: Knopf, 1946), p. 239.

331 **Surveying American public opinion** Note by Paul J. Patrick, 25 Sept. 1942 in Nicholas Mansergh, ed., *The Transfer of Power,* vol. 3 (London: HMSO, 1971), pp. 30, 31; Lord Alexander Cadogen to Cyril Radcliffe, 29 Sept. 1942, FO 371/30660, The National Archives, UK.

331 **"almost hysterical"** "The India League of America," 7 Oct. 1943, f. 89, India Office Records, 262/35, L/P&J/12/487.

331 **When Nehru's two nieces** See Dorothy Dix's column of 12 Aug. 1943, *Shreveport Journal,* 12 Aug. 1943, p. 14; Nayantara Sahgal, *Prison and Chocolate Cake* (New York: Knopf, 1954), pp. 121, 130.

331 **The British spy** Report on 9 Aug. 1943 India League meeting, f. 51, India Office Records, 262/35, L/P&J/12/487.

331 **Her short book** "Frances Gunther has finally written her first book," noted *Variety,* adding that "Husband, John Gunther, a number of books ahead of her, however." *Variety,* Oct. 1943, p. 54.

331 **Worse, it had created** FFG, *Revolution in India,* p. 11.

331 **"Isn't this rather"** FFG, "England Without India," *Common Sense,* Jan. 1943, p. 437.

332 **The dynamic** An "implacable dependence," in Memmi's words, joined the colonizer to the colonized. Albert Memmi, *The Colonizer and the Colonized,* trans. Howard Greenfeld (New York: Orion Press, 1965 [1957]), p. ix. The influence of Frantz Fanon here is also critical.

332 **"the slaves of the waves"** FFG, *Revolution in India,* p. 55.

332 **What evidence** "Answering You," 19–22 Aug. 1943, BBC TS "The British Commonwealth," FFG Papers, file 282.

332 **Would most of them even** FFG, "England Without India," p. 438.

332 **"they are not good Europeans"** FFG, Empire TS, FFG Papers, file 266.

332 **"By Our Own"** FFG, *Revolution in India,* p. 65.

332 **"mine of exact information"** T. A. Bisson, "India Is Still There," *Nation,* 5 Aug. 1944, p. 159. See also John Chamberlain, "Books of the Times," *NYT,* 6 May 1944, p. 13.

332 ***Common Sense* issued** Frederic Babcock, "Among the Authors," *Chicago Tribune,*

29 July 1945, p. 61. "Highly emotional," charged her critics, especially in Britain, where Americans' strong feelings about India, it was feared, might threaten the Atlantic partnership. It was a "cold douche thrown full in the face of those who would try by some mystic process to equate force and freedom," judged the *New York Times*'s reviewer. As much as he agreed with her diagnosis of the situation, he doubted her solution. It seemed to him that Mrs. Gunther wasn't being at all practical. Could the British simply let India go now? And if not, couldn't she "try to persuade her English and her Indian friends" to a compromise?

333   **The British authorities** See Gov't of Bengal Office of the D.C.P. (Sp. Br.) File No. M603/44 II [Bengal State Archives], dated 17 June 1944, quoted in *Towards Freedom: Documents on the Movement for Independence in India, 1942–1944*, Part I, ed. Partha Sarathi Gupta (New York: Oxford University Press, 1998), p. 818.

333   **Why hadn't she been** Oswald Villard to FFG, 1 June 1944, Oswald Garrison Villard Papers, B MS Am 1323, file 1436, Houghton Library, Harvard.

333   **She'd come to the United States** Hannah Pakula, *The Last Empress: Madame Chiang Kai-Shek and the Birth of Modern China* (New York: Simon & Schuster, 2009). On Madame Chiang and the foreign correspondents, Leland Stowe, *They Shall Not Sleep* (New York: Knopf, 1944), pp. 40–41.

333   **When Frances visited** FFG, Notes from conversation with Mme. Chiang Kai-shek, Jan. 1943, FFG Papers, file 219.

333   **Or was it too personal** FFG, Notes from conversation with Mme. Chiang Kai-shek, 23 May 1943, FFG Papers, file 219.

333   **What Frances wrote had such life** FFG, Notes from conversation with Mme. Chiang Kai-shek, Jan. 1943.

334   **"What is she doing at Yale?"** JN to Chandra Pandit, 30 May 1944, FFG Papers, file 316.

334   **But when she got hamstrung** FFG, note, on paper scrap, FFG Papers, file 26.

334   **"What kind of man are you"** JG, diary entry, 20 Oct. 1942, JG Papers II, Box 19.

334   **"I have never known her to compromise"** JG, "About Frances Gunther," FFG Papers, file 229. Reprinted (in part) on the dust jacket of *Revolution in India*.

334   **"If he had added the phrase"** JG, diary entry, 3 May 1947, JG Papers II, Box 19.

334   **"Jews and Hindus"** JG, diary entry, 26 Jan. 1942, JG Papers II, Box 19.

335   **Both Gandhi and Nehru** See P. R. Kumaraswamy, *India's Israel Policy* (New York: Columbia University Press, 2010).

335   **The Jews had only one** FFG to JN, March 1938, FFG Papers, file 315.

335   **She helped Jabotinsky's** Kook credited JG but it was FFG's effort. Monty Noam Penkower, "Vladimir (Ze'ev) Jabotinsky, Hillel Kook–Peter Bergson, and the Campaign for a Jewish Army," *Modern Judaism* 31, no. 3 (Oct. 2011): 340.

335   **She served** Note that in an interview conducted in 1973, Bergson claimed that FFG was principally a figurehead treasurer who had "blind faith" in the Boys. David Wyman and Rafael Medoff, *A Race Against Death: Peter Bergson, America, and the Holocaust* (New York: Norton, 2002), p. 111. Alexander Rafaeli gave her substantially more credit, and the surviving records of the Emergency Committee indicate her active (and sometimes combative) participation in council meetings. Telephone interview with Judith Baumel-Schwartz, 30 June 2020. See also N. Shlomo, "Frances Gunther, The Tale of a Marvelous Life Story," *Herut*, 8 April 1964; Yoseph Charif, "She Was Devoted to Israel's Independence," *Ma'ariv*, 8 April 1964. (Translations by Gil Engelstein.)

335   **After the first press** Given the controversy at the time, the subject of Bergson and the Emergency Committee has inevitably generated a large and disputatious literature. Among others, see Louis Rapaport, *Shake Heaven and Earth: Peter Bergson and the Struggle to Rescue the Jews of Europe* (Jerusalem: Gefen, 1999); Judith

Tydor Baumel, *The "Bergson Boys" and the Origins of Contemporary Zionist Militancy,* trans. Dena Ordan (Syracuse: Syracuse University Press, 2005 [1999]); Monty Noam Penkower, "In Dramatic Dissent: The Bergson Boys," *American Jewish History* 70, no. 3 (March 1981): 281–309.

335 **"bring a Madison Square Garden"** Quoted in Hoffmann, *Ben Hecht,* p. 153. Planning meetings for the pageant were held in Frances's apartment. See Meyer Levin, *In Search* (New York: Horizon, 1950), p. 303.

336 **The audience for a special** See Hoffmann, *Ben Hecht,* p. 155.

336 **The Emergency Committee's office** Penkower, "In Dramatic Dissent," p. 306.

336 **For a ragtag group** On the centrality of media campaigns and PR efforts to the Bergson Boys, Baumel, *"Bergson Boys,"* esp. chs. 3 and 4.

336 **"Externally she seemed the shyest"** JG, "About Frances Gunther."

337 **The hearing on the rescue resolution** Establishment of a Commission to Effectuate the Rescue of Jewish People of Europe (H. Res. 350 and 352, 78th Cong., 1st Sess.), 23 Nov. 1943, House Committee on Foreign Affairs, Selected Executive Session Hearings of the Committee, 1942–50, vol. II, *Problems of World War II and Its Aftermath, Part 2* (Washington, D.C.: U.S. Gov't Printing Office, 1976), pp. 62–65, 95–139.

337 **His voice squeaked** Gloria Lubar and Edward F. van der Veen, "Bergson Admits $1,000,000 Fund Raised, Vague on Its Use," *Washington Post,* 3 Oct. 1944.

337 **The hearing devolved** Gloria Lubar and Edward F. van der Veen, "Bergson Admits His Committee Has No Right to Collect Funds," *Washington Post,* 4 Oct. 1944.

337 **Was the subject** Bergson's testimony, Establishment, 23 Nov. 1943, p. 100; see Wyman and Medoff, *Race,* pp. 141–55.

337 **The accusation was taking hold** Lucy Dawidowicz, *The Jewish Presence: Essays on Identity and History* (New York: Holt, Rinehart and Winston, 1977), pp. 277–78.

337 **She wasn't accustomed** FFG's testimony, Establishment of a Commission, 24 Nov. 1943, pp. 141–46.

338 **"Awful! Awful!"** FFG's testimony, p. 142.

338 **"We cannot sit by"** FFG's testimony, p. 144.

338 **"little prejudices"** FFG's testimony, p. 145.

339 **"You are expressing"** FFG's testimony, p. 146.

339 **"One of mine, too"** FFG's testimony, p. 145.

339 **Too little** See FFG, Emergency Ctte. re. disbandment, 14 May 1945, Emergency Committee to Save the Jewish People of Europe, Reports, Jabotinsky Institute Archive, HT11-13/1, 1/12/11n.

339 **"You know your son"** Hackett, quoted in John Gunther, *Death Be Not Proud* [*DBNP*] (New York: Harper & Brothers, 1949), p. 11.

340 **"Now we buy our fish"** Johnny and FG to JG, 20 Aug. 1943, JG Papers II, Box 6.

340 **He was taking lessons** Johnny to JG, 24 July ny [1943], JG Papers II, Box 6.

340 **They'd planted** Johnny to JG, 17 Aug. 1943, JG Papers II, Box 6.

340 **John said the decision** On Deerfield, John McPhee, *The Headmaster: Frank L. Boyden, of Deerfield* (New York: Farrar, Straus and Giroux, 1966), pp. 6, 17, 19; Melissa Bingmann, *Prep School Cowboys: Ranch Schools in the American West* (Albuquerque: University of New Mexico Press, 2015), p. 52.

340 **"That is the hardest duty"** FFG to JN, 17 June 1942, Jawaharlal Nehru Papers, vol. 30.

340 **"I try to be spontaneous"** Johnny to FFG, Tuesday ny [1944], JG Papers II, Box 6.

340 **John was angry about it** JG, diary entry, 7 April 1944, JG Papers II, Box 19.

340 **Part of the problem** FFG, notes re. Dr. Levy and Karen Horney, 1940s, FFG Papers, file 24.

341 **"What do you want me"** JG, diary entry, 7 April 1944, JG Papers II, Box 19.

341 **Your shoes are worse** JG, diary entry, 2 July 1943, JG Papers II, Box 19.

341 **In Washington, John got** Little more than a week after he arrived in North Africa, an American officer whom he'd never seen before blurted out the whole thing. The invasion would start on the southern coast of Sicily, the man told him, with paratrooper landings followed immediately by a huge amphibious assault. Under different circumstances, the indiscretion would have been a jackpot, but to be in possession of such information, as an accredited correspondent, was mostly a hassle. John had to remember to play dumb when the conversation in the mess hall, inevitably, turned to the subject. JG, *D-Day: What Preceded It, What Followed* (New York: Harper & Brothers, 1944), p. 38.

341 **John could feel the real** JG, diary entry, 5 July 1943, JG Papers II, Box 19.

341 **"We can't all be great"** JG, diary entry, 21 July 1943, JG Papers II, Box 19. See Steven Casey, *The War Beat, Europe: The American Media at War Against Nazi Germany* (New York: Oxford University Press, 2017), p. 149.

342 **Consider yourself members** JG, *D-Day*, p. 44.

342 **Like any good city editor** JG, *D-Day*, pp. 44–48.

342 **"So you're the only U.S. correspondent"** JG, *D-Day*, pp. 71–72.

342 **"Guess won't die in poorhouse"** JG, *D-Day*, p. 72 and JG, diary entry for 7 July 1943, JG Papers II, Box 19. Note that quote attributed to Montgomery in the published version isn't in the diary entry for that day.

342 **Champion of the little guy** Ernie Pyle, *Brave Men* (New York: H. Holt, 1944).

343 **In his book on the Sicilian** "Gunther Covers the War," *Akron Beacon Journal*, 19 March 1944, p. 37; "Book Reviews," *Morning Call* (Allentown, Pa.), 14 May 1944, p. 6; Lafayette L. Marchand, "How Invasion Works," *Boston Globe*, 8 March 1944, p. 15.

343 **It was less a war book** The book, confusingly, is entitled *D-Day*, which was the name that the Sicily invasion was given before it was superseded by the Normandy battle, which became the famous example of a "D-day," or surprise attack.

343 **Unlike Pyle** Pyle won the Pulitzer for his 1943 war correspondence.

343 **"feuilletonist of genius"** JG, "Here Is Your America, Seen by Ernie Pyle," *NYHT*, 25 May 1947, p. E5.

343 **While he worried** JG, diary entry, 2 Aug. 1944, JG Papers II, Box 19.

343 **Their ration boxes** JG, *D-Day*, p. 67.

343 **"Finito Benito"** JG, "How Sicily Learned of Duce's Fall," *Fort Worth Star-Telegram*, 29 July 1943, p. 1.

343 **John worried** JG, diary entry, 26 Jan. 1942, JG Papers II, Box 19.

343 **They sat together at the glass** JG, diary entry, 8 May 1943, JG Papers II, Box 19.

344 **"I *went*. I went from myself"** JG, diary entry, 8 May 1943, JG Papers II, Box 19.

344 **"You bastard"** JG, diary entry, 22 Sept. 1943, JG Papers II, Box 19.

344 **"I have never been fonder of her"** JG, diary entry, 21 Oct. 1943, JG Papers II, Box 19.

344 **An entire infrastructure** Nelson Manfred Blake, *The Road to Reno: A History of Divorce in the United States* (New York: Macmillan, 1962), pp. 152–58; Anita Watson, "Fading Shame: Divorce Stigma in American Culture, 1882–1939" (unpub. Ph.D. diss., University of Nevada, 1997).

344 **Although she denied the charge** See divorce papers granted 7 March 1944, JG Papers II, Box 23; "Gunther Wins Divorce on Desertion Charge," *Democrat and Chronicle* (Rochester, N.Y.), 9 March 1944, p. 3.

345 **While in the Gunthers' circle** On divorce between the 1920s and the 1940s, see esp. Kristin Celello, *Making Marriage Work* (Chapel Hill: University of North Carolina Press, 2009), ch. 1. Between 1940 and 1944, the American divorce rate

increased more than 50 percent. See Steven Mintz and Susan Kellogg, *Domestic Revolutions: A Social History of American Family Life* (New York: Free Press, 1988), p. 171.

345 **Frances didn't want any alimony** FFG to JG, 1 Nov. 1944, JG Papers II, Box 23. Though earlier, JG diary entry for 21 Sept. 1941 (JG Papers II, Box 19), she'd made extravagant financial settlement demands.

345 **He wouldn't make her choose** JG, diary entry, 23 Oct. 1943, JG Papers II, Box 19.

345 **He hardly had any stories** AK to JG, Sat. the 17th nd [1944], JG Papers II, Box 22.

345 **They talked about the asparagus** JG, diary entry for 2–20 May 1944, JG Papers II, Box 19.

345 **"I'll always dominate the private"** FFG to JG, undated, 1944, JG Papers II, Box 23.

CHAPTER FIFTEEN

349 **"Hitler's greatest psychological"** Dorothy Thompson, *Listen, Hans* (Boston: Houghton Mifflin, 1942), p. 23.

349 **She envisioned a European Continent** DT, *Listen, Hans,* pp. 54–61.

350 **Part of what Dorothy had** Clayton D. Laurie, *The Propaganda Warriors: America's Crusade Against Nazi Germany* (Lawrence: University Press of Kansas, 1996).

350 **"vast dirty brown wave"** DT, *Listen, Hans,* p. 239.

351 **Both the U.S. Army and the civilian** Mandler, *Return from the Natives,* pp. 56–68, 139.

351 **"Such a psychological confusion"** DT, *Listen, Hans,* p. 20.

351 **The solution was to harness** DT, *Listen, Hans,* pp. 62–80.

351 **"three meals"** DT, *Listen, Hans,* p. 78.

351 **"To believe that Nazism"** DT, *Listen, Hans,* pp. 109–10.

352 **In a much-quoted** DT, "Who Goes Nazi?" *Harper's Magazine,* Aug. 1941, pp. 237–42.

352 **"somewhat macabre parlor game"** DT, "Who Goes Nazi?" p. 237.

352 **"she is looking"** DT, "Who Goes Nazi?" p. 239.

352 **"But the frustrated and humiliated"** DT, "Who Goes Nazi?" p. 242.

352 **Don't start** Dorothy Cremin, "Dorothy Thompson Scores the Nazis in 'Listen Hans,'" *Atlanta Constitution,* 3 Jan. 1943, p. 49.

353 **"one of the most remarkable"** Carl J. Friedrich, "Broadcast to Germany: Dorothy Thompson Speaking," *Atlantic Monthly,* Jan. 1943, p. 138; Malcolm Cowley, "Listen, Dorothy," *New Republic,* 28 Dec. 1942, pp. 861–62; John Chamberlain, "Books of the Times," *NYT,* 28 Nov. 1942, p. 11. The rare negative review was Melchior Palyi's "'Listen, Hans' Is Pretty Mild for Bellicose Miss Thompson," *Chicago Tribune,* 20 Dec. 1942, p. 109; balanced by the same paper's positive review by Fanny Butcher, 2 Dec. 1942, p. 21.

353 **As disturbed** Kurth, *American Cassandra,* p. 364.

353 **"amorphous ass"** DT to Robert Sherwood, 22 Aug. 1947, cited in Kurth, *American Cassandra,* p. 365. For DT's view, "On the Record: Playing into Goebbels' Hand," *Fort Worth Star-Telegram,* 8 Oct. 1944, p. 12.

353 **The fact that Americans** "Our old friend Dorothy Thompson is picking this moment to nauseate and disgust people by yapping for a soft peace at the very moment when I think we should be toughest. I think she's gone mashuga." Bennett Cerf to Donald Klopfer, 6 Sept. 1944, in *Dear Donald, Dear Bennett* (New York: Random House, 2002), p. 172.

353 **"Neither your personal life"** DT address to the Volunteer Land Corps, Twin Farms, 29 Aug. 1942, DT Papers, Box 36.

353 **"I was not going to live"** Quoted in DT, "My Husband, Maxim Kopf: The Artist in the Twentieth Century" in *Maxim Kopf* (New York: Frederick A. Praeger, 1960), p. 24.

354 **Then when he got out** Kurth, *American Cassandra*, pp. 349–57. See Philip Hamburger, "Talk of the Town: Mr. Kopf," *New Yorker*, 25 Nov. 1944, pp. 20–21; DT, "My Husband."

354 **By 1941, courtesy of Jan Masaryk** DT, "My Husband," p. 25.

354 **That same night, his shoes in hand** Described in Kurth, *American Cassandra*, pp. 351–52.

354 **"The world crowds in"** DT to Maxim Kopf, Private Collection, undated but 1942/3, cited in Kurth, *American Cassandra*, pp. 352–53.

354 **"My Great Woman"** Cited in Kurth, *American Cassandra*, p. 353.

354 **"What you need a cock"** JG, diary entry, 30 July–6 Aug. 1947, JG Papers II, Box 20.

354 **"always tried to marry"** DT to JG, 1 Nov. 1943, JG Papers II, Box 35.

354 **He knew how to** DT, "My Husband," p. 23.

354 **He was very, very good** RW to Marion Sanders, 20 March 1973, Houghton Mifflin Company Records. Just after DT's marriage, RW wrote Ben Huebsch, 22 July 1943, to say: "I do hope Dorothy's marriage is going to be a success. It cannot anyway be worse than the others!" *Selected Letters of Rebecca West*, p. 181.

354 **"Mr. Thompson"** See for instance JG to Billie, 7 Jan. 1946, JG Papers II, Box 24, folder labeled Family Letters.

354 **It used to be that the world** JG, diary entry, 16–18 June 1943, JG Papers, Box 19.

355 **The FBI spent a few weeks** "Allegation Regarding Dorothy Thompson's Husband," 65-5464201, referenced in FBI Report on DT, undated [1946?].

355 **"I'm just the janitor"** Peter Kurth interview with Dinah Sheean, cited in Kurth, *American Cassandra*, p. 356.

355 **"I make myself recriminations"** DT to Carl Zuckmayer, 16 Nov. 1944, quoted in Sanders, *Dorothy Thompson*, p. 310.

355 **"How can anyone know"** Helmuth von Moltke to Freya von Moltke, 21 Oct. 1941, in *Letters to Freya, 1939–1945*, ed. and trans. by Beate Ruhm von Oppen (New York: Knopf, 1990), p. 175.

355 **He never knew** Kurth, *American Cassandra*, p. 523, fn. 11.

355 **He was chagrined** Rev. H. D. Knickerbocker to HRK, 26 Oct. 1932, HRK Papers, Uncatalogued correspondence, Box 3—folder 1932; Rev. H. D. Knickerbocker to HRK, 17 May 1933, Box 4—folder 1933.

356 **"discipline and restraint"** Rev. H. D. Knickerbocker to Knick, 22 April 1933, HRK Papers, Uncatalogued correspondence, Box 4—folder 1933.

356 **"I am rid of that incubus"** HRK to AK, 17 July nd [1943], JG Papers II, Box 22.

356 **"At least, they say they are"** HRK, "Paris Delighted as Yankee Army Approaches City," *The Daily Times* (Davenport, Iowa), 11 Aug. 1944, p. 2.

356 **The Norwegian maid** Leonard Lyons, "Broadway Medley," *Times* (San Mateo, Calif.), 29 Sept. 1944, p. 8.

357 **But she denied doing** JG, *Indian Sign*, p. 139. In the version of the story Agnes wrote years later for her children, she edged even further from responsibility. The vengeful Danish nanny, she recounted, had fished torn-up scraps of love letters out of the wastebasket and presented the pasted-together documents to Knick when he returned from Europe. AK, TS Memoir, p. 38.

357 **God, the Knickerbockers** Leonora Schinasi Hornblow to JG, Wednesday, no date, [1945?], JG Papers II, Box 22.

357 **To mollify him** JG, diary entry, 22 Jan. 1945, JG Papers II, Box 19.

357 **"We've got a human"** JG, diary entry, 31 Jan. 1945, JG Papers II, Box 19.

357   **"You're well out of it"** JG, diary entry, 10 Feb. 1945, JG Papers II, Box 19.

358   **It also represents the culmination** JG, *Indian Sign*, p. 82. See also the advertisement, JG Papers II, Box 31: "Pertaining to the Novel the Indian Sign."

358   **All "capital"** See note dated Feb. 1952, JG Papers II, Box 1, Diary Scraps, 1952, New York & London.

358   **"a large part of me"** JG, *Indian Sign*, p. 152.

358   **He'd gotten himself** Officers over the age of thirty-eight were being released. JVS, *This House Against This House* (London: Macmillan, 1947), p. 323.

358   **He'd arrived in Europe** On the spread of the Ernie Pyle style of war reporting, which mentioned the names and hometowns of individual soldiers, Sheean, *This House*, p. 324.

358   **He hadn't met** JVS, "Without Hate, Without Love," p. 74.

358   **Here, Jimmy agreed** See, among many others, DT, "What Juvenile Crime Reflects," *LHJ*, Oct. 1946.

359   **"Look at their faces"** JG, diary entry, 9 Jan. 1946, JG Papers II, Box 20.

359   **"mental cruelty"** "Vincent Sheean's Wife Wins Reno Divorce," *The Pittsburgh Press*, 10 Jan. 1946, p. 17.

359   **He could hardly believe** JVS, diary entry, 17 Jan. 1946, JVS Papers, WHS, Box 1, folder 38, diary, 1944–46.

359   **"reconstructing myself"** JG to Leonora Schinasi, 9 May 1945, Leonora and Arthur Hornblow Papers, Special Collections, Margaret Herrick Library, folder 3.

360   **But *Inside U.S.A.*** He'd made the decision to organize the book by regions, then a new concept in political science but one that made a sort of intuitive sense to a reporter schooled in the politics of European nationalities.

360   **Who *really* runs** JG, *Fragment*, p. 53.

360   **"What do you believe in most"** JG, *Inside U.S.A.*, p. xv.

360   **To Sinclair Lewis** Sinclair Lewis, diary entry, July 18, 1942, Minnesota Diary— Sinclair Lewis Papers, folder 856, Beinecke Library; also JG diary entry, 26–28 July 1947, JG Papers II, Box 20.

360   **Just to say something** JG, diary entry, 17 Dec. 1942, JG Papers II, Box 19.

360   **At the end of the war** JG, *Fragment*, p. 48.

360   **Starting in the 1930s** Sarah Igo, *The Averaged American: Surveys, Citizens, and the Making of a Mass Public* (Cambridge, Mass.: Harvard University Press, 2008), p. 150.

361   **In Bloomington, Indiana** Julia A. Ericksen, "With Enough Cases, Why Do You Need Statistics? Revisiting Kinsey's Methodology," *The Journal of Sex Research* 35, no. 2 (May 1998): 132–40.

361   **Four hundred thousand** JG, *Inside U.S.A.* (New York: Harper & Brothers, 1947), p. 42. For JG's research materials, see more generally JG I, Box 30.

361   **There were fifty million** JG, *IUSA*, p. 248.

361   **Americans ate** JG, *IUSA*, p. x.

361   **What about the 37** JG, *IUSA*, p. 641.

361   **"a somewhat shady"** JG, *IUSA*, p. 605.

361   **"If a man's from Texas"** JG, *IUSA*, p. 818.

362   **"preposterous and flamboyant"** JG, *IUSA*, p. xi.

362   **"out-ghettoes"** JG, *IUSA*, p. 680.

362   **A "cancer"** JG, *IUSA*, pp. 704, 916.

362   **Inferiority or superiority** JG, *IUSA*, pp. 682–84.

362   **"Brown Brethren"** JG to FFG, 30 April 1945, file 175.

362   **He took her to dinner** JG, diary entries, 5 Feb. 1945, 21 Jan. 1946; also 18 Dec. 1945, 12 Jan., 8 Feb. 1946, JG Papers II, Boxes 19 and 20.

363 **As it turned out** Scott Farris, *Inga: Kennedy's Great Love, Hitler's Perfect Beauty and J. Edgar Hoover's Prime Suspect* (Guilford, Conn.: Lyons Press, 2016).

363 **He couldn't really afford** JG, diary entry, 29 May 1944, JG Papers II, Box 19.

363 **There was even a barn** For Sale notice for the Inside House, undated [1947], Bill Shirer, Dated Correspondence, 1940–1943.

363 **Sometimes it struck him** JG, diary entry, 12 Jan. 1946, JG Papers II, Box 20.

363 **Your son has a very fine** Frank L. Boyden to FFG, 14 July 1945; also 15 Jan. 1946, JG Papers I, Box 44, folder 6. Similarly, Boyden to JG, 14 July 1945, JG Papers II, Box 24, CDE Correspondence, 1941–45.

363 **"Um," he said** JG, *DBNP,* p. 13.

363 **"He is a grand boy"** Frank Boyden to JG, 12 April 1946, JG Papers II, Box 25, Correspondence 1947 & 1948, some earlier A-F.

363 **Did the headmaster think** JG to Boyden, 18 April 1946, JG Papers II, Box 25.

364 **"Say nice things"** Johnny, diary entry for Wednesday [1945], in *DBNP,* p. 232.

364 **He was doing exercises** Johnny to FFG, Tuesday [1945], Johnny, diary entry, Tues., summer of 1945, *DBNP,* p. 231.

364 **Hadn't she been** See Johnny, Summer, 1945 diary, FFG Papers, file 309.

364 **I do remember the advice** Johnny to FFG, 19 April 1945, JG Papers II, Box 6.

364 **The next month, he wrote** JN to FFG, 25 July 1945, FFG Papers, file 316.

365 **Once he returned home** JN to FFG, 5 Sept. 1945, *SWJN,* Series 1, vol. 14, p. 582.

365 **He sent her a piece** JN to FFG, 12 Jan. 1946, FFG Papers, file 316.

365 **"But I shall take the risk"** JN to FFG, 4 Dec. ny [1945], FFG Papers, file 316.

365 **John had gotten hold** On Putnam, Lewis P. Rowland, *The Legacy of Tracy J. Putnam and H. Houston Merritt: Modern Neurology in the United States* (New York and Oxford: Oxford University Press, 2009).

365 **"Well, for goodness' sake!"** JG, *DBNP,* p. 30.

366 **Her mind was racing** FFG, Notes about Johnny's sickness, April 1946, JG Papers II, Box 23.

366 **"I know it can't"** JG, *DBNP,* p. 34.

366 **Later that evening** JG, *DBNP,* p. 30.

366 **He wouldn't know much** JG, *DBNP,* p. 41.

366 **The operation lasted** JG, "Johnny," 1946 diary [after 6 May entry], JG Papers, Box 20.

366 **"Is he your only child?"** JG, *DBNP,* p. 38.

366 **"Where are the parents?"** FFG, Notes about Johnny's sickness.

367 **The rest had fingered** JG, *DBNP,* p. 42.

367 **He was testing** JG, *DBNP,* pp. 45–46.

367 **"You are truly Machiavellian"** JG, *DBNP,* p. 52.

367 **They were alone** JG, *DBNP,* p. 51.

367 **"How shall we break it"** JG, *DBNP,* p. 5.

367 **Such tumors** JG, *DBNP,* p. 64. *Encyclopaedia Britannica,* 14th ed., vol. 4, Brain to Casting (London and New York: Encyclopaedia Britannica, 1929), see "Brain, Surgery of," p. 21.

CHAPTER SIXTEEN

368 **It would be better** JG, *DBNP,* p. 53.

368 **Putnam tried** Putnam had a child of his own, nineteen and a sophomore at Vassar. A Boston Brahmin and a Harvard man, Putnam was divorced and remarried; with his first wife, the psychoanalyst Dr. Irmarita Kellers, he'd been in analysis in Amsterdam in the 1920s. He was dismissed from his post as director of the Neu-

rological Institute in 1946, by his account because he refused to fire the Jews in his department, many of them emigrés. In December 1947, his daughter died from a fall out her dormitory window. See Rowland, *Legacy*, chs. 6–8.

368 **The situation wasn't** JG, Note, JG Papers I, Box 44, folder 11.

368 **He'd left the skull** JG, *DBNP*, p. 54.

369 **And John replied the same** JG, *DBNP*, p. 55.

369 **The rest of his workshop** JG, *DBNP*, p. 66.

369 **She bought him colorful scarves** JG, *DBNP*, p. 102.

369 **He was nearly broke** JG, diary entry, 23 July 1946, JG Papers II, Box 20.

369 **On the weekends, he came** FFG, Notes about Johnny's sickness, 16 Aug. 1946.

369 **His parents sent for** JG, *DBNP*, pp. 86–87.

369 **His subject would be** Johnny Gunther, Harvard application, JG Papers I, Box 44, folder 20.

369 **"You don't understand"** FFG, Notes about Johnny's sickness, Sunday A.M.

369 **His eyes were affected** JG, *DBNP*, p. 71.

370 **Edgar's mother** Bertha Brenner to JG, 19 Feb. 1949, JG Papers I, Box 44, folder 22.

370 **But to leave him** JG, *DBNP*, p. 50.

370 **John wrote or telephoned** See correspondence in JG Papers I, Box 44, folder 8.

370 **According to a short article** JG, *DBNP*, pp. 77–79.

370 **From a friend** Raymond Swing to JG, 18 June 1946, JG Papers II, Box 35.

370 **"If I could die for him"** FFG, Notes about Johnny's sickness, 27 July 1946.

370 **"All the things I want to do!"** FFG, Notes about Johnny's sickness, 7 Aug. 1946.

370 **"Another fine day"** FFG, Notes about Johnny's sickness, 11 Aug. 1946.

370 **He depended on her** FFG, Notes about Johnny's sickness, 4 Aug. 1946.

370 **It showed astounding** FFG, Notes about Johnny's sickness, 25 Aug. 1946.

370 **"Feeling wonderful"** FFG, Notes about Johnny's sickness, 25 Aug. 1946.

371 **She and Johnny talked** JG, *DBNP*, p. 81.

371 **"Ask parents what you can do"** Johnny, diary entry, 11 Nov. 1946, FFG Papers, folder 52.

371 **"Pray for a miracle"** JVS, diary entry, 31 July 1946, JVS Papers, WHS, Box 1, folder 39—Diary, 1946–1947.

371 **John had already** DT to Helen Reid, 8 Aug. 1946, Helen Reid Papers.

371 **"God and nature do not waste"** DT to JG, 2 Aug. 1946, JG Papers II, Box 35.

371 **"I feel rather like the American"** JVS to JG, 21 July 1946, JG Papers II, Box 35.

371 **But to divide the Allies** JVS, *This House*, esp. Part III.

371 **"One Worlder"** On Wendell Willkie's "One World," Samuel Zipp, *The Idealist: Wendell Willkie's Wartime Quest to Build One World* (Cambridge, Mass.: Harvard University Press, 2020). Willkie was a friend of Gunther, Sheean, and Thompson. See Cohen, "The Geopolitical Is Personal."

372 **White had known** Walter White, *A Man Called White* (New York: Viking Press, 1948), p. 317.

372 **When a young Black** For an analysis of this case, Gail Williams O'Brien, *The Color of the Law: Race, Violence and Justice in the Post–World War II South* (Chapel Hill: University of North Carolina Press, 1999).

372 **He deployed his forces** On the Highway Patrol, O'Brien, *Color*, pp. 162–67.

372 **"While trying to escape"** JVS, "Present-Day American Tragedy," *NYHT*, 27 Sept. 1946, p. 18.

373 **"They would appear to be"** JVS, "A Social Question Outlaws Law," *NYHT*, 1 Oct. 1946, p. 26. On Nuremberg and the trial at Lawrenceville, compared, "The Trial in Tennessee," *NYHT*, 2 Oct. 1946, p. 30.

373 **The person Jimmy** JVS, "Social Question."

373 **"Did you write this"** The word was "son of a bitch," according to Paul L. Montgomery, "Vincent Sheean, Journalist, Dies at 75," *NYT,* 17 March 1975, p. 32.

373 **"Any good word"** "Witness Calls Sheean a Liar at Tennessee Trial," *NYHT,* 4 Oct. 1946, p. 7.

373 **He couldn't cash** JVS, Interviews with Carl Johnson, Dec. 1971, cited in "Twentieth-Century Seeker," pp. 489, 493.

373 **"lousy pinks"** JVS, "Lawrenceburg Verdict Assessed," *NYHT,* 7 Oct. 1946, p. 11; for the DA statement, O'Brien, *Color,* p. 49.

373 **For Walter White** White, *Man,* pp. 317–18; Walter White, "People, Politics and Places: Incredible Acquittal," *Chicago Defender,* 19 Oct. 1946, p. 15. For a critique of JVS's point about the possibility of the South reforming itself without intervention from outside, see "Bilbo Must Go!: Mr. Sheean's Mirage," *Pittsburgh Courier,* 19 Oct. 1946, p. 6.

374 **"For once I have done"** JVS, diary entry for 8 Oct. 1946. The NAACP's lawyer echoed Jimmy's analogies between the Tennessee authorities and the Nazi regime, likening the mistreatment of prisoners to the wartime massacre of the Czechs at Lidice.

374 **The man is a crackpot** JG, diary entry, 19 July 1946; also 21 Sept. 1946, JG Papers II, Box 20.

374 **How did I get here?** FFG, Notes about Johnny's sickness, 11 Sept. 1946.

374 **At the start of the regimen** On the Gerson regime, *DBNP* and Raymond Swing, broadcast TS, JG Papers I, Box 44, folder 23.

374 **Frances left it** JG, diary entry, 16 Sept. 1946, JG Papers II, Box 20.

374 **That fall, John** JG, diary entry, 19 Sept. 1946, JG Papers II, Box 20.

374 **He had to borrow money** Telegram from Miriam Hopkins to JG, 15 June 1946, JG Papers II, Box 22, Letters—Miriam Hopkins.

375 **Thank God** JG, diary entry, 29 Sept. 1946, JG Papers II, Box 20.

375 **Canfield looked worried** JG, diary entry, 1 Oct. 1946, JG Papers II, Box 20.

375 **For months, he hadn't** JG to Clare Boothe Luce, 17 Oct. 1946, JG Papers II, Box 34.

375 **She rolled up** FFG, Notes about Johnny's sickness, 1 Nov. 1946.

375 **"Maybe I will be a historic"** FFG, Notes about Johnny's sickness, 11 Dec. 1946.

375 **Johnny asked Frances** FFG, Notes about Johnny's sickness, 5 Nov. 1946.

375 **"Got Father's"** Johnny, diary entry, 17 Nov. 1946, FFG Papers, folder 52.

375 **She's been simply** JG to Mr. and Mrs. Julius Schoeninger, 7 April 1947, JG Papers II, Box 24, folder labeled Family Letters.

375 **When he called her up** FFG, Notes about Johnny's sickness, 6 Jan. 1947.

375 **"Unity line"** A phrase usually reserved for diplomacy and politics. The reference is to a point of common agreement and was used in 1940 to refer to accords among neutral nations (see "House Puts Okeh Upon 20 Million Finn Loan," *Austin American,* 29 Feb. 1940, p. 1) as by the *San Bernardino Daily Sun,* eight years later, to refer to the need for common ground within a political party. ("Gov. Warren to Speak in S.B., Colton Today," 26 Oct. 1948, p. 24.)

376 **"disorderly life"** FFG to JG, undated [likely April 1947], FFG Papers, folder 26. See FFG, Notes about Johnny's sickness, 11 April 1947—"Furies—Leave alone—to John."

376 **But she apparently** There's a copy of the letter in her papers, but not in his. Since he seems to have thrown little away, not even the damning or painful stuff, she probably didn't send the letter.

376 **"God deliver me"** FFG, Notes about Johnny's sickness, 6 Jan. 1946.

376 **"every doctor in the western"** JVS, diary entry, 11 Dec. 1946, JVS Papers, WHS, Box 1, folder 39—Diary, 1946–1947.

376 **"Tell Pop"** FFG, Notes about Johnny's sickness, 12–13 Dec. 1946.

376 **For Christmas** FFG, Notes about Johnny's sickness, 24 Dec. 1946.

376 **When Rebecca West** RW to Henry Andrews, nd [March 1947], RW Papers, Yale, GEN 105, Series 1, Box 2, folder 36.

376 **Rebecca had been reporting** 21 of them in the dock, 3 were tried in absentia.

376 **"a high-grade lynching party"** Harlan Stone to Louis Lusky, 13 Nov. 1945, quoted in Alpheus Mason, *Harlan Fiske Stone: Pillar of the Law* (Hamden, CT: Archon Books, 1968), p. 716 and discussion pp. 715–18.

376 **At Nuremberg, innovative** On the International Military Tribunal, see, among others, Kevin Jon Heller, *The Nuremberg Military Tribunals and the Origins of International Criminal Law* (New York: Oxford University Press, 2011); Arieh J. Kochavi, *Prelude to Nuremberg: Allied War Crimes Policy and the Question of Punishment* (Chapel Hill: University of North Carolina Press, 2000); Ann Tusa and John Tusa, *The Nuremberg Trial* (New York: Atheneum, 1984); Bradley F. Smith, *The Road to Nuremberg* (New York: Basic Books, 1981); Bradley F. Smith, *Reaching Judgment at Nuremberg* (New York: Basic Books, 1977); Telford Taylor, *The Anatomy of the Nuremberg Trials: A Personal Memoir* (New York: Knopf, 1992); Michael Robert Marrus, *The Holocaust at Nuremberg* (Toronto: Faculty of Law, 1996); Gary Jonathan Bass, *Stay the Hand of Vengeance: The Politics of War Crimes Tribunals* (Princeton: Princeton University Press, 2014).

377 **The notion of a "crime against humanity"** On this point and the history of "genocide" versus "crimes against humanity," Philippe Sands, *East West Street: On the Origins of "Genocide" and "Crimes Against Humanity"* (New York: Knopf, 2016).

377 **Rebecca went to Nuremberg** RW, "The Birch Leaves Falling," *New Yorker*, 26 Oct. 1946, p. 93. In a letter to Harold Ross, she said that Sir Hartley Shawcross, the British attorney general, had asked her to write a book on Nuremberg along the lines of the trial pieces she'd previously written for the *New Yorker*. RW to Harold Ross, 28 Aug. 1946, *New Yorker* Records, Box 66, file 9, folder 2.

377 **"My left hand's power"** RW to Rowse, Dec. 1947, cited in A. L. Rowse, *Glimpses of the Great* (Lanham, Md.: University Press of America, 1985), pp. 128–29.

377 **He was an old friend** RW to Podge, nd [1946], Copies of RW's Letters to Mother, RP 6367, British Library; RW to Ross, 20 Nov. 1946, *New Yorker* Records, Box 66, file 10, folder 2.

377 **He put her in the bedroom** Described in RW to Harold Ross, 28 Aug. 1946.

377 **The affair with Biddle** RW to Emanie Arling, 13 Aug. 1946, *Selected Letters of RW*, pp. 214–15.

377 **With her left hand** Ravit Reichman, *The Affective Life of Law: Legal Modernism and the Literary* (Stanford: Stanford University Press, 2009), ch. 4.

377 **"abscesses of cruelty"** RW, *Train of Powder*, p. 60.

377 **"a dirty old man"** RW, *Train of Powder*, p. 5.

378 **"the head of a ventriloquist's dummy"** RW, *Train of Powder*, p. 6.

378 **The former head** RW, *Train of Powder*, p. 5.

378 **As in *Black Lamb*** RW, *Train of Powder*, compare pp. 53 and 55.

378 **"he was a devil"** RW to Emanie Arling, 13 Aug. 1946, in *Selected Letters*, p. 214.

378 **At the same time, she found** RW, *Train of Powder*, p. 51. The trial was of a piece with the "oddity of the world," not separate from it.

378 **"small Allied island"** Genêt [Janet Flanner], "Letter from Nuremberg," *New Yorker*, 16 March 1946, p. 92. Flanner was critical of the American prosecution and her "Letter from Nuremberg," *New Yorker*, 5 Jan. 1946, sounds some of the same notes as RW about the boredom of the trial.

378 **"A man's world"** RW, "The Birch Leaves Falling," pp. 92–95. She edited out that refrain when she published the essay in *A Train of Powder*. Her theme was conso-

nant with the sort of international feminism (e.g., Jane Addams or the Women's International League for Peace and Freedom) that conceived of wars as pathologies of men, though West didn't share their pacifism.

379 **She'd asked Dorothy** Immediately after Hiroshima, Dorothy started calling for universal disarmament and the establishment of a world state. The tribunal at Nuremberg seemed to her pure hypocrisy. Would the American attacks on Hiroshima and Nagasaki also be prosecuted as war crimes? Unless the trial marked the start of a new epoch of "humanistic international law," it was nothing better than a victor's verdict, a lynching. DT, "On the Record: Law Demands Definitions," *Knoxville Journal,* 8 Oct. 1946, p. 6.

379 **Rebecca wanted the pretext** RW to DT, 31 Aug. 1946, DT Papers, Box 33.

379 **But then the New York** RW to Henry Andrews, 21 April ny [1947], Rebecca West Papers, Yale, GEN 105, Series I, Box 2, folder 36.

379 **By some miracle** Untitled autobiographical sketch, Rebecca West Papers, Yale, GEN 105, Series III, Box 38—Diary for 1946.

379 **The first course** TS draft of Rovere profile of JG, *New Yorker* Records, Run/Killed Files, Series 6.2.

379 **He told her about Agnes** RW to Henry Andrews, no date, [April 1947], Rebecca West Papers, Yale, GEN 105, Series I, Box 2, folder 36.

379 **"The boy had seemed"** RW to Henry Andrews, 21 April ny [1947].

379 **He was talking** JG, diary entry, 20 Feb. 1947, JG Papers II, Box 20; JG to Dean Gummere at Harvard, 17 June 1947, JG Papers II, Box 26.

379 **John bought him a Harris tweed** JG, diary entry, 17 March 1947, JG Papers II.

380 **"I got two handfuls"** JG, *DBNP,* p. 151.

380 **That next afternoon** RW to Henry Andrews, nd but recv'd 7 May 1947, GEN 105, Series I, Box 2, folder 36. Also JG to RW, 31 July 1962, Rebecca West Papers, Yale, GEN 105, Series 1, Box 9, folder 335; Brock Baker, Interview with RW, 25 April 1975, JG Papers II, Box 2.

380 **His son is dying** JG, diary entry, 26 May 1947, JG Papers II, Box 20.

381 **"Nobody who saw it"** JG, *DBNP,* p. 168.

381 **This was a very peculiar** JG, diary entry, 23 June 1947, JG Papers II, Box 20.

381 **"I can't bear to see him"** FFG, Notes about Johnny's sickness, 15 June 1947.

381 **"Father, I hope"** JG, diary entry, 28 June 1947, JG Papers II, Box 20.

381 **"I sure will miss him"** JG, diary entry, 30 June 1947, JG Papers II, Box 20.

381 **The funeral was** Betty Hotchkiss to FFG, 1 March 1949, FFG Papers, file 58.

382 **It's nobody's fault** JG, diary entry for 30 July 1947, JG Papers II, Box 20.

382 **For dinner, she had** FFG, Notes about Johnny's sickness, 7 July 1947.

382 **"Remember your destiny"** FFG, Notes about Johnny's sickness, 5 Jan. 1948.

382 **Why hadn't she** FFG, Notes about Johnny's sickness, 22 July 1947.

382 **Not that many fathers** FFG, Notes about Johnny's sickness, Wedn. 10:45 July nd [1947].

382 **"How can I speak"** FFG, Notes about Johnny's sickness, 5 Jan. 1948.

CHAPTER SEVENTEEN

383 **In the month before** Bertha Brenner to FFG and JG, Wednesday nd [July 1947], JG Papers 1972 Add., Box 144, folder 6.

383 **Mixing psychoanalytic ideas** Joshua Loth Liebman, *Peace of Mind* (New York: Simon & Schuster, 1946); Andrew R. Heinze, "Peace of Mind (1946): Judaism and the Therapeutic Polemics of Postwar America," *Religion and American Culture* 12, no. 1 (Winter 2002): 31–58.

383 **"psychologically mature"** Liebman, *Peace,* p. 174.

384 **"must be sanity"** Cited in Anne Harrington, *Mind Fixers: Psychiatry's Troubled Search for the Biology of Mental Illness* (New York: Norton, 2019), p. 86. (According to Harrington, Truman's statement was likely written by William Menninger.) Ran Zwigenberg, "Healing a Sick World: Psychiatric Medicine and the Atomic Age," *Medical History* 62, no. 1 (Jan. 2018): 27–49.

384 **"the whole region"** JG, *IUSA,* p. 669.

384 **"a lucky country"** JG, *IUSA,* p. 920.

384 **Harper & Brothers** Richard Rovere, "Inside," *New Yorker,* 23 Aug. 1947, p. 31. Of that run, 375,000 went to the Book-of-the-Month Club.

384 **His characterizations of Houston** For example, "Spotlight on Texas: Gunther's 'Inside' Series Now Turns to the U.S.A.," *Fort Worth Star-Telegram,* 1 June 1947, p. 23; Stanley E. Babb, "John Gunther's 'Inside U.S.A.,' A Graphic Exploration of Contemporary America," *The Galveston Daily News,* 1 June 1947, p. 20; Ethel Gillett Whitehorn, "Palm Springs' Great Role," *Desert Sun* (Palm Springs), 6 June 1947, p. 10.

384 **Was Indianapolis** Among others, Lowell Nussbaum, "The Things I Hear," *Indianapolis Star,* 18 May 1947, p. 23.

384 **He received reams** JG Papers I, Box 32, folders 2–20; Box 33, folders 1–6.

384 **Apart from the matter** A survey of newspapers.com gives some indication of the reach of the book: more than two thousand articles in 1947 (some of which are local tabulations of bestsellers).

384 **Heavy hitters such as the American** Arthur M. Schlesinger, Jr., "Mr. Gunther Discovers America," *Atlantic Monthly* (June 1947), pp. 120–22; Henry Steele Commager, "Mr. Gunther Surveys the U.S.A.," *NYT,* 1 June 1947, p. 1.

384 **"three dimensional"** Commager, "Mr. Gunther," p. 25. See also Richard Watts, Jr., "It's a Big Country, Mister," *New Republic,* 2 June 1947, pp. 25–26.

385 **According to *Time*** "Gunther's America," *Time,* 2 June 1947.

385 **"ingenuous amazement"** J. M. Lalley, "Of the Inner Man and the Ineffectual Angel," *New Yorker,* 31 May 1947, p. 74.

385 **Richard Rovere, the young** Note from Rovere to accompany Leigh White letter, Rovere Papers, WHS, USS Mss. 75AF, Box 17.

385 **"So you're the hatchet"** JG, *DBNP,* p. 156.

385 **The more time Rovere** Rovere, "Inside."

385 **"But of course"** Rovere, "Inside," p. 33. JG felt he'd been misquoted re. superficiality (diary entry, 11 Aug. 1947).

385 **"The entire planet"** Rovere, "Inside," p. 30.

385 **"Gunther, to me"** Leigh White to Richard Rovere, 27 June 1948, Rovere Papers, Box 17.

386 **Ten of John's books** See "John Gunther, Biographical Memo," 1962, JG Papers II, Box 2.

386 **For people who fancied** On the Book-of-the-Month Club, Janice Radway, *Feeling for Books: The Book-of-the-Month Club, Literary Taste, and Middle-Class Desire* (Chapel Hill: University of North Carolina Press, 1997), esp. chs. 7 and 8 and her description of "middlebrow personalism" and the BOMC's preference for characters (pp. 227–28).

386 **"Agnes, who?"** JG, note, 29 May 1947, JG Papers II, Box 22.

387 **"This is the finest"** JG, diary entry, 20 April 1947, JG Papers II, Box 20.

387 **It had been more than** He'd called Agnes on the phone in Oct. 1946 to tell her about Johnny. See JG, diary entry for 11 Oct. 1946, JG Papers II, Box 20.

387 **"Can Russia Be Part"** "Noted Writers Are Engaged for Debate on Russian Issue," *Cincinnati Enquirer,* 6 Oct. 1946, p. 65.

387 **"full of classical erudition"** HRK to Horsley Gantt, 18 Jan. 1947, Alan Mason

Chesney Medical Archives, Johns Hopkins University. For a sense of Knick's anti-Communism, HRK to Immigration and Naturalization Service, 10 Jan. 1949, Leopold Schwarzschild Collection, Leo Baeck Institute Archives.

387 **It turned out his life** HRK to Horsley Gantt, Gantt Papers, 15 Jan. 1948.

387 **"Oh, if only I hadn't"** 16 Dec. 1947, 1947/8 notes, JG Papers II, Box 22.

387 **He spent a day** JG, diary entries,16, 22 July 1947, JG Papers II, Box 20.

387 **His own letters** JG to Johnny, 6 Oct. 1940; 26 Jan. 1941, FFG Papers, file 173.

388 **She'd nearly lost** JG, diary entry, 25–26 July 1947, JG Papers II, Box 22.

388 **Makes God a son** JG, diary entry, 26–28 July 1947, JG Papers II, Box 22.

388 **A wife—indeed, three** Dinah Sheean to Ernestine Evans, 30 July 1947, Box 1, folder 13, Ernestine Evans Papers, Rare Book & Manuscript Library, Columbia University.

389 **Dorothy's acceptance speech** JG's trip to Twin Farms is detailed in JG, diary entry for 30 July–6 Aug. 1947, JG Papers II, Box 20.

389 **Jimmy had lost** JVS to Clare Boothe Luce, 30 July 1947, Box 760, folder 1, Clare Boothe Luce Papers, Library of Congress.

389 **Jimmy's hair** Dinah Sheean to Ernestine Evans, 22 Nov. 1947, Ernestine Evans Papers, Box 1, folder 10.

389 **Dorothy cabled Dinah** Dinah Sheean to Ernestine Evans, 14 July 1947, Ernestine Evans Papers, Box 1, folder 10.

389 **Jimmy objected to the way** JVS, diary entry, 20 Aug. 1946, Diary, 1946–7, JVS Papers, WHS, Box 1, folder 39. On DT and the USSR, diary entry, 14 March 1946, Box 59, folder 5; Bill Shirer, diary entry, 14 April 1946, Shirer Papers, Looseleaf Box—Diary, 1946–9; DT to RW, 16 Dec. 1947, Rebecca West Papers, Yale, GEN 105, Series 1, Box 16, folder 823.

390 **"He's still alive"** DT to JG, no date [July 1947], JG Papers II, Box 35.

390 **"Has any one supposed"** Walt Whitman, "Song of Myself," section 7.

390 **"I need hardly tell you"** JVS to FFG, 5 Aug. 1947, FFG Papers, file 229.

391 **"the religions, separately"** Quoted in Vincent Sheean, *Lead, Kindly Light* (New York: Random House, 1949), p. 167.

391 **Jimmy had cut back** JVS to Clare Boothe Luce, 9 Aug. 1947, Clare Boothe Luce Papers, Box 760, folder 1.

391 **At night, he stared** JVS to DT, 11 Sept ny [1947 or 1948?], DT Papers, Box 28.

391 **The British were cutting** Among others, Yasmin Khan, *The Great Partition* (New Haven: Yale University Press, 2007); Vazira Fazila-Yacoobali Zamindar, *The Long Partition and the Making of Modern South Asia: Refugees, Boundaries, Histories* (New York: Columbia University Press, 2007).

391 **However bad** JVS, *Lead, Kindly Light,* p. 167.

392 **"cave of winds"** JG, diary entry for 30 July–6 Aug. 1947, JG Papers II, Box 20.

392 **"Wagnerian mists"** Dinah Sheean to Ernestine Evans, 30 July 1947.

392 **"forces of history"** Dinah Sheean to Ernestine Evans, 14 July 1947.

392 **Jimmy detailed** JVS, "The Pakistan Case," *NYHT,* 16 Jan. 1948, p. 22.

393 **Nehru was living** JVS, *Lead, Kindly Light,* p. 180; Nayantara Sahgal, *Jawaharlal Nehru: Civilizing a Savage World* (London: Penguin, 2010), p. 82.

393 **Point by point** Vincent Sheean, *Nehru: The Years of Power* (New York: Random House, 1960), p. 270.

393 **"Well, this is more"** JVS, *Lead, Kindly Light,* p. 191.

394 **It would have been unbearable** JVS, "Gandhi's Last Days: A Report by Vincent Sheean," *NYHT,* 8 Feb. 1948, p. 1.

394 *"How can such things"* JVS, *Lead, Kindly Light,* p. 204.

394 **After Johnny's death** For these letters, see FFG Papers, files 310–314; JG Papers 1972 Add., Box 144, folders 6–9.

394 **Even people who were** Morris Ernst to JG, nd [July 1947], FFG Papers, file 313. Ernst was JG's lawyer. Among many others, see Dr. Maurice William to JG, 2 July 1947, Bill Ormerod to JG, 2 July 1947, Francis Biddle to FFG & JG, 6 July 1947, Bill Shirer to JG, 2 July 1947, Jamie Hamilton to JG, 9 July 1947, Jennie Lee and Aneurin Bevan to FFG & JG, 8 July 1947, JG Papers 1972 Add., Box 144, folder 6; David E. Lilienthal to JG, 2 July 1947, Box 122, JG folder, David E. Lilienthal Papers, Mudd Manuscript Library, Princeton; card from Maggie Case, JG Papers 1972 Add., Box 144, folder 5.

394 **"In the presence of such grief"** Felix Frankfurter to JG, 19 July 1947, JG Papers II, Box 34.

394 **"I'm terrified"** Mickey Hahn to Frances, no date [July 1947], FFG Papers, file 310.

395 **John's thought** JG to Whit Burnett, 24 July 1947, JG Papers II, Box 6; also JG, Memo for the University of Chicago, Confidential, Nov. 1960, JG Papers 1972 Add., Box 138, folder 11.

395 **John started the book** JG, diary entry, 28 Dec. 1947; 15 Jan. 1948, JG Papers II, Box 20. See Gretchen Marie Krueger, "Death Be Not Proud: Children, Families, and Cancer in Postwar America," *Bulletin of the History of Medicine*, vol. 78 (Winter 2004): 836-63.

395 **By February, he'd** Lewis S. Gannett to JG, 27 Feb. 1948, JG Papers I, Box 44, folder 22; DT to Miss Barnett, 19 Feb. 1948, Box 44, folder 23; Bill Shirer to Cass Canfield, 9 Feb. 1949, JG Papers I, Box 119, folder 4.

395 **Dr. Traeger thought** Traeger's notes, JG Papers I, Box 44, folder 17; JG, diary entry, 14 Feb. 1948, JG Papers II, Box 20.

395 **Frances gave John** Annotated TS of *DBNP*, FFG Papers, file 56.

395 **Maybe Johnny would have** See, for instance, DT's point, JG, diary entry, 30 July–6 Aug. 1947.

396 **"I wish I could say"** "A Word from Frances," *DBNP*, p. 259.

396 **"caring more and more"** "A Word," p. 260.

396 **John had been searching** Jane's comments, as written out by JG, nd [1948], JG Papers I, Box 44, folder 18; see also Box 44, folder 17. At the time, Jane Gunther also thought Frances's afterword was too personal to be published.

397 **On the book's jacket** Memo for the University of Chicago, Confidential, Nov. 1960.

397 **There were Victorian autobiographical** For example, Catharine Tait's memoir of the death of five of her children from scarlet fever. See *Catharine and Craufurd Tait, Wife and Son of Archibald Campbell, Archbishop of Canterbury: A Memoir*, ed. Rev. William Benham (London: Macmillan, 1879). After the First World War, there were as well many "in memoriam" volumes produced about fallen soldiers, elegizing the character and unfulfilled promise of a dead son or brother.

397 **Narratives of illness** In Louis Kaplan, ed., *A Bibliography of American Autobiographies* (Madison: University of Wisconsin Press, 1961), there are forty-five titles that concerned physical disabilities and fourteen that dealt with illness.

397 **"has not taken"** Virginia Woolf, "On Being Ill," *The Criterion*, Jan. 1926, p. 32. More generally, Ben Yagoda, *Memoir: A History* (New York: Riverhead, 2009).

397 **The magazine was deluged** Bea Gould to JG, 4 March 1949, JG Papers I, Box 44, folder 22. More broadly, on revelation and privacy, Igo, *Known Citizen*, pp. 26–34, 102–8, 311–12; Philip Cushman, *Constructing the Self, Constructing America: A Cultural History of Psychotherapy* (Reading, Mass.: Addison-Wesley, 1995).

397 **What good could possibly** H.H.A. to JG, 6 March 1949, JG Papers I, Box 45, folder 1; see also, for example, C.F. to JG, 6 Feb. 1949, Box 45, folder 10; Mrs. W.O.H. to Mr. and Mrs. JG, 2 Feb. 1949, Box 46, folder 4; M.M. to Mrs. Gunther, 11 Feb. 1949, FFG Papers, file 58.

398 Nevertheless, it was like eavesdropping [Sylvia Norman], "Promise Unfulfilled," *TLS*, 27 May 1949, p. 348.

398 "The book is just as breathtaking" A.B., "Dying Boy's Courage Humbling," Hartford, Conn. *Times*, 5 Feb. 1949. Neither of the Book-of-the-Month Club's reviewers thought it should be chosen as a selection. According to one, "the book is a terrible experience . . . sheer agony all the way through." See YCAL MSS 278, Box 37, f. 310, Beinecke Library.

398 They sent photos of their dead For example, Mrs. H.V.A. to JG, undated [1949], JG Papers I, Box 45, folder 1.

398 Dear Mr. Gunther Mother to JG, 29 Jan. 1949, JG Papers I, Box 45, folder 2. I have anonymized this family's identifying details and used pseudonyms. I refer to the other DBNP correspondents by their initials.

400 They'd been sitting G.D. to JG, 14 Feb. 1949, JG Papers I, Box 45, folder 6. Similarly, H.J. to JG, 22 Jan. 1959, Box 46, folder 6.

400 "You see, your story" F.K. to JG, 2 Feb. 1949, JG Papers I, Box 46, folder 7.

400 My minister has told T.C. to JG, nd [1949], JG Papers I, Box 45, folder 5.

400 A mother whose baby Mrs. K.K. to JG, 1 April 1949, JG Papers I, Box 46, folder 8.

400 Parents felt guilty Mrs. H.M.E. to JG, 8 Feb. 1949; Mrs. H.C. to JG and FFG, 13 March 1950, JG Papers I, Box 45, folder 6.

400 Their sons had died H.K. to JG, 1 April 1949, JG Papers I, Box 46, folder 8.

400 Mothers sent letters to say A.D. to JG, 2 Feb. 1949 and Mrs. R.B. to JG, 31 Jan. 1949, JG Papers I, Box 45, folder 3; J.K.C. to JG, 17 March 1949, Mrs. A.L.C. to JG, 27 Jan. 1949, Box 45, folder 5; Z.D.H. to JG, 9 March 1949, Box 46, folder 5.

400 I am going to see a psychiatrist F.J.F. to Mrs. Gunther, 27 Feb. 1949, FFG Papers, file 59.

400 Visitors arrived asking to see Frank Boyden to JG, 7 March 1949, JG Papers I, Box 44, folder 22.

401 John tried to acknowledge Memo for the University of Chicago, Nov. 1960.

401 "Bringing Christ to the Nations" J.B. to JG, 24 March 1949, JG Papers I, Box 45, folder 3.

401 Cancer is caused M.B. to JG, 5 July 1949, JG Papers I, Box 45, folder 4.

401 "separation of his procreators" Mrs. G.C.H. to JG, 22 Jan. 1949, JG Papers I, Box 46, folder 4.

401 "a human life could be" DT, "Memorial to a Son," *Boston Globe*, 11 Feb. 1949, p. 22; DT to JG, 14 Feb. 1949, JG Papers II, Box 35.

402 "Little that was human" DT, "The Old Outcasts."

402 Jane would have been FFG, diary entry, April 1948, FFG Papers, folder 16.

402 She made Jane a present FFG, diary entry, nd [April/May 1948], FFG Papers, folder 16; DC interview with Jane Gunther, New York, 23 May 2018.

402 She was preparing to leave FFG to JVS, 14 March 1948, FFG Papers, file 229.

402 Maybe she'd even get JN to FFG, 24 May 1947, *SWJN*, series 2, vol. 2, pp. 634–35.

402 "glowed at me" JVS to FFG, 19 Jan. 1948, FFG Papers, file 229.

402 "You must say" FFG, diary entry, 10 Jan. 1948, FFG Papers, folder 16; FFG to Dr. Levy [Johnny's psychiatrist], draft letter, undated [1948], FFG Papers, file 283.

402 After the founding of Israel Frances Gunther, Background Notes, FFG Papers, file 1; diary entry for 12 Nov. 1948, FFG Papers, folder 16.

403 "You are the mother of a hero" JVS to FFG, 14 May nd [1949], JG Papers I, Box 44, folder 23.

403 "complete freedom of action" "Onze Amerikaanse gasten," *De Locomotief,* 15 June 1949, p. 1.

403 "I need to beg you" HRK to Agnes Knickerbocker, 16 June 1949, Private Collection.

403 **He was back in the headlines** "Amerikanen Zien Indonesië," *Algemeen Handelsblad*, 4 July 1949, p. 1.

404 **"It is fun to be back"** HRK to Agnes Knickerbocker, 2 July 1949, Private Collection.

404 **The rain had been ferocious** "45, Including 13 Americans, Killed," *Standard-Speaker* (Hazleton, Pa.), 13 July 1949, p. 22.

404 **I've provided the world** Milton Marmor, "Premonitions of Fatal Crash" and "Knickerbocker's Voice on Air Again," *Daily American*, 13 July 1949, p. 2.

EPILOGUE

405 **At least not until** Dinah Sheean to Carolyn Amussen, 19 Sept. 1971, JVS Papers, WHS, Box 2, folder 17.

405 **She could tell you who** JVS to Joyce Hartman, 17 Sept. 1971, JVS Papers, WHS, Box 2, folder 17.

405 **a "Manhattanese coolie"** JVS to Joyce Hartman, 16 Sept. 1971, JVS Papers, WHS, Box 2, folder 17.

406 **a "nothing, a nebbish"** Dinah Sheean to Carolyn Amussen, 19 Sept. 1971.

406 **"She's a meddler"** JVS to Joyce Hartman, 16 Sept. 1971.

406 **Mrs. Sanders reported** Carolyn Amussen to Joyce Hartman, nd [1971], JVS Papers, WHS, Box 2, folder 17.

406 **Imagine living without** Dinah Sheean to Carolyn Amussen, 19 Sept. 1971.

406 **"Poor Jimmy—he's finished"** Carolyn Amussen to Joyce Hartman, nd [1971].

406 **Mrs. Sanders's visit** Dinah Sheean to Carolyn Amussen, 19 Sept. 1971.

407 **Jimmy was "expendable"** Dinah Sheean to Carolyn Amussen, 19 Sept. 1971; also Dinah Sheean to Marion Sanders, 19 Sept. 1971.

407 **John Gunther, with his astounding** JVS on FFG, see Brock Baker's interview with JVS, Dec. 1974, New York, JG Papers II, Box 2.

407 **Knick dying an honest-to-god** "John Gunther Interviews Vincent Sheean," *NYHT* Weekly Book Review, 31 July 1949.

407 **Jimmy should take more pains** "John Gunther Interviews Vincent Sheean."

407 **But when he reached** Dinah Sheean to Ruth Falkenau, 4 July 1975, Sheean/Falkenau Correspondence, file 5.

407 **"I'm so old!"** Dinah Sheean to Joyce Hartman, 4 July 1970, Houghton Mifflin Records, bMS Am 2105 (228), folder 20.

408 **"He lived it"** Thornton Wilder to Dinah Sheean, 14 Sept. 1970, JVS Papers, WHS, folder 37.

408 **Too bad you didn't** JVS to DT, 12 June 1955, DT Papers, Box 28.

408 **"most representative form"** DT, "Writing Contemporary History," *Saturday Review of Literature*, 20 May 1939, p. 13.

408 **"congeries of eccentrics"** Albert Hubbell, "The World Was My Oyster," *New Yorker*, 23 March 1957 reviewing Farson's *A Mirror for Narcissus* (1956), p. 145.

408 **The advent of the jet** Hamilton, *Journalism's Roving Eye*, p. 214; see also Howard K. Smith, "The Dubious Phoenix," *Nation*, 14 Nov. 1953, p. 400.

408 **As the United States sought** DT, "The Old Outcasts," DT Papers, Box 100; Ulf Hannerz, *Foreign News: Exploring the World of Foreign Correspondents* (Chicago: University of Chicago Press, 2004); John Simpson, *We Chose to Speak of War and Strife: The World of the Foreign Correspondent* (London: Bloomsbury, 2017).

409 **It was because of** Walter Cronkite to Dinah Sheean, 21 May 1975, JVS Papers, WHS, Box 2, folder 36.

409 **By contrast, the New Journalists** On the New Journalism, Everette E. Dennis and William L. Rivers, *Other Voices: The New Journalism in America* (New Bruns-

wick, N.J.: Transaction Publishers, 2011 [1974]); Marc Weingarten, *The Gang that Wouldn't Write Straight: Wolfe, Thompson, Didion, and the New Journalism Revolution* (New York: Crown, 2006); Michael J. Arlen, "Notes on the New Journalism," *Atlantic,* May 1972, pp. 43-47.

409 **Eight publishers vied** Sanders, *Dorothy Thompson,* p. 348.

409 **"Mighty pretty country"** DT to Malcolm Lovell, 1 July 1959, cited in Kurth, *American Cassandra,* p. 456.

409 **Jimmy stewed** Dinah Sheean to Thornton Wilder, 1 Nov. 1970, Thornton Wilder Papers, Box 56, folder 1539.

409 **For years she labored** Ernestine Evans to DT, 3 June 1953, DT Papers, Box 10.

410 **When he wrote fiction** JG, *Fragment of Autobiography.*

410 **"Save for Autobiography"** "Titles," JG Papers II, Box 30.

410 **It depends on who kicks** JVS to Agatha Brooks Young, 25 Sept. nd [1962?], JVS Papers, Berg.

410 **That was the question** JVS to Dinah, 8 July nd [1952?], JVS Papers, WHS, Box 1, folder 3.

410 **And some of them worked** DT to RW, 30 June 1955, GEN 105, Series 1, Box 16, folder 824.

410 **Dorothy's ability to separate** Schorer, *Sinclair Lewis,* p. xviii.

410 **If his book had a heroine** Dale Warren, "I Remember Dorothy," *The Courier* (Syracuse University Library Associates) 4, no. 2 (Summer 1964), p. 23.

410 **She wasn't about to undertake** DT to RW, 30 June 1955, Rebecca West Papers, Yale, GEN 105, Series 1, Box 16, folder 824.

410 **Nevertheless, in a long** DT, "The Boy and Man from Sauk Centre," *Atlantic* 206 (November 1960): 39–48.

410 **"Lewis was an American genius"** Cited in Joyce Hartman Memo to Paul Brooks, Dale Warren, Dorothy de Santillana, 14 June 1961, Houghton Company Records, bMS Am 2105 (245), folder 4.

410 **"I hope I can get through"** JVS to Jane Gunther and JG, 23 June [1953?], JG Papers II, Box 35.

411 **"suppressed homosexuality"** JVS to Dinah Sheean, 8 July [1952?], JVS Papers, WHS, Box 1, folder 3, Correspondence with Dinah, 1950–52; also RW to DT, 16 June 1953, DT Papers, Box 33.

411 **"obituarians"** Dinah Sheean to Ruth Falkenau, 29 May 1975, Sheean/Falkenau Correspondence, file 5. [The "Tormentor" here, too.]

411 **"like saying goodbye"** JVS, *Dorothy and Red,* p. 267.

411 **The title of the book** JVS to JG, 24 May nd, JG Papers II, Box 35.

411 **She wasn't even writing** Joyce Hartman Memo to Paul Brooks and Lovell Thompson, 28 Feb. 1962, Houghton Company Records, bMS Am 2105 (245), folder 2.

411 **"necrology"** JVS to Agatha Brooks Young, 25 Sept. [1962?].

412 **That would take** JVS to Joyce Hartman, 5 Feb. 1963, Houghton Company Records, bMS Am 2105 (228), folder 4.

412 **Moreover, he didn't give** Robert Neville, "A Talk with Vincent Sheean," *NYT,* 17 Nov. 1963, p. 63 in Book Review Section.

412 **Writing about one's own** Among other frank memoirs of marriage are the actress Peggy Hopkins Joyce's *Men, Marriage and Me* (1930), the chorus girl Carolyn Green Rothstein's *Now I'll Tell* (1934), and the account by Sinclair Lewis's first wife, Grace Hegger Lewis's *With Love from Gracie: Sinclair Lewis, 1912–1925* (New York: Harcourt, Brace & Co., 1955), the nonfiction version of her 1931 novel, *Half a Loaf.* Given Lewis's commitment to realism, it's fitting that he became the subject of two separate marriage memoirs.

412 **At Houghton** TNB to Dorothy de Santillana, Houghton Company Records, bMS Am 2105 (228), folder 4.

412 **Nevertheless, it had to go** JVS to Joyce Hartman, 7 Feb. [1963], Houghton Company Records, bMS Am 2105 (228), folder 4.

412 **Her sister, her executors** Peggy Wilson to JVS, 18 Nov. 1963, Houghton Company Records, bMS Am 2105 (228), folder 10; on JG, Neville, "A Talk."

412 **"It may well be the frankest"** See *Harper's* advertisement, 1 Sept. 1963, p. 116; quote on the cover of the paperback edition.

412 **"extraordinary thing"** "Teller of Tales," *Time,* 15 Nov. 1963, p. 119.

412 **Just as many** William Hogan, "Sheean's Odd Record of Dorothy and Red," *Daily Journal* (Franklin, Ind.), 11 Nov. 1963, p. 6. For a suggestion that DT's lesbian diary was an attempt at fiction, Holmes Alexander, "People Should Know Limitations," *Marshall News Messenger* (Marshall, Tex.), 16 Dec. 1963, p. 4.

412 **It was the real-life version** Ida L. Compton, "Two Literary Dynamos Joined in Wedlock," *Berkshire Eagle,* 21 Dec. 1963, p. 16.

413 **"It is the story of virtually"** Neville, "A Talk."

413 **Laura Knickerbocker's** JG to Miss Ford, 12 Sept. 1963, JVS Papers, WHS, Box 2, folder 9; JVS to Joyce Hartman, 29 Sept. [1963], bMS Am 2105 (228), folder 8.

413 **"A Mrs. Joseph"** JVS to JG, 14 Nov. 1963, JG Papers II, Box 35.

413 **"a sponging Hungarian cad"** JVS to Dorothy de Santillana and Joyce Hartman, 9–10 Jan. ny [1964], Houghton Company Records, bMS Am 2105 (228), folder 14. JVS objected to the notion he'd use such a tasteless, moth-worn phrase, joking to JG that he'd sue *Time,* too. JVS to JG, 11 Jan. 1964, JG Papers II, Box 35.

413 **"like a surprised spaniel"** JVS to Miss Ford, 11 Jan. [1964], Houghton Company Records, bMS Am 2105 (228), folder 14.

413 **"A little late for my vices"** JVS to Dinah, 19 Jan. 1963, JVS Papers, WHS, Box 1, folder 15, Letters to Dinah, 1963.

414 **"Why do you have to have"** JVS to JG, 27 March, Sunday [nd, 1955?], JG Papers II, Box 35.

414 **An anti-imperialist** JG to RW, 2 July 1951 [misdated 1941], Rebecca West Papers, Yale, GEN 105, Series 1, Box 9, folder 335.

414 **He wrote a biography** JVS to Dinah Sheean, 11 Aug. ny, JVS Papers, WHS, Box 1, Folder 3—Correspondence with Dinah, 1950–52.

414 **He wore a white** DC Interview with Stephen Graubard, New York, 28 January 2017.

414 **"People never do look"** JVS to DT, 1 Dec. 1952, DT Papers, Box 27.

414 **He and Dinah** See JVS Papers, WHS, Box 1, folders 2–24; also Straus, *Showcases,* pp. 140–58.

414 **In 1970, she returned** Johnson, "Twentieth-Century Seeker," pp. 705–6.

414 **In those last years** Dinah Sheean to Ruth Falkenau, 29 May 1975.

414 **"Jimmy is a hazard"** Dinah Sheean to Carolyn Amussen, 19 Sept. 1971.

414 **They came to New York** "Sheean, Noted Author, Dies," *Dispatch* (Moline, Ill.), 17 March 1975, p. 2; Israel Shenker, "Vincent Sheean at 75 Ponders His and the World's State," *NYT,* 6 Dec. 1974, p. 83.

415 **"state of the world"** Dinah Sheean to Leland Stowe, 10 Jan. 1976, Leland Stowe Papers, Box 23, Wisconsin Historical Society; Dinah Sheean to Thornton Wilder, 10 April 1975, Thornton Wilder Papers, Box 56, f. 1543.

POSTSCRIPT

417 **His coolness** FFG, diary entries, 21 April 1950, 3 and 6 May 1950, FFG Papers, folder 9.

417 **"wrath of the Israeli"** FFG to Frances Wickes, June 1952, Frances G. Wickes Papers, Library of Congress, Box 2, folder 9.

417 **"What you need"** Edgar Snow, *Journey to the Beginning* (London: Lowe and Brydone, 1958), p. 412.

418 **"just got into a rut"** JVS to JG, 5 July 1959, JG Papers II, Box 35.

418 **Sometimes Jimmy said** Irita Van Doren, Note, 1960, Irita Van Doren Papers, Box 8.

418 **"And by the way, only statesmen"** Goebbels, diary entry, 14 Oct. 1942.

418 **Rebecca West lived** Marina Warner's Interview with RW, *Paris Review*, no. 79 (Spring 1981), p. 119.

418 **"I've nothing good to say"** Brock Baker's Interview with RW, London, 25 April 1975, JG Papers II, Box 2.

419 **Of her startlingly frank** The subject of p. 238 is a conversation between Charles Boxer and his then wife, Ursula, as relayed by Boxer to his pregnant lover, Mickey.

419 **"I don't care"** Ken Cuthbertson to DC, 20 March 2021.

PERMISSIONS

—

DEBORAH COHEN GRATEFULLY ACKNOWLEDGES THE FOLLOWING copyright holders for permission to quote from unpublished materials:

The late Jane Gunther (John Gunther)
Miranda Knickerbocker de Kay (Agnes and Hubert Renfro Knickerbocker)
Jane Morton (Dinah and Vincent Sheean)
Carola Vecchio (Emily Hahn)
Mary von Euler (Frances Fineman Gunther)
The late Denis Fodor (Marcel W. Fodor)
McIntosh and Otis, Inc. and the Syracuse University Special Collections
    Research Center (Dorothy Thompson)

PHOTO CREDITS

1. Newberry Library 2. DN-0080461, *Chicago Sun-Times/Chicago Daily News* collection, Chicago Historical Society 3, 6, 11, 12, 13, 22, 23, 25, 31, 35, 36. Schlesinger Library 4, 8, 34. Syracuse University Special Collections Research Center 5, 7, 26, 27, 32, 33, 37. Private Collection 9. Estates of Barbara Ker-Seymer and John Banting, Christie's Image/Bridgeman Images (my thanks to Max Ker-Seymer) 10, 15, 16. Rare Book & Manuscript Library, Columbia University frontispiece, 14. Denis Fodor 17, 20, 21. Special Collections Research Center, University of Chicago 19. Granger Historical Picture Archive 24. Lilly Library, Indiana University 28. *Time* magazine 29. *Scarsdale Inquirer* 30. Keystone via Getty Images

INDEX

DEBORAH COHEN is the Richard W. Leopold Professor of History at Northwestern University. She's written books about veterans in Britain and Germany after the First World War (*The War Come Home*), British consumerism (*Household Gods*), and families (*Family Secrets*). She writes regularly for *The Atlantic* and has published reviews in *The New York Review of Books,* the *London Review of Books,* and *The Wall Street Journal.* Raised in Louisville, Kentucky, she lives in Chicago.

deborahcohen.com

A B O U T   T H E

T Y P E

This book was set in Caslon, a typeface first designed in 1722 by William Caslon (1692–1766). Its widespread use by most English printers in the early eighteenth century soon supplanted the Dutch typefaces that had formerly prevailed. The roman is considered a "workhorse" typeface due to its pleasant, open appearance, while the italic is exceedingly decorative.